D1252257

The Culinary Professional

Third Edition

John Draz, CEC, CCE

Executive Research Chef
Ed Miniat, Inc.
South Holland, Illinois

Christopher Koetke, MBA, CEC, CCE, HAAC

Vice President School of Culinary Arts
Kendall College
Chicago, Illinois

Publisher
The Goodheart-Willcox Company, Inc.
Tinley Park, Illinois
www.g-w.com

Cover image: Westend61/Westend61/Getty Images

Introduction

The Culinary Professional is the first step on the path to a career in the culinary field. It will provide you with the necessary skills for more advanced class work and expose you to the world of professional cooking.

The foodservice industry, which employs most culinary professionals, is large and diverse. This text begins with an introduction to that industry's opportunities and challenges. You will learn what it takes to succeed in this growing field.

Before you begin to cook, you should know how to be safe in the kitchen. Early chapters will explain how to protect your health and safety as well as that of your coworkers and customers. You will learn how to find a job and what is expected of you as an employee. A new chapter explores concepts and practices that promote sustainability in the kitchen.

Chefs use many tools and select from an immense array of ingredients when preparing dishes. *The Culinary Professional* supplies a generous number of photos and clear descriptions of the tools and ingredients used in the professional kitchen. Step-by-step directions for basic culinary skills and cooking methods appear throughout the text. The presentation of your food is nearly as important as the preparation, and for this reason, a full chapter covers the principles of plating, design, and garnishing. A new chapter explains how to analyze cuisines and explores various international cuisines.

Successful chefs must be able to do more than simply prepare delicious dishes. You will learn about the importance of working with other departments and managing resources.

Welcome to the first step on your path to a career in culinary!

About the Authors

Chef John Draz received his associate's degree from The Culinary Institute of America in Hyde Park, New York in 1981 and was the recipient of the Edward T. Hanley Scholarship. He also holds a bachelor's degree in culinary management from Kendall College in Evanston, Illinois. During his nearly 30 years in the field, Chef Draz has worked at numerous restaurants including The Ritz-Carlton Chicago, The Winnetka Grill, The Ninety-Fifth, and Café Provencal. In 1983, Chef Draz was featured in the PBS television series Great Chefs of Chicago.

Chef Draz was a founding faculty member of the Kendall College School of Culinary Arts. While serving on the faculty, he taught a wide variety of subjects related to professional cookery. Chef Draz served as chair of the culinary department from 1988 to 1991, supervising all aspects of instruction and college foodservice. He has earned certifications from the American Culinary Federation including Certified Executive Chef and Certified Culinary Educator.

In addition, Chef Draz has experienced entrepreneurship as chef/owner of a 300-seat fine-dining restaurant. He has extensive consulting experience lending his talents to numerous independent restaurants, corporations, and marketing organizations. Chef Draz currently serves as Executive Research Chef for Ed Miniat, Inc., a manufacturer of cooked meat products. In this position, he develops products and menu items for the frozen food industry and national restaurant chains.

Chef Christopher Koetke is currently Vice President of the School of Culinary Arts Kendall College. Prior to this, he served as dean of the School of Culinary Arts of Kendall College. Before being named dean, he was a chef instructor for six years, specializing in sauce making, charcuterie, and ice carving. Chef Koetke has been cooking professionally since 1982 in some of the best restaurants and pastry shops in France, Switzerland, and the United States. Before coming to Kendall College in 1998, he was the executive chef of Chicago's critically acclaimed Les Nomades restaurant.

Chef Koetke has received numerous industry awards including Chef of the Year by the Chicago chapter of the International Food and Wine Society, ACF culinary competition medals, and third place in the US finals of the Bocuse d'Or. For several years, Christopher was a contributing editor to *Chef*, *Chef Educator Today*, and *Fancy Food* magazines. He currently sits on numerous boards nationally, is an elected commissioner of the American Culinary Federation Foundation Accrediting Committee, serves as a consultant to numerous foodservice enterprises, judges national culinary competitions, and frequently presents at professional conferences and various international culinary forums. Chef Koetke is often a guest on TV and radio broadcasts in Chicago and has produced numerous educational DVDs. He is also host of his own TV show called *Let's Dish!* on the Live Well Network.

Chef Koetke has an MBA from Dominican University, BA in French Literature from Valparaiso University, and a Certificat de la Langue Française from the Sorbonne in Paris.

Acknowledgments

The authors and Goodheart-Willcox Publisher would like to thank the following professionals who provided valuable input:

Contributing Author

Harry J. Crane, Executive Chef
Kraft Foods Inc., Madison, WI
Past president and chef member, Research Chefs Association; chef member, American Culinary Federation; adjunct faculty, School of Culinary Arts at Kendall College

Additional Acknowledgments

The Beef Checkoff
Carrie Conway
George J. Corneille and Sons
Steve Ells
Eric Futran
Intelligentsia Coffee & Tea, Inc.
Kendall College Administration
Jack Klasey

Todd Menaker, CRC
The Plitt Company
Alisa Ann Ruch Burn Foundation
The Seafood Merchants, Ltd.
Oehme Soule, RD, LDN
Stock Yards Packing
Todd and Holland Tea Merchants
US Foodservice

Reviewers

Chef Allen Bild, CEPC
Culinary Arts Instructor
Hammond Area Career Center
Hammond, Indiana

Brenda Cavins
Former Hospitality Instructor
Tulsa Technology Center
Tulsa, Oklahoma

Julian Cribb
Journalist, Editor, and Science Communicator
Principal, Julian Cribb & Associates

Holly D. Elmore
Waste Reduction Specialist
Founder & CEO, Elemental Impact

Frederick L. Kirschenmann
Distinguished Fellow, Leopold Center for Sustainable Agriculture at Iowa State University (Ames, IA)
President, Stone Barns Center for Food and Agriculture
Pocantico Hills, New York

Melissa Kogut
Executive Director, Chefs Collaborative

Richard S. McKinney
Culinary Arts Instructor
Rindge School of Technical Arts
Cambridge, Massachusetts

Susan M. Moberg
Culinary Arts Instructor
Moses Lake High School
Moses Lake, Washington

Judy Moon
Academy Coordinator/Instructor
International Hospitality and Tourism Academy
Concord, California

Chef Lou Rice, MA, CCC, CHE
Director Culinary Arts/Hospitality
Northwest Arkansas Community College
Bentonville, Arkansas

Cindy Railing, APR
Foodservice Industry Sustainability Specialist
Principal, Railing & Associates

Dan Rosenthal
President of The Rosenthal Group, Inc.
Founder of the Green Chicago Restaurant Coalition

Chef David Ross, CCC
Department Chair, Culinary Arts
Helms College
Augusta, Georgia

Richard Young
Energy and Water Conservation Specialist
Senior Engineer/Director of Education
Food Service Technology Center

Contents in Brief

Table of Contents

Unit Three
Ingredients, Preparation, and Presentation

Unit Five
Beyond Cooking

Features

The Science of...

INDUSTRY INSIGHTS

SANITATION & SAFETY

A SERVING OF HISTORY

CHEF'S ETHICS

Hints from the Chef

Culture & Cuisine

Culinary Trends

Chef Speak

SCIENCE & TECHNOLOGY

SUSTAINABLE CULINARY

Mix In Math

Nutrition Connection

TECHNIQUES

Video Clips

Video

Approachable Writing and Design Engage Reader

Pilaf Method

Pilaf (also spelled "pilaw" or "pilau") can be traced back to ancient Persia, an...

TECHNIQUE
Preparing Pilaf

1. Heat a small amount of fat in a heavy saucepan and sweat the appropriate aromatic ingredients.

2. Add the measured amount of rice and stir to coat grains with the fat.

3. Add the measured amount of seasoned liquid to the rice and bring to a boil.

4. Cover saucepan with a tight fitting lid and place in a 350°F (180°C) oven for the correct cooking time. Large batches can be cooked in the oven in a covered hotel pan.

5. When all of the liquid has been absorbed, remove the rice from the oven, uncover and fluff with a fork.

Design focuses
attention and guides reader.

Cherimoya (Custard Apple)
Cherimoya is a fruit native to South and Central America that looks like a stout green pinecone with creamy white flesh. It has a sweet fragrant flavor and black seeds.

Guava
Guava is a golf ball-sized fruit with green skin and pink or yellow flesh. This fragrant fruit is desirable for its juice, which is used in tropical drinks, sauces, and preserves.

Kiwano (Horned Melon)
The kiwano is a spiked oval orange fruit with thick skin and a tart juicy interior.

Kumquat
The kumquat is a small thumb-sized citrus fruit with virtually no juice. The rind and flesh of this fruit are eaten and provide a fragrant and tart citrus flavor.

Lychee
Lychee is a small reddish-skinned fruit that has a white inner flesh with sweet, juicy, subtle flavor. Originally grown in China, it is popular in Asian cuisines.

Passion Fruit
Passion fruit is a small round fruit with a thick bumpy purple skin and an interior

Beef Loin Foodservice Cuts

Strip Loin, boneless, IMPS# 180
The strip loin is a boneless cut. When used whole, it is typically roasted. It is more commonly fabricated into steaks.

Strip Loin Steak, boneless, IMPS# 1180
The strip loin steak is also known as the *New York strip steak*. This cut is commonly grilled or broiled.

Tenderloin, peeled, side muscle on (PSMO), IMPS# 189A
Tenderloin PSMO has had the fat layer peeled off. This boneless cut is typically roasted.

Tenderloin Steak, IMPS# 1190
The tenderloin steak is also known as *filet mignon*. It is typically grilled or broiled.

Bottom Sirloin Butt Steak, IMPS# 1185B
The bottom sirloin butt steak is a boneless steak cut from the ball tip. It is served grilled or broiled.

Porterhouse Steak, IMPS# 1173
The porterhouse steak, similar to the T-bone steak, contains the strip loin and a section of the tenderloin. It is served grilled or broiled.

Sirloin Butt Tri-Tip, IMPS# 185D
The sirloin butt tri-tip is a tender, flat muscle that is typically roasted, grilled, or broiled.

Inviting presentation
captures attention and generates interest.

Mediterranean

Characteristics of Cuisines
The Mediterranean basin encompasses lands surrounding the Mediterranean Sea. Due to similarities in climate and geography, the cuisines of this region share many characteristics. The Mediterranean enjoys a temperate climate with hot, dry summers and mild, wet winters. The region is ringed by mountain ranges with desert regions on the African side. Throughout history, European Christian and North African Muslim food traditions have influenced foodways of this area.

The region's agriculture is a legacy of the crops that the ancient Greeks and Romans spread through the region, including wheat, olives, and grapes. Summer vegetable crops such as tomatoes, peppers, beans, squash, artichokes, and eggplant grow well throughout the region. Generous use of garlic and herbs is characteristic. Mediterranean orchards provide oranges, lemons, figs, almonds, and pistachios. Rice is also a staple of the Mediterranean cuisine. Lamb and pork are the most common meats and the sea provides an abundance of fish, shellfish, and crustaceans.

Ratatouille (France)
Eggplant and zucchini stewed with peppers, tomatoes, onions, herbs, and garlic.

Pasta Marinara (Italy)
Pasta mixed with tomato sauce flavored with garlic and herbs.

Souvlaki (Greece)
Cubes of pork or lamb skewered and grilled.

Harira (North Africa)
Spiced legume soup usually with lentils or chickpeas and tomatoes.

Paella (Spain)
Short-grain rice flavored with saffron and cooked in an open pan with vegetables, chicken sausage, and shellfish.

Activities Prepare for College and Career

Reading Prep
improves reading skills and challenges student to explore a range of informational texts.

Online Resources
reinforce learning.

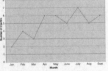

Core Skills
apply writing, reading, speaking, listening, and math to chapter content.

Critical Thinking
challenges student to use higher-level thinking skills.

Technology
use and explore technologies related to content.

Teamwork
develops ability to collaborate and interact with others in a productive manner.

Chef's E-portfolio
builds your e-portfolio for use when exploring volunteer, education and training, or career opportunities.

Relevant Features Capture Attention

Sustainable Culinary

focuses on sustainable concepts and practices in the culinary industry.

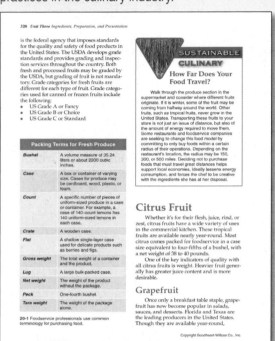

320 Unit Three Ingredients, Preparation, and Presentation

is the federal agency that imposes standards for the quality and safety of food products in the United States. The USDA develops grade standards and provides grading and inspection services throughout the country. Both fresh and processed fruits may be graded by the USDA, but grading of fruit is not mandatory. Grade categories for fresh fruits are different for each type of fruit. Grade categories used for canned or frozen fruits include the following:

- US Grade A or Fancy
- US Grade B or Choice
- US Grade C or Standard

SUSTAINABLE CULINARY

How Far Does Your Food Travel?

Walk through the produce section in the supermarket and consider where different fruits originate. If it is winter, some of the fruit may be coming from halfway around the world. Other fruits, such as tropical fruits, never grow in the United States. Transporting these fruits to your store is not just an issue of distance, but also of the amount of energy required to move them. Some restaurants and foodservice companies are seeking to change this food model by committing to only buy foods within a certain radius of their operations. Depending on the restaurant's location, the radius may be 150, 300, or 500 miles. Deciding not to purchase foods that must travel great distances helps support local economies, ideally lessens energy consumption, and forces the chef to be creative with the ingredients she has at her disposal.

Citrus Fruit

Whether it's for their flesh, juice, rind, or zest, citrus fruits have a wide variety of uses in the commercial kitchen. These tropical fruits are available nearly year-round. Most citrus comes packed for foodservice in a case size equivalent to four-fifths of a bushel, with a net weight of 38 to 40 pounds.

One of the key indicators of quality with all citrus fruits is weight. Heavier fruit generally has greater juice content and is more desirable.

Grapefruit

Once only a breakfast table staple, grapefruit has now become popular in salads, sauces, and desserts. Florida and Texas are the leading producers in the United States. Though they are available year-round,

Packing Terms for Fresh Produce	
Bushel	A volume measure of 35.24 liters or about 2200 cubic inches.
Case	A box or container of varying size. Cases for produce may be cardboard, wood, plastic, or foam.
Count	A specific number of pieces of uniform-sized produce in a case or container. For example, a case of 140-count lemons has 140 uniform-sized lemons in each case.
Crate	A wooden case.
Flat	A shallow single-layer case used for delicate products such as berries and figs.
Gross weight	The total weight of a container and the product.
Lug	A large bulk-packed case.
Net weight	The weight of the product without the package.
Peck	One-fourth bushel.
Tare weight	The weight of the package alone.

20-1 Foodservice professionals use common terminology for purchasing food.

Copyright Goodheart-Willcox Co., Inc.

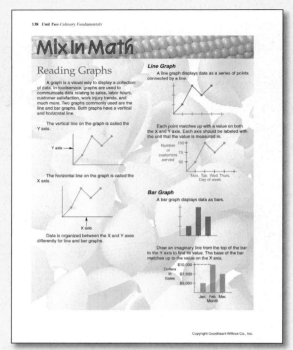

138 Unit Two Culinary Fundamentals

Mix In Math

Reading Graphs

A graph is a visual way to display a collection of data. In foodservice, graphs are used to communicate data relating to sales, labor hours, customer satisfaction, work injury trends, and much more. Two graphs commonly used are the line and bar graphs. Both graphs have a vertical and horizontal line.

The vertical line on the graph is called the Y axis.

Y axis

The horizontal line on the graph is called the X axis.

X axis

Data is organized between the X and Y axes differently for line and bar graphs.

Line Graph

A line graph displays data as a series of points connected by a line.

Each point matches up with a value on both the X and Y axis. Each axis should be labeled with the unit that the value is measured in.

Number of customers served — 100, 75, 50 — Mon. Tue. Wed. Thurs. Day of week

Bar Graph

A bar graph displays data as bars.

Draw an imaginary line from the top of the bar to the Y axis to find its value. The base of the bar matches up to the value on the X axis.

Dollars in Sales — $10,000, $7,500, $5,000 — Jan. Feb. Mar. Month

Copyright Goodheart-Willcox Co., Inc.

Mix In Math

reviews math skills commonly used in foodservice.

The Science...

simplifies fundamental food science concepts and relates them to culinary success.

Unit One
Introducing the Foodservice Industry

1. Welcome to the Foodservice Industry
2. Understanding Foodservice Operations
3. Culinary History
4. Workstations in the Professional Kitchen
5. The Professional Chef
6. Entering the Workforce

The Science of Flavor— Maillard Reaction

What gives cooked meat that tantalizing appearance, irresistible aroma, and unmatched flavor? When meats are cooked at high temperatures, a chemical reaction occurs that produces these desirable results. The name for this science behind the flavor is the *Maillard reaction*.

The Maillard reaction is the result of basic elements of the food combining, which yields the distinctive brown color. For this reason, it is also called the *browning reaction*. In addition to lending color, the by-products of this reaction produce wonderful flavors that are the trademark of many roasted and grilled meats.

The Maillard reaction occurs in foods such as cooked meats, toasted breads, and beer. These foods contain the necessary elements for the reaction to take place—proteins and sugars. The chemistry behind the reaction is quite complex, but luckily it is not necessary to understand the chemistry to prepare delectable dishes.

1. Describe the discernible changes to food brought about by the Maillard reaction.
2. List two elements that must be present in a food for the Maillard reaction to take place.

Visual Elements Reinforce Concepts

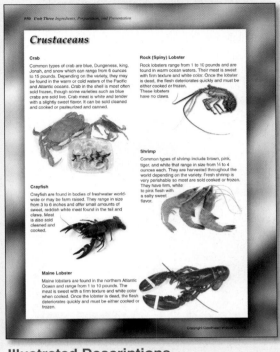

Step-by-Step Techniques show key preparation stages and changes in the food's appearance.

Illustrated Descriptions identify foods and equipment used in commercial kitchens.

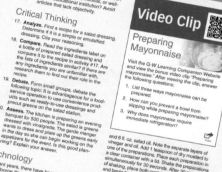

Video Features sprinkled throughout text link to author demonstrations of culinary techniques.

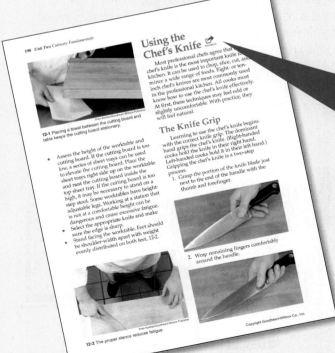

Animations bring chapter concepts to life.

G-W Integrated Learning Solution

The G-W Integrated Learning Solution offers easy-to-use resources for both students and instructors. Digital and blended learning content can be accessed through any Internet-enabled device such as a computer, smartphone, or tablet. Students spend more time learning, and instructors spend less time administering. While studying, look for the activity icon ⤴ in the text to access hands-on interactivity and study anywhere, anytime at www.g-wlearning.com.

G-W Learning Companion Website/ Student Textbook

The G-W Learning companion website is a study reference that contains photo identification and matching activities, animations and videos, In Review questions, vocabulary exercises, recipes, and more! Accessible from any digital device, the G-W Learning companion website complements the textbook and is available to the student at no charge.

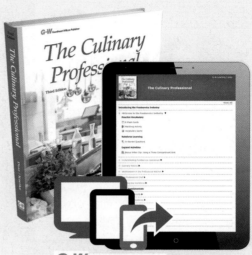

Online Learning Suite

Available as a classroom subscription, the Online Learning Suite provides the foundation of instruction and learning for digital and blended classrooms. An easy-to-manage shared classroom subscription makes it a hassle-free solution for both students and instructors. An online student text and workbook, along with rich supplemental content, brings digital learning to the classroom. All instructional materials are found on a convenient online bookshelf and are accessible at home, at school, or on the go.

Online Learning Suite/ Student Textbook Bundle

Looking for a blended solution? Goodheart-Willcox offers the Online Learning Suite bundled with the printed text in one easy-to-access package. Students have the flexibility to use the print version, the Online Learning Suite, or a combination of both components to meet their individual learning style. The convenient packaging makes managing and accessing content easy and efficient.

Online Instructor Resources

Online Instructor Resources provide all the support needed to make preparation and classroom instruction easier than ever. Available in one accessible location, support materials include Answer Keys, Lesson Plans, Instructor Presentations for PowerPoint®, ExamView® Assessment Suite, and more! Online Instructor Resources are available as a subscription and can be accessed at school or at home.

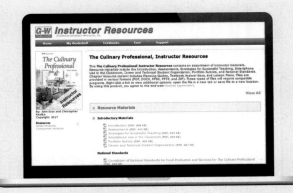

G-W Integrated Learning Solution

For the Student:

Student Textbook (print)
Study Guide (print)
Lab Manual (print)
G-W Learning Companion Website (free)
Online Learning Suite (subscription)
Online Learning Suite/Student Textbook Bundle

For the Instructor:

Instructor's Presentations for PowerPoint® (CD)
ExamView® Assessment Suite (CD)
Instructor Resources (CD)
Online Instructor Resources (subscription)

Precision Exams Certification

Goodheart-Willcox is pleased to partner with Precision Exams by correlating **The Culinary Professional** to the Standards, Objectives, and Indicators for Precision Exams Food Service/Culinary Arts exam. Precision Exams were created in concert with industry and subject matter experts to match real-world job skills and marketplace demands. Students who pass the exam and performance portion of the exam can earn a Career Skills Certification™. To see how **The Culinary Professional** correlates to the Precision Exam Standards, please visit www.g-w.com/culinary-professional-2017 and click on the Correlations tab. For more information on Precision Exams, please visit www.precisionexams.com.

I earned a CAREER SKILLS™ Certificate in FOOD SERVICE CULINARY ARTS. You can earn one too!

Ask your instructor how you can earn a CAREER SKILLS™ Certificate for your résumé.

800.470.1215   PRECISION EXAMS   precisionexams.com

Unit One
Introducing the Foodservice Industry

marco mayer/Shutterstock.com

2

The Science of Flavor—
Maillard Reaction

What gives cooked meat that tantalizing appearance, irresistible aroma, and unmatched flavor? When meats are cooked at high temperatures, a chemical reaction occurs that produces these desirable results. The name for this science behind the flavor is the *Maillard reaction*.

The Maillard reaction is the result of basic elements of the food combining, which yields the distinctive brown color. For this reason, it is also called the *browning reaction*. In addition to lending color, the by-products of this reaction produce wonderful flavors that are the trademark of many roasted and grilled meats.

The Maillard reaction occurs in foods such as cooked meats, toasted breads, and beer. These foods contain the necessary elements for the reaction to take place—proteins and sugars. The chemistry behind the reaction is quite complex, but luckily it is not necessary to understand the chemistry to prepare delectable dishes.

1. Describe the discernible changes to food brought about by the Maillard reaction.

2. List two elements that must be present in a food for the Maillard reaction to take place.

While studying, look for the activity icon  **to:**

- Build vocabulary with e-flash cards and matching activities.
- Expand learning with video clips, photo identification activities, animations, and interactive activities.
- Review and assess what you learn by completing end-of-chapter questions.

Welcome to the Foodservice Industry

Reading Prep

Before reading, observe the objectives for this chapter. As you read, focus on how the chapter is structured. Does this structure make points clear, convincing, and engaging?

Culinary Terminology Build Vocab

foodservice, p. 5
hospitality, p. 6
cuisine, p. 7
home meal replacements, p. 9
culinary, p. 12
culinarian, p. 12

Academic Terminology Build Vocab

trends, p. 7
sustainable products and practices, p. 9
living wage, p. 10

Objectives

After studying this chapter, you will be able to

- summarize the foodservice and hospitality industries.
- recall current trends in the foodservice industry.
- recognize challenges facing the foodservice industry.
- understand the role of the culinary profession in the hospitality industry.

Many people believe the key to happiness is finding a job they love. Often people who work in commercial kitchens find great happiness in their work. Professional chefs get fulfillment by combining their creativity with a love of good food to delight their customers. As you begin to explore this exciting and rewarding career, it is important to understand the industry that offers cooks and chefs the chance to practice their craft.

An Overview of the Industry

Foodservice is the business of making and serving prepared food and drink. It includes restaurants, hotels, clubs, catering, school and business feeding, healthcare facilities, convenience stores, airlines, railroads, and cruise lines. Foodservice is a service industry. In recent years, the economy has seen greater growth in service industries than in manufacturing jobs.

The size and scope of the foodservice industry is so large that it is hard to grasp. According to the National Restaurant Association, foodservice operations sell over $1.8 billion in meals, snacks, and beverages each day. Consider how many meals your family eats away from home in an average week. You may have dinner at your favorite restaurant. Maybe you and your friends go out for pizza. Count the lunches you eat in your school cafeteria. Do you stop for fast food or buy a snack from a vending machine? All these meals are part of the foodservice industry. This industry employs about 13 million people. It is the second largest employer in the United States after the federal government. Chefs, cooks, servers, bartenders, cashiers, and managers are all employed in foodservice. In 2013, the restaurant industry generated over $660 billion in sales. Foodservice is important to the world economy as well. Globally, the foodservice industry is expected to reach a value of almost $2.1 trillion in 2015.

Foodservice is one part of the larger hospitality industry. **Hospitality** means welcoming guests and satisfying their needs. Hospitality is based on guest or customer service, and quality guest service anticipates guests, needs and delivers beyond their expectations. Since the need for nourishment is important, foodservice plays a large role in hospitality. The International Council on Hotel, Restaurant, and Institutional Education (ICHRIE) divides the hospitality industry into five segments, 1-1. The hospitality industry is an important part of the US and global economies.

Growth and Employment Prospects

The foodservice industry continues to grow. Americans are consuming more meals away from home than ever before. Some reasons for the growth include more dual-career families, busy schedules, an increasing number of older adults who are unable or choose not to prepare their own meals, and the overall increase in travel. In addition, food continues to be an important part of celebrations and special events.

The growth of the industry means more job opportunities. The foodservice industry is a great place to begin a career. Twenty-seven percent of adults had their first work experience in restaurants. Opportunities for advancement are plentiful. Individuals with a degree in hospitality or foodservice management have the best job opportunities. Eighty percent of restaurant owners began their careers as hourly employees. The industry is projected to grow nearly 10 percent from 13.1 to nearly 14.4 million employees by 2023.

Segments of the Hospitality Industry	
Segment	**Examples**
Food	Quick-service, carryout, specialty and fine-dining restaurants; private clubs; banquet operations; coffee shops and dining rooms in hotels and lodging facilities; delis; gourmet shops; nightclubs; catering companies; foodservice operations in businesses, schools, colleges and universities, stadiums, convention centers, state and national parks, hospitals
Lodging	Hotels, motels, resorts, conference centers, inns, senior living facilities, time-shares, bed-and-breakfasts
Recreation	Theme parks and attractions, marinas, campgrounds, parks, casinos
Travel-related	National and international air travel, cruise lines, railroads, tour operators, travel agencies, tourism marketing
Convention and Meeting	Meeting planning, convention center management, event planning and management, exhibition and trade show planning, management and convention services in hotels
Source: International Council on Hotel, Restaurant, and Institutional Education (ICHRIE)	

1-1 The goal of all hospitality industry segments is serving the customer.

Trends in Foodservice

Trends are new practices or conditions that point to the way things will be in the future. There are always new trends in foodservice. Trends in foodservice are driven by larger influences such as economic conditions, political developments, social changes, and scientific and technological advancements. Some of the current trends in foodservice are globalization of cuisine, increased use of technology, adoption of sustainable practices, and the development of new markets.

Global Cuisine

The world of food is becoming smaller every day. Today, diners are rarely limited to local dishes and food products. **Cuisine** (kwih-ZEEN) is the French word for "kitchen," but in English it means a style of cooking. Global cuisine is a blend of ingredients and cooking techniques from around the world.

Through travel and the media, diners are exposed to an ever-widening range of dishes from around the world. Restaurateurs and chefs are constantly exploring the world of food for new and interesting items to put on their menus.

Foodservice professionals must be familiar with a wider variety of foods than ever before. Classical cuisine remains the foundation for most professional chefs. However, to meet the demands of modern diners, a good knowledge of Asian, Mediterranean, and Latin American cuisines is also needed, 1-2.

Technology

Like many areas of life, technology is changing foodservice. Technology creates more efficient ways to work. Tedious tasks are reduced. A company's ability to make money is improved. Foodservice remains labor-intensive with many traditional methods still being used, but technology is making dramatic changes in the way work is done.

Foodservice was slower to utilize computers than other industries. However, many tasks are now computerized. Technology has become part of the fabric of the hospitality industry. Foodservice professionals must be able to use spreadsheets and

Draz-Koetke/Goodheart-Willcox Publisher
1-2 Culinarians need to be experienced in cuisines and cooking methods of cultures around the world.

word processing. These are essential tools for management and communication. Many workers use computer systems designed for the foodservice industry. These systems allow servers to take and send orders to the kitchen. Some systems manage tasks in the kitchen and provide cooks with instructions on cooking techniques. Managers also use computer systems to manage labor and inventory.

Video technology allows chefs to monitor more than one location at a time. Managers use cell phones, pagers, and walkie-talkies to maintain contact with staff throughout a large facility.

Technology has made kitchen equipment more accurate and efficient. Equipment with programmable cooking cycles allows cooks and chefs to produce food at the perfect

doneness. Advances in cooking equipment allow food to be cooked faster and better than ever before.

The Internet is a means for diners to access restaurant information and menus as well as make reservations. Social media is an important means of promotion for many foodservice operations. Cell phone text paging can be used to notify guests their table is ready.

Food science and technology have gained greater roles in professional kitchens in recent years. Chefs now regularly make use of ingredient technology creating dishes with new flavors and textures by using ingredients such as gels, gums, flavor extracts, and concentrates as well as other functional ingredients that were once only used by food scientists. In striving for new and creative cooking methods, cutting edge chefs now employ technologically advanced equipment such as vacuum sealers, low-temperature circulating water bath cookers, liquid nitrogen tanks, dehydrators, and distillation equipment, 1-3.

Culinary Tourism

This growing subset of cultural tourism involves the pursuit and enjoyment of prepared food and drink. Culinary tourism often involves the actual preparation of foods as well. The food acts as a link between the land you are visiting and the culture of the area. Many in the industry believe the growing interest is due in large part to the increase of food-focused television programs. Examples of culinary tourism might include the following:

- touring an organic farm and dining on the harvest at the farm's restaurant

- an open-hearth cooking demonstration and meal in an historic inn's kitchen

- a spa retreat to learn about raw and vegan foods

- shopping at an authentic foods market and eating at its adjacent restaurant

- taking a cooking class from a local chef or expert while visiting a particular area

margouillat photo/Shutterstock.com

1-3 The use of technology is evident in some modern cuisine.

Sustainability

The foodservice industry is concerned about the environment. The amount of products purchased, utilities used, and waste created by the industry has a significant impact on the environment. Foodservice is an energy-intensive industry. There is a growing interest in utilizing products and practices that are sustainable. **Sustainable products and practices** can be produced or carried out over a long period of time without a negative effect on the environment.

Foodservice operations are adopting more sustainable practices when selecting food products, managing energy use, and dealing with waste, 1-4.

New Markets

The foodservice industry is moving into new areas of daily life to offer prepared meals. Americans are eating more meals that are prepared outside of the home. Busy lifestyles leave many people with no time to prepare their own food. According to the National Restaurant Association, foodservice's share of the dollars spent on food has risen from 25 to 48 percent since 1955.

Draz-Koetke/Goodheart-Willcox Publisher

1-4 Composting is a sustainable practice employed in many foodservice operations.

Following the trend, many foodservice operations offer home meal replacements. **Home meal replacements** are meals that are consumed at home but professionally prepared elsewhere. To respond to this demand, more restaurants now offer carryout meals. Take-home meals can also be found in supermarkets, office buildings, train stations, and airports. Some businesses operate strictly on a delivery basis with orders placed by phone or over the Internet. With more people working outside the home and longer hours, home meal replacements fill an increasingly important need.

In response to the rising cost of building and staffing a traditional restaurant, many chefs and restaurateurs are seeking out nontraditional venues to serve diners. Pop-up restaurants set up a temporary restaurant in a location for a short period of time and invite diners through social media. Many chefs and restaurateurs have launched food trucks. Food trucks are popular in densely populated cities. The trucks bring a limited menu of unique food products directly to the customers. Both pop-ups and food trucks are a means for operators to do business without many of the costs associated with traditional restaurants.

Challenges Facing the Foodservice Industry

All industries face challenges. Young people entering the industry should be aware of these challenges. As their careers develop, they will be called on to find solutions to these problems.

Meeting Labor Demands

As with most areas of the hospitality industry, foodservice is labor-intensive. Given the rapid growth of the industry and employee turnover, finding enough trained workers to fill all the jobs is difficult. This is one of the greatest challenges the industry faces. Attracting people to careers in food-service is one part of the problem. Keeping trained, experienced people involved in the industry is the other part.

One outcome of the industry's labor shortage is a growing reliance on nontraditional workers. Instead of full-time workers, many businesses rely more on part-time workers. Older adults are another group being recruited by some firms, 1-5. Recent immigrants from many countries play a critical role in meeting foodservice labor demands.

Living Wage

Many hospitality careers are rewarding and profitable. There are also many jobs that do not pay well. Some positions do not pay enough to support an individual. These people require another job to supplement their wages. A **living wage** is one that allows someone working full-time to support his or her family above the poverty level. The more training, education, and experience a person has, the better his or her earning potential.

CandyBox Images/Shutterstock.com

1-5 Many employers value the experience, responsibility, and skills older workers bring to the workplace.

Federal law sets a minimum hourly wage. However, it is not always a living wage. Some parts of the country have a higher cost of living than others. In these areas, people working for minimum wage may not be able to support their families above the poverty level.

Mix In Math

Percents

In the foodservice industry, as in other industries, percents are used frequently. Percents are used to describe the cost of ingredients for a menu item, a company's financial performance, popularity of a menu item, nutrient content of food items, industry trends, and much more.

Percent means part of a hundred. Therefore, if 15 out of every 100 guests order coffee with their meal, you would say 15 percent of guests order coffee. If your restaurant makes 5 cents profit on every dollar (100 cents) customers spend, you would say the company has a 5 percent profit.

There are three ways to write percents—using the percent sign, as a fraction, or as a decimal. No matter which way the percent is written, it is describing the same thing.

Percent Sign

The percent sign (%) is the symbol or shorthand for percent. You would write 15% to describe 15 guests out of 100 order coffee.

Fraction

The popularity of coffee can be written as a fraction as well. The 15% of guests who order coffee could be written 15/100 guests order coffee.

Decimal

To write 15% as a decimal, you simply move the decimal point two places to the left and get rid of the percent sign. As a decimal, 15.0% is written 0.15.

To convert a decimal to a percent, you multiply the decimal by 100, or move the decimal two places to the right, and add the percent sign. For example,

$$0.15 \times 100 = 15\%$$

Foodservice managers are challenged to come up with ways to pay higher wages and still meet the customers' demands for lower prices.

Nutrition Concerns

Americans are more aware of the effects of diet on health. As knowledge of the role that nutrition plays in health increases, so do demands for healthier menu options—low-fat, low-calorie, and vegetarian. Since people are consuming more meals away from home, the foodservice industry is challenged to meet these demands. Some people argue that foodservice operators—not the diner—should be held responsible for their diners' nutrition-related health.

When nutrition is not an issue, creating great tasting food that customers will buy is easier. The challenge is to produce food that is both satisfying and healthy. Knowledge of nutrition is constantly growing and changing. As this knowledge evolves, so does the definition of a healthful diet. The industry continues to struggle with what responsibility chefs and restaurateurs have for the health of their guests, 1-6.

In response to nutrition concerns, several trends have emerged. A number of high-profile chefs have used their celebrity to help educate consumers on the topic of healthful eating. Many restaurants are offering customers nutritional information for the items on their menus. In some cases, posting nutritional information is voluntary, but many foodservice operations are required to do so by law.

Draz-Koetke/Goodheart-Willcox Publisher

1-6 Chefs often work with dietitians to create healthful menus.

The Culinary Profession

The word *culinary* comes from the Latin word *culina* meaning "kitchen." **Culinary** refers to matters related to the preparation or cooking of food. A **culinarian** is a term for a cook or someone who prepares food.

Making sure that guests are well fed is at the core of any sense of hospitality. Therefore, the culinary arts are effectively the heart of the hospitality industry. Many in the hospitality industry refer to the kitchen as the "heart of the house."

A Wide Culinary Spectrum

The culinary arts offers a wide variety of employment options. Whether the job is fast-food employee or master chef managing a multi-restaurant resort, the goal is the same. The essential mission for all culinarians is to prepare safe and satisfying food for guests.

The number of cuisines and styles of cooking is vast. This great variety means culinarians always have something new to taste and learn. For those who always seek to improve and grow, the profession is never boring. Due to the wide array of cuisines and food products, no one can know all there is to know about food and cooking. For this reason, chefs often specialize in a particular cuisine such as Italian or Thai.

Culinarians may also choose to concentrate on one segment of foodservice such as casual dining, catering, institutional cooking, or pastries.

It's a Tough Profession

A celebrity chef prepares an artfully garnished dish to the applause of the TV studio audience. This is often the stimulus for a young person to consider a career as a chef. Many people outside the industry see only the glamour and fame that a few well-known, successful chefs enjoy. Those outside the profession are often unaware of the years of hard work, study, and sacrifice those chefs paid for their success. Often chefs that work in rewarding positions out of the public eye go unrecognized, 1-7.

1-7 Foodservice professionals often work long hours in busy kitchens with little recognition.

Work experience exposes new hires to the true rigors of the field. The physical demands of the culinary profession are great. The job requires the physical stamina to work in hot, noisy kitchens and stand for long periods of time while continuing to move quickly. Meeting deadlines can be stressful. Lifting and carrying are a large part of the job. The risk of cuts, burns, slips, and falls is always present. This field often requires working long hours, nights, weekends, and holidays. These schedules can place great demands on an individual's personal life.

The Real Rewards

With all the drawbacks of working in a professional kitchen, why does anyone choose a career in this field? Just as it is difficult for someone outside the industry to recognize the demands of this career choice, it is also difficult to see the rewards. A job in the kitchen offers the chance to be creative. The ability to see and taste what you create is unique to this profession. Additionally, many in the field derive great pleasure from the sense of hospitality found in satisfying diners, 1-8. Combined with these rewards is the love of good food. A driving passion for good food is what motivates most successful chefs and restaurateurs. In this profession, job satisfaction is high for those who love good food and enjoy sharing that passion with others.

Draz-Koetke/Goodheart-Willcox Publisher

1-8 Many culinarians find satisfying the needs of guests rewarding.

Summary Points

- Foodservice is the business of making and serving prepared food and drink. It is part of the larger hospitality industry and the second largest employer in the United States. Foodservice is an important part of the US and global economy.

- Foodservice trends are driven by larger influences such as economic conditions, political developments, social changes, and scientific and technological advancements.

- Important challenges facing the foodservice industry include meeting the increasing need for workers, balancing fair wages with customers' demands for low prices, and providing healthier foods.

- The culinary profession covers a wide range of cuisines and specialties. It is a physically demanding job but culinarians find satisfaction in the creativity the job offers and satisfying their customers.

In Review
Assess

1. How many Americans are employed in the foodservice industry?

2. List five segments that are included in the larger hospitality industry.

3. Identify three influences that drive trends in foodservice.

4. The foundation for most professional chefs is _____ cuisine.

5. Based on content in the chapter, what larger influence contributed to the pop-up restaurant and food truck trends?

6. Name five examples of how technology is used in foodservice.

7. How are foodservice operations adopting sustainable practices?

8. Why is there a growing demand for home meal replacements?

9. If there is a law setting a minimum hourly wage, why is a living wage for foodservice employees a concern?

10. List three challenges and three rewards of a culinary career.

Core Skills

11. **Math.** In this chapter, you learned that the foodservice industry's share of dollars spent on food is 48%. Convert 48% to a decimal.

12. **Speaking.** Pick a figure in this chapter, such as Figure 1-1, 1-2, or 1-3. Working with a partner, tell and then retell the important information being conveyed by that figure. Through your collaboration, develop what you and your partner believe is the most interesting verbal description of the importance of the chosen figure. Present your narration to the class.

13. **Writing.** Choose a trend or challenge in foodservice. Research the topic and write a two-page paper explaining why you think this trend or challenge is important. Identify factors that have created and shaped this trend or challenge. Predict where this trend or challenge will be in 5 years and in 10 years. Provide evidence to support your prediction.

14. **Speaking.** Prepare and give a speech about a time when you experienced hospitality. How were you made to feel welcome? Which of your needs were satisfied and how? Did the experience meet or exceed your expectations? Cite specific examples in order to convey your perspective.

15. **Reading.** Read an article or profile on a professional chef. How and when did he or she get started in the hospitality industry? What segment of the hospitality industry do they work in now? What rewards or challenges have they experienced in their career?

16. **CTE Career Readiness Practice.** Complete an oral history by interviewing a person who has worked in the foodservice industry. If you are unable to interview someone, read one or more case studies about working in the foodservice industry from reliable Internet or library resources. How does the information you learned from the interview

or reading compare to information presented by the authors of your text? Write a detailed summary of your interview or reading, describing how working in the foodservice industry affected the person's life.

Critical Thinking

17. **Predict.** Identify a current economic or social trend that you think will influence how or what people eat. In what ways could this affect the foodservice industry globally, nationally, and in your community?

18. **Organize.** Form small groups and debate the following topic: The foodservice industry has a responsibility for the nutritional health of its patrons. Organize evidence to support your argument.

19. **Analyze.** How have images of chefs in the media (television, magazines, newspapers, Internet) influenced your interest in culinary arts?

Technology

Use a spreadsheet program to calculate the value of US foodservice for each of the next ten years. Assume the value of the US foodservice industry is currently $657 billion and it is projected to grow 10 percent each year. Create a graph to show the results.

Teamwork
Teams That Work

Teams are formed to perform work, solve a problem, or achieve a goal. Teams may be short-term or ongoing. Regardless of the time frame, it is essential that a team is effective.

Effective teamwork requires

- contributing team members
- good communication skills
- organization and focus
- problem-solving and decision-making skills

Contributing team members—Team members fill many important roles. A leader is needed to focus the team, encourage participation,

assign responsibilities, and summarize decisions. Members perform essential duties such as analyzing problems, brainstorming solutions, completing tasks, and evaluating results.

Good communication skills—Team members must listen well, observe behaviors to deepen understanding, confirm understanding, and provide useful, respectful feedback.

Organization and focus—The leader must ensure the team stays focused on the task, meets deadlines, and fully participates.

Problem-solving and decision-making skills— To solve problems and make decisions, team members must define the problem, identify the root cause, offer possible solutions or alternatives, evaluate the alternatives, select an alternative, implement the decision, and evaluate the results.

Form a small team and apply what you have learned about effective teamwork to a simple task such as selecting a team name. You will have opportunities in future chapters to apply and develop your teamwork skills further.

Chef's E-portfolio
Creating a Portfolio

A portfolio is a selection of materials that you collect and organize to show your qualifications, skills, and talents. When you interview for a job, community service, or admission for college, you will need a portfolio to showcase your qualifications for the opportunity for which you are applying.

There are two types of portfolios that are commonly used—print portfolio or an e-portfolio. An e-portfolio is also known as a digital portfolio. Go to the Internet and search for an e-portfolio. Write an overview of how to create one. Build an e-portfolio and upload the overview you created to your new e-portfolio. Ask your instructor where to save your file. This could be on the school's network or a flash drive of your own. Name your portfolio document *FirstnameLastname_Portfolio Ch#.docx* (i.e., JohnSmith_PortfolioCh01.docx). You will be adding content to your e-portfolio throughout the class.

While studying, look for the activity icon ⬆ to:

- Build vocabulary with e-flash cards and matching activities.
- Expand learning with video clips, photo identification activities, animations, and interactive activities.
- Review and assess what you learn by completing end-of-chapter questions.

G-WLEARNING.com

LI CHAOSHU/Shutterstock.com

Understanding Foodservice Operations

2

Culinary Terminology Build Vocab

commercial foodservice, p. 17
noncommercial foodservice, p. 17
full-service restaurant, p. 18
catering, p. 19
chain restaurants, p. 23
franchise restaurants, p. 24

Academic Terminology Build Vocab

lucrative, p. 19
free enterprise, p. 21
sole proprietorship, p. 21
authority, p. 22
partnership, p. 22
corporation, p. 22
entrepreneur, p. 24

Objectives

After studying this chapter, you will be able to

- recognize various foodservice segments.
- compare and contrast the different forms of business ownership.
- summarize government's involvement in regulating foodservice operations.
- explain the different ways foodservice businesses are organized.
- summarize the risks and rewards of entrepreneurship.

Foodservice is a large industry that offers a wide range of jobs. Trained culinarians have many different opportunities to practice their craft. This chapter explores the many facets of the foodservice industry.

Foodservice Segments

When meals are consumed away from the home, it is often professional cooks preparing the meals. These are often purchased from businesses in the commercial foodservice segment. **Commercial foodservice** includes businesses with the primary goal of preparing and selling food to make money. Many other culinarians find work in the noncommercial foodservice segment. **Noncommercial foodservice** (also referred to as *institutional foodservice*) describes operations providing foodservice as a secondary activity for the business in which it is found. For example, a food concession in a baseball stadium is

Courtesy of Ballogg Photography

2-1 The elegant décor of this fine-dining restaurant matches the quality of food and service it offers.

secondary to the business of sports entertainment. There is some overlap between these two segments and some businesses may have features of both segments.

Commercial Foodservice

The commercial segment includes restaurants, hotels, clubs, and catering. Restaurants are the most familiar segment of the foodservice industry. Many people eat at restaurants every day. Restaurants can be categorized as full service or quick service.

Full-Service Restaurants **Full-service restaurants** employ servers to take the

customers' orders and bring the meals to their tables. Full-service restaurants span a range of styles from fine dining to casual.

Fine-dining restaurants offer elegantly prepared food, served by highly trained waitstaff, 2-1. Linen napkins and tablecloths, fine china, and crystal are used to create a refined atmosphere. Food served in fine-dining restaurants is of the highest quality. Menu prices in these restaurants are typically high. Fine-dining restaurants are popular for special occasions and business entertaining.

Casual restaurants offer simply prepared foods in less formal surroundings. There are many more styles of restaurants that fall somewhere between fine dining and casual.

These restaurants serve a wide variety of cuisines. Casual restaurants typically have moderate menu prices and therefore, enjoy repeat business from their patrons.

Quick-Service Restaurants   Quick-service or fast-food restaurants offer speed, convenience, and reasonable prices. Customers typically place their orders at a counter and serve themselves. Before the 1950s, the quick-service segment of the foodservice industry was very small. Today, fast food accounts for 38 percent of dollars spent on dining out in the United States. McDonald's and Subway® restaurants are leaders in the fast-food industry.

Quick-service restaurants usually offer limited menus. In this business, efficiency is the key to success. Quick-service restaurants are some of the most lucrative, or wealth producing, operations in the industry despite their lower menu prices.

Hotels   Travelers need lodging and a place to eat; therefore, hotels offer meals to their guests. Though smaller motels may not supply more than vending machines or perhaps a continental breakfast, large hotels often offer guests a variety of dining choices. These choices may include restaurants of varying styles and cuisines. The variety gives guests options when dining within the hotel property. Quality hotel restaurants serve the registered guests, but may also be popular dining spots for the community.

Along with restaurants, many hotels operate room service and banquet facilities. Room service delivers meals to guests in their rooms. Most large hotels have a number of banquet and ballrooms where they cater business and social events.

Clubs   Private clubs provide their members with certain activities. Country clubs offer golf and tennis. Other clubs may offer polo or yachting. Most private clubs maintain clubhouses with restaurant and banquet facilities for members. Members expect fine cuisine and excellent service for their high membership fees.

City clubs are often formed around social or professional organizations. Members use the club's dining rooms to conduct business as well as for entertaining. The cuisine at most city clubs rivals that of the finest restaurants in the area. Many clubs have foodservice operations of equal size and scope to hotels.

Catering   Catering is providing food and service for groups. Catered events are often held in a hall or banquet facility. Frequently, catered events are held in locations where food is not normally served, 2-2. Catering

A SERVING OF HISTORY

A Brief History of Restaurants

Taverns, an early form of restaurant, began to appear during medieval times. Taverns served a daily meal, or "ordinary," for a reasonable price to their patrons. *Traiteurs* (cookshops) also began to show up during this time. These were places where prepared foods, particularly cooked meats, could be purchased for carryout.

In 1765, the first dining establishment to be called a restaurant was opened in Paris. The owner's name was Boulanger. The word *restaurant* was coined from the restorative properties that Boulanger claimed his soups had. This first restaurant became immensely popular and was soon widely copied.

In the eighteenth and nineteenth centuries, Europe saw the rise in popularity of *cafés* (coffeehouses). These businesses sold the popular new drink imported from the Americas. In the British Isles, tearooms were similarly popular. These cafés and tearooms soon expanded their menus to include food and then full meals.

By the end of the 1800s, restaurants had become fully established. The practice of dining out was fashionable for all social classes.

Courtesy of Calihan Catering, Chicago, Illinois

2-2 Off-premise catering can take place in unique settings such as an airplane hangar.

these special locations is known as *off-premise catering*. Chefs who work in catering must be extremely organized when preparing for large numbers of guests.

The demand for catered events has grown in recent years. Social gatherings such as weddings, anniversaries, family reunions, balls, and proms are commonly catered. Business events, such as meetings and conventions, are also important to the catering industry.

Noncommercial Foodservice

Many cooks and chefs have careers in noncommercial foodservice. Noncommercial foodservice supplies meals onsite for businesses and organizations. These employers want to provide their clients and employees a place to eat without leaving the premises. Institutional foodservice fills that need. This segment of the industry is a source of many jobs.

Noncommercial Foodservice Settings

Corporations—Factories and office buildings often provide dining facilities for employees and clients. Catering the business' events is often an important duty of the foodservice departments.

Schools—Elementary schools and high schools maintain cafeterias to feed students and faculty.

Colleges and universities—Dining halls, restaurants, faculty clubs, and event catering are all part of most college foodservice operations.

Hospitals and nursing homes—Along with supplying meals for staff and visitors, healthcare foodservice has the responsibility of preparing food for patients with dietary restrictions.

Military—Many bases find it more effective to hire civilian contractors to provide foodservice. Officers' clubs are commonly staffed by civilian foodservice personnel.

Travel—Providing meals for passengers on airlines, railroads, and cruise ships is a sizeable sector of the industry. Foodservice outlets in airports and terminals are also important.

Parks and recreation—National, state, and local parks, and other recreational facilities offer concessions and full-service restaurants.

Stadiums and sports arenas—Along with concessions for snack foods, most stadiums operate dining rooms and skybox catering.

Convention centers—Large exhibition halls provide foodservice outlets for visitors as well as catering.

Prisons and correctional facilities—Employees and inmates must be fed with a variety of special meal requests and diet restrictions being accommodated.

2-3 Noncommercial foodservice is provided in a wide variety of settings.

Many cooks and chefs find fulfilling work in noncommercial settings, 2-3. Many of these positions offer better hours and benefits than restaurant jobs. Many of these foodservice operations are run by large companies called *contract foodservice*.

Legal Forms of Business Ownership

The economic system in the United States is based on free enterprise. **Free enterprise** recognizes and promotes a person's right to own a business and manage it with little intervention by the government. In this system,

few restrictions are placed on purchase of goods, sale of products and services, and form of ownership.

As with any business, foodservice operations can take different forms of ownership. The form of ownership affects how the business is run. It influences how decisions are made within the business. It can affect financing for start-up or expansion and ultimately how profitable the business is. The main forms of business ownership are sole proprietorship, partnership, and corporation.

Sole Proprietorship

A **sole proprietorship** is a business in which one person owns and often operates the business. The owner of this type of business is personally responsible for all debts of the business. Decision making in this type of business is simple. Sole proprietors have final authority, or control over, all decisions.

Partnership

A partnership is a business in which ownership is shared by two or more people. Partners should have a legal contract known as a partnership agreement. The agreement spells out the responsibilities of each partner and how profits (or losses) will be divided. In a partnership, each owner is personally responsible for all the debts of the business. Legally, the partnership is ended when one or more partners dies or leaves the business.

Corporation

Most businesses are formed as corporations. A corporation is granted a charter from the state, which recognizes it as a separate entity with legal rights. Ownership of the corporation is divided among investors in parts called *shares*. The number of shares owned is determined by the amount of money each shareholder invests.

Unlike sole proprietorships and partnerships, shareholders are not responsible for the debts of the corporation. The corporation has most of the rights and responsibilities of a real person. Therefore, the business is responsible for its debts. In addition, a corporation does not end when a shareholder dies or leaves. Corporations generally pay more taxes than other forms of ownership.

Foodservice Laws and Regulations

In addition to the legal form of ownership, there are many laws and regulations affecting the operation of a foodservice establishment. Laws and regulations are rules governing how a restaurant or other foodservice operation can conduct business. These rules may be enforced by one of three levels of government—federal, state, or local.

The federal government enforces laws and regulations covering
- employment and hiring practices
- workplace safety
- environmental issues

State governments dictate the largest part of how a business operates including such aspects as
- chartering a corporation
- establishing a sanitation code
- regulating pay and benefits

Local governments, either county or municipality, often enforce state health and sanitation codes through inspections. They also oversee
- zoning
- licensing and permit issues, such as business licenses
- building inspections
- liquor licenses

INDUSTRY INSIGHTS

NATIONAL
RESTAURANT
ASSOCIATION

Advocate for an Industry— The National Restaurant Association

The National Restaurant Association (NRA) is the leading US business association for the foodservice industry. The NRA has more than 60,000 member companies.

The NRA works to establish laws that benefit the industry. It promotes the industry and its contribution to the economy. The NRA supports industry research and provides information to its members on trends and business practices.

The NRA Education Foundation provides training for industry employees. It supports mentoring programs and funds scholarships.

Local governments often have more restrictive rules for local businesses than the larger state. Businesses must abide by the law or regulation which is most strict. The National Restaurant Association (NRA) and the state restaurant associations work to help government enact laws that are fair and beneficial to foodservice operators and their customers, 2-4.

Foodservice operators are responsible for obeying all federal, state, and local laws. To do so, it's wise to seek the counsel of a licensed attorney. There are many attorneys that specialize in legal issues related to the hospitality industry.

Organization of Foodservice Businesses

Once legal form of ownership is decided, there are other decisions to be made. Foodservice businesses can be organized in many ways. Each type of organization has its advantages and disadvantages. This section explains the different types of business organization commonly seen in the industry.

Independent Restaurants

An independent restaurant is a restaurant that is not a part of a group. Each independent restaurant is a unique operation with different ownership. They may have fewer resources than larger organizations, but they can quickly adapt to meet the needs of the guest.

Chains

Chain restaurants are a group of restaurants owned by the same company. Chain restaurants are often referred to as "multi-unit foodservice operations." A chain uses the same menu, décor, and management practices in each location. Outback Steakhouse restaurants are an example of a successful chain, 2-5. Successful chains work hard to make the food and service consistent among all their units.

The size of restaurant chains gives them an advantage. Purchasing for many restaurants allows chains to buy products for less

Laws and Regulations Affecting Foodservice			
	Source		
Area of Law or Regulation	Federal	State	Local
Hiring and Employment	•	•	
Worker Safety	•	•	
Food Safety and Sanitation	•	•	•
Zoning			•
Building Codes		•	•
Environmental Protection	•	•	
Smoking Ordinances		•	•
Liquor Laws		•	•

2-4 Foodservice operations must comply with a number of laws and regulations.

Courtesy of Outback Steakhouse

2-5 Chain restaurants often have distinctive themes.

INDUSTRY INSIGHTS

Marketing

Successful foodservice operators understand the importance of marketing. Marketing plans must include "the four Ps"—product, price, place, and promotion. In foodservice, the four Ps are

- **Product.** The restaurant or operation itself and the guest experience are the product with the menu playing a central role. Marketing plans define and ensure that the operation and its menu meet the expectations of guests.

- **Place.** It's long been said that the three most important keys to a restaurant's success are "location, location, and location." Choosing the right location for a restaurant or other foodservice operation is perhaps the most important part of the marketing plan.

- **Price.** Properly pricing the menu is essential for financial success in any foodservice operation. Pricing strategy must balance the cost of the product with the diner's perception of value.

- **Promotion.** Promotion is the means by which restaurateurs make their operations and menus known to potential customers. It includes advertising, public relations, signage, publicity, and communications.

Before a business opens, a marketing plan should be created based on detailed research and analysis. The marketing plan requires ongoing monitoring, evaluation, and possible adjustments.

cost than a single restaurant can. Chains can also benefit from centralizing training and administrative costs. On the other hand, it can be more difficult for chains to implement changes because there are multiple units.

Franchises

Franchise restaurants are independently owned restaurants that are part of a larger restaurant chain. The owner who pays for the right to operate a franchise is called a *franchisee.* The franchisee pays the franchise company for the right to use the brand name, concept, logo, and advertising. The franchise company requires the franchisee to use its products and operate the restaurant by its standards.

McDonald's is one of the most successful restaurant franchises. The majority of the McDonald's restaurants around the world are owned by franchisees.

Entrepreneurship

An **entrepreneur** is someone who organizes a business and assumes the risk for it. The foodservice industry offers many prospects for people wanting to open their own businesses. Culinarians are well prepared to

A SERVING OF HISTORY

Historic Entrepreneurs in US Foodservice

The Delmonico Brothers

The Swiss-born Delmonico brothers opened their restaurant in New York City in 1827. Delmonico's introduced the à la carte menu to America. Before that time, restaurants in the United States were taverns, inns, or hotels offering a table d'hôte menu. Delmonico's also made it acceptable and fashionable for proper society to dine in public. Delmonico's remained a New York institution until 1923. The restaurant introduced American diners to famous dishes such as the Delmonico steak, Lobster Newburg, Chicken à la King, and Baked Alaska.

Fred Harvey

Fred Harvey was an American entrepreneur credited with starting the first restaurant chain. In 1873, Harvey opened three restaurants along the Kansas Pacific Railroad. He later opened and operated more Harvey House restaurants and hotels along the route of the Atchison, Topeka, and Santa Fe railroad. Eventually, there were 84 Harvey Houses throughout the United States. Fred Harvey became known as "the civilizer of the West." Harvey House restaurants operated into the 1960s.

Howard Johnson

A Massachusetts businessman, Howard Johnson, created the first restaurant franchise in the 1930s. Howard Johnson was the first operation to allow franchisees to use the name, logo, and standardized food and supplies for a fee. The company was the first restaurant chain to establish centralized purchasing and a commissary system to distribute prepared food to the restaurants. The chain grew through the 20th century by capitalizing on the growing importance of the automobile and the highway system. Its easily recognized roadside locations with distinctive orange roofs offered travelers quality food and consistent service. Nicknamed "HoJo's," the business grew to over 1,000 restaurants and 500 motor lodges by the 1970s.

Colonel Harlan Sanders

In 1930, Harlan Sanders opened a restaurant in Corbin, Kentucky. The restaurant featured his unique method for preparing fried chicken. The chicken was cooked in a pressure fryer which was much quicker than the traditional pan-fried method. Sanders gained notoriety for his "secret recipe" and his restaurant prospered for years. In the 1950s, the interstate highway system bypassed his restaurant resulting in reduced business. He began to seek out restaurants to franchise his chicken recipe. Sanders, a great promoter with a dedication to food quality, ended up creating the Kentucky Fried Chicken chain. Today "KFC" is one of the most recognized brands worldwide with 15,000 restaurants in 105 countries.

Ray Kroc

Ray Kroc was a salesman for a milk shake mixer company when he saw a promising opportunity with one of his customers. The customer was a drive-in restaurant in San Bernadino, CA owned by the McDonald brothers. In 1954, Kroc became the franchise agent for the McDonald brothers. In 1961, he purchased the company from the brothers and launched the most successful restaurant company in history. Through strictly enforced standards for food and service, Kroc grew the simple hamburger stand into a franchise system that serves 68 million customers daily in 119 countries.

INDUSTRY INSIGHTS

Business Plan for Success

A business plan is a well-written guide for starting and running a business. This document is a valuable planning tool for the business owner. The business plan is also necessary when applying for a business loan. It introduces and explains your company to potential lenders and investors. A well-written and researched business plan will clearly inform interested parties about your operation and its potential.

A professional business plan begins with a cover sheet, statement of purpose, and table of contents. The body of the business plan typically includes the following sections:

Description of business. This section describes what your business is about. Be sure to include a description of your product or service and your customer. Describe your competition and how your business compares. Provide your business location and your rationale for choosing it. Include your goals for your business and how you will promote and grow your business to achieve them.

Management. This section should include the form of business ownership—proprietorship, partnership, or corporation. Provide an organizational chart including planned staff additions as business grows. Explain the responsibilities and experience of partners and employees.

Financials. Explain how much money is required to start and run the business for the next five years. Describe how the money will be used. List all sources from which you intend to receive financing. Describe your processes for budgeting and controlling costs. Include forecasts of sales and profits.

Production. This section should explain how the product will be made or the service delivered. List the facilities, suppliers, labor, equipment, and technology that will be used.

Documents. Include all the documents needed to support the information provided in the business plan such as résumés, budgets, copies of leases, research, and so on.

Studying business plans for existing businesses in the industry is a good way to learn more about this process. There are many resources available on the Internet such as the US Small Business Administration.

run their own restaurants. According to the NRA, most restaurants are independent operations. Seven out of ten of these companies have fewer than 20 employees. Small businesses require less money to start up and are easier to manage. Therefore, many entrepreneurs are attracted to foodservice businesses.

Chefs who succeed in business beyond the kitchen are often called chef-entrepreneurs. Successful chef-entrepreneurs possess more than great culinary skills. They enhance their culinary talents with business management expertise. These chefs must possess an ability to see the larger business environment and new opportunities.

Chefs who own their own restaurants are the most common example of chef-entrepreneurs. Many chefs aspire to be restaurant owners. Their desire is to impact not only the food being served, but also the dining experience. Many chefs use their culinary skills to develop catering businesses, cooking schools, and even food manufacturing companies. Other chefs publish cookbooks or produce their own television shows. Business opportunities involving food are nearly limitless.

Risks and Rewards

Most entrepreneurs are motivated by the hope of financial gain. Many also like the sense of being in charge and the excitement of starting a new business. But what happens if the business fails?

The entrepreneur often assumes a large part of the responsibility for repaying the debts of the failed business. Paying off the debts of an unsuccessful business can often take years. Given the fact that restaurants have one of the highest failure rates of any business, foodservice entrepreneurs take on a significant risk.

Being your own boss is one of the most obvious rewards of entrepreneurship. The experience of being involved in all aspects of the business and the contacts that you make will benefit you in all future endeavors. Successful entrepreneurs benefit financially as well. However, personal and professional pride in a successful business is probably the most valued reward.

INDUSTRY INSIGHTS

Chef Entrepreneur, Steve Ells

One of the most successful examples of chef entrepreneurship is Steve Ells, the founder, chairman, and CEO of Chipotle Mexican Grill®. Steve's success can be traced to his understanding of classic cooking methods and the importance of choosing the best ingredients—a philosophy he calls "Food with Integrity." After graduating from the Culinary Institute of America in 1990, he moved to San Francisco and spent two years working in the kitchens of Stars restaurant for noted chef, Jeremiah Tower.

During his time as an hourly line cook, he often ate at many of the modest Mexican restaurants in San Francisco's Mission District. Steve Ells was struck with an idea. In order to make enough money to finance his dream of a fine-dining restaurant, he would open a burrito shop.

Steve returned to Colorado. With a loan from his father, he rented a space for his restaurant and renovated it himself. His entrepreneurial risk paid off. Chipotle opened in July of 1993 with $450 in sales the first day. Within six months, sales had grown to $3,000 a day. A year and a half later, Steve opened a second restaurant. Within three years, there were seven restaurants.

Not long after this, executives from McDonald's Corporation took notice of Chipotle's popularity, focus on a limited core menu, and quality food. In 2001, McDonald's became the majority owner of Chipotle providing the company the expertise and capital to grow. By 2005, the number of Chipotle restaurants had grown to 500.

Today, Chipotle is an independent company whose stock is traded on the New York Stock Exchange. The chain has over 1,300 company-owned restaurants and over 2.2 billion dollars in sales. For Steve Ells, Chipotle's success is not only financial. He takes great pride in the quality of the food Chipotle serves, pointing out the use of naturally raised meats and poultry, the slow-cooking process of their signature pork carnitas, and the freshness of the food they serve.

Summary Points

- Foodservice operations are often categorized as either commercial or noncommercial.

- Restaurants can be categorized as full service and quick service. Full-service restaurants can be fine dining or casual. Quick service is also called *fast food*.

- Noncommercial foodservice supplies meals for businesses and organizations that want to provide foodservice for employees and clients.

- Foodservice businesses can take one of the following forms of ownership—sole proprietorship, partnership, or corporation. Each of the forms of ownership has pros and cons.

- Foodservice businesses need to operate under laws and regulations of the federal, state, and local governments.

- Independent restaurants are not part of a group. Chains are groups of restaurants with the same menu and décor. Franchises provide independent owners with a uniform foodservice operation for a fee.

In Review
Assess

1. Explain why hospital foodservice is considered noncommercial.

2. List three characteristics each of a fine-dining and casual restaurant.

3. List four ways hotels might provide food for guests.

4. What types of clubs commonly provide foodservice for their members?

5. True or false. Caterers provide food and service for large gatherings.

6. Events held in locations that do not regularly serve food is _____ catering.

7. True or false. A benefit of being a sole proprietor is that you have no personal responsibility for the debts of the business.

8. What are the owners of a corporation called?

9. If the county's health code is more strict than the state's, which must a foodservice operator follow?

10. Describe the difference between a chain and a franchise.

Core Skills

11. **Speaking.** Assume you are opening a restaurant. Decide whether your restaurant will be independent or a franchise. Outline the reasons for your choice and present to the class.

12. **Reading.** Research to learn the local government agencies and departments that regulate health inspections, building inspections, zoning, business licenses, and liquor licenses for restaurants in your community.

13. **Math.** You and a partner own a restaurant together. According to the partnership agreement, you are entitled to two-thirds of the profits (or losses) and your partner to one-third. Your restaurant did well this year and you and your partner are splitting $20,250 in profits. What is your share?

14. **Writing.** Write a brief paper about your favorite chain or franchise restaurant. Research and gather relevant information from a variety of sources. Explain the restaurant's form of ownership and history. Cite significant facts or quotations from your research.

15. **Reading.** Read a biography of a famous entrepreneur in the food industry. Based on your reading, identify the risks and challenges the entrepreneur faced. How long did it take for them to realize success?

16. **Speaking and Listening.** Divide into groups of four or five students. Each group should choose one of the following noncommercial foodservice segments: corporations, schools, colleges and universities, hospitals and nursing homes, military, travel, parks and recreation, stadiums and sports arenas, convention centers, or prisons and

correctional facilities. Using your textbook as a starting point, research your segment and prepare a report on the size of the segment, employment opportunities, typical work environment, and so on. As a group, deliver your presentation to the rest of the class. Take notes while other students give their reports. Ask questions about any details that you would like clarified.

17. **Reading and Speaking.** Select either a current or proposed law or regulation that affects foodservice. Conduct research to learn why the law or regulation came into being or was proposed. Identify what level of government enforces it. Consider the impact the law or regulation has on the foodservice business as well as the customer. Make a list of new vocabulary and learn their definitions. Prepare and give a presentation to share what you learned with the class. Adjust the style and content of your presentation to your audience. Use digital media to add visual interest and improve understanding.

18. **Listening.** Listen carefully as classmates deliver their presentations from the preceding activity. Take notes on important points and write down any questions that occur to you. Later, ask questions to obtain additional information or clarification from your classmates as necessary.

19. **CTE Career Readiness Practice.** Making small improvements in the way things are done can bring about great benefits. Do an Internet search for culinary entrepreneurs. Choose three individuals and explain how they used innovation to start a new culinary business or improve an existing business.

Critical Thinking

20. **Conclude.** If the fast-food segment continues to capture more of the dining market, do you believe fine-dining operations will exist in the future?

21. **Analyze.** Select a foodservice operation and describe its marketing strategy using the four Ps of marketing.

22. **Evaluate.** Do you believe a franchisee is truly an independent owner? Why?

Technology

Research a large hotel or resort's website to learn about the food and catering services offered. Select two of the services (for example room service and restaurant) and prepare a spreadsheet that compares the two. Download menus, pricing, hours and days of service, and other information for your comparison. How do the services differ in offerings and price? How are they similar? Which service appeals to you most as a potential customer?

Teamwork

Work with a small group of classmates to identify a foodservice business to open. Create a simple business plan that includes a basic description of the business, form of ownership, and the products and services offered. Include a brief marketing plan addressing the four Ps. Present your business and marketing plan to the class. Assign each member a portion of the presentation.

Chef's E-portfolio
Business and Marketing Plan

Upload the business and marketing plans created in the Teamwork activity to your e-portfolio. Ask your instructor where to save your file. This could be on the school's network or a flash drive of your own. Name your portfolio document *FirstnameLastname_ Portfolio Ch#. docx* (i.e., JohnSmith_PortfolioCh02.docx).

While studying, look for the activity icon ➲ to:

- Build vocabulary with e-flash cards and matching activities.
- Expand learning with video clips, photo identification activities, animations, and interactive activities.
- Review and assess what you learn by completing end-of-chapter questions.

G-WLEARNING.com

jsp/Shutterstock.com

Culinary History

Reading Prep

As you read the chapter, determine the purpose of the author. What aspects of the text help to establish the purpose?

Culinary Terminology
Build Vocab

grande cuisine, p. 36
indigenous foods, p. 37
classic cuisine, p. 37
haute cuisine, p. 37
nouvelle cuisine, p. 38
fusion cuisine, p. 38

Academic Terminology
Build Vocab

eclectic, p. 31
vacuum, p. 34
Renaissance, p. 35

Objectives

After studying this chapter, you will be able to

- explain why it is important to study culinary history.
- understand influences on culinary practices from ancient times through the 1900s.
- summarize the progression of the various styles of cuisine.
- explain the origins of American cuisine.

Understanding the past helps you to understand the present. Culinary history is a large subject; after all, people have been cooking for over 10,000 years. Studying culinary history reveals much about a people's social customs, ingenuity, values, and religious beliefs. By studying culinary history, chefs learn about past culinary practices. This knowledge gives chefs a better understanding of the present state of cuisine and where it is headed in the future.

This chapter gives a brief summary of culinary history in Europe and North America. This review of culinary history begins in the Mediterranean basin, travels through Europe, and finishes in America. Because the United States was settled largely by Europeans, there is a strong link between American and European culinary history. As the United States grew, its cuisine was influenced by every ethnic group that came to its shores. These worldwide influences coupled with the traditions of the Native Americans, shaped and continue to shape a new cuisine. The result is a cuisine that is **eclectic**, or composed of the best aspects of various cuisines.

Ancient Cooking

Throughout history, the job of the cook has been to prepare nutritious, digestible, flavorful food. In early times, cooks, hunters, and gatherers assured human survival. As agriculture developed, the endless struggle to find food was eased. Small cities appeared and people's standards of living rose. More complex cooking practices developed.

Though ancient cultures are often thought of as primitive, many of these cultures made major culinary breakthroughs with limited resources.

Early Asian Culinary History

Asian cultures also have a long and illustrious culinary history. At the time of ancient Greece and ancient Rome, Chinese chefs were preparing elaborate meals for the emperor. Through the centuries, China and India influenced the culinary traditions of many Asian countries through military campaigns and the spread of Buddhism and Hinduism.

For instance, rice, soybeans, and tea originated in China. Rice became a staple crop for much of Asia and tea became its universal beverage. Soybeans were turned into many products such as soymilk, tofu, and soy sauce. In a similar manner, the Indian use of spices influenced the cuisines of Southeast Asia and Indonesia.

While Chinese and Indian cuisines influenced much of Asia, each individual country developed its own unique cuisine. Often, differences between cuisines reflect different climates, religious views, and customs.

- Beef would not be eaten in India because the cow is considered sacred.
- In tropical Asia, dishes might be flavored with spices, tropical fruits, fermented fish sauce, and coconut.
- Parts of Asia that border the ocean subsist on seafood.
- Inland areas focus on using every part of the animal.
- In areas where it is too cold to plant rice, wheat is the dominant grain.
- In areas with large populations and little firewood, people learned how to cook items quickly over high heat in a wok.

The study of Asian cuisines is an enormous project!

Ancient Egypt

This journey through culinary history begins in ancient Egypt from about 3100 BC to 300 BC. Early writings reveal that the ancient Egyptians made yeast-raised and flat breads, tended bees, cooked assorted fishes from the Nile River, and raised animals for both their milk and meat.

Ancient Greece

Ancient Greece (750 BC–146 BC) rose to power as ancient Egypt declined. The cuisine of ancient Greece was simple, 3-1. It focused on food products, rather than on elaborate cooking techniques. Therefore, much effort was put into sourcing the best quality foods. Cooking techniques centered around spit roasting, boiling, baking, and grilling. As with present-day Greek cuisine, olives, honey, cheese, seafood products, grain products, lamb, and wild herbs were the mainstays of the ancient diet.

Ancient Rome

Ancient Rome (625 BC–476 AD) followed ancient Greece as the dominant power. Much has been written about the excesses of ancient Roman cuisine. As with many societies, there was a social elite that delighted in a refined cuisine that sometimes veered toward excess. At the same time, the largest part of the population existed on simple ingredients prepared simply. One such item was a porridge made from ground grains.

Bridgeman Art Library

3-1 Ancient Greek pottery gives clues to the cuisine of that time.

For chefs of Rome's elite, the wealth of ancient Rome allowed them to develop their art. They had a wide variety of imported and rare products at their disposal. Game animals and seafood products of all shapes and sizes were prepared in sometimes very complex ways. The chef's pantry contained many costly spices from Asia and Africa. Hams were imported from France and oysters imported from the British Isles. In summer, snow from mountaintops was rushed to Rome so chefs could prepare frozen desserts and cool beverages.

The most famous culinary name of ancient Rome is undoubtedly Apicius,

A SERVING OF HISTORY

Epicurius

The Greek philosopher, Epicurius (ehp ih KUHR ee us) (341 BC–270 BC), believed that there was no God and no afterlife. As a result, he believed that mankind's duty was to maximize pleasure. His philosophy, Epicureanism, has become associated with those in search of fine food. To that end, gourmets are sometimes referred to as Epicureans.

who lived during the first century AD. His cookbook, *De re coquinaria*, is the first complete Western cookbook. It was subsequently revised over the next several hundred years and remained the most important cookbook until the Middle Ages. Apicius' book describes challenging culinary dishes with complex flavor profiles. Many recipes call for scores of different herbs and spices. Honey, the common sweetener, is added to many of the savory recipes. Garum, a liquid that was produced from salted fermented fish, is routinely used for flavoring. It probably resembled the fish sauces used in many Asian countries today.

Cooking of the Middle Ages

With the fall of Rome to invading armies in 476 AD, Europe entered the Middle Ages. The Middle Ages lasted for at least 1,000 years. During these years, Europe was carved into smaller kingdoms that wrestled one another for power.

The Religious Influence

The Catholic Church filled the power **vacuum**, or void, and influenced European life and dining habits. For instance, the Catholic Church enforced many meatless and fast days. Catholic monasteries scattered throughout Europe preserved records of ancient cooking practices. These monasteries also preserved and improved the art of baking as well as cheese, wine, and beer making.

The Influence of Arab Culture

Another important power during the Middle Ages was the Arabs. They invaded and ruled southern Europe and northern Africa for hundreds of years. With the Arab culture came many new ingredients such as almonds, eggplant, citrus fruits, assorted spices, sugar, and rice. The invading Arabs also brought with them new recipes, techniques, and culinary traditions such as distillation and the addition of sugar and ground nuts to many savory dishes. With time, Arabian ideas and customs influenced food traditions throughout Europe.

Meals for the Masses

One common trait of societies during the Middle Ages was a rigid class structure. In general, societies consisted of a small aristocracy and a large majority of common people. The common people subsisted on local agricultural products, which each family grew for themselves. Their limited products were often cooked using simple techniques. For example, many homes kept a cauldron of soup constantly simmering above a fire. As vegetables and meats became available, they were added to the soup. Thus, there was always a soup ready to be eaten at any meal. In the winter months, survival became difficult as less food, especially fresh food, was available.

Meals for Royalty

Royalty, on the other hand, often ate well and employed many cooks to create lavish banquets. In the royal courts, dishes laden with costly spices were the norm. Sugar, which was very rare and considered a spice, was added to savory dishes. Acidic ingredients such as vinegar countered the added sweetness to create a sweet and sour effect. Complex edible visual creations were displayed or paraded at these banquets. Despite the grandeur of these meals, people in the Middle Ages ate with only a knife, and occasionally a spoon. The fork had not yet made its appearance; instead people ate their food on stale or roasted pieces of bread called *trenchers*.

Cooking of the Renaissance

Starting in the 1400s and ending in the 1600s, Europe was slowly transformed by the Renaissance, 3-2. The **Renaissance**, which means "the rebirth," marked the end of the Middle Ages. During this period, changes in science, art, thought, and music transformed Europe. Similarly, the culinary practices of the Middle Ages gave way to new ideas within the cooking for the aristocracy. Sauces became lighter and more refined. Dishes were streamlined and simpler to prepare. Cooking for the masses tended not to change that much.

During the Renaissance, the exchange of culinary traditions between France, Spain,

Morphart Creation/Shutterstock.com

3-2 During the sixteenth century, bread served as both a food when fresh and as a plate when it became stale.

and Italy increased greatly. As a result, the culinary arts practiced in the courts of the nobles became more refined. A significant event was the marriage of Caterina de Medici, daughter from a wealthy Italian family, to King Henry II of France in 1533. This added to the slow and steady refining of French cooking that would eventually lead to the popularity of French cuisine around the world in the following centuries.

Cooking Ingredients Crisscross Continents

The most important change to Western cooking resulted from the first voyages to the Americas. Early explorers traveled from Europe to find a cheaper route to buy expensive Asian and Indian spices. Instead, these explorers landed in the New World. From that moment, European and American culinary experiences would never be the same. New products such as tomatoes, potatoes, peppers, corn, chocolate, beans, and vanilla traveled from the New World to Europe. Other products such as wheat, citrus fruit, sugar, cattle, and pigs made the voyage from Europe to the New World.

Cooking of the 1700s and 1800s

During the 1700s and 1800s, cooking changed greatly. The first major shift occurred as the result of the French Revolution. Prior to the beginning of the French Revolution in 1789, chefs worked in the homes of the wealthy. As many of these wealthy elite either lost their lives or fled France, chefs lost their jobs. To find work, they turned to a new idea—the restaurant. Prior to the French Revolution, restaurants were nothing more than simple roadside stops for travelers. After the French Revolution and during the years that followed, restaurants became the main source of jobs for chefs, 3-3.

Bridgeman Art Library

3-3 Cafés were popular because they were light and spacious compared to average living quarters of the time.

It was during these two centuries that one of the most renowned chefs practiced his art. Antonin Carême (ahn tohn IN kahr EHM) lived from 1783 to 1833. He was a private chef to the social elite and royalty of his day. He did not work as a chef of a restaurant. Carême designed elaborate buffets and edible centerpieces, and managed the many cooks needed to prepare such meals. Indeed, many chefs still consider Carême to be among the greatest chefs of all time.

While renowned as a great chef, Carême was also the author of several famous and large cookbooks. In these books, Carême refined and systemized the grande cuisine. Grande cuisine was an elaborate and time-consuming style of cooking popular in the early 1800s that was often practiced in the homes of the rich. Despite this, Carême's

menus could still easily include 10 to 20 dishes. He was able to detail every aspect of cooking because Carême was also a famous pastry chef. Carême's written works would be the most important culinary books for the next 100 years.

The US Melting Pot

While Europe changed under the influences of the French Revolution and Carême, the United States began to change the face of North America. Early European settlers interacted with the Native Americans. They learned culinary techniques from each other and shared American and European food products. From these relationships, new dishes were created that took advantage of the best of both worlds.

Culture & Cuisine

Contributions from Africa

The one group of immigrants who came to America against their will was the millions of Africans brought here as slaves. This group had a significant impact on America's regional cooking. Slaves brought products such as watermelon, black-eyed peas, and okra from Africa. The slaves cooked on plantations and in doing so became talented chefs. The slaves also became the experts of Southern barbeque and developed a cuisine of their own called soul food. Soul food was based on the foods that the slaves cooked for themselves. Often, the slaves were given the least desirable cuts of meat or had to hunt animals such as raccoon and squirrel.

As the United States grew, waves of new immigrants added to the unique fabric of the new country. Each immigrant group brought their own culinary traditions. Each of these traditions affected what people would refer to as a "melting pot cuisine." The term *melting pot* comes from the image of putting all the different culinary traditions into one pot to create a new one. The result does not look like any one culinary tradition, but instead resembles them all.

Being a large country, various regional cuisines slowly developed within the United States. These regional differences resulted from the merging of the following factors:

- cooking traditions of local Native American tribes
- cooking traditions of the immigrant groups who settled in a particular region
- a region's climate, which favored only certain types of agriculture
- an area's **indigenous** (ihn DIH gehn us) **foods**, or those foods that were native or traditional to the particular geographic region or ethnic population

Food Safety and Availability

During the 1800s, many other important culinary advances took place. Long-term preservation of food by canning became commonplace during this century. Louis Pasteur (pahs TUHR) explained fermentation and bacteria, and invented pasteurization. As farming practices became more efficient, populations increasingly moved from the country to the city. As a result, advances in food transportation and refrigeration became necessary to feed growing city populations. For the first time in history, food products could be reliably frozen or refrigerated at any time of the year. It was also during this century that the first stoves were invented and popularized.

Cooking of the 1900s

The 1900s began under the influence of one of the most revered chefs, Auguste Escoffier (ehs kawf EEAY). Escoffier lived from 1846 to 1935. He spent his professional career as chef of some of the greatest hotels in France and England. Escoffier's contributions to cooking were many, 3-4. He reformed the professional kitchen into its modern organization. Escoffier stressed that cooks and chefs should always act as professionally as possible so they would be respected as professionals.

Escoffier simplified the still extravagant grande cuisine of Carême by serving fewer numbers of less complicated dishes. His famous book, *Le Guide Culinaire*, systemized classic cuisine. **Classic cuisine** was defined by orderly menus organized by courses that were served tableside by waiters in hotels and restaurants. *Le Guide Culinaire* continues to be a reference for chefs worldwide and is routinely studied by culinary students.

In the years following Escoffier, France continued to be at the forefront of haute (OHT) cuisine. **Haute cuisine** refers to the highest level of the culinary arts in which the most challenging dishes are prepared. Ferdinand Point

Mary Evans Picture Library

3-4 Auguste Escoffier began his career when he was 12 years old and retired at 74 years of age.

(1897–1955) and his restaurant La Pyramide in southern France popularized regional cooking.

Culinary Experimentation

Some of the chefs who trained at La Pyramide went on to challenge classical French cuisine in the 1960s. They introduced nouvelle (noo VEHL) cuisine, which means "new cuisine." **Nouvelle cuisine** was a style of cuisine that highlighted individual ingredients that were simply prepared and served in small portions on artistic plates. Nouvelle cuisine was a reaction against classic cuisine which, if poorly prepared, was overly rich and lacked inspiration.

Many of the chefs who introduced nouvelle cuisine were influenced by Asian food traditions. Contact between chefs on opposite sides of the world became increasingly common with air travel. As a result, many chefs turned to studying foreign

cuisines as a source of inspiration. Their travels allowed them to experience other food traditions firsthand.

In the late 1960s and early 1970s, Americans began watching cooking demonstrations on TV for the first time. Television chef stars such as Julia Child popularized French cooking. Other chefs in the 1980s and into the 1990s introduced more ethnic cuisines to the American palate. Thai, Mexican, Cajun, and Italian cuisines became increasingly popular. Some chefs then mixed the different cuisines to create various fusion cuisines. **Fusion cuisine** is the merging of two or more ethnic cuisines into one cooking style. Other chefs explored traditional regional American cuisines by creating variations of traditional favorites such as crab cakes and pot roast.

Culinary and Technology

A discussion of the 1900s would be incomplete without discussing technology. The last few decades of the 1900s and the beginning of the 21st century brought technological advances that dramatically changed the commercial kitchen. Increased air travel resulted in greater numbers of new food products arriving from all over the world. The kitchen environment changed with inventions such as the microwave, food processor, convection ovens, and induction cooking. The rise of the computer benefited chefs. Computers provided easy access to large amounts of information. Powerful software aided the chef in managing food and labor costs.

Technology also expanded communications media. Mass media such as magazines and television popularized wide interest in food and dining. As a result, the culinary profession enjoyed unprecedented visibility. This celebrity allowed a small number of chefs to become media stars and to create a brand name on everything from packaged food products to cookware to multiple restaurants in cities around the world.

A SERVING OF HISTORY

Historical Cookbooks

A number of cookbooks have been responsible for shaping culinary history. These cookbooks also give us a better understanding of the culinary practices of their time period. The following list represents some of the most influential cookbooks in Western culinary history:

- *Hedypatheia* by Archestratus, around 330 BC, ancient Greece. These fragments of an ancient poem describe different foods and preparations.
- *De re coquinaria* by Apicius, first century AD, ancient Rome. This classic ancient Roman text lists hundreds of diverse recipes.
- *Le Viandier* by Taillevent, late 14th century, France. This is the classic medieval text written by the chef to King Charles VI of France.
- *Le Cuisinier François* by La Varenne, 1651, France. This book represents a break from medieval food traditions in favor of lighter and less complicated cuisine.
- *La Cuisine Bourgeoise* by Menon, 1746, France. This cookbook was designed to cater to the new upper middle class in France.
- *American Cookery* by Amelia Simmons, 1796, United States. This is the first truly American cookbook. It lists recipes using American products and some preparations inspired by Native American traditions.

- *L'Art de la Cuisine Francaise au XIXeme Sieçle* by Antonin Carême, 1833, France. This enormous work was the foundation of grande cuisine in the 1800s.
- *The Epicurean* by Charles Ranhofer, 1893, United States. The chef of the Delmonico Restaurant in New York City wrote this book. It is very large and details haute cuisine as it was practiced in America.
- *Le Guide Culinaire* by Auguste Escoffier, 1902, France. This book was written for professionals and details the many dishes of classical French cuisine.
- *The Joy of Cooking* by Irma S. Rombauer and Marion Rombauer Becker, 1931, United States. This is the classic American cookbook that has been reprinted many times. It contains many recipes that reflect both international and American specialties. Many chefs often refer to it as a reference guide.
- *Mastering the Art of French Cooking* by Julia Child, Simone Beck, and Louisette Bertholle, 1961, United States. This book was behind the public interest in cooking upscale foreign cuisines. Its descriptions of classic and regional French cooking allowed amateur cooks to cook dishes previously only made by professional chefs. A second, equally important volume followed.

Summary Points

- Three ancient cultures—Egypt, Greece, and Rome—laid the foundations of Western culinary practices.

- The Middle Ages was marked by influence from the church and a rigid class structure that determined the foods that people ate. During the Middle Ages, Arab invasions into the Mediterranean basin changed Europe's eating habits.

- Exploration during the Renaissance resulted in changes in the food customs in Europe and the Americas.

- During the 1700s and 1800s, restaurants began to flourish. In America, a melting pot cuisine began to develop.

- In the 1900s, Chef Auguste Escoffier introduced classic cuisine. French chefs combined influences from their regional cuisines and others outside of France. In the United States, chefs started to explore American traditions.

In Review
Assess

1. Identify which ancient civilization (Egypt, Greece, or Rome) is associated with the culinary practices described in the following:
   A. The social elite enjoyed culinary excesses. Chefs cooked with imported spices, hams, oysters, and snow rushed from the mountaintops.
   B. Yeast-raised and flat breads were prepared. Domesticated animals were raised for meat and milk and bees were tended for honey.
   C. Focus was on simple preparation of quality foods rather than elaborate cooking techniques. Olives, honey, cheese, seafood, grains, lamb, and wild herbs made up large parts of their diet.

2. True or false. The first complete cookbook in Western civilization was written by Apicius in first century AD.

3. Explain how the Catholic Church influenced European food practices during the Middle Ages.

4. List four foods that Arabs introduced into Europe during the Middle Ages.

5. True or false. During the Renaissance, France was the source of culinary change.

6. Discovery of the _____ _____ during the Renaissance changed American and European culinary experiences forever.

7. Why did restaurants begin to flourish after the French Revolution?

8. American culinary tradition is often described as _____ _____ _____ because it is a combination of the culinary traditions of each immigrant group that has come to this country.

9. Antonin Carême is associated with _____ cuisine.

10. List three technological advances in the last decades of the 1900s that had significant impact on the professional kitchen.

Core Skills

11. **Writing.** Write a two-page paper on the history of a food ingredient that came to Europe from the New World (i.e., peppers, corn, potatoes, chocolate, etc.). Where did the food originate? How was it adopted in European cuisine?

12. **Math.** Create a time line to show a pictorial culinary history. Use one or more poster boards or a long sheet of roll paper to allow space to place pictures of the items at their proper locations on the time line. For each item you include, find out the year or century (for older items) in which the item was introduced. Then decide on a scale for the time line. For example, you may decide to allow 10 inches for every 10,000 years. Label the time line accurately according to your scale. Place the items at their correct locations on the time line.

13. **Speaking.** Choose a historic period that interests you. Prepare and give a two-minute presentation to your class about the food customs of that era.

14. **Listening.** Interview an older adult about foods they ate in their youth. What factors,

such as ethnic customs, where they lived, or economics influenced what they ate? Identify three ways that their diet was different than the foods you enjoy today.

15. **Math.** Spices were very expensive in the 1400s. Typically, master carpenters worked an 11 hour day during that time. It took 2¼ days' wages for a master carpenter to buy one pound of cinnamon. Today, it would take 20 minutes' wages for a master carpenter to buy the same amount of cinnamon. Based on the number of minutes worked, how many times more expensive was cinnamon during the 1400s than today?

16. **Reading.** Read a historic cookbook. Choose a unique recipe and update it for modern kitchens and contemporary diners.

17. **Reading and Speaking.** Identify a famous chef who practiced his or her craft during a different time in history. Conduct research to learn about the chef and prepare a presentation to share what you learn with the class. Adjust the style and content of your presentation to your audience. Use digital media to add visual interest and improve understanding.

18. **CTE Career Readiness Practice.** Regional differences influence local cuisines. You are opening a new restaurant in the United States that is to be unique and very representative of that particular region of the country. Select a region of the United States in which the restaurant will be located and research the area's history and resources. Draw conclusions about how these factors could be incorporated into the restaurant's menu. Write the menu based on your research and provide support for your decisions.

Critical Thinking

19. **Research.** Draw, trace, or download the outline of the continents on a world map. Highlight locations mentioned in this chapter as being influential to the development of

cuisine including Egypt, Greece, ancient Rome, India, China, Italy, and France. Research and chart overland and ocean spice routes between Europe and Asia.

20. **Conclude.** Why do you think that many culinary histories focus on the food practices of royalty and the wealthy?

21. **Infer.** Would it be correct to assume that cooks of ancient Rome would have made tomato sauce for Italian dishes such as pasta? Explain.

22. **Propose.** Part of being a chef is to anticipate future trends within foodservice. What are some trends that you think will be popular in the next five years?

Technology

Research the accomplishments of 19th century inventor Nicolas Appert and the influence of his invention on food. Cite another invention that changed what or how people eat. Compare and contrast its influence to that of Appert's invention.

Teamwork

Working in a small group, create a plan for a historical dinner based on a particular historical period. Create a menu, describe the service, sketch the décor and table settings, and present the plan in class.

Chef's E-portfolio
Recipe Collection

Begin your recipe collection. Upload the recipe you revised from the historic cookbook in the earlier activity to your e-portfolio. Ask your instructor where to save your file. This could be on the school's network or a flash drive of your own. Name your portfolio document *FirstnameLastname_Portfolio Ch#.docx* (i.e., JohnSmith_PortfolioCh03.docx).

While studying, look for the activity icon  **to:**

- Build vocabulary with e-flash cards and matching activities.
- Expand learning with video clips, photo identification activities, animations, and interactive activities.
- Review and assess what you learn by completing end-of-chapter questions.

erwinova/Shutterstock.com

Workstations in the Professional Kitchen

Reading Prep

Recall all the things you already know about how work in professional kitchens is organized. As you read, think of how the new information presented in the text matches or challenges your prior understanding of the topic. Think of direct connections you can make between the old material and the new material.

Culinary Terminology
Build Vocab

brigade, p. 43
executive chef, p. 45
banquet chef, p. 45

Academic Terminology
Build Vocab

hierarchy, p. 45
cross training, p. 46

Objectives

After studying this chapter, you will be able to

- recall the names and roles of workstations in the traditional brigade.

- recognize modern variations on the classical brigade.

- explain how the kitchen interacts with other departments to satisfy guests.

- summarize recent trends in foodservice to reduce labor.

Walking into a professional kitchen during a mealtime, you are struck by how busy it is. The pace of work and the variety of tasks is often astonishing. The amount of work done to prepare for the meal is astounding. So how do chefs and cooks organize the activities in a professional kitchen? Like any large job, the running of a big kitchen is broken down into many, smaller jobs. In this chapter, you will learn how the wide variety of jobs in the professional kitchen is organized.

The Brigade

Prior to the second half of the nineteenth century, most hotels were small inns. In the 1900s, classical cuisine was introduced to the professional kitchen at the same time very large grand hotels came into being. Grand hotels required grand kitchens. For the first time, chefs were preparing fine cuisine in commercial kitchens on a large scale.

Fine cuisine requires a large number of trained cooks to perform a wide variety of tasks. Coordinating the efforts of so many workers in a large kitchen required structure and leadership. Armies and navies were experts at organizing large numbers of people to accomplish a central task. Chefs chose the military's brigade system as a model. Large kitchen staffs became known as brigades because they were organized like the military. The **brigade** used a chain of command—each workstation had a leader and each leader reported to the head chef—to complete a task, 4-1.

In the brigade system, similar tasks and products were assigned by station. Most modern kitchens don't employ all the stations of a classical brigade. However, the

Brigade System

Workstation Positions	Duties
Chef de cuisine (shef deh kwih-ZEEN)	*Chef de cuisine* literally means "chief of the kitchen." The chef supervises all the positions in the kitchen. He or she is responsible for the quality of the food and the safety of the guests and cooks.
Sous chef (SOO shef)	*Sous* means "under" in French. The sous chef is the second in command. In the absence of the chef, the sous chef assumes the authority and responsibility of the chef.
Chef de garde (shef deh GAHRD)	Chef de garde is the night chef. In a large operation that operates 24 hours a day, the chef de garde is in charge of the kitchen after the chef has left for the evening.
Chef de partie (shef deh pahr-TEE)	A chef de partie is the position in charge of any of the particular workstations in the kitchen. In American kitchens, the chef de partie may be called a *station chef*. The number of cooks working in each station varies with the size of the kitchen and scope of the menu.
Saucier (saw-see-YAY)	As the name of the position implies, the saucier is responsible for making sauces. The saucier also prepares any sautéed or panfried items.
Poissonier (pwah-sawn-YAY)	Poisson is French for "fish" and the poissonier is the fish cook. This position is responsible for the preparation of all fish and shellfish items. In many kitchens, the poissonier is not under the direction of the saucier, but is the head of his or her own workstation.
Garde manger (gahrd mohn-ZHAY)	The garde manger is in charge of the cold food station. This position makes salads, dressing, fruit plates, and many types of cold appetizers and buffet platters.
Butcher	The butcher cuts and trims meats and poultry for other stations in the kitchen.
Rotisseur (roh-teess-UHR)	This position is charged with roasting meats and poultry and preparing pan sauces or gravies to accompany them. The rotisseur also carves these roasted items.
Grill cook	All grilled and broiled meats, poultry, and fish are cooked by the grill cook.
Fry cook	Deep-fried items are prepared and cooked by the fry cook. Since grilled items often have deep-fried garnishes, some kitchens combine the jobs of grill cook and fry cook.
Entremetier (ehn-treh-meh-tee-YAY)	The entremetier oversees the preparation and cooking of vegetables, starches, egg dishes, and hot appetizers.
Potager (poh-tahj-AY)	The potager makes all stocks, soups, and mother sauces.
Légumier (lay-goo-mee-YAY)	The légumier prepares and cooks vegetables. In some kitchens, the tasks of the potager and légumier are combined and known as the *preparation station*.
Pastry chef	The pastry chef is the head of the baking and pastry department. He or she oversees the work of specialists in that station.
Pastry cook	Pastry cooks prepare primarily sweets and pastries. These cooks work in the bakeshop during the daytime.

(Continued)

4-1 The brigade system organizes work in the kitchen to enhance productivity.

Brigade System *(Continued)*	
Workstation Positions	**Duties**
Baker	The baker makes breads. Duties of a baker may also include breakfast pastries. Bakers typically work during the night and early morning hours so breads are fresh for the beginning of the workday.
Decorator	Many bakeshops have a specialist who decorates cakes and pastries. The decorator also makes chocolate carvings or sugar sculptures for pastry displays. This job requires artistic ability.
Tournant (toor-NAHN)	The tournant is also called the *swing chef* or *roundsman*. This position fills in for other staff members on their days off. A versatile and talented individual is required to perform a different job each day.
Commis (koh MEE)	In addition to cooks, a department may also have one or more commis (koh MEE) or "assistants."
Communard (com-muh-NAHR)	In large operations, one person is assigned the task of preparing meals for the staff. This position is referred to as the *communard*.
Expeditor	In restaurants, the expeditor reads the servers' food orders to the cooks. This position then organizes the finished dishes so servers can deliver them promptly.

traditional names are often used for specific jobs in the kitchen.

The traditional brigade operated as a **hierarchy**, an organization based on rank and ability. This chain of command approach is still used in many large kitchens, 4-2.

Organization of Modern Kitchens

One hundred years ago, larger staffs were needed to work in kitchens than are needed today. Fewer cooks are needed to staff today's smaller operations equipped with modern conveniences and more limited menus. Despite the reduced staff size, a chain of command and the organization of tasks by stations still exist.

A foodservice operation's menu is the most important factor for determining the staff size and organization of a kitchen. A seafood house requires a large fish station, grill station, and fryer station. However, this

operation may have no need for a rotisseur. On the other hand, a restaurant specializing in steaks and prime rib of beef will have large rotisseur and grill stations. This business may need little or no staff to prepare fish.

Many large hotels and resorts operate a number of restaurants. Each restaurant has its own chef de cuisine and brigade. The hotel or resort employs an **executive chef** to coordinate the operation of the restaurants and departments. Many of the duties of an executive chef are managerial. However, an executive chef must also be an excellent cook in order to oversee the work of other cooks and chefs. Successful executive chefs interact often with all members of their team and even periodically work alongside them.

Most hotels have a special department that prepares banquets or meals for large groups. This department is headed by the banquet chef. The **banquet chef** oversees a staff of cooks that prepares meals for large groups.

The Classical Brigade

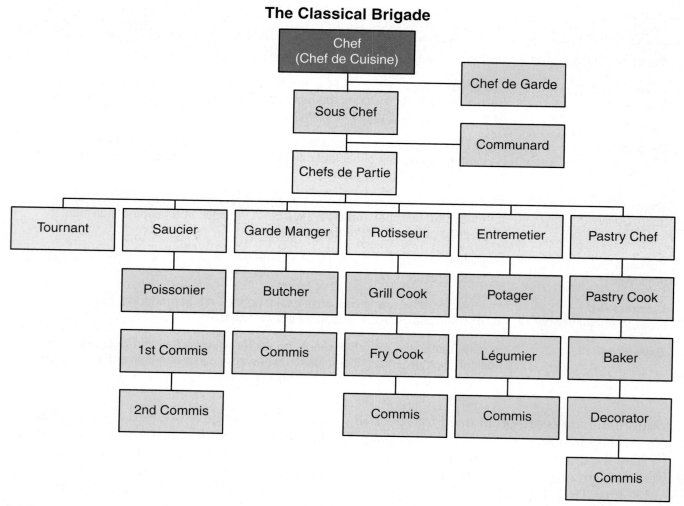

4-2 The organizational chart of a classical brigade illustrates how the department is ordered.

Cross Training

The traditional way of organizing work in kitchens created specialists. A cook performed one specific job and became expert at it. This narrow focus made very intricate food preparations possible. It also made labor hard to manage. What happens when the expert fish cook is out sick? Who works the position?

Cross training became popular because it solved this problem. **Cross training** teaches staff to do more than one job in the kitchen. Scheduling staff is easier when employees are cross trained. The chef has more flexibility in assigning jobs. If a cook is sick or quits, another employee can perform his or her job. Cross

training also eases the boredom associated with performing the same task every day.

Some restaurants take the concept of crossing training one step further. These businesses cross train employees to do all the jobs in the restaurant. This type of cross training has restaurant staff cooking, serving guests, or cashiering with equal ease.

Working with Departments Beyond the Kitchen

Foodservice operations in large restaurants, hotels, clubs, and resorts

INDUSTRY INSIGHTS

Teamwork in the Brigade

Luis, the banquet chef in a large private club, is preparing for an upscale wedding banquet. The hosts have chosen *Beef Wellington* for their main course. *Beef Wellington* is beef tenderloin baked in pastry with mushrooms and liver pâté served with a truffle sauce. Preparation of this dish demonstrates how stations in a large kitchen must work together.

Luis must work with other stations to assemble components of this dish. After receiving the menu for the party from the executive chef, he sees the butcher to get the beef tenderloin needed for the banquet. In the banquet kitchen, the banquet cooks brown the tenderloins as the first step in the preparation of the dish.

Luis sends one of his commis to the garde manger chef to get several pounds of liver pâté.

The pâté will be stuffed into the middle of the tenderloins. Luis also gets several pounds of mushroom duxelle that was prepared by the entremetier. The duxelle is spread over the surface of the tenderloins.

Once the tenderloins are seared, stuffed, and covered with mushroom duxelle, one of the banquet staff takes them to the pastry department. In the pastry department, one of the pastry cooks wraps each tenderloin in puff pastry.

The saucier prepares Madeira sauce with truffles and delivers it to the banquet kitchen. As time for the banquet meal gets closer, the banquet chef bakes the tenderloins. At service, Luis' staff slices the finished *Beef Wellington* and serves it with the sauce. The meal is a success because the brigade worked together as a team.

are complex. The kitchen must work with other departments to be successful. Efforts must be coordinated between the kitchen and the stewarding, dining room, catering, room service, and purchasing departments.

Stewarding

The stewarding department's primary task is sanitation. Warewashing—the cleaning of dishes, glasses, and serviceware—is done by this department. They also wash pots and pans. This department is often responsible for cleaning the kitchen as well. In addition to cleaning, people who work in stewarding store, inventory, and transport serviceware.

Because many tasks in the stewarding department require unskilled labor, its importance is often overlooked. Yet, this department is key to a good foodservice operation. Imagine a cook trying to serve a meal and there are no clean plates. Consider the impact of a kitchen being shut down by a health inspector due to poor sanitation. In all foodservice operations, cleanliness is crucial.

Dining Room

No matter how good food tastes, if not served properly the diner will not be satisfied. The kitchen works closely with the dining room to ensure that the carefully prepared food is served to the guest in a pleasing manner. Timing the cooking and serving of food is the most critical interaction between the kitchen and servers. If the food preparation takes too long or the food is cold, guests will be dissatisfied. Additionally, food must be served correctly and with a friendly attitude, 4-3.

4-3 The dining room staff works with the kitchen to provide excellent customer service.

Catering

In large operations that do banquets and catering, the sales staff and chefs must work closely to plan events. Chefs are consulted to create menus for large events. Communication between the sales, kitchen, and service staffs for large affairs is crucial to the success of catered events. During an event, banquet chefs consult often with the sales staff and servers to discuss timing of the meal service and special requests from guests.

Room Service

Larger hotels offer guests the option to dine in their rooms. Special staff is assigned to take room-service orders and serve them in guests' rooms. The food is prepared in one of the hotel's restaurants. In some cases, the hotel has a separate kitchen for room service. No matter where the food is prepared, good communication and timing between the kitchen and room-service staffs are essential to please in-room diners.

Purchasing

Many large operations have staff whose job is to purchase, receive, and store the food and supplies used by foodservice. The chef works closely with the purchasing staff to ensure the right products and correct quantities are being purchased. The staff issues food and supplies out of the storeroom to the kitchen staff as needed.

Culinary Trends

Cooking Under Vacuum

Vacuum packing has been used in commercial food production since the 1960s. Now sophisticated restaurant kitchens are using this method also known as *sous vide* (soo VEED). Sous vide is a technique that combines fresh ingredients in vacuum-packed pouches. These pouches are then cooked in a water bath or steamer. The pouches are then cooled and stored for future use. The vacuum packing seals in juices and the cooking process pasteurizes the food product. Sous vide is growing in popularity with chefs. It gives them freedom to prepare food to their specifications in advance and leave someone else in charge at service time. The end result is also very pleasing to diners as well. Due to the long, slow-cooking technique, special health and sanitary guidelines are often required.

Labor Saving Trends

The size of the kitchen staff needed to create fine cuisine in the 1900s is too costly for a modern kitchen. If the same number of staff were needed today, only the wealthy would be able to afford fine cuisine. Labor is one of the largest costs in the foodservice industry. The trend in foodservice is to reduce labor costs. Chefs have been successful using technology and prepared foods to control labor costs. This trend will undoubtedly continue.

Technology

Advances in the technology of food-service equipment have made great labor savings in the commercial kitchen possible. Food processors and grinders allow one cook to do the chopping and puréeing that used to take many cooks to do by hand. Vegetable cutting machines eliminate many hours of knife work. Roll-in rack ovens allow one cook to load and remove hundreds of portions from the oven quickly and easily.

Some kitchens prepare entrées for the entire week and vacuum-pack them in special plastic bags. During service, one cook can reheat and plate meals that used to take several cooks to prepare.

Prepared Foods

Many prepared food products designed to decrease labor in the kitchen are available to chefs today. Though these products cost more than the basic ingredients needed to make the item, less labor is used. Labor can be one of the largest costs for a foodservice operation. The labor savings means lower cost to diners. The labor savings is usually greater than the increased product cost. Prepared foods also contribute to product consistency. Some common labor-saving items in commercial kitchens include the following:

- Portion-controlled meats and fish
- Precut vegetables
- Trimmed and washed lettuce and greens
- Prepared sauces and soups
- Powdered soup base and sauce mixes
- Frozen precooked meats and vegetables
- Ready-made breads and pastries

Summary Points

- The kitchen brigade creates a chain of leadership and responsibility.

- The professional kitchen is organized into workstations to keep similar jobs and food products together.

- The staffing and number of stations is determined by the menu and size of the business.

- Cross training teaches staff to do more than one job in the kitchen. This gives the chef flexibility in assigning tasks.

- The kitchen brigade relies on other departments in a foodservice operation, such as stewarding and dining room staff.

- Chefs use technology and prepared food products to save labor and reduce kitchen staff.

In Review
Assess

1. Why did chefs use the military as a model for organizing the work in their kitchens?

2. What station takes charge of the kitchen in the absence of the chef?

3. List three responsibilities the saucier has.

4. Which station in the traditional brigade would perform the following tasks?
   A. Poach salmon filets.
   B. Portion a loin into steaks.
   C. Bake rye bread.
   D. Clarify a broth for soup.
   E. Cook dauphine potatoes.
   F. Fill cream puffs with whipped cream.

5. The _____ chef coordinates the operation of restaurants and departments at hotels and resorts.

6. What is an advantage of cross training?

7. True or false. The stewarding department purchases, receives, and stores food and supplies for the operation.

8. Why is timing between the kitchen staff and servers important?

9. List four prepared food products that decrease labor in the kitchen.

Core Skills

10. **Math.** Commercial food processors save time spent processing vegetables. Currently, three cooks each work 8 hours per day at a rate of $10.50 per hour processing vegetables. Only one cook will be needed to work the food processor for 8 hours per day at $10.50 per hour. If a food processor costs $5,376, how many days will it take before the cost of the food processor is paid for in labor savings?

11. **Reading.** Read a biography of Auguste Escoffier. Describe the organization of kitchens in his era. What experiences in his life influenced him to organize his hotel kitchens following the brigade system?

12. **Speaking.** Choose a restaurant or other foodservice operation and review its menu. Based on the menu and type of operation decide whether specialized workstations or cross training is best for the operation. Prepare and give a two-minute presentation to the class about your decision and the reasons behind it.

13. **Math.** A 40-pound case of butternut squash costs $14.00. After trimming and removing the seeds and dicing, 70 percent usable product is left. A cook earning $12.50 per hour works 45 minutes to prepare the squash. Peeled and precut squash is available from the produce company in a 20-pound case for $11.50. Which product is most cost effective? Find the overall cost of each product and show your work.

14. **Listening.** Interview someone who works in a large foodservice operation. How is the operation organized? What other departments does the department interact with? What would he or she change to improve how the operation functions?

15. **Speaking.** Working in a group, brainstorm ideas for creating classroom tools (posters, flash cards, and/or games, for example) that will help your classmates learn and remember the different workstation positions and duties in the brigade system. Choose the best idea(s), then delegate responsibilities to group members for constructing the tools and presenting the final products to the class.

16. **CTE Career Readiness Practice.** Working in a professional kitchen allows you the opportunity to work with a diverse group of people. Productively working with others who have a background different from yours may require that you learn to treat others as they wish to be treated. Conduct research on the Internet about cultural differences related to personal space, time, gestures/body language, and relationship toward authority figures. Create a T-chart that shows the difference on the left and ways you would adapt your interactions to account for that difference on the right.

Critical Thinking

17. **Organize.** Some employees resist cross training. Organize evidence and write a persuasive paper to convince those employees that cross training benefits them.

18. **Evaluate.** Managing labor cost is one of a chef's most important responsibilities. If a chef based his staffing decisions only on saving labor cost, how might this impact his operation?

19. **Recognize.** Identify equipment and food products that save labor hours in your kitchen at home.

Technology

Sous vide cooking technique uses technology to make kitchen work more productive. Research and report on the special equipment needed to execute this technique.

Teamwork

Working in groups of three, organize the foodservice for a hotel or resort with two restaurants and a catering department. Assign each team member a restaurant or the catering department and create an organizational chart showing staffing for each. Work together to combine these three charts in a larger organization chart that shows the hierarchy and departmental organization of the entire foodservice organization including purchasing, stewarding, and dining room staffs.

Chef's E-portfolio
Brigade System

Upload your *Chef's Journal* from *The Brigade System Lab Activity*. Ask your instructor where to save your file. This could be on the school's network or a flash drive of your own. Name your portfolio document *FirstnameLastname_Portfolio Ch#.docx* (i.e., JohnSmith_PortfolioCh04.docx).

While studying, look for the activity icon to:

- Build vocabulary with e-flash cards and matching activities.
- Expand learning with video clips, photo identification activities, animations, and interactive activities.
- Review and assess what you learn by completing end-of-chapter questions.

G-WLEARNING.com

Yuri Arcurs/Shutterstock.com

The Professional Chef 5

Reading Prep

In preparation for reading this chapter, locate and complete a personality test online to begin to understand your personality type, strengths, and weaknesses. As you read, consider whether your personality might be compatible with a career in culinary.

Culinary Terminology Build Vocab

apprenticeship, p. 64
American Culinary Federation (ACF), p. 64
certification, p. 64

Academic Terminology Build Vocab

resource, p. 55
professionalism, p. 57
diversity, p. 57
attitude, p. 58
stress, p. 60
conflict, p. 60
active listening, p. 67
registered dietitian (RD), p. 71

Objectives

After studying this chapter, you will be able to

- explain the various roles a professional chef must fulfill.
- understand the professional traits of successful culinarians.
- recognize personal behaviors that contribute to a successful culinary career.
- explain the various types of knowledge and expertise that a chef's job requires.

- summarize training and education options available to those seeking a career in culinary arts.
- recognize how essential leadership skills are developed.
- recall professions that require knowledge and skills similar to those of a chef.

The word *chef* is French for "chief." The title is short for *chef de cuisine*, or "chief of the kitchen." Any successful chef will tell you that the path to becoming a professional chef requires both study and hard work. One without the other makes an unformed and uninformed cook. Success also requires someone with special characteristics and motivation. This chapter explores what it takes to become a success in the culinary arts.

The Chef's Many Roles

The title of chef implies someone who can prepare creative, tasty dishes and has the skills and knowledge needed to run a commercial kitchen. The chef must fulfill many roles to accomplish these feats.

Cook

Cooking is the basis of skills and knowledge needed by a chef. No one can become a chef without first being an experienced cook. In order to oversee all the food being prepared in a kitchen, the chef must have experience at each position of the brigade. The chef must be knowledgeable of all the tasks each position in the kitchen must perform.

The chef must be able to judge the quality of food products being prepared by the cooks. This ability comes with experience. Without cooking skills, corrections and refinements to the work in the kitchen and the food being prepared are merely guesswork. In the end, the quality of the food being produced in a kitchen is often only as good as the experience of its chef.

Leader

The chef is at the top of the kitchen's chain of command and is the leader of all the cooks in his or her brigade. As leader, the chef organizes and directs the efforts of the kitchen staff to achieve his or her vision of cuisine.

The chef also assumes responsibility for the health and safety of the members of the staff. Often, the chef must enforce a policy or discipline a staff member. Fairness is the key to dealing with these difficult situations. When all members of the staff are treated with equal fairness, authority can be exercised without destroying the morale of the kitchen team.

The chef sets the professional standards for the kitchen. The most powerful way to influence behavior is by example. The chef serves as a model to those in the brigade. In the end, the level of professionalism the leader demonstrates by his or her actions is the level to which the kitchen staff will aspire.

INDUSTRY INSIGHTS

A Day in the Life of a Chef

José Luna comes from a family of chefs. He has six family members who currently work as chefs. He began cooking in his family's restaurant in his native Jalisco, Mexico at the age of 17. He has been a chef since 1979.

Chef Luna is Executive Chef of White Eagle Golf Club, a private golf club near Chicago. The club has 600 members. Chef Luna oversees a staff of 19.

Chef Luna is a Certified Executive Chef and a member of the American Academy of Chefs. He is actively involved in his local chapter of the American Culinary Federation.

The hours and responsibilities of Chef Luna's job are typical of most chefs managing a busy operation. The following is a typical workday for the chef:

10:00 A.M. On his arrival at the club, Chef Luna walks through the kitchen and greets his staff. His sous chef opens the kitchen earlier in the morning so the staff is already at work. Chef Luna has a brief meeting with the a.m. sous chef to review menu specials and parties for lunch.

(Continued)

INDUSTRY INSIGHTS

Continued

10:30 A.M. Chef Luna changes into his uniform and returns to the kitchen to check the staff's mise en place for the lunch menu. He tastes soups, sauces, and other prepared items to be sure they are up to standards.

11:00 A.M. Chef Luna meets with the dining room manager and the service staff to review the day's lunch specials and discuss the service of banquets for that day.

11:30 A.M. As lunch service begins, the chef spends time working with whichever station needs help. Once lunch service is in full swing, Chef Luna spends time as the expeditor calling orders to the various stations in the kitchen and coordinating the pickup of food with the servers. As expeditor, he also checks to be sure that the quality of food leaving the kitchen meets his standards.

1:00 P.M. The lunch rush is over and service has slowed down. Chef Luna has time to check his mailbox for notes on changes to upcoming banquets and functions. The chef makes a quick check of the food stores to determine what is in house to be used for dinner specials. He meets with the p.m. sous chef to write the list of specials for dinner.

1:30 P.M. Chef Luna makes an inventory of the coolers and storeroom. He determines what needs to be ordered and then places orders with his suppliers.

2:30 P.M. The chef checks on preparations for dinner with the p.m. sous chef and supervises preparation for the evening's banquets.

4:30 P.M. The chef and kitchen staff break for a "family" meal to eat and relax before dinner service.

5:00 P.M. Chef Luna meets with the line cooks to review specials for the dinner menu. He tastes prepared items to be sure that they meet club standards.

5:15 P.M. The chef has a preshift meeting with the dining room staff. He explains the ingredients and preparations of dinner specials, and servers get a chance to sample the specials.

5:30 P.M. The dining room opens for dinner. The chef helps his crew do prep work for the following day.

6:30 P.M. During dinner service, Chef Luna expedites and visits the dining room to speak with club members when his presence is requested. He checks regularly with the dining room manager to assure that diners are served promptly and satisfied with the food they are served.

9:00 P.M. The chef does a walk-through of the kitchen to be sure that everything is in order. He returns to his office to return phone messages and respond to e-mails.

10:00 P.M. Chef Luna makes a final check with the p.m. sous chef and leaves the club for the day.

Manager

As leader of the kitchen, the chef's role is to manage resources. A **resource** can be supplies, money, or staff that a company needs to do business. The most important resource a chef manages is the staff. Although the chef may delegate some authority to sous chefs and chefs de partie, the chef is ultimately held accountable for the performance of the kitchen.

Management has been defined as "getting things done through other people."

INDUSTRY INSIGHTS

Effective Teamwork

Teams are formed to perform work, solve a problem, or achieve a goal. Teams may be short-term or ongoing. Regardless of the time frame, it is essential that a team is effective.

Effective teamwork requires
- contributing team members
- good communication skills
- organization and focus
- problem-solving and decision-making skills

Contributing team members—Team members fill many important roles. A leader is needed to focus the team, encourage participation, assign responsibilities, and summarize decisions. Members perform essential duties such as analyzing problems, brainstorming solutions, completing tasks, and evaluating results.

Good communication skills—Team members must listen well, observe behaviors to deepen understanding, confirm understanding, and provide useful, respectful feedback.

Organization and focus—The leader must ensure the team stays focused on the task, meets deadlines, and fully participates.

Problem-solving and decision-making skills—To solve problems and make decisions, team members must define the problem, identify the root cause, offer possible solutions or alternatives, evaluate the alternatives, select an alternative, implement the decision, and evaluate the results.

1. What is required for a team to be effective?
2. List three duties of a team leader and of a team member.

The chef alone cannot perform every task that needs to be done in the kitchen. Other people must carry out the chef's concept of cuisine and the chef must manage their work. To be effective, the chef must
- communicate objectives and how they will be achieved
- check work while in progress and test finished products
- provide feedback
- give a clear and fair evaluation of the staff's performance

The chef is also charged with managing the nonlabor resources of the foodservice operation. These resources include food, nonfood products, equipment, and facilities. Making sure that these items are used properly and efficiently is one of the primary responsibilities of the chef.

Eliminating waste is critical to controlling costs. Cost control is essential for a business to make money. If a foodservice operation does not make enough money to at least cover its costs, it will go out of business. If the business closes, neither the chef nor the employees will have jobs. The chef's ability to manage resources impacts everyone.

Artistic Innovator

Many people are drawn to culinary arts because it gives them an outlet for their creativity. A cook has limited opportunities to be creative. It is the job of cooks to carry out the creative visions of the chef. The opportunity to exercise creativity is typically realized only by culinarians who are more experienced in the professional kitchen.

Chefs regularly need to create new dishes for daily specials and market menus. Occasionally, the chef needs to create an entirely new menu. Extensive knowledge of food ingredients and cooking methods is the starting point for a chef's creativity. Additionally, the chef must master the principles of presentation in order to create new items that are attractive as well as tasty. Finally, the chef must understand customer preferences for his or her creations to be successful.

Being in touch with current fashion and trends in food is essential for being able to create effective menus. Chefs continually read food periodicals to keep current. Dining out to sample the creations of other chefs is another way that chefs feed their creative interest.

Kzenon/Shutterstock.com

5-1 Successful chefs share their knowledge with staff.

Teacher and Mentor

Any successful chef is, by necessity, also a good teacher. A chef's success is largely dependent on his or her ability to train their staff. The chef teaches the staff cooking skills, management skills, how to deal with people, and more, 5-1. A chef requires good communication skills to be an effective trainer.

Aside from the benefit to the business from training their cooks, many chefs also feel a personal responsibility for teaching their staff. Sharing knowledge with the next "generation" is common among chefs. Many believe it is a way to repay the debt owed to those who trained and mentored them. There is perhaps no greater professional satisfaction than seeing someone who you mentored succeed in the profession.

Professional Traits of a Successful Chef

Culinarians are judged for the professionalism they display. **Professionalism** refers to the positive behaviors and appearance exhibited by an individual who is committed to a career in the culinary arts. Certain behaviors or traits are key for success in the professional kitchen.

Respectful

Demonstrating respectful behavior is recommended when beginning a career in the culinary arts. This shows that you have a genuine desire to become a professional. Respecting your coworkers and supervisors is essential for getting along in a busy, stressful professional kitchen. Without due respect, colleagues will be unwilling to share their hard-earned knowledge and skills.

One part of respect concerns diversity. **Diversity** means being composed of or including different elements. People with diverse religious beliefs, ethnic backgrounds, work experiences, educational levels, and languages work in foodservice. This diversity can add to the richness of a work setting. People from varied cultures share their native cuisines and lend input. To create a healthy work environment, diversity must be respected.

Cooks and chefs interact with many people during the course of a day. They must show respect to everyone. Respect for customers is at the core of hospitality. The true professional demonstrates respect for the food, kitchen facilities, and equipment as well.

CHEF'S ETHICS

Introduction to Ethics

Ethics are the principles of conduct governing an individual or a group. These principles deal with right and wrong behavior. As a professional in the foodservice industry, you will be expected to follow a code of ethics, or rules and procedures of professional conduct.

In all areas of life, you may face ethical challenges from time to time. How can you determine if the decisions you make conform to principles of good behavior? Ask yourself the following questions before taking action:

- Does my plan follow my employer's code of ethics and/or code of professional conduct?
- Is my plan fair, honest, and legal?
- Can I live with myself if following through with this course of action?
- Would I publicize my plan?

Punctual and Dependable

Timing and promptness are big factors in a foodservice operation's success. Prompt customer service results when staff members work together as a team. When a team member is late, it can disrupt the entire operation. Being punctual and ready for your scheduled shift is necessary if you want to keep your job and succeed.

Dependability tops every chef's list of traits needed for success. An employee is expected to report to work when scheduled unless he or she is physically unable to do so. If you are not on the job, another employee must assume your duties. Your supervisor must call in a replacement, or another employee must do your work as well as their own. People who play team sports know the best teammates are those you can count on when problems arise. The professional

kitchen is no different. Chefs and cooks prefer working with coworkers on which they can rely.

Everyone has instances when they cannot work their scheduled shift. Dependable workers inform their supervisors as soon as possible, if they will be absent or late. This gives the chef time to reassign the absent employee's duties.

Positive Attitude

Your outlook on life is reflected in your attitude. An **attitude** is how you think and feel about other people and situations. A cook with a positive attitude is an asset in the professional kitchen. He or she is more likely to achieve success. A popular quote states, "Success in life is ten percent what happens to you and ninety percent how you respond to it." How you respond to what happens in your life depends on your attitude. A positive attitude is key to success in any effort. The foodservice industry is no different.

A professional attitude requires a positive outlook, 5-2. The culinary field presents many challenges. Individuals who are easily discouraged do not last long in foodservice. The ability to maintain a "can do" attitude during difficult times is an invaluable quality in this field. Treating failures as learning experiences helps to foster a positive attitude. This approach to mistakes builds knowledge and advances careers.

The attitude and pride of successful chefs is evident in even the most basic tasks such as washing pots or peeling vegetables. The goal of a chef is to achieve the best results no matter how menial the job. This professionalism is seen in the pursuit of continuous improvements in quality and efficiency.

Flexible

When a chef enters the kitchen, he or she must be focused and mentally alert. The foodservice business is unpredictable. A

perform their jobs the same way they did when they entered the profession. A positive attitude toward change can lead to learning and advancement. Being receptive to new techniques, foods, and working conditions makes a better chef. Professional growth is inevitable when you are open to adopting innovations and change.

Productive

Kitchens are fast-paced places to work. Customers expect to receive their meals in a timely manner. Chefs expect their cooks to work skillfully. A skilled cook demonstrates a combination of speed, accuracy, and safety. Working efficiently comes with experience. Working quickly and efficiently leads to increased productivity. High productivity with matching quality is one of the marks of a professional. Chefs understand that beginning cooks do not work fast at first. Beginning culinarians should strive to increase their speed every day but never at the expense of quality or precision.

A part of contributing to the productivity of the kitchen team is initiative. *Initiative* means being able to start things independently. When you have been trained in a particular job, rather than waiting to be prompted on the next task, starting the next step independently is part of being productive. Even when you are unsure of the next step, asking "what needs to be done next" demonstrates initiative.

Productivity requires more than just the ability to work quickly. Time management also contributes to productivity and the ability to be effective on the job. *Time management* involves identifying the tasks that need to be accomplished, prioritizing these tasks, and then allotting an amount of time to be spent on each. Effective time management is useful not only on the job, but also in your personal life. It contributes to efficiency and productivity, and can help reduce anxiety.

Eric Futran/ChefShots

5-2 A professional chef demonstrates a positive attitude and takes pride in his or her work.

successful culinarian must be flexible enough to respond to unexpected events and adjust plans as needed. For instance, more guests arrive at a banquet than expected. Or the kitchen is overwhelmed by the early reservations arriving late and the late reservations arriving early. A flexible chef is mentally prepared to respond to any circumstance.

Chefs must be prepared to adapt their cooking methods or menu to fluctuations in resources. Chefs and cooks often deal with seasonal and market variations in food products. Good training and experience give chefs the flexibility to adjust and prepare a quality product.

In addition to being flexible mentally and with food preparation, good chefs adapt to and even welcome change. Few chefs

Personal Behaviors of a Successful Chef

The previous section discussed the work behaviors and traits that make a successful chef. However, there are personal behaviors that contribute to success as well. These are lifestyle traits that play a big part in building and sustaining a successful culinary career.

Maintain Balance

Burnout is common in the culinary profession. Some people quit their jobs or leave the field because the work can be physically and mentally overwhelming. Other less fortunate individuals stay in the field but turn to alcohol or drugs to help them cope.

Balance is key to achieving and maintaining success. A life that is devoted solely to career and professional activities is unbalanced. This is a sure path to professional burnout. Time spent on career training and advancement must be balanced with other interests and activities. Hobbies, reading, family, and community activities serve as relief from the pressures of work, 5-3. Balancing work and personal life can be challenging. The demanding work schedule common in the culinary field adds to the challenge.

StockLite/Shutterstock.com

5-3 Chefs who learn to balance work life with family and community are less likely to experience burnout.

Reflection is a great tool to help achieve balance. One outcome of this reflection is the ability to put life's matters in perspective. This perspective sheds light on the issues of balance or imbalance in your life.

Manage Stress

Everyday people experience differing levels of stress. **Stress** is a physical, mental, and emotional response to external pressures. Pressures can be caused by change, deadlines, or confrontation. Not all stress is bad. Some level of stress is necessary to keep life interesting and urge people to action. Levels of stress that are too high can negatively impact health and damage relationships.

The hospitality business is a stressful work environment. Culinarians must perform skillfully under substantial pressure. Deadlines are frequent and short. Customer expectations leave little room for error. The job requires long hours of physically demanding work. The work schedule often includes evenings, weekends, and holidays. It is easy to understand why stress is a concern in this field.

Because stress is part of the foodservice business, cooks and chefs must learn how to manage it in a healthy way. Long-term, unmanaged stress leads to health problems—depression, high blood pressure, insomnia, and others. Alcoholism, drug abuse, and smoking are examples of unhealthy ways of relieving stress. These behaviors are harmful to the individual, his or her family and friends, and coworkers. People who feel they cannot cope with stress should seek professional help.

Identifying the cause of and your reaction to stress is key to managing it. In order to reduce stress, you must eliminate what is causing it. This may require discussing work conditions or expectations with a supervisor. It may also mean settling a **conflict**, or disagreement, with a coworker. If stress levels do not improve, it may be necessary to find a new job with manageable stress levels.

Balance on the Plate

The demands of working in the culinary industry can be overwhelming. A culinary professional's health is affected when these demands create prolonged stress. Eating a well-balanced diet is one way to combat the effects of stress on the body. Nutrients that play a role in building immunity are protein, vitamins A, C, and E, and zinc. A daily meal plan should include whole grains, fruits, vegetables, low-fat dairy products, lean meats, and small amounts of unsaturated oils. These foods provide a balance of nutrients the body needs to maintain good health. Limit the amount of solid fats and added sugars that come from cakes, cookies, sodas, and ice cream. Many of these foods provide a lot of calories but very little nutrients.

Individuals working in the hospitality industry must find healthy ways to manage stress. Each person manages stress differently. Some positive ways include meditation, talking to a friend, exercise, reading, or hobbies. Stress management classes offer a more focused approach. Many schools, agencies, and sometimes employers offer these classes. Stress management classes are helpful because they teach you how to deal with stress before it becomes a problem.

Maintain Health

Working in a professional kitchen is physically demanding. Good health is necessary to do the job well. Like professional athletes, chefs must be in good physical condition to perform their best.

Younger culinarians often fail to get enough rest. The temptation to do too much on too little sleep is sometimes irresistible. Without proper rest, workers are less effective and more likely to be injured. Fatigue is a leading cause of accidents in the kitchen.

Regular physical exercise is key to maintaining health, 5-4. It is also effective for relieving stress. Working in a professional kitchen involves a great deal of physical activity. However, this work does not exercise all the muscle groups or the heart and lungs which is needed to be fit. An exercise routine should also include stretching to improve flexibility. Flexibility makes it easier to perform physical tasks in the kitchen without injury.

A healthy diet is another important element in maintaining health. Professional chefs receive extensive training in nutrition as part of their schooling. However, many chefs find that practicing healthy eating habits is one of the most difficult aspects of the job. It is hard to resist the temptation of the delicious, rich foods that are always

Diego Cervo/Shutterstock.com

5-4 Regular physical exercise helps chefs perform their job well and deal with stress.

present in the professional kitchen. Many chefs give in to the temptation. The fact that a chef's job requires tasting the numerous dishes the kitchen produces to ensure quality, adds to the problem. Maintaining a balanced, appropriate intake of food requires a conscious effort for chefs and cooks.

A Chef's Knowledge and Expertise

To be successful as a chef, an individual must be multifaceted. In addition to cooking expertise, a chef must be well versed in a number of other areas in order to keep the kitchen running safely, smoothly, and profitably.

Cost Accounting

Keeping a foodservice business running profitably is one of the most important tasks the chef has. Financial reports are compiled to determine how effective his or her efforts are. Chefs are responsible for providing the cost data for an operation's income statement. They must also be able to read and understand financial documents. Knowledge of basic mathematics and common bookkeeping procedures are needed for the job. These skills are essential when trying to control costs and increase sales for a successful operation.

Sanitation

The chef is the person who is ultimately responsible for sanitary conditions and the safety of the food products served. Understanding microbiology and basic chemistry is the foundation for sanitation management.

Knowledge of sanitation laws and regulations are a requirement of the chef's job. This knowledge is verified through sanitation certification. A chef must remain current in this area since periodic testing is required to maintain sanitation certification.

Laws of the Foodservice Industry

As with other businesses, restaurants and other foodservice establishments must operate within the law. Chefs must know and understand the laws that affect the foodservice industry. Every day, chefs must operate within the laws that govern the hiring and managing of employees. Transactions between restaurants and their suppliers or customers are also regulated by laws. Chefs must operate within the Truth-in-Menu laws as they write and prepare their menus.

Chefs who are business owners deal with an even broader range of legal issues. These issues may include building and zoning codes, liquor laws, and tax laws. It is not necessary to be a lawyer in order to own a restaurant, however, some training in hospitality law is recommended.

Food Science

At a basic level, cooking is simply a matter of following procedures. The ability to cook a wide variety of dishes and exercise creativity requires deeper knowledge. Understanding how foods react chemically and physically during the cooking process allows chefs to be better cooks, 5-5. When working with new food products or creating known dishes under new conditions, this knowledge allows chefs to achieve the flavor and appearance they want.

Nutrition

The role food plays in maintaining good health gains more attention every day. Chefs in all segments of the foodservice industry are called upon to accommodate diners' dietary requests. Since nutrition is a rapidly evolving science, new information on diet and health is regularly being made known. Chefs need to stay current with the latest information on nutrition to meet the demands of their guests.

Mike Liu/Shutterstock.com

5-5 Crème brûlée illustrates the use of food science to create a flavorful dish.

Knowledge of nutrition is also important because chefs must be able to communicate with dietitians and nutritionists. Chefs often work with nutrition experts to create menu items that fit various dietary restrictions.

Purchasing and Storekeeping

A large part of the chef's job involves selecting, receiving, and storing the food used in the kitchen. The position of chef requires someone with experience and knowledge of food products. Chefs also deal with vendors to negotiate the price and payment for supplies. Once those products are purchased, the proper receiving and storage of the products requires another skill set. Much of this knowledge comes from experience, but much more can be gained through study and training.

Food and Beverage Service

Since a diner's experience is impacted greatly by the quality of service, knowing the rules and procedures of table service is critical for chefs. In many operations, chefs are often the most knowledgeable about table service. Chefs often give guidance to the service staff about which plates and utensils should be used with particular dishes or the procedures of service for particular dishes.

Knowledge of beverages is also an important element of the chef's job. Chefs are often required to suggest appropriate beverages to accompany the dishes they create.

Equipment Maintenance

Equipment maintenance is an ongoing concern for chefs. Imagine a kitchen staff ready to prepare a meal with no working ranges on which to cook. Keeping the kitchen equipment up and running is an important task and the cost of repairs can be high. Chefs need to manage preventive maintenance on stoves, ovens, refrigerators, and appliances. They also need to know when to call in maintenance professionals.

Public Relations

Chefs often take on the role of spokesperson for their restaurants. Part of a chef's job involves visiting the dining room to interact with diners. A restaurant's marketing and promotions often center on the chef. This role is often called on to participate in charity events, give cooking classes, and appear in advertising.

In recent years, it has become common for some chefs to become celebrities. The public has developed a fascination with the culinary profession. Chefs receive requests to speak with food writers about their specialties or give cooking demonstrations on local television shows. Today, a chef must work on perfecting his or her communication and appearance to be comfortable when dealing with the media.

Education and Training Options

You may have the personal skills necessary for a culinary career, but you must pursue the education and training needed to succeed. You can choose from several options beginning at the high school level. The more education and training you have, the greater your career opportunities will be.

Apprenticeship

In times past, parents would decide what career was suitable for their child. If the career choice was a trade or craft, the family would seek out a master in that craft who was willing to teach their child the trade. The young person worked for food, lodging, and clothing while learning their trade. This training arrangement was known as an apprenticeship. An apprenticeship is a method of training in which a person learns a trade under the guidance of skilled tradespeople. After a standard period of time, usually seven years, the apprentice became a journeyman with intermediate skill in the craft. Journeymen received pay for their work.

Today, a culinary apprenticeship is an entry-level job, which incorporates a long-term, formal training program. The apprentice learns the trade from a skilled worker. The standard term of the apprenticeship is three years. At the end of an apprenticeship, the apprentice is tested to assure he or she is prepared to practice the trade.

The American Culinary Federation (ACF) is the largest professional organization for culinarians in the United States. The US Department of Labor has charged the ACF with the task of administering professional certification for cooks and chefs. Along with structured on-the-job training, the ACF requires classroom work in sanitation, nutrition, and management. After successful completion of the ACF apprenticeship, classwork, and testing, the apprentice receives the first level of professional certification as a certified cook or pastry cook. Certification confirms that a culinarian possesses certain knowledge, skill level, and experience, 5-6.

Formal Education

Historically, the art and craft of the professional kitchen was taught in apprenticeships. In the last fifty years, culinary arts has gained acceptance as a subject taught in schools. In the past, culinary programs were limited to career tech or trade schools. Today, the spectrum of culinary training and education has broadened to include high schools, colleges, and universities.

High Schools and Career and Technical Centers   Career and technical centers have been training young people for skilled jobs

Certification Levels for Culinarians
Certified Culinarian (CC)
Certified Sous Chef (CSC)
Certified Chef de Cuisine (CCC)
Certified Executive Chef (CEC)
Certified Master Chef (CMC)
Personal Certified Chef (PCC)
Personal Certified Executive Chef (PCEC)
Certified Pastry Culinarian (CPC)
Certified Working Pastry Chef (CWPC)
Certified Executive Pastry Chef (CEPC)
Certified Master Pastry Chef (CMPC)
Certified Culinary Administrator (CCA)
Certified Secondary Culinary Educator (CSCE)
Certified Culinary Educator (CCE)

5-6 American Culinary Federation certification is recognized as the benchmark for excellence in the industry.

for many years. The primary focus of these programs has been training students to be successful in their chosen careers. Career and technical centers offer classes in technical jobs such as computer systems and automotive repair. These schools have also included culinary arts and hotel and lodging management training in their mission for a long time. Internships and work-based experience are part of career and technology programs. Various industry certifications are obtained upon successful completion of the program and passing a written test.

Some career and technical programs are offered to students who attend traditional high schools. In recent years, high schools have begun to offer culinary and hospitality training. Many have redesigned their family and consumer sciences courses. Food preparation has been taught in these classes for many years. Now, many of these classes are career focused. These classes introduce students to opportunities in the culinary and hospitality fields. Entry-level positions can often be obtained on completion of these courses.

Associate's Degree Institutions of higher learning began offering a degree in culinary arts in the late 1940s. These were associate's degrees because the course of study for most culinary programs was no longer than two years. The value of a degree versus on-the-job training was debated for many years. Today, this degree is well established. Many consider it to be the standard level of education for culinary management positions.

Bachelor's and Advanced Degrees

Schools were not offering bachelor's degrees in culinary arts until recently. Previously, if a student wished to pursue a higher degree in culinary arts, he or she studied hospitality management. The evolution of culinary education from vocational

training to bachelor's degree recognizes how complex the field is. The job of a chef requires great skill and knowledge. Chefs are now regarded as professionals rather than tradespeople.

Currently, there are no degrees beyond a bachelor's degree in culinary arts. Individuals wishing to continue their studies must do so in the broader field of hospitality management. This discipline offers both master's and doctoral degrees.

On-the-Job Training

Many successful chefs have no formal training or apprenticeship. Due to the mobile nature of employment in the foodservice industry, the details of the chef's job can be learned by working in a series of different kitchen positions. The position of chef can be achieved based strictly on work experience.

Work experience is also an important part of formal culinary education. School alone does not give students the skills they need to be successful culinarians. Most recognized culinary programs include an internship or work experience component.

Which Option Is Best?

Many training options exist for individuals who want to become chefs. There is no one option that guarantees success more than another. An individual's personality and educational opportunities impact which option is best for him or her. Most successful chefs achieve their positions through a combination of formal training and on-the-job experience.

Lifelong Learning

Lifelong learning is essential for all culinary professionals. This is true for seasoned veterans as well as those just entering the field. A chef's job is complex. Trends in dining are constantly changing. New products for the professional kitchen are being introduced.

INDUSTRY INSIGHTS
Culinary Competition

Photo courtesy of Eric Futran/Chef Shots

Some people are motivated by competition. For chefs who wish to test their abilities against other professionals, there are many opportunities for culinary competition. For most chefs, the reason for competing is not for the awards but for the learning experience. Culinary competitions are a good way to keep skills honed. Competitions also showcase culinary innovations and promote professionalism.

Many professional competitions are sanctioned by the American Culinary Federation (ACF). The ACF standardizes rules, judging criteria, and the qualification of judges in keeping with internationally recognized standards. Culinary competitions may be staged for individual competitors or for teams of chefs.

While these dynamic conditions make the field exciting and interesting, they also require a commitment to continued learning.

Successful chefs expand their professional knowledge and skills through seminars, classes, travel, dining, culinary competitions, and trade shows. They make a point of reading cookbooks, magazines, and professional journals to remain current in their field.

Developing Leadership Skills

The chef is the leader in a kitchen operation. To lead a kitchen staff, chefs must develop skills in communication, decision making, and problem solving.

Not everyone is born with leadership qualities but they can be developed. Leadership skills are gained through experience. Many high schools and technical schools have career and technical student organizations (CTSO) that provide leadership opportunities for students.

Communication

To be successful, chefs must be able to communicate with those around them. This requires effective oral and written communication skills. Speaking and writing are classified as *verbal communications*. Good leaders know that *nonverbal communications* are also important—appearance, posture, gestures, and facial expressions all send a message.

A chef must be able to speak clearly and confidently with employees, customers, and suppliers on a daily basis. In addition, a chef's job often includes delivering informal as well as formal presentations. He or she must be able to plan a presentation that successfully communicates the intended message to the audience. Whether it is to inform employees about a new procedure or to share a best practice with a group of peers, a presenter should address a few basic guidelines when creating a presentation, 5-7

Presentation Guidelines

- *Identify the purpose.* Are you trying to inform, persuade, make a request, or give instructions? Answering this question will help focus your presentation.
- *Understand your audience.* Is the audience knowledgeable in the topic being discussed or unfamiliar with the subject? This understanding should guide your level of detail and vocabulary choices.
- *Know your time limit.* Prioritize and adjust the amount and type of information you share to fit the allotted time. Consider providing supporting details or facts in the form of handouts or visual aids.
- *Gather information.* Determine and obtain the information needed to support the purpose of the presentation. Be sure to cite sources where appropriate.
- *Choose a delivery method.* If you plan to use technology to enrich your presentation, be sure the necessary equipment will be available and that you know how to use it.

5-7 Successful presentations require planning.

Writing a Procedure

First Step: Collect Information

- Obtain information from sources such as operations or owner's manuals, individuals who are currently or who will be performing the procedure, and maintenance or service personnel.
- Record all the information you gather.
- Organize the information using a flowchart or mind map.

Second Step: Write the Procedure

- Write the procedure steps in sequential order.
- Be specific, but not wordy.
- Use active rather than passive voice.
- Use words the reader will understand.

Third Step: Format for Ease of Reading

- Include images or graphics to enhance understanding.
- Use bullets or numbered lists when appropriate.
- Employ white space and indents to improve readability.

Fourth Step: Edit, Review, and Revise

- Edit for accuracy and clarity.
- Recruit end users to review the procedure.
- Incorporate feedback.
- Proofread the procedure before distributing.

5-8 Procedures should be relevant, accurate, and easy to read.

Writing letters, e-mails, procedures, menus, product specifications, and other documents is a regular part of managing a foodservice operation. Effective writing is based on the "4 Cs of communication"—clear, concise, courteous, and correct. This is rarely achieved in a first draft. The writer must always edit and revise written communications to refine the message. When writing procedures or product specifications, the first step should be collecting information, 5-8.

Effective communication includes both sending and receiving information. Listening is as important to good communication as is speaking and writing. The best leaders use the technique of active listening. **Active listening** signals to the speaker that what he or she is saying is understood. These signals may include a forward posture, nodding in agreement, and maintaining eye contact.

Likewise, if the message is not understood, an active listener asks questions.

Decision Making and Problem Solving

As leaders, chefs are continually making decisions and solving problems. The decisions are made both consciously and unconsciously. Good decision making relies on analysis of

INDUSTRY INSIGHTS

Use Reliable Information for Decision Making

Before accepting and using new information to make decisions at school and at work, it is important to determine the reliability and validity of research sources. To determine the reliability of print or Internet research sources, ask the following questions:

- **Information:** Is the information what you need? What is the date of the information (is it current)? Can you document the accuracy of the information from other reliable sources (educational institutions, professional and trade organizations, government)? Is the information from a popular source (magazine, newspaper, Internet) or scholarly source (academic institution, trade journal, professional organization journal)? Is the information researched well? Are assumptions and conclusions supported with evidence? Is the information authoritative? Does the information carry endorsements from an educational institution or professional organization?

- **Author:** Who is the author and what are his/her credentials (degree, work experience, previous writings)? What are the author's qualifications and affiliations? What is the author's intent for the research (inform, instruct, persuade, entertain, sell)?

- **Bias/Objectivity:** Does the research address other points of view? Is any important information omitted? Is the writing style emotional or does it promote a certain viewpoint? Is the article or publication sponsored or endorsed by a political entity or special interest group? Is the author's bias obvious?

- **Publisher:** Is the publisher known as an educational, commercial, or trade publisher of quality or scholarly materials? What can you find out about the publisher from its website? What instructions does the publisher give potential authors for submitting book proposals and manuscript?

- **Quality:** Is the information presented in a logical sequence or structure? Can you clearly identify key points? Do the key points support a main idea? Is the text easy to read and does it flow well? Does the text use good grammar and correct spelling and punctuation?

---

the facts, weighing available alternatives, and implementing a plan of action.

Similarly, problem solving is a process:
- problem is identified
- the situation is analyzed to determine the cause or causes
- possible solutions are identified and evaluated
- a decision is made on which solution is best
- solution is implemented
- feedback is collected and analyzed to determine if the solution was successful

One form of problem solving that regularly arises for leaders is conflict resolution. *Conflict resolution* is solving differences between individuals or groups peacefully.

Conflicts regularly arise in the high-energy, fast-paced environment of the professional kitchen. Resolving conflicts is a skill chefs need in order to be successful. Conflicts are often resolved through compromise. Good leaders consider both sides of a conflict and deal with issues—not personalities. Successful conflict resolution maintains positive feelings of those involved and treats all parties fairly.

Career and Technical Student Organizations

Career and technical student organizations (CTSO) provide students with opportunities to develop their leadership skills. Family, Career and Community Leaders of America (FCCLA) and SkillsUSA are two CTSOs in which culinary students may participate.

FCCLA is a national CTSO for students in family and consumer sciences education through twelfth grade. FCCLA promotes personal growth and leadership development through family and consumer sciences education. The group also offers opportunities for training in Food Production and Services, and Hospitality and Tourism.

FCCLA stages competitive events for members enrolled in culinary arts and foodservice training programs. In these competitions, student teams produce meals using commercial equipment and professional techniques.

SkillsUSA is a national organization for high school and college students who are preparing for careers in technical, skilled, and service occupations. SkillsUSA was formerly known as VICA (the Vocational Industrial Clubs of America). It provides education experiences for students in leadership, teamwork, citizenship, and character development. Its programs also help to establish industry standards for job skills training in the lab and classroom. SkillsUSA promotes community service as well.

SkillsUSA programs include local, state, and national competitions in which students demonstrate work-related and leadership skills, 5-9. Contests in culinary arts and commercial baking require each student to prepare a multicourse meal or a series of baked goods to professional standards.

Allied Professions

There are many foodservice professions that require knowledge and skills similar to those of a chef. Many times chefs collaborate with these professionals. Some chefs find that their career paths may lead them into one of these related fields.

Photo courtesy of Lloyd Wolf for SkillsUSA

5-9 SkillsUSA offers culinary competitions in which students demonstrate their culinary preparation and presentation skills.

Research Chef

After gaining years of experience in the professional kitchen, some chefs are employed by food manufacturers as research chefs. These chefs create recipes for mass-produced food products. Most research chefs work in conjunction with food scientists to develop products that can be produced in a manufacturing plant rather than a restaurant kitchen. Typically, the food technologists solve the problems of manufacturing and packaging and the research chef assures that the flavor, texture, and appearance are as close to restaurant quality as possible.

INDUSTRY INSIGHTS

Professional Organizations

There are a number of professional organizations serving the culinary and foodservice industry. The following is a list of some of the better known:

American Culinary Federation (ACF). The ACF is the largest professional chef's organization in the US. It has been promoting the professionalism of chefs since 1929. Its mission includes certification, accrediting culinary schools, and holding culinary competitions.

American Academy of Chefs (AAC). The AAC is the honor society for members of The American Culinary Federation. These chefs have the highest standards and demonstrate the highest professionalism.

American Personal and Private Chef Association. This association provides education and networking opportunities for those working as personal chefs.

Asian Chef Association. The mission of this group is to create a community for Asian culinary professionals and its supporters to promote, support and inspire the art of Asian cooking.

BCA. This group is dedicated to creating exposure and providing educational and professional opportunities for culinary and hospitality professionals of color.

Bread Baker's Guild of America. This group is devoted to advancing artisan bakers, their suppliers, and specialists in the science of baking and baking ingredients.

International Association of Culinary Professionals (IACP). IACP is a professional association that provides education and networking for members engaged in culinary education, communication, and the preparation of food and drink.

Les Dames d'Escoffier International. Les Dames d'Escoffier is a culinary organization composed of women who have achieved professional success. Its mission is to elevate the profession through mentoring members and helping worthy students succeed in their culinary careers.

Multicultural Foodservice & Hospitality Alliance (MFHA). The focus of this organization is multicultural training and advocacy in the food and hospitality industry.

Research Chefs Association (RCA). The RCA membership is comprised of chefs and food scientists working in food manufacturing, chain restaurants, hotels, ingredient supply houses, consulting, and academia. It also includes other food professionals in R&D, sales, marketing, manufacturing, distribution, and the media.

Vatel Club. The Vatel Club is an organization of French speaking chefs and cooks. It assists members in finding employment and maintains, promotes and upholds the French Culinary tradition in the US.

World Association of Chefs' Societies (WACS). WACS is a nonpolitical professional organization, dedicated to maintaining and improving the culinary standards of global cuisines. This international body has 72 official chefs associations as members.

Women Chefs and Restaurateurs. The mission of Women Chefs and Restaurateurs is to promote the education and advancement of women in the restaurant industry and the betterment of the industry as a whole.

Personal Chef

Personal chefs are paid professional culinarians who regularly cook for the same individual, family, or group. Though personal chefs do not often cook on the same scale as chefs in commercial food-service operations, they still must exercise professional cooking and management skills.

Restaurant Consultant

Restaurant consultants are foodservice professionals who offer their expertise to other foodservice operators for a fee. They can help with many of the difficult aspects of the hospitality business such as business planning and restaurant start-ups. Some consultants specialize in menu development, marketing, and advertising. Restaurant consultants are often called into a struggling operation to troubleshoot and make suggestions to improve an operation's efficiency and profitability. Certain consultants specialize in helping restaurants find and hire chefs and managers.

Marketing and Sales

Being able to sell products to chefs requires a great understanding of the challenges that chefs face. People who market and sell to the foodservice industry must have detailed knowledge of how their products are used in various operations. Some of the best people in this field have substantial culinary training and experience. Many companies that make products for the foodservice industry hire former chefs and managers because of their knowledge and experience. Jobs in this field include sales representative, marketing and promotions, and technical support.

Culinary Instructor

The task of training professional chefs and cooks is growing. More individuals seeking a career in culinary arts choose some sort of formalized training. The ability to teach culinary arts combines two important qualities—a high level of culinary skill and the ability to teach in a structured educational setting. Culinary instructors are employed in high schools, technical centers, colleges, and the military. Additionally, many large foodservice companies run their own culinary training programs.

Registered Dietitian

Chefs often rely on nutrition professionals to verify nutrition information and analyze nutritional content of recipes. **Registered dietitians (RD)** are nutrition professionals who have completed at minimum a bachelor's degree in dietetics, an internship, and passed a national exam. They are also required to complete ongoing continuing education to maintain their registration.

In addition to training in nutrition, registered dietitians have extensive knowledge in food science, meal preparation, service, and management. Those nutrition professionals who work with foodservice clients need a working knowledge of the professional kitchen. Some dietitians work to increase the public's food knowledge and culinary skills to improve nutrition and health status.

Food Writer

Media coverage of food and cooking is growing. Writers specializing in food topics write for newspapers, magazines, television, and cookbooks. Along with a love of food and knowledge of cooking, most food writers have a journalism background or a degree in English.

Summary Points

- Running a kitchen requires a chef to fulfill more roles than just cook.

- Respectful behavior, punctuality, dependability, a positive attitude, flexibility, productivity, and speed are traits of successful culinarians.

- For a successful career in culinary arts, an individual must balance personal and work life, manage stress, and maintain good health.

- A wide range of knowledge and expertise is required to keep a kitchen running safely, smoothly, and profitably.

- Options for education and training in the culinary field include apprenticeship, formal education, or on-the-job training.

- Individuals who are training to be chefs can develop leadership skills as members of career and technical student organizations.

- Chefs have many career options in professions that require similar knowledge and skills.

In Review
Assess

1. Name the role that is being fulfilled by the following actions:
   A. Creating new daily specials or menus.
   B. Sharing knowledge of various skills.
   C. Influencing behavior by example.
   D. Getting things done through other people.
   E. Judging the quality of food produced by other staff.

2. What impact does punctuality have on a foodservice operation?

3. List four strategies that help prevent professional burnout.

4. True or false. All stress is bad.

5. List six areas other than cooking that a chef must have expertise in to keep the kitchen running safely, smoothly, and profitably.

6. What group oversees culinary apprenticeships and certification in the United States?

7. The _____ degree is considered the standard level of education for culinary management positions.

8. List two practices of chefs who are committed to lifelong learning.

9. True or false. Listening is as important to good communication as is speaking and writing.

10. Name two organizations that provide opportunities for culinary students to develop leadership skills.

11. A career that requires knowledge and skills similar to those of a chef is called a(n) _____ _____.

Core Skills

12. **Math.** You have recently been hired as chef of a large commercial kitchen. Part of your job involves managing the repair and maintenance costs for the kitchen equipment. Repair bills for the past 12 months were as follows: $435.92, $894.90, $237.07, $386.12, $444.20, $705.55, $289.00, $663.80, and $278.55. None of these repairs would have been necessary if preventive maintenance (PM) had been done on the equipment. You have decided to look into getting a PM contract for your kitchen equipment. A vendor has submitted a proposal to provide you with maintenance and repair on your equipment at a rate of $325.00/month. Apply the decision-making process to determine whether you should pay for monthly service. Show your work.

13. **Writing.** Write a one-page paper describing your personal career goal and your plans for achieving it. In your plan, identify your career goal and the level of education and/or training required to achieve it. Identify schools, training centers, and work experiences that will prepare you for your career. Include information about tuition and supply costs as well as earning potential. Research to learn about scholarships and grants that are available to help offset these costs. Use multiple resources when performing your research and cite them in your paper. Edit and revise your paper to ensure it meets the 4 Cs of communication.

14. **Speaking.** Find a communication activity online that demonstrates some aspect of communication discussed in this chapter. Adapt the activity if necessary to fit your audience and location. Lead the class through the activity. Following the activity, lead the class in a discussion about what was learned during the exercise.

15. **Reading.** Read a short biography of a well-known leader whom you admire. Identify three qualities that made that person an effective leader. Which of those qualities might be effective for a chef leading a large kitchen team?

16. **Speaking.** Research to learn about different types of stress such as positive stress (eustress) and harmful stress (distress). Use the guidelines in Figure 5-7 as you prepare an informative presentation for your classmates explaining different types of stress, the body's response to it, possible health effects, and ways to effectively deal with stress. Use digital media to enhance understanding and provide interest.

17. **Writing.** Use time management to plan your home and school responsibilities for one week. List your responsibilities, assign each a priority, and then allot an amount of time you will spend on each. At the conclusion of the week, write a few paragraphs summarizing this experience. Reflect on the impact, if any, on your energy level. Identify aspects that worked well and ways you could improve the process.

18. **CTE Career Readiness Practice.** Imagine it is five years in the future and you are starting your first full-time job. You know the work is fast-paced and demanding. Your goal is to maintain health and wellness by developing a plan for handling workplace stress. Investigate and evaluate the resources on the *National Institute for Occupational Safety and Health* link on the Centers for Disease Control (CDC) website. Then write your plan for preventing job stress.

Critical Thinking

19. **Analyze.** Select an individual whom you respect and admire. Describe how he or she displays professionalism in his or her chosen field.

20. **Problem Solve.** Working in small groups, select a problem that arises frequently in your class. Use the problem-solving steps discussed in this chapter to find a solution. Document how the group arrived at the solution and a brief evaluation of how well the process worked. Present your results in class.

21. **Identify.** To discover the impact of a positive attitude and respect for others, observe your friends, family, teachers, and employees and customers at the supermarket or mall for a few days. Make notes of instances of both positive and negative attitudes as well as respect you observe. Next to each instance, indicate how people responded to one another. For those negative instances, describe how the same situation could have been handled in a positive way.

Technology

Use the Internet to research culinary professional organizations listed in this chapter. Which of these organizations would you most likely join and why? How does the organization you chose promote professionalism? Does that organization have any activities for students or apprentices? How does the organization's website (design, ease of use, etc.) reflect its message?

Teamwork

Form a small team to organize and implement a community service project such as a food drive or working at a food depository. Write a brief summary describing the process and the role teamwork played in accomplishing the task. Consider any professional skills that you were able to enhance during this process.

Chef's E-portfolio
Career Plan

Upload your career plan that you developed in activity #13. Ask your instructor where to save your file. This could be on the school's network or a flash drive of your own. Name your portfolio document *FirstnameLastname_Portfolio Ch#.docx* (i.e., JohnSmith_PortfolioCh05.docx).

While studying, look for the activity icon **to:**

- Build vocabulary with e-flash cards and matching activities.
- Expand learning with video clips, photo identification activities, animations, and interactive activities.
- Review and assess what you learn by completing end-of-chapter questions.

Deklofenak/Shutterstock.com

Entering the Workforce

Reading Prep

In preparation for the chapter, research one of the laws discussed in this chapter. Keep in mind the main purpose and provisions of this law as you read.

Culinary Terminology
Build Vocab

culinary apprenticeship, p. 87

Academic Terminology
Build Vocab

goals, p. 75
reference, p. 77
résumé, p. 77
cover message, p. 80
work ethic, p. 84
benefits, p. 87
on-the-job training, p. 87
probation period, p. 87
progressive discipline, p. 88
Fair Labor Standards Act (FLSA), p. 90
minimum wage, p. 90
Equal Employment Opportunity Commission (EEOC), p. 90
sexual harassment, p. 91
workplace diversity, p. 91

Objectives

After studying this chapter, you will be able to

- understand how to prepare for a job search.
- recall sources for finding job opportunities.
- explain factors to consider when submitting a résumé.

- summarize the importance of completing a job application form.
- understand effective behaviors when interviewing.
- explain what employers expect from workers.
- recall what employees can expect from their employers.
- summarize various laws and conditions of employment in this country.

How do you see your future in the foodservice industry? The ultimate objective might be to become a professional chef. The process of becoming a chef involves a number of career stages over a period of years. The first stage is entering the foodservice workforce.

Preparing for a Job Search

To enter the foodservice workforce, you must find a job. Before you begin your job search, there are a few tasks you should complete to be prepared.

Identify Desired Job

You must know the type of job you are searching for before you can apply for it. Depending on education and experience, there are different basic levels of jobs in professional kitchens, 6-1. The job you are searching for today is probably not the job you want to do for the rest of your life. You can improve your life by setting goals. **Goals** are the aims you

Career Steps in a Professional Kitchen

Job	Description	Minimum Education and Experience Requirements
Cook's Helper	Assists cooks and chefs with various jobs such as cleaning counters, equipment, and floor. May clean vegetables, slice fruit, and prepare simple items.	No education or experience required. Most skills learned on the job.
Prep Cook	Works under the direction of line cooks and sous chef to do basic kitchen tasks including cleaning produce, cutting food ingredients, measuring or weighing ingredients, portioning finished products, and making sure the kitchen and equipment are sanitary.	No education or experience required. A high school education or basic reading and math skills usually required to perform many tasks. Most skills learned on the job.
Line Cook	Responsible for a specific area of the kitchen such as broiler, grill, fry, sauté, bakery or pantry. Prepares product and cooks food for service.	Many line cooks learn by being a cook's helper or a prep cook. Some line cooks begin after attending a career and technical high school or two-year college program.
Sous Chef	Acts as second-in-command of the kitchen. Directs cooks and other kitchen employees under supervision of chef. May perform other duties as delegated by the chef, such as ordering supplies.	Sous chefs may work their way up from line cook positions. Some sous chefs have attended career and technical high schools, two-year or four-year college programs. Some work in an apprenticeship with a chef.
Chef	The manager of all the employees in a professional foodservice kitchen.	Chefs may work their way up the ranks from line cook through sous chef. Some chefs have attended career and technical high schools, two-year or four-year college programs. Some work as an apprentice with a chef and then work their way up through the different steps.

6-1 Experience and education will help you advance in your career

strive to reach. Securing a particular job in the next few months is a *short-term career goal*. Becoming the executive chef of a large hotel, owning your own restaurant, or competing in an international culinary competition are examples of *long-term career goals.*

Ideally, jobs you consider in your search should help you achieve your career goal. The types of positions you hold and experiences you gain in the workplace are possibly the most important factors in achieving long-term career goals. You must assess your experience and skill level in order to determine the job that is appropriate for you. Even though many individuals would like to start out their career

at a top-level job, years of education and experience are needed to qualify for those positions. An honest self-assessment of your skill level will help you identify jobs that you can apply for with the greatest chance of success.

Determine Contacts and References

Develop a list of people that you can contact to help you in your job search. Examples of contacts might include school career counselors, parents or other relatives, and friends that know about or work in the

INDUSTRY INSIGHTS
Developing Goals

The ability to set and achieve goals is key to success. Well-defined goals meet certain criteria. They must be specific (S), measurable (M), attainable (A), realistic (R), and timely (T). Use the acronym SMART to remember how to create effective goals.

A specific goal is unambiguous. It should describe precisely what you intend to achieve. A specific goal answers the questions who, what, when, where, why, and how.

A goal that is measurable allows you to track your progress. For instance, setting target dates for completing various stages is one way to measure your progress.

An attainable goal is one that you can achieve. Nearly any goal can be achieved with enough thought, planning, and effort. For example, if you lack certain skills necessary to achieve the goal, part of your goal must include a plan for acquiring those skills.

Realistic goals are practical. An unrealistic goal may simply require further development. For instance, a goal to be an executive chef at a Michelin 3 star restaurant immediately after graduating from high school is not realistic. This goal needs to be divided into incremental goals such as acquiring an associate's in culinary arts from an accredited program, completing an apprenticeship, and passing the certification exam.

A timely goal will have an appropriate time frame for completion. Using the previous example, a timely goal might be to acquire an associate's in culinary arts in two years.

1. Write a goal that is specific, measurable, attainable, realistic, and timely.
2. Use callouts to show where each of the SMART criteria is met in your goal statement.

valuable. Personal contacts go a long way in convincing an employer to hire a job applicant.

As you build your list of contacts, you should also ask appropriate contacts if you could use them as a reference. A **reference** is a person that knows and can discuss your work history and personal qualities. Examples of references are coaches, teachers, and former employers. Relatives should not be used for references. Before looking for a job, find three adults that agree to serve as references and ask for permission to use their names. Write down each reference's name, phone number, address, and why he or she is a reference in order to be ready to provide the information when asked. During the application or interview process, you may be asked to provide a list of references.

Write Your Résumé

Most employers ask applicants to provide a résumé. A **résumé** is a summary of the important information about an applicant. It provides an employer with a brief outline of an applicant's work history, education, and other relevant information such as awards, certificates held, and languages spoken. Résumés must be easy to read because a typical reader scans a résumé.

A good résumé is neat, accurate, and concise, 6-2. When writing your résumé include the following:

- Your full name and contact information including an address, telephone number, and e-mail address.
- An objective describing the type of job you want or your career goal.
- A work history listing jobs held, internships, or other relevant experience such as volunteer positions.
- Information about the location of the employer, relevant duties, and dates of employment should be given.
- Education information listing the names and addresses of schools attended, programs of study, grade average, and

foodservice industry. These contacts may have personal knowledge of job opportunities in the field. A personal introduction to someone seeking to fill a position is very

Andrea S. Jones
2638 Orrington Avenue
Evanston, IL   60201
Home: 190.534.2368
Mobile: 190.444.2368
E-mail: ajones@xxxx.net

Job Objective	To obtain a line cook position in a hotel fine-dining restaurant.
Work History	
6/11 to present	Pantry Station Cook, Ritz-Carlton, Chicago, IL
	Responsible for cold food production (mainly salads and sandwiches) for lunch and dinner in the hotel's casual restaurant, The Café.
9/09 to 9/11	Volunteer, HELP, Inc., Evanston, IL
	Cooked weekly Sunday dinner at a home for victims of domestic violence.
Education	
6/11 Associate of Applied Science, Culinary Arts	Kendall College, The School of Culinary Arts, Chicago, IL
	GPA: 3.5/4.0; Externship: Ritz-Carlton, Chicago Illinois
Certifications	Illinois State Sanitation Certificate
Honors and Scholarships	President's Scholarship, Kendall College, 1/10
	2nd Place–American Culinary Federation Student Culinary Salon, 9/10
Special Skills and Interests	Computer: Microsoft Office Suite including Word, Excel, PowerPoint, and Access
	Language: Fluent in French

6-2 Your résumé is a potential employer's first impression of you.

graduation date, as well as any individual workshops or courses related to the position.

- Other information such as awards, activities, memberships, licenses, certificates, and skills and interests that relate to the job.

A résumé is an opportunity to make a good first impression. It is a primary tool for getting an interview with a potential employer. Paper versions of your résumé should convey a businesslike image. Printing your résumé on good quality white paper is recommended. Avoid colored or embellished paper and exotic type faces. Potential employers are interested in what your résumé says not its style.

Keeping an electronic version of your résumé is necessary as potential employers may request that you submit your résumé electronically or via e-mail. You can also post your electronic résumé to online job-search sites. Be sure that your electronic résumé is formatted on software that is accessible and readable from the operating systems most common to businesses. If in doubt, check with your schools information technology specialist.

Your Portfolio

A portfolio is a selection of materials that you collect and organize to prove your qualifications. Qualifications are qualities and skills that confirm you are suitable for a job. Portfolios for chefs commonly include awards, menus, press clippings, and examples of work such as photos of plate and buffet presentations.

There are two types of portfolios that are commonly used—print and electronic- or e-portfolios. Print portfolios are often bound in a book or case that can be taken to job interviews. An e-portfolio is also known as a *digital portfolio*. E-portfolios are often maintained on a website. An electronic résumé is a key component of your e-portfolio. Likewise, if your portfolio is accessible via a website,

the web address can be included on your résumé.

The beginning of the job search process is a good time to review and update your portfolio. To help you create your own portfolio this textbook has an activity in each chapter titled "Chef's E-portfolio."

Finding Job Opportunities

The next step is to find the jobs to which you can apply. Begin by communicating with the individuals you identified as your job-search contacts, this is also called *networking*. Let your contacts know that you are looking for employment, the type of job you are looking for, and give them a copy of your résumé.

Other good sources of information on job opportunities are professional publications such as newsletters, magazines, and newspapers published for the foodservice industry. Sources of these publications are schools that train people for foodservice jobs. The public library and Internet can be useful in identifying these publications. Many of these publications also have websites that can be accessed by the public. Daily newspapers have a classified advertisements section that may be a source of employment opportunities.

Another option is to research and contact an employer directly. You can do this using telephone books or business directories. If there is a business you are interested in working for, send them a résumé and letter expressing your interest in employment with their company.

Using the Internet for a job search is also effective, 6-3. The benefits of an online search are that it can be done at any time of the day or night, provides you with a broad range of options, and demonstrates your proficiency with technology to potential employers. There are many job search websites that specialize in restaurant, foodservice, and hospitality jobs. Available positions can be

Elena Elisseeva/Shutterstock.com
6-3 The Internet is an effective way to search for jobs and research potential employers.

searched based on criteria such as location, experience, and salary.

The most effective job search would use all of the sources discussed in this section. Failing to pursue one or more of these sources may result in missed job opportunities.

Submitting Your Résumé

Once you have identified a job opportunity, your résumé should be submitted promptly. Many positions require you to submit your résumé online, often by e-mail. Be sure to read the company's directions for how résumés should be submitted and carefully follow them.

A résumé should be accompanied by a cover message. A **cover message** is a letter or e-mail that introduces yourself, indicates why you are contacting a potential employer, and provides a sample of your writing ability. This letter is also the chance for you to highlight your qualifications. Match your qualifications to those the employer is looking for but do not simply repeat information from the résumé. A good cover message should also demonstrate that you have researched the company. You could mention experience with their cuisine, a recommendation from someone who works there, or that you are familiar with their reputation, 6-4.

A good cover message is short and to the point. Close the message with a "Thank you" and an action statement indicating how and when you will follow-up with the employer.

Job Application Form

Many companies ask you to complete a job application form when you apply for a job. The form may request information that is on your résumé in addition to other information required by the employer. Application forms often request information about your education, references, and work experiences. Therefore, it is important to bring your list of references and a summary of your work experience and dates of employment, as well as, schools you have attended, degrees, and dates of attendance.

If the company is not hiring at this time, the form is kept on file for future hiring needs. If the individual is hired, the form becomes part of his or her record of information that the employer maintains for each employee.

Hiring managers typically review the prospective employee's résumé as well as the job application form when deciding whether to interview the individual. Prospective employees are judged by the content as well

Sample Cover Message

Andrea S. Jones
2638 Orrington Avenue
Evanston, IL   60201
190.534.2368
E-mail: ajones@xxxx.net

September 9, 20XX

Mark Hopkins
Human Resources Manager
Nationwide Hotel Group
San Francisco, CA 94128

Dear Mr. Hopkins:

I am submitting my résumé for the position of Line Cook in the Point Reyes Room that was advertised in the San Francisco Chronicle. I plan to relocate to the Bay area and am excited about the opportunity to work at a restaurant with such an outstanding reputation.

My fine-dining experience as a student in The Dining Room at Kendall College and working in The Café at the Ritz-Carlton in Chicago provide me with the skills and background to make a significant contribution at the Point Reyes Room. In addition to my fine-dining culinary skills, I have taken courses in computerized inventory management and worked with the chef with online ordering for The Café.

My résumé provides more information on my education and work experience. I would like to discuss my qualifications for the position with you at your earliest convenience. Toward that end, I will call at the end of this week to determine if you have reviewed my résumé and to schedule a time when we can discuss my qualifications.

Thank you,

Andrea S. Jones

6-4 A good cover message convinces an interviewer to read a résumé.

as how the form is filled out. Therefore, it is important to be neat when filling out the form. Unless told otherwise, the form should be printed in ink or typed. The form should have no stains and be free from dirt. Some organizations require the job application to be filled out electronically, either online or at a computer terminal at their location. This makes management of numerous applications easier for the employer and also allows them to screen applicants for basic computer skills.

There are a few additional points to consider when filling out a job application.

- Read the form completely before beginning to fill in the information.
- Match information given on the résumé to questions asked on the job application.
- Answer all required questions on the form. Failing to answer all the questions raises concerns.

A properly completed job application form does not guarantee an interview. A form that is sloppy, dirty, or incomplete may eliminate the possibility of getting an interview.

Interviewing

The interview is a personal meeting between you and a potential employer. The person conducting the interview may be the person for whom you would work such as the chef in a kitchen. The interviewer may be a manager or human resources professional trained to conduct interviews. The interview is an opportunity for both parties to learn about one another. The employer wants to determine if the applicant is qualified for the job. The applicant wants to learn more about the prospective employer.

Whether you are the interviewer or interviewee, it is important to remember that interviewers are prohibited from asking applicants certain types of questions, 6-5. Questions should be focused on determining the applicant's ability to perform the job. Often when interviewers ask an illegal

question it is because they have not been properly trained on interviewing techniques. Your best response to an illegal question is to phrase your answer so that it confirms your ability to do the job.

Some interviews may be conducted in an office and be more structured. Other interviews may be conducted while the interviewer is working on the job. Or, a busy chef might take a few minutes and sit with an applicant in the dining room. Whatever the circumstances of the interview, there are several ways an applicant can present his or her best image.

- Prepare for the interview by learning enough about the employer to discuss why you want to work there.
- Dress appropriately and look clean, well groomed, and professional.
- Introduce yourself and give a firm handshake.
- Answer the interviewer's questions as specifically as possible. When possible, provide examples of your experience or work that indicate you would be right for the job.

Prohibited Interview Questions

- How old are you? What is your date of birth?
- Are you married? With whom do you live?
- Are you pregnant? Do you expect to become pregnant? What are your child care arrangements?
- How tall are you? How much do you weigh?
- Do you have any disabilities? How is your family's health?
- Where were you born? Are you a US citizen?
- Have you ever been arrested?
- What clubs or social organizations do you belong to?
- Any question about race, color, or religion.

6-5 An interviewer should ask questions only to determine your ability to perform the job.

INDUSTRY INSIGHTS

Common Job Interview Questions

- How did you become interested in working in a kitchen?
- Tell me about yourself.
- What are your major strengths and weaknesses?
- What (course, activity, club) did you like best about school?
- If you could change one thing about yourself, what would it be?
- Why do you want to work for us?
- What do you see yourself doing in five years?
- Why should we hire you?

- Ask questions, if appropriate, that are positive such as "Are there opportunities for advancement from this position?"

When the interview is over, thank the person for his or her time. Always send a thank-you letter or note, 6-6. The letter should be short, thanking the interviewer and indicating your interest in the job.

What Employers Expect

An employer provides pay and benefits and in return expects the employee to perform in a specific manner and assume the responsibility that is appropriate for the position. As an employee, there are many aspects of your job that you cannot control. You are able, however, to control how you perform within the framework of your job. This is called *self-management*. Demonstrate self-management by performing work assignments to the best of your ability. Show up to

work rested and ready to focus. Rather than complain, offer solutions.

An employer expects an employee to display a positive attitude and work ethic. A **work ethic** is how you feel about your job and how much effort you put into it. Though a good work ethic is demonstrated in on-the-job performance, it is more clearly seen in an employee's attendance, punctuality, honesty, cooperation and teamwork, and ability to accept criticism.

Good Attendance

Attendance is important. Simply put, employees who are excessively absent will not keep their jobs long. Foodservice operations work around the meal schedules of their diners. Unlike other jobs, work that is not performed today cannot be completed tomorrow.

Knowing when you are scheduled to work is your responsibility. Put your job first and plan social events around your work schedule. When situations arise where you

CHEF'S ETHICS

Employee Theft

Foodservice managers report that employee theft can be a problem. How does employee theft occur in the foodservice industry? The following includes a few examples:

- cheating on his or her time card by asking other employees to punch in or out
- taking food or beverages from the establishment
- not charging customers for food or beverages with hopes of increasing tips

In all circumstances, employee theft is wrong. Theft is a violation of personal ethics for right behavior and moral obligation. Employee theft is grounds for immediate termination. If you are a witness to employee theft, report the incident to your supervisor right away.

Sample Thank-You Letter

Andrea S. Jones
2638 Orrington Avenue
Evanston, IL 60201
190.534.2368
E-mail: ajones@xxxx.net

September 26, 20XX

Mark Hopkins
Human Resources Manager
Nationwide Hotel Group
San Francisco, CA 94128
Dear Mr. Hopkins:

Dear Mr. Hopkins:

Thank you for taking the time to discuss the Line Cook position with me last Wednesday. I am excited to learn more about the position and believe I could make a positive contribution to the Point Reyes Room.

During the interview, you mentioned the importance of selecting a candidate who has both fine-dining experience and an understanding of how restaurants operate as an integral part of a quality hotel's offerings to the guest. My current position at The Café in the Ritz-Carlton in Chicago has provided firsthand experience in this important aspect of how a fine-dining restaurant contributes to the overall hotel experience.

Again, thank you for your time and considering me for this position. Please feel free to contact me if you need any additional information.

Thank you,

Andrea S. Jones

6-6 A thank-you letter or e-mail should be sent immediately after the interview.

must be absent, let your supervisor know as soon as possible. This shows consideration for both your employer and coworkers.

Punctuality

Being punctual means that you are at your station and ready to work when your shift begins. Punctual workers allow extra travel time to deal with unforeseen delays. Cooks must be on time for a kitchen to operate smoothly.

Honesty

Honesty is an important character trait and a primary expectation of employers. Lying and stealing are the most obvious forms of dishonesty and both are grounds for immediate dismissal. It may be difficult to admit mistakes, but being honest about your actions and capabilities is always best.

Not all forms of dishonesty are as obvious as lying and stealing. When an employee does not give his or her full and best effort at work or wastes the resources of the establishment, these are also forms of dishonesty. Remember that most dishonest actions are eventually discovered and a reputation for dishonesty can follow you throughout your career.

Cooperation and Teamwork

Following set rules and procedures demonstrates cooperation with the management. Following policies and procedures is a workplace necessity and failing to do so can be cause for termination. Beyond formal policies and procedures, cooperation also extends to following verbal instructions from the chef, managers, and supervisors.

Cooperating with coworkers is the basis of teamwork. Kitchens perform as a team. Employers expect employees to be team players. In the professional kitchen, as in most other jobs, a group working together can achieve

more than its members can individually. Maintaining a cheerful attitude and acting with consideration for other team members is the foundation for teamwork, 6-7. Kitchen teams work together to solve problems and continually improve performance. Goals such as improved customer service or controlling costs are often best achieved through teamwork.

Ability to Accept Criticism

Any job is a learning experience. Part of the learning process is getting feedback from those who train or supervise you. Whether criticism comes in the form of a review or simply as verbal corrections, it is important to receive the criticism with a positive attitude. Treat the criticism as an opportunity to learn rather than a personal attack.

This is often hard for chefs and cooks because they are passionate about their work and cuisine. Still, if you can develop the ability to accept criticism in a positive manner, it will aid you throughout your culinary career. Chefs regularly hear criticism from diners. Being able to respond to criticism constructively is one of the highest forms of professionalism.

What Employees Can Expect

Employment is a give-and-take relationship. Just as an employer can expect certain behaviors from employees, employees have certain expectations of their employer.

Job Description

A job description helps you understand what is expected of a particular position. Job descriptions are usually included in a job posting. Employers develop these written summaries to ensure that applicants and employees understand their roles and responsibilities.

6-7 Employers value employees who work well with others and maintain a positive attitude.

Well written job descriptions include:
- purpose
- responsibilities
- essential tasks and methods involved
- work conditions
- the relationship of the job to others in the organization
- qualifications needed

Pay

In exchange for their work, employees can expect to receive pay from their employer. Pay scales in the foodservice industry are determined by the number of people available to fill jobs and the skills required for a job. An entry-level job that requires little training and no experience will pay low wages. Jobs that require more education, training, and experience will pay more.

The foodservice industry tends to have lower paying jobs than other industries for entry-level jobs. As workers progress in ability and assume more responsibility, salaries rise. Executive chefs earn high salaries in exchange for their experience, training, and level of responsibility.

Benefits

In addition to pay, employees can often expect to receive benefits from their employers. Benefits are non-wage, financial extras provided by employers to their employees. Benefits would include extras such as paid time off, retirement plans, and health and life insurances. The benefit programs vary widely from one employer to the next. This can be an important consideration when comparing job offers. Many small, independent operators do not offer a wide range of benefits to workers. In contrast, many national chain restaurants, major hotel companies, and contract feeding companies provide a broad range of benefits. Asking about benefits is appropriate during a job interview.

Work Schedules

Employees in the foodservice industry generally work long hours. It is not unusual to work six days per week with one day off. Employees in entry-level jobs usually work forty hours per week. Many employees like the foodservice industry because there are opportunities to earn additional money. If employees work more than forty hours, they are generally paid at a higher rate for the additional hours.

Some foodservice operators are open twenty-four hours a day and employees have an option to work at night rather than during the day. There are also many opportunities in foodservice to work part-time.

Many workers consider the ability to work flexible schedules a benefit of the industry. Students, for example, can choose a work schedule that fits with a changing school calendar, 6-8. However, some employees do not like working the holidays, evenings, and weekends that are a necessity in foodservice.

Training and Probation Period

Training programs that are offered through high schools, career and technical schools, and colleges teach universal culinary skills and techniques that are used across the industry. Most foodservice operations provide on-the-job training to instruct new employees on the specific skills or procedures that are unique to the operation while they are working.

In the case of entry-level jobs, some operations may have formal on-the-job training that teaches general culinary skills as well as tasks specific to the job. In today's foodservice industry, an entry-level job combined with a formal training program is called a culinary apprenticeship.

Even where there is no apprenticeship program, most operations have on-the-job training provided by one employee to another. Because each foodservice operation is unique, approaches to on-the-job training are likely to differ as well.

Some foodservice operations, as well as other industries, have a probation period. A probation period is a length of time during which the supervisor observes a new employee to see if he or she is able to perform the job. This period can be as little as one day or as long as three months or more. Generally, an employee may be terminated more easily during this trial period than an employee who is past the probation period.

During the probation period, new employees may not be eligible for benefits provided by the employer. Each benefit could also have different periods of eligibility. For

©BananaStock Ltd.

6-8 Many students work evenings and weekends in entry-level foodservice jobs.

example, new employees may start earning credit for paid time off as soon as they begin working but may not be able to use it until they have completed the probation period. However, a new employee may have to work three months to be eligible for health insurance and one year to earn retirement benefits. Asking if there is a probation period and about benefits is appropriate during a job interview. If the job is covered by a union contract, these terms of employment will probably be described in the contract.

Policies and Procedures

Businesses must have effective policies and procedures established in order to be successful. When communicated and followed, policies and procedures contribute to productivity, profitability, and employee and customer satisfaction, 6-9. A company's policies and procedures are often found in employee handbooks and union contracts. However, some companies' policies may be informal and verbal. Procedures describe how specific tasks are to be performed. Policies explain the company's pay and benefits, general workplace rules, safety and security, attendance, performance evaluations, and how disciplinary issues are handled.

The manner in which discipline is handled varies from one business to the next, but generally progressive discipline is recommended. **Progressive discipline** is a method for dealing with unacceptable job-related behavior in a step process. The goal of this

©BananaStock Ltd.

6-9 Regular staff meetings communicate policies and keep workers informed

process is to give the employee feedback so he or she can correct the problem. Steps in a progressive discipline process usually include the following:

- Counsel the employee about performance issue for clear understanding.
- Verbally warn employee for poor performance.
- Provide written warning if poor performance continues.

- Suspend employee from work to consider his or her desire for continued employment with the company.
- End the employment of employee who refuses to improve.

Documentation of the employee's progression through this process is important in the event of legal action. Although laws and work rules vary from state to state and by employer, all employees should be aware of the rules of employment where they work.

Laws and Conditions of Employment

There are many local, state, and federal laws that both employers and employees must follow. These laws were passed to set minimum standards for wage and prohibit job discrimination in the United States. Other laws address safe working conditions in the workplace.

Fair Labor Practices

The **Fair Labor Standards Act (FLSA)** was passed in 1938 to protect workers from unfair treatment by employers. Most full-time and part-time workers in this country are covered by this act. This act establishes minimum wage, overtime pay, and child labor standards. States may also have laws regarding these issues. When both the state law and the FLSA apply, the law that sets the higher standard must be observed.

Minimum Wage   The FLSA requires employers to pay covered employees minimum wage or more. **Minimum wage** is the lowest hourly rate of pay that an employee can be paid legally. Some states have established their own minimum wage, but it cannot be lower than the minimum wage established by the federal government.

Employers may not be required to pay certain types of employees minimum wage. For example, foodservice workers who earn tips can be paid less than minimum wage. Tips may be considered part of the employee's wages but the employer must make up the difference if the tips combined with the hourly rate do not equal at least minimum wage. Employers are also allowed to pay new employees less during a training period.

Overtime Pay   The FLSA also establishes standards for overtime pay to covered employees. An employer must pay at least 1½ times the employee's regular rate of pay for all hours worked over 40 in a work week.

For example, if an employee's rate of pay is $7.50 per hour, the overtime rate is 1½ times $7.50, or $11.25 per hour. An employee is paid at the overtime rate only for those hours over 40 in the workweek. Therefore, if this employee works 42 hours in a week, he or she will be paid $7.50 per hour for the first 40 hours plus $11.25 per hour for the 2 hours overtime. These overtime standards may be different for certain employees. For example, healthcare workers often have different agreements with their employers regarding overtime payment.

The FLSA does not limit the number of hours in a day or the number of days in a week that an employer may require an employee to work as long as the employee is at least 16 years old.

Child Labor Standards   The FLSA regulates the employment of child labor. Individual state's laws may be stricter. The goal of the child labor standards is to protect the health and educational opportunities of young people who choose to work. For this reason, the FLSA prohibits the employment of children in jobs that are considered hazardous.

The standards also restrict the hours that individuals ages 14 and 15 can work. Fourteen- and fifteen-year-olds can work in acceptable jobs for the following hours:
- After 7 a.m. and until 7 p.m. (Hours are extended to 9 p.m. June 1–Labor Day)
- Up to 3 hours on a school day
- Up to 18 hours in a school week
- Up to 8 hours on a nonschool day
- Up to 40 hours in a nonschool week

Equal Employment Opportunities
The Equal Pay Act of 1963 is an amendment to the FLSA. This law requires employees of either sex who are working for the same employer under similar conditions to receive equal pay. This law is enforced by a US agency called the **Equal Employment Opportunity Commission (EEOC)** which is responsible for the oversight and

coordination of all federal equal employment opportunity regulations, practices, and policies.

Title VII of the Civil Rights Act of 1964 is also enforced by the EEOC. This law makes it illegal to discriminate against any individual due to such factors as race, color, sex, national origin, or religion. More recently, laws have been passed to protect people from discrimination for other reasons, such as disabilities, age, and marital status.

Sexual harassment is an example of a violation of Title VII of the Civil Rights Act of 1964. **Sexual harassment** is any unwelcome sexual advance, request for sexual favor, and other verbal or physical conduct of a sexual nature that affects a person's ability to work. Employers must let employees know that this behavior is not tolerated. Providing sexual harassment training to employees and a process for complaints sends the message that this behavior is unacceptable. If a complaint is received, quick and appropriate action must be taken.

When equal opportunities for employment exist, workplace diversity is possible. **Workplace diversity** means valuing and respecting the contributions of coworkers who are different from you. A diverse workplace is important to US companies that want to remain competitive. A company that values diversity can benefit from higher morale and increased productivity and creativity.

Family and Medical Leave

The Family and Medical Leave Act of 1993 (FMLA) is a federal law requiring employers with 50 or more employees to provide up to 12 weeks unpaid, job protected leave to qualified employees to

- care for a new child by birth, adoption or foster care
- care for a seriously ill family member
- recover from serious illness
- care for an injured service member in the family
- deal with issues related to a family member's military deployment

Employers are required to maintain employee benefits including health insurance and to restore the employee to the same or equal position upon their return.

Conditions of Employment

Some employers require that you meet certain conditions before you are hired. Some of these are required by law in various states and for certain jobs. To verify that you meet these conditions, you may be asked to take tests, provide documentation, or sign a release. When a job offer is extended to you by a company, it may be conditional based on the results of one or more of the following:

- preemployment drug screening
- verification of degrees and work experience
- criminal background checks
- employment eligibility verification (I-9 form)
- credit history check
- minimum age requirements

Summary Points

- Preparing for a job search requires identifying the type of job you are looking for, make a list of possible contacts and references, writing your résumé, and assembling a portfolio.

- Pursue all possible sources to be effective in your job search.

- Read and follow the company's instructions when submitting your résumé.

- Be complete, accurate, and neat when filling out job application forms.

- Present your best image to the potential employer during an interview.

- Employers expect employees to demonstrate a positive attitude and good work ethic in return for pay.

- Foodservice employees can expect a job description, pay, benefits, nontraditional work schedules, training, and information on the company's policies and procedures.

- Workers benefit from knowing the various laws that regulate employment in the United States.

In Review
Assess

1. List three examples of appropriate references.

2. List four points of information that a résumé should include.

3. True or false. Using the Internet to locate jobs demonstrates your proficiency with technology to potential employers.

4. A résumé should always be accompanied by a _____ _____.

5. True or false. Potential employers evaluate job application forms only for content and not for neatness or ability to follow directions.

6. List four ways an applicant can present their best image during an interview.

7. List five ways employees can demonstrate a good work ethic.

8. True or false. Every company offers the same benefits.

9. The Fair Labor Standards Act established which of the following:
   A. Minimum wage
   B. Overtime pay
   C. Child labor standards
   D. All of the above.

10. Give three examples of conditions of employment that companies may require.

Core Skills

11. **Math.** An employee earns $7.40 per hour and works 46 hours in one week. Assuming the overtime rate is 1½ times regular pay, calculate how much money this employee will earn.

12. **Writing.** Research the annals of the US Department of Labor online to learn about the passage of the FLSA. Write a brief summary of your findings that answers the questions: What were the economic and social conditions that led to the passage of the law? Who promoted the law? What were the immediate results of the FLSA?

13. **Listening.** Interview someone who conducted a successful job search. What sources did she use to identify job opportunities? How did she describe the interview process? How did her expectations before being hired compare to her experiences on the job? How will this interview influence your job search?

14. **Math.** Locate the history of the federal minimum wage rate on the US Department of Labor website. Create a time line showing the minimum wage rate from 1938 to present. Next to each rate, note the percentage change from the previous rate in parentheses. Make the time line to scale.

15. **Reading.** Read a book about child labor such as Barbara Greenwood's *Factory Girl*. Write a brief review of the book to present in class.

16. **Writing.** Select two culinary related careers to research on O*NET. Read the summary reports for these careers, especially the knowledge, skills abilities, and interests required to do the work. Analyze whether your personal interests, skills, and abilities

are a logical fit with one or both careers. Write a summary explaining why you think you are well-suited for either career.

17. **Writing and Speaking.** Working in small groups, write a script for a sketch that depicts the effect of attitude and work ethic on the workplace. Include one or more characters who demonstrate self-management. Perform your play in class.

18. **Listening.** In small groups, discuss with your classmates—in basic, everyday language—your knowledge and awareness of the job search process. Conduct this discussion as though you had never read this chapter. Take notes on the observations expressed. Then review the points discussed, factoring in your new knowledge of the job search process. Develop a summary of what you have learned and present it to the class using the terms that you have learned in this chapter.

19. **CTE Career Readiness Practice.** Most employers value employees that can set and achieve reasonable, attainable goals. Think about your short- and long-term career goals. In writing: identify your short- and long-term career goals, determine how you will measure achievement of these goals, and identify a deadline for meeting each.

Critical Thinking

20. **Conclude.** You are reviewing the résumé of someone who has applied for a job and notice several misspelled words in their résumé. What does that tell you about this individual?

21. **Determine.** You will be interviewing an applicant for an entry-level job who has never worked in a professional kitchen. What are three questions you would ask to assess if this individual could be successful working in foodservice?

22. **Research.** Select an employer that you might be interested in working for some day. Use the Internet, library, or other sources to research this company and write a paragraph sharing your results. Include any history of the company, type of ownership, their benefits, mission statement, how many

people they employ, what states and countries they do business in, opportunities for growth, and so on. Explain why you are interested in working for this company.

Technology

Find three job search websites that list restaurant or hospitality jobs in your state. Which site had the most listings for your state? Which site provided the most information on the jobs listed? Which site was easiest to use? Write a brief summary of your findings.

Teamwork

In groups of three, role-play an interview for an entry-level position in a kitchen. One student assumes the role of interviewer, a second student is the interviewee, and the third videos the role-play. Team members should rotate through each role. The team should view each video and collaborate on a written critique of each interview. The critiques should include constructive, meaningful feedback. Consider the interviewer's and interviewee's word choices, tone, and nonverbal communication in the critiques.

Chef's E-portfolio
Résumé

Prepare and upload your résumé. Ask your instructor where to save your file. This could be on the school's network or a flash drive of your own. Name your portfolio document *FirstnameLastname_Portfolio Ch#.docx* (i.e., JohnSmith_PortfolioCh06.docx).

Unit Two
Culinary Fundamentals

Barbro Bergfeldt /Shutterstock.com

The Science of Texture—
Denaturation and Coagulation

When proteins such as eggs, meat, or fish are exposed to certain chemical or physical elements, it causes changes in their structure. This is called *denaturation*. Another name for the process in which food is exposed to chemical or physical elements is *cooking*. For instance, when raw fish is soaked in an acid such as lime juice or eggs are placed in hot water, the bonds that are invisible to the human eye—but essential to the protein's structure—are broken. As a result, newly "freed" parts of the denatured proteins are exposed and ready to make new bonds. When these denatured proteins create new bonds with other denatured proteins in the food, it is called *coagulation*. As coagulation takes place, the new bonds form a net that captures and holds moisture. The food that results is changed not only visibly, but also to touch. When this process (cooking) is done properly, the result is a texture or density that is pleasing. However, if the process goes on too long, the new bonds become tighter and tighter. Not surprisingly, as the bonds become tighter the moisture they once held in the food is squeezed out. Now you can understand why overcooking food results in a tough, dry product.

1. During cooking, what happens to the bonds responsible for a protein's structure?

2. How can you apply this knowledge to improve your food preparation skills?

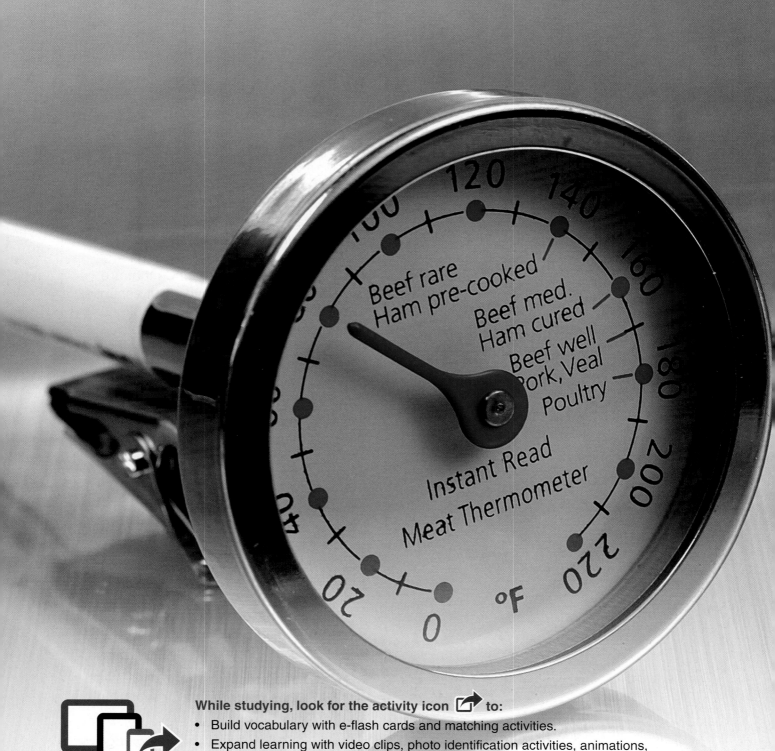

While studying, look for the activity icon ↱ to:

- Build vocabulary with e-flash cards and matching activities.
- Expand learning with video clips, photo identification activities, animations, and interactive activities.
- Review and assess what you learn by completing end-of-chapter questions.

G-WLEARNING.com

Sanitation Hazards

7

Reading Prep

Review the chapter headings and use them to create an outline for taking notes during reading and class discussion. Under each heading, list any term highlighted in yellow. Write two questions that you expect the chapter to answer.

Culinary Terminology Build Vocab

foodborne illness, p. 98
contamination, p. 98
sanitation, p. 98
biological hazard, p. 99
time and temperature control for safety (TCS) food, p. 99
spore, p. 100
infection, p. 100
intoxication, p. 100
toxin mediated infection, p. 100
temperature danger zone, p. 102
virus, p. 104
yeast, p. 105
mold, p. 105
parasite, p. 106
chemical hazard, p. 107
physical hazard, p. 108
cross-contact, p. 109

Academic Terminology Build Vocab

pathogen, p. 99
bacteria, p. 99
aerobic bacteria, p. 100
anaerobic bacteria, p. 100
facultative bacteria, p. 100
pH, p. 102
water activity (a_w), p. 104
leach, p. 107
material safety data sheets (MSDS), p. 108
allergen, p. 109

Objectives

After studying this chapter, you will be able to

- summarize the importance of working with food safely.
- differentiate among biological, chemical, and physical hazards.
- classify the sources of biological hazards and ways to control their growth.
- recognize chemical hazards and explain how to prevent them.
- explain physical hazards and how to prevent them.
- recognize eight common food allergens.

When considering a career in the culinary arts, people rarely think about the importance of cooking food safely. Instead, they envision the lights, glamour, and success of famous chefs. The images of superstar chefs are everywhere—on TV, in magazines, and in newspapers. These chefs did not become stars overnight. Behind their success are years of training and a firm understanding of the basics.

Culinary training begins with one of the most important skills—knowing how to prepare safe food. This may not seem as fun as cooking. Students want to learn how to prepare mousses or roast Cornish hens right away. Those skills are taught in future chapters. This chapter addresses preparing safe food.

Building a career in the culinary arts is like building a house. The first step is laying a solid foundation. No one ever sees the foundation, but the house will not stand without it. Learning about illness caused by food and how to prevent it is the basis for a successful career.

SANITATION & SAFETY
Foodborne-Illness Estimates

According to the Centers for Disease Control and Prevention (CDC), it is estimated that every year in the United States there are

- 47.8 million cases of foodborne illness

- 127,839 hospitalizations from foodborne illness

- 3,037 deaths linked to unsafe food

Unfortunately, these numbers are only estimates. The Centers for Disease Control and Prevention estimates that only 1 out of 38 cases of *Salmonella* is reported to them. As you can see, foodborne illness is no little matter, and costs hundreds of thousands of dollars.

Importance of Safe Food Handling

Why should you study correct food-handling procedures? Imagine how you feel after eating a delicious meal. Then imagine that within hours or days you start feeling a little queasy. Perhaps you become feverish and weak. Perhaps you begin vomiting or suffer from serious diarrhea. You might need to be hospitalized to avoid permanent injury or even death. This scenario can happen when food is not handled correctly. Handling and preparing food safely is essential and must be taken seriously.

Improper food handling can result in foodborne illness. **Foodborne illness** is sickness caused by eating unsafe food. An outbreak is when two or more people eat the same food and get the same sickness. An outbreak is the result of a foodborne illness.

Foodborne illness outbreaks happen to people just like you. Not only do outbreaks harm the customer, they can result in employees being fired or demoted, businesses getting sued, and reputations being ruined. The bad publicity caused by an outbreak can lead to the establishment going out of business.

Anyone who works in a professional kitchen must know how to serve safe food. One mistake can result in unsafe food. Serving food that is free of contamination must be the goal of all foodservice workers. **Contamination** refers to the presence of unsafe substances or levels of dangerous microorganisms in food.

Proper sanitation prevents contamination. **Sanitation** is the creation and practice of clean and healthy food-handling habits. Food that does not have dangerous levels of contamination is said to be safe. Contamination can result from biological,

SANITATION & SAFETY
Foodborne-Illness Outbreaks

Food poisoning outbreaks can be local, regional, national, or even international. Outbreaks can affect large numbers of people. Any outbreak, no matter what the size, has just one source. A few examples of outbreaks follow:

- In 2011, a multistate outbreak of *Listeria monocytogenes* infections linked to whole cantaloupes resulted in 150 illnesses and 33 deaths.

- In 1998 in Illinois, an outbreak of *Salmonella* occurred at a catered event. Of the 400 guests, 43 contracted *Salmonella*.

- In 1996, 646 inmates at a county jail fell ill due to *Clostridium perfringens* poisoning.

- In 1993, a multistate outbreak of *E. coli* occurred when a fast-food chain served undercooked hamburgers. Over 500 people became ill and 4 died as a result.

chemical, or physical hazards. Other hazards that cause allergic reactions for some individuals may either naturally occur in foods or be introduced.

Biological Hazards

Biological hazards are harmful organisms that cause foodborne illness. This source of contamination is the most troublesome for foodservice. The illness that results can range from mild discomfort to life threatening.

Most biological hazards are too small to see with the naked eye. In some cases, you cannot detect them by smell or taste. To make matters worse, there is not just one type. These biological hazards, or pathogens, include harmful bacteria, viruses, fungi, parasites, and fish toxins. A **pathogen** is an organism that causes illness in humans. Each of these pathogens behaves uniquely.

There is a war in the kitchen every day—foodservice workers versus biological hazards. Before you can fight these pathogens, you must understand them. You must know how they behave. You must know each pathogen's strengths and weaknesses. Once you understand these hazards, you can develop a plan for safe food handling.

Bacteria

A type of pathogen responsible for many foodborne-illness outbreaks is bacteria. **Bacteria** are single-celled organisms that reproduce by dividing. They are everywhere. They surround us by the billions. They are on your clothes, in your hair, on your hands, and in the air you breathe. You can only see them with a microscope.

How Bacteria Grow

Bacteria have many of the same needs that humans do to live and grow. Bacteria need water, food, and favorable temperatures to thrive. To limit the growth of pathogens or the formation of their dangerous by-products, these factors must be controlled for certain foods. These foods are referred to as **time and temperature control for safety (TCS) foods**, or TCS foods. TCS foods were formerly called *potentially hazardous foods*. Controlling the time these foods are exposed to unsafe temperatures helps to limit bacterial growth. Foods that are high in protein provide a very favorable environment for rapid bacterial growth. However, there are many other foods with low protein content that can result in foodborne illnesses, 7-1.

SANITATION & SAFETY

Friendly Bacteria?

From the time you were very young, you have been warned about the dangers of bacteria. Let's set the record straight. The fact is that the vast majority of bacteria are not harmful to humans. Some bacteria are even desirable. For example, without bacteria, there would be no cheese, vinegar, or yogurt!

Time/Temperature Control for Safety (TCS) Food
Raw or cooked animal products such as meat, poultry, milk, and eggs
Cooked plant food such as corn and rice
Cut melons
Raw seed sprouts such as bean sprouts
Cut leafy greens such as spinach and lettuce
Cut tomatoes and tomato mixtures such as salsa
Garlic-in-oil mixtures
Source: FDA Food Code 2009

7-1 Time/temperature control for safety foods support bacterial growth if not handled properly.

Unlike humans, not all bacteria need oxygen to live and grow. Bacteria that require oxygen are called **aerobic bacteria**. Those that thrive without oxygen are called **anaerobic bacteria**. Bacteria that can grow either with or without oxygen are called **facultative bacteria**.

When bacteria have all their needs for growth met, they reproduce rapidly. Bacteria reproduce by dividing. If conditions are ideal, they can divide every 20 minutes. At that rate, one cell can turn into over 250,000 bacterial cells in six hours, 7-2. As the number of bacteria increase in food, so does the possibility of a foodborne illness.

Luckily, bacterial growth rate is not constant. When introduced to a new food source, bacteria take one to four hours to adjust to the new surroundings. Growth is slow during the beginning phase, called the *lag phase*. Next, the bacteria enter the *log phase* during which there is rapid growth. During this stage, bacteria become increasingly dangerous due to their growing numbers. After awhile, the number of bacteria level off, marking the beginning of the *decline phase*. During this final phase, an increasing number of bacteria die.

Some bacteria have an added survival mechanism—the ability to form spores. A **spore** is a thick-walled, "supersurvival unit." If conditions threaten the bacterium's existence, it may produce a spore. The spore can survive conditions that might kill the bacterium. Once the environment improves, the spore will become a normal, functioning bacterium.

Pathogenic bacteria cause foodborne illness in humans in one of the following ways:
- **Infection** is illness resulting from live bacteria. These bacteria must be ingested to be a threat.
- **Intoxication** is illness resulting from ingestion of toxins left behind by bacteria. Toxins are poisonous substances that are harmful to humans. To become ill, you do not need to ingest the bacteria, but simply their toxic residue. Toxins are troublesome because

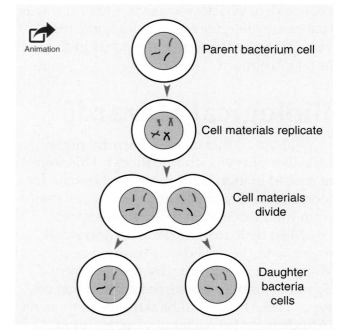

| Parent bacterium cell |
| Cell materials replicate |
| Cell materials divide |
| Daughter bacteria cells |

| Reproduction Rate of Bacteria ||
Time Elapsed	**Number of Cells**
0	1
1 hour	8
2 hours	64
3 hours	512
4 hours	4,096
5 hours	32,768
6 hours	262,144

7-2 Bacteria reproduce by dividing and, under ideal conditions, they can multiply rapidly.

you may succeed at killing the bacteria without affecting the toxins. Some toxins are both difficult to detect and deadly.
- **Toxin mediated infection** occurs when bacteria are ingested and then produce harmful toxins while in the human digestive tract.

Certain pathogens are commonly found in foods. These pathogens often differ in the symptoms that result and the means of transmission, 7-3.

Common Foodborne Pathogens

Pathogen	Category	Symptoms	Transmission
Bacillus cereus	Toxin mediated infection, forms spores	Diarrhea, abdominal cramps, vomiting *Onset:* 30 minutes–15 hours after eating	Produce, meat, fish, milk, cooked rice dishes
Clostridium botulinum (botulism)	Intoxication, forms spores	Weakness, blurred or double vision, difficulty breathing, possible death *Onset:* 18–36 hours after eating	Improperly handled foods in an anaerobic environment such as cans and vacuum-packed bags; garlic-in-oil mixtures
Campylobacter jejuni	Infection	Fever, diarrhea, bloody diarrhea, cramps *Onset:* 2–5 days after eating	Improperly cooked meat and poultry
Clostridium perfringens	Toxin mediated infection, forms spores	Diarrhea, cramping *Onset:* 8–24 hours after eating	Meat, poultry, meat-containing stews and gravies
Escherichia coli 0157:H7 (E. coli)	Toxin mediated infection	Severe diarrhea, cramping, possibly severe kidney problems and death *Onset:* 3–4 days after eating	Improperly cooked meats, particularly ground meats; produce
Listeria monocytogenes (Can reproduce at refrigeration temperatures.)	Infection	Fever, muscle aches, possible diarrhea and nausea, may affect the central nervous system, can be fatal *Onset:* 2 days–3 months	Fruits, vegetables, dairy products, improperly cooked meat and poultry, hot dogs, deli meats
Salmonella Enteritidis	Infection	Nausea, vomiting, abdominal cramps, diarrhea, fever *Onset:* 6–72 hours	Poultry, eggs, produce
Salmonella Typhimurium	Infection	High fever; lethargy; abdominal pain, diarrhea or constipation; headache; appetite loss; achiness *Onset:* 1–3 weeks	Contaminated drinking water, raw vegetables grown using contaminated irrigation water
Shigella	Infection	Weakness, flue-like symptoms, abdominal pain, diarrhea *Onset:* 8 hours–4 days	Raw produce, potato, tuna, macaroni, shrimp, and chicken salads.
Staphylococcus aureus	Intoxication	Nausea, vomiting, headache, stomach cramps, diarrhea *Onset:* 1–6 hours	Potato, tuna, macaroni, shrimp, and chicken salads; deli meats; cream-filled bakery products
Vibrio vulnificus and *Vibrio parahaemolyticus*	Infection	Diarrhea, vomiting, abdominal pain, fever, chills *Onset:* 12 hours–21 days	Consuming shellfish from infected waters
Yersinia enterocolitica	Infection	Fever, abdominal pain, and bloody diarrhea *Onset:* 4–7 days after eating	Consuming undercooked pork, especially chitterlings; unpasteurized milk

7-3 A variety of pathogens can cause foodborne illness.

Controlling Growth of Bacteria

Now that you know how bacteria grow, what strategies would you use to keep them from reproducing in food? In general, creating an unfriendly environment slows down bacterial growth or kills them. Unfavorable conditions can be created by controlling any or all of the following factors:

- *Food source.* High protein and other TCS foods must be handled carefully to limit contamination from bacteria. Protein in particular is a favored food source of bacteria.

- *pH.* The measure of acidity or alkalinity of a substance is called the **pH**. The pH is measured on a scale of 1 to 14. Pure water is neutral with a pH of 7. Something is neutral when it is neither acidic nor alkaline. A pH of 1 to 6 is acidic, with 1 being the most acidic. A pH of 8 to 14 is alkaline, with 14 being the most alkaline. Bacteria remain active in a pH range of 4.6 to 7. Most bacteria function best close to a neutral pH. Therefore, adding acidic ingredients such as vinegar, lime juice, or lemon juice to foods discourages bacterial growth and prevents spoilage. Acids can help preserve food.

- *Temperature.* Bacteria need warm conditions to grow. They reproduce rapidly in the **temperature danger zone** which is between 41°F and 135°F (5°C and 57°C), 7-4. Above the temperature danger zone, biological hazards begin to die. However, some bacteria form heat-protective spores. Many toxins produced by bacteria are not destroyed by heat either. Below the temperature danger zone, bacteria reproduce at an increasingly slower pace. These temperatures slow bacterial growth but

SCIENCE & TECHNOLOGY

pH Values

The acidity or alkalinity of an element or compound is measured using the pH scale. It ranges from 0 to 14. Pure water is neutral with a pH of 7.

Most foods are neutral or slightly acidic. As a point of comparison, the pH values of some common foods are:

Highly Acidic	0		
	1	limes	1.8–2.0
	2	vinegar	2.0–3.4
		cranberry	
	3	juice	2.3–2.5
Acidic	4	apples	3.3–3.9
	5	yogurt	3.8–4.2
	6	tomatoes	4.2–4.3
Neutral	7	beef	5.1–6.2
	8	cabbage	5.4–6.0
	9	chicken	6.2–6.4
	10	milk	6.3–6.5
Alkaline	11	egg yolks	6.4
	12	fish	6.6–6.8
	13	distilled water	7.0
Highly Alkaline	14	egg whites	7.0–9.0
		baking soda	8.4

pH values derived from U.S. Food & Drug Administration Center for Food Safety & Applied Nutrition, Foodborne pathogenic Microorganisms and Natural Toxins Handbook

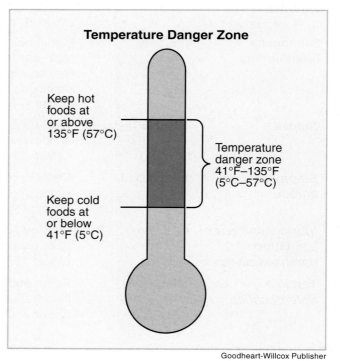

Temperature Danger Zone

Keep hot foods at or above 135°F (57°C)

Temperature danger zone 41°F–135°F (5°C–57°C)

Keep cold foods at or below 41°F (5°C)

Goodheart-Willcox Publisher

7-4 The time food spends in the temperature danger zone must be monitored and limited.

do not kill the bacteria. Therefore, once a product enters the temperature danger zone again, bacteria will begin to reproduce once more.

- *Time.* The amount of time food spends in the temperature danger zone must be limited. The longer bacteria spend between 41°F and 135°F (5°C and 57°C), the more numerous and dangerous they become. TCS foods should not be kept in the temperature danger zone for more than four hours. Those four hours are cumulative so procedures must be in place to monitor times. For example, suppose a raw chicken breast is in the temperature danger zone for two hours and then placed in the cooler for several hours. It is still well within the four-hour limit. If the chicken breast is removed from the cooler and spends three more hours in the temperature danger zone, it is no longer safe to eat. It has spent a total of five hours in the temperature danger zone.

- *Atmosphere.* Most bacteria are aerobic so removing oxygen from their atmosphere stops their growth. Many products are sold in special plastic bags to reduce the amount of oxygen available to bacteria. Vacuum packing removes all air from the plastic bag. *Modified atmosphere packaging (MAP)* replaces air inside the plastic bag with an inert gas such as carbon dioxide or nitrogen, 7-5. Unfortunately, removing oxygen favors anaerobic bacteria. For this reason, many health departments do not allow foodservice establishments to make their own vacuum packaged or MAP foods. Never use, open, or taste a bulging vacuum-packed product as this could indicate contaminated food. If in doubt about any MAP or vacuum-packed product, ask a supervisor.

Mix In Math

Temperature Scales

Temperature can be measured using either a Fahrenheit or Celsius scale. In the United States, people primarily use the Fahrenheit scale. Scientists and most other countries use the Celsius scale. It is convenient for a chef to know how to convert recipe temperatures from one scale to another.

Convert Fahrenheit to Celsius

1. Subtract 32 degrees from Fahrenheit temperature.
2. Multiply by 5.
3. Divide by 9.

   Example:

   Convert 74 degrees Fahrenheit (°F) to degrees Celsius (°C)

   74°F − 32 = 42
   42 × 5 = 210
   210 ÷ 9 = 23.3°C

Convert Celsius to Fahrenheit

1. Multiply the Celsius temperature by 9.
2. Divide by 5.
3. Add 32.

   Example:

   Convert 7 degrees Celsius (°C) to degrees Fahrenheit (°F)

   7°C × 9 = 63
   63 ÷ 5 = 12.6
   12.6 + 32 = 44.6°F

Draz-Koetke/Goodheart-Willcox Publisher

7-5 These products are examples of modified atmosphere packaging (MAP) and vacuum packing.

SANITATION & SAFETY

Botulism—A Life and Death Matter

Botulism is perhaps the deadliest foodborne illness that foodservice will encounter. The bacteria *Clostridium botulinum* is an anaerobic bacteria that causes an intoxication. The toxin this bacteria produces can be fatal even in small amounts. Botulism result from consuming improperly canned products. This explains why foodservice operations are not permitted to can their own food. Foodservice operations also are not allowed to use home-canned foods. Never open or taste any damaged or bulging cans.

- *Water.* Removing water from food stops bacterial growth. Foods with low water content such as crackers, beef jerky, and raisins don't support bacterial growth, 7-6. The amount of water available for microbial growth in a product is called **water activity (a_w)**. Bacteria are quite sensitive to water activity and require a high level for growth. The processes of freeze-drying and dehydrating foods act to lower the water activity and discourage bacterial growth. If water is added back, growth occurs once again.

Viruses

Bacteria are small, but viruses are even smaller. A **virus** is a very small organism that invades another cell and causes it to reproduce the virus. Without a cell host, viruses can survive but cannot reproduce.

Draz-Koetke/Goodheart-Willcox Publisher

7-6 Foods are freeze-dried and dehydrated to preserve them for later use.

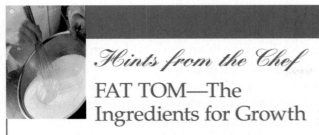

Hints from the Chef

FAT TOM—The Ingredients for Growth

Chefs use a trick to remember the six "ingredients" bacteria need to grow. They simply must remember the words FAT TOM:

F-food
A-acidity (pH)
T-temperature
T-time
O-oxygen (atmosphere)
M-moisture (water)

Once a virus forcibly takes over a cell, the virus transfers its genetic material to the captive cell. The cell then reproduces the virus' genetics. Often, the invaded cell is damaged or dies in the process.

Most viruses are destroyed by high heat. However, some viruses are unaffected by heat. Unlike bacteria, viruses are not affected by water activity or pH.

Two viruses that concern foodservice are hepatitis A and Norovirus (Norwalk virus). Hepatitis A causes liver damage. According to the Centers for Disease Control and Prevention (CDC), Norovirus is estimated to be responsible for 48% of foodborne illness outbreaks in the United States. These viruses are excreted in the feces of infected people. Individuals become sick when they consume contaminated water or foods. The foods most often causing outbreaks of these viruses include raw or undercooked shellfish and raw salad ingredients. These viruses can be destroyed by heat.

Contamination of foods by infected workers in food processing plants and restaurants is often to blame for outbreaks. Viral contamination can be avoided by

- practicing excellent personal hygiene
- washing raw vegetables before preparation and eating

- avoiding shellfish harvested from polluted waters
- purchasing food only from the most reputable suppliers

Fungi

There are many types of fungi. Edible mushrooms are a type of fungi that are highly valued in the professional kitchen. Other types of fungi, such as poisonous mushrooms, yeasts, and molds, can cause food contamination.

Most mushrooms farmed in America pose no threat. Some restaurants purchase wild mushrooms, which can be very expensive. Always purchase wild mushrooms from a reputable source. If you do not recognize a wild mushroom, ask a supervisor. Never pick your own mushrooms because many have poisonous counterparts, which share a similar appearance.

Yeast

Yeast is a microscopic fungus that consumes sugar and expels alcohol and carbon dioxide gas. This process is called *fermentation*. Fermentation is necessary to make beer, wine, or bread. While specific yeasts can be beneficial, wild yeasts growing unintentionally in food can be a problem. A yeast contamination is characterized by slime, discoloration, bubbles, and an alcoholic or "off" smell. Though not dangerous to humans, fermenting food is unattractive and unappetizing. Yeast is easily killed when heated above 136°F (58°C).

Mold

The green-blue powdery fuzz you find on a piece of old fruit or container of leftover food is mold. **Mold** is the name for a large family of single-cell fungi. Mold grows on most foods and in many conditions. Some molds are used to manufacture foods such as blue cheese. Most molds are not poisonous but can make food unappealing. There are a few molds that produce toxins that are dangerous to humans. Temperatures above

SANITATION & SAFETY

Irradiating Food

Various forms of irradiation have been approved for use on food since 1985. It is used extensively by NASA to ensure that no food containing pathogens goes into space. The effects of food irradiation have been studied extensively for 40 years.

Irradiation is a process in which food is treated with small levels of radiation. Radiation kills the pathogen, but does not stay in the food. Parasites are quickly killed by low doses of irradiation. Killing bacteria requires more irradiation. Unfortunately, viruses are resistant to amounts of irradiation approved for use on foods.

You can identify foods that have been irradiated by the green "radura" symbol on the package.

140°F (60°C) kill molds but their toxins may not be affected. To be safe, moldy food should always be discarded. Using foods in a timely manner will prevent mold infestations.

Parasites

A **parasite** is an organism that lives in and feeds on the body of another live creature. Parasites can be found in meat and fish. When humans eat food infested with live parasites, the parasites may be transmitted to the human host. Illness may result.

One of the better-known parasites in foodservice is *Trichinella spiralis*. This parasite causes the disease called *trichinellosis* (trek ihn ell OH sis). This illness is marked by fatigue, extreme digestive discomfort, and in rare instances, death. *Trichinella spiralis* is not visible to the

naked eye. In the past, this illness was often the result of eating undercooked pork. Today, *trichinellosis* is rarely from pork and more often from eating improperly cooked game meats such as bear. To prevent trichinellosis, cook whole cuts of pork to an internal temperature of 145°F (63°C) allowing a three minute rest. Whole cuts and ground game should be cooked to an internal temperature of 160°F (71°C).

Fish also harbor parasites. Parasites such as *anisakis*, and certain varieties of *cestodes* (tapeworms) and *trematodes* (flukes) can be dangerous. Some of these parasites are not easily visible. These parasites may be present in some raw fish. They can be passed to a human host if they are not killed during processing. The only way to kill these parasites is by cooking fish to an internal temperature of 140°F (60°C). Freezing infested fish at −31°F (−35°C) for 15 hours or −4°F (−20°C) for seven days also kills fish parasites.

Fish Toxins

As with fish parasites, the danger of fish toxins is gaining more widespread attention as fish becomes a larger part of the American diet. Fish toxins are poisons within the fish's flesh. These toxins may not harm the fish, but can cause illness when eaten. Two illnesses caused by fish toxins that concern foodservice are *ciguatera* and *scombroid poisoning*.

Ciguatera results when small fish eat certain algae that contain the toxin *ciguatoxin*. Larger fish then eat the smaller fish and the poison is passed along. Humans become ill when they eat the larger fish containing the toxins. Fish commonly associated with this toxin include red snapper, grouper, and barracuda.

Scombroid poisoning occurs when specific species of fish are left in the temperature danger zone for too long. Dangerous levels of toxins called *histamines* build up in the flesh during this time. Humans can have serious reactions after eating affected fish. Affected fish often include yellowfin tuna, skipjack, bonito, and mackerel.

Unfortunately, there is no easy way to detect if fish have ciguatoxins or histamines. The best line of defense is to buy fish from reputable sources.

Chemical Hazards

Chemicals are part of the foodservice environment. In many cases, they aid the foodservice worker. Any chemical that contaminates food is considered a **chemical hazard**. There are many possible sources of chemical contamination in the kitchen.

Metals

Certain metals found in cookware can become a chemical hazard. For instance, copper is used to make some of the best cookware. However, copper from cookware can **leach**, or seep, into food and chemical contamination can result. To avoid this problem, copper pans are lined with another metal that does not react with food. Some copper pans are lined with tin. Over time, the tin can be damaged or wear off, 7-7. If this happens, the pan must be discarded or repaired before it is safe to use again.

Galvanized steel is another metal that should never be used in food preparation. Galvanized metal contains zinc. Zinc can

Draz-Koetke/Goodheart-Willcox Publisher

7-7 If the lining wears off a copper pot, the pot is unsafe to use for food preparation.

leach into acidic foods and pose a health threat. Chipped enamel cookware is another source of metal poisoning. For this reason, enamel pots are not recommended in the commercial kitchen.

Not all metal contaminations happen in the kitchen. Food contaminated by chemical hazards may be delivered to a kitchen. Fish from polluted waters can contain unsafe levels of heavy metals such as mercury. There is no way to identify heavy metal levels unless scientific testing is done. The only way to avoid this danger is to purchase fish from reputable sources.

Agricultural Chemicals

Insecticides, pesticides, and herbicides may be found on the exterior of fruits and vegetables. These contaminants cannot be seen with the naked eye. Washing and peeling produce is the best prevention against this chemical contamination.

Kitchen Chemicals

Every kitchen contains dangerous chemicals. Chemicals such as cleaning supplies, bleach, grease cutters, and polishes are found in many kitchens. These chemicals

SANITATION & SAFETY
When in Doubt...

If you work in a commercial kitchen, eventually you will hear someone say, "When in doubt, throw it out." This is one of those classic kitchen expressions that is worth remembering. It is better to be overly cautious when faced with a situation that could result in food contamination and illness.

are potential sources of contamination. While contaminations from chemical sources are more rare than those from biological sources, they can be extremely serious. Most often, chemical contamination results from employee carelessness or improper working habits. Following these safety precautions can prevent most chemical contamination:

- Store chemicals in clearly marked containers or leave them in their original containers.
- Do not store food in containers that previously held chemicals.
- Only use chemicals according to the manufacturer's instructions.
- Store chemicals in an area separate from food preparation or storage.
- Never randomly mix chemicals as certain chemicals can react to create highly poisonous substances.
- Dispose of chemicals in accordance with manufacturer's directions.
- If uncertain about how to use a chemical product, ask a supervisor.
- In the event of ingestion, call a poison control hotline immediately, refer to material safety data sheets, and notify a supervisor. **Material safety data sheets (MSDS)** list the composition of a chemical product, proper procedures

for storage and handling, and what to do in the case of an emergency. MSDS indicate what protective equipment should be worn when working with the chemical and possible health effects. All chemicals delivered to the professional kitchen come with MSDS. By law, these sheets must be current and displayed in a visible, accessible place in the kitchen, 7-8.

Physical Hazards

Glass, staples, part of a plastic bag, and toothpicks are examples of physical hazards. **Physical hazards** are solid materials that pose a danger to the consumer when present in food.

Physical hazards can be as dangerous as biological or chemical hazards. As with chemical hazards, physical hazards are easily prevented. Often, physical contamination is the result of carelessness. Many physical hazards are visible to the naked eye. The best prevention is to be aware of potential problems and to pay close attention to food being prepared and served.

SANITATION & SAFETY
Glass—Looks like Ice

Have you ever seen a person dip their glass into an ice bin and then fill it with a beverage? Hopefully you have not, but it happens. Aside from being unsanitary, it is very dangerous. What if a small piece of glass breaks off into the ice? Ice does not look any different than glass. Someone could then swallow a small piece of glass. NEVER scoop ice with a glass!

Draz-Koetke/Goodheart-Willcox Publisher

7-8 By law, restaurants must store MSDS in an easily accessible area in the kitchen.

Some of the more common physical hazards in the commercial kitchen include the following:

- *Glass.* Broken glass is particularly dangerous because it is not easily seen. Even a small piece of glass is dangerous if swallowed. Do not store glass high on shelves in food preparation areas. Do not use glass drinkware in the kitchen. If glass breaks in the kitchen, all food that might possibly be contaminated must be thrown out. Do not take chances!
- *Staples.* Many food delivery boxes are sealed with large staples. Be careful when removing food from boxes and breaking down boxes so that staples do not mix in with food.
- *Metal shards.* Commercial can openers that are not working properly can tear little pieces of metal from the can during operation. The metal shards then contaminate the can's contents.
- *Toothpicks.* Toothpicks are often used for hors d'oeuvres or sandwiches. Be sure to use toothpicks that the customer can easily see. It is a safe practice to use colored toothpicks or those with plastic frills at one end.

Food Allergens

You probably know someone who suffers from allergies. An allergy occurs when the body interprets a normally harmless protein as a dangerous substance. An **allergen** is the misinterpreted protein, 7-9. The body's immune system then reacts against the allergen. These reactions range from skin irritations to difficulty breathing. In some instances, death can result. Allergies are different from other biological hazards since they do not affect all people in the same way.

Food allergies need to be treated seriously by everyone in foodservice. When a customer alerts a restaurant server to an allergy, the kitchen staff must analyze everything that is served to that customer. Even trace amounts of an allergen could be life

Nutrition Connection

Going Gluten-Free

For people with a gluten intolerance or celiac disease, eating gluten-free is not a fad, it is a necessity. Gluten protein found in many grain products can damage the gastrointestinal tract of those who are intolerant or allergic to it. When cooking or preparing gluten-free items, wash hands, all utensils, and workstations to prevent cross-contamination. Substitute gluten-free flours in breads, pastas, sauces, gravies, and other baked goods. Investigate other foods that contain gluten to determine the need for a safe alternative. This may involve testing recipes to find the best substitute ingredient.

threatening. For instance, if a customer is allergic to peanuts, the cooks must make sure that no peanut or peanut-based ingredients are added to the food. The cooks must avoid peanut oil when sautéing, or frying foods. All utensils previously used with peanut ingredients must be thoroughly cleaned. When an allergen is transferred from its food of origin to a food that does not contain the allergen, it is called **cross-contact**.

Common Food Allergens

- dairy products
- wheat products, including flour
- fish
- shellfish
- peanut and peanut products
- soy and soy derivatives
- eggs
- seeds such as poppy, sunflower, and sesame
- tree nuts such as walnuts and almonds

7-9 Most people with food allergies have reactions to one or more of these allergens.

Summary Points

- Contamination can lead to outbreaks of foodborne illness. Such outbreaks are serious events. Every kitchen employee must practice good sanitation to prevent contamination.

- Biological hazards are the result of live organisms such as bacteria, viruses, fungi, or parasites. Biological hazards also include toxins produced.

- Bacteria is the biological hazard that causes many foodborne illnesses. There are many types of bacteria. Bacteria can be controlled or killed by creating an unfavorable environment.

- Foodservice workers routinely use chemicals for cleaning and sanitizing the kitchen. Other possible sources of chemicals include metals from cookware or the food supply, and agricultural chemicals. When these chemicals are ingested or come in contact with the food supply, they become a chemical hazard.

- Physical hazards are solid materials that pose a danger to the consumer when present in food. Physical hazards are preventable by paying close attention to the food that is being served since many physical hazards are visible.

- Kitchen staff must be familiar with menu items that contain potential food allergens.

In Review

Assess

1. True or false. Contamination is the creation and practice of clean and healthy food-handling habits.

2. List five biological hazards.

3. Explain the difference between infection and intoxication.

4. Grapes spoil more quickly than raisins because grapes have _____ water activity.

5. What is the temperature danger zone?

6. True or false. Most bacteria are killed in the temperature danger zone.

7. Name two practices that protect against viral contamination in foodservice.

8. What information is included in a material safety data sheet (MSDS)?

9. List two metals that could result in chemical contamination if used for cooking or storing food.

10. True or false. Most physical hazards cannot be seen with the naked eye.

11. List six common allergens found in foods.

Core Skills

12. **Math.** A food product in your kitchen has been contaminated with one bacteria cell. Assume conditions are ideal and bacteria are dividing every 20 minutes. At this rate, how many bacteria cells will there be after 1 hour and 40 minutes?

13. **Speaking.** Prepare and present an in-service to educate foodservice workers about a common foodborne pathogen. Integrate multiple sources of information and use diverse formats and media to present your information. Provide a list of your sources at the end of your in-service.

14. **Speaking.** Select one of the three metals listed in this chapter as chemical hazards. Prepare and give a brief presentation in class. In your presentation, locate the metal on the periodic table, give its chemical symbol, and discuss the symptoms of poisoning from this metal.

15. **Writing.** Place equal samples of several different food ingredients in petri dishes with growth medium and observe the results over the period of a week. What differences in the microbial growth did you observe? What factors might contribute to those differences? Write a brief summary of your observations.

16. **Reading.** Read the material safety data sheet (MSDS) for one of the cleaning chemicals used in your instructional kitchen. How does the way you have used and stored the product compare with MSDS recommendations?

17. **Speaking.** Select one category of biological hazard (bacteria, viruses, fungi, parasites, or toxins) discussed in this chapter. Prepare an

informative presentation regarding a specific type within that category (for example, Norovirus or *Shigella*) and the associated foodborne illness it causes. Adjust the style of delivery, vocabulary, use of visual aids, and length of presentation based on your audience. Give your presentation in class.

18. **Writing.** Write five questions related to your presentation in activity #17. Provide the answers to the questions as well. As a class, pool the questions for use in a quiz show game. Play the game periodically throughout the semester to prepare for the food sanitation test. Add more questions as you learn more about kitchen sanitation and safety.

19. **Speaking.** Debate the topic of irradiating food for safety. Divide into two groups. Each group should gather information in support of either the "pro" argument (irradiation should be used on foods) or the "con" argument (irradiation should not be used on foods). Use definitions and descriptions from this chapter to support your side of the debate and to clarify word meanings as necessary. You will want to do further research to find expert opinions, alternative treatments, and other relevant information.

20. **CTE Career Readiness Practice.** Use reliable Internet or print resources to investigate how the body's immune system reacts against a food allergen. Organize your findings in graphic form to share with the class.

Critical Thinking

21. **Infer.** What are some reasons a restaurant might have to close after causing a large foodborne illness outbreak?

22. **Consider.** Who might be affected by a well-publicized outbreak?

23. A shipment of chicken is delivered to the restaurant. The chef checks and discovers that the temperature of the chicken is 90°F (32°C). Instead of refusing the chicken, the shrewd chef bargains with the deliveryman and agrees to purchase it for half price. The chef immediately cooks the chicken to an internal temperature of 165°F (74°C), and

then rapidly chills it. Once the chicken is cold, he slices it, places it on sandwiches, and within 20 minutes serves it to a luncheon party. By the next day, all of his customers who ate the sandwiches are sick.
   A. **Analyze.** What went wrong?
   B. **Conclude.** Was it worth it for the chef to buy the questionable chicken?

Technology

Food professionals traditionally use sample cultures to detect the presence of pathogens in food products and food preparation environments. Use the Internet to research new DNA-based detection technologies such as polymerase chain reaction (PCR). How does this technology work? Do you think chefs might ever use it in a professional environment?

Teamwork

In a small group, observe food-handling situations at home, school, or at a restaurant. Make a list of sanitation hazards observed. Next to each hazard indicate the type—biological, chemical, or physical—and how it should be controlled or corrected. Present your findings in class.

Chef's E-portfolio
Foodborne Pathogen In-service

Upload your foodborne pathogen in-service from activity #13. Ask your instructor where to save your file. This could be on the school's network or a flash drive of your own. Name your portfolio document *FirstnameLastname_Portfolio Ch#. docx* (i.e., JohnSmith_PortfolioCh07.docx).

While studying, look for the activity icon to:
- Build vocabulary with e-flash cards and matching activities.
- Expand learning with video clips, photo identification activities, animations, and interactive activities.
- Review and assess what you learn by completing end-of-chapter questions.

Muriel Lasure/Shutterstock.com

Sanitation Procedures

8

Reading Prep

In preparation for the chapter, research the food code that applies to your school foodservice. As you read this chapter, compare the sanitation and cleaning recommendations to those of your local code.

Culinary Terminology
Build Vocab

cross-contamination, p. 118
clean, p. 119
sanitary, p. 119
food-contact surface, p. 119
three-compartment sink, p. 122
pest control operator (PCO), p. 129
Hazard Analysis Critical Control Point
   (HACCP), p. 129
critical control point (CCP), p. 130

Academic Terminology
Build Vocab

harbor, p. 119

Objectives

After studying this chapter, you will be able to

- understand the role of federal, state, and local government agencies in food safety.
- apply time and temperature control when handling food.
- summarize how cross-contamination occurs and how to prevent it.
- explain the difference between clean and sanitary.
- apply proper procedures when cleaning and sanitizing food-contact surfaces in the kitchen.

- explain the various aspects of personal hygiene that are important in foodservice.
- understand the importance of proper pest control and waste management to food safety.
- summarize how a HACCP plan works.
- understand the role of the health inspector.

In the previous chapter, you learned that biological, chemical, and physical hazards put the health of foodservice employees and customers at risk. However, biological hazards pose the greatest threat to foodservice. Preventing chemical and physical hazards is a matter of being careful. Preventing biological hazards is more complicated. So how exactly do you combat the bacteria, viruses, parasites, and fungi that pose a risk to safe food every day? What are the steps you must follow to prevent pathogens from multiplying in your food? In this chapter, you will learn the issues foodservice professionals focus on to ensure safe, healthy food.

Government's Role in Food Safety

Many government agencies are involved in keeping the US food supply safe and preventing foodborne illness. The Food and Drug Administration (FDA) and the US Department of Agriculture (USDA) are two of the federal government agencies that play key roles. These agencies inspect food and create recommendations for food safety regulations. The FDA publishes the

FDA Food Code which outlines recommendations for food safety.

State and local agencies create their own food safety regulations. As of 2013, 50 states, two territories, and the Indian Health Service had voluntarily adopted codes patterned after some version of the *FDA Food Code*. State and local agencies are responsible for enforcing their regulations and performing inspections in

- restaurants
- grocery stores
- correctional facilities
- vending operations
- schools
- day-care centers
- nursing homes
- hospitals

Since food codes can vary by state and local agency, you must learn what regulations apply to your foodservice operation.

Time and Temperature Control

Both time and temperature must be controlled to prevent pathogen contamination of food. This principle is key to food safety. To keep food safe, you must ensure the following:

- *Time.* When food must be in the temperature danger zone, limit the time to no more than four cumulative hours.
- *Temperature.* Make sure food is either above or below the temperature danger zone [41°F–135°F (5°C–57°C)] whenever possible.

Kitchen workers follow these two principles every day as they perform their job. Time and temperature control is crucial to common kitchen operations such as thawing, cooking, hot holding, cooling, storing, and reheating.

Thawing

Often, frozen food is thawed in an unsafe manner. Leaving a frozen item on the counter to thaw is not safe. The outside of the item is in the temperature danger zone long before the center of the item is completely thawed.

The FDA suggests the following three ways to thaw food safely:

1. *Thaw the product under cold running water.* The water temperature should be less than 70°F (21°C), 8-1.

SANITATION & SAFETY

The Importance of Thermometers

Part of most chefs' attire is a small thermometer sticking out of a pocket. Maintaining proper temperatures is one of the chef's main defenses against bacterial growth. You will frequently see a chef checking temperatures of refrigerators, freezers, dishmachines, warmers, and food. These temperatures are recorded and a file maintained. Temperatures that do not meet standards must be addressed immediately.

Draz-Koetke/Goodheart-Willcox Publisher

8-1 Food should be completely submerged when thawing with running water.

2. *Thaw the product in the refrigerator.* This takes longer than the running water method. This method is useful for products that cannot be submerged in water. The refrigerator temperature must be below 41°F (5°C) to keep the product out of the temperature danger zone.
3. *Cook product directly from a frozen state without first thawing.* It is important to note that the product must be cooked to the proper internal temperature and not simply thawed. The product may be thawed in a microwave if it is to be cooked immediately following thawing.

Cooking

As food cooks, heat destroys the biological hazards that are present in the food. Internal temperatures of cooked food must be high enough to kill pathogens. Most time and temperature control for safety (TCS) food is cooked to an internal temperature higher than 145°F (63°C).

Foodservice professionals use instant-read thermometers to measure the temperature of food. The thermometer must be placed in the center, or thickest part of the food to get a true reading, 8-2. FDA recommends cooking food to the following minimum internal temperatures:

- 165°F (74°C) for poultry, stuffings/stuffed food products, and leftovers.
- 155°F (68°C) for hot-held eggs, and ground meats and fish.
- 145°F (63°C) for whole muscle meats and fish, and raw eggs that are broken and immediately cooked to order.

There are exceptions to these general temperature guidelines. Follow your local food code and supervisor's instructions for each food preparation.

Hot Holding

In professional foodservice, it is often necessary to hold cooked food and keep it hot until it is needed. According to the FDA, food held hot must maintain an internal

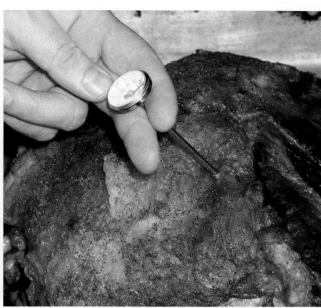

Draz-Koetke/Goodheart-Willcox Publisher

8-2 Thermometers are used to check the internal temperatures of food.

temperature of at least 135°F (57°C). Warming ovens and steam tables are designed to do this. If proper holding temperatures are not maintained, food can venture into the temperature danger zone. If food is in the temperature danger zone for too long, the food is no longer fit to be served. Food in a steam table should be stirred frequently and the temperature checked so it does not fall below 135°F (57°C), 8-3.

Cooling

Many time and temperature abuses happen during cooling. Hot, fully cooked food must be cooled rapidly so it does not spend more than six hours in the temperature danger zone. Cooked foods must be cooled from 135°F (57°C) to 70°F (21°C) in two hours or less. In less than a total of six hours, the food must be cooled to 41°F (5°C) or less. Foods prepared from ingredients at room temperature must be cooled to 41°F (5°C) within four hours. If food is not cooled properly, it becomes a breeding ground for biological hazards.

Draz-Koetke/Goodheart-Willcox Publisher

8-3 Foods held in a steam table must be stirred frequently to keep the top of the food out of the temperature danger zone.

Techniques for chilling food safely and rapidly include the following:

- *Place food in shallow pans for cooling.* This increases the surface area and speeds up cooling, 8-4. For example, it takes a stockpot of soup many hours to cool in the refrigerator. If the soup is ladled into shallow pans and placed in the refrigerator, it cools more quickly. If too many pans of hot product are placed in the refrigerator, it could raise the temperature of the refrigerator. This may cause other food in the refrigerator to spoil. Over time, cooling too much food this way can damage the refrigerator.

- *Place the container of hot food in an ice water bath and stir the ingredients frequently.* Water transfers heat—and thus cold— much more efficiently than air. For example, you could stand outside in 32°F (0°C) weather wearing just shorts and a T-shirt for maybe 15 minutes before becoming uncomfortable. But if you were to jump into 32°F (0°C) water, you would

Draz-Koetke/Goodheart-Willcox Publisher

8-4 As hot food is spread out in shallow containers, more surface area is exposed and the cooling process is faster.

be in serious danger within minutes. When placing a pot in ice water, place it on a perforated pan to allow water to circulate beneath the pot.

- *Place food in a blast chiller or other rapid cooling equipment.* Blast chillers are designed to chill food quickly, 8-5. They work by continually "blasting" freezing air over the food. If food is left too long in a blast chiller, it will freeze.

Storing

TCS food must be stored at or below 41°F (5°C). At refrigeration temperatures, pathogen growth is slowed greatly. However, in time the food will spoil at these temperatures. Freezer temperatures below 0°F (–18°C) stop pathogen growth. Freezing kills some biological hazards, but more often that is not the case. Instead, freezing simply renders them dormant.

8-5 Blast chillers cool food quickly with cold, circulating air.

All coolers and freezers should have a thermometer installed or placed in the warmest location of the unit. Routinely verify cooler and freezer temperatures to ensure food is being held at a safe temperature. It is important not to overload or otherwise restrict airflow to encourage the movement of cold air around food items.

Reheating

In foodservice, it is often necessary to reheat chilled food. Proper sanitation procedure must be followed when reheating food. Reheated food must be heated to an

SANITATION & SAFETY
What Went Wrong?

During the afternoon shift, a foodservice worker made 10 gallons of thick split pea soup. When the soup was done, it was left to cool at room temperature for three hours in the same container. The soup was barely steaming when the worker put the soup in the refrigerator on a shelf. The next day, the same foodservice worker took the soup from the refrigerator. He noticed there were small bubbles on the surface of the soup. He also noticed the center of the soup was still slightly warm. He reheated the soup and served it to customers. The customers complained the soup tasted sour. What went wrong?

The soup spent many hours in the temperature danger zone while cooling at room temperature and later in the refrigerator. During this time, pathogens multiplied in the soup. The bubbles and sour flavor were caused by the bacteria. The soup should never have been served to the customers. The soup had to be discarded, which hurts the restaurant's profit. This was an obvious example of spoiled food. Remember that not all spoilage is easily recognized.

Draz-Koetke/Goodheart-Willcox Publisher

internal temperature of 165°F (74°C) for at least 15 seconds. It must reach 165°F (74°C) within no more than two hours. Food may be reheated only once.

Cross-Contamination

Animation

Another important factor that poses a risk to safe food is cross-contamination. Cross-contamination occurs when harmful microorganisms are transferred from one product to another by hands, utensils, equipment, or other physical contact, 8-6. This is one of the largest sources of foodborne illness. Cross-contamination is often the result of negligence or ignorance on the part of the foodservice worker.

Cross-contamination happens in a variety of ways. Hands are often the vehicles that transfer a contaminant. For instance, if a worker does not wash his or her hands after handling raw chicken and before preparing cold sandwiches, contamination can occur. In this scenario, the worker transfers bacteria from the chicken to the sandwiches. In the same way, scratching your skin or head and

Draz-Koetke/Goodheart-Willcox Publisher

8-6 Using the same cutting board to prepare raw chicken and a ready-to-eat sandwich will result in cross-contamination.

then touching lunchmeat can result in cross-contamination. Hands must be washed properly and often throughout the workday to prevent cross-contamination.

Utensils such as knives and cutting boards can contribute to cross-contamination. Consider the following scenario:

Joe is cutting pork steaks on a cutting board. Mary, the pantry cook, needs to cut up a large amount of salad greens and is in a hurry. She asks Joe to help her cut some lettuce. Joe, eager to help a fellow cook, quickly wipes off his cutting board and knife using a side towel. He takes half of the lettuce and cuts it using the knife and cutting board that he just wiped off.

Do you see the problem? The cutting board and knife were not cleaned and sanitized. Any pathogens present in the meat were transferred to the lettuce. That is not the only problem; another opportunity for cross-contamination was created. Bacteria were transferred to the side towel when it was used to wipe the knife and cutting board. The side towel could later become a vehicle for further cross-contamination. Utensils must be cleaned and sanitized between tasks to prevent transfer of contaminants.

Cross-contamination can happen in the refrigerator. For instance, a container of raw fish stored above a container of ham salad could drip into the salad, 8-7. To prevent cross-contamination, store raw meat, poultry, and fish separate from ready-to-eat foods. If it is not possible to store separately, store ready-to-eat foods above the raw products.

To further guard against cross-contamination, food should be stored in leak-proof containers, covered, and labeled with the item name and date. If raw meat, poultry, and fish must be stored together, place the item with the lowest minimum internal cooking temperature at top. For instance, beef roast has a minimum cooking temperature of 145°F (63°C) so it should be stored above chicken, which has a minimum cooking temperature of 165°F (74°C).

8-7 These raw chickens are improperly stored above ready-to-eat food (lettuce).

Clean Versus Sanitary

Have you ever seen a beautifully clean kitchen? Maybe it is the cafeteria kitchen in your school before the cooks begin their day. Maybe it is the kitchen on TV or your kitchen at home. While these kitchens may look clean, they may not be sanitary.

There is a difference between clean and sanitary. **Clean** describes a condition of being free of dirt, grease, or grime. A counter or piece of equipment may be clean, but may not be sanitary. **Sanitary** refers to an environment that is free from pathogens. Remember that biological hazards are often not visible to the naked eye. A kitchen can look clean and still be unsanitary.

Professional kitchens have many areas that need to be routinely cleaned and sanitized. Any surface such as a table, cutting board, or piece of equipment that comes in contact with food is considered a **food-contact surface**. Food-contact surfaces can **harbor**, or be home to, pathogens and lead to cross-contamination.

Food-contact surfaces must be both cleaned and sanitized before food preparation takes place. To be effective against biological hazards, both steps must be performed. Completing only one of these steps is not enough.

Step One: Cleaning

The first step toward a sanitary work environment is cleaning, or the removal of any visible dirt, grime, or pieces of food. Proper cleaning requires the use of hot water and detergents or grease cutters. Care must be taken when using chemical cleaning agents.

Clean all food-contact surfaces after completing a task and before starting a new one. Foodservice operations should have cleaning schedules and policies to ensure that facility cleanliness is maintained.

Step Two: Sanitizing

Once the cleaning is complete, it is time for step two, sanitizing. Sanitizing kills pathogens. Foodservice workers have two powerful sanitizing strategies—heat and chemicals. When used correctly, heat or the appropriate chemicals kill most pathogens.

Heat Sanitizing

To heat sanitize a food-contact surface, it must be soaked in water that is at least 171°F (77°C) for 30 seconds. Many dishmachines rely on hot water for the sanitizing step. The final sanitizing rinse in these machines must be at least 180°F (82°C). Small pieces of equipment that fit into a dishmachine can be effectively heat sanitized. Heat sanitizing large

SUSTAINABLE CULINARY

Green Cleaning

Across the United States, restaurants use chemicals to clean and sanitize every day. As the environmental impact of some of these chemicals is better understood, restaurateurs and chefs are evaluating the environmental effect these chemicals have. There are now many ecofriendly chemicals that clean and sanitize effectively. To learn more, investigate which chemicals are used in your school or at the restaurant where you work. For additional resources, visit the Green Seal organization's website or search the Environmental Protection Agency's (EPA) website for environmentally preferable purchasing for cleaning products.

Using Cleaning and Sanitizing Products

- Ask the supervisor how and where to use each product—specific products have specific jobs.

- Never randomly mix products. To avoid toxic by-products, follow manufacturer's instructions on the label.

- Wear protective clothing, such as gloves, aprons, and eyewear, as needed.

- Dilute chemicals to proper strength with water. Improper dilution can make the product ineffective or dangerous. Use the proper chemical test strips to measure the dilution strength.

- Mix chemicals with water at the correct temperature.

- Allow surface to air-dry.

- In the event of an emergency, consult material data safety sheets (MSDS) and call a poison control center immediately.

8-8 Always read the label on cleaning and sanitizing supplies before using.

pieces of equipment and countertops is not effective and can be dangerous.

Chemical Sanitizing

Chemical sanitizing is the most common sanitizing technique in the professional kitchen. A variety of chemicals can be used for chemical sanitizing. These chemicals are only effective when used properly. Factors such as water temperature, hardness of water, concentration of sanitizer, detergents, food residue, and contact time influence effectiveness. Some of these chemicals are dangerous if used improperly. Precautions must be taken when using chemical sanitizers, 8-8.

Cleaning and Sanitizing the Entire Kitchen

There are many different types of food-contact surfaces in the kitchen. Each requires a slightly different technique for cleaning and sanitizing. While the technique may

be different, the result is always the same—to remove visible dirt and kill pathogens. Food-contact surfaces are divided into the following categories:
- work surfaces
- small equipment and dishes
- large equipment

Work Surfaces

Counters and workstations need to be cleaned and sanitized when a task is completed or after four hours of continuous work. For instance, while cutting meat or fish on a cutting board, the worktable also becomes soiled. Once the job is done, or after four hours of continuous work, the counter needs to be cleaned and sanitized. Similarly, if an item such as a box of produce or chef's toolbox is placed on a worktable, the table must be sanitized once the item is removed. Work surfaces are usually sanitized using a chemical sanitizer. Each workstation in the kitchen should have sanitizing solution on hand. Sanitizing solution can be dispensed from a spray bottle or from a bucket using a wiping towel. In either case, the container of sanitizer must be clearly labeled and prepared according to manufacturer's directions. The sanitizing solution must be checked periodically to ensure effectiveness and replaced as needed.

Small Equipment and Dishes

Dishes and small equipment must be cleaned and sanitized after each use or every four hours of continuous use. Professional

SANITATION & SAFETY
Common Chemical Sanitizers

There are many different brand names for chemical sanitizers used in commercial kitchens. The active ingredient in most chemical sanitizers is typically one of the following:
- Iodine
- Chlorine
- Quaternary Ammonium ("QUAT")

TECHNIQUE
Sanitizing a Counter or Worktable

1. Clear table or countertop for cleaning. Dirty objects must be cleaned and sanitized separately.
2. Wash the table with hot water and detergent. Apply pressure to remove any dirt or stuck-on food.

3. Rinse table using hot water and a clean towel.

4. Apply sanitizer using either a spray bottle or a special sanitizing bucket. Be certain the sanitizer is diluted following the manufacturer's specifications.

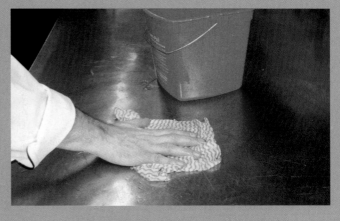

5. Allow to air-dry

foodservice workers use a combination of chemicals and heat to clean and sanitize dishes and small equipment. Dishes and small equipment are cleaned and sanitized in dishmachines or three-compartment sinks.

Dishmachine A dishmachine can be found in every professional kitchen. Dishmachines have a wide range of capacity. Some are small and can wash only one rack of dishes at a time. Others can be very large using a conveyor belt to move numerous racks of dishes through the machine, 8-9. The dishmachine uses three cycles to clean and sanitize. The first cycle removes physical objects and grease. The second cycle rinses off detergent used in the first cycle. The final cycle sanitizes. It relies on either water over 180°F

(82°C) or a chemical sanitizer to accomplish this task. You will need training before using a particular dishmachine for the first time.

Three-Compartment Sink

Health code requires that most commercial kitchens have a three-compartment sink. A **three-compartment sink** consists of three adjacent sinks used to clean, rinse, and sanitize small equipment and utensils. In addition, there is a work area on each side of the three-compartment sink. The work area next to the wash sink is where dirty equipment is placed before washing. The work area next to the sanitizing sink is a drain board used for air-drying cleaned and sanitized equipment. Many restaurants have systems that dispense the correct amount of detergent for the size

Eric Futran/ChefShots

8-9 A dishmachine should be an adequate size to meet the needs of the operation.

TECHNIQUE
Using a Dishmachine

1. Presoak flatware to loosen encrusted food.
2. Scrape or use a high-powered sprayer to remove any visible pieces of food off dishes, equipment, flatware, or glassware before placing into the machine.

3. Place the items to be washed in the appropriate dish rack.

4. Load the rack into the dishmachine.
5. When the cleaning and sanitizing cycles are complete, remove from the dishmachine and allow to air-dry.

of the sink, 8-10. Three-compartment sinks are often used for washing small equipment such as pots and pans. They are rarely used for cleaning and sanitizing dishware.

Regardless the method used, small equipment and dishes must be properly stored in a designated area after cleaning and sanitizing to protect them from contamination. To protect cleaned and sanitized items, store them

- at least six inches from the floor
- on or in cleaned and sanitized drawers, trays, or carts
- with handles of utensils and flatware facing up
- upside down (glassware and cups)

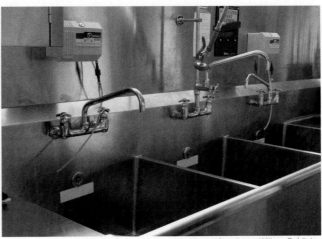

Draz-Koetke/Goodheart-Willcox Publisher

8-10 Often detergent or sanitizer dispensing systems are attached to the wall above the appropriate sink compartment.

TECHNIQUE
Using a Three-Compartment Sink

1. Scrape large food particles from dirty equipment into a garbage can or disposal. If needed, wipe excess grease from item with disposable towels first.
2. Fill the first compartment with hot water and an appropriate detergent. It may be necessary to wear protective gloves if the hot water or detergent irritates the skin. Change the water once it becomes dirty, greasy, or cool.

3. Fill the middle sink with hot water. Rinse the equipment from the first sink in the middle sink. Change the water once it becomes slightly dirty or cool.
4. Fill the third sink with a chemical sanitizer and water dilution following manufacturer's instructions. Leave the equipment in the sanitizing sink for the specified time. Heat sanitizing is rarely used in the three-compartment sink since it is difficult to keep the water at the proper temperature and can be dangerous for workers.
5. Place sanitized equipment on the drain board next to the sanitizing sink to air-dry. A drying rack may be necessary for certain items.

Never leave knives, glass, or sharp objects in a sink. Serious injury could result if an unsuspecting worker reaches into the water.

SANITATION & SAFETY
That Dirty Towel

The counters have just been cleaned and sanitized when the cook grabs a soiled side towel to dry the counter. Have you ever seen this bad habit? Everything may look clean, but using a dirty towel negates any sanitizing. It is best to simply let surfaces air-dry.

Large Equipment

Large equipment cannot be washed in a dishmachine or three-compartment sink due to size constraints. Electrical equipment cannot be cleaned and sanitized in a dishmachine or three-compartment sink either. However, large kitchen equipment such as mixers, slicers, and grinders must still be cleaned and sanitized. Clean and sanitize large equipment after each use or after four hours of continual use. Equipment should be covered to protect it from contamination until the next use.

Since each piece of large equipment is unique, you should receive training before cleaning it for the first time. Some large equipment has parts that can be removed and washed either in a dishmachine or three-compartment sink. Certain steps and safety precautions should always be followed when cleaning and sanitizing equipment.

Cleaning and Sanitation Schedule

In order to ensure that no part of kitchen cleaning is overlooked, kitchens should follow a cleaning schedule. The cleaning schedule lists
- areas and equipment to be cleaned
- when the cleaning should be done

SANITATION & SAFETY

Mind the Can Opener

One piece of equipment that is frequently overlooked at cleanup is the can opener. Can openers used in professional kitchens are different from those found in the home. The blade and handle need to be cleaned and sanitized every four hours when in use. This will ensure that food does not build up and lead to a biological hazard.

- who performs the cleaning
- procedures to follow

Items may need to be cleaned after each use, every several hours, each shift, daily, weekly, or monthly. When cleaning is completed, time and date is noted on the schedule.

To further ensure that sanitation standards are maintained, many kitchens do regular self-inspections. Applying the criteria of the state or local food codes helps assure there are no deficiencies when the actual health inspection takes place.

Personal Hygiene

Do you know you are one of the main vehicles for food contamination? The human

TECHNIQUE
Cleaning and Sanitizing Large Equipment

Do not clean any equipment until you have been trained on its use and cleaning.

1. Unplug electrical equipment before beginning to clean.
2. Wear cut-resistant gloves if washing a sharp piece of machinery like a slicer or grinder.

3. Disassemble equipment as needed. Clean and sanitize small parts in a dishmachine or three-compartment sink.
4. Wash with hot water and detergent to remove visible grime and pieces of food.

5. Rinse with hot water.
6. Dry using a clean towel or paper towels.
7. Sanitize using sanitizing solution. Follow manufacturer's instructions to determine dilution.

body is a perfect environment for breeding and carrying biological hazards. Good personal hygiene helps you avoid being a source of contamination in the kitchen.

Hands

Hands look innocent, but are the most likely source of contamination on the human body. Every time you touch or work with food, your hands become contaminated. Every time you use the restroom, touch your hair, or scratch your skin, bacteria are transferred to your hands. Fingernails, jewelry, and open cuts or burns on your hands can harbor dangerous bacteria. Foodservice professionals must pay close attention to their hands! This includes proper handwashing, use of disposable gloves, attention to small injuries, and care of fingernails. During food preparation, the only jewelry that should be worn on an employee's hands or arms is a plain wedding band.

Handwashing

Handwashing seems simple enough. You have been washing hands your whole life, but properly washing your hands with soap requires close attention to detail. You need to know where and when to wash your hands, 8-11. (See the technique box to learn how to wash your hands properly.)

Disposable Gloves

Many states require the use of disposable gloves when handling ready-to-eat foods.

Proper Handwashing

Where

- designated handwashing stations stocked with soap, disposable towels, and a fingernail brush
- *not* food preparation sinks

When

- before beginning a work shift
- after using the restroom
- after eating, drinking, smoking, or taking a break
- at the end of each job task
- after handling toxic chemicals
- after taking out the trash
- after handling dirty dishes or linens
- after coughing or sneezing
- after touching hair or skin

Draz-Koetke/Goodheart-Willcox Publisher

8-11 Proper handwashing is essential in foodservice.

While gloves can play an important role in preventing the spread of biological hazards via hands, they are not the cure-all. Gloves can give a false sense of security. Improper glove use can actually lead to an increased risk of contamination. Guidelines for using gloves include the following:

- Properly wash hands using soap before putting on a pair of gloves.
- Change gloves if sweat starts to drip out from under the gloves. Be sure to wash hands before putting on new pair.
- Change gloves after every work task.
- Change gloves if they become even slightly torn or punctured.
- Change gloves at least every four hours.
- Never wash gloved hands.

Hand Injuries

Kitchens are fast-paced work environments and can be dangerous. Small hand injuries such as cuts or burns are common. Foodservice workers must not work with open wounds. Open wounds are an ideal breeding ground for pathogens. All wounds must be adequately dressed with bandages and covered with a glove or finger cot. All kitchen injuries should be reported to a supervisor to determine if it is safe to work with food.

Fingernails

Pathogens can hide under fingernails. Fingernails must be clean when working with food. A fingernail brush is needed to clean under fingernails. Nails must also be trimmed short. Nail polish and artificial nails are possible physical hazards and are not permitted in the professional kitchen.

Hair

Hair is a notorious breeding ground for bacteria. Hairs found in food are repulsive. Hair restraints should be worn in professional kitchens to prevent foodservice workers from touching their hair while working. Hair restraints also keep hair out of food. Restraints can be anything from a chef

TECHNIQUE
Proper Handwashing

1. Use water that is as hot as is comfortable—at least 110°F (43°C).
2. Roll up sleeves and wet your hands. Add soap and lather hands, including the backs and wrists, and up to the elbows.

3. Scrub for 20 seconds and use a nailbrush to scrub under the fingernails. Wash well between fingers.

4. Rinse under hot, running water.

5. Dry hands and arms with a single-use paper towel or air dryer. Do not dry hands on a communal towel or apron.
6. Use paper towel to turn water off and open bathroom door, then throw towel away.

hat to a hairnet. If hair falls below the collar, it should be tied back and a hair restraint used. Beards that are not well trimmed should be covered with a beard net.

Bathing

All foodservice workers should bathe or shower daily before coming to work. Using cologne or perfume is not a substitute for daily bathing. Deodorant is recommended in addition to bathing, but strongly scented deodorant and colognes should be avoided.

Clothing

At the beginning of every workday, foodservice employees should put on a clean uniform. If during the course of the day the uniform becomes heavily soiled, it should be changed. Ideally, the work uniform should not be worn to work. Employers prefer that employees change into their uniform at work before starting their shift.

Smoking, Drinking, and Eating

Smoking, drinking, and eating are not allowed in the professional kitchen. These activities should only take place in designated areas. Drinking cups should not be at workstations. Some states allow squeeze bottles in work areas. Remember to wash hands after smoking, eating, or drinking. Tasting food is permissible and part of a cook's job. Be sure not to use fingers when tasting food. Proper procedure requires use of a disposable or sanitized spoon. A spoon used for taste testing should never be reused because this could contaminate the food.

Illness

Foodservice workers should not work with or around food if they have a contagious illness. Employees should notify their supervisor if they are ill. Illnesses resulting from

SANITATION & SAFETY
Beware of Boxes

Kitchens are not always perfect places. Sometimes, foodservice workers practice poor sanitation. One bad habit is not cleaning and sanitizing a work surface after a box has been placed on it. Many times, boxes have been placed on floors at vegetable markets, meatpacking houses, or in trucks. Sometimes boxes are set on sidewalks or in streets. Don't forget, even if the box looks clean, it most likely is not sanitary.

certain foodborne pathogens should be reported to local health departments.

Insect and Rodent Control

Pests are a subject that people do not like to consider. The mere mention of a kitchen infested with insects or rodents is enough to destroy a restaurant's business.

Insects and rodents spread biological hazards in a couple of ways. Their urine and feces contain pathogens. When pests leave their droppings, they also deposit pathogens. Insects and rodents also spread these hazards with their feet and bodies. When they touch garbage and then crawl over work surfaces, they contaminate the area. The insects that pose the greatest health risk are flies and cockroaches. Mice and rats are the most problematic rodents to foodservice operations.

The most important step in pest control is to keep a clean and sanitized facility. An unclean facility provides food and breeding areas for pests. If the facility is not clean, it is difficult to practice effective pest control.

Foodservice facilities should be designed to prevent pests from entering the building. Window and door screens keep out insects and rodents. Some facilities have special blowers installed above doors so that when the door is open, a powerful curtain of air blows across the opening. Flying insects are not able to fly through this air curtain. Some insects, such as cockroaches, enter the kitchen in delivery boxes. Always inspect boxes for signs of insects or their egg sacs. To prevent rodents from entering a facility, make sure doors and windows seal tightly and ensure that the building's foundation is free of holes and cracks.

In addition, many city or county health departments require regular visits from a pest control operator. A **pest control operator (PCO)** is a licensed professional who uses various chemicals, sprays, and traps to prevent or eliminate infestations. Questions concerning specific pest problems should be addressed to the PCO.

Waste Control

Every kitchen produces waste during the workday. Garbage is a perfect breeding ground for bacteria and attracts insects and rodents. Waste is placed in garbage containers that are lined with sturdy plastic bags. When these containers are full or at the end of the workday, they are emptied into dumpsters outside the restaurant. The dumpster is regularly emptied by a professional garbage collecting service, 8-12. Remember to wash hands after handling garbage.

Many kitchens separate recyclable waste and compostable waste. Clearly marked containers should be designated for metal cans, plastic, and paper which can be recycled. Compostable materials can be decomposed by natural bacteria and used for fertilizer, saving landfill space. Some operations separate items such as fruit and vegetable scraps, and some paper products from the waste stream so they can be composted. Just as with garbage containers, recycling and compost containers need to be kept covered and should be cleaned regularly.

Guidelines for Waste Control

- Empty indoor containers frequently.
- Garbage should not come in contact with food preparation surfaces as it is being transported to the dumpster.
- Garbage containers should be regularly cleaned, both inside and out.
- Garbage containers should be leak and pest proof, and covered when not in use.
- Recyclables should be separated according to local recycling plans.
- Grease should be collected separately instead of being placed with the rest of the garbage.
- Dumpsters need to be large enough so the lid can close completely. (Even small spaces between the lid and dumpster can attract insect and rodent pests.)
- Lids need to have covers that fit snugly. The lids should also be locked shut to discourage vandalism.
- Dumpsters need to be emptied as soon as they are filled.
- Dumpsters must be periodically washed.

8-12 Foodservice operations must manage their waste to maintain a pest-free kitchen.

Hazard Analysis Critical Control Point

HACCP is a food safety program that was developed nearly 30 years ago. **Hazard Analysis Critical Control Point (HACCP)** is a system that identifies and manages key steps in food handling where contamination is most likely to occur. HACCP was developed to guarantee that a safe food supply was sent with astronauts into space. This system now has widespread use in the foodservice industry.

The HACCP system involves analyzing food-handling procedures to identify potential hazards which pose threats to the food's wholesomeness. Those hazards may be present at any point along the journey the food takes, 8-13. HACCP pays particular attention to the temperature danger zone and minimum internal temperatures.

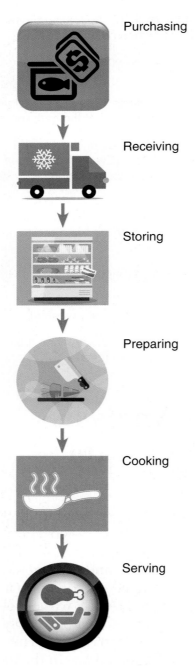

Purchasing

Receiving

Storing

Preparing

Cooking

Serving

8-13 Food may be exposed to hazards at every step on the path to the customer's plate.

HACCP plans rely on predetermined critical control points. A **critical control point (CCP)** is a step in food handling at which control can be applied to prevent or eliminate a food safety hazard. Often, the CCP is the cooking step at which sufficiently high internal temperatures kill pathogens. Other critical control points include the length of time a product is held in storage and at what temperature. A HACCP plan consists of seven steps, 8-14.

Increasingly, restaurants are implementing HACCP programs. Restaurants that successfully create and follow HACCP programs reduce the possibility of an outbreak. State and local health departments review and approve HACCP plans.

The Health Inspection

Local health departments monitor compliance with health codes. An official of

Seven Steps to a HACCP Plan

1. Analyze how foods move through the establishment.

2. Determine which steps are critical control points (CCP).

3. Define the limits for each CCP needed to achieve safety. Limits might include maximum time in the temperature danger zone or minimum internal temperatures.

4. Establish monitoring procedures for employees to implement and record CCP data.

5. Establish plan for corrective action when limits for CCP are not met.

6. Establish procedures to verify the HACCP system is working.

7. Establish record keeping and documentation procedures.

8-14 Chefs use HACCP plans to improve food handling in their kitchens.

the health department periodically inspects all foodservice establishments. The frequency of the inspections is determined by a number of factors

- size of the foodservice operation
- operation's prior inspection results
- risk level of customer base
- workload of health department

Health inspectors are responsible for protecting the public health. They make sure that the public is being served safe food by making unannounced inspections.

Contrary to what many chefs feel, health inspectors are not the enemy, 8-15. When a health department official inspects a food-service operation, be open and honest with them. Do not try to hide things from them. Instead, ask health inspectors questions and advice. View health inspectors as expert resources ready to help keep your workplace free from biological, chemical, and physical hazards. If there are sanitation questions that arise between inspections, you can always call the local health department for guidance.

Draz-Koetke/Goodheart-Willcox Publisher

8-15 Health inspections are performed on foodservice operations on a regular basis.

Summary Points

- Federal agencies recommend food safety regulations, but state and local agencies write and enforce their own regulations.

- Time and temperature control is essential to ensuring safe food.

- Cross-contamination occurs when harmful microorganisms are transferred from one product to another by hands, utensils, equipment, or other contact.

- A food-contact surface must first be cleaned and then sanitized.

- Small equipment is cleaned and sanitized in a three-compartment sink or dishmachine. Dishes are cleaned and sanitized in a dishmachine. Large equipment is cleaned and sanitized in place.

- Personal hygiene is important to the sanitary practices of a kitchen.

- Insect and rodent control is part of sanitation.

- Waste must be disposed of properly so it does not become a breeding ground for bacteria or an attraction to insects and rodents.

- A HACCP plan identifies and manages key points in food handling where contamination is most likely to occur.

In Review

Assess

1. True or false. The *FDA Food Code* serves as the model for most state's food safety regulations.

2. What are three approved methods for thawing out food safely?

3. List three ways to cool food safely.

4. True or false. Cross-contamination is one of the most common causes of foodborne illness.

5. Explain the difference between clean and sanitary.

6. Describe the function of each compartment in a three-compartment sink.

7. The final sanitizing rinse in dishmachines that rely on hot water for sanitizing must be at least _____°F or higher to sanitize.

8. List the steps for washing hands correctly.

9. Explain how rodents and insects spread biological hazards.

10. True or false. A HACCP plan analyzes food-handling procedures to identify opportunities for cost savings.

11. What is the principle responsibility of a health inspector?

Core Skills

12. **Writing.** Write a paper that supports or opposes the argument for a federally mandated, uniform food code across all states, counties, and cities.

13. **Math.** You have a recipe from a French colleague that you would like to use but all the temperatures are Celsius. The recipe requires a 177°C oven temperature. Convert 177°C to Fahrenheit. Show your work.

14. **Speaking.** Research a foodborne-illness outbreak and present your findings to the class. Use at least three sources of information for your research. In your presentation, provide a brief evaluation of the credibility and accuracy of each source, noting any discrepancies between the sources.

15. **Math.** Calculate the cost per fluid ounce for sanitizing solutions using chlorine or quaternary ammonium given the following information (Hint: 1 gal. = 128 fl. oz.):
    A. Undiluted chlorine—price: $6.75/1 gal., dilution: 0.5 fl. oz./1 gal. of water
    B. Quaternary ammonium—price: $35.50/2.5 gal., dilution: 0.25 fl. oz./ 1 gal. of water

16. **Speaking.** Prepare an in-service on basic kitchen sanitation and professional hygiene. Identify the audience for which your in-service is intended (for example, volunteers at the food pantry or a middle school foods class). The presentation should include a demonstration of how to properly clean

a piece of kitchen equipment and proper handwashing technique. Your appearance should reflect the professional grooming and hygiene standards discussed in the text. Adjust the style of delivery, vocabulary, use of visual aids, and length of presentation based on your audience.

17. **CTE Career Readiness.** Suppose your restaurant supervisor presents your team the following dilemma: your produce supplier has just delivered your weekly supply of potatoes and half of the load is green so you will be unable to use them to make mashed potatoes for a large catering event that evening. Your team assignment is to develop a creative and innovation plan for solving this problem. Use the problem-solving process to create your plan:
    A. Analyze the problem.
    B. Apply past learning/brainstorm possible options.
    C. Gather new information.
    D. Organize and compare data.
    E. Choose a solution.
    F. Summarize the actions necessary to solve the problem.

Critical Thinking

18. **Apply.** In pairs, assume the roles of chef and health inspector and perform a health inspection of your school's kitchen. If possible, utilize the same criteria as your local health department. Report your findings.

19. **Assess.** HACCP is one of the most effective tools foodservice has to ensure food safety. Do you believe it is foolproof? Explain.

20. **Debate.** Debate the following topic in small groups: In foodservice, wearing disposable gloves is safer than clean, bare hands.

Technology

Use the Internet to find health department food-service sanitation inspections posted for public review. What are the most common violations noted? Do you think posting scores influences diners' decisions about where to eat?

Teamwork

Working in small groups, select a subpart from the *FDA Food Code* to compare to the state or local food code for your area. Work collaboratively to understand the subpart content. Present your findings to the class making strategic use of digital media to enhance interest and understanding. Use presentation style and word choice appropriate to the audience and content matter.

Chef's E-portfolio
Health Inspection

Upload your health inspection findings from activity #18. Ask your instructor where to save your file. This could be on the school's network or a flash drive of your own. Name your portfolio document *FirstnameLastname_Portfolio Ch#.docx* (i.e., JohnSmith_PortfolioCh08.docx).

Video Clip

Using a Three-Compartment Sink

Visit the G-W Learning Companion Website and view the bonus video clip "Setting up a three-compartment sink." After viewing the clip, answer the following questions:

1. What is placed in the middle sink of a three-compartment sink?

2. How do you know if the sanitizing solution is the correct strength?

3. True or false. Sanitized items should be allowed to air-dry.

Video

While studying, look for the activity icon to:

- Build vocabulary with e-flash cards and matching activities.
- Expand learning with video clips, photo identification activities, animations, and interactive activities.
- Review and assess what you learn by completing end-of-chapter questions.

G-WLEARNING.com

Sideways Design/Shutterstock.com

Safety in the Kitchen 9

Reading Prep

Before reading the chapter, skim the photos and their captions. As you are reading, determine how these concepts contribute to the ideas presented in the text.

Culinary Terminology
Build Vocab

kitchen hood fire suppression system, p. 147

Academic Terminology
Build Vocab

Occupational Safety and Health Administration (OSHA), p. 135
heat exhaustion, p. 141
heatstroke, p. 141
cardiopulmonary resuscitation (CPR), p. 143
automated external defibrillator (AED), p. 144
prudent, p. 145
fire extinguisher, p. 145

Objectives

After reading this chapter, you will be able to

- summarize the roles of government, employers, and employees in creating a safe workplace.
- explain how the professional culinary uniform promotes safety.
- recall common kitchen injuries and summarize steps to prevent or respond to accidents in the kitchen.
- implement basic fire prevention and safety practices.
- recognize content to include in an emergency readiness plan.

Any seasoned foodservice professional will tell you the kitchen can be a dangerous place. Most chefs can tell stories of injuries that they or their coworkers have sustained on-the-job. The kitchen is a fast-paced and stressful place. Add sharp knives, powerful machines, open flame, steam, and boiling liquids to this setting and the risk for an accident increases.

Safety issues are not limited to the kitchen. Foodservice workers must be prepared to respond to emergency situations that arise while serving customers. Foodservice and hospitality industries include environments from the dining room to room service. The safety information presented in this chapter is not limited to the kitchen or even the dining room. Safety is serious business.

The Safe Workplace

Who is responsible for a safe workplace? According to the US government, it is the employer's job to provide a safe workplace. Employers are required to train and supervise their employees in safe work practices. To ensure this happens, the government established the Occupational Safety and Health Administration in 1970. **Occupational Safety and Health Administration (OSHA)** is the governmental agency that defines and enforces safe working conditions. Employers can contact OSHA for safety advice. Employees can contact OSHA to report an unsafe working environment. By law, all workplaces must post OSHA's safety and health poster and maintain a yearly log of work-related injury and illness.

Every professional kitchen has safety policies and procedures. Before you begin work, you should be familiar with the safety policies and procedures of the kitchen. These policies and procedures are usually shared with new employees during an orientation session. Periodically, ongoing employees are given a review of procedures for safety, sanitation, and hazardous materials. Pay close attention during safety training because you will be held responsible for all safety information presented. Records of employees' attendance at these and other training sessions are kept in their files along with any certifications.

When an accident or injury occurs, a supervisor must be informed. The supervisor will ask the injured employee and any witnesses to fill out an incident report form. Forms should be completed accurately and promptly. The employer keeps these forms on file permanently for future reference. The forms can be used to trend injuries in

the workplace. Employers use the report to identify the problem and prevent it from happening again. Reports should also be created and filed for accidents involving customers.

The employer is not the only party responsible for safety. Foodservice employees must also take an active role in workplace safety. Safety begins by

- understanding everyday dangers in the kitchen.
- taking steps to prevent accidents.
- knowing what to do in the event of an accident or emergency.
- knowing who to contact in an emergency.

Most importantly, safety requires every foodservice employee to be alert and aware while at work. This is the first step to preventing accidents. Many accidents happen due to carelessness.

Dress for Safety

The chef uniform is a mark of professionalism. However, the uniform also contributes to working safely in the kitchen. The modern chef uniform is designed to provide maximum protection and comfort.

The Chef Jacket and Pants

The chef jacket is designed to protect the cook from burns. The long sleeves protect the arms from splatters of hot grease or the intense heat of a grill. The sleeves can be turned up when needed. If they hang too low, they could catch fire, drag in food, or get caught on machines. The traditional jacket is also double-breasted for a reason. When a cook stands in front of a hot stove or oven, the double layer protects the chest from the heat. The traditional jacket is white. White reflects heat, which helps keep the cook cool.

Professional cooks and chefs always wear long pants in the kitchen. Long pants protect the legs from burns. The traditional black and white checked pants also hide stains, 9-1.

CHEF'S ETHICS

Ethics and Accountability

According to Webster's dictionary, accountability is an ethical obligation or willingness to accept responsibility for your actions. Everyone is responsible for their actions, especially in how they treat others. Because the focus in the foodservice industry is serving others, accountability is an important employee trait. For instance, foodservice managers are accountable for the safety and well-being of employees and patrons of the establishment. Likewise, foodservice employees are responsible for treating customers well and also protecting their safety and security.

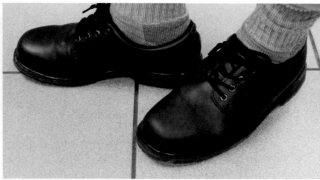
Draz-Koetke/Goodheart-Willcox Publisher

9-2 Sturdy, nonslip, close-toed shoes should be worn in the kitchen.

Draz-Koetke/Goodheart-Willcox Publisher

9-1 The chef's uniform is designed for safety and comfort.

Sturdy, comfortable shoes reduce fatigue and accidents. Some shoes are available with nonslip soles. This is ideal since kitchen floors are often slippery. At no time should open-toed shoes or sandals be worn in the kitchen. These shoes provide no protection against a falling knife or heavy object. Many European chefs wear clogs, which are open-heeled shoes. Clogs keep feet cool. Unfortunately, they can also cause accidents if the worker's heel slips off the clog.

Jewelry

Jewelry does not belong in the kitchen. Rings, necklaces, earrings, and bracelets can get caught on moving equipment and cause serious injury. Small pieces of jewelry, such as those used in piercings, can fall into food unobserved and become a physical hazard.

Kitchen Injuries

The kitchen can be a dangerous place. There are many ways in which workers can be injured. Most kitchen injuries are minor, heal quickly, and do not require additional medical care. If there is any doubt about the severity of an injury, play it safe and get medical attention.

Every professional kitchen should have a supervisor who is trained in basic first aid and lifesaving techniques. Every kitchen should also have an accessible first aid kit

The Apron

The apron is the least understood piece of clothing. Aprons certainly keep employees clean and looking good. Aprons are not to be used for wiping hands, as this could be a source of cross-contamination. The most important function aprons fulfill is protecting cooks from spills. If a hot liquid spills on an apron, the employee can immediately lift the apron away from the body to minimize any burns.

Footwear

Footwear is often overlooked when considering safety. Cooks spend most of the workday on their feet. Shoes need to be solid, well constructed, and comfortable, 9-2.

Mix In Math

Reading Graphs

A graph is a visual way to display a collection of data. In foodservice, graphs are used to communicate data relating to sales, labor hours, customer satisfaction, work injury trends, and much more. Two graphs commonly used are the line and bar graphs. Both graphs have a vertical and horizontal line.

The vertical line on the graph is called the Y axis.

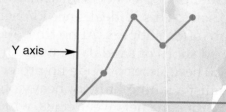

The horizontal line on the graph is called the X axis.

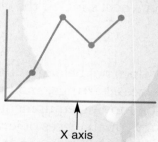

Data is organized between the X and Y axes differently for line and bar graphs.

Line Graph

A line graph displays data as a series of points connected by a line.

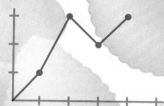

Each point matches up with a value on both the X and Y axis. Each axis should be labeled with the unit that the value is measured in.

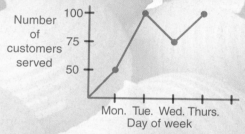

Bar Graph

A bar graph displays data as bars.

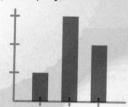

Draw an imaginary line from the top of the bar to the Y axis to find its value. The base of the bar matches up to the value on the X axis.

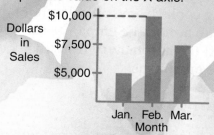

and phone numbers for emergency services posted. First aid kits need to be properly stocked at all times, 9-3. All employees should know the location of the first aid kit. They should also know what it contains. Never use anything in the first aid kit that you have not been trained to use. In the event of an injury, always alert a supervisor before applying first aid.

Preventing accidents requires a team effort. Many accidents are the result of carelessness. Paying close attention to what you and your coworkers are doing is the best prevention.

Cuts

There are many sharp knives and cutting machines in kitchens. It is not surprising that cuts are one of the most common injuries. Taking the following precautions can help to reduce the frequency and severity of cuts:

- Practice correct knife cutting skills.
- Always carry a knife by your side and pointed downward.
- Announce when you are carrying a knife so that others are aware of the danger.
- Never leave a knife or sharp object in a dishwashing sink.
- Never gesture with a knife.
- Never try to catch a falling knife. It is better to damage a knife than sustain a serious injury.
- Use only sharp knives. Dull knives cause injuries.
- Use knives only for appropriate tasks— do not use knives for opening cans or as a hammer.

In the event of a cut, first contact the supervisor. If the cut is small, apply first aid. The cut should be cleaned, disinfected, bandaged, and a protective finger cot should be worn, 9-4. Deeper cuts may require stitches and prompt medical treatment.

Contents of a Basic First Aid Kit

• activated charcoal (use only if instructed by Poison Control Center)	• gauze pads and roller gauze (assorted sizes)
• adhesive tape	• hand sanitizer
• antiseptic ointment	• plastic bags
• adhesive bandages (assorted sizes)	• scissors and tweezers
• burn gel or spray	• small flashlight and extra batteries
• cold pack	• ipecac syrup (use only if instructed by Poison Control Center)
• disposable gloves	
• eyewash bottles	• triangular bandage

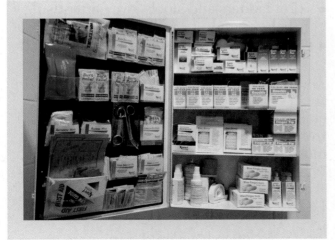

Draz-Koetke/Goodheart-Willcox Publisher

9-3 Every kitchen must have a properly stocked first aid kit.

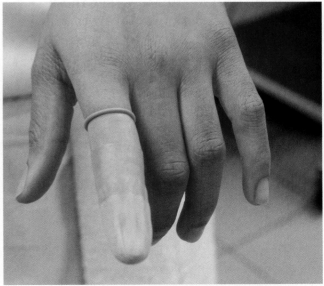

Draz-Koetke/Goodheart-Willcox Publisher

9-4 Finger cots help keep cuts clean and dry.

SANITATION & SAFETY
Limit Exposure

Foodservice employees may be exposed to health risks when cleaning up or responding to accidents involving another person's blood or other body fluids. Exposure may occur when assisting an injured coworker or when cleaning up after a customer who has become ill in the dining room. An operation's safety program should include cleaning procedures and training for employees to limit their exposure and risk. Training should include

- how diseases are passed in blood and body fluids
- cleanup procedures
- proper use and removal of gloves
- proper handwashing
- how to report an exposure incident

Draz-Koetke/Goodheart-Willcox Publisher

9-5 Items on the floor pose serious tripping hazards.

Puncture Wounds

Puncture wounds warrant close attention. They can be dangerous and may require further medical treatment. Often, these injuries look less serious than an open cut. Punctures can deposit bacteria deep in the skin where it is hard to wash. This can lead to infection. Fish fins are frequent causes of puncture wounds.

Puncture wounds must be washed well and an antibacterial product should be applied. If the wound is deep, seek medical attention. If the injury becomes red and painful, seek medical help immediately.

Falls

Slipping on a wet floor or tripping over a box can result in injuries ranging from bruises to broken bones. The kitchen has many hazards that can cause falls, 9-5. A fall

becomes more dangerous if heavy, sharp, or hot items are being carried. The following measures will prevent many falls:

- Make sure spills are promptly wiped up and a wet floor sign is displayed until the floor is dry.
- Clean greasy floors immediately.
- Do not place items such as stockpots or cases of food on the floor.
- No matter how busy you are, do not run or push in the kitchen.
- Apply nonslip treads or place removable rubber mats wherever the floor is slippery.
- Keep aisles clear; never store equipment or boxes in aisles.
- Wear shoes with nonslip soles.
- Put ladders and stools away after using them.
- Be aware of items such as purses or backpacks that customers place on the floor.

In the event someone falls, alert your supervisor. It may be necessary to call for emergency help. In the event of a serious fall from which the victim cannot get up, do not move the victim unless absolutely necessary. Wait for emergency help to arrive.

Burns

Cooks often have mild burn scars on their forearms and hands. Most burns are minor and heal readily, though some can be serious. If the following rules are used, burns can be prevented:

- Never use a damp or wet towel as a hot pad.
- Be sure that a hot pad is sufficiently thick to properly protect your hand from a hot pan.
- Never place a hot pan at a dishwashing station without alerting the dishwashing staff.
- When carrying a hot pan or liquid through the kitchen, loudly warn others by saying "HOT!"
- Never attempt to move anything hot that you cannot comfortably carry or lift.
- Avoid contact with steam when opening the door of a steamer or lifting the lid off a pot of boiling liquid. Steam burns quickly and seriously.

Burns are some of the most painful injuries. If a burn causes the skin to redden or blister, place the burned part of the body in cold water, 9-6. The cold water stops the burning process. Alert a supervisor. Do not place in ice water. Ice can damage injured skin. After 10 to 15 minutes, remove the injured area from the water, dry gently, and cover loosely with a bandage.

Burns can become infected. Burns must be treated properly to avoid infection. Leave blisters intact. Do not apply creams, butters, or other ointments to a burn. Seek medical attention in the following circumstances:

- The burn is larger than two to three inches in diameter.
- The burn is deep or the skin peels.
- The burn becomes infected.

Heat Exhaustion

Kitchens are famous for being hot and the work fast paced. This combination can lead to heat exhaustion. **Heat exhaustion** is a heat-related condition that results when the body loses too much water and salt. Drinking plenty of water is the first step in preventing heat exhaustion.

If a person is experiencing symptoms of heat exhaustion, have him or her rest in a cool location. Seek emergency medical help if needed. Always alert a supervisor.

Serious heat exhaustion can lead to heatstroke. **Heatstroke** is a more severe heat-related condition in which the body's usual ability to deal with heat stress is lost. Heatstroke is potentially life threatening and requires immediate medical attention. If heatstroke symptoms occur, move person into a cool location and seek medical attention immediately, 9-7. Cool the person by spraying with cool water or fanning.

Draz-Koetke/Goodheart-Willcox Publisher
9-6 Minor burns should be placed in cold water immediately.

Signs and Symptoms	
Heat Exhaustion	**Heatstroke**
• muscle cramping • lack of sweat • dizziness • unusual tiredness • nausea • vomiting • fainting	• irritability, confusion, or unconsciousness • fainting • very hot skin • lack of sweat • rapid, shallow breathing • fast pulse • dilated pupils

9-7 Be familiar with the signs and symptoms of heat exhaustion and heatstroke.

Back and Muscle Injuries

Many back and muscle injuries result from improper lifting. When lifting a heavy object, do not bend your back. This can result in painful back injuries. Instead, keep your back straight and bend your knees. This allows the strong leg muscles to do the lifting instead of the back muscles. Get assistance when lifting heavy or bulky items. This is also true for servers who may need to carry a tray of heavy plates. If it is too heavy, divide the plates on two trays until the load is comfortable to carry. In the event of a muscle strain, seek medical assistance before continuing to work, 9-8.

Repetitive Motion Injuries

Frequently performing the same action over a long period of time can cause repetitive motion injuries. For instance, performing the same butchery procedure for long periods each day can lead to a repetitive motion injury. Some repetitive motion injuries require long rehabilitation periods. To prevent this type of injury, vary tasks during the workday. If you notice pain associated with a repetitive movement or job in the kitchen, alert your supervisor.

Choking

Choking occurs when an object becomes stuck in the throat and blocks the airway and the victim cannot speak, cough, or breathe, 9-9. This is a life-threatening event and requires immediate action. Not only do cooks need to know how to respond to this, but also anyone who works with customers in a dining setting such as dining room

Draz-Koetke/Goodheart-Willcox Publisher

9-8 (A) Lift safely by bending at the knees instead of the back. (B) Get assistance if the item is too heavy to lift alone.

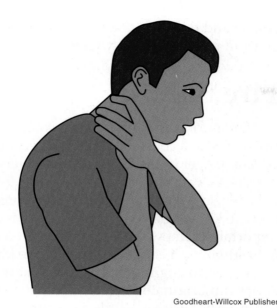

9-9 The symbol for choking is universal.

or room service. The American Red Cross recommends the following "five-and-five" response:
1. Ask the person if they are choking and need help. Have someone call 9-1-1. Once you have his or her consent, lean person forward and give five sharp back blows between the shoulder blades.
2. If the object does not dislodge, give five quick abdominal thrusts using the following procedure:
   A. Stand behind the person who is choking and wrap your arms around his or her waist.
   B. Make a fist and place the thumb side of the fist between the victim's navel and rib cage.
   C. Place your other hand over the fist of the first hand.
   D. Quickly and forcefully thrust your hands upward into the victim's abdomen.
3. Continue the cycle of back blows and abdominal thrusts until the object is forced out, the person can breathe or cough, or becomes unconscious. If the person becomes unconscious, carefully lower him or her to the ground and verify 9-1-1 or other local emergency number was called.

The American Heart Association (AHA) recommends that you obtain the victim's consent and then begin with Step 2 above. These methods are to be used only on conscious individuals over the age of one year. Infants and people with certain medical conditions require different responses. It is recommended that you obtain training from either American Red Cross or the AHA so that you can respond appropriately in an emergency.

Allergic Reaction

Allergic reactions can be deadly. Allergic reactions are sensitivities to a substance that a victim has swallowed, touched, or inhaled. Signs of allergic reactions can include
- profuse sweating
- hives or skin rash
- difficulty breathing
- dizziness
- swelling
- unconsciousness

If you notice someone suffering from an allergic reaction, call 9-1-1. If the victim has allergy medication, assist the victim in taking the medication, if necessary.

Cardiac Arrest

Cardiac arrest means the heart has stopped beating. When someone collapses due to cardiac arrest, it is a serious situation requiring a quick response. If action is not taken immediately, the victim's chance of survival diminishes quickly. **Cardiopulmonary resuscitation (CPR)** is a rescue procedure that combines chest compressions with blowing into the victim's mouth, simulating the beating of the heart and breathing of the lungs. The American Heart Association (AHA) and American Red Cross suggest anyone can use the Hands-Only™ CPR method. This method involves applying chest compressions at a rate of about 100 per minute. The first step is to call 9-1-1 so emergency professionals can be dispatched as quickly as possible.

SANITATION & SAFETY
When to Go to the Emergency Room

An injury has occurred. Should 9-1-1 be called? How do you know if an injury is serious enough to warrant a trip to the emergency room?

Call 9-1-1 if

- The person hits their head and passes out. Don't move a person with a possible neck injury unless their life is in danger.
- The injured party develops chest pain or shortness of breath.
- There is brisk bleeding in spite of elevating the injured part of the body and putting pressure on the wound.
- A victim goes into shock or is unable to calm down emotionally.

Go to the emergency room if

- There is muscle or fat visible in the cut. An X-ray may be needed to determine if something has broken off inside the injury.
- The injured body part is numb.
- The injury is a deep puncture wound, which has greater risk for infection.
- The injured person has diabetes or HIV, or takes steroids. These individuals have decreased ability to fight infection.

The best way to avoid a trip to the hospital is to practice safety. Be wise in the kitchen!

Some work and public environments have **automated external defibrillators (AED)**. These devices automatically detect the type of heart rhythm and deliver an electric shock if appropriate. AEDs are designed so people with little to no training can use them.

The AHA and American Red Cross provide basic CPR courses that provide training on performing CPR and using an AED. These courses are recommended for everyone. If, however, you are involved in a rescue and have not taken such a course, you can still use Hands-Only CPR and the AED.

Fire Safety

For as long as man has been cooking food, fire has been a constant danger. Fire continues to be a danger in the kitchen today. Every year, restaurants are destroyed by fire, 9-10. Foodservice professionals have a responsibility to know how to prevent a fire. It is also important to know what to do if a fire occurs to ensure the safety of everyone in the kitchen.

Fires can begin in many different ways. A fire can originate from candles, electrical cords, or hot grease. While the source may vary, the following three ingredients must always be present to produce a fire:

- *Fuel.* A substance such as paper, wood, or grease that actually burns.
- *Oxygen.* All fires need oxygen to burn.
- *Heat.* Enough heat must be available to raise the temperature high enough to ignite the initial fire.

If even one of these ingredients is missing, a fire will not start. If one of these ingredients is removed from a burning fire, the fire will go out. For instance, if a sauté pan catches fire, covering the pan will extinguish the fire because oxygen is no longer available.

Preventing Kitchen Fires

Fires can be prevented if the proper procedures and practices are followed. Some of the most common preventable causes of foodservice fires include

- improperly cleaned hood ventilation system
- excessive grease buildup on equipment
- failure to turn off all heat sources at closing
- use of damaged or improper size electrical cords
- unsteady, loose-fitting candleholders
- failure to extinguish candles at closing
- unextinguished cigarette butts in the garbage

Draz-Koetke/Goodheart-Willcox Publisher

9-10 Fire safety is critical in the foodservice industry to avoid injury and loss.

Some fires are not easily prevented. For instance, faulty electrical work can be difficult to detect and could result in a fire inside a wall.

What to Do If Fire Occurs

Consider the following scenarios. A sauté pan of oil gets too hot and suddenly catches fire. The fire spreads to another pan. A broiler full of steaks dripping fat suddenly bursts into flames. The flames shoot out the back of the broiler and into the ventilation system. When should you call the fire department? When should you reach for a fire extinguisher? When should you evacuate?

The first step in dealing with any fire is to quickly assess the severity of the fire. If the fire is spreading rapidly or you feel that your safety is in question, evacuate immediately.

Once your safety is assured, call 9-1-1. Often, fire departments are called too late. It takes time for the fire department to arrive on the scene, and by then a fire may be out of control. Most areas in the United States have

a 9-1-1 emergency phone number. Find out whether 9-1-1 or another emergency phone number applies to your area and post it in a visible location.

If a fire spreads beyond its initial source, calling 9-1-1 would be **prudent**, or wise. In the earlier example, if the contents of a sauté pan catch fire, the fire department need not be called. Simply covering the pan will probably put out the fire. But, if the fire spreads to a greasy wall, the fire department should be called immediately. Even if the fire is brought under control by foodservice staff, the fire department should still inspect the damage. Sometimes fires restart or may be smoldering behind walls or in ventilation ducts.

Fire Extinguishers Animation

By law, all commercial kitchens must have fire extinguishers. A **fire extinguisher** is a pressurized canister filled with a substance that puts out fires. Every foodservice operation should have several fire extinguishers placed at strategic points in

SANITATION & SAFETY

Drugs and Alcohol in the Kitchen

Students may be expelled from school for not adhering to the school's drug and alcohol policies. Employees can be fired for alcohol or drug use while on the job. These substances act to slow the reaction time and distort reality for the employee who is using them. This creates a dangerous environment for the employee and his or her coworkers when performing kitchen work. Employees must be aware that even over-the-counter medications and prescriptions can result in an unsafe condition. Medications may cause a light-headed or dizzy effect that is unsafe when working with equipment commonly found in a professional kitchen. If an employee begins to feel dizzy or ill, he or she should cease working. Any equipment being used should be turned off and the supervisor notified immediately. If the employee is feeling faint, it is best to sit down rather than risk falling down.

9-11 Select the fire extinguisher that is best for the type of fire.

the facility. Always know where fire extinguishers are located before a fire begins. Never block access to a fire extinguisher with equipment or boxes of food.

Not all fire extinguishers are the same. Each type of fire extinguisher is effective against a specific type of fire. Using the wrong extinguisher on a fire can be dangerous. Always match the fire extinguisher to the type of fire, 9-11. The class K fire extinguisher is recommended for commercial foodservice. Class K extinguishers are designed to put out vegetable-based oil and grease fires. They can also be used on other types of fires. However, class K extinguishers are expensive to recharge after use so some operations may restrict their use

to the oil and grease fires they are designed to extinguish. Use the multipurpose ABC extinguishers when appropriate.

Fire extinguishers must be inspected periodically to be sure they are in working order. Only professional services should inspect fire extinguishers. If a fire extinguisher is used, it must be refilled and recharged by a specialist. The tag attached to the extinguisher's nozzle records the last time the extinguisher was inspected, 9-12.

Fire extinguishers are designed to put out small, contained fires. If a fire is spreading rapidly, evacuate and let the fire department fight the fire. If the fire is localized, a fire extinguisher can be used.

Before using a fire extinguisher

1. Confirm that the fire department has been notified.
2. Position yourself with your back to an exit. If the fire spreads, you will still have a safe exit.

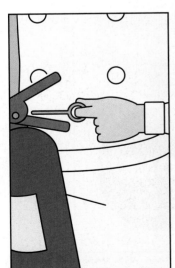

9-12 The tag on a fire extinguisher shows when it was last inspected.

3. Verify that you have the correct extinguisher for the type of fire.

Follow the four-step PASS technique when using a fire extinguisher, 9-13.

1. **P**ull the pin at the top of the fire extinguisher. The pin keeps the fire extinguisher from accidentally discharging.

2. **A**im at the base of the flames. Do not aim at the flames, but rather their source.

3. **S**queeze the handle.

4. **S**weep back and forth so the entire base of the fire is covered repeatedly. Continue to spray until the fire is out. It may be necessary to spray after the fire is out to prevent the fire from restarting. Monitor the extinguished fire closely in case it restarts.

Kitchen Hood Fire Suppression Systems

Every commercial kitchen has nozzles that hang in the hoods above fryers, stoves, griddles, and grills. These nozzles are connected to pipes that lead to a pressurized fire extinguisher canister. Those nozzles, pipes, and canisters make up the kitchen hood fire suppression system. A **kitchen hood fire suppression system** is an installed, comprehensive fire-fighting system that automatically puts out a fire before it spreads, 9-14. If equipment under the system is moved or relocated, the suppression system nozzles must be repositioned.

Suppose a grease fire on a grill begins to burn out of control. The sensor links in the

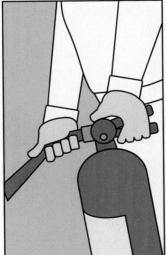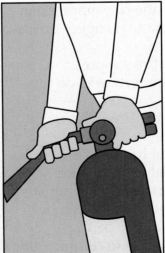

9-13 Fire extinguishers are most effective when the four-step PASS technique is used.

Courtesy of Fox Valley Fire and Safety

9-14 In commercial kitchens, most cooking equipment is located under kitchen hood fire suppression systems.

fire suppression system detect the prolonged high temperatures coming from the fire. This triggers an automatic release of a fire-fighting chemical that smothers the fire.

Fire suppression systems are also equipped with a backup manual trigger. If pulled, this will activate the fire suppression system. Never pull the manual trigger unless there is an emergency.

In the event that the fire suppression system is engaged, it is important to do the following:

* Assess the fire. Call the fire department if necessary.
* Discard any food that has been contaminated by the chemical extinguisher.
* Call the health department. They must inspect the kitchen before food can be prepared or served.
* Call a licensed technician to recharge the fire suppression system.

Clothing on Fire

It is a rare but serious event when someone's clothes catch on fire. If this happens to you or someone else, immediately

* *Stop* where you are.
* *Drop* to the ground, covering your face with your hands.
* *Roll* on the ground to smother the flames, 9-15.

Others can assist smothering the flames by using a blanket or tablecloth. Call emergency help immediately if necessary.

Fire Inspections

All foodservice operations are inspected periodically by the local fire department. The fire inspector checks for possible fire hazards. When the inspector arrives, assist

©Alisa Ann Ruch Burn Foundation

9-15 Stop, drop, and roll if your clothes catch on fire.

them in any way possible. Fire inspections help reduce the number of kitchen fires.

Natural Gas Leak

The blue flames you see on cookstoves are from burning natural gas. Natural gas can be very dangerous because it is explosive. Many stoves and ovens in commercial kitchens rely on natural gas. Many times, a small natural gas leak results from an unlit pilot light. The pilot light is a small, continuous flame that lights the burners when they are turned on. If you smell natural gas, it is important to alert a supervisor immediately.

Emergency Readiness Plans

Every kitchen should have an emergency readiness plan that guides action to take in the event of various emergencies such as fire, loss of power, or natural disaster. The plan should
- identify various emergencies that may disrupt the operation
- include procedures to follow
- be communicated to staff
- be practiced during drills
- be re-evaluated periodically and revised if needed

For instance, every kitchen should have a fire evacuation plan. Employees must be trained and the plan posted in a visible place in the kitchen. Every fire evacuation plan should list different exit paths. Be sure to familiarize yourself with all the escape routes. If there is a fire, one or more of the escape routes could be blocked by fire. Always keep escape routes free of obstructions. Additionally, there should be periodic

SANITATION & SAFETY
Design and Construction Features

When planning or renovating a foodservice operation, designers must think about more than how many customers will be served and what equipment will be needed. The design and construction must also promote proper sanitation and a safe work environment. They must design work and dining areas that are readily accessible to and usable by persons with disabilities. Some examples of design and construction features that address safety and sanitation include:

- Having at least two exits in each room in case of fire
- Building a space or short wall between a deep fryer and gas stove to minimize the chance for fire
- Creating a dishwashing space separate from food preparation areas
- Creating a receiving area separate from the food preparation area to minimize cross-contamination
- Installing nonslip flooring to minimize falls
- Selecting equipment that meets sanitation and safety design standards
- Constructing ramps and entryways that accommodate wheelchairs

fire drills to practice the fire evacuation plan. Drills ensure that everyone knows what to do if a fire alarm goes off, how to get the customers out, and where to meet.

Summary Points

- The employer is responsible for creating and maintaining a safe workplace. It is each employee's responsibility to practice safe working habits.

- The professional cook's uniform is designed to promote personal safety.

- Kitchen injuries such as cuts, falls, and burns are not uncommon. Employees must work safely to prevent these injuries and know how to respond to accidents when they occur.

- Cooks use fire to prepare food every day. Foodservice professionals must know how to prevent fires and respond to a fire emergency.

- Emergency readiness plans serve as a guide for actions to take in the event of various emergencies that may disrupt a foodservice operation.

In Review Assess

1. Explain OSHA's role in workplace safety.

2. Why is it important for employees to fill out an incident report?

3. List three safety features of the traditional chef jacket.

4. True or false. Open-heeled clogs can be dangerous in the kitchen.

5. True or false. If your knife is falling, you should try to catch it so the blade is not damaged.

6. List five ways to prevent kitchen falls.

7. In the event of a burn, place the affected area in _____ water immediately.

8. Describe how to care for a person experiencing symptoms of heat exhaustion.

9. List the three ingredients necessary to produce fire.

10. What are the four steps of the PASS technique for using a fire extinguisher?

11. List four elements that an emergency readiness plan should address.

Core Skills

12. **Writing.** Many different types of emergencies can affect a foodservice operation's ability to function. Emergencies can range from a brief interruption in power to flooding from a hurricane. Select an emergency and write a readiness plan for a fictional foodservice operation. Be sure to include a brief description of the operation (for example, "fast-food restaurant").

13. **Math.** Use the graph below to answer the following questions: How many injuries were logged in June? Is the number of injuries trending up or down?

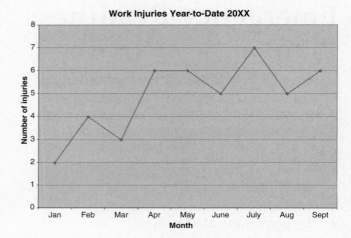

14. **Speaking.** Tom, the kitchen supervisor, is convinced he trains his employees well in all areas of safety regarding use of kitchen chemicals. This training consists of a rigorous full-day in-service for each employee at the beginning of employment. Tom does not believe any further training is necessary. Prepare and present an argument either supporting or refuting Tom's opinion. Support your position using credible sources.

15. **Writing.** Write a brief paper summarizing the history of OSHA, important milestones, who is covered under this law, and any new initiatives.

16. **Math.** Search online to learn the average annual employment and the incidence rate of nonfatal occupational injuries and illnesses for food services and drinking places. If the average cost is $22,417 for these types of

injuries, calculate the estimated total cost of nonfatal injuries and illnesses for employees of food services and drinking places.

17. **Speaking.** Prepare an in-service on basic kitchen safety. Assume the in-service will be viewed by newly hired restaurant employees. Adjust the style of delivery, vocabulary, and length of presentation based on your audience. Use visual aids and demonstrations to enhance your presentation and add interest.

18. **Writing.** Create a kitchen safety checklist based on what you read in this chapter. Obtain permission to use the checklist to assess the school's kitchen for safety hazards and workplace conditions. Include corrective action for any problems you note.

19. **CTE Career Readiness Practice.** Act as a responsible and contributing citizen and employee. Locate the instructional video on either the American Heart Association or the American Red Cross websites and learn how to perform Hands-Only CPR in the event of an emergency.

Critical Thinking

20. **Evaluate.** Suppose you work in a commercial kitchen. Safe actions are important to prevent employee injuries. In an effort to promote employee safety and health, the company strictly follows a random drug testing policy. One of your coworkers often brags to you about his off-hours alcohol and drug use—the effects of which showed in his near-accident recently. You question whether his actions are responsible, especially in light of the type of work and equipment used on the job. What is the responsible way to handle such situations?

21. **Debate.** Form small groups and debate the following topic: A foodservice employee shares equal responsibility with the employer for workplace safety.

22. **Identify.** You observe another employee's workplace accident. The employee does not want to report the accident because it is his or her third this month. Should you report the accident to your supervisor? What are the potential consequences of your action or inaction?

23. **Evaluate.** A fire in the broiler has set off the fire suppression system in the hood and appears to have extinguished the fire. The owner does not want to call 9-1-1 or the health department because it will cause a loss of business. Evaluate the owner's reasoning.

24. **Assess.** You are the catering manager responsible for organizing an outdoor catering event in August. Consider the injuries to staff or guests that might occur. Make a list of first aid supplies to have on hand for each possible injury. What preventive measures could you take to avoid as many injuries as possible?

Technology

Research AEDs and write a procedure outlining their use on a victim of cardiac arrest. Find out if your school or place of work supplies an AED. What is the policy regarding its use?

Teamwork

Form a small team to create a fire evacuation plan. Select a leader and assign responsibilities to each member. The team will need to locate all fire exits, types and locations of fire extinguishers, alarm pulls, and hood fire suppression system manual pull (if applicable). Use this information to create and label a map of the kitchen. Write a procedure for your plan. The leader is responsible to coordinate the final report and ensure it is complete and accurate.

Chef's E-portfolio
Dress for Safety

Find a photo of a chef in uniform. Use callouts to label the safety features of his or her uniform. Upload the image to your e-portfolio. Ask your instructor where to save your file. This could be on the school's network or a flash drive of your own. Name your portfolio document *FirstnameLastname_Portfolio Ch#.docx* (i.e., JohnSmith_PortfolioCh09.docx).

While studying, look for the activity icon to:
- Build vocabulary with e-flash cards and matching activities.
- Expand learning with video clips, photo identification activities, animations, and interactive activities.
- Review and assess what you learn by completing end-of-chapter questions.

Yuri Arcurs/Shutterstock.com

Sustainability in the Kitchen

10

Reading Prep

As you read the chapter, think about the advantages and disadvantages of adopting sustainable practices in foodservice. Do you think these practices help or hurt the foodservice industry? Use examples from the text to support your opinion.

Culinary Terminology
Build Vocab

food miles, p. 156
heirloom variety, p. 157

Academic Terminology
Build Vocab

sustainability, p. 153
biodiversity, p. 157
ecofriendly, p. 158
energy efficient, p. 159
low-flow aerators, p. 163
composting, p. 165
biodegradable, p. 166
reusable, p. 167
recycling, p. 167

Objectives

After studying this chapter, you will be able to

- understand why adopting sustainable practices is important in the foodservice industry.
- analyze purchasing decisions in foodservice for sustainability.
- recognize opportunities to conserve energy usage in foodservice.
- identify ways to reduce water usage in the kitchen.
- outline a sustainable plan to reduce foodservice waste and its negative impact on the environment.
- recognize the role of foodservice in social sustainability.

Feeding people requires large amounts of food, energy, and water. These resources are used at every step of growing, transporting, purchasing, delivering, preparing, and serving meals. Additionally, this activity produces much waste. This affects not only a foodservice operation, but the world as a whole. As a result, chefs have a substantial duty to make responsible, informed choices in their daily work.

Sustainability in Foodservice

Addressing sustainability may seem like just one more item on an already long list of responsibilities for a busy chef. However, it is not so much an added task as it is a guide when making decisions and choices. Sustainability is the adoption of practices that either preserve or improve the condition of Earth for future generations.

While the definition for sustainability is rather straightforward, the details are sometimes not so clear. To better understand the different facets of sustainability, it can be divided into the following categories: purchasing, energy, water, waste, and social considerations.

Sustainability also makes good business sense and can improve profitability, or ability of a business to make money and thrive. For instance, buying an energy efficient piece of equipment can save money in the long run by using less energy or water. Many times decisions based on sustainability cost more initially, but yield significant savings over time. Additionally, restaurants that pursue sustainable objectives are viewed favorably by customers. This means that sustainable restaurants can attract more like-minded customers.

Purchasing

Foodservice operations purchase large amounts of food to cook and serve every day. They also buy nonfood items such as cleaning products, disposables, serviceware, tables, chairs, and equipment. Increasingly, sustainability is becoming a factor in purchasing decisions.

Food

Practicing sustainability when purchasing food is complex. This is challenging because there are many variables in the ways food is produced and transported. As a result, making sustainably sound buying decisions requires constant research and good relationships with suppliers. There are many credible organizations that provide current information on sustainable food issues to which chefs can turn, 10-1.

Sustainably produced food often costs more than traditional industrially produced foods. There are numerous factors that increase the cost. For instance, sustainable foods may require more labor to produce or have lower yields because the farmer is trying to put less stress on the soil, livestock, and water supply. The farmer may not have access to common distribution systems used to transport food to markets. This may result in higher transportation costs. Since the price of food is critical to a restaurant's profitability, chefs must use

Sustainability Resources	
Segment	**Examples**
Construction	• US Green Building Council
Energy Conservation & Alternative Energy	• ENERGY STAR® • Food Service Technology Center • National Restaurant Association Conserve • US Environmental Protection Agency (EPA)
General	• Conservation International • Green Seal™
Sustainable Agriculture	• Leopold Center for Sustainable Agriculture • Stanford University School of Earth Sciences Sustainable Choices • Stone Barns Center for Food & Agriculture • USDA Alternative Farming Systems Information Center
Sustainable Food	• Sustainable Food Laboratory • Yale Sustainable Food Project
Sustainable Seafood	• Chefs Collaborative • National Oceanic and Atmospheric Administration (NOAA) Fisheries • Save the Oceans- Monterey Bay Aquarium • Shedd Aquarium
Waste Stream Reduction	• American Forest & Paper Association • US Composting Council
Water Conservation	• American Water Learning Center • USGA Water Science School

10-1 There are many resources available to help chefs operate a sustainable kitchen.

different strategies to offset the higher prices paid for sustainable food products. Some chefs promote a dish as made with sustainable products and pass the added cost on to the customer in the form of higher menu prices. Others keep costs down by sourcing produce when it is in season, fresh, and cheap. The ability of a restaurant to market sustainable foods can also draw more customers helping to increase sales. Another strategy is to serve smaller (and more healthful) portion sizes.

To make sustainable decisions, chefs need to know where the food comes from and how it was raised or grown and harvested. Figure 10-2 defines some of the most important concepts around sustainable food.

Sustainability Concepts		
TERM	**Applies to**	**DEFINITION**
Antibiotic-free	Meat and dairy products	An animal that has either never received antibiotics or sufficient time has lapsed for the drugs to clear out of the animal's system. Some animals are given antibiotics to counteract the effects of crowding, stress-inducing conditions, and unnatural diets. Most antibiotics are given to healthy animals. As much as 80%–90% of antibiotics given to animals and humans are passed through the body and into the water system. They interact with bacteria and can form more antibiotic-resistant strains that pose a risk to both humans and animals.
Aquaculture	Seafood	The farming of fish in fresh or saltwater under controlled conditions. There are many varieties of aquaculture. Some methods cause damage to the environment from waste, chemical treatments, or abnormally high concentrations of fish. Other methods, called *closed systems*, raise fish in containers which can be sustainable if discharged water does not harm the ecosystem.
Barn-roaming	Poultry, eggs	A new term used in the United States referring to birds that are restricted to a barn, rather than a cage.
Biodynamic	Produce	A cultivation method that considers the farm to be a living thing, or organism. This method includes the use of fermented manure, minerals, and herbs to enhance soil health. Soil health influences the nutrient content, quality, and flavor of the food grown in it. Originally, biodynamic meant that a farm was completely self-contained and everything used on the farm originated there.
Cage-free	Poultry, eggs	Often used with "free-range," this means that domestic fowl (chickens, ducks, etc.) are not raised in cages. It is not a legally defined term.
Carbon Footprint		The amount of climate-changing carbon emissions from a system or activity often referred to as *greenhouse gases*. The foodservice industry accounts for about one-third of all human greenhouse emissions. These emissions are generated during the transport, production, and consumption of food.
Free-range	Beef cattle, sheep, goats, pigs, dairy cattle, and particularly poultry	A USDA definition meaning that animals have access to the outside.

(Continued)

10-2 Practicing sustainability requires an understanding of the vocabulary.

	Sustainability Concepts *(Continued)*	
TERM	**Applies to**	**DEFINITION**
Genetically Modified Organisms (GMO)	Produce and animals	Plants or animals that have had genes introduced, rearranged, or eliminated to make them more resistant to pests and other elements that endanger the crop and reduce yield. (The USDA includes plants or animals altered through traditional breeding methods in this definition.)
Grass-fed	Cattle, sheep, goats, and bison	Grass-fed cattle consume the majority of their nutrients from grass as opposed to grain, soy, or corn. This label does not limit the use of antibiotics, hormones, or pesticides.
Hormone-free	Meat and dairy products	Foods are free of hormones given to stimulate growth and milk production. Although the USDA and FDA deem them safe for human consumption, the European Union considers them a risk to human health
Local	All foods	There is no strict definition for this term, but its use implies the food is produced close to the restaurant. Some foodservice operations define sustainable as a 50- or 150-mile radius.
Monocrop	Produce	This is a high-yield system that grows a single crop year after year on the same land instead of rotating with other crops. It is economically efficient, but controversial as it can damage soil ecology, and lead to increased chemical use and pest resistance.
Organic	All foods	Foods with this certification meet the requirements for production and labeling established by the Organic Foods Production Act. These foods must be produced without the use of synthetic fertilizers, sewage sludge, irradiation, and genetic engineering. Only natural products and methods that promote and protect the environment can be used. Products can be labeled either *100 Percent Organic* or *Organic*.
Seasonal	Produce and some meats and seafood	This term refers to food at the time of year when it is at its peak, either in terms of harvest or flavor. This is also the time when the item is the cheapest and freshest on the market. For instance, berries purchased in the Midwest in December have traveled a long distance, were picked before their peak sweetness, and are expensive. Some ingredients, such as specialty produce or certain seafoods, are not available out-of-season. Cooking with seasonal ingredients requires planning—promising a seasonal menu item today for a party six months from now could be a problem if it is out of season and unavailable.
Wild-caught	Seafood	Seafood that is harvested in the wild environments of the ocean, lakes, and rivers. There are many harvesting techniques that vary with the type of seafood being harvested. Some protect fish stocks and other destroy them and the ecosystems.

Choosing which foods to purchase is not simply a matter of understanding how they were raised or grown, and harvested. How products are transported to the restaurant is also a factor to consider. Energy is required to move food around the world. The more energy used to move food, the less sustainable it is. **Food miles** is a measure of the amount of energy needed to move food from its point of harvest to its final destination. This is not simply the distance the food travels from one point to another, but rather a measure of the energy used to get it there. For instance, moving perishable food by

Chef Speak

Terms with No Definition

The concept and practice of sustainability is relatively new and still evolving. As a result, some terms commonly used in the discussion of sustainability may not yet be legally defined. For instance, it is not uncommon to see foods labeled "natural." At this time there is no legal definition for "natural." The Food and Drug Administration (FDA) does not object to its use as long as the food does not contain added color, artificial flavor, or synthetic substances. Similarly, "local" has no standard definition. While some agricultural experts agree that a 150-mile radius is the limit, some chefs and restaurant chains have crafted their own definition of "local." These definitions may stretch to include foods grown within a radius of 300 to 500 miles of a restaurant. When you see "local" on a menu, ask what their definition is.

airplane consumes much more energy than moving food by train. Trains are so energy efficient it is possible to move large quantities of food long distances by train more sustainably than smaller quantities of food shorter distances by truck or pickup, 10-3. Therefore, purchasing locally sourced food may not always be the most sustainable decision if food miles are considered.

Other possible drawbacks to locally sourced foods include inconsistent availability or lower quality than the same food grown in other parts of the country or world. There are also many reasons to buy local ingredients. For instance, locally sourced foods contribute to local economies. Locally sourced foods can also be fresher than foods sourced further away and offer a greater degree of biodiversity. **Biodiversity** is the variety of forms of animal and plant life in a particular area. Just as species of animals are nurtured and protected to prevent their extinction, the same must be true of food sources. For instance, some of the most common varieties of apples found in stores were developed to travel well, produce a consistent size for ease of packing, and have a long shelf life. If reliance becomes too heavy on this uniform apple hybrid and other apple varieties are not perpetuated, the

diversity is diminished. Over the last decade, heirloom varieties of apples have become more popular. **Heirloom varieties** are plants grown from seeds that have been unchanged for several to many generations. Heirloom plants have genetics that remain constant and reflect a long heritage. This is not the case with plants grown from hybrid seeds. Heirloom seeds have been grown for many decades and are valued for their superior flavor. These heirloom variety apples may not fit well in the factory-farm system that seeks uniformity, but their flavor is incomparable. Depending on the circumstances, locally

Mayskyphoto/Shutterstock.com

10-3 Trains can be an energy-efficient method of transporting food.

sourced foods could be more or less expensive than similar foods that are shipped long distances.

Cleaning Products

Foodservice involves a great deal of cleaning every day. Dishes, pots and pans, food-contact surfaces, carpets, windows, bathrooms, and floors need to be cleaned on a regular basis. This is not only important from a visual standpoint, but also to ensure proper sanitation. Some of these traditional cleaning products, while effective, are not ecofriendly and are potentially unhealthy. Some can cause serious health concerns such as cancer and lung disease and may be

an occupational hazard for people who use them daily. **Ecofriendly** refers to products or practices that do not damage the environment. This is not a legal definition in the United States and is open to interpretation. Some independent organizations have been created to address ecofriendly standards and develop certifications. Since there is no legal definition, it is important to research and verify whether the product is actually ecofriendly or "green." There are many products available that do not damage the environment and still perform well.

Before using any of these ecofriendly products, it is important to read the instructions carefully. Sometimes the way the products are used is different from conventional products. For instance, they may be used at different concentrations or require more time to work effectively, 10-4. Chefs can learn about ecofriendly cleaning products through research and discussions with trusted purveyors.

Other Purchasing Decisions

Restaurants purchase many items besides food and cleaning supplies. With each of these decisions, it is important to consider sustainability. Some common purchasing decisions to evaluate for sustainability include
- **Laundering**. Most restaurants have some level of laundry needs. While some foodservice establishments do their own laundry, most choose to use a service. Laundry services clean uniforms, tablecloths, and cloth napkins. When choosing a laundry service, learn about their sustainability practices and the types of cleaning chemicals they use.
- **Interior design elements**. Foodservice establishments make choices about furniture, carpet, and wall coverings when building a new restaurant or updating an established one. Part of the selection criteria should be how ecofriendly

SCIENCE & TECHNOLOGY

Genetically Modified (GM) Foods

Genetically modified (GM) food is produced from a genetically modified organism (GMO) such as a plant or animal. GM foods generate controversy worldwide. Some groups warn about potential negative health and environmental concerns. Other groups believe the benefits of GM foods include the ability to feed an expanding global population while reducing environmental impact. The USDA's position is that GMOs are "substantially equivalent" to parent crops and do not require labeling. The position of the Center for Science in the Public Interest (CSPI) is that GM crops in the United States are safe to eat and provide some benefits, but regulation is necessary and needs improvement. Many public interests groups and consumers in the European Union continue to express concerns over the impact GM foods may have on both human health and the environment. It is important to understand the views of each side and supporting science before taking a position on GMOs.

CandyBox Images/Shutterstock.com

10-4 Ecofriendly cleaning products must be used properly to be effective.

a product is. For instance, some of these elements may contain dangerous chemicals called *volatile organic compounds (VOC)* that diffuse into the air at room temperatures.

- **Pesticides**. All restaurants use pest control operators (PCO) to prevent pest infestations. Information should be obtained about the types and toxicity of chemicals being used at this level of exposure before choosing a PCO.
- **Chafing dish fuel**. The foodservice industry uses a lot of chafing dish fuel to keep food warm on buffets. Ecofriendly options should be considered when making this purchase.

Energy

Energy is needed to cook, chill, and freeze food, heat or cool dining areas, and provide lighting and ventilation. Energy is an essential part of running a foodservice operation. According to the Environmental Protection Agency (EPA), restaurants use five to seven times more energy than office buildings or retail stores. Quick-service establishments' energy usage can reach ten times that of other commercial buildings. A typical electric deep-fat fryer uses more than 11,000 kilowatt-hours (kWh) and costs about $1,100 per year to operate—more than $90 per month for just one piece of equipment. For these reasons, foodservice operations must be as energy efficient as possible. Equipment and systems that are **energy efficient** use less energy to perform work than conventional alternatives. For instance, using light-emitting diode (LED) lighting as opposed to conventional incandescent lighting to illuminate a room reduces energy consumption by about 80 percent. The room can be satisfactorily lit by both bulbs, but the amount of energy required is vastly different.

Energy efficiency also makes sense from a business standpoint. If a restaurant consumes less energy to complete the same task, then less money is spent on energy. Saving money helps increase overall profits and is good business practice.

When considering the financial impact of energy efficiency, long-term thinking is critical. For instance, spending more on a piece of equipment because it is energy efficient may seem like a bad business decision. However, the savings from lower energy usage over the life of the equipment can greatly exceed the initial higher price.

There are many ways to save energy in a foodservice operation. Some of the most common ones include lighting, hot water pipes, maintenance, equipment selection, and employee training.

Lighting

Traditionally, incandescent bulbs have been used for lighting. Compact fluorescent lamps (CFLs) represented the next generation with ten times the life span and an energy savings of 75 percent compared to incandescent. The newest product is LED lighting with three to five times the life span of CFLs and closer to 50 times that of incandescent bulbs, 10-5. LED lighting costs more initially, but is 80 percent more energy efficient than incandescent lighting and 20 percent more efficient than CFLs. LED lamps also do not contain mercury which is a concern with many CFLs. LED light quality can also be far superior and many are dimmable—perfect for front-of-the-house ambient lighting. Another way to reduce lighting energy is to install occupancy-sensor light switches. There are many places in a foodservice operation that do not need to be lit at all times. Occupancy-sensor switches turn on lights when someone is in the room and turn them off when motion is no longer detected. Storerooms, closets, breakrooms, offices, and employee bathrooms are ideal locations to use this technology.

Another type of lighting deserves special attention—neon lighting. This type of lighting, often used for eye-catching signs and advertising, consumes large amounts of energy. For this reason, turn on neon signs only when needed. Additionally, there are LED alternatives to neon lighting.

maxstockphoto/Shutterstock.com

10-5 (*Left to right*) Incandescent, CFLs, and LEDs vary in cost and energy efficiency.

Hot Water Pipes

Foodservice operations use large quantities of hot water on a daily basis. Energy is required to heat the water. The heated water travels in pipes to faucets. As the water moves through or is held in the pipes, the heat energy escapes into the atmosphere and the water cools. The water must be reheated when hot water is required again. Wrapping the water pipes with insulation improves energy efficiency and is easy and inexpensive to do.

Maintenance

Poor equipment maintenance also contributes to energy waste. As equipment is used, it is subjected to general wear and tear. All foodservice operations should have a preventive maintenance schedule to ensure proper care of the facility. The following are some common maintenance issues that need regular attention to improve energy efficiency:

- *Refrigerator doors*. As a result of daily use and abuse, cooler doors may fail to close or seal properly. The gaskets around the cooler doors must be checked regularly for damage. If a cooler door is not closing or sealing properly, the cooling unit must work harder to maintain the temperature as cool air leaks out. This wastes large amounts of energy and wears out the cooling units prematurely, 10-6.
- *Coils in cooling units*. The cooling mechanism of refrigerators uses coils to transfer the heat out of the unit. Air must be able to circulate freely around the coils in order for them to do their job efficiently. Over time, the coils can become dirty which impedes their ability to work. The coils must be cleaned on a regular basis to operate efficiently, 10-7.

Equipment Selection

More and more, cooking equipment is being designed to be energy efficient. For this reason, a foodservice professional should learn about a piece of equipment's energy

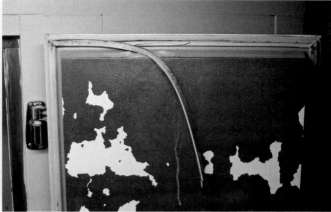

10-6 Poorly maintained refrigerator doors and gaskets result in energy inefficiency and unnecessary wear on the equipment.

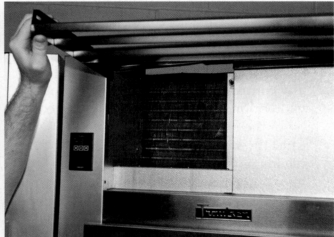

10-7 Compare the dirty, clogged coils of the cooling unit on the left to the clean coils on the right. Which piece of equipment do you think operates more efficiently?

efficiency before making a purchase. The EPA and the US Department of Energy (DOE) jointly sponsor a program called ENERGY STAR®. ENERGY STAR qualifies equipment that meets their criteria for energy efficiency. The testing of this equipment is performed by the PG&E Food Service Technology Center which is an excellent resource for information on energy and water conservation within the foodservice industry.

Great strides have been made in energy-efficient alternatives for two pieces of equipment that receive heavy usage in commercial kitchens—stovetops and dishmachines.

- **Stovetops.** Stovetops use energy to heat the pots and pans which then transfer the heat to the food. Many foodservice operations have gas stovetops. Although many chefs like gas heat, it is very inefficient. About 30 percent of the heat generated by the flame actually gets transferred to the food. The remaining 70 percent is lost and must be ventilated out of the kitchen. Since stovetops are in use many hours every day, the losses add up quickly. Induction ranges are a great energy-efficient alternative. About 90 percent of the heat generated by induction is transferred to the food. In addition, it is possible to regulate the heat quickly and generate large amounts of heat on demand.

- **Dishmachines**. Advances are also being made to improve the energy efficiency of dishmachines. Most foodservice operations use dishmachines to clean flatware, serviceware, and glasses. Like stovetops, they are used many hours each day. Improvements such as adding insulation to prevent heat from escaping the dishmachine have increased energy efficiency. Other improvements include capturing the steam that previously escaped from the dishmachine and using it to maintain water at safe sanitizing temperatures.

- **Ventilation**. Removing hot, grease-laden or smoke-filled air is essential for any commercial kitchen. Conventional ventilation systems are usually turned on in the morning and remain on until the kitchen closes, 10-8. This means no matter how much cooking is happening, the ventilation system operates at 100 percent. More energy-efficient, "on-demand" ventilation systems are available that continuously regulate the amount of ventilation based on how much is needed to clear the air. These systems operate only when there is a need.

Employee Training

There is one last area of energy efficiency that costs little to implement and can be effective in reducing energy consumption— employee behavior. Without meaning to, people sometimes act in ways that waste energy. Employers can train their employees to act with energy efficiency in mind. Actions employees can take to be more energy efficient include:

- Turning off lights when leaving a room.

Eric Futran/ChefShots

10-8 Hood ventilation systems located above large kitchen equipment often operate all day, regardless of need.

- Turning on cooking equipment (ovens, steamers, deep-fryers, steam tables, etc.) only when needed. Often these items are turned on hours before they are actually needed and left on when not in use.
- Turning on kitchen ventilation only when needed unless the kitchen has on-demand ventilation.

Water

Foodservice operations also use much water every day. Water is served to customers and used for cleaning and cooking. Some equipment, such as steamers, can use large amounts of water. Water is not a limitless

INDUSTRY INSIGHTS

Farm-Raised Seafood

The increasing global population and a growing appetite for seafood's health benefits are putting pressure on this food source. Wild harvest of seafood is believed by many to be at maximum sustainable usage. This leaves farm-raised seafood to fill the gap between supply and demand. However, farm-raised methods, or aquaculture, can vary greatly in sustainability. There are many types of aquaculture including ponds, tanks, raceways, net pens, open ocean, and aquaponics. These methods vary in the types of fish that can be farmed and environmental impact.

Smokedsalmon/Shutterstock.com

10-9 Restaurants can avoid wasting water needlessly by asking customers if they would like water before serving it.

resource, and in some areas, water shortages have become increasingly common. Across the United States and around the world, the amount of clean drinking water is being depleted. As the world population increases, water will continue to become increasingly scarce. Regardless the location, foodservice operations have a responsibility to conserve water. As with energy, this makes good business sense since water costs money. As water becomes scarcer, the price will increase, which will affect profitability.

Some steps that can be taken to conserve water in a foodservice operation include:

- **Water service**. Millions of gallons of clean water are wasted each year from untouched drinking water served to customers. Ask customers if they want water, rather than serving it automatically, 10-9.
- **Equipment**. Kitchen equipment can use vast quantities of water, often inefficiently. When purchasing new kitchen equipment, consider its water usage. Great progress has been made to decrease water usage in dishmachines,

steamers, and ice machines. For instance, an ice machine that is air-cooled uses less water than a water-cooled unit.
- **Maintenance**. Normal, daily use causes equipment to function less optimally and results in wasted water. This is often seen as a drip. Drips seem minor, but can amount to thousands of gallons of wasted water in a year. Because they seem so unimportant, drips often go unrepaired for long periods. Often, they can be fixed quickly with a couple of turns of a wrench. Toilets and urinals that are stuck in a "flow" position can waste hundreds of gallons of water per day and should be fixed immediately.
- **Reducing flow**. There are a number of devices that can reduce the amount of water used without effecting how a job is completed. These water-efficient devices are critical in the strategy to consume less water. For instance, handwashing sinks can be outfitted with low-flow aerators. **Low-flow aerators** reduce the amount of water that comes from a faucet while directing the water stream so as not to reduce its effectiveness. Low-flow, pre-rinse spray valves in the dishroom can

dramatically reduce the amount of water used to rinse dirty dishes, 10-10. In the bathroom, low-flush toilets and urinals are increasingly common. Waterless urinals are also being installed in more restaurants.

- **Cleaning.** Water is an important part of cleaning. When cleaning, consider how to use a minimal amount of water without sacrificing proper sanitation standards. Cleaning outdoor spaces with a high-powered sprayer is a common misuse of water. Sweeping with a broom is just as effective and less wasteful.
- **Thawing.** Thawing food under cold running water is a safe method, but it is not water efficient. In fact, thawing just

Food Service Technology Center

10-10 Low-flow sprayers can be used to conserve water in the dishroom.

one product under cold running water for 45 minutes per day, 365 days per year would waste about 90,000 gallons of clean water. A much more water-efficient way to thaw food is in the refrigerator. This method takes longer and requires planning, but saves a considerable amount of money and water.

Waste

Every day, restaurants prepare large amounts of food, use large quantities of water and energy, and produce large amounts of waste. Traditionally, much of this waste is hauled away and dumped into a landfill. Landfills are basically large holes in the ground into which refuse is dumped, 10-11. Once full, it is covered with dirt and plants, and another landfill is dug somewhere else. What happens in the landfill over time may surprise you. Foods decompose very slowly. Potentially harmful substances leach into the ground and ground water. Methane gas is produced and escapes into the atmosphere, causing damage there. Millions of tons of precious nutrients are lost forever in landfills.

There are better ways to deal with waste that are more responsible to the environment and safer. The National Restaurant Association (NRA) has estimated that 90 percent of restaurants' waste could be diverted from landfills. To do this, food-service waste must be sorted into different containers for food waste, recycling, and refuse. These receptacles should be well-marked and positioned throughout the foodservice operation. Employees and even quick-service restaurant customers must be educated how to sort waste properly.

Food Animation

Decreasing the amount of food a kitchen wastes makes sense financially and can help improve profits. The EPA suggests the following strategy for reducing food waste:

Picsfive/Shutterstock.com

10-11 Restaurants produce large amounts of waste that ends up in landfills.

1. Source Reduction–Reduce the volume of food waste generated.
2. Feed People–Donate extra food to food banks, soup kitchens, and shelters.
3. Feed Animals–Provide food to farmers for use as animal feed.
4. Industrial Uses–Provide fats for rendering and food discards for animal feed production.
5. Composting–Convert food scraps into a nutrient-rich soil amendment.
6. Incineration or landfill–Use as a last resort to dispose of food waste.

The strategy lists steps for keeping food out of the waste stream in order of preference, 10-12. For instance, the first step limits waste by controlling the amount of food that must be discarded in the first place. This may require better planning or better management and rotation of food. Reducing the amount of food that is purchased or prepared unnecessarily, reduces costs and improves a restaurant's profitability.

If food still remains, the next step should be to repurpose it for human consumption if possible. This might involve creating a new menu item from leftovers or donating to food pantries and shelters.

The third and fourth steps may be more difficult to implement, but can be done. The EPA's website provides useful information on how to use food waste for animal feed or industrial uses.

Food waste can also be addressed sustainably with composting. **Composting** is the process by which some food and other organic matter (leaves, grass clippings, paper, and so on) decay to form a highly fertile growing substance. All biodegradable substances can be composted.

Food Recovery Hierarchy

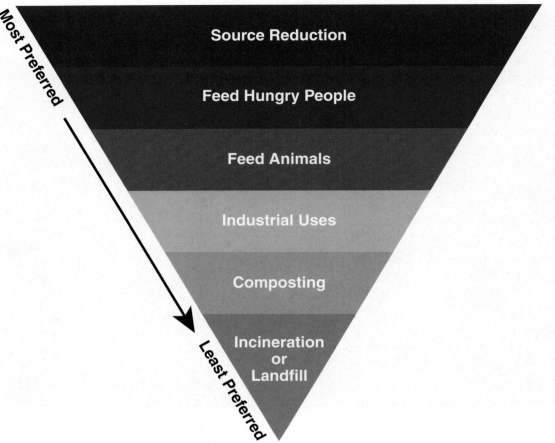

US Environmental Protection Agency

10-12 The Food Recovery Hierarchy suggests alternatives to dumping food waste in landfills.

Biodegradable means something can be broken down into harmless products by living things such as worms, insects, and bacteria. Walking through a forest or park, you will see composting happening all around you. When leaves fall to the ground, they biodegrade into a dirtlike substance that serves as food for growing plants. Composting is an essential part of the life cycle. When food is put into a landfill, it is taken out of this cycle. The following are three basic ways that foods decompose:

- **Vermicomposting**. Uses worms, along with other bacteria, fungi, and insects to break down the waste into a high-quality fertilizer. This method is typically recommended for food scraps, excluding animal proteins and dairy foods.

- **Aerobic/Windrow composting**. Exposes the organic matter to bacteria and plenty of oxygen through frequent mixing. The result is the matter gets hot (up to 160°F, 71°C) and breaks down into a rich, fertile substance. This is typically recommended for lawn clippings and leaves. Food scraps, excluding dairy and animal proteins, may be added to the mix.

- **Anaerobic composting**. This occurs when a large pile of organic matter is simply heaped up and not mixed. This is what happens in a landfill. This process takes longer to break down organic matter and a different kind of bacteria (anaerobic) grows in this oxygen-depleted environment. This process produces methane gas, which is damaging to the atmosphere. While anaerobic composting in a landfill hurts the environment, there are new technologies being employed to produce valuable products instead. These technologies use anaerobic composting in a controlled environment called an *anaerobic digester*. The anaerobic digester turns food waste into renewable energy and soil amendment by quickly breaking down the materials and capturing the methane gas for use as fuel. The remaining solid materials are added back into soil.

Not all areas of the country provide composting resources to foodservice. This is changing as cities realize that making compost is more beneficial and less damaging to the environment than creating more landfills. Commercial composting companies meet state permitting requirements that ensure foods are decomposed in a safe way. Which foods can be composted varies from location to location. As a result, each foodservice operation should research the composting possibilities available to them.

Reuse

A strategy to reduce the overall amount of waste is to consider reuse instead of disposal. A **reusable** item can be repurposed and kept out of the waste stream. For instance, pieces of unwanted or used furniture can be donated to various organizations. Plastic packaging containers can be cleaned and used for storage of nonfood items or given to a local nursery or school to use as seed planters. There are many options—all that is required is creative thinking.

Recycle

There are a growing number of products that can be recycled. **Recycling** is the process by which something is reformulated to be used again. Recycling not only conserves resources, but also reduces the

amount of waste that goes into landfills. It is also energy efficient. Many communities across the United States have successful recycling programs. Check with your local recycling source to learn if recycled items need to be sorted or cleaned. Some of the most commonly recycled items are

- **Plastic**. There are seven basic types of plastics. Plastic containers are typically stamped with a number that corresponds to the type of plastic from which they were made, 10-13. Recycling programs may accept some or all of these types. For instance, most plastic wrap used in kitchens is not recyclable due to food residue. Yet plastic film used in transport packaging, especially shrink wrap on pallets received in large operations, is recyclable. This type of wrap is valued when sufficient quantities are collected.
- **Aluminum**. Most aluminum containers and cans are recyclable. Aluminum foil is typically not recyclable due to food residue.
- **Glass**. All forms of glass jars and bottles are recyclable. In some communities, different colors of glass must be separated.
- **Paper**. Most paper can be composted or recycled. Exceptions include paper that is soiled with food or oil and wax-coated paper. Such paper is no longer pure paper and cannot be recycled. Most paper beverage cups have a film lining making them unsuitable for recycling.
- **Oil**. Many foodservice operations have special containers for collecting spent oil. Cooking oil recyclers collect the oil and turn it into a wide range of products.
- **Ink cartridges from printers**. These cartridges can either be refilled for reuse or recycled into new plastic.
- **Computers and other electronic devices**. Some components of a computer can be reclaimed and recycled. This service is becoming increasingly available in cities across the country. Some cities are even banning electronics from landfills.

PET or PETE (Polyethylene terephthalate)—All two-liter soda bottles and most plastic containers that have replaced glass.

HDPE (High-density polyethylene)—Detergent, liquid-bleach, milk, and engine-oil containers.

V (Vinyl, polyvinyl chloride)—Meat wrappers and many other translucent and transparent wraps and containers.

LDPE (Low-density polyethylene)—Shopping and garment bags, bread wrappers, and most shrink-wrap packaging.

PP (Polypropylene)—Margarine tubs, straws, plastic bottle caps, twine, and rope.

PS (Polystyrene)—Foam cartons, packing peanuts, clear plastic bowls, plates, and utensils.

OTHER (Nonrecyclables)—Plastics, such as some squeezable bottles.

10-13 Plastic containers and packaging are stamped with universal symbols to aid in recycling.

Hazardous Waste

Material that cannot be composted or recycled ends up in the refuse, or garbage, container. This waste eventually enters the landfill. To prevent hazardous waste from entering the landfill, it should never be discarded in refuse. Instead, hazardous materials waste should be taken to specific locations capable of disposing these substances safely and in a way that is eco-conscious. Some communities sponsor hazardous waste collections periodically to keep these materials out of landfills, 10-14. Additionally, mixing hazardous substances such as chemicals can be potentially dangerous and should be avoided. Common hazardous materials include:

- oil-based paint and paint thinners
- fluorescent lightbulbs
- batteries
- cleaning materials
- pesticides

Social Considerations

Many decisions made in the foodservice industry affect the lives of people within the organization, community, nation, and world. Social sustainability requires that, as these decisions are being made, consideration be given to

- diversity which includes cultural sharing, education, and inclusion of all groups
- social resources, such as community programs, social justice, and health
- equal opportunity as it relates to employment, housing, labor rights, and education
- supply issues such as food, clothing, product safety, and shelter
- poverty

As in other areas of sustainability, social sustainability is about maintaining a balance between economic development—business—and the welfare of society so both can survive and flourish. More and more companies are developing corporate social responsibility (CSR) programs. These programs benefit not only society, but also the company by polishing the company's image in the eyes of those who would buy from them.

spirit of america/Shutterstock.com

10-14 Hazardous waste collections help keep unsafe materials out of landfills.

The following are some areas in which the foodservice industry can have a meaningful social impact:

- *Food Waste.* It is estimated that half the food produced in the United States is thrown away. When there are people experiencing hunger every day, there is an obligation to use food resources wisely and thoughtfully. Foodservice in the United States has also taken a leadership role in trying to alleviate hunger.

- *Obesity.* As overweight and obesity threaten the health and welfare of citizens and future generations, the culinary community is ideally positioned to set the "food fashion" that can improve the way people eat.

- *Purchasing.* When evaluating companies to purchase from, consideration should be given to the value placed on employees, and the importance placed on the wholesomeness of the food they sell and the methods used to raise or grow it. Organizations such as Fair Trade USA certify products that meet social sustainability standards.

- *Public policy.* Staying informed about current topics and voicing an opinion is the social responsibility of all citizens.

- *Diversity.* Whether hiring, designing work spaces, providing service, or even writing menus, the diversity of the community must be considered. Diversity encompasses differences in ethnicity, gender, gender-orientation, as well as, those with disabilities.

Summary Points

- Adopting sustainable practices not only helps preserve the condition of Earth, but also is good business practice.

- When foodservice operators purchase food, cleaning supplies, and other items, sustainability is part of the decision-making process. There are many variables that affect a particular food's sustainability.

- Foodservice operations can save energy in many ways. Lighting, hot water delivery, maintenance, equipment purchases, and ventilation are common areas where energy can be saved. Changing behaviors can also result in energy savings.

- Water is not a limitless resource and foodservice uses large amounts every day. There are many ways that foodservice can save water including at service, equipment selection, proper maintenance, and cleaning.

- Reducing the amount of waste going to landfills makes good environmental and business sense. Food waste can be minimized through good planning. Reusing and recycling can reduce waste going to landfills. Hazardous waste must be handled in such a way as to keep it from landfills.

- Social issues are part of a sustainable future. Foodservice operations should consider social issues in their decision making.

In Review
Assess

1. Explain why foodservice operations have a responsibility to act sustainably.

2. Give several reasons why food that is produced sustainably may cost more than foods that are raised or produced using industrial or modern agriculture methods.

3. Explain what is required for food to be certified organic in the United States.

4. Why is biodiversity of food crops and animals important?

5. What is the best way to identify truly ecofriendly cleaning products?

6. Compare and contrast LEDs, CFLs, and incandescent lighting in terms of cost, life expectancy, and energy efficiency.

7. What are two common maintenance issues that need regular attention to improve energy efficiency of refrigeration equipment?

8. List five ways to reduce water consumption in a foodservice operation.

9. Compare the three types of composting.

10. How can you identify what type of plastic a product is made from?

11. List four ways that foodservice can have a positive impact on social sustainability.

Core Skills

12. **Math.** If a water faucet drips at a rate of one drip per minute and a drip from a faucet is ¼ mL, how many ounces of water would be wasted in one day? (*Hint: 30 mL = 1 fl. oz.*)

13. **Writing.** Use multiple, authoritative sources to learn more about genetically modified foods and form an opinion. Assess the strengths and limitations of each source. Write an opinion paper citing sources to support your opinion.

14. **Speaking.** Prepare an electronic presentation explaining the different types of aquaculture and their potential effects on the environment. What types of fish can be farm-raised? What percent of the world's seafood supply is farm-raised? Make strategic use of audio, visual, or other elements to add interest. Share your presentation with the class.

15. **Reading.** Find articles in various culinary (or related) industry publications, journals, and websites to learn more about sustainability trends in restaurants. Write a brief summary listing your sources and significant trends you identify.

16. **Math.** A full-size gas convection oven costs $3,429. A similar ENERGY STAR qualified gas convection oven costs $5,213. If the ENERGY STAR qualified oven saves $360

in gas annually, how long before the price difference is paid for in gas savings? (*Round answer up to the nearest whole number.*)

17. **Writing.** Search for corporate social responsibility (CSR) programs online to serve as examples. Imagine you are the owner of a foodservice operation and craft a corporate social responsibility (CSR) program for your company. Present your CSR in class.

18. **Reading.** With a partner, choose two words from Figure 10-2 to compare. Create a Venn diagram to compare your words and identify differences. Write one term under the left circle and the other term under the right. Where the circles overlap, write three characteristics the terms have in common. For each term, write a difference of the term for each characteristic in its respective outer circle.

19. **CTE Career Readiness Practice.** Clean, pure drinking water is not available to many people in various parts of the world. Identify key areas where this is a problem. What are some cost-effective ways to provide clean, pure drinking water? What are the social and economic impacts of countries failing to provide basic water purification for its citizens? Write a report of your findings to share with the class.

Critical Thinking

20. **Assess.** Research recycling and composting policies in your area. Identify central issues or barriers that might discourage or prevent a foodservice operation from reducing their contribution to the waste stream through implementation of a recycling and composting program. Suggest a possible solution for each issue or barrier you identify.

21. **Analysis.** Organize evidence to support or refute the following topic and debate in class: This generation has a responsibility to future generations and other regions of the world to implement sustainable practices.

22. **Evaluate.** Select three organizations that promote sustainability. Judge the credibility of each organization. Prepare a brief summary of your conclusions and the reasoning behind each.

Technology

Use the Internet to find foods that are grown or raised within a 150-mile radius of your school. Write a brief summary including the name of the website(s) you used and your list of locally grown foods. List the pros and cons of purchasing locally in your area. Conclude the level of ease with which an area restaurant might be able to source locally grown food.

Teamwork

Working in teams, perform a survey of your school kitchen or lab. Identify areas where waste control could be improved and suggestions for how this could be done. Create a list of products that could be recycled or composted. Research and identify environmentally friendly cleaning products that could be used in place of current products. Include a cost comparison of the current and proposed products. Create an electronic presentation of your findings and share with the class.

Chef's E-portfolio
Water Conservation in the Kitchen PSA

Produce a public service announcement (PSA) explaining how to conserve water in the kitchen. Video yourself as you survey the faucets in your home or school kitchen to check for leaks or drips. Provide a list of simple steps to conserve water. Upload the PSA to your e-portfolio. Ask your instructor where to save your file. This could be on the school's network or a flash drive of your own. Name your portfolio document *FirstnameLastname_Portfolio Ch#.docx* (i.e., JohnSmith_PortfolioCh10.docx).

While studying, look for the activity icon ➜ to:

- Build vocabulary with e-flash cards and matching activities.
- Expand learning with video clips, photo identification activities, animations, and interactive activities.
- Review and assess what you learn by completing end-of-chapter questions.

G-WLEARNING.com

Knives and Hand Tools in the Professional Kitchen

11

Reading Prep

Before you read the chapter, interview someone in foodservice. Ask the person why it is important to know about the chapter topic and how this topic affects the workplace. Take notes during the interview. As you read the chapter, highlight the items from your notes that are discussed in the chapter.

Culinary Terminology
Build Vocab

carbon steel, p. 173
stainless steel, p. 174
high-carbon stainless steel, p. 174
tang, p. 174
bolster, p. 177
steel, p. 177
whetstone, p. 177
Parisienne scoop, p. 183
spider, p. 184

Academic Terminology
Build Vocab

synthetic, p. 177

Objectives

After studying this chapter, you will be able to

- explain the elements of knife construction and how they relate to quality.
- apply techniques to sharpen and maintain an edge on a knife using a steel and whetstone.
- implement proper storage and safety practices when using knives.
- recognize various knives and hand tools used in the professional kitchen.

Every trade, art, or craft has its own assortment of tools or implements used to practice the discipline. This chapter explores the qualities of a well-made knife and identifies the types of knives and hand tools found in professional kitchens. You will also learn how to sharpen knives and keep them sharp.

Knives

No tool is more identified with the chef's profession than the knife, and for good reason. The knife is the chef's most important tool. Many chefs have favorite knives they have used for years. The right knife for the job becomes an extension of the chef's hand. A sharp, well-constructed knife makes the cutting task seem almost effortless, 11-1. One of the most important things an aspiring chef can do to develop his or her culinary skill is to invest in a good quality chef's knife. Cutting boards are nearly as important and must be used to keep the knives in good condition.

Construction and Selection

A key factor to consider when judging the quality of a knife is the type of metal used for the blade. Kitchen knives are usually made from one of three types of metals— carbon steel, stainless steel, or high-carbon stainless steel.

Carbon steel has been used to make knives for hundreds of years. A blade made from **carbon steel** is the easiest to sharpen to a finely honed edge, but loses its shine and

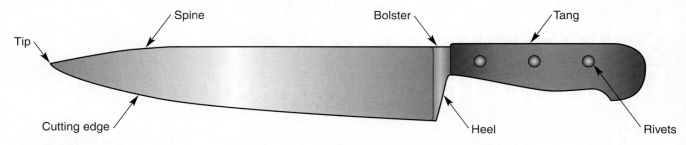

Tip

Spine

Bolster

Tang

Cutting edge

Heel

Rivets

11-1 Understanding how knives are constructed aids a chef when selecting a quality knife.

discolors quickly after its first use. These knives rust if left wet or in a damp place. As a result, this type of blade sometimes transfers a metallic flavor to foods, especially acidic foods. It also causes certain foods such as lettuce and avocados to discolor more rapidly.

To solve the rust and discoloration problems with carbon steel knives, knife makers introduced stainless steel chef knives. **Stainless steel** does not pit, rust, or discolor, and does not affect the flavor of foods. The disadvantage of stainless steel is that it is a much harder metal than carbon steel. Because stainless steel is so hard, these blades are more difficult to sharpen and keep sharp.

By the 1980s, cutlery manufacturers had arrived at a solution that combined the best properties of both carbon and stainless steels. This improved combination is called **high-carbon stainless steel**. Today, most good quality professional knives are made with high-carbon stainless steel. These knife blades are easier to sharpen and maintain, and do not rust or discolor.

Another feature to consider when selecting a quality knife is the tang. **Tang** is the term used to describe the portion of the knife blade that extends into the handle of the knife. The best made knives have a *full tang*. A full tang extends all the way to the end of the handle as one continuous piece of metal. Less durable knives have what is called a *rattail tang*. This tang consists of a thin piece of metal—like the handle of a rattail comb—that extends into the handle of the knife, 11-2. Knives with a rattail tang may be less expensive, but the blade and the handle often become loose with wear. A knife with a loose blade is not safe to use. When choosing a chef's knife, select one with a tang that extends at least three-fourths the length of the handle.

Knife handles can vary in material and weight. Handles are often made from hardwoods such as rosewood and maple. Other common materials used to make handles include plastic, rubber, and composite materials. If the handle is molded onto the tang, it is hard to know the length of the tang. When choosing a knife, the material the handle is made of is important and so is the weight. The weight of the handle should be balanced with the weight of the blade. A balanced knife is more comfortable to grip and easier to use.

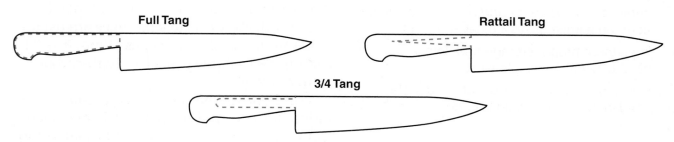

Full Tang

Rattail Tang

3/4 Tang

11-2 There are a variety of tangs used in knife construction.

Knives and Their Uses

Chef's Knife

The chef's knife or French knife is the most used knife in any chef's knife kit. It is used for chopping, slicing, and most other cutting tasks. Lengths vary between 8 and 14 inches. The 10-inch blade is the most popular. The blade is wide enough for the gripping hand to clear the work surface when cutting and chopping. The blade tapers to a point at the tip. This design allows the knife to be used for chopping by rocking it on the curved part of the blade.

Utility Knife

A utility knife is a smaller version of the chef's knife and is designed for lighter kitchen work. Typically, utility knives have blades between 5 and 7 inches long. Its blade is more flexible and usually not wide enough to use for chopping tasks.

Boning and Filet Knives

The blade of a boning or filet knife is approximately 6 inches long and narrower than a chef or utility knife. Styles vary in the shape, thickness, and flexibility of the blade. The knives with the wider, more rigid blades are called *boning knives*. Boning knives are used for separating muscle from bone on meat or poultry. The thinner, more flexible blades are called *filet knives* and are often used for filleting and portioning fish.

Slicers

A slicer is a knife with a long, narrow, flexible blade. Using a light sawing motion with this knife allows you to cut cooked meat and poultry into thin, even slices. Its length also makes it useful for many other jobs.

Serrated Slicer

A serrated blade has teeth like a saw. A serrated slicer is a long knife with a serrated blade. This knife is useful when cutting breads and pastries which might crumble or be crushed with a smooth blade.

Paring Knives

Paring is the act of cutting away skin or peel. Paring knives are the small, short-bladed knives designed to accomplish this task. They are also useful for cutting intricate garnishes and other detail work.

Images courtesy of R. H. Forschner, a division of Swiss Army Brands, Inc.

(Continued)

Knives and Their Uses (Continued)

Tourné Knife

A tourné is a vegetable that has been cut into a small barrel or football shape. This variation on the paring knife with its inwardly curved blade makes the job of cutting these shapes easier.

Clam Knife

A clam knife is a short knife with a 1-inch-wide blade. The blade tapers to an edge, but is not honed sharp. This knife is not used for cutting. The blade is wedged between the top and bottom shells of the clam and acts like a wedge to open it.

Scimitar

Sometimes called a *butcher's knife*, the scimitar has a long, thick, highly curved blade. This knife is excellent for cutting steaks from large cuts of meat.

Cleavers

A cleaver is easily identified by its large, rect-angular blade. It is used for chopping. Heavier cleavers can chop through bones.

Palette Knives and Spreaders

Palette knives and spreaders come in various lengths and widths. They have flexible blades, but are not sharp. They are designed to spread coatings on foods but may also be used as a spatula to turn items while cooking them.

Oyster Knife

An oyster knife is a small knife with a narrow, rigid blade. It is not sharp, but the pointed tip is used to pry apart the top and bottom shells of oysters.

Images courtesy of R. H. Forschner, a division of Swiss Army Brands, Inc.

More expensive knives are constructed with a bolster. A **bolster** strengthens the blade by forging it with a thick, metal collar that runs from the heel of the blade to the handle. The bolster makes the knife heavier, therefore, many chefs prefer a knife without this feature. The purpose of the bolster is to strengthen the blade at a stress point where knife blades often crack or chip. Even with the added strength of a bolster, a chef's knife should be used only on tasks for which it was designed. Knives should not be used to crack hard bones or open metal cans.

Cutting Boards

Traditionally, chefs have preferred the use of cutting boards and butcher's blocks made from hardwoods such as maple and oak. In the 1980s, health departments began requiring cutting boards made from **synthetic**, or man-made materials, instead of wood boards. The wood boards were thought to be less sanitary because wood is porous. Recently, studies have shown that hardwoods are less likely to allow bacterial growth than synthetic boards. As a result, wooden cutting boards have returned to commercial kitchens.

Today, the decision to use wood or synthetic cutting boards is a matter of personal preference and cost. Synthetic boards are much cheaper than wood. Synthetic boards can be purchased in a range of colors. Each color is then restricted to a specific use to help avoid cross-contamination. Whichever type or color board you choose, clean and sanitize it after each use. Cutting boards come in contact with many foods and have potential for being vehicles for cross-contamination.

Sharpening Knives

Once you select a good quality knife, it is important to learn how to keep it sharp. A dull knife is more dangerous than a sharp knife because it is harder to control and requires more force to make the desired cuts.

Some confusion exists over the roles of the two tools used to sharpen knives in the professional kitchen—the steel and the whetstone. Simply put, the **steel** is a rod used to keep the blade sharp as you work, 11-3. The **whetstone** is a flat, abrasive stone used to sharpen a knife once its edge is dull and worn.

The Steel

The steel is a rod designed to remove the very small, rough metal irregularities on the edge of the blade and to realign it. The steel requires only a moderate amount of force to hone the edge of the blade to a smooth and even cutting surface. When using the steel, the following two things are important to remember:

1. Hold the blade at the proper angle to the steel.
2. Use only moderate force when stroking the steel.

There are two ways to steel a knife blade. Both methods require that the full length of the blade, from heel to tip, be honed evenly and on both sides.

Images courtesy of R.H. Forschner, a division of Swiss Army Brands, Inc.

11-3 Steels may vary slightly in design.

TECHNIQUE
Using a Steel
Method One

1. Begin by holding the steel in front of you and parallel to your body. Place the heel of the blade at the top end of the steel being sure the edge of the knife is at a 20-degree angle to the steel.

2. By rotating the wrist of your knife hand downward, gently draw the length of the blade across the steel, ending with the tip.

3. Repeat the process several times on each side of the blade until the edge has a fine finish.

Method Two

1. Place the tip of the steel on the cutting board and grasp the handle so the steel is vertical, butt side up.

2. Place the heel of the blade at the top of the steel keeping the edge of the knife at a 20-degree angle to the steel.

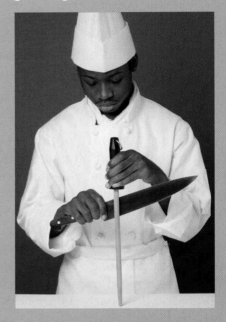

3. With even pressure, draw the blade across the steel to the tip maintaining the 20-degree angle.

4. Repeat the process several times on each side of the blade until the edge has a fine finish.

Mix In Math

Measuring Angles

Lines are measured in inches or centimeters. Angles are measured in degrees. A full circle measures 360 degrees (°).

There are many angles that make up that full circle. Try picturing a clock instead of a circle and you will be able to see and measure the angles better.

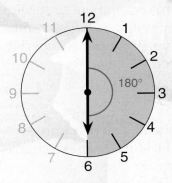

The hands of this clock create a 180° angle.

The hands of this clock create a 90° angle.

The hands of this clock create a 45° angle.

The hands of this clock create a 20° angle.

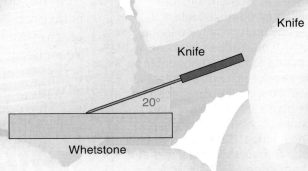

Knives must be held at a 20° angle to either a whetstone or steel when sharpening.

Culture & Cuisine

Asian Cuisine—A Different Approach to Knives

In the Chinese kitchen and in most other Asian cuisines, the knife of choice is a cleaver. A Chinese cleaver has a rectangular shape with a slightly curved blade to accommodate a rocking motion. In Asian kitchens, the cleaver is used for a wide range of tasks including boning chicken, peeling carrots, mincing garlic, and chopping scallions. Cleavers are even used as spatulas.

The Chinese cleaver is gripped and handled the same way as the chef's knife. However, Asian chefs believe that its heavier weight requires less effort than a chef's knife for cutting and chopping. Chinese cleavers come in a range of sizes for different tasks. Carbon steel is the preferred metal for Chinese cleavers because of its sharpening ability, but they must be kept clean and dry to avoid rusting.

Image courtesy of R. H. Forschner, a division of Swiss Army Brands, Inc.

Japanese chefs utilize styles of knives that are less often seen in Western kitchens. The santoku knife is an all-purpose knife with a flat cutting edge. They are typically no longer than 8 inches (20 cm). The blades of Japanese knives are usually honed to have a thinner blade profile. Japanese knives for fish and vegetables are also unique because they are sharpened on only one side of the blade with the other side remaining flat. In contrast, Western-style knives are sharpened on both sides. Santoku knives are traditionally made from carbon steel and are honed to a razor sharp edge.

The Whetstone

The whetstone, or sharpening stone, is used to sharpen the edge of a blade that has become dull with use. Stones are made from a variety of abrasive mineral materials such as carborundum, carbide, sandstone, or ceramic. These materials act to grind and hone your knife to a sharp edge. Most stones have two sides—one rough and the other fine. The rougher side is used first to grind an edge on the blade, then the finer side is used to hone it. A *tri-stone* is a three-sided stone with a holder and lubricant reservoir. There are also machines that perform this process more quickly and companies that provide knife-sharpening service. This equipment or service can be costly. However, with a small amount of practice and an inexpensive stone, superior results can be achieved.

Lubricants

When using a stone to sharpen knives, most chefs lubricate the stone to make sharpening easier. The lubricant also helps to remove the filings of metal and mineral that are created during the sharpening process. Water and mineral oil are the lubricants typically used for sharpening in the professional kitchen. Water is a less effective lubricant than oil, but it is readily available. Mineral oil is favored because it does not become sticky or gummy from friction like vegetable oil does. Because mineral oil is digestible, there is no fear of chemically contaminating foods as with petroleum-based oils.

Sharpening stones are porous and, therefore, they absorb some lubricant. For this reason, once oil is used on a stone, water will not work as a lubricant on that stone.

Knife Storage and Safety

Storing knives correctly accomplishes two goals—protects the knife and keeps cooks

TECHNIQUE
Using a Whetstone

1. Place the sharpening stone on a wet towel or rubber mat to prevent it from slipping during the sharpening process. Begin with the coarsest side of the stone.

2. If you are using a lubricant, saturate the surface of the stone with an even layer of water or mineral oil.

3. Hold the knife at a 20-degree angle to the surface of the stone.

4. Maintain a 20-degree angle as you begin with the heel of the blade in the upper left-hand corner of the stone.

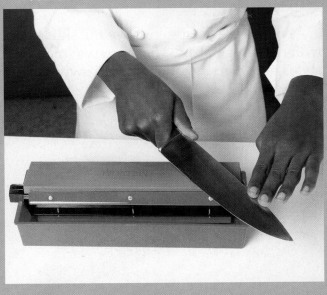

5. Draw the knife down and across the stone until the tip of the knife is on the lower right-hand corner of the stone. Be sure to maintain even pressure on all parts of the blade throughout the process.

6. Repeat the process on the other side of the blade. Begin with the heel in the upper-right corner of the stone and finish with the tip in the lower-left corner.

7. Repeat the process 5 to 10 times depending on the dullness of the blade. Apply equal pressure to all parts of the blade and an equal number of strokes to each side of the blade.

8. Turn the stone to its finer side, lubricate it, and repeat steps three through six.

9. To finish the edge, hone it on the steel as illustrated previously.

safe. Before any knife is stored, it is important that the knife is cleaned, rinsed, sanitized, and completely dry. Some knives may be washed in a commercial dishmachine. This is often done with lower-priced knives. High-quality knives should never be washed in a dishmachine to avoid damage over time.

Knives should not be stored loose in a drawer. This is unsafe and knives become dull from contact with other knives. Knives should be stored in a

- drawer with a knife sheath on each knife
- knife roll with a sheath on each knife in case the knife falls out when the roll is opened
- knife holder which can be cleaned and sanitized
- knife cabinet

Knife holders must be cleaned and sanitized on a regular basis. Some knife cabinets are available that emit UV rays which sanitize the knives as they are stored. Some of these options can be locked for added security.

Knives are a necessary part of working in a professional kitchen. They are also dangerous if not handled correctly. One of the most important safety considerations in a commercial kitchen is keeping the cutting tools in top condition. Beginner cooks may be afraid of a razor-sharp chef's knife, however, it is much safer than a dull knife. A sharp blade means the knife cuts more cleanly and accurately. Most importantly, with a sharp knife the cook has greater control. Most accidents with knives occur when the user loses control because the blade slips or bounces off the surface being cut. A sharp knife also requires less force to cut the desired product, which also aids in control and reduces fatigue.

Before working with a knife, be sure that you are trained on proper technique and safety by a supervisor. The supervisor should verify that each employee has been trained and demonstrated proper use of each piece of kitchen equipment, including knives, 11-4. This written record is kept on file by the employer.

Safe Knife Handling

Do:
- Keep knives sharpened and let other staff know when knives are newly sharpened.
- Use a knife only for its intended purpose.
- Use the appropriate knife for the job.
- Carry knives with the cutting edge slightly away from your body.
- Store knives properly in racks or knife sheaths.

Don't:
- Touch knife blades.
- Try and catch a falling knife—let it fall.
- Hand a knife to someone. Put it down on the counter and let him or her pick it up.
- Leave a knife soaking in a sink of water.
- Talk to people while using a knife.

Source: Occupational Safety & Health Administration

11-4 Safe knife handling is essential in the professional kitchen.

Hand Tools

A wide variety of hand tools are used in commercial kitchens. These devices perform many useful tasks. Foodservice professionals must be able to identify and use these tools.

Peelers

Peelers are used to remove the skins of fruits and vegetables. There are two main styles of peelers—stationary and swivel.

The stationary peeler is a slit blade with a sharpened edge mounted on a handle. The blade of most stationary peelers can also be used to core apples. Swivel peelers have their blade mounted to the handle so they swivel or rock. The ability to swivel makes it easier to keep the blade in contact with the surface of the item being peeled.

Whips and Whisks

The terms *whip* and *whisk* are both used to refer to an implement of looped wire attached to a handle. The purpose of this tool is to incorporate air into a mixture or blend ingredients. Whips or whisks come in a variety of sizes. Their wires may be flexible for incorporating more air into a thinner substance, or rigid for mixing thicker substances. Most kitchens should have a variety of sizes and styles for a variety of jobs.

Tongs

Metal spring tongs are used widely in the professional kitchen. Tongs act as an extension of the hand for handling food items of all sorts.

Parisienne Scoops

Home cooks call this scoop a melon baller. Professional cooks refer to this utensil as a **Parisienne scoop**. The name is derived from the classical preparation of potatoes Parisienne, which are scooped into small balls. Parisienne scoops are available in a variety of sizes and can form a great number of foods into appealing garnishes.

Meat Fork

A heavy-duty fork with two long tines is used by chefs to turn large pieces of meat during cooking and to hold the meat when carving. The fork is also used to test for doneness.

Image courtesy of R.H. Forschner, a division of Swiss Army Brands, Inc.

Images courtesy of R. H. Forschner, a division of Swiss Army Brands, Inc.

Spiders

A **spider** is a long-handled tool used to strain items or lift them out of liquid. The name comes from the fact that the mesh disc at the end of the handle resembles a spider's web.

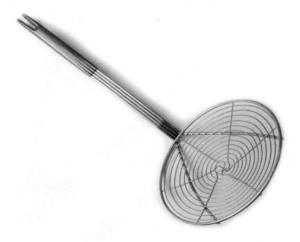

Ladles

Ladles are used for portioning liquid products and come in a wide range of sizes. The volume capacity of a ladle is usually imprinted on its handle.

Skimmer

The flat, perforated disk on the working end of a skimmer is designed to remove impurities that form scum on the surface of simmering liquids. It can also be used to perform the same tasks as a spider.

Kitchen Spoons

Sturdy stainless steel spoons can be solid, slotted, or perforated. Slotted and perforated spoons are used for draining wet products.

Offset Spatulas

One of the most commonly used tools in the kitchen, this metal spatula has a wide blade with an offset handle. The offset spatula, or hamburger turner, is used to lift, turn, and carry food items. They are available in a variety of sizes and thicknesses. Some models are perforated to allow for draining a food product.

Garnishing Tools

Chefs utilize a number of small devices or gadgets designed to prepare decorative food garnishes.

Zester　A zester is a tool that is designed to remove fine strips of the outer rind of citrus fruits.

Images courtesy of R. H. Forschner, a division of Swiss Army Brands, Inc.

Channel Knife　Channel knives are tools that cut a decorative groove in the surface of fruits and vegetables.

Images courtesy of R. H. Forschner, a division of Swiss Army Brands, Inc.

Spatulas and Scrapers

A spatula is a flexible blade on a long handle. Blades may be made from silicon, rubber, vinyl, or other materials. This hand tool helps the cook when removing food product from a container. Heat-resistant spatulas are also used for cooking in nonstick pans to avoid scratching their finish. Bakers and pastry chefs also utilize a plain plastic blade without a handle called a *scraper*. This tool is particularly useful for scraping down large mixing bowls.

Garnishing Knives　Garnishing knives are V- or U-shaped chisels that are used to carve decorations from fruits and vegetables.

Images courtesy of R. H. Forschner, a division of Swiss Army Brands, Inc.

Summary Points

- Knives are the most often used tools in the commercial kitchen. Choosing the right knife for a particular cutting job makes the task safer and easier.

- Maintaining a sharp blade on knives is essential for safety. Knives can be kept sharp using a whetstone and steel.

- Storing knives correctly protects the knives' blades and the cook's safety.

- Knife safety is an important topic in the kitchen on which employees should receive training.

- Chefs use a wide variety of hand tools. Using the right tool for a particular job saves time and effort.

In Review Assess

1. True or false. The bolster is the most important factor in judging the quality of a knife.

2. A knife blade made from _____ _____ is easiest to sharpen.

3. Explain what makes a balanced knife.

4. Identify the best knife to use for the following tasks:
   A. dicing an onion
   B. cutting steaks from a loin of beef
   C. splitting a sponge cake into layers
   D. making radishes into flower garnishes
   E. spreading icing on a cake

5. True or false. Studies have shown that hardwood cutting boards are less likely to allow bacterial growth than synthetic boards.

6. The _____ is used to sharpen a dull, worn knife blade.

7. List the two lubricants that are used on whetstones in the professional kitchen.

8. Explain which oil is the best to use as a whetstone lubricant and why.

9. A knife should be held at _____ angle to the whetstone or steel when sharpening or honing.

10. List three ways to correctly store knives.

11. Identify five rules of knife safety.

12. Describe tasks each of the following hand tools might be used for:
    A. spider
    B. skimmer
    C. slotted spoon
    D. offset spatula

Core Skills

13. **Math.** According to a local knife shop, every time a knife is sharpened there, 0.5 millimeters (mm) of blade is removed on average. If the knife is sharpened 2 times a year, how long will it take for 1 centimeter (cm) of blade to have been removed? (Hint: 10 mm = 1 cm)

14. **Writing.** A restaurant manager uses lecture and demonstration to instruct new employees on proper and safe use of equipment. After this instruction, the employees are expected to use the equipment in their daily work. Despite this training, the manager finds there are still too many work injuries due to improper use of equipment. Write an assessment of the manager's training program. Include any root problems identified and recommendations for improvements.

15. **Writing.** Prepare a document to record various equipment and safety training and assessments that you have completed. Have your instructors sign off on this record. Revise and add to it as you continue your education and training. Include as much detail as possible.

16. **Math.** Use a protractor to create a cardboard triangle with a 20-degree angle. Use the triangle as a guide to practice holding a knife at a 20-degree angle to either a steel or whetstone.

17. **Speaking.** Imagine you are a sales representative for a company that sells knives

and hand tools for use in professional kitchens. Select one of the knives or hand tools discussed in this chapter and prepare a sales demonstration. Assume your audience consists of foodservice professionals. Adjust the style of delivery, vocabulary, use of visual aids, and length of presentation based on your audience. Video your presentation and show it in class.

18. **CTE Career Readiness Practice.** Research silicon and its use in hand tools such as flexible spatulas. What characteristics make silicon a good material for this use? When did silicon first begin to be used in kitchen hand tools and why? Prepare and give a presentation to share your findings. Use digital media to enhance the understanding and add interest. Consider the audience when making word choices and organizing information.

Critical Thinking

19. **Consider.** You observe a culinary student cutting a loaf of fresh bread with her chef's knife. What is your instruction to her?

20. **Determine.** Which knives do you consider essential and which are supplemental? Provide a rationale for your answer.

21. **Assess.** Use the Internet, catalogs, or other sources to identify ways that professional chefs store knives. Which method do you think is most effective? Why?

Technology

Use the Internet and other sources to research the knife sterilizing cabinet discussed in this chapter. How does this technology work? What are the pros and cons of this technology? Give a brief presentation of your findings to the class.

Teamwork

As a group of students, visit a cutlery store or assemble a collection of knives of varying degrees of construction quality from the school kitchen. Examine the construction of each knife and record the group's observations in a chart. Next, handle each knife to assess its balance. Record these results in the chart. As a group, rank the knives for construction and comfort based on your observations. Provide a brief summary of how the group functioned. How does the group's ranking compare with what is considered quality construction? Was there significant variation among group members about perceived comfort level and balance? How did the group arrive at a consensus on ranking the knives?

Chef's E-portfolio
Record of Safety Training and Assessments

Upload the record of safety training and assessments you created in activity #15. Add to this record as your education, training, and career progress. Ask your instructor where to save your file. This could be on the school's network or a flash drive of your own. Name your portfolio document *FirstnameLastname_ Portfolio Ch#. docx* (i.e., JohnSmith_PortfolioCh11.docx).

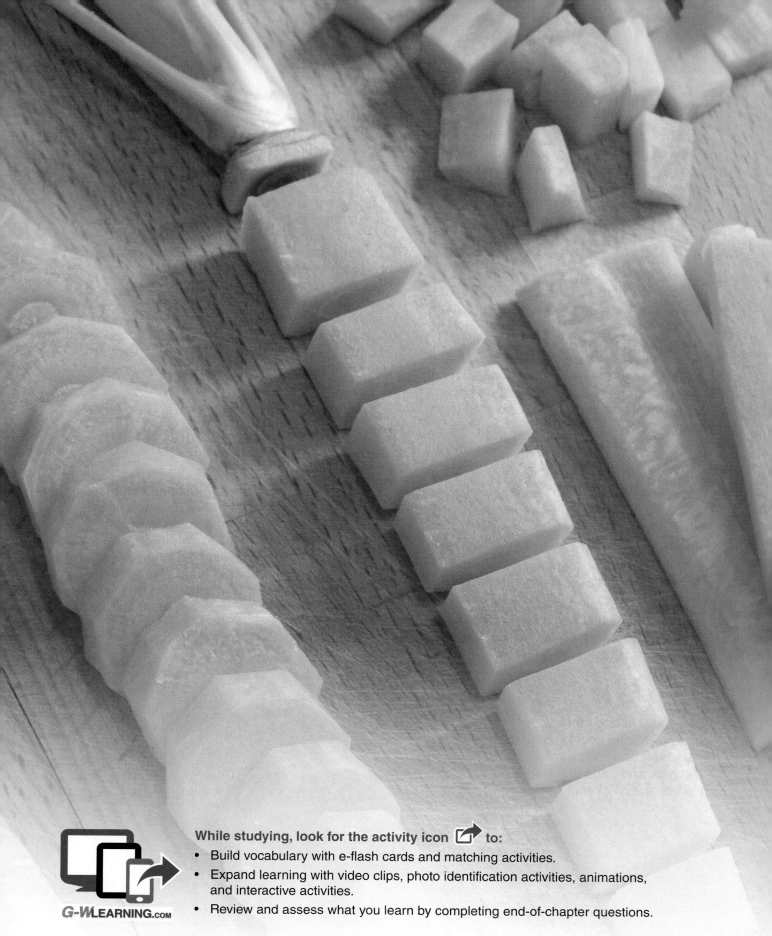

While studying, look for the activity icon to:

- Build vocabulary with e-flash cards and matching activities.
- Expand learning with video clips, photo identification activities, animations, and interactive activities.
- Review and assess what you learn by completing end-of-chapter questions.

Knife Skills

Reading Prep

Write all of the chapter terms on a sheet of paper. Highlight the words that you *do not* know. Before you begin reading, look up the highlighted words in the glossary and write the definitions.

Culinary Terminology Build Vocab

rondelle, p. 192
batonnet, p. 193
julienne, p. 193
large dice, p. 193
medium dice, p. 194
small dice, p. 194
brunoise, p. 194
paysanne, p. 194
mincing, p. 194
tourné, p. 196

Academic Terminology Build Vocab

proficient, p. 192

Objectives

After studying this chapter, you will be able to

- prepare a workstation for knife work.
- execute the proper technique for cutting with a chef's knife.
- execute the three basic knife cuts.
- apply the correct techniques for using a boning knife.
- demonstrate the correct use of a paring knife.
- implement the proper technique when using a slicer or serrated bread knife.

Simply being able to identify the knives that are commonly used in the professional kitchen is not sufficient. Now you must learn how to use those knives correctly. This chapter describes proper knife technique for the following types of knives: chef, boning, paring, the slicer, and serrated bread.

A word of caution is in order before beginning your first knife lesson. You have probably seen chefs wielding knives with lightning speed. This is one of the hallmarks of a seasoned chef. Such knife skills are not learned casually or quickly. Speed should never be the first goal when learning to use a knife. Going too fast can lead to a lack of knife control followed by injuries. The first step is to master the basic technique. Once the proper technique is learned, the second goal is accuracy and consistency. With time and practice, your speed will increase naturally.

Preparing the Workstation

The first step in learning knife skills is to set up a workstation. An improper workstation slows down production and can lead to accidents. Preparing a workstation consists of the following steps:

- Select a cleaned and sanitized cutting board.
- Place a damp towel between the cutting board and worktable to prevent the cutting board from shifting during knife work, 12-1.

Draz-Koetke/Goodheart-Willcox Publisher

12-1 Placing a towel between the cutting board and table keeps the cutting board stationary.

- Assess the height of the worktable and cutting board. If the cutting board is too low, a series of sheet trays can be used to elevate the cutting board. Place the sheet trays right side up on the worktable and nest the cutting board inside the top sheet tray. If the cutting board is too high, it may be necessary to stand on a step stool. Some worktables have height-adjustable legs. Working at a station that is not at a comfortable height can be dangerous and cause excessive fatigue.
- Select the appropriate knife and make sure the edge is sharp.
- Stand facing the worktable. Feet should be shoulder-width apart with weight evenly distributed on both feet, 12-2.

Draz-Koetke/Goodheart-Willcox Publisher

12-2 The proper stance reduces fatigue.

Using the Chef's Knife

Animation

Most professional chefs agree that the chef's knife is the most important knife in the kitchen. It can be used to chop, slice, cut, and mince a wide range of foods. Eight- or ten-inch chef's knives are most commonly used in the professional kitchen. All cooks must know how to use the chef's knife effectively. At first, these techniques may feel odd or slightly uncomfortable. With practice, they will feel natural.

The Knife Grip

Learning to use the chef's knife begins with the correct knife grip. The dominant hand grips the chef's knife. (Right-handed cooks hold the knife in their right hand. Left-handed cooks hold it in their left hand.) Gripping the chef's knife is a two-step process.

1. Grasp the portion of the knife blade just next to the end of the handle with the thumb and forefinger.

2. Wrap remaining fingers comfortably around the handle.

Placing the thumb and forefinger on either side of the blade provides maximum stability because the knife cannot slip or rotate out of your hand. Gripping the knife in any other manner is less safe and is not recommended, 12-3.

The Guiding Hand

Once the grip is mastered, the focus shifts to the other hand. This hand is called the guiding hand because it guides the knife during the cutting process. In addition to guiding, this hand also holds the product during cutting.

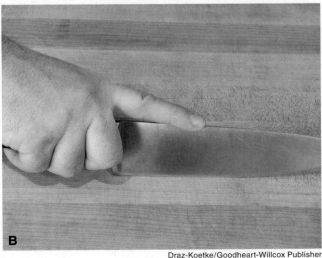

Draz-Koetke/Goodheart-Willcox Publisher

12-3 Placing either the (A) thumb or (B) index finger on top of the blade is an improper grip.

When positioning the guiding hand, remember the following guidelines:
1. Fingertips should be curled under slightly. This protects the fingertips from being cut accidentally.
2. The thumb and pinkie finger are behind the other fingers where they help grasp the object during cutting.

To become comfortable with the grip, practice grasping foods of different sizes and shapes. Do not start cutting until you are able to position the guiding hand correctly.

The Cutting Motion

The knife stroke that is used with the chef's knife is a combination of a downward and forward motion. The stroke begins with the tip of the knife pointed toward the cutting board. In one unbroken motion, the knife glides smoothly forward as the handle of the knife descends toward the cutting board. This basic cutting stroke is not a sawing motion or a stroke in which the knife is drawn backward.

The guiding hand steers the knife to where it should cut. During the knife stroke, the hand that grips the knife supplies the power and the guiding hand aids with the accuracy. For the two hands to work together, the knife must touch the middle joint of the front fingers of the guiding hand. This may seem dangerous but it is safe. The knife is touching the guiding hand, which acts to steer it away from the hand and prevent injury.

The best way to learn the technique for cutting with a chef's knife is to practice on an imaginary object. Cut slowly and deliberately at first. As your comfort level increases, cut small potatoes or celery stalks. Don't worry about how the cuts look or if they are all the same size. First, focus on mastering the correct cutting technique.

Basic Knife Cuts

Once you are comfortable with the basic cutting technique, it is time to learn to produce specific knife cuts. Foodservice professionals must be able to consistently produce shapes that are exactly the same size. This level of accuracy is the mark of a professional. Accuracy begins with learning and practicing the three basic knife cuts—slice, stick, and dice. Chefs become **proficient**, or skilled, at producing basic knife cuts with practice.

Foodservice professionals have names for the different sizes of slices, sticks, and dices. Understanding what each of these names means allows cooks to communicate easily and effectively. For instance, if a chef asks a cook to make a medium dice carrot, that cook will know exactly what size the chef wants the end product to be.

Slices

Most knife cuts begin by cutting slices. If the slices are cut correctly, they should all be the same thickness. One specific type of slice is called a *rondelle*. A **rondelle** (rahn DEHL) is a round slice cut from round food such as carrots, 12-4. It is often ¼-inch (6 mm) thick. To keep the food stationary during cutting, part of the round surface may be lightly trimmed flat. The side of the food is shaved slightly so that it does not roll during cutting.

TECHNIQUE
Cutting with the Chef's Knife

1. **Position the guiding hand on one or several smaller objects. Be sure that the thumb and pinkie are holding the object(s) securely and are behind the other fingers. Be sure that the front fingers are curved. The position of these fingers determines the location of the cut.**

2. **Place the flat side of the chef's knife against the middle joint of the front fingers of the guiding hand. The knife blade should be resting on the object(s).**

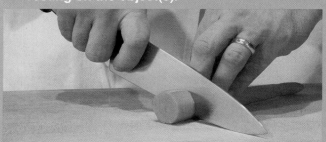

3. **Gently glide the chef's knife in the proper forward and down motion until the entire blade of the chef's knife is resting on the cutting board. The object(s) should be completely cut.**

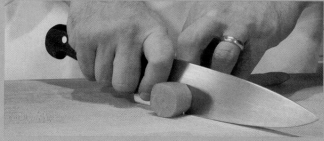

4. **Lift the back end of the knife so the tip remains pointing down. Slide the guiding hand back to the location of the next cut. Verify the position of the guiding hand and begin again at step one.**

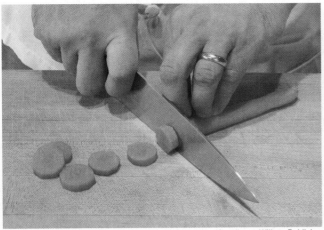

Draz-Koetke/Goodheart-Willcox Publisher

12-4 A skilled chef can cut rondelles of consistent thickness.

Sticks

Foods cut into sticks of various sizes are often used in the professional kitchen. The most common stick cuts are

- **Batonnet** (bat ohn AY)—2 × ¼ × ¼ inches (50 × 6 × 6 mm)

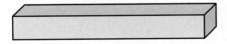

- **Julienne** (joo lee EHN)—2 × ⅛ × ⅛ inches (50 × 3 × 3 mm)

Dices

The dice cut is a continuation of the stick-cut technique. To make a dice, simply cut across stick cuts to make cubes. The most common five dice cuts are

- **Large dice**—¾ × ¾ × ¾ inches (2 × 2 × 2 cm)

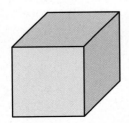

TECHNIQUE 🔗 Animation
Preparing Stick and Dice Cuts

1. Trim the food item so it is flat on one side. This keeps the food steady while you are cutting it and forms the first side of a rectangle.
2. Trim the other five sides of the food to create a rectangular box.
3. Cut lengthwise slices according to the thickness required for the specific stick cut.

4. Cut each slice lengthwise into uniformly sized sticks based on the dimensions of the desired stick cut.

5. Cut sticks into cubes to create dice cuts.

- **Medium dice**—½ × ½ × ½ inches (13 × 13 × 13 mm)

- **Small dice**—¼ × ¼ × ¼ inches (6 × 6 × 6 mm)

- **Brunoise** (broon WAHZ)—⅛ × ⅛ × ⅛ inches (3 × 3 × 3 mm)

- **Paysanne** (pay ZAHN)—½ × ½ × ¼ inches (13 × 13 × 6 mm) (This is technically not a dice as all the sides are not equal.)

Mincing

In addition to cutting, the chef's knife is also used for mincing foods such as fresh herbs, garlic, and olives. **Mincing** is the process of chopping food into very fine pieces.

During mincing, some foods stick to the side of the blade. Periodically, push the food off the blade by dragging a finger from the back of the knife toward the edge. Also during mincing, food spreads out on the cutting board. Push the food back into a neat pile by dragging the blade of the knife across the cutting board.

SANITATION & SAFETY
Cut-Resistant Gloves

Wearing cut-resistant gloves in the kitchen is increasingly common. These gloves are made from metal or cut-resistant fibers. When using a cut-resistant glove, keep the following precautions in mind:

- Do not purposely try to cut through the glove.
- Cut-resistant gloves rarely protect against puncture wounds like those received from a fish fin or the tip of a knife.
- Wash and sanitize gloves between every use.

TECHNIQUE
Mincing

1. **Place the tip of the knife on the cutting board. Place the guiding hand on the back of the tip of the knife. Keep the fingers of the guiding hand away from the blade.**

2. **To mince a product, lower and raise the chef knife repeatedly while pivoting the knife on the rounded front section of the blade.**

Using the Boning Knife

The boning knife is one of the most important knives in the kitchen because it is used to cut meat, poultry, and fish. All boning knives have a thin, pointed blade that is designed to work around bones and in between muscles. Boning knives vary in flexibility. Some blades are quite flexible while others are more rigid. Flexible boning knives are designed to maneuver easily around bones. For many chefs, the degree of flexibility is a matter of personal preference.

Gripping a boning knife is different from gripping a chef's knife. The nature of the job and the chef's preference usually determine which of the following methods are used:

- All the fingers grip the handle of the knife as if shaking someone's hand.

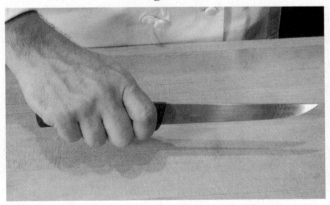

- All the fingers except the index finger grip the handle. The index finger rests on the back of the blade. This method gives maximum flexibility.

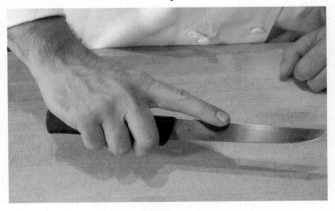

- All the fingers wrap around the handle with the blade pointing down. This method is often used when cutting large pieces of meat as it delivers maximum power.

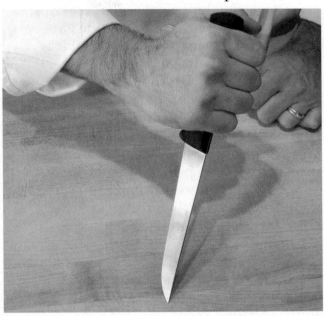

The guiding hand does not directly guide the boning knife during cutting as it does with the chef's knife. The guiding hand manipulates the fish or meat during the cutting process. When using a boning knife, never cut toward your guiding hand. A cut-resistant glove may be worn on the guiding hand to lessen the chance of an accident, 12-5.

12-5 Cut-resistant gloves prevent injury.

Using the Paring Knife

The paring knife is the smallest knife in the kitchen. It is used for a wide variety of small tasks such as carving vegetables, peeling pearl onions, and trimming mushrooms.

Before the invention of the vegetable peeler, paring knives were used to peel vegetables and fruits, 12-6. Using a paring knife for peeling requires more skill than using a vegetable peeler. Still, paring knives are preferred for peeling certain vegetables with thick skins. When using a paring knife for peeling, remove as little skin as necessary.

Paring knives are also used to make the classical knife cut called a *tourné*. A **tourné** (toor NAY) is a seven-sided football shape. Tourné-shaped vegetables are common in high-end restaurants. A tourné or bird's beak paring knife is helpful, although not essential, when cutting the tourné shape. Making the perfect tourné requires much practice and patience.

Draz-Koetke/Goodheart-Willcox Publisher

12-6 Some chefs prefer to use paring knives to peel fruits and vegetables rather than peelers.

TECHNIQUE
Preparing Vegetable Tournés

1. Cut the vegetable to the approximate desired length of the tourné.
2. Hold the trimmed vegetable in the guiding hand.
3. Place the thumb of the knife hand on or near the end of the vegetable. Starting at the top of the vegetable, draw the paring knife toward the bottom of the vegetable in a slightly rounded fashion. It is important that one continuous cut is made so that the tourné does not look jagged.

4. Turn the vegetable 1/7th revolution and make another cut. Right-handed cooks turn the vegetable counterclockwise, while left-handed cooks turn the vegetable clockwise. Tourné should have seven equal sides.

Using the Slicer and Serrated Bread Knife

The slicer and serrated bread knife are used in similar manners. The hand is wrapped around the handle, like a hand-shake, with none of the fingers on the blade.

Depending on the job, the guiding hand may or may not guide the knife. Because these knives have long, thin blades, the knife stroke consists of a long, sawing motion. Apply minimal downward pressure while sawing. The knife hand should be relaxed and not tense during slicing. Correct slicing should never smash the product, 12-7.

12-7 The (A) slicer and (B) serrated bread knives are used to saw through many different foods.

Summary Points

- Before beginning any knife work, the work-station must be set up properly. You should also maintain the correct stance during knife work.

- The chef's knife has many uses and requires a special grip. Fingertips of the guiding hand are curled under for safety and accuracy. The guiding hand guides the knife as it makes uniform cuts using a smooth, forward and down motion.

- The chef's knife is used to make basic cuts and most of the classical knife cuts. The chef's knife is also used for mincing.

- The boning knife is widely used for cutting meats, poultry, and fish. There are several ways of gripping the boning knife. During cutting, the guiding hand does less actual guiding and more maneuvering of the meat, poultry, or fish.

- The paring knife is the smallest knife and is suited for peeling, trimming, and making the classical tourné.

- The slicer and bread knife are used for slicing. Slicing relies on a sawing motion with little downward pressure. Correct slicing cuts delicately without smashing the product.

In Review
Assess

1. Why is a damp towel placed between a cutting board and the worktable prior to beginning knife work?

2. Most professional chefs agree the _____ knife is the most important knife in the kitchen.

3. Describe the position of the guiding hand when cutting vegetables with a chef's knife.

4. True or false. The basic cutting stroke when using a chef's knife is a sawing motion.

5. List the three basic knife cuts.

6. Why may you want to trim one side of a round vegetable before beginning to cut it into various shapes?

7. True or false. A julienne is smaller than a batonnet.

8. The _____ knife has a thin, pointed blade designed to cut between bones.

9. True or false. Before the invention of the vegetable peeler, the boning knife was used for peeling vegetables.

10. True or false. A paring knife is most often used to carve vegetables.

11. Describe the slicing motion when using a slicer or serrated bread knife.

Core Skills

12. **Math.** How many ¼-inch rondelles can be produced from a peeled and trimmed 5½-inch carrot?

13. **Math.** How many small dice can be cut from a squared off piece of potato measuring 2 inches × 2 inches × 3 inches? After you calculate the answer, reproduce this problem with a real potato. Create a potato rectangle measuring 2 inches × 2 inches × 3 inches then cut into small dice cuts. Do you produce the same number of dice cuts as you predicted in the calculation?

14. **Speaking and Listening.** With two class-mates, role-play a situation in which you are the légumier responsible for vegetable prep. You have been assigned two apprentices to train on one of the knife cuts described in this chapter. Adjust your vocabulary as necessary while responding to their questions and clarifying information. Then switch roles. Each "légumier" should train on a different knife cut or technique.

15. **Math.** Brie and Tomas are each assigned to cut 18 pounds (36 pounds total) of carrots into rondelles. Brie uses the chef's knife properly by cutting with one continuous

stroke, down and forward. Tomas uses the chef's knife improperly by drawing the knife forward and back for each cut. Brie can cut one pound of carrots into ¼-inch rondelles in five minutes. It takes Tomas twice as long as Brie to cut the carrots. Both cooks are paid $9.00 per hour. How much will the restaurant need to pay Tomas and Brie respectively for completing this task?

16. **Reading.** Review the lists of Culinary and Academic Terminology at the beginning of this chapter. Use mnemonics (memory tricks) to help you remember terms that are unfamiliar. The following is an example of a mnemonic to remember when Christopher Columbus reached America: "In fourteen ninety-two, Columbus sailed the ocean blue." Share your mnemonics with the class.

17. **CTE Career Readiness Practice.** Culinary work often involves many hours of repeated motions such as knife work. Use valid, reliable sources to research repetitive motion injuries. Write a brief summary of what repetitive motion injuries are common to the foodservice industry. Investigate and evaluate suggestions for preventing this type of injury. Then write a personal plan for avoiding this injury as you progress in your career.

Critical Thinking

18. **Conclude.** Many names for knife cuts come from the French language. Why do you think that it is necessary for all cooks to know these terms?

19. **Analyze.** When cutting carrots with a chef's knife, why is it safer for the knife to be touching the fingers of your properly positioned guiding hand instead of not touching your guiding hand?

20. **Compare.** What are the advantages and disadvantages of using a flexible versus a rigid boning knife?

Technology

In the foodservice industry, time is money. Sometimes, it is more economical to use an industrial machine for cutting. Research to learn other technology that is used for cutting and processing food. Compare and contrast the results of these technologies to the knife skills of a professional chef.

Teamwork

Form teams and assign each member a responsibility. Obtain four similar apples, two paring knives, and two peelers. Assign two members the task of peeling two apples each. Each member should peel one apple using a paring knife and a second apple using a peeler. Another member should be responsible for weighing the peelings from each of the four apples. Assign a fourth team member to record the weights of the peelings from each of the four apples, being sure to label them. As a team, observe the finished products and evaluate the weights of the peelings that were created. Did the members assigned to the peeling task find one method easier than the other? Was one of the finished products more attractive than the other? Record the team's observations and conclusion.

Chef's E-portfolio
Knife Skills—Dice Cut

Upload a photo of the small dice cut you produced in activity #13 to your e-portfolio. Ask your instructor where to save your file. This could be on the school's network or a flash drive of your own. Name your portfolio document *FirstnameLastname_Portfolio Ch#.docx* (i.e., JohnSmith_PortfolioCh12.docx).

While studying, look for the activity icon  **to:**
- Build vocabulary with e-flash cards and matching activities.
- Expand learning with video clips, photo identification activities, animations, and interactive activities.
- Review and assess what you learn by completing end-of-chapter questions.

Chris Hill/Shutterstock.com

Smallwares

13

Reading Prep

Before reading this chapter, review the highlighted terms and definitions to preview the new content. Building a culinary vocabulary is an important activity to broadening your understanding of new material.

Culinary Terminology Build Vocab

smallwares, p. 201
pot, p. 201
pan, p. 201
rondeau, p. 203
sauteuse, p. 203
sautoir, p. 204
hotel pans, p. 205
sheet pans, p. 205
bain marie, p. 206
china cap, p. 210
colander, p. 210
chinois, p. 210
mandoline, p. 212
buffalo chopper, p. 214

Academic Terminology Build Vocab

conduction, p. 201

Objectives

After studying this chapter, you will be able to

- recognize various smallwares used in commercial kitchens.
- recall the properties of various materials used to make pots and pans.

- identify proper equipment for various measuring and portioning tasks, and various cooking methods.
- summarize proper storage of smallwares.
- explain proper safety procedures when using smallwares and preparation equipment.

A variety of smallwares and preparation equipment is used in kitchens to make work more efficient. **Smallwares** are the pots, pans, and other hand tools used to prepare food. Cooks have a wide range of equipment to choose from when preparing menu items. However, using the right tool for the job not only makes work easier, but also turns out a better end product.

Pots and Pans

There is a wide variety of cookware used in the professional kitchen. Choosing the right pot or pan to cook a certain dish may be critical to a good finished dish. Although many people use the words *pot* and *pan* interchangeably, there is a difference between the two. A **pot** is a cooking container that is as tall, or taller, than it is wide. A **pan** is wider than it is tall.

Materials Used in Cookware

Pots and pans are available in a variety of materials. Different materials have different properties which affect how well foods cook. One of the most important factors to chefs is conduction. **Conduction** is how well pots and pans transfer heat from the burner or oven to the food they contain. The most common cookware materials in commercial kitchens are copper, stainless steel, and aluminum.

Copper Copper has long been considered the best material for pots and pans because it is an excellent conductor of heat. As a result, cookware made with copper cooks items quickly and evenly. It has a number of drawbacks as well. Copper cookware is expensive and rather heavy. Extra work is needed to keep it clean and shiny because it tarnishes. Another disadvantage is that copper reacts with certain foods. For this reason, most copper cookware is lined with another metal such as stainless steel.

Aluminum Aluminum is a widely used material for commercial cookware. Its main advantage is that it costs less than copper or stainless steel. Additionally, aluminum cookware usually weighs less than pots and pans made with copper and stainless. It is a good conductor of heat, though it does not conduct heat as well as copper. Thick-gauge aluminum pots heat more evenly than thin-gauge aluminum pots. One disadvantage of aluminum is that it can discolor some preparations.

Stainless Steel Pots and pans made from stainless steel are slightly less expensive and a bit lighter than copper cookware. One benefit of stainless steel is that it does not tarnish like copper. However, stainless does not conduct heat as well as copper or aluminum. It is a poor heat conductor and creates a cooking surface with hot spots, or uneven heating. The best stainless cookware has heavy copper or aluminum bottoms for better conduction.

Other Materials Used in Cookware Carbon steel, also known as *black steel*, is used to make sauté, frying, and roasting pans. It conducts heat well but rusts if left wet. Carbon steel can also give off a metallic taste if used to cook acidic foods.

Another material sometimes used in cookware is cast iron. It is an excellent conductor of heat. The most frequent use of cast iron is in frying pans. Unfortunately, cast iron is extremely heavy and may crack or chip if dropped. Like carbon steel, it is prone to rusting if not cared for properly.

In the professional kitchen, pots and pans get heavy use and rough handling. Due to their fragile nature, glass and ceramic cookware are rarely used in commercial kitchens. Whatever material you choose, look for well-made pots and pans with thick-gauge metal and sturdy construction. Thinner metal results in uneven heating and buckles over time. Handles should be attached with strong rivets or welds to extend the useful life of the cookware and prevent leaking.

Types of Pots and Pans

In addition to the material used, the size and shape of the cookware is an important

Types of Pots and Pans

Stockpot

A stockpot is a large, tall-sided pot used mainly for cooking stocks and soups. Stockpots may have a spigot or valve at the base for easier draining.

Saucepot

A saucepot is like a stockpot but not as wide or tall. This straight-sided pot may come with one long handle or two looped handles. Saucepots are used for a wide variety of cooking tasks.

Saucepan

A saucepan is smaller than a saucepot. It has a single long handle. A saucepan may have either straight sides or flared sides.

Rondeau

A **rondeau** (rahn DOH) is a wide pan with 6- to 8-inch (15 to 21 cm) sides and two looped handles. It can accommodate a large amount of product and is especially useful for braising.

Double Boiler

A double boiler is a set of two nesting pots. The lower pot is used to heat water, which warms or cooks the ingredients in the top pot. Double boilers are used to cook ingredients that require indirect or gentle heat.

Sauteuse

A **sauteuse** (saw-TOOZ) is a sauté pan with sloped or rounded sides. Its shape makes it easy to toss or flip products when sautéing.

(Continued)

Types of Pots and Pans (Continued)

Sautoir

A sauté pan with straight sides is called a **sautoir** (saw TWAHR). Its shape makes it most effective for panfrying.

Cast-Iron Skillet

A cast-iron skillet is a frying pan made of heavy cast iron. Some chefs call it a "Griswold." It is excellent for panfrying.

Wok

A wok is a bowl-shaped pan of Asian origin used for stir-frying. Its shape makes it possible to achieve intense heat at the cooking surface and cook with a small amount of oil. Most traditional woks are made of black steel and must be brushed with oil and stored dry when not in use.

Roasting Pan

A roasting pan is a large rectangular metal pan with 2- to 5-inch (5 to 12 cm) sides used for roasting and baking.

Braising Pan

A braising pan, or braisière, is a high-sided square or rectangular pan with a tight-fitting lid. It is designed for cooking items first on the rangetop and then covered in the oven.

consideration. Chefs must be familiar with the many different pots and pans and their intended uses.

Hotel Pans

Hotel pans, also called *steam table pans,* are rectangular stainless steel pans used to hold food in steam tables, warmers, and refrigerators. The standard full-size hotel pan measures 12 × 20 inches (30.5 × 51 cm). Hotel pans are available in depths of 2½, 4, and 6 inches (5, 10, and 15 cm). Pans that are a fraction of the size of a full pan are also available for purchase, 13-1. These smaller pans can be purchased in any of the three depths discussed. Commercial foodservice equipment is designed to accommodate the standard dimensions of hotel pans.

Nutrition Connection

Getting an Iron Boost

According to the World Health Organization, iron deficiency is the most common nutrient deficiency in the world. Iron is a trace mineral needed for red blood cell production. Food sources include meats, fortified cereals, soybean, nuts, spinach, and wheat bran. Some foods cooked in cast iron increase in iron content because they absorb some of the iron from the pan. These include acidic foods with high moisture content, such as spaghetti sauce, citrus or tomato juices, and vinegar. Simmering these foods for longer periods of time or using a newer cast iron skillet increases the amount of iron that is absorbed.

Sheet Pans

Large, shallow pans called sheet pans are used for baking and food storage. A standard-size sheet pan is 18 × 24 inches (45 × 60 cm). Sheet pans are most often made of aluminum. Commercial ovens, refrigerators, and carts are designed to accommodate sheet

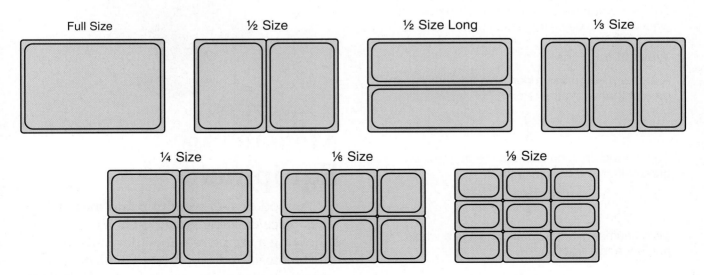

Full Size   ½ Size   ½ Size Long   ⅓ Size

¼ Size   ⅙ Size   ⅑ Size

13-1 There are many ways these pan sizes can be combined to fit in the standard opening for a steam table.

pans. A half-size sheet pan, 18 × 12 inches (45 × 30 cm), is also commonly used.

Bowls

Commercial kitchens need a variety of sizes of bowls for mixing and storage of products. Mixing bowls are made of stainless steel for durability and to avoid reaction with acidic ingredients.

Bain Marie Inserts

A **bain marie** (bay mahr Ee) is a hot water bath used to cook foods gently. The food to be cooked is placed in an insert. The insert is placed in a steam table or ice bath. Typically the inserts are tall, cylinder-shaped containers made of stainless steel.

Mix In Math

Fractions

Most cooks must use fractions when converting or preparing recipes.

What is a fraction?

$\frac{4}{5}$ = numerator
= denominator

The denominator represents the number of equal parts into which the whole unit is divided. The numerator describes how many parts of the whole unit are being counted.

Types of fractions

A proper fraction has a denominator that is greater than the numerator.

$$\frac{3}{4}$$

An improper fraction has a numerator that is greater than the denominator.

$$\frac{7}{5}$$

Mixed numbers are a combination of a whole number and a fraction.

$$4\frac{1}{8}$$

Measuring Equipment

A good deal of weighing and measuring takes place in commercial kitchens. Following a recipe requires that ingredients be measured accurately. Chefs have a variety of measuring equipment to help them perform their job.

Measuring Cups and Pitchers

Containers used for measuring volume come in a variety of sizes and shapes. Their capacities range from one cup to several gallons.

Measuring Spoons

A set of graduated measuring spoons typically consists of spoons ranging in capacity from an eighth of a teaspoon up to one tablespoon. Sets of measuring spoons are useful for measuring small amounts of ingredients such as herbs and spices.

A SERVING OF HISTORY

Bain Marie

Chefs did not invent the bain marie. Alchemists—people who tried to make gold from other metals—were the first ones to use the device. Bain marie means "Mary's Bath." Some historians say that it was named for Moses' sister Mary who was an alchemist. Today in commercial kitchens, the term *bain marie* has a number of meanings. Most often it refers to the gentle heat that a simmering water bath can provide. The term is also used to describe the following:

- double boiler—a pot nested on top of another pot that is filled with simmering water.
- steam table—a metal table with cutouts containing wells filled with simmering water into which pans are placed to keep warm.
- steam table insert—pans or cylindrical containers used to hold foods in a steam table well.
- water bath for baking—a pan about one-third full of water into which food items in baking dishes are placed. The pan is then placed in the oven. This method is used for food that requires slow, gentle baking.
- ice bath—a pan filled with ice or cold water into which containers of food are placed in order to cool more quickly.

Scales

Portioning product by weight is one of the most important tasks in a professional kitchen. There are a variety of different types of scales used in commercial foodservice.

Portion Scale A portion scale is a small scale used for weighing smaller quantities and individual ingredients. Portion scales are available as mechanical spring-type scales or as electronic scales with digital readout.

SCIENCE & TECHNOLOGY

Weighing Ingredients

The term *tare weight* means the weight of the container used to hold a product that is to be weighed. The tare might be the weight of a cardboard box holding loins of beef or the weight of a bowl holding flour. Most scales make the task of weighing easier by allowing you to adjust for the tare weight. Place the empty container on the scale and reset the scale to zero. When you place the product to be weighed on the scale in the container, the scale reading will reflect only the product weight and not the container weight. This method eliminates the chance for math errors that could result when subtracting the tare weight from the total weight.

Balance-Beam Scale   A balance-beam scale is a scale with two balanced platforms. Ingredients to be weighed are placed on one platform and counterweights are placed on the other. This type of scale is popular with bakers and pastry chefs because of its capacity to weigh large amounts of dry ingredients.

Receiving Scale   Most foodservice operations use a large-capacity scale to weigh big quantities of products when they are delivered. Some receiving scales have a capacity of several hundred pounds. These scales are available in both mechanical and electronic models.

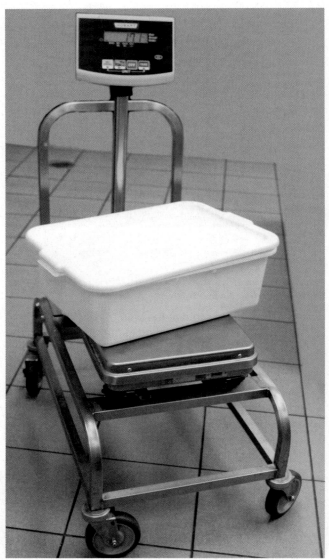

Thermometers

Thermometers are used to measure temperatures during cooking, holding, and cooling. This tool is essential for ensuring safe food-handling practices. Several types of thermometers are commonly used in professional kitchens.

Bimetallic-Coil Thermometer Bimetallic-coil thermometers use a coil made from two metals contained in the probe to measure temperature. These thermometers are available as oven safe or instant read. The oven-safe thermometer takes one to two minutes to register the temperature and is often used for roasts or large pieces of meat. An instant-read thermometer is a smaller thermometer that registers temperature within a few seconds. It is widely used for a variety of temperature monitoring tasks. Its temperature range is 0°F to 220°F (–18°C to 104°C).

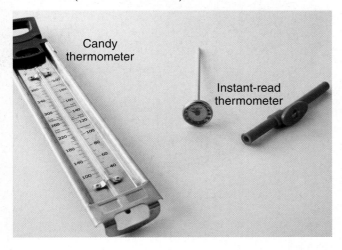

Candy thermometer

Instant-read thermometer

Candy Thermometer A candy thermometer, also known as a *deep-fat thermometer*, is used to measure the higher temperatures used when cooking sugar and deep-frying. This class of thermometers measures temperatures as high as 400°F (204°C).

Infrared Thermometer Infrared thermometers work by aiming a beam of laser light onto a small spot on the surface of an object.

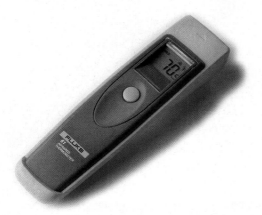

The infrared energy reflected from that spot is reflected back through the lens of the thermometer to measure the surface temperature. Temperatures can be measured from a distance without touching the product. One limitation of infrared thermometers is that they only measure the temperature on the surface and not internally.

Thermocouple Thermometer One area where technology has made its way into the commercial kitchens is in the use of electronic devices to measure and record temperatures. The thermocouple thermometer is a style of instant-read thermometer that utilizes a probe which is connected to an electronic meter which digitally displays the temperature. Some thermocouple probes can be placed in an oven and the meter placed outside where the cooking process can be continually monitored.

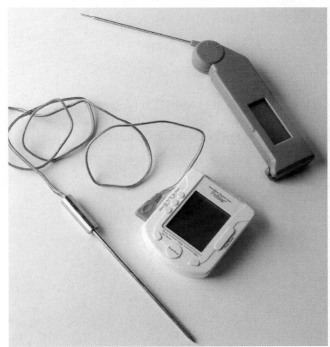

Straining Equipment

Smallwares designed to strain and drain food products come in many interesting shapes and sizes. These tools help chefs separate solid from liquid, larger particles from smaller, and sometimes change the product consistency.

Straining Equipment

China Cap

A **china cap** is a cone-shaped strainer used to remove lumps and particles from liquids such as sauces. They are typically made from stainless steel. China caps can range in overall size as well as the size of the holes used to strain the product.

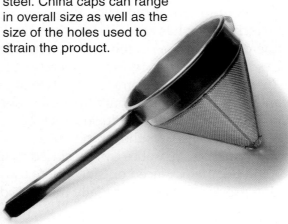

Colander

A **colander** is a large bowl-shaped strainer used to drain large quantities of product.

Chinois

A **chinois** (SHEEN wah) is a type of china cap that has a finely woven, metal mesh. It is used for removing small particles from sauces.

Strainer

There are many different shapes and sizes of handheld sieves made of mesh or perforated metal.

(Continued)

Straining Equipment (Continued)

Drum Sieve

A drum sieve is a metal or nylon mesh screen stretched over a circular metal or wooden frame. It is used for sifting large quantities of dry ingredients or for straining puréed foods to remove lumps.

Ricer

A ricer is a cylindrical, metal sieve with an attached plunger. Cooked foods, usually potatoes, are placed in the sieve and forced through with the plunger to form small rice-shaped pieces.

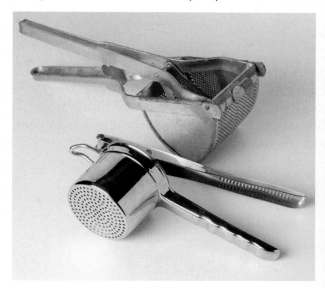

Cheesecloth

Cheesecloth is a cotton, gauze-like material. It is sometimes used in place of a chinois. Small pieces of cheesecloth are also used to make bags to hold herbs and spices for flavoring stocks and other foods.

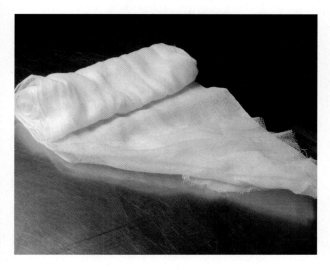

Food Mill

A food mill is a strainer used to purée soft foods. A hand-cranked paddle pushes the food through a strainer. Most food mills have interchangeable strainers of varying sizes.

Cutting and Processing Equipment

Chefs serve foods in many different sizes, shapes, and consistencies. They use a range of tools to help them produce that variety.

Graters

A grater is a single plate with a series of teeth or a hollow, metal box with different size teeth on each side. It is used for shredding vegetables, cheese, chocolate, citrus peel, and spices.

A rasp is a handheld grater that is becoming more and more popular. This tool is useful for zesting citrus fruits. It is often used to very finely grate spices, hard cheeses, baking chocolates, or garlic.

Mandoline

A mandoline is a device used to slice food by pushing the food onto and across a sharp metal blade. The plate on which the product is pushed into the blade can be adjusted to increase or decrease the thickness of the slice. Additionally, teeth can be added to the slicing blade to create stick cuts or juliennes. Mandolines come equipped with a carriage or hand guard for safely holding the product while slicing.

Food Processors

A food processor is a tabletop machine with a motorized base and a variety of bowls and blade attachments. This equipment is used primarily to grind, purée, and blend. However, cutting attachments can be used that produce shredded, julienned, and diced foods in a wide range of sizes.

Blenders

There are various types of machines that employ high velocity blades for mixing, puréeing, and liquefying fluid or semifluid foods. Commercial blenders come in two basic designs—bar blenders and immersion blenders.

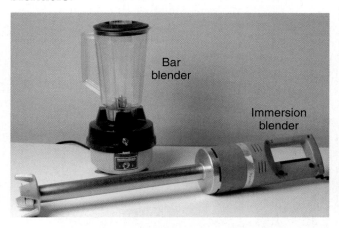

Bar blender

Immersion blender

Bar Blender   A bar blender is a two-part machine consisting of a motorized base and a covered container. The blades that process the product are located in the bottom of the container. The food to be processed is placed in the container and a lid covers the top to prevent splash.

Hints from the Chef

Sharp Blades!

One of the keys to maintaining food-processing equipment such as slicers, grinders, choppers, and food processors in peak performance is keeping the blades sharp. Blades should be sharpened regularly since a dull blade will produce a poor product. Most slicers have a sharpening device attached to them. Many others need to be sent to a professional sharpening service.

Immersion Blender   An immersion blender, or stick blender, is a one-piece machine consisting of a motorized shaft with blades on the end. The shaft and the blades are immersed in a container of liquid such as a pot of soup. This handheld blender mixes or purées the product in the container in which it was prepared.

Meat Grinder

A meat grinder is a machine or attachment used to grind meat or other foods into various textures. An auger forces the food through a feed tube, past a rotating

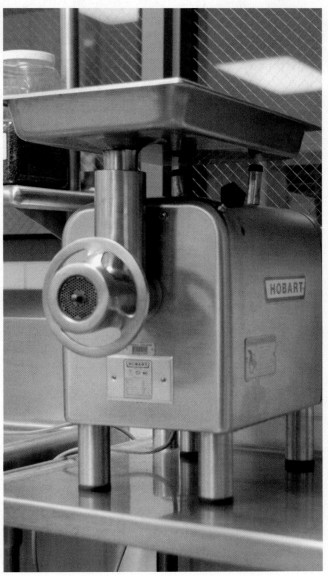

blade, and through the holes of the die, 13-2. Different size dies can be used to produce the desired end product, 13-3. Never use your hands to push product into the feed tube. A plastic plunger should always be used for this task.

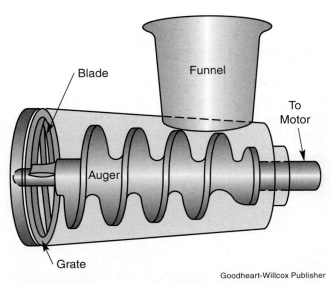

Goodheart-Willcox Publisher

13-2 This diagram shows how the parts of a meat grinder work.

Draz-Koetke/Goodheart-Willcox Publisher

13-3 Different size dies can be used to produce foods of various textures.

Buffalo Chopper

A **buffalo chopper** is a machine used for chopping large quantities of food. The machine consists of a rotating bowl into which the food is placed. The bowl then passes under a set of rotating blades that chop the food into small pieces.

Slicer

A slicer uses a rotating blade to slice foods thinly and evenly. A carriage holds the food being sliced to allow hands to stay

clear of the blades. Care should be taken when using, assembling, or cleaning slicing machines due to the risk of injury.

Smallwares Storage

Before storing any smallwares, they must be properly cleaned, rinsed, sanitized, and allowed to dry. Often, smallwares are hung up in a kitchen to make them easily accessible. They may also be stored in drawers or on shelves. If they are stored in drawers, be sure the drawers are labeled to make the small-wares easy to find which is important in the fast-paced kitchen. If bowls, pots, and pans are stored on a shelf, they must be inverted. Also, be sure that any drawers and shelving units are routinely cleaned and sanitized.

Kitchen Equipment Safety

Just as with knives, there are many pieces of equipment in the kitchen that are dangerous if improperly used. According to OSHA regulations, people under 18 years of age are not permitted to operate, clean, or repair power equipment such as meat slicers or bakery mixers. Before working with any dangerous equipment, be sure to

- get trained on its proper use and safety
- wear any personal protective equipment provided by the employer
- use any machine guarding provided
- ask for help if you are not sure how to do something
- be aware that age restrictions exist for workers under the age of 18 for using or cleaning certain equipment
- follow the manufacturer's instructions for machine use and cleaning

The employer should verify that each employee has been trained and demonstrated proper use of each dangerous piece of equip-ment. A written record of the training is kept on file by the employer.

OSHA suggests following some general safety recommendations to identify and avoid possible hazards when working with kitchen equipment, 13-4. Report any malfunctions—never try to fix machine jams or malfunctions yourself. Disconnect the power source, follow the lockout/tagout procedure, and report problems immediately to a supervisor. The *lockout/tagout procedure* describes the steps taken to label equipment that is malfunctioning and prevent its use.

Kitchen Equipment Safety

Mincers, Choppers, Dicers, Slicers:

- Always use push sticks or tamps to feed or remove food from these types of machines. DO NOT use your hands to feed smaller pieces of meat through slicers.

- Make sure you use any machine guarding that is provided to prevent access to cutter blades. DO NOT bypass safety guards.

- DO NOT open up or put your hands into an operating machine to stir contents or guide food.

- Turn off and unplug a machine before disas-sembling and cleaning.

Food Processors and Mixers:

- DO NOT attempt to remove items (for example, a spoon that falls into the mixture) from dough while the machine is mixing.

- DO NOT open up the lids of processors to stir contents while food is processing.

- Make sure the processor is off before opening the lid or adding items.

- Turn off and unplug machinery before cleaning or removing a blockage.

- Use any machine guards provided.

Source: Occupational Safety and Health Administration

13-4 Always obtain training on equipment before using it.

Summary Points

- Selecting the right piece of equipment is important when preparing food. Chefs must consider the material used in the cookware as well as the type of pot or pan best suited to the job.

- Many pieces of equipment exist that help cooks measure weights, volumes, and temperatures.

- Straining equipment varies depending on the size particles to be strained out and the end product desired.

- Cutting and processing equipment can range from simple, handheld tools to complex, motorized machines.

- Smallwares should be clean, sanitized, and dry before storing in a clean location.

- Individuals should receive training on the safe use of a piece of equipment before using it.

In Review
Assess

1. True or false. An important factor to chefs when selecting cookware is how well the pot or pan transfers heat from the source to the food.

2. Carbon steel is a good conductor of heat but gives off a metallic taste when used to cook _____ foods.

3. List the professional names for the following pots and pans:
   A. straight-sided sauté pan
   B. sauté pan with sloped sides
   C. cone-shaped strainer
   D. tall, cylindrical containers placed in steam tables or ice baths

4. A square or rectangular piece of cookware with high sides and a tight-fitting lid that is designed for cooking items first on the range top and then covered in the oven is a _____.
   A. braising pan
   B. colander
   C. hotel pan
   D. stockpot

5. True or false. A portion scale is preferred by bakers and pastry chefs for weighing large amounts of dry ingredients.

6. Cheesecloth is sometimes used in place of a _____ for straining out fine particles.

7. True or false. A mandoline is a piece of equipment commonly used to purée foods.

8. Identify the tool(s) a chef would use to do the following:
   A. shred cheese
   B. purée cooked carrots
   C. cook a soup
   D. sauté diced vegetables

9. A(n) _____ blender is used to mix or purée food in the container in which it was prepared.

10. True or false. Pots and pans should be stored on a shelf right-side up.

11. List three safety recommendations to follow when operating food processors or mixers.

Core Skills

12. **Math.** Calculate how many 3-inch square brownies can be cut from a standard sheet pan. Draw a picture illustrating how you came to your answer.

13. **Math.** You have a half-size hotel pan of sliced beef and you need to record the weight of the beef on the production sheet. The pan and beef together weigh 13¼ pounds. The tare weight of the pan is ¾ pound. The scale does not allow you to reset the scale for tare weight. How much does the beef weigh?

14. **Writing.** Obtain permission to tour the school kitchen or another commercial kitchen. Create a list noting all the equipment a new employee should be trained on before operating. Next to each piece of equipment on the list, give your reason for including it.

15. **Speaking.** Choose a pot or pan from your home or school kitchen. Prepare and give an informative speech identifying the materials

used to make the cookware, the strengths or weaknesses in the design and construction, and the gauge of metal used if applicable.

16. **Writing.** Research to learn what materials other than metal cultures have used to construct cooking vessels. For instance, some cultures have been known to use baskets or stones as cooking vessels. Write a one-page paper about the culture and why this material was chosen for cooking. Do you think the cookware influenced the culture's cuisine?

17. **CTE Career Readiness Practice.** Different types of thermometers may be better suited to various uses. Consider all the aspects of foodservice that require measurement of temperature such as receiving, storing, and cooking food. Draw conclusions about which type of thermometer discussed in this chapter might be best suited for different activities in the kitchen. Give examples to support your conclusions and share them with the class.

Critical Thinking

18. **Recognize.** What factors should be considered when selecting a tool, pot, or pan for a particular task?

19. **Analyze.** Bimetallic-coil thermometers have about a 2-inch space between the end of the thermometer and a small dimple on the stem. The thermometer must be inserted up to the dimple into the food for the reading to be accurate. Thermocouple thermometers register the temperature at the tip only of the thermometer. Why do you think that many chefs prefer to use a thermocouple thermometer instead of a bimetallic-coil thermometer?

20. **Evaluate.** If you had to set up a kitchen and could choose only four pots and pans, which ones would you choose? Why?

21. **Identify.** Why would it be a problem if a thermometer only reads the external surface of food?

Technology

Much of the world uses the metric system and measure temperatures in degrees Celsius. Create a Fahrenheit to Celsius converter using spreadsheet software. Use your converter to convert the following temperatures to degrees Celsius: 32°F, 41°F, 125°F, 140°F, 165°F, 180°F, 210°F, 350°F. (Hint: the conversion formula is $°F - 32 \times 5/9 = °C$)

Teamwork

Form teams of three students. Find three pots that are the same size but each made with a different material—copper lined with stainless steel, stainless steel, and aluminum. Measure equal amounts of water into each pot (should be at least three inches deep). Place each pot on a stovetop burner set at the same setting. Using a watch or timer, record how long it takes each pot of water to reach a rolling boil. Record your results. Which pot of water reached a boil first? Is this the result you expected? Write a summary of the team's observations and conclusions.

Chef's E-portfolio
Temperature Conversions Spreadsheet

Upload the temperature conversion spreadsheet you created for the Technology activity. Ask your instructor where to save your file. This could be on the school's network or a flash drive of your own. Name your portfolio document *FirstnameLastname_Portfolio Ch#.docx* (i.e., JohnSmith_PortfolioCh13.docx).

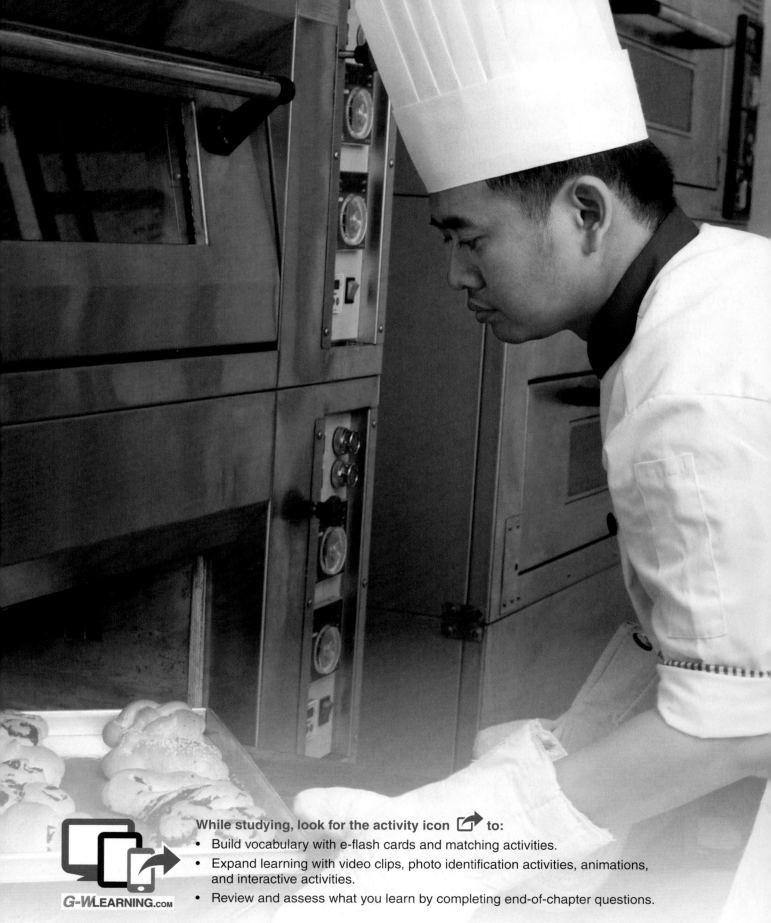

While studying, look for the activity icon to:

- Build vocabulary with e-flash cards and matching activities.
- Expand learning with video clips, photo identification activities, animations, and interactive activities.
- Review and assess what you learn by completing end-of-chapter questions.

G-WLEARNING.com

OtnaYdur/Shutterstock.com

Reading Prep

In preparation for reading the chapter, read a foodservice equipment journal and make a list of significant topics and content. As you read the chapter, evaluate how the topics on the list relate to the chapter content.

Culinary Terminology Build Vocab

open-burner range, p. 220
induction range, p. 220
griddle, p. 221
flattop range, p. 221
thermostat, p. 222
convection oven, p. 222
combination oven, p. 223
steam-jacketed kettle, p. 226
broiler, p. 227
salamander, p. 227
grill, p. 227
preventive maintenance schedule, p. 230

Academic Terminology Build Vocab

oscillate, p. 220

Objectives

After studying this chapter, you will be able to

- identify various pieces of large equipment used in commercial kitchens.
- recognize marks that certify equipment is designed to meet safety and sanitation standards.
- explain properties of design and construction and how they relate to functionality.

- differentiate proper equipment for various cooking tasks.
- compare the different types of refrigeration units.
- understand the importance of proper equipment maintenance for safety and controlling costs.

One of the most intimidating aspects of a commercial kitchen to a newcomer is the strange array of cooking apparatus. This chapter introduces you to some of the most common pieces of large equipment cooks use. The size, speed, capacity, and durability of commercial equipment are what sets this equipment apart from the home appliances with which you are familiar. As with any equipment, you should be trained in the use of equipment before cooking on it. Know the proper operating procedures, safety features, and temperature settings to avoid injuries and ensure a properly cooked product.

Cooking Equipment

The equipment in a commercial kitchen may not look like yours at home, but the basic function of applying heat to food is the same. Cooking equipment may vary in the location of the heat source in relation to the food. Some equipment uses dry heat while others use moist heat. Some equipment is valued for the long, slow cooking process it provides and others are prized for their speed and high temperatures. The challenge is to select the right cooking equipment for the job.

Cooking equipment should be selected that is designed with safety and sanitation in mind. Much of the foodservice equipment used in professional kitchens is NSF and Underwriters Laboratories (UL) certified. Equipment with these certifications can be identified by their respective marks, 14-1. NSF International tests and certifies that various products and equipment meet public health and safety standards. UL tests and certifies equipment for safety. Many local laws require that all equipment in professional kitchens be NSF and UL certified.

Most cooking equipment is somewhat dangerous since heat is being generated and applied. The Occupational Safety and Health Administration (OSHA) mandates that all employees are properly trained to use this equipment and are provided the proper equipment to work safely. This could include items such as hot pads or heat protective gloves. Some local or state labor laws may prohibit workers under 18 years old from using certain equipment.

Ranges

The term *range* refers to a cooktop or stove. The types of ranges commonly found in commercial kitchens are open-burner ranges, griddles, and flattops.

Open-Burner Range   The most common type of commercial cooktop is the **open-burner range**. When using these cooktops,

pots or pans are placed on trivets directly over a gas flame burner or on an electric element. Each burner can be adjusted individually giving this range the advantage of instant heat control.

Courtesy of Middleby Corp.

Induction Range   An induction range is less common in professional kitchens than gas or electric burners. An **induction range** uses electromagnetic energy to heat special pots and pans. This option is becoming more popular due to its energy efficiency, very high heat, and precise control. The technology used in an induction range causes molecules in the cookware to **oscillate**, or move back and forth very rapidly. The movement of the molecules creates heat to cook the food, 14-2. For the technology to work, the cookware used must contain a magnetic metal. For instance, aluminum pots and pans are not suitable for use on induction ranges.

NSF International   Underwriters Laboratories

14-1 The NSF and UL marks can only be displayed on equipment these organizations have certified.

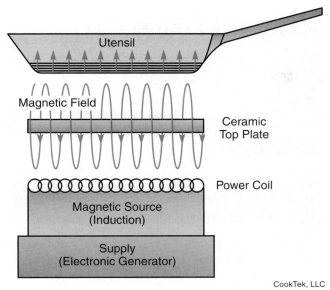

CookTek, LLC

14-2 An induction range cooks using electromagnetic energy.

In addition to its energy efficiency and instant heat control, the induction range is safer because it remains cool to the touch. It does not heat up the kitchen or require special ventilation. However, it does require access to an electrical outlet that can handle the equipment's electrical requirements.

Griddle   A **griddle** is a polished stainless steel cooktop. Food is cooked directly on the griddle, without pots or pans. The cooking surface is pitched slightly to allow grease to run off and collect in a container away from the heat source. Griddles are especially popular for fast-paced, short-order establishments.

Courtesy of Imperial Manufacturing

Flattop Range   A **flattop range** has a heavy cast-iron top which has a heat source located underneath it. Pots and pans are placed on the flattop and heated by conduction. Flattops need several minutes or longer of preheating before they are ready for cooking. Pots and pans are moved to hotter or cooler spots on the flattop to regulate heat instead of turning the temperature setting up or down. While a flattop stove doesn't offer instant heat control, it can hold more pots and pans than an open-burner range. A ring-top range is a type of flattop range. A ring-top range has concentric rings within the cooking surface that can be removed to place large pots over direct flame.

Courtesy of Blodgett Corp.

INDUSTRY INSIGHTS

Gas Versus Electric in the Commercial Kitchen

Most commercial kitchen equipment is available in electric or gas models. The choice of which fuel to use is based on a number of factors.

1. Cost of operation—Depending on what utilities are available in the location of your establishment, the cost of natural gas, liquefied petroleum gas, or electricity may vary greatly.
2. Performance—Many chefs prefer a gas flame to an electric burner because the flame is more responsive. A gas burner heats up more quickly and shuts off immediately. Electric burners take time to both heat up and cool down.
3. Local codes and regulations—Local building laws and fire codes may have great influence on what fuel is used in a commercial kitchen.

Draz-Koetke/Goodheart-Willcox Publisher

14-3 A thermostat knob on the outside of the oven is used to set the thermostat.

the thermostat is set. When the temperature falls below the thermostat setting, the burner is reignited until the proper temperature is reached.

Courtesy of Blodgett Corp.

Ovens

An oven is an enclosed compartment in which heat is applied to roast, bake, or thaw food. Various ovens differ in the heat sources they use to cook the food and how quickly they cook.

Conventional Ovens   A conventional oven is simply an insulated box or compartment in which air is heated. When food is placed in the oven, the hot, dry air circulates around the food and cooks it. This method of heat transfer is called *convection*. Ovens have thermostats that regulate the heat, 14-3. A **thermostat** is a device that responds to temperature changes and either turns the burner on or off. The burners turn off when the heat reaches the temperature to which

Convection Ovens   Convection ovens work in the same manner as conventional ovens with one exception. A **convection oven** has a fan that helps circulate the air inside the oven. This forced circulation allows cooking at lower temperatures with better results. Foods cook more evenly and brown faster in convection ovens. Recipes written for use with a conventional oven often need to be revised for use with convection ovens. The revised recipe should call for a lower oven temperature (typically 25°F–50°F lower) or for a shorter cooking time.

Courtesy of Middleby Corp.

Cook-Hold Ovens   Ovens designed to cook at lower temperatures [180°F–225°F (82°C–107°C)] are useful for roasting large pieces of meat or poultry. The lower cooking temperature results in less shrinkage. An oven called a *cook-hold oven* is designed especially for this task.

SCIENCE & TECHNOLOGY

British Thermal Unit (BTU)

BTU is a measure of energy, specifically, the amount of energy needed to raise the temperature of one pound of water one degree Fahrenheit. Among other things, BTU's are used to compare the power of various cooking appliances. A burner or oven with a higher BTU rating has more heat output and should cook items more quickly than one with a lower rating.

A sensitive thermostat allows precise temperature control. A programmable timer allows items to be roasted for hours or even overnight. When the programmed roasting time is through, the oven switches to holding mode. The holding mode maintains the items at the correct temperature until service.

Combination Ovens   A combination oven uses a combination of convection heat and steam to cook foods. This oven, also known as a *combi* or *combo oven*, is essentially a convection oven with injected steam. The moisture of the steam makes heat transfer more effective and greatly reduces cook time. The steam also reduces moisture loss in the cooked foods. These ovens can operate as a convection oven, combination mode, or as a convection steamer. In some combi ovens, the amount or percentage of steam can be precisely regulated and the cooking cycles can be programmed.

Courtesy of Blodgett Corp.

Microwave Ovens   Microwave ovens operate by bombarding food with microwave radiation. The radiation causes the water molecules in the food to vibrate and create heat. The resulting heat cooks the food. Even though commercial microwave ovens have a higher power output than their household counterparts, the size of the oven is roughly the same. Due to their limited capacity, microwaves are used primarily for reheating or thawing individual portions in foodservice operations. Follow safety guidelines when using microwave ovens to prevent accidents, 14-4.

Microwave Oven Safety

- **Make sure** the microwave is located at approximately waist level and within easy reach, to provide for ease in the lifting of hot foods.

- **Follow** manufacturer's instructions for operating microwave ovens.

- **Cover** foods cooked in microwaves to avoid splattering.

- **Use** caution when opening tightly covered containers. Open containers away from your face because they may be under pressure and could be extremely hot.

- **Use** appropriate personal protective equipment such as hot pads when removing foods from microwave.

- **Make sure** door seals are in good condition and free from food or grease buildup.

- **Do not** use a microwave if it has a door that is damaged or does not lock properly. Damaged ovens may emit harmful radiation.

- **Do not** microwave metals, foil, or whole eggs.

- **Keep** the interior of the microwave clean to avoid splattering and popping.

- **If** you notice any sparking inside the microwave, immediately turn off the microwave, unplug it, report it to the supervisor, and do not use it.

- **Be advised** that microwaves may interfere with the workings of pacemakers.

- **Be aware** that food cooked in the microwave can remain hot long after the microwave turns off.

Source: Occupational Safety and Health Administration

14-4 Follow safety guidelines when operating a microwave oven.

Steamers

Steamers use water that is heated to the point of vaporizing to apply heat to food. This is a moist method of cooking that is not suitable for all foods.

Convection Steamers   A convection steamer is an oven that cooks by directing jets of steam at the food placed in it. Food is usually cooked in perforated hotel pans to allow free circulation of the steam and for the condensing moisture to drain off.

Courtesy of Cleveland Range

Pressure Steamers   As with the convection steamer, food is cooked in an oven with injected steam. A pressure steamer's chamber is tightly sealed and pressure is allowed to build. Steam under pressure holds more

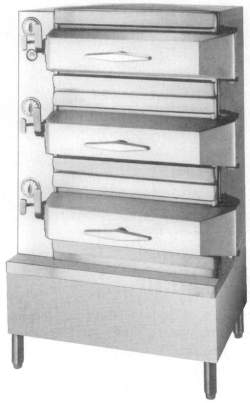

Courtesy of Cleveland Range

heat energy and cooks food more quickly. Food cooked in a pressure steamer cannot be removed until the chamber is depressurized and the sealed door is unlocked. This type of steamer is used in high-volume, institutional kitchens. Pressure steamers tend to overcook some foods, so many chefs prefer the gentler heat of a convection steamer.

Improper use of steamers can result in severe burns. To reduce accidents, OSHA provides guidelines for the safe use of steamers and pressure cookers, 14-5.

Steamer and Pressure Cooker Safety

For steamers and pressure cookers:

- **Do not** open the door while the steamer is on, shut off the steam, and then wait a couple of minutes before releasing the pressure and opening.

- **Clear** the area around the steamer before opening.

- **Open** the steamer door by standing to the side, keeping the door between you and the open steamer.

- **Use** oven mitts to remove hot trays from the steamer.

- **Place** hot, dripping steamer trays on a cart to transport. If trays are carried by hand, they will drip on floors and create a slip hazard.

- **If** a steamer is stacked, remove the tray from the top steamer first, then the lower one, to prevent burns from rising steam.

For pressure cookers:

- **Shut off** the steam supply and wait for the pressure to equalize before opening the lid of the pressure cooker.

- **Stand** to the side and open the pressure cooker away from yourself, keeping the open lid between you and the pressure cooker.

Source: Occupational Safety and Health Administration

14-5 Follow safety guidelines to avoid injury when operating steamers.

Kettles

Kettles are essentially a large pot with a self-contained heat source. They function in the same way as a pot or pan on the stove would. The kettles found in commercial kitchens are much larger than those found in homes. Their larger capacity makes them suitable for large batches of product.

Steam-Jacketed Kettles   Steam-jacketed kettles are permanently fixed, large pots with double-walled construction. The gap between the two walls fills with steam and the heat is conducted to the inside surface of the kettle. The kettle is a quick and efficient way to heat large quantities of liquid because the interior is heated with the pressurized steam. Kettles can have capacities of up to 100 gallons (379 L). Steam-jacketed kettles are most common in high-volume operations. Some types of steam kettles are drained through a valve at the bottom of the kettle called a *spigot*.

Others have a mechanism that tilts the kettle so it can be drained from the top; this type is sometimes called a *trunion kettle*.

Tilt Braiser   One of the most versatile pieces of equipment in large production kitchens is a tilt braiser. This piece of equipment is also known as a *Swiss braiser*, *tilting skillet*, and *bratt pan*. It is designed to stew or braise large quantities of product. It can also be used as a griddle for sautéing and pan-frying, or for simmering and poaching. Tilt braisers have a large rectangular heated base, 6- to 8-inch (15 to 20 cm) high sides, and a tight-fitting lid. They are emptied by being tipped or tilted forward to pour out their contents. Tilt braisers are available in capacities ranging from 8 to 40 gallons (30 to 151 L).

Grills and Broilers

The glow of intense heat from a flame or electric element is radiant heat. This searing heat can produce flavorful foods with beautiful caramelization. Both grills and broilers cook with this type of heat, but in slightly different ways.

Foods to be cooked in either a broiler or grill are usually placed on a metal rack or grate. However, when a radiant heat source is placed above the food to be cooked, the device used is called a **broiler**. Broilers typically allow the grate on which the food is

Courtesy of Imperial Manufacturing

placed to slide under the heat or be pulled out and away from the heat. This equipment is sometimes referred to as an "upright broiler," and is available in single- or double-deck models. Many broilers also have a finishing oven above the burners. Upright broilers employ heat as high as 1600°F (871°C) on the burner surface to cook foods quickly. A smaller, less powerful broiler used for browning food rather than fully cooking it is called a **salamander**. The name *salamander* is believed to be associated with the browned food changing color in much the same way a salamander changes the color of its skin.

When the radiant heat source is located below the food and rack, the cooking appliance is called a **grill** or char-grill. There are many designs for grills. Some use a gas flame or electric element to radiate heat directly to

Salamander

Courtesy of Blodgett Corp.

the food. Others use a burner to heat materials such as ceramic tiles or lava that give off an even glowing heat. Still others use charcoal or hardwoods to produce intense heat and a smoky flavor. Whichever style is used, grilled foods are popular with American diners because of the unique flavor the searing heat gives to all types of foods.

Courtesy of Middleby Corp.

Fryers

With the popularity of fried foods, this piece of equipment is a familiar sight in most kitchens from fast food to fine dining.

Deep Fryers Deep fryers are designed to cook foods by submerging them in hot fat. The deep fryer's thermostat maintains the fat at a constant temperature allowing for a consistently cooked product. Deep fryers are classified by the amount of fat they hold. Most common are fryers that hold 35 to 50 pounds.

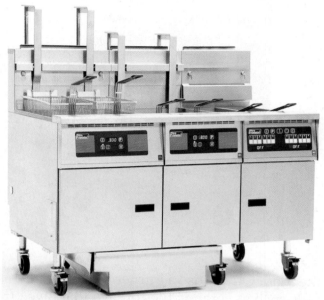

Courtesy of Middleby Corp.

Pressure Fryers A fry kettle with a tightly sealed lid is known as a *pressure fryer* or *broaster*. The pressurized kettle fries food rapidly, even at lower temperatures. These fryers are widely used for fast-food fried chicken.

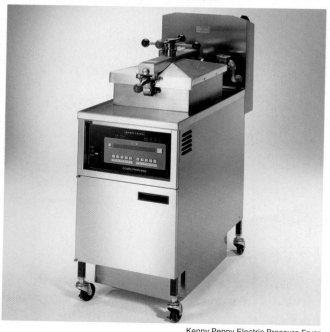

Kenny Penny Electric Pressure Fryer

Holding Equipment

Once food is cooked, it is essential that it is held at a temperature that keeps it safe, healthy, and appealing. Holding equipment serves that purpose.

Steam Tables

A large water bath designed to keep food in hotel pans and metal inserts hot by surrounding them with hot water and steam is called a *steam table*. This equipment is sometimes referred to by the French term *bain marie*. Steam tables are available heated by gas or electric and come in a variety of sizes. They are placed in the area of the kitchen where food is plated for service.

Warming Cabinets

A warming cabinet is an enclosed cabinet designed to hold food. The cabinet is heated by an electric element with thermostatic controls. Some cabinets have a feature that maintains moisture in the cabinet. Some warming cabinets are mobile and can be moved to different locations. When not in use, they should be stored cleaned and sanitized, and in a designated, safe location.

It should never be stored in a hallway or other area where the cabinet may become an obstacle to safe exit during an emergency.

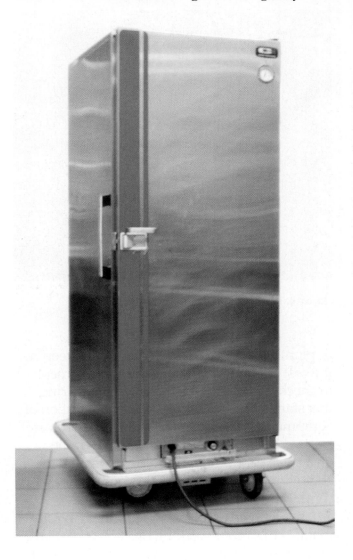

Refrigeration

Refrigeration is some of the most important equipment in the commercial kitchen. It is typically located throughout the kitchen. Refrigeration stores foods below 41°F (5°C). This keeps food out of the temperature danger zone until it is ready to be cooked or served. Refrigeration works by removing heat from the refrigerator compartment. A chemical coolant circulating through tubes inside the refrigerator acts to remove the heat and transfer

SUSTAINABLE CULINARY

Buying Sustainably

Large foodservice equipment uses vast amounts of energy and water to cook, cool, and hold food. The more energy and water a piece of equipment uses, the more negatively it impacts the environment and more expensive it is to use. As a result, foodservice professionals increasingly consider energy and water usage when buying equipment. To help with these choices, the US Environmental Protection Agency (EPA) and US Department of Energy (DOE) sponsor a program called ENERGY STAR. If a piece of equipment meets the ENERGY STAR guidelines, then it is awarded the ENERGY STAR logo. For more information, visit the ENERGY STAR website and find the Small Business Guide for foodservice and restaurants.

it out of the compartment where food is stored. When the coolant passes outside the compartment, it releases the heat with the help of a fan or cool water.

Refrigerators are defined by their size. For example, *walk-in refrigerators* are the size of a room and tall enough to walk in. *Reach-in refrigerators* are smaller units placed at various cooking stations. They are often located under counters or work-tables, 14-6. Though smaller in size, reach-in refrigerators in commercial kitchens are still large enough to fit standard-size hotel pans.

Freezers work in the same manner as refrigerators but are designed to hold foods at 0°F (–18°C) for long-term storage. Freezers may be either walk-in or reach-in.

Keeping food products at proper temperatures is essential in foodservice. Repairs to refrigeration equipment are costly.

Eric Futran/ChefShots

14-6 Refrigerators and freezers can be either large enough to walk in or located under counters.

Kitchen staff can help maintain refrigerators and freezers in good working order. The following guidelines help keep refrigeration equipment working properly:

- Don't use the refrigerator or freezer to cool hot product.
- Don't overload refrigerators, allow for free airflow.
- Keep interior fans and coils free from obstructions.
- Store boxes or trays so that ventilation is not obstructed.
- Keep doors tightly closed whenever possible.

Maintaining Equipment

Commercial kitchen equipment is more sturdy than home kitchen equipment because it must withstand heavy use. Keeping the wide array of equipment found in commercial kitchens in top working order is a daunting task for an executive chef or kitchen manager. Chefs are not expected to be mechanics, electricians,

or plumbers, but they play a key role in keeping the cost of equipment repair and replacement in check. The chef is responsible for ensuring that staff is properly trained on the operation of equipment. As part of this training, records are kept verifying an employee has been trained on a piece of equipment and demonstrated ability to use it safely. Misuse is one of the most common causes of equipment failure.

Before using a piece of equipment, be sure that it is in proper working order. If a particular piece of equipment is not working correctly, it is everyone's responsibility to alert their supervisor to the problem. In the event of equipment failure or malfunction, the lockout/tagout procedure should be followed to prevent other employees from using the equipment.

Chefs are also responsible for making sure each piece of equipment has a preventive maintenance schedule and that the schedule is followed. A **preventive maintenance schedule** is a list of tasks to be performed to ensure that equipment stays in proper working order. The schedule also outlines how often those tasks should be performed, 14-7. The schedule is often

Sample Maintenance Schedule			
Equipment:	**Make:**	**Model:**	**Location:**
Meat slicer	Acme	500	Main kitchen
Daily:			
–Disconnect power.			
–Disassemble, clean, and sanitize blade and carriage.			
–Sharpen blade.			
Weekly:		**Date**	**Performed by**
Lubricate carriage slide rods with mineral oil.			
Monthly:			
Oil guage plate with mineral oil.			
Yearly:			
Lubricate motor bearings.			
(see owner's manual)			

14-7 Maintenance schedules help keep equipment in working order and prolong its life.

based on the manufacturer's recommendations. This is one reason chefs must be able to comprehend a variety of texts such as operations and training manuals. Maintenance schedules should include the following:
- a description of daily cleaning of the equipment
- weekly or monthly checks and adjustments such as lubrication of mechanisms and detailed cleaning
- monthly, quarterly, or annual service such as calibration of thermostats and maintenance of motors

Long-term maintenance of equipment is often a job for professional service personnel. To control the cost of service calls, many foodservice operations purchase service contracts with equipment service companies. A service contract allows the operator to prepay a flat fee for future maintenance on equipment. This way the operator knows how much to budget for equipment repairs.

SUSTAINABLE CULINARY

An Invaluable Resource

For over two decades, the Food Service Technology Center has provided information about foodservice equipment to foodservice professionals. Their engineers test equipment from a sustainability standpoint and provide large amounts of data. This data helps managers make good business and sustainability decisions. Visit the Food Service Technology Center website and read their Energy Efficiency Case Studies to learn more about this resource.

Summary Points

- Foodservice equipment should bear marks to certify the design meets safety and sanitation standards.

- Commercial rangetops are available in a variety of styles.

- Ovens vary based on the method of heat transfer and the speed of cooking.

- Kettles usually handle large volumes of food and are flexible pieces of equipment.

- Steamers are made in convection and pressure steam designs.

- Broilers differ from grills based on the location of the heat source.

- Deep fryers and pressure fryers allow chefs to prepare large quantities of fried foods quickly and with consistent quality.

- Hot foods are held for service in steam tables and warming cabinets.

- Refrigeration equipment is some of the most important in the commercial kitchen because it keeps food out of the temperature danger zone.

- Foodservice operations must manage the high cost of equipment repair. All employees are responsible to alert their supervisor to malfunctioning equipment.

In Review
Assess

1. True or false. OSHA tests and certifies that foodservice equipment meets public health and safety standards.

2. The open-burner range has the advantage of instant _____ control.

3. Compare the flattop range and the griddle.

4. True or false. The device that regulates heat in an oven is called a *salamander*.

5. List two modifications you could make to a conventional oven recipe in order to prepare it using a convection oven.

6. What piece of equipment would you use to roast a large cut of beef with the least amount of shrinkage?
   A. microwave oven
   B. cook-hold oven
   C. conventional oven
   D. broiler
   E. convection steamer

7. True or false. In a broiler, the radiant heat source is placed above the food to be cooked.

8. Deep fryers are classified by the amount of _____ they hold.

9. List two types of equipment used to hold hot foods.

10. Why is refrigeration equipment some of the most important equipment in the commercial kitchen?

11. List five things kitchen staff can do to help keep refrigerators and freezers working properly.

12. True or false. A preventive maintenance schedule is a tool chefs use to help them manage the repair and replacement of equipment.

Core Skills

13. **Math.** You are preparing to bake using a convection oven. Your recipe calls for a 375°F conventional oven. To what temperature should you preheat the oven?

14. **Reading and Writing.** Select a piece of large equipment discussed in this chapter. Find the operations or owner's manual online or in print to learn how to properly maintain the equipment. Write a preventive maintenance schedule for the piece of equipment you selected.

15. **Reading and Writing.** Using the owner's manual from activity #14, write a procedure for the use of this piece of equipment. Review the information on writing a procedure from Chapter 5.

16. **Reading.** Locate either a print or digital food-service supplies catalog that features large kitchen equipment. List all the various certifications you find for large equipment. Select one certification and write a brief summary about it. Include the certification mark in your summary.

17. **Math.** Energy efficient equipment can reduce costs. Suppose an energy efficient steamer costs $500 more to purchase than a traditional one. It costs $1,000 per year to operate the traditional steamer and the energy efficient steamer saves 25% on energy per year. How long will it take for energy savings from the energy efficient steamer to offset its higher purchase price?

18. **CTE Career Readiness Practice.** Suppose you want to buy a griddle for $1,500.00 on credit. Investigate what the credit terms would be if you
    A. obtained credit from the seller
    B. procured a cash loan
    C. used a credit card

    Find out about finance charges, annual percentage rate, monthly payments, length of repayment period, and late payment charges. Which option would give you the best deal? Why? What benefit would you have from delaying your purchase and pay with cash?

Critical Thinking

19. **Consider.** Look through a catalog or on the Internet for a particular piece of commercial foodservice equipment. Note differences in models with regards to capacity, size, power, and cost. What factors are most important when choosing a piece of equipment? Why?

20. **Assess.** Identify options in your area for powering cooking equipment in a commercial kitchen (natural gas, liquefied petroleum gas, electric). What are the advantages and disadvantages of each?

21. **Conclude.** When choosing equipment for a commercial kitchen, how is selection affected by the operation's menu, kitchen space, staff, and volume?

22. **Analyze.** The chef observes a new cook who has just completed making a large batch of stock in a steam-jacketed kettle. The cook is pouring the hot stock into large, deep stockpots and placing them in a reach-in refrigerator to cool. What is wrong with this scenario? What should the chef instruct the cook to do with the stock?

Technology

Research to learn how a refrigerator works. Use presentation software to describe the process to the class. Make strategic use of visual and interactive elements in your presentation to enhance understanding and add interest.

Teamwork

Working in small teams, write a procedure that includes who, what, when, and how students will be trained on equipment. Perform an inventory of the equipment that requires training. Create a spreadsheet to record and track students' training. Present your procedure to the class.

Chef's E-portfolio
Preventive Maintenance Schedule

Upload the preventive maintenance schedule you created for activity #14. Ask your instructor where to save your file. This could be on the school's network or a flash drive of your own. Name your portfolio document *FirstnameLastname_Portfolio Ch#.docx* (i.e., JohnSmith_PortfolioCh14.docx). Be sure to update your record of safety training and assessments with any new equipment on which you passed an operational checkout or examination. If you have not yet initiated a record in your e-portfolio, upload the spreadsheet created in the Teamwork activity.

While studying, look for the activity icon to:

- Build vocabulary with e-flash cards and matching activities.
- Expand learning with video clips, photo identification activities, animations, and interactive activities.
- Review and assess what you learn by completing end-of-chapter questions.

G-W LEARNING.com

Tyler Olson/Shutterstock.com

Using Recipes

Reading Prep

In preparation for reading the chapter, print off and read a standardized recipe from the USDA recipes for schools. As you read the chapter, highlight parts of the recipe that are being discussed.

Culinary Terminology
Build Vocab

recipe, p. 235
tare weight, p. 238
standardized recipe, p. 240
yield, p. 242
portion size, p. 242
product specification, p. 243
conversion factor, p. 244

Academic Terminology
Build Vocab

prevalent, p. 235

Objectives

After studying this chapter, you will be able to

- apply common units of measure for weight and volume.
- execute accurate ingredient measurements for a recipe.
- understand the value and characteristics of standardized recipes.
- apply a conversion factor to ingredient lists to adjust recipe yields.

Imagine going on a trip to a place you have never been without a map or instructions on how to get there. A **recipe** is like a map that guides the chef to a particular finished food product and allows others to arrive at exactly the same place as well. Recipes are important in any kitchen to assure a consistent finished product each and every time a dish is prepared. A recipe is a list of products and the amounts needed to prepare a dish followed by preparation instructions. Many professional recipes also include the time required to prepare the dish and specifications on what equipment should be used.

Units of Measure

Just as a map is displayed in yards, meters, miles, or kilometers, a recipe is expressed in units of measure. This section introduces common units of measure used in recipes in both standard US measures and the more **prevalent**, or widely accepted, metric system. Proficiency with units of measure is essential for working in the kitchen. It is a prerequisite for being able to properly measure ingredients for any recipe. Knowing equivalents of various measurements is necessary for adjusting and converting recipes.

Units of Weight

Weight is the preferred way to measure ingredients in the professional kitchen. Weight is more accurate and consistent than measuring by volume. When preparing recipes repeatedly, amounts vary less when they are measured by weight than if measured by volume. Weight measurements can be scaled up or down with more accuracy. Professional chefs measure ingredients by weight whenever possible.

The US system of measurement has two basic units of weight—ounces and pounds. The metric system measures weight in grams. The prefix *kilo* comes from the Greek word for "one thousand." Therefore, a kilogram is one thousand grams, often called a "kilo" for short, 15-1.

You may be more familiar with either the US system or the metric system. Today, it is necessary for chefs to understand recipes in both systems and be able to convert measurements from one system to another. Recipes often use approximate conversions from the US system to the metric system so that the numbers are easier to measure and adjust.

Units of Volume

In the US system, the basic unit of measure for volume is the ounce. It is often referred to as the *fluid ounce* to distinguish it

Mix In Math

Converting Measures

Use the bridge method to convert from one unit of measure to another.

Suppose you have 9 teaspoons and you want to convert to tablespoons. First step is to take the number you want to convert and place it over one. This does not change its value. If the number is a fraction, turn it into a decimal and then place it over one.

$$\frac{9 \text{ tsp.}}{1}$$

Next, you multiply by the conversion factor. In this example, you are converting teaspoons to tablespoons. As you learned, 1 tablespoon equals 3 teaspoons. The unit you are converting to (in this example it is tablespoons) should always be on top in the conversion factor. Your conversion factor will be

$$\frac{1 \text{ Tbsp.}}{3 \text{ tsp.}}$$

Multiply the measure you want to convert by the conversion factor.

$$\frac{9 \text{ tsp.}}{1} \times \frac{1 \text{ Tbsp.}}{3 \text{ tsp.}}$$

The teaspoon units cancel out, then multiply what remains.

$$\frac{9 \text{ tsp.}}{1} \times \frac{1 \text{ Tbsp.}}{3 \text{ tsp.}} = \frac{9 \text{ Tbsp.}}{3}$$

Divide the top number by the bottom number and you have your conversion.

$$3 \text{ Tbsp.}$$

This method can also be used to convert from the US system of measurement to the metric system.

Suppose a recipe calls for 224 grams of flour but your scale weighs in ounces and pounds. You learned that 1 ounce equals 28 grams. The conversion would look like this

$$\frac{224 \text{ g}}{1}$$

$$\frac{224 \text{ g}}{1} \times \frac{1 \text{ oz.}}{28 \text{ g}}$$

$$\frac{224 \text{ g}}{1} \times \frac{1 \text{ oz.}}{28 \text{ g}} = \frac{224 \text{ oz.}}{28}$$

$$8 \text{ oz.}$$

Measuring Weights			
	Unit of Weight	**Abbreviation**	**Equivalent**
US System	ounce	oz.	
	pound	lb. or #	1 lb. = 16 oz.
Metric System	gram	g	
	kilogram	kg	1 kg = 1000 g
Conversions*			
1 oz. = 28 g		1 lb. = 454 g	
1 g = 0.035 oz.		1 kg = 2.2 lb.	
* US/metric conversions are approximate			

15-1 Chefs must be able to use both US and metric systems of measurement.

from the ounce measure for weight. Volume units smaller than an ounce are the teaspoon, which is one-sixth ounce; and the tablespoon, which is one-half ounce. In the US system, there are many units of measure that are larger than an ounce such as cup, pint, quart, and gallon.

The metric system measures volume with the base unit of the liter. Latin prefixes denote a fraction of a liter. Therefore, a deciliter is one-tenth liter, a centiliter is one-hundredth liter, and a milliliter is one-thousandth liter. Of these units, the liter and milliliter are most often used, 15-2.

Measuring Volumes			
	Unit of Volume	**Abbreviation**	**Equivalent**
US System	fluid ounce	fl. oz.	
	teaspoon	tsp.	1 tsp. = ⅙ fl. oz.
	tablespoon	Tbsp.	1 Tbsp. = 3 tsp.= ½ fl. oz.
	cup	c.	1 c. = 8 fl. oz.
	pint	pt.	1 pt. = 16 fl. oz. = 2 c.
	quart	qt.	1 qt. = 32 fl. oz. = 4 c. = 2 pt.
	gallon	gal.	1 gal. = 128 fl. oz. = 16 c. = 8 pt. = 4 qt.
Metric System	milliliter	mL	
	liter	L	1 L = 1000 mL
Conversions*			
1 fl. oz. = 30 mL	1 qt. = 0.95 L	1 gal. = 3.8 L	
1 mL = 0.033 fl. oz.	1 L = 33.8 fl. oz.		
* US/metric conversions are approximate			

15-2 Measuring volume requires different units of measure than weight measurements.

Units by Container

Food is often purchased in containers. While these containers have specific volume or weight measures, they are often referred to by name in professional kitchens. For instance, a chef may request a flat of strawberries (a flat case containing a single layer of fruit), a jib of oil (35 pounds), or a #10 can (12 cups) of tomatoes. Sometimes, what seems simple is not. For instance, not all cases are the same size and can vary depending on their content. Learning the different names for these common food containers takes time and is essential for professional communication.

Correlation of Weight and Volume

Measuring ingredients by volume is avoided because there is more variation in quantity when an ingredient is measured this way. For example, a cup of flour that is densely packed contains more flour than a cup of flour that is sifted and airy. Therefore, the densely packed cup weighs more than the sifted cup. The difference in measuring packed flour one time and sifted flour another can be enough to ruin the final product in a recipe that uses flour.

Although measuring by weight is preferred over measuring by volume, there are some instances where the two methods are interchangeable. Those instances are when you are measuring water or liquids with a similar density as water. Some of those liquids are stock or broth, juice, and milk. With these liquids, one fluid ounce is equal to one ounce in weight. Another way to remember this fact is the old rhyme "A pint is a pound the world around."

The metric system also correlates weight and volume measure with liquids such as water. When measuring water, one milliliter

is equal to one gram; and one liter is equal to one kilogram. Knowing this correlation can save time and make measuring liquid ingredients easier.

Measuring Ingredients
Animation

In order to have a recipe turn out right each time you make it, accuracy in measurement is key. Two mistakes that cause recipes to fail are not accounting for tare weight and not using level volume measures.

Tare weight is the weight of the container that holds the ingredients being measured. To be sure that you are measuring only the ingredients, place the empty container on the scale. With the container on the scale, reset the weight indicator to read zero. Now you can place the ingredients in the container and weigh them for a true indication of their weight, 15-3. Most scales are designed to be reset to adjust for tare weight. For those that are not, weigh the empty container and subtract its weight from the gross weight of the container and ingredients.

Level volume measurements are important when measuring dry ingredients by volume. To improve accuracy when dry ingredients are measured by volume, select the appropriate size measuring container, overfill the container, and then scrape off any ingredients that are above the rim of the measure. With liquid ingredients, place the measuring container on a level surface in order to be sure that the liquid is the desired level. Bend down if necessary so that the measuring container is at eye level, 15-4. Clear measuring containers make it easier to see liquid levels for accurate measure.

Standardized Recipes

Have you ever returned to a favorite restaurant and ordered an item that you enjoyed on a previous visit, only to be

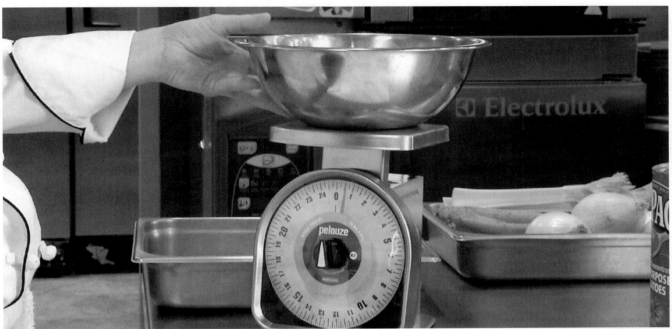

15-3 This scale is tared by placing the empty bowl on the scale and resetting it to zero.

15-4 Liquid measurements must be viewed at eye level to be accurate.

disappointed because the dish did not meet your expectations? Perhaps the portion size was smaller than before. Maybe the quality of the food was inferior. Maybe the seasoning and flavor were not the same.

Whatever the difference, it is not a satisfying experience and it may keep you from ever returning to that restaurant again.

Any successful foodservice operation builds its reputation on repeat business.

The key to creating repeat business is creating quality products, while the key to maintaining repeat business is consistency. The most successful companies in the hospitality industry have made a mission of delivering a consistent product to their customers each and every visit. The tool that chefs and managers use to create a dish that is uniform each time it is prepared is the standardized recipe, 15-5. A **standardized recipe** is an accurate list of the ingredients, their quantities, and the preparation methods needed to prepare a particular menu item in a consistent manner every time.

Draz-Koetke/Goodheart-Willcox Publisher

15-5 Chefs use standardized recipes during food preparation.

The Value of Standardization

Standardization is the process of making things uniform or the same. In a commercial kitchen, standardization relates to the food products used, how much is used, and the method in which the products are cooked. The ability to create a consistent, finished dish time and again is one of the most challenging tasks in the foodservice industry. The goal is for different cooks—possibly in multiple locations—to present a consistent menu item to customers.

When working in a professional kitchen, it is important that the recipes being used are as clear and accurate as possible. This is key to producing the same quality product time after time, regardless of who is preparing it. A well-written and clearly formatted recipe also saves time and effort by allowing the cook to have all necessary ingredients ready when needed and by clearly explaining the steps in preparing the dish. When comparing a recipe written for a home cook with a standardized recipe written for a professional kitchen, the differences are evident, 15-6.

A foodservice operation may keep their standardized recipes in a book, card file, or computer database. In a well-managed kitchen, the standardized recipe is read and followed each time a recipe is prepared by anyone in the kitchen. This is true for the first time the recipe is prepared as well as for the thousandth time the item is being made.

Anatomy of a Recipe

The standardized recipe has certain characteristics that distinguish it from the home recipe. Most chefs consider the following elements when writing or evaluating a recipe, 15-7.

Name   The name of the recipe is consistent with the way it will be written on the menu.

Home Recipe

Take one chicken and place in a pot with some cold water. Add 1 chopped onion, 2 chopped carrots, and 1 piece of chopped celery. Cover and simmer for one and a half hours. Remove the chicken from the pot and pick the meat from the bones. Add the meat back to the pot along with 1/3 package of noodles. Simmer 2 minutes more. Add 1 teaspoon salt, and 1/2 teaspoon pepper and chopped parsley.----serves six

15-6 A home cook might use a recipe like this one.

Recipe No.	Name		Category
25.1	Chicken Vegetable Soup		Soup
Yield	**Portion Size**		**No. Portions**
1 gal. (3.8 L)	8 fl. oz. (240 mL)		16
US Quantity	**Metric Quantity**	**Ingredient**	**TCS**
2 lb.	900 g	chicken pieces (breast, legs, thighs)	•
8 oz.	225 g	carrot, diced	
1 lb.	450 g	onion, diced	
8 oz.	225 g	celery, diced	
8 oz.	225 g	parsnips (optional)	
1 gal.	3.8 L	water or chicken stock	•
1 ea.		*sachet:*	
2 ea.		bay leaves	
2 tsp.	10 mL	dried thyme leaf	
1 tsp.	5 mL	black peppercorn	
To taste		salt and white pepper	
Method			**CCP**
1. Place all ingredients in a stockpot.			
2. Bring to a boil over medium heat.			
3. Skim to remove all scum. Simmer about 1 hour until the chicken is tender and reaches 165°F (74°C).			CCP
4. Remove the chicken and allow it to cool briefly until it can be handled easily.			
5. Remove meat from the chicken bones and tear or cut into bite-sized pieces. Place the chicken back in the pan and bring the soup back to a simmer.			CCP
6. Remove sachet and season with salt and pepper. Moments before serving, mix soup with minced parsley.			

Portion (g)	Calories	Fat (g)	Protein (g)	Carbohydrate (g)	Cholesterol (mg)	Sodium (mg)	Fiber (g)
225	117	3.39	10.36	10.83	22.89	791.53	1.26

15-7 Standardized recipes are used in professional foodservice operations.

Yield The yield is the quantity or number of portions the recipe will produce. It is shown at the top of the recipe so that the cook knows immediately how much the recipe will make. Yield may be expressed in volume, weight, or number of portions. To create a smaller or larger yield, scaling the quantities of ingredients is necessary.

Portion Size The portion size indicates the serving size the chef expects to be served to the customer. It is frequently expressed in ounces, cups, or by count. Portioning is more accurate when tools such as ladles, scoops, and scales are used. Consistency in portion size is important for customer satisfaction and controlling costs.

Category A kitchen's recipe file or book is often organized in categories such as appetizers, soups, salads, main courses, and desserts.

Recipe Number To avoid confusion and for filing purposes, each recipe is assigned a number which makes it easier to find or identify.

Ingredients Ingredients are separate from the preparation instructions, which makes gathering the necessary products easier. Ingredients should be listed in the order in which they are used in the recipe. The list of ingredients is as specific as possible including key descriptions such as size, cut, type, or even specific brand necessary to create a consistent product every time.

If a chef has implemented a hazard analysis critical control point (HACCP) program, the recipe may also indicate if an ingredient requires time and temperature control for safety (TCS).

Quantity The quantities of products are measured by weight whenever possible. Small quantities of ingredients such as spices and herbs are often measured in teaspoons or tablespoons.

Method The directions for preparation are written clearly and concisely using professional terminology. Steps are numbered to make the directions easier to follow. Steps also help the cook work in a sequential way which helps ensure a proper outcome. Some recipes list the amount of time it takes to prepare and cook the final product. This helps the cook manage his or her time effectively. Cooking and holding times and temperatures are clearly stated to assure proper sanitation, serving temperature, and product quality. Those steps that are critical control points (CCP) in the preparation are labeled.

Plating Instructions A standardized recipe often includes the specific way in which the dish is to be presented to the diner. This may

Nutrition Connection

Recipe Makeovers

Chefs may need to adjust their recipes to meet consumer demand for healthy alternatives. Reviewing recipe ingredients and their functions helps identify how to modify the recipe without compromising the quality of the product. For instance, chefs can cut the sugar by one-third in some baked goods without altering the finished product. In addition, they substitute

- cholesterol-free egg products for whole eggs
- reduced-fat cheeses for their full-fat counterparts
- reduced-sodium broth for the regular version
- herbs and spices for salt
- lean ground beef or turkey for regular ground beef
- low-fat yogurt for sour cream in dips and some creamy sauces

Many ingredients allow chefs to make over recipes from the traditional version to a healthier alternative.

include a standard portion size, type of plate it will be served on, and how the items are to be arranged and garnished. Photos and a diagram of the presentation are sometimes included in the recipe.

As nutrition concerns become a greater challenge for foodservice professionals, nutrient analyses become a more important element of recipes, 15-8.

Product Specification

Suppose a cook is preparing a shrimp appetizer from a standardized recipe card. The recipe calls for "shrimp." While gathering ingredients, the cook finds three different types of shrimp in the seafood cooler. One type is a jumbo shell-on shrimp; the second is small, peeled and deveined

15-8 Recipes can be more easily written and modified using recipe software.

shrimp pieces; and the third type is tiny, cooked shrimp. Clearly, the choice of which shrimp to use will have a significant impact on how the finished dish will look and taste, and how much it will cost to produce.

When ingredients are listed in a standardized recipe, it is very important that their description be as accurate as possible. That is why recipes use product specifications to describe the ingredients. A **product specification** is a detailed description of a product used in a foodservice operation. It is called a "spec" for short. Following product specs ensures that the same size, quality, and type of product is used, contributing to a consistent finished product. Product specifications for food products often include the following:

- product
- market form (fresh, frozen, dried, etc.)
- size
- grade
- brand

Beyond the kitchen, product specification is also essential to the purchaser. The spec tells the purchasing agent exactly what product the chef wants. The chef has created the menu and recipes with certain quality and cost levels in mind and requires the correct product to achieve those, 15-9.

Increasingly, foods that are partially or fully prepared are being used in professional kitchens. For instance, bread may be purchased partially baked and may only need to be browned in the oven before serving. Frozen vegetables or canned beans may be used in place of raw vegetables or dried beans. These foods offer convenience to the chef as they require less time and attention to prepare. There can be considerable variation among different prepared products, making it critical to specify the brand of the product.

Sometimes, chefs and purchasers need to substitute one ingredient for another if the desired ingredient is not available. If you need to substitute ingredients in a recipe, first consult your supervisor. Not all ingredients can be easily substituted. Substitutions

Sample Product Specifications

Product	Purchase Unit	Pack Size	Grade/Brand	Weight/ Count	Detailed Requirements
Tomatoes, salad, fresh	Case	2 layer	U.S. No. 1	5×6	Uniform round shape, pink to light red color, free from defects and decay.
Tomatoes, plum, fresh	Case	25 lb.	U.S. No. 1	bulk	Roma variety tomatoes light red to red color, firm, free from decay and sun scalding.
Tomatoes, diced, canned	Case	6/#10 cans	U.S. Grade A	6 lb., 10 oz.	½″ diced California tomatoes in juice, with min. 60 oz. drained wt., no extraneous material or green pieces.
Tomato juice	Case	12/46 oz. cans	California Red Brand	46 oz.	California Red Brand, no substitutes.
Tomato paste	Case	6/#10 cans	U.S. Grade A / Fancy	6 lb., 15 oz.	Good tomato flavor and color, min. 35% tomato solids, smooth texture free of defects.

15-9 Product specifications are essential for controlling quality and cost.

Converting Fractions to Decimals

Suppose you want to convert ¾ to a decimal. Set up your fraction as a division problem. The denominator is divided into the numerator.

$$4\overline{)3}$$

Because the 3 is smaller than 4, you will need to add a decimal and some zeroes.

$$4\overline{)3.00}$$

Now, start dividing.

```
      .75
  4 )3.00
     2.80
      .20
      .20
        0
```

The resulting quotient is your decimal.

may require changes to the rest of the recipe. Substitutions may also introduce potential allergens that were not part of the initial recipe. This could be life threatening to a customer or another employee.

Changing Recipe Yields

Chefs often need more or less yield than a standardized recipe produces. A chef must be able to adjust the quantities of the ingredients to produce the desired yield. For example, a chef using the recipe for chicken vegetable soup in Figure 15-7 can prepare 1 gallon or 16 portions. If the chef is preparing the same soup for a banquet of 140 guests, he or she must adjust the recipe to yield 140 portions. In order to adjust the recipe, the chef needs to determine the conversion factor. The **conversion factor** is a multiplier that adjusts the quantity of each ingredient in the original recipe to determine the quantities needed for the revised recipe.

The conversion factor is calculated by using the following formula:

New Yield ÷ Old Yield = Conversion Factor

Using the example of the chicken vegetable soup, the new yield is the 140 portions needed for the banquet. The old yield is the 16 portions that the original recipe yielded. The conversion factor is the quotient that results from this equation.

140 portions ÷ 16 portions = 8.75 conversion factor

The process can also be used to decrease the quantity produced. Suppose in our previous example that the chef needs to make a small batch of soup for a tasting. If the chef needs only 6 portions instead of 16, the same formula is used to adjust the recipe yield.

6 portions ÷ 16 portions = 0.375 conversion factor

The next step is to apply the conversion factor to the original recipe. Use the following formula to convert the original recipe amounts to the new recipe amounts:

$$\text{Old Quantity} \times \text{Conversion Factor} = \text{New Quantity}$$

This formula must be used on every ingredient in the recipe in order to increase or decrease the recipe yield, 15-10.

Changing Recipe Yields

Increasing Yield

Ingredient	Old Quantity	×	Conversion Factor	=	New Quantity
chicken pieces	2 lb.	×	8.75	=	17.5 lb.
onions, small dice	8 oz.	×	8.75	=	70 oz.
celery, small dice	4 oz.	×	8.75	=	35 oz.
carrots, small dice	4 oz.	×	8.75	=	35 oz.
clarified butter	1 oz.	×	8.75	=	8.75 oz.
chicken stock	3 qt.	×	8.75	=	26.25 qt.

Decreasing Yield

Ingredient	Old Quantity	×	Conversion Factor	=	New Quantity
chicken pieces	2 lb.	×	0.375	=	0.75 lb.
onions, small dice	8 oz.	×	0.375	=	3 oz.
celery, small dice	4 oz.	×	0.375	=	1.5 oz.
carrots, small dice	4 oz.	×	0.375	=	1.5 oz.
clarified butter	1 oz.	×	0.375	=	0.38 oz.
chicken stock	3 qt.	×	0.375	=	1.13 qt.

15-10 These examples show how conversion factors are used to adjust recipe yields.

Summary Points

- Knowing units of measure and their equivalents is essential for following a recipe in the professional kitchen.

- Units of measure are different for weights and volumes. Chefs must be familiar with both the US system and the metric system.

- Weight and volume measures must be performed accurately in order for recipes to turn out right.

- Standardized recipes are used in professional kitchens and are different from recipes used in the home. Standardized recipes give accurate, clear instructions that help create a consistent finished product time after time.

- A yield for a professional recipe can be increased or decreased by multiplying ingredient quantities by a conversion factor.

In Review

Assess

1. List the basic units of measure for weight in
   A. the US system
   B. the metric system

2. List the basic units of measure for volume in
   A. the US system
   B. the metric system

3. Convert the following to the equivalent quantities in the US system:
   A. 1 L
   B. 750 mL
   C. 1 mL
   D. 1 kg
   E. 1 g

4. Convert the following to the equivalent quantities in the metric system:
   A. 1 oz. (weight)
   B. 1 lb.
   C. 1 fl. oz. (volume)
   D. 1 qt.
   E. 1 gal.

5. Can one gallon of water be measured accurately using a scale? Explain.

6. Why is weight the preferred method of measuring ingredients in the professional kitchen?

7. Explain why adjusting a scale for tare weight is important.

8. True or false. Professional kitchens use standardized recipes in order to produce consistent menu items no matter which cook has prepared the item.

9. If a cook wants to know how many portions a recipe makes, he or she should look at which part of the recipe?
   A. method
   B. recipe number
   C. yield
   D. ingredients

10. True or false. The list of ingredients in a recipe should appear in alphabetical order.

11. What is the formula for calculating a conversion factor to scale a recipe?

12. If the conversion factor is less than one, will the new yield be larger or smaller than the old yield?

Core Skills

13. **Math.** The chef hands you a recipe that serves 30 portions and asks you to prepare 165 portions. What conversion factor will you use to change the recipe yield?

14. **Reading and Writing.** Write a simple three-item menu. Find recipes for the items on your menu. Write a step-by-step plan describing how you will produce your menu. Your plan should include every step in the process, for example: purchasing needed ingredients, thawing items if necessary, identifying equipment needed, verifying equipment is in working order, gathering serving dishes, chopping and dicing, cooking, plating the finished product, and so on. Assign an estimate of how long each task will take. Include dates and times you will perform each task. Write a brief summary of this experience.

15. **Reading.** Read and analyze some of the recipes found in Escoffier's *Le Guide Culinaire*. Are these recipes easy to understand from an ingredient and method standpoint? For what type of audience do you think these recipes were written? Provide reasoning to support your answer.

16. **Math.** Charles, the prep cook, determines he needs 156 oz. of flour for his recipe. He decides to use a pound scale to measure the flour. How many pounds of flour will he need? Provide your answer in pounds and ounces. If your answer includes a fraction of a pound, convert the fraction to ounces.

17. **Writing.** Choose a recipe from a magazine. Rewrite this recipe to create a standardized recipe using the guidelines in this chapter.

18. **Writing.** Select one ingredient from the recipe in activity #17. Write a product specification for the ingredient using Figure 15-9 as a guide.

19. **CTE Career Readiness Practice.** Search the Internet for new technologies in recipe conversion tools or programs. Choose one of interest and determine the following: What are the benefits of using the technology to enhance productivity? What are some disadvantages or risks of using the new technology? What actions could you take to mitigate the disadvantages or risks? In your opinion, for what applications will this new technology most likely be used? Create a digital report to share your findings with the class.

Critical Thinking

20. **Assess.** Identify a situation when more than one member of the class prepared the same recipe with different results. What might have caused the difference?

21. **Determine.** When working with recipes, what math skills do chefs need?

22. **Consider.** The chef is in the kitchen tasting the various cooks' dishes before service. A new cook has prepared a dish that is traditionally quite popular with customers. The chef notices the dish tastes and looks significantly different. What is likely to be the first question the chef asks the cook?

Technology

Using spreadsheet software, create a tool that scales recipes up or down. Test your tool by using it to scale a simple recipe from 20 to 120 portions.

Teamwork

Assemble a group of three students and assign each member a role. Perform the following experiment to determine the possible impact of measuring by weight compared with measuring by volume:

A. Gather flour, a one-cup measure, knife, sifter, spoon, and a small scale.

B. Fill the cup measure with flour and tap the cup repeatedly on the counter to pack the flour down. Add more flour as necessary to fill cup. Use the knife to scrape off the flour above the top of the cup measure.

C. Weigh the flour and cup measure and record the weight.

D. Sift the flour.

E. Use the spoon to gently fill the cup measure with the sifted flour. Scrape excess off with the knife.

F. Weigh the flour and cup measure and record the weight.

Did each cup of flour weigh the same? Calculate the percent difference between the packed and the sifted cups of flour. Explain. Record your results, observations, and summary of your findings to present in class. For an additional challenge, prepare a recipe first using the weighed measure and again using the volume measure. Note the differences in the final products.

Chef's E-portfolio
Scaling Recipes

Upload the tool you created for scaling recipes in the Technology activity. Ask your instructor where to save your file. This could be on the school's network or a flash drive of your own. Name your portfolio document *FirstnameLastname_Portfolio Ch#.docx* (i.e., JohnSmith_PortfolioCh15.docx).

While studying, look for the activity icon ⬀ to:
- Build vocabulary with e-flash cards and matching activities.
- Expand learning with video clips, photo identification activities, animations, and interactive activities.
- Review and assess what you learn by completing end-of-chapter questions.

Basic Preparations —Mise en Place

16

Reading Prep

In preparation for reading the chapter, reflect on how you prepare to perform a task or project. Is this method effective for you? Do you often achieve your desired results? As you read about mise en place, consider how this compares to your process of preparing to perform a task.

Culinary Terminology

Build Vocab

mise en place, p. 249
chiffonade, p. 253
concassé, p. 255
clarified butter, p. 258
mirepoix, p. 259
white mirepoix, p. 259

Academic Terminology

Build Vocab

remedy, p. 250

Objectives

After studying this chapter, you will be able to

- summarize mise en place and its role in the professional kitchen.
- execute the techniques for peeling, julienning, and dicing an onion.
- execute the techniques for mincing parsley.
- explain the chiffonade technique.
- execute the techniques for preparing leeks.
- execute the techniques for peeling, seeding, and dicing tomatoes.
- execute the techniques for peeling and mincing garlic.

- explain how to make clarified butter.
- explain how to prepare mirepoix and its role in the professional kitchen.

Every profession has its unique set of basic preparations or skills. These basics are the backbone of more advanced techniques. Mastering any profession begins with learning basic preparations and skills. Once these skills are mastered, a student can progress to more challenging preparations.

This chapter addresses the foundational preparations that are employed in professional kitchens every day. Take the time to practice these basic building blocks of the culinary profession until you can prepare them with accuracy and speed.

Mise en Place

A common term used in professional kitchens is *mise en place* (meez ahn PLAHS). It is a French phrase that translates loosely as "put in place." In the kitchen, **mise en place** refers to having all foods and equipment ready for a specific preparation before beginning it. Mise en place also refers to a state of mental readiness.

Reading and understanding a menu or recipe is an essential part of mise en place. Before beginning to work, the recipe should be reviewed to ensure needed ingredients are available and that each preparation step is understood. Reviewing the recipe in advance also helps the chef to prepare mentally by having a clear vision of the scope of the task, 16-1. With a full understanding of what needs to be done, the chef is better able to manage his or her time and sequence the work that must be accomplished. Failing to review the recipe in advance can result in confusion and errors during preparation when it may be too late to **remedy**, or correct. Ultimately, this could mean a less than successful dish.

Assembling all the ingredients necessary for a recipe is part of mise en place. Any processing of the ingredients to prepare them for the recipe is done at this time. For instance, chopping onions and mincing herbs may be part of the mise en place for a soup recipe. Verifying that all the necessary pieces of equipment are available and in working order is also part of mise en place. Even setting up your station prior to service is considered mise en place.

Mise en place ensures that kitchen work is orderly and carried out efficiently. It is critical to a well organized and productive kitchen. Coordinating efforts of many different cooks requires mise en place. For instance, to make 100 plates for a banquet, one cook might be responsible to have the vegetables ready at the appointed time. Similarly, other cooks may be assigned to prepare the fish, sauce, starch, and garnish. When the entire staff knows the end goal and the plan to get there, success is more

likely. Many of the basic skills covered in this chapter are frequently part of mise en place.

Peeling, Slicing, and Dicing Onions

Onions are one of the most commonly used vegetables in the professional kitchen. They require their own cutting techniques due to their unusual structure.

Before slicing or dicing onions, the onion must be peeled. During peeling, the inedible parts of the onion such as the skin, stem, and root ends are removed.

Sliced onions are also known as julienned onions. Julienned onions are part of many dishes from Italian sausage to French onion soup. Whether thick or thin, it is crucial that the knife cuts are consistent when slicing onions.

Possibly a more common ingredient than julienned onions, are diced onions. Dicing an onion is routine in the professional kitchen. Diced onions, of many different sizes, are ingredients in most recipe categories.

All cooks must become skilled at peeling, slicing, and dicing onions.

Draz-Koetke/Goodheart-Willcox Publisher

16-1 Reviewing the recipe before beginning preparation is an essential part of mise en place.

CHEF'S ETHICS

Work Ethic

Having a strong work ethic in today's society is crucial to achieving workplace success. For employers, people with a strong work ethic add value to the company by providing quality work that meets or exceeds expectations. People with a strong work ethic have a positive attitude, work well with other team members, and take on additional tasks as needed. They are assertive and self-directed. For employees, the reward not only comes in the form of monetary compensation, but also an internal satisfaction of doing a job to the best of his or her ability.

TECHNIQUE
Peeling an Onion

1. Cut the ends off the onion being careful to remove only a small amount of each end. If too much is cut off, the onion will fall apart and be difficult to cut properly. Notice that the onion has two distinct ends—the stem and root end.
2. Cut the onion in half by cutting lengthwise through the stem and root end of the onion. If onion rings are desired, then this step is skipped.
3. Remove the peel from the onion using a paring knife.

TECHNIQUE
Preparing Julienne Onions

1. Place peeled onion halves cut side down on the cutting board.
2. Remove the remaining root of the onion. The root is removed by making a small triangular cut with the tip of the chef knife or paring knife.

3. Slice the onion into ⅛-inch wide slices using the proper knife technique.

4. As you slice the onion, it becomes increasingly harder to hold in place. When the onion becomes too small to hold, lay it face down on the cutting board and continue slicing.

INDUSTRY INSIGHTS
Precut Vegetables

In many foodservice operations, commonly used vegetables such as onions may be purchased already cut into various sizes. Precut vegetables are stored in the refrigerator until needed, although they may have a shorter shelf life than whole vegetables. Precut vegetables may be preferred in kitchens that prepare large amounts of food, have limited preparation space, or lack enough cooks.

TECHNIQUE
Dicing Onions

1. Place the peeled onion half cut side down on the cutting board.

2. Place your guiding hand on top of the onion half. Be sure that the root end of the onion faces away from the knife. If the root end is facing the knife, the onion will fall apart during dicing.

3. Position the guiding hand as needed for slicing. Slice the onion lengthwise by drawing the knife backward instead of in the usual forward motion. The slice should begin just short of the root end of the onion so that the root end remains intact. Do not cut through the root end core of the onion either.

4. Continue slicing until the onion has been evenly sliced except for the small area on the root end of the onion.

5. Reposition the guiding hand so that it is placed on top of the onion either as shown or with the palm of the hand resting on top of the onion. Be sure that the fingertips are up and out of harm's way. The knife blade will be parallel to the cutting board to make the next slices. Drawing the knife backward, cut slices that are parallel to the cutting board. These slices begin at the stem end and stop before cutting through the root end.

6. Reposition the guiding hand on the onion. Slice the onion crosswise, perpendicular to the previous cuts and beginning at the stem end. As the onion becomes difficult to hold safely, lay it down on the cutting board. Cut this small piece of onion into a dice by slicing and then cutting across the slices.

7. By changing the width of the cuts in steps 3, 4, and 5, you can adjust the size of the finished dice.

Mincing Parsley

Minced parsley is a familiar sight in many professional kitchens. It is frequently sprinkled on food as a garnish. It is also added to preparations such as sauces, soups, stews, and dips. Unlike most herbs, parsley is often not only minced but also wrung out to extract excess moisture. Freshly minced parsley is wet and sticky. Removing moisture makes parsley easy to sprinkle and increases its shelf life. Removing moisture also prevents parsley's green color from bleeding into other foods.

Parsley is not wrung out for all preparations. Removing moisture also removes some flavor. For recipes that rely on a strong parsley flavor, wringing out parsley is not recommended.

Chiffonade
Animation

Certain leafy vegetables and fresh herbs can be cut into a chiffonade. A **chiffonade** (shif on AHD) refers to thinly cut strips of leafy greens. To make a chiffonade, stack five to six leaves on top of each other. Tightly roll the stack. Cut thin slices across the roll, 16-2. Unroll the cuts to reveal the chiffonade.

Draz-Koetke/Goodheart-Willcox Publisher

16-2 Chiffonade cut greens can be used as a garnish or ingredients in a recipe.

TECHNIQUE
Mincing Parsley

1. Wash the parsley in cold water. Dry between paper towels or in a salad spinner.
2. Separate the parsley leaves from the stems.
3. Roll the leaves into a tight ball. Cut finely with a chef's knife.

4. Mince the parsley using the same technique as for garlic.
5. To wring out the parsley, place the minced parsley in a piece of cheesecloth. Gather the ends of the cheesecloth together and twist the cheesecloth tightly. Green parsley juice should drip from the cheesecloth.

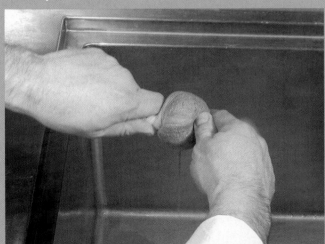

6. Store parsley in a covered container in the refrigerator until needed.

TECHNIQUE
Preparing Leeks

Trimming Leeks

1. Remove the dark green leaves one at a time using a paring knife. Only cut each leaf where the dark green begins.

2. Trim the root end of the leek.

Washing Leeks

Leeks are unique because dirt is found inside the vegetable as well as on the outside. Simply rinsing the outside of a leek does not remove the dirt trapped inside. There are two techniques for washing a trimmed leek.

For leek halves or quarters:

1. Cut the leek in half lengthwise stopping short of completely cutting through the root end. If the leeks are very large, it may be necessary to cut the leek lengthwise into quarters.

2. Place the leek, cut end up, under cold running water. Open the leek as the water is running on it to remove the dirt that is trapped between the leaves.

3. After washing, verify that all the dirt has been removed from between the leaves.

For chopped or julienned leeks:

1. Cut the leek completely in half lengthwise. Cut the leeks according to the desired shape.

2. Place the cut leek in a large container of cold water. Agitate the water to loosen dirt from the leeks. Let the leeks sit undisturbed in the water for 10 to 15 minutes. During this time, the dirt settles to the bottom of the container.

3. Scoop the leeks off the top of the water using a spider. Do not agitate the water any more than is necessary. Never pour the leeks and water into a colander to avoid depositing the dirt back on top of the clean leeks.

4. Verify that leeks are free from dirt before using.

Washing and Cutting Leeks

Leeks are members of the onion family. Leeks are less well-known than their bulb-shaped counterparts, but often used in a wide assortment of recipes. The techniques for handling leeks are unique and deserve special attention.

The white and light green portion of the leek is the part that is used most often. It is the mildest and most tender portion of the leek. The dark green leaves have a strong flavor and tougher texture. The dark green leaves are often reserved for stocks and some soups.

Peeling, Seeding, and Dicing Tomatoes

From pizza sauce to salad, tomatoes are part of an astonishing array of dishes. While tomatoes can be purchased canned or sun-dried, it is essential to know how to peel, seed, and dice fresh tomatoes.

Peeling tomatoes requires a special technique because tomatoes are soft and the skin is very thin. Using a knife or vegetable peeler is impossible. The only way to efficiently peel tomatoes is to briefly place them in boiling water and then into ice water.

In addition to peeling, many recipes call for seeded tomatoes. Removing the seeds from the tomatoes also removes excess juice.

There are two techniques for dicing tomatoes. The first technique is called a *concassé*. The term **concassé** (kon kah SAY) refers to roughly dicing or chopping a product. Concassé tomatoes are an integral ingredient in many dishes. The second technique is a uniform dice that is ideal for garnishing.

TECHNIQUE
Peeling Tomatoes

1. **Remove the tomato's core using the tip of the paring knife. Cut an "X" through the skin of the opposite end of the tomato.**

2. **Plunge the tomatoes in boiling water for 30 seconds. Scoop the tomatoes from the boiling water using a spider or pair of tongs and place them in ice water.**

3. **When the tomatoes are cold, remove them from the ice water. Using a paring knife, pull the skin from the tomato by grabbing the skin where the "X" was initially cut in the tomato. If the skin of the tomato does not come off easily, repeat step 2. This may be necessary if the tomatoes are not ripe.**

TECHNIQUE
Seeding Tomatoes

1. Cut the tomato (most often tomatoes are peeled first) in half. Do not cut through the core, but rather through the middle of the tomato.
2. Squeeze the tomatoes gently so as to push seeds and excess moisture from the tomatoes. Inspect each tomato half to be sure that the seeds have all been removed.

TECHNIQUE
Dicing Tomatoes

Technique 1: Concassé

1. Flatten a peeled and seeded tomato half slightly with the palm of the hand.

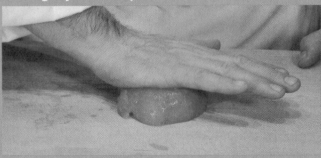

2. Cut into strips and then dice using a chef's knife.

Technique 2: Fine Dice

1. Using a small knife, trim the flesh from a tomato that has been peeled but not seeded. As the flesh is trimmed off, the seeds should remain inside the tomato.

2. Cut each of these trimmed pieces into strips and then dice. The center of the tomato can be seeded and cut into a concassé.

Peeling and Mincing Garlic

Garlic's flavor is intense when used raw, mild when cooked, and sweet when roasted. Along with onions, garlic is one of the most common flavorings in foodservice.

While garlic can be purchased either peeled and separated into individual cloves or pre-minced, it is important to know how to process an intact head of garlic.

Like onions, garlic has a unique structure. As a result, there are a series of specialized techniques for processing garlic.

TECHNIQUE
Peeling and Mincing Garlic

1. Place the head of garlic on its side on a cutting board. Position the palm of your hand on the head of garlic. Press firmly until the head breaks apart into individual cloves.

2. To peel the garlic, place a clove on the cutting board. Place the side of a chef's knife on the clove. Press firmly on the knife until the clove breaks. It may be necessary to tap the side of the knife with the guiding hand. Remove the loosened skin from each clove.

3. Cut each clove in half and remove the germ if it has a green tint. If not removed, the garlic will taste bitter. Also, trim a small amount of the root end of the garlic if brown.

4. To mince garlic, begin by coarsely chopping the peeled cloves. The garlic is then minced using the mincing technique.

5. Some recipes call for garlic paste. To make a paste, sprinkle the minced garlic with a pinch of salt. Using the side of the knife, reduce the garlic to a paste by repeatedly dragging the knife across the garlic. The salt acts as an abrasive and helps make the paste.

Clarified Butter Animation

Another kitchen staple is clarified butter. **Clarified butter** is the fat portion of the butter, which has been separated from the water and milk solids. Many people think of butter as pure fat. However, butter is actually on average 80 percent fat, 18 percent water, and 2 percent milk solids.

The water and milk solids in butter can be problematic when butter is used for high temperature cooking. At high temperatures, the water sputters, which can be dangerous. In addition, the solids in hot butter quickly turn from brown to black. Black, or burned butter, is very bitter and cannot be used.

Clarified butter is ideal for higher temperature cooking. The easiest technique for clarifying butter is to place a metal container of butter in lightly simmering water. As the butter melts, the water and some of the milk solids sink to the bottom of the container. The rest of the milk solids—in the form of white foam—float. Do not stir the butter during the clarifying process, as this slows down the separating process. It takes one pound (454 g) of whole butter to yield 12 ounces (340 g) of clarified butter. This is a 75 percent yield.

When the butter is completely melted, skim the foam off the top using a ladle. After the foam is removed, gently lift the container of butter out of the water. Carefully pour the fat from the container into another container. Stop pouring when the water becomes visible. Ladle any remaining fat from the water's surface. This pouring process that separates one liquid from another liquid or solid is called *decanting*, 16-3.

Draz-Koetke/Goodheart-Willcox Publisher

16-3 Clarified butter is made by decanting the fat from the water and milk solids in butter.

In most foodservice operations, butter is clarified in large quantities. The clarified butter is stored in the refrigerator until needed. If covered, it keeps for at least three to four weeks in the refrigerator.

Mirepoix

Mirepoix (mir eh PWAH) is a French culinary term that is recognized around the world. **Mirepoix** is a vegetable-based seasoning made of two parts chopped onion, one part chopped carrot, and one part chopped celery. It is used extensively for making sauces, stocks, soups, braises, stews, and roasts. A variation of mirepoix, **white mirepoix** contains two parts chopped onion, one part chopped leek, and one part chopped celery. As you will learn in later chapters, there are specific uses for both types of mirepoix, 16-4.

When chefs talk about "parts" in mirepoix, they are referring to a weight measurement. However, in many kitchens, it is rare to see mirepoix actually weighed. Most chefs and cooks find it is easy to approximate the amounts visually by volume. After you have prepared several mirepoix by weight, you too will be able to prepare a mirepoix without weighing.

The size of the mirepoix varies depending on how it will be used. In general, the longer a mirepoix will cook, the larger it can be. It is important that the three vegetables are cut to the same size. If the vegetables are cut to different sizes, the mirepoix will cook unevenly.

Draz-Koetke/Goodheart-Willcox Publisher

16-4 Mirepoix (left) and white mirepoix (right) are used to add flavor to many preparations.

Summary Points

- Mise en place is an important concept for ensuring a well-organized and efficient kitchen.

- Onions are a frequently used vegetable with a unique structure. Cooks must know how to peel, julienne, and dice onions.

- Parsley is used as a garnish and an ingredient in many recipes. Freshly minced parsley can be wet and sticky. There is a technique for wringing out parsley.

- A chiffonade is a cut used on leafy vegetables and fresh herbs.

- Leeks are members of the onion family but require unique preparation before use.

- Tomatoes are used in a wide array of dishes in many different forms. Cooks must know how to peel, seed, and dice fresh tomatoes.

- Garlic is a favored flavoring in the kitchen. There are specialized techniques for processing garlic.

- Clarified butter is the fat portion of the butter that is separated from water and milk solids.

- Mirepoix is used to flavor sauces, stocks, soups, braises, stews, and roasts.

In Review
Assess

1. List five activities that would be considered mise en place.

2. Why do onions require a cutting technique that is different from most vegetables?

3. True or false. The stem end of the onion prevents the onion from falling apart during the dicing technique.

4. If the germ of a garlic clove is _____, it must be removed to avoid a bitter taste.

5. List three reasons to wring out parsley.

6. Describe how to prepare a chiffonade.

7. True or false. The dark green leaves of the leek have a strong flavor and tough texture.

8. Describe the technique for peeling tomatoes.

9. A _____ is made up of _____ part(s) chopped onion, _____ part(s) chopped carrot, and _____ part(s) chopped celery.

10. When do chefs use clarified butter in the professional kitchen?

Core Skills

11. **Math.** The chef asks you to prepare six pounds of clarified butter to replenish the supply kept on hand in the refrigerator. How much whole butter will you need in order to yield six pounds of clarified butter?

12. **Writing.** Write a step-by-step description of mise en place to prepare a bacon, lettuce, and tomato sandwich (BLT).

13. **Speaking.** Research the science behind clarifying butter. Why does it separate into the three layers? Why does the water portion fall to the bottom layer? Include drawings or molecular structures as needed to illustrate. Prepare an electronic presentation to share your findings with the class.

14. **Math.** Calculate how many ounces each of chopped onion, carrot, and celery are needed to prepare three pounds of mirepoix?

15. **CTE Career Readiness Practice.** Research to learn about work sequencing. Prepare and give a presentation explaining what work sequencing is and how it is done. Include examples of how work sequencing can be used effectively in foodservice.

Critical Thinking

16. **Discover.** Research and write a few paragraphs explaining why leeks have dirt inside the vegetable as well as on the outside.

17. **Conclude.** One day when peeling a case of tomatoes, you notice that the skins loosen after 30 seconds in boiling water. The next day, you clean another case of tomatoes.

This time, the skins take 1 minute in the boiling water before they loosen. What might account for the difference in time needed to loosen the tomatoes' skins from one day to the next?

18. **Infer.** Search cookbooks and the Internet for recipes that use mirepoix. Find additional recipes that call for white mirepoix. After studying the recipes, why do you think some recipes call for mirepoix and others for white mirepoix?

19. **Evaluate.** Suppose you are assigned to prepare a bacon, lettuce, and tomato sandwich without the opportunity to perform the mise en place you wrote for activity #12. Predict what effect this would have on performing your assignment. Based on this analysis, identify the benefits of mise en place in the professional foodservice setting.

Video Clip

Peeling and Mincing Garlic and Parsley

Visit the G-W Learning Companion Website and view the bonus video clip "Peeling and mincing garlic and parsley." After viewing the clip, answer the following questions:

1. When mincing with a chef's knife, where is the guiding hand placed?

2. True or false. To peel garlic, drop it into boiling water briefly and then into ice water.

3. List three reasons to remove moisture from minced parsley.

Video

Technology

Create a document using word processing or spreadsheet software to map out the steps needed to prepare a grilled chicken sandwich. The sandwich consists of toasted bread, grilled chicken, raw onion slices, raw tomato slices, mayonnaise, and mustard. Assume that nothing has been done to the foods (i.e. the chicken is raw, bread untoasted, vegetables unsliced, mayonnaise must be prepared). Be sure to also consider sanitation steps. Also, indicate next to each step about how long it would take (estimate) to complete the task for 10 sandwiches. Identify which workstations would be involved and coordinate their activities.

Teamwork

Working in small teams, select two ripe tomatoes that are similar in size. One member will use a paring knife to core and peel the first tomato. The second member will core the second tomato and cut an "X" on the other end using a paring knife. The second tomato is then dropped into boiling water for 30 seconds, removed, and placed immediately into ice water. When the tomato is cold, the second member should remove it from the water and use the paring knife to pull the skin from the tomato. The third team member is responsible for weighing and recording observations and results. Which method was easier? Which method had the least waste?

Chef's E-portfolio
Mise en Place Photo

Select a recipe and prepare the mise en place. Take a photo of yourself with the mise en place and upload it to your e-portfolio. Ask your instructor where to save your file. This could be on the school's network or a flash drive of your own. Name your portfolio document *FirstnameLastname_Portfolio Ch#.docx* (i.e., JohnSmith_PortfolioCh16.docx).

While studying, look for the activity icon to:

- Build vocabulary with e-flash cards and matching activities.
- Expand learning with video clips, photo identification activities, animations, and interactive activities.
- Review and assess what you learn by completing end-of-chapter questions.

Krzysztof Slusarczyk/Shutterstock.com

Reading Prep

In preparation for reading the chapter, locate one or more reliable references for food ingredient substitutions. As you learn about the various kitchen staples, consult the substitution references for possible alternatives. Do the alternatives seem reasonable?

Culinary Terminology Build Vocab

herbs, p. 265
spices, p. 272
marinade, p. 272
rub, p. 272
condiment, p. 277
pickles, p. 279
relish, p. 280
chutney, p. 280
capers, p. 280
olives, p. 281
anchovies, p. 281

Academic Terminology Build Vocab

permeate, p. 272

Objectives

After studying this chapter, you will be able to

- recall the basic seasonings used in professional kitchens and explain their uses in professional cookery.
- recognize the sources, various forms, and uses of herbs and spices in professional kitchens.
- differentiate between marinades and rubs.
- recall various starches and their uses.

- explain the various sources of sweeteners and their qualities.
- recognize the role of acid ingredients in the kitchen and the types commonly used.
- recall various forms of tomato products and how they are classified.
- recognize commonly used condiments.

Any chef or cook can walk into any professional kitchen with the expectation of finding certain essential ingredients. These ingredients are used so often and in so many different preparations that they are referred to as *staple ingredients*. This chapter discusses these kitchen staples and their uses.

Basic Seasoning

A chef may follow a recipe exactly, cook an item perfectly, and present it artistically. However, if seasoning is missing or not in proper balance, that dish may be an unsatisfying failure. Most dining tables are set with salt and pepper. These are the primary seasonings and, therefore, a good place to begin.

Salt

The chemical name for salt is sodium chloride (NaCl). Sodium chloride is a compound of two minerals necessary for maintaining health. Most Americans consume much more salt than is needed to meet their sodium requirements. The taste for salt is an individual preference. Having an acceptable level of salt is important for the taste of any savory dish. Seasoning with salt not only gives a dish a salty taste, but also accentuates other flavors. A dish that lacks salt will seem especially bland.

There are three types of salt commonly found in commercial kitchens—table salt, kosher salt, and rock salt.

Table salt   Kosher salt   Rock salt

Table Salt   Table salt is often referred to as granulated salt because it is in the form of fine granular crystals. These crystals are small enough to flow through a shaker and dissolve quickly in liquids. Most granulated salt has anticaking agents, which keep it from forming into lumps under humid conditions. Iodine, an essential mineral, is often added to salt for nutrition.

Kosher Salt   Kosher salt has slightly larger crystals than granulated salt. It was originally made for salting meats to make them fit according to Jewish dietary law, or kosher. It is used to season clear broths or consommés because it has no additives. Kosher salt does not cloud clear liquids as granulated salt might. Additionally, many chefs prefer to use it when sprinkling seasoning with their fingers. The larger grains are easier to feel and therefore, easier to measure.

Rock Salt   Rock salt consists of still larger crystals—about the size of fine gravel. Rock salt is not used to season foods. Baked shellfish are often served on a bed of rock salt to keep them from rocking and spilling their flavorful juices. In these dishes, the rock salt is also heated to help keep the shellfish hot.

Chef Speak

Other Salts in the Kitchen

There are an increasing variety of salts at the disposal of the creative chef. These salts are either mined or made from evaporated seawater. What makes these salts unique (and sometimes quite expensive) is that they contain small amounts of other substances besides salt. These other substances add a complex flavor and even unusual colors. The flavor complexities are subtle and are best used as a last minute sprinkle on a cooked ingredient. For example, using these salts to season a pot of boiling water, would be wasteful. Widely appreciated by chefs, fleur de sel (flower of salt) is a premium sea salt collected from specific coastal areas of France and naturally evaporated in the sun.

Pepper

Pepper is the other half of what most chefs consider basic seasoning. It is thought to be one of the first spices used by man and is still widely in use today. Pepper supplies a sharp flavor that adds character to most savory dishes.

Black Pepper   The ground black pepper found on dining tables is made by grinding peppercorns. Peppercorns are the berrylike fruit of a plant cultivated in tropical Asia. The berries are picked when underripe and dried in the sun. Peppercorns have been valued throughout history for the sharp, spicy flavor they add to foods. They were

Black peppercorns   White peppercorns

so valuable that they were even used for currency during the Middle Ages.

Whole black peppercorns are used to flavor stocks and sauces and are removed before serving. To season foods directly, peppercorns are also used crushed, cracked, or ground. Ground pepper loses its pungency, or sharp flavor, quickly if not stored in a sealed container.

White Pepper   White peppercorns come from the same plant as black pepper, but the berries are allowed to fully ripen. Their outer skins are then removed before drying. White pepper is widely used in professional kitchens because it adds pepper flavor without the visible black specks. White pepper's flavor has less aroma and is sharper than black pepper. White pepper is used as whole peppercorns or finely ground.

Herbs and Spices

Herbs are the green leafy parts of aromatic plants that are used to flavor foods. Fresh herbs are more flavorful and often preferred to dried.

Herbs and Their Uses

Basil

Basil has delicate, pointed green leaves and a sweet, aromatic flavor. Opal basil has purple leaves and lighter flavor. It is essential for pesto and tomato sauces, and popular in Mediterranean cuisines.

Chervil

Chervil has delicate, lacy leaves and a light licorice flavor. It is popular as a garnish and used in sauces.

Bay Leaf (Laurel)

Bay leaf is a stiff, green oval leaf used to flavor stocks, soups, stews, and other savory dishes.

(Continued)

Herbs and Their Uses (Continued)

Chives

Chives are long, hollow grasslike leaves. It is a member of the onion family and has a delicate onion-garlic flavor. Chopped chives are used as a garnish for many savory dishes.

Cilantro (Chinese parsley)

Cilantro has flat green leaves with serrated edges, similar to flat parsley. It has a strong flavor with citrus tones and is commonly used in salsas. This herb is important to Latin American and Asian cuisines. Its seeds are a spice called *coriander*.

Dill

Dill has dark green, feathery leaves. It is often used in pickling and is excellent with fish. This herb is important to Scandinavian and Eastern European cuisines.

Marjoram

Marjoram has small round leaves and a flavor similar to a combination of thyme and oregano. It is used in meat and vegetable dishes and is important to Mediterranean cuisines.

Mint

Mint has pointed leaves with serrated edges. Both peppermint and spearmint are commonly used. This herb is a classic garnish for desserts and is also used with lamb and in Middle Eastern cuisines.

Oregano

Oregano has small oval leaves. It is actually wild marjoram. Used in tomato sauces, it is popular in Italian, Greek, and Mexican cuisines.

(Continued)

Herbs and Their Uses (Continued)

Parsley (Curly)

Curly parsley has tight, curly leaves and fresh, green flavor. It is a classical garnish for fish and poultry.

Parsley (Flat-leaf or Italian)

Flat-leaf parsley has flat, jagged leaves. This herb is used much the same as curly parsley. It is most commonly used in Southern European cuisines.

Rosemary

Rosemary has stiff needles on a woody stem and a pinelike aroma. It is excellent with poultry, pork, lamb, and game.

Sage

Sage has oval leaves with a dusty green color and a velvety texture. It is popular in stuffings and sausages, and goes well with poultry, pork, and game.

Tarragon

Tarragon has long stems with long, narrow leaves and a slight licorice flavor. It is used with fish, chicken, eggs, salad dressings, and is an essential ingredient of béarnaise sauce.

Thyme

Thyme has very small, oval leaves on thin, fibrous stems. It is a basic savory flavoring for stocks, soups, and stews.

Spices and Their Uses

Allspice

Allspice is from the dried berries of a Caribbean tree; also known as *Jamaican pepper*. It has the flavor of nutmeg, cinnamon, and cloves. It is used for forcemeats, pickling, and baking.

Anise

Anise is from the seeds of a small annual plant that originated in Egypt. Anise has a strong licorice flavor. It is used in liquors and for baking.

Caraway Seeds

Caraway seeds are the brown crescent-shaped seeds of a plant that is widely grown in Europe and Asia. It is used in breads, soups, and stews, and is popular in Germanic and Eastern European cuisines.

Cardamom

Cardamom is the light green, pointed seeds of a plant grown in India. It is used in curries, breads, and pastries and is a common ingredient in Indian and Scandinavian cuisines.

Cayenne Pepper

Cayenne, or red, pepper is not a member of the peppercorn family, but is a product of chile peppers. Cayenne peppers ripen to a bright red color. They are dried and finely ground. Cayenne pepper is very strong and adds a hot, spicy flavor to dishes. It is often used for seasoning soups and sauces. Cayenne pepper is also used in the form of crushed chile flakes and is the main flavoring agent in hot pepper sauces.

Celery Seed

Celery seed is the small, brown seed of the celery plant that is commonly used in pickling and relishes. It is also ground and mixed with salt to make celery salt.

Chile Powder

Chile powder is ground red chile peppers. It is often combined with other spices and herbs such as cumin. Chile powders come in varying levels of intensity and are commonly used in chilies and stews. It is a popular ingredient in Mexican and south-western cooking.

(Continued)

Spices and Their Uses (Continued)

Cinnamon

Cinnamon is the bark of a tropical tree, dried and rolled up. Its sweet flavor makes it extremely popular in pastries and fruit dishes.

Cumin (Cumino)

Cumin is the slender brown seed of an annual plant that originated in the Middle East often used in chilies and curries. It is popular in Mexican, Indian, and Middle Eastern cookery.

Cloves

Cloves are the sun-dried buds of a tropical tree. They have a strong sweet aroma and are frequently used for pickling, marinades, and in baked goods.

Curry Powder

Curry powder is a mixture of a dozen or more spices commonly used in curries and stews. These blends vary in flavor and intensity according to regional and individual taste. Indian and other south Asian cuisines use curry powder.

Coriander

Coriander is the round, pale seed of the coriander plant. It has a slight citrus aroma and is used for pickling, marinades, and baking.

Dill Seed

Dill seeds are the light brown, oval seeds of the dill plant and are a popular herb for pickling.

(Continued)

Spices and Their Uses (Continued)

Fennel Seed

Fennel seed is the greenish-brown pointed seeds of the fennel plant whose bulb is used as a vegetable. It has a licorice flavor and is often used in sausages and pork dishes. It is popular in Italian cuisine.

Ginger

Ginger is the root of a tropical plant grown in Asia and the Caribbean. It is available as fresh ginger root, dried powder, or preserved with sugar. Powdered ginger is used in baking and pastries. Fresh root is widely used in Asian cuisines.

Juniper Berries

Juniper berries are the round brownish-purple berries of an evergreen tree. They are good with game and are used to flavor gin, marinades, and stews.

Mace

Mace is the red, veiny middle layer of the same large tropical seed that produces nutmeg. It has an intense spicy flavor and is used in desserts, baking, and some savory dishes.

Mustard

Mustard is the small, round seed of the mustard plant. There are black, brown, and yellow varieties produced. Mustard has a sharp, burning flavor and is a main ingredient in prepared mustards. It is also used for pickling and sauces.

Nutmeg

Nutmeg is the woody inner seed of the same tropical plant that produces mace. It has a wide number of uses including baking, pastries, vegetables, and potatoes.

(Continued)

Spices and Their Uses (Continued)

Paprika

Paprika is a powder ground from a variety of different red chile peppers and is classified as sweet or hot. It is used in a wide variety of soups, stews, and sauces for color and flavor. Paprika is popular in Hungarian and Spanish cuisines.

Sesame Seeds

Sesame seeds are pale-colored seeds of an annual plant native to India. The seeds are ground to a paste (tahini) or can be made into oil. They are commonly used in breads, pastries, and vegetable dishes. Sesame seeds are used in Middle Eastern, Asian, and African cuisines.

Poppy Seeds

Poppy seeds are the small, black seeds of the poppy flower. They have a slightly nutty flavor and are used in breads and pastries.

Star Anise

Star anise is the star-shaped fruit of a tree grown in China. This spice is important in Chinese cuisine.

Saffron

Saffron is the stigma, or center, of the crocus flower and is expensive because it is handpicked. It gives foods a bright yellow color and subtle flavor. It is used in rice dishes, sauces, and seafood, and is very important in Mediterranean cuisines.

Turmeric

Turmeric is the root of a lily native to Southeast Asia. It is used for the bright yellow color it gives dishes and is often an ingredient in rice dishes, curries, pickling, and prepared mustard.

Today, chefs have a wide variety of fresh herbs available to them through produce suppliers. Many kitchens grow an herb garden so fresh herbs are available all the time.

Professional kitchens have traditionally relied on dried herbs. Dried herbs are cheaper, easier to store, and last longer than fresh herbs. When herbs are dried, sometimes their flavors change. Dried basil, for example, is much less flavorful than fresh.

Not every recipe turns out the same if substitutions are made. In most cases, fresh and dried herbs are interchangeable. Remember the flavor of dried herbs is more concentrated. As a rule of thumb, use half the amount of dried herbs by volume as you would fresh, or twice as much fresh herb as dried. Dried herbs usually need to be cooked for some time to release their flavor so they should be added near the beginning of the cooking process. Most fresh herbs release their flavors much more quickly and should be added at the end.

Fresh herbs should be stored in the refrigerator. Many chefs like to store them in plastic bags with their stems wrapped in a piece of wet paper towel. This keeps the herbs from drying out. Dried herbs are stored in tightly sealed containers in a cool dry place. Humid conditions may cause them to mold.

Spices are the woody parts of plants, including seeds, bark, berries, buds, and roots that are used to flavor foods. Some recipes call for dried, whole spices to be toasted before being added to a recipe. This toasting helps the spice develop a more complex and aromatic flavor.

In commercial kitchens, spices are typically used in a ground, powdered form. Ground spices should be stored in tightly sealed containers to help preserve their flavor.

Marinades and Rubs

Creating great flavored food is often a matter of combining different ingredients to achieve an overall delicious flavor. Marinades and rubs are two flavoring strategies used by chefs to impart flavor to their dishes. Sometimes a marinade is used first, followed by a rub.

Marinades

A **marinade** is a liquid that is infused with different ingredients, in which foods are soaked in order to impart flavor before cooking. The liquid may consist of combinations of different oils, wines, vinegars, beers, or fruit juices. Many different condiments, salt, sweeteners, herbs, spices, vegetables, or fruits may be added to the liquid for additional flavors. Acidic marinades are especially important in meat preparation. The acid in the marinade acts to tenderize tough meat. Marinades are prepared two ways: by simply mixing the ingredients together or cooking to combine the ingredients. Because they are a liquid-based, marinades are able to **permeate**, or spread throughout, the food.

Rubs

A **rub** is a combination of seasonings that are massaged into a food product to impart flavor. Rubs generally consist of many different ingredients such as spices, herbs, salt, and sweeteners. They are applied to the outside of food and season only the exterior of the food.

Starches

Starches perform many roles in a commercial kitchen or bakery. They are used to make doughs and batters. They are important as binders and thickening agents and also as coatings. You will learn more about the many uses of starches in later chapters.

Flour

Flour is a finely milled grain. Wheat is the grain most commonly used to produce flour. The bakery or pastry shop has a variety of wheat flour to produce various textures of baked goods. These flours are discussed in the baking chapters.

All-Purpose Flour   Used as a thickening agent or coating, all-purpose flour is the type of flour used most often. All-purpose flour is made from a blend of soft and hard wheats. This combination means that it is neither extremely light and starchy nor heavy and gummy. Its moderate qualities make it appropriate for general purpose baking and cooking.

Semolina   Pasta is made using a combination of all-purpose and semolina flours, or using them individually. Semolina flour is made from hard durum wheat and gives the finished pasta a firm texture.

Rice Flour   Some kitchens prefer rice flour because its starch lends a very light texture to sauces and coatings. It is used for preparations such as tempura batter or as a thickening agent.

Cornmeal

Cornmeal is coarsely ground dried corn. It is used as a coating and in baking. Cornmeal is milled from both yellow and white corn. Another form of cornmeal, masa harina, is ground hominy that has been dried into a powder. It is used in the preparation of many Latin dishes such as tamales. (Hominy is mature corn kernels that have been treated with a lye solution.)

Cornstarch

Cornstarch is a finely powdered starch milled from corn. Its main use is as a thickening agent. It can also be used as an ingredient in batters or doughs.

Arrowroot

Arrowroot looks identical to cornstarch. It is produced from a tropical root and functions as a thickening agent.

Bread Crumbs

Bread crumbs can be used as a coating, topping, and thickening or binding agent.

Leftover bread and crusts are dried and ground up to make dried bread crumbs. They are the most common type of bread crumbs used in foodservice. Some kitchens purchase them; others make their own from leftover bread.

Some recipes call for fresh bread crumbs. Fresh bread crumbs are prepared by trimming the crusts from fresh bread and grinding or sieving them into fine crumbs. Fresh bread crumbs give dishes a lighter texture than dried.

Panko or Japanese-style bread crumbs have become popular with chefs. These bread crumbs are crisp and white. They have a very flaky texture that makes them desirable for coating fried foods, 17-1.

Sweeteners

Sweeteners are an important ingredient in the pastry shop, but they also play a significant role in the kitchen. Sugar and other sweeteners are often used in sauces and to balance or enhance the taste of many savory dishes.

Draz-Koetke/Goodheart-Willcox Publisher

17-1 Different types of bread crumbs vary in texture.

When a sweetener is called for in a dish, chefs have a number of options. Sugar imparts only a sweet taste to dishes it is used in. Other sweeteners may add a distinctive flavor in addition to their sweet taste.

Sugar

Sugar is also known by its scientific name *sucrose*. It can be refined from either the sugarcane plant or sugar beets. In the kitchen, granulated sugar is used most often. In cooking, sugar is primarily used to add a sweet flavor to dishes. More details about the various types of sugar and their uses can be found in the baking chapters.

Molasses

Molasses is the liquid that is leftover after refined sugar is extracted from sugarcane juice. Some sugar is left in the molasses, but it is less sweet than sugar. Molasses can be light or dark. The more molasses is processed to remove the sugar, the darker it gets.

Honey

Honey is formed from flower nectars gathered by bees. The type of flowers from which the nectar is gathered affects the honey's flavor. The most common types of honeys are clover, alfalfa, and orange blossom. Honeys can

Molasses

Honey

Maple syrup

Corn syrup

Dark corn syrup

Agave nectar

Dark brown sugar

Light brown sugar

Sugar

be made from hundreds of different flowers including wildflowers, lavender, and buckwheat. Honey is often blended to achieve a consistent flavor and color.

Honey is slightly sweeter than sugar. In most cases, it can be substituted equally by weight for sugar, although in baking this may not be true. Substituting honey for sugar gives a finished dish the distinctive flavor of the honey.

Brown Sugar

Brown sugar was originally partially refined sugar. Today, brown sugar is made by adding molasses back into refined sugar to create a consistent product. Light and dark brown sugars are the result of the quantity and intensity of the molasses used.

Maple Syrup

Maple syrup is a traditional American staple made from the sap of maple trees. The process for making maple syrup begins with collecting the sap during late winter or early spring. The maple sap is cooked to evaporate the water and concentrate its natural sugars. Thirty to fifty gallons of sap are required to make one gallon of syrup. For this reason, pure maple syrup is a rather expensive ingredient.

Maple syrup is graded on color, clarity, and flavor. Light or amber syrup is most valued. Due to the cost of real maple syrup, many pancake syrups are actually corn syrup with artificial maple flavor.

Corn Syrup

Corn syrup is extracted from the starchy part of corn. Many foodservice professionals refer to it as *glucose syrup*. In its purest form, it is very thick and difficult to scale or measure. Some corn syrups are made thinner so they are pourable and easier to handle. Light corn syrup is clear and has a neutral sweet flavor. Cane by-products and caramel coloring are added to lend color and a more robust flavor to dark corn syrup.

Corn syrup is used as table syrup, in baking, sausage making, beverages, and many other recipes. It is often favored because it does not crystallize like some other sweeteners.

Agave Nectar

Agave nectar is made from the centers of large agave plants. When the juice is extracted from the agave plant, it has a level of sweetness comparable to honey but is much thinner than honey.

Acid Ingredients

Acid is an often overlooked element in cookery. It is an important factor in balancing the taste of many dishes. Acid ingredients play other roles in the kitchen; they can be a preservative and also a coloring agent. When preparing an item that calls for an acid ingredient, chefs have many options.

Vinegar

Vinegar is one of the oldest cooking ingredients known to man. Vinegar comes from the Latin term for "sour wine." Indeed, that is exactly how vinegar is made. Specific types of bacteria consume the alcohol in wine and turn it into acid. Vinegar can be made from any alcoholic beverage. Vinegar is used in marinades, salad dressings, sauces, and pickling. Vinegars differ in strength of acidity from four to seven percent. Most mass-produced vinegar is five percent acid. Most specialty vinegars are higher, ranging from six to seven percent acid content.

The most common vinegars in commercial kitchens include the following:
- *Distilled vinegar* is produced from industrial alcohol. It is clear, acidic, and neutral in flavor. It is the least expensive vinegar and preferred for pickling because of its clear color.
- *Cider vinegar* is made from fermented apple cider. It has an amber color and its

| Sherry wine vinegar | Malt vinegar | Balsamic vinegar | Rice vinegar |

| Distilled vinegar | Cider vinegar | Red wine vinegar | White wine vinegar |

subtle apple flavor makes it good to use in dressings and fruit dishes.

- *Red wine vinegar* is distinctive for its reddish color. It is highly aromatic and widely used in dressings, sauces, and savory dishes.
- *White wine vinegar* does not give dishes the purple color that red wine vinegar does. It imparts a distinct aromatic quality. White wine vinegars are made from generic white wines as well as champagne and sherry wine. Their colors range from a light golden straw color to amber.
- *Balsamic vinegar* is a specialty of Modena, Italy. It is made from cooked grapes giving it a distinctive dark brown color. The vinegar is fermented and aged in a series of different wood barrels for several years. This aging accounts for its complex and aromatic flavor. True balsamic vinegar is highly prized as a condiment and very expensive. Far less expensive forms of balsamic vinegar are made using a faster and less costly process and are used for salad dressings and cold sauces.

- *Malt vinegar* is distilled from the alcohol of fermented barley or beer. It has a brown color and pleasant flavor. It is often used as a condiment to fried foods in English cuisine.
- *Rice vinegar*, made from rice wine, is clear and typically low in acid. Seasoned rice vinegar has salt and sugar added. Rice vinegar is a traditional seasoning in Asian cuisines. It is essential for the preparation of sushi rice.
- *Flavored vinegars* are infused with additional ingredients to give them a unique flavor. The most common items used to flavor vinegars are fruits, herbs, and spices. Popular fruit vinegars include raspberry, blackberry, peach, and cherry. Tarragon, rosemary, garlic, and chile peppers are also commonly used to flavor vinegars.

Lemon and Lime Juice

Bottled lemon and lime juices are staple items in many kitchens. Freshly squeezed or bottled lemon or lime juice may be used interchangeably in many recipes. The acid content of both bottled and fresh is relatively the same. Bottled lemon or lime juice costs less and requires no preparation time. Freshly squeezed lemons and limes have a much better lemon and lime flavor, but are more expensive and require more labor.

Tomato Products

Tomatoes are used in a great number of dishes to add natural sweetness combined with a tangy acidity. They are also important for the deep rich color they add to dishes. Tomatoes are used in basic stocks, sauces, stews, and vegetable dishes. Canned tomato products, rather than fresh, are often used in cooking because they offer a more consistent flavor and lower cost.

Canned tomato products are classified according to their concentration. Concentration is measured by the amount of tomato solids the product contains. Chefs may substitute one type of tomato product for another, adjusting quantities to account for the difference in concentration. It is important to note that within a category there may be a significant range of the amount of tomato solids. One brand of tomato purée, for example, may be noticeably thicker or thinner than another, 17-2.

Solids Content of Various Tomato Products	
Product	**Percent Solids**
Fresh tomatoes	5.4%
Tomato juice	5.5%–8%
Tomato purée	8%–23%
Tomato sauce	11% solids, with added seasonings and vegetables
Tomato paste	24%–35%

17-2 The percentage of solids influences the choice of tomato product to use in a preparation.

Canned tomatoes can be purchased in many forms other than juices, sauces, purées, and pastes. Whole tomatoes, diced, strips, and crushed tomatoes are some of the most popular forms used in commercial kitchens. All forms may be packed in juice, purée, or sauce. The liquid in which the tomatoes are packed affects both the price of the product and how it is best used in the kitchen.

Condiments

Condiments are flavorings or seasonings served with foods to enhance their flavor. Although typically served at the table, condiments are also important ingredients in many recipes. Condiments include cooked or prepared sauces, relishes, and pickles.

Ketchup

Tomato ketchup is perhaps America's favorite condiment. Ketchup is made from tomatoes, corn syrup, vinegar, and spices. The sweet and sour taste makes it popular in salad dressings, cocktail sauce, barbecue sauce, and many other dishes.

Mustard

Mustard seeds are one of the oldest spices and prepared mustard is one of the oldest condiments. All varieties of prepared mustard are based on ground mustard seed combined with acid, salt, and spices. Mustard is essential in making mayonnaise, salad dressings, sauces, and glazes. The more mustard is cooked, the milder its flavor becomes. Therefore, mustard is usually added to cooked recipes at the end to preserve its sharp flavor.

The most commonly used styles of mustards include the following:
- *Yellow mustard*, or "salad-style" mustard, is America's favorite mustard. It is a mild mixture that gets its color from turmeric. Finely ground yellow mustard seeds, vinegar, and salt are combined with the yellow turmeric to create this condiment.

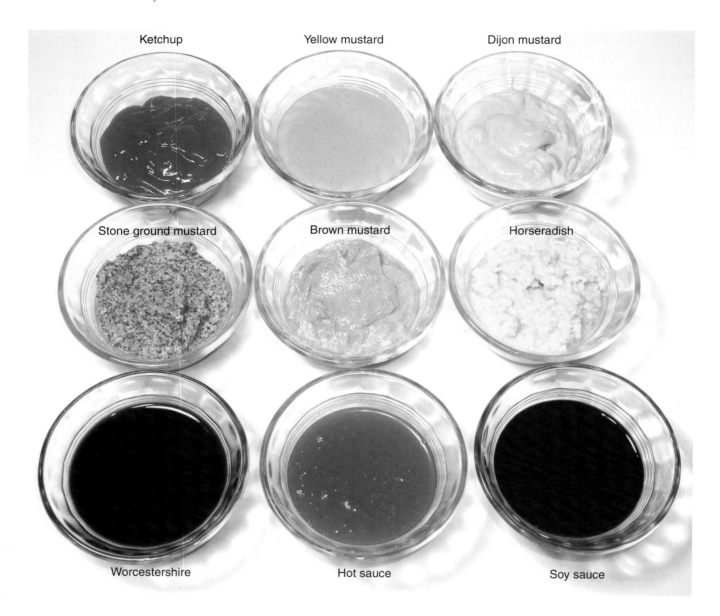

Ketchup   Yellow mustard   Dijon mustard

Stone ground mustard   Brown mustard   Horseradish

Worcestershire   Hot sauce   Soy sauce

- *Dijon mustard* is named for the French city of Dijon where it was first made. It is strongly flavored mustard made from finely ground mustard seed, white wine, herbs, and spices.
- *Stone ground mustard* refers to any number of mustards that are coarsely ground with bits of mustard seed still visible. One of the best-known stone ground mustards is moutarde de Meaux produced near Dijon.
- *Brown mustard*, also known as Düsseldorf-style mustard, is a darker mustard that has a spicy and slightly sweet flavor.

Horseradish

Horseradish is a root that looks like a large, woody white carrot. It is finely grated and mixed with vinegar and salt. This condiment's strong burning flavor goes well with rich, fatty meats. Prepared horseradish is also used to flavor sauces, dressings, and other dishes. Like mustard, the more it is cooked, the milder its flavor becomes.

Worcestershire Sauce

The recipe for Worcestershire sauce was brought back to England by a former governor of Bengal, India. This classic condiment was reproduced by two chemists named Lea and Perrin. The exact original recipe is a secret, though many companies now make their own version.

Worcestershire is thin, murky, and dark brown in appearance. It gives a distinct pungent flavor to foods. This flavor is derived from dozens of ingredients but most distinctive are vinegar, tamarind (pods of a tree grown in India), anchovies, and pepper. Worcestershire sauce is a favorite with grilled and roasted meats. It can also be used to finish sauces, soups, and dressings.

Hot Sauce

As the taste for spicier foods grows, hot sauces are becoming more and more popular. There are many different brands of

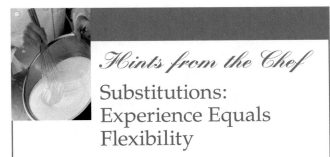

Hints from the Chef

Substitutions: Experience Equals Flexibility

Chefs are often faced with situations where substituting one product for another becomes necessary. A missed delivery, a discontinued or out-of-stock product, or a significant rise in the price of a product could all be reasons to substitute one product for another. Experienced chefs know the characteristics of the food products in their recipes well. They also know the characteristics of many other products. Their knowledge helps them decide if a substitution can be made, and if so, what additional adjustments are needed in a recipe.

Making substitutions when cooking at home is a good way to experiment and learn more about various food products. On the contrary, in commercial foodservice operations, where product consistency is of the utmost importance, always ask the chef or a supervisor before making a substitution to standardized recipes.

hot sauce with diverse intensities of flavor and taste. Despite this variety, all hot sauces are basically made of the same ingredients— vinegar flavored with hot chile peppers and salt. Hot sauce can be used as a substitute for cayenne pepper or other hot chiles in recipes where acid is appropriate. It is often used in hollandaise sauce, salad dressings, or salsa recipes.

Soy Sauce

Soy sauce is a condiment of Chinese origin. It is brewed from fermented soybeans and wheat. Soy sauce comes in different potencies—light, medium, and black. The flavor of the sauce is stronger, thicker, and more intense when more soybeans and less wheat are used to brew the sauce. Japanese-style soy sauce (shoyu) is generally lighter. Chinese-style soy sauce is generally heavier and darker. Tamari is a type of soy sauce brewed with little or no wheat at all.

Soy sauce is used to flavor a variety of dishes. Along with its distinctive salty flavor, soy sauce adds a complex satisfying element to all types of dishes.

Pickles and Relishes

Pickles are foods that have been saturated with acid, usually vinegar, in order to preserve them, or have been fermented. Pickles can be made from any number of fruits and vegetables. Cucumbers are the vegetable most often used to make pickles because they react so well to the pickling process. Pickled cucumbers are used as a garnish on cold plates, and as an ingredient in salads and sandwiches.

The brine, or liquid, in which the pickles are preserved can be flavored in many different ways. Some brines are highly acidic, while others are balanced with sugar or salt. A number of spices, herbs, and aromatic vegetables can be used to flavor pickles.

The most common pickles used in American kitchens are the following:

- *Kosher dill pickles* are pickling cucumbers that are fermented with dill, garlic, and other spices. Dill pickles may be purchased whole, in spears, or slices.
- *Sweet gherkins* are small cucumbers pickled in a sweet brine with spices.
- *Cornichons* are tiny cucumbers that are pickled in a strong vinegar brine flavored with tarragon. Cornichons are the classical garnish for pâtés and often used in sauces and appetizers.

A **relish** is a condiment made of a mixture of chopped or diced ingredients preserved in an acidic liquid. As with pickles, relishes are made of a wide variety of fruits and vegetables. The most common relish is pickle relish made from chopped cucumbers.

Pickle relish is used as a condiment and an ingredient in cold sauces and salad dressings.

Chutney is a condiment made of preserved fruits and vegetables with an acidic, sweet and spicy flavor. It is a traditional condiment in Indian cuisine and comes in many different forms.

Capers

Capers are the bud of a bush that grows near the Mediterranean. These unopened flowers are pickled in vinegar and salt. Some capers are simply packed in salt to preserve them. Capers are sorted by size with the smallest buds being most desirable. Capers are used to garnish sauces, salads, and a variety of cold and hot entrées. Capers should be rinsed to remove some of their

Ripe olives

Green olives

Kalamata olives

Anchovies

Pickle relish

Chutney

Capers

Kosher dill

Cornichons

Sweet gherkins

strong brine before using them in a recipe. The caper bush also produces a berry that looks like a small green olive and has a flavor similar to capers.

Olives

Olives are the fruit of the olive tree that is native to the Mediterranean region. They may be green (picked underripe) or black (picked mature). Olives are treated with salt or lye to remove their bitter flavor. Olives are preserved in brine, often with spices and other flavoring ingredients.

There are hundreds of different varieties and methods of preserving olives. Olives are a common garnish for sandwiches and salads and are often an ingredient in sauces, stuffings, stews, and other dishes. The most common olives used in American kitchens include the following:

- *Green olives* are typically from Spain and are packed in an acidic brine. They are often pitted and stuffed with pimento, olives, or anchovies. The Manzanilla olive is most commonly sold as green olives.
- *Ripe olives* are black olives with a mild salty flavor. They are produced in California from a number of different varieties. Lye curing gives them their mild flavor.

- *Kalamata olives* are a traditional specialty of Greece. Ripe cured olives are preserved in a vinegar brine. They have a salty and acidic flavor.
- *Niçoise olives* are small black olives from the south of France with a nutty, assertive flavor.
- *Alfonso olives* are large, soft, purple olives.
- *Black oil cured olives* are typical of Morocco and look like shriveled black olives. Because they are harvested at peak ripeness, their flavor is pungent, salty, and fruity.

Anchovies

Anchovies are a small, oily ocean fish preserved by salting. Though anchovies can be purchased as whole salted fish, they are mostly sold as fillets canned in oil. Anchovies are a popular ingredient in Mediterranean cuisines. Many chefs utilize less expensive anchovy paste in recipes that call for chopped or puréed anchovies because anchovies are rather expensive.

Fillets are used to garnish salads, pizza, and seafood dishes. Chopped anchovies are added to sauces, stews, and salad dressings.

Summary Points

- Salt and pepper are the essential basic seasonings for most savory dishes.

- Herbs and spices add complexity to cooking. Chefs have the option of using whole or ground spices and fresh or dried herbs in their cooking.

- Marinades and rubs are ways to impart flavor to foods.

- Starches perform many roles in the kitchen. It is important to know which starch is best suited for each role.

- A variety of sweeteners are used in the professional kitchen. Sweeteners differ in their flavor and form.

- Common acid ingredients used in cooking include vinegar and lemon juice.

- Tomato products are used in many different forms to provide color and a sweet, tangy flavor to dishes.

- Condiments are used to enhance the flavor of dishes. They may be used as an ingredient or served at the table.

In Review
Assess

1. Why do some chefs prefer to use white pepper instead of black?

2. When substituting fresh herbs for dried herbs in a recipe, you must use _____ as much fresh herb as dried.

3. True or false. Spices and dried herbs should be stored in tightly sealed containers.

4. Identify the following as either an herb or a spice:
   A. basil
   B. cinnamon
   C. curry
   D. tarragon
   E. thyme

5. Identify the following recipes as either a marinade or a rub:
   A. olive oil, lemon juice, oregano, garlic, and pepper
   B. soy sauce, ginger, sesame oil, brown sugar, and garlic
   C. brown sugar, paprika, garlic powder, onion powder, cayenne pepper, and dry mustard

6. True or false. Cornmeal and cornstarch are the interchangeable food products.

7. How does brown sugar differ from white?

8. List three roles acid ingredients have in cookery.

9. Which ingredient has a more concentrated tomato flavor—tomato purée or tomato paste?

10. List two cuisines that commonly use soy sauce as a seasoning.

11. What is the acid ingredient typically used to pickle vegetables?

Core Skills

12. **Math.** Arrowroot is approximately three times the cost of cornstarch and cornstarch is approximately five times the cost of flour. If cornstarch is $1.50 per pound, calculate the price per pound for arrowroot and flour.

13. **Writing.** Saffron is the world's most expensive spice. Write an informative paper that explains where it comes from, its history, dishes in which it is used, and current pricing.

14. **Speaking.** Trace the history of a food-related expression such as "worth one's salt." Use presentation software to share your findings with the class.

15. **Reading.** Read a book about the history of the spice trade. Write a brief review of the book and share with the class.

16. **Math.** If the tomato juice your restaurant is purchasing contains 8% tomato solids, how much tomato solids would be in a 500 gram glass of tomato juice

17. **CTE Career Readiness Practice.** Research one of the kitchen staples discussed in this chapter. What are its origins? How is this ingredient commonly used? What is an appropriate substitute? Provide a recipe that includes this ingredient. Use presentation software to share your findings with the class in an oral report. Have a classmate video your presentation so you can review it to identify opportunities to improve your presentation skills.

Critical Thinking

18. **Evaluate.** Choose several recipes and discuss whether dried and fresh herbs can be interchanged without affecting the quality of the final product.

19. **Judge.** Compare the cost of sugar, honey, maple syrup, and corn syrup from the school's purveyor. How might this affect where and when each sweetener might be used?

20. **Compare.** Cilantro and coriander both come from the same plant. Compare their uses, differences, and similarities.

21. **Analyze.** Suppose you have been hired to run a restaurant in a small resort located in the mountains. Due to the remote location, you receive food deliveries only once a week. Additionally, the kitchen has very limited refrigerated storage. How would these factors affect your kitchen staples purchasing decisions? Share your reasoning.

Technology

Black pepper grows in India, as well as some other countries. During the Middle Ages, it was a precious spice partly because of the journey it made. If you lived in Madrid, Spain during the Middle Ages, how many miles would the pepper have to travel to reach you from Mumbai, India? Find a map of the spice trade routes on the Internet. Trace the route the pepper would have travelled to reach Madrid. What bodies of water and types of terrains does this route include?

Teamwork

Working in small groups, develop an experiment to investigate how using dry versus fresh herbs impacts a food preparation. Be sure to include your purpose, hypothesis, list of equipment and supplies, procedure, data and observations, and conclusion. Share your experiment and findings with the class.

Chef's E-portfolio
Presentation Video

Effective presentation skills are important to your success in a career. Upload the video of your class presentation from activity #17 to your e-portfolio. This video can be used as a yardstick to measure how you grow and improve as a speaker in the future. Ask your instructor where to save your file. This could be on the school's network or a flash drive of your own. Name your portfolio document *FirstnameLastname_Portfolio Ch#.docx* (i.e., JohnSmith_PortfolioCh17.docx).

While studying, look for the activity icon [➜] to:

- Build vocabulary with e-flash cards and matching activities.
- Expand learning with video clips, photo identification activities, animations, and interactive activities.
- Review and assess what you learn by completing end-of-chapter questions.

dotshock/Shutterstock.com

Cooking Principles 18

Reading Prep

In preparation for reading the chapter, find a full-service restaurant menu online and print it off. As you read the chapter, identify the cooking method used for each menu item.

Culinary Terminology
Build Vocab

cooking, p. 285
gelatinization, p. 287
caramelization, p. 287
sautéing, p. 289
sweating, p. 289
panfrying, p. 289
deep frying, p. 289
grilling, p. 290
broiling, p. 290
gratiner, p. 290
roasting, p. 290
baking, p. 290
poaching, p. 291
simmering, p. 292
boiling, p. 293
steaming, p. 293
braising, p. 293

Academic Terminology
Build Vocab

conduction, p. 288
convection, p. 288
radiation, p. 288

Objectives

After studying this chapter, you will be able to

- understand the reasons food is cooked.

- explain what happens to food when it is cooked and overcooked.

- classify various methods of cooking by the process of heat transfer.

- explain basic cooking methods.

Understanding the basic science involved in the cooking process will make you a better cook. The knowledge of how heat is applied and affects various food products allows chefs to be more flexible. They are better prepared to adapt to unfamiliar cooking appliances or new foods. Identifying cooking methods correctly is important when communicating in the kitchen or writing recipes and menus. In this chapter, various cooking processes are identified and explained.

What Is Cooking?

Cooking is the process of preparing food for eating by applying heat. Soon after prehistoric man harnessed fire, cooking was possible. Food was placed on or near the fire with dramatic results. The act of cooking food was an important step in the development of the human race. The ability to cook food meant a longer, healthier life. Foods are cooked for several reasons.

- *Cooked food is safer to eat.* The most important reason for cooking is food safety. As you have learned, heat kills microorganisms that cause spoilage and illness.

- *Cooked food is more digestible.* The fibrous structure of vegetables and connective tissues in meats are broken down when cooked. The cooking process makes it easier for the human body to extract nutrients from many foods.

- *The texture, taste, aroma, and appearance of foods are improved.* Cooking adds variety and interest to food, 18-1. Food products take on different appearances, flavors, aromas, and textures based on how they are cooked.

What Happens to Foods When They Are Cooked?

What happens to the raw food product when heat is applied? Understanding what heat does to the different elements of food is key to understanding the cooking process and becoming a better chef.

Bochkarev Photography/Shutterstock.com
18-1 Roasting enhances the appeal of this dish.

Microorganisms Are Destroyed

Most bacteria, fungi, and molds are killed at temperatures above 135°F (57.2°C). Most foods are cooked to temperatures higher than this. Once food is cooked to the appropriate temperature, it must be held at or above 135°F to keep it safe. This temperature is key to ensuring that foods are safe when cooked by any of the methods discussed in this chapter.

Connective Tissue in Meats Breaks Down

Heat is necessary to make tough pieces of meat and poultry tender and easier to eat. Connective tissues are the tough fibers that hold muscles together. Much of the connective tissue in meat becomes tender when it is properly cooked.

Proteins Coagulate

When proteins are heated, many solidify or become firm. This is called *coagulation*. Coagulation is the reason the texture of many foods change when cooked. Consider the difference in texture between raw and cooked chicken breast or the difference between raw and cooked egg.

Fibers in Vegetables Break Down

The fibers that make up the cell structure of most plants are broken down with heat. This makes cooked vegetables tender and releases certain nutrients.

Starches Absorb Liquid

Starches such as flour and cornstarch are used to thicken liquids such as sauces and soups. Many starches must be heated in order for the thickening process to take place.

When starches combine with hot liquid, they absorb the liquid like a sponge and swell in a process called gelatinization. This process is used in many preparations in the kitchen and bakeshop.

Flavors Blend and Change

The most obvious change when raw food is cooked is the change in flavor. Flavor changes in foods happen in several ways. The most common flavor change is the caramelization of sugars. Caramelization is the browning that occurs when sugars are heated, resulting in a richer, more complex aroma and flavor. Sugars are found in some quantity in most ingredients; they are the building block for starches.

The flavors of proteins are also changed by heat. Amino acids which make up proteins change when heated, creating new flavors.

Not only does cooking change the flavor of foods, it also helps to blend or marry the flavors of multiple ingredients. Consider the way a combination of meat, vegetables, spices, and seasonings in a long-simmered stew creates a single flavor, 18-2.

Effects of Overcooking

While the application of heat to food causes many favorable changes, the cooking process must be done to the proper degree. Monitoring timing and temperature is essential to achieve the proper degree of doneness. When foods are cooked to excessive temperatures or for too long, the following problems may occur:
- Texture is destroyed and foods become mushy and disintegrate, or tough and stringy.
- Proteins can curdle or toughen.
- Moisture is lost and foods become dry.
- Sugars burn, causing foods to taste bitter.
- Green vegetables lose their color and become brown.
- Nutrients are lost or destroyed.

margouillat photo/Shutterstock.com

18-2 The flavors of a variety of foods combine to produce a single rich flavor in this stew.

Methods of Heat Transfer

The transfer of heat to food products is the essence of cooking. How heat is transferred to the food has a distinct effect on how the finished product turns out. Different appliances and utensils transfer heat in different manners. Consider the difference in taste and appearance between a chicken cooked on a rotisserie and one simmered in liquid. Understanding how heat energy is conveyed is the key to distinguishing between different cooking methods. Cooking methods use conduction, convection, or radiation to transfer heat to food.

Conduction

Conduction is the transfer of heat energy from one object to another through direct contact. Heat energy travels through solid substances from one molecule to adjacent molecules by means of the vibration of electrons. This is much the same way electricity travels through a wire.

In cooking, heat is conducted from the heating element through pots and pans to the food. The material the pot or pan is made of determines how well it conducts heat. Copper is an excellent conductor, while ceramic is a relatively poor conductor. The food product itself can be a conductor. Heat is transferred from the outside of the product to the inside. This is particularly evident when cooking a large roast.

Convection

Convection is the manner in which heat energy travels through liquids and gases. Natural convection occurs when warm air (a gas) rises to the top of an oven or when warmer liquid rises to the top of a pot. The cooler air or liquid descends to the bottom and creates a circular flow.

By mechanically circulating the gas or liquid, the transfer of heat can be sped up. This is done when a convection oven circulates air with a fan. Another example is when a pot of liquid is stirred.

Radiation

Radiation is the transfer of heat energy through waves. No conductor is necessary to cook with radiation. The glowing flames of a broiler, for example, transfer heat to food being cooked by means of radiation.

Microwaves also cook food by radiation, though not heat radiation. In microwave cooking, microwaves pass through the food causing the water molecules in the food to heat.

Nutrition Connection

Healthy Cooking Techniques

Cooking techniques can affect the nutrient content of food. For instance, deep frying at high temperatures can destroy heat-sensitive vitamins. Frying also adds calories and fat. Choose roasting, baking, grilling, broiling, poaching, sautéing, braising, steaming, and stir-frying instead. These healthier cooking alternatives help retain important nutrients and avoid unwanted fat and calories.

Cooking Methods

Methods used to cook in the professional kitchen can be classified as dry-heat methods, moist-heat methods, or combination methods. Combination methods of cooking combine both dry heat and moist heat in the same recipe. These methods can produce some of the most flavorful and complex dishes in the professional kitchen. The various cooking methods transfer heat to food by conduction, convection, or radiation. Some cooking methods transfer heat using two or more of these.

Dry-Heat Methods

Dry-heat methods transfer heat to food by conduction, hot air convection, or radiation. Many dry-heat methods begin with a high temperature to create browning and improve flavor, 18-3. Although these methods may use higher temperatures, they do not break down fibers or connective tissues as well as moist methods. For this reason, dry-heat cooking methods are most often used with tender products. Dry-heat cooking methods include sautéing, panfrying, deep frying, grilling, broiling, roasting, and baking.

Sautéing Quickly cooking an item in a small amount of hot fat over high heat is

Dry-Heat Cooking Temperatures

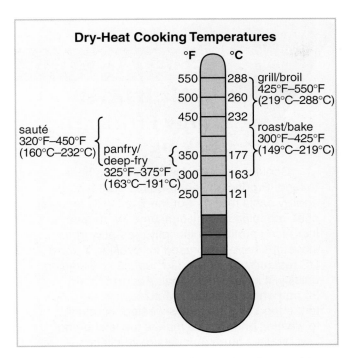

18-3 The temperatures used for dry-heating cooking vary depending on the method used.

called **sautéing**. This method requires only enough fat to coat the bottom of the pan. In French, the word *sauté* means "to jump." Often sautéed items are tossed or made to jump in the pan to flip them. Though sautéing is traditionally done in a sauteuse, it can also be done on a griddle or in a wok. Meat, poultry, seafood, vegetables, and starches can all be sautéed. Foods to be sautéed are cut in small, uniform pieces. Larger cuts of meat are generally cut into pieces before sautéing. Sautéing transfers heat by conduction.

The Asian technique of stir-frying is similar to sautéing. Small, evenly cut pieces of food are cooked quickly in a small amount of fat. Stir-frying is typically done in a wok rather than a sauteuse. As with sautéing, the pieces of food are regularly stirred or tossed for even cooking.

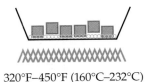

320°F–450°F (160°C–232°C)

Animation

Home cookbooks often instruct the cook to "sauté items over a low heat." A culinarian refers to this as sweating. **Sweating** is cooking food in a small amount of fat using low heat in order to soften the food without browning. Sweating is typically used with onions, mirepoix, and garlic. The browning brought about by the higher heat of sautéing changes the flavor and appearance of these ingredients and, therefore, impacts the finished dish as well.

Panfrying   Panfrying, like sautéing, uses hot fat to cook a food item. However, **panfrying** cooks the food in enough hot fat to cover it halfway. The food is turned during the cooking process in order to cook both sides evenly. Panfrying may also be called *shallow-fat frying*. Large or thick pieces of meat, fish, or poultry may be panfried and then finished in the oven. Heat is transferred to the food primarily by conduction with this method.

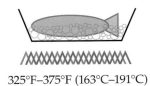

325°F–375°F (163°C–191°C)

Animation

Deep Frying   **Deep frying** is a method that cooks food in enough hot fat to fully cover the item. Enough fat must be used to ensure proper cooking. If too little is used, it is difficult to maintain the fat's high temperature when food is added for cooking. The result from deep-frying in fat that is not consistently hot enough is a finished product that is limp and greasy rather than crisp. Most deep-fried foods are coated with flour, breading, or batter before being fried. This method transfers heat by convection.

Deep frying on the stovetop is dangerous and should be avoided. Deep frying is best

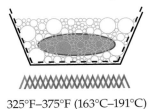

325°F–375°F (163°C–191°C)

Animation

done in a deep-fat fryer, an appliance that precisely regulates the temperature of the fat.

Grilling   **Grilling** is a cooking method that uses radiation from a heat source located below the food. A metal grate holds the food over the heat source. Grilled foods can be cooked over a variety of heat sources; gas flames, electric burners, charcoal, or hard woods are all commonly used in commercial kitchens. Juices dripping from the food being grilled into the heat source create smoke, which adds flavor to the food. Grilling is a popular cooking method because of the robust flavor the cooking process imparts. It is also a healthy way to cook because melted fat from the food drips away during cooking.

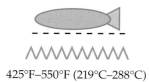

425°F–550°F (219°C–288°C)

Animation

Broiling   **Broiling** uses radiation from a heat source located above the food. The food being cooked is placed on a pan or a grate and then placed under the heat source. The heat for broiling is usually intense in order to sear or brown the food.

Often broiling is used as a finishing process to brown cooked foods. **Gratiner** (grah tehn AY) means to brown a food product. Product can also be gratinéed in a hot oven. Browned foods are often described by the French term *au gratin* (OH grah tehn).

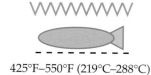

425°F–550°F (219°C–288°C)

Animation

Roasting   Originally, roasting was done by turning meat placed on a spit or skewer over the radiant heat of a fire. Today, most roasting is done in the oven. **Roasting** is a method that cooks a food by surrounding it with hot air. During roasting, the food is uncovered so any moisture released can evaporate. The product to be roasted is often

cooked on a rack so air can circulate evenly on all sides and fat can drip away.

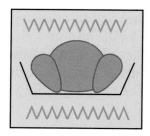

300°F–425°F (149°C–219°C)

Animation

Baking   Similar to roasting, baking is done in the oven. However, **baking** is the method used to cook foods with a certain amount of added moisture. The moisture might be stock, sauce, or custard. Baked products are often cooked covered to keep the moisture in the product.

The subtle difference between baking and roasting is often important when

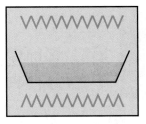

300°F–425°F (149°C–219°C)

Animation

describing foods in menus or recipes. For example, a pork loin (cooked in the oven uncovered) would be described as *roasted*, while lasagna (with the moisture of a sauce) would be described as *baked*. Both baking and roasting use a combination of convection and radiation to transfer heat to foods.

Some products that require a gentle heat are baked in a water bath. To make a water bath, use a container that is larger than the pan holding the food. Partially fill the container with water. Place the pan of food inside the container of water and place in the oven. The water bath regulates the heat so the product cooks very slowly. Baking in a water bath is also called baking *au bain marie* (oh bay mahr EE).

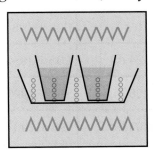

Animation

Moist-Heat Methods

Moist-heat methods use liquid or steam in the cooking process. It envelops and penetrates food products during the cooking process. Even at lower temperatures, moisture is more effective at heat transfer than air. For example, you could easily reach your bare hand into an oven heated to 350°F (177°C), but you would never dream of sticking your hand into a pot of liquid simmering at 180°F (82°C). Moist methods are best used for tougher cuts of meats and fibrous vegetables.

Each of the following moist-heat methods has a specific temperature range, 18-4. The temperatures are noted here to provide a point of comparison. Professionals rarely need to use a thermometer to judge the temperature of a cooking liquid. The motion and appearance of the cooking liquid is an accurate indicator of its temperature. When using moist-cooking methods, observe how rapidly the liquid bubbles.

Poaching   Cooking food in a liquid at a relatively low temperature is called **poaching**. The liquid used is often flavored. Poaching is used for delicate products that might fall apart if cooked at a higher temperature. The temperature range for poaching is 160°F to 180°F (71°C to 82°C). At the proper temperature, the liquid for poaching barely moves and some small bubbles occasionally break the surface. The poaching liquid transfers heat to the food by convection.

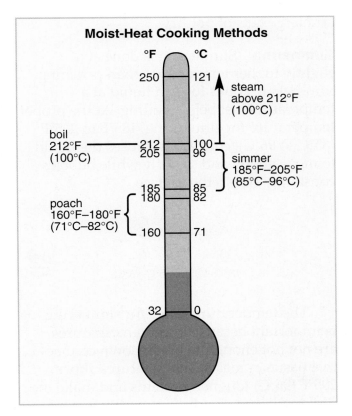

18-4 Moist-heat methods employ lower temperatures for cooking than dry-heat methods.

A properly poached product maintains its shape and delicate texture. Its taste is enhanced by the flavor of the poaching liquid.

There are two distinct techniques for poaching—shallow poaching and deep poaching. With shallow poaching, a small amount of liquid, usually stock, is used. The liquid is often not enough to cover the product halfway. When the poaching is complete, the liquid in which the food was poached, has a concentrated flavor. That liquid is then used to create a sauce.

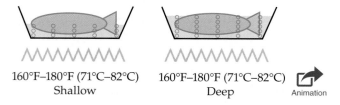

160°F–180°F (71°C–82°C)　　160°F–180°F (71°C–82°C)
　　Shallow　　　　　　　　　　　　Deep
　　　　　　　　　　　　　　　　　　　　Animation

With deep poaching, enough liquid is used to fully cover the product being cooked. The liquid used for deep poaching is not used to create a sauce. Deep poaching is often used for items such as eggs, whole fish, and large cuts of poultry.

Simmering　Simmering is done at a slightly higher temperature than poaching. **Simmering** cooks food in liquid at a temperature just below boiling. At the proper temperature for simmering, 185°F to 205°F (85°C to 96°C), convection causes the liquid to move gently and steadily while bubbles constantly rise to the surface.

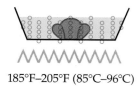

185°F–205°F (85°C–96°C)
　　　　　　　　　　　Animation

The temperature range for simmering is important because lower temperatures are not hot enough to break down connective tissue in meats. Temperatures above 205°F (96°C) toughen proteins and make the cooking liquid cloudy. Simmering is used to make stocks and broths as well as for cooking tough cuts of meat and poultry.

SCIENCE & TECHNOLOGY

The Atmosphere for Moist Cooking

Moist cooking is dependent on atmosphere. The atmospheric pressure surrounding the cooking process has an impact on heat transfer. There are two situations that require adjustment to cooking times due to atmospheric pressures—boiling at altitudes above sea level and cooking with steam under pressure. When boiling at high altitudes, water changes to steam at a lower temperature, therefore, boiled items usually take longer to cook to compensate for the lower temperature.

Altitude	Boiling temperature
Sea level	212°F (100°C)
1,000 ft. (305 m)	210°F (99°C)
2,000 ft. (610 m)	208°F (98°C)
5,000 ft. (1524 m)	203°F (95°C)
7,500 ft. (2286 m)	198°F (92°C)
10,000 ft. (3048 m)	194°F (90°C)

When steam is put under pressure in a pressure steamer or pressure cooker, the gas becomes denser and holds more heat energy. Items cooked under pressure take much less time to cook. Pressure is measured in *pounds per square inch (psi)*.

Amount of pressure	Temperature of steam
5 psi	220°F (105°C)
10 psi	235°F (115°C)
15 psi	250°F (120°C)

Boiling Boiling is cooking in liquid at its highest possible temperature. At sea level, water boils at 212°F (100°C). Boiling liquids move rapidly creating a vigorous rolling motion and large bubbles, transferring heat to the food by convection. If liquids are heated above 212°F, they will turn to steam.

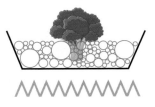

Animation

212°F (100°C)

Boiling should not be used for protein foods such as meat, poultry, eggs, or fish because the higher temperature makes them tough. Many so-called "boiled" dishes are actually simmered. Boiling is most often used for vegetables, starches, and grains.

Steaming Steaming is a moist method that cooks a food product by surrounding it with steam vapor. The temperature of steam is hotter than boiling water. Steaming can be done in a covered pot with food placed on a rack above boiling liquid. Steam vapor rises and surrounds the product being cooked.

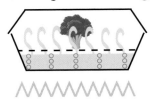

Animation

above 212°F (100°C)

Steaming may also be done in a steamer or steam oven. These appliances create steam and then direct the vapor at the food through jets. Some steamers use a fan to create a more rapid convection. Pressure steamers use a tightly sealed compartment with pressurized steam for even greater heat transfer. The heat energy contained in steam vapor increases greatly under pressure.

Combination Methods

Once you understand the process and reason for dry and moist techniques, you can more easily understand combination methods. Combination cooking methods apply both dry-and moist-heat techniques to the same food.

Braising The process of braising combines browning and simmering. When braising, first the food is browned on all sides, usually in a small amount of fat. Next, liquid is added and then it is simmered. Braising has the advantage of being able to tenderize tough cuts of meat or poultry like simmering. It also has the richer flavor and color of sautéed items.

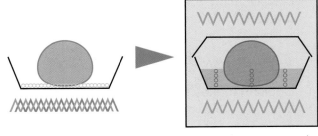

Animation

The first part of the braising process is usually done on the stovetop over high heat in a small amount of fat. After the product is browned, liquid is added and brought to a simmer. The item is covered and may then be cooked either on the stovetop or in the oven. The cooking liquid from a braised dish is typically rich in flavor and is often used to make a sauce to accompany the braised item.

Stewing Strictly speaking, stewing is not a unique cooking method. Either the braising or simmering technique can be used to make a stew. Stews are different from braised or simmered dishes because the ingredients are cut in smaller pieces. The ingredients for a stew cook in enough liquid for them to float freely during the cooking process. The slow simmering of a stew is excellent for combining the flavors of many different ingredients in one dish.

Animation

Summary Points

- Food is cooked to make it safer to eat, easier to digest, and more appetizing.
- Understanding how heat impacts the different elements of food will make you a better chef.
- Heat can be transferred by conduction, convection, or radiation.
- Cooking methods can be classified as dry, moist, or combination methods. Within each classification, the heat may be transferred to the food in different ways.

In Review
Assess

1. Cooking makes foods safer to eat because it kills _____ that cause spoilage and illness.
2. True or false. When proteins are heated, they caramelize, which changes their texture.
3. _____ allows starches to absorb liquids.
4. Identify the method of heat transfer in the following cooking methods:
   A. broiling
   B. simmering
   C. roasting
   D. sautéing
5. Identify the following as dry-, moist-, or combination-cooking methods:
   A. grilling
   B. poaching
   C. braising
   D. stewing
6. Explain how panfrying and deep frying differ.
7. Au gratin potatoes get their name from gratiner, which means to _____ a food.
8. Identify if you would bake or roast the following items:
   A. tuna casserole
   B. whole turkey
   C. leg of lamb
9. True or false. Professionals can judge the temperature of cooking liquid by observing how rapidly the liquid bubbles.
10. Braising is a combination of which two cooking methods?

Core Skills

11. **Math.** Pressure cooking methods can reduce cooking time to as little as one-third the time as nonpressurized methods. If a food product usually requires 1¼ hours to cook, how long would it take to cook using a pressure cooking method? (Round your answer to the nearest whole minute.)

12. **Reading.** Read a book about the history of food and cooking. Prepare a summary of the theories as to how and why people started cooking food.

13. **Speaking.** The microwave is one of the most used kitchen appliances in the home. Prepare an electronic presentation about how a microwave works and its proper use. How is the radiation generated? How does the radiation heat food? Why is there a turntable in many microwaves? What types of foods can be cooked in a microwave? Be sure to address any safety considerations. Share your presentation with the class.

14. **Math.** A chef must be able to produce all the dishes for a particular table at the same time. Suppose the guests at a table order the following entrées:
    - sautéed chicken dish (10 minutes to prepare)
    - poached salmon dish (12 minutes to prepare)
    - braised beef dish (20 minutes to reheat)
    - vegetable stir-fry (5 minutes to prepare)

    Using the preparation times given in parentheses, when should the chef instruct each cook to start making their dish? Assume the chef wants the food ready to serve to the table at 6:10 p.m.

15. **CTE Career Readiness Practice.** The director of the food pantry at which you volunteer asks you to prepare an informational handout to send home with the clients. The director gives the following guidelines for preparing the handout:

- explains a cooking method that is effective with low-cost ingredients
- written in a style appropriate to the purpose and the audience
- lists foods on which this cooking method can be used
- promotes healthful eating
- includes one or more suggested recipes

Critical Thinking

16. **Compare.** What differences in the cooking process and final product might you observe between grilling and broiling a boneless breast of chicken?

17. **Assess.** Should printed menus describe the cooking method used for different dishes? Why?

18. **Relate.** Some chefs determine the doneness of a steak by touch. Steaks that are softer to the touch are more rare and those that are firmer to the touch are more well done. What happens during the cooking process that would explain why this method works?

19. **Analyze.** In previous centuries, eating meat was considered a privilege and was quite expensive. Often times, older work animals were consumed at the end of their lives. Why was it that simmering, braising, and stewing were commonly used for these animals?

Technology

Pressure cooking is an increasingly popular way of cooking as it shortens cooking times dramatically. Learn about how a pressure cooker works. How has this technology been improved in recent years? What types of foods can be cooked in a pressure cooker? Prepare a brief summary of your findings to share with the class.

Teamwork

Working in small teams, perform a lab to compare different dry-heat cooking methods on chicken. Select three boneless, skinless chicken breasts of similar size and shape. Each chicken breast must be cooked to an internal temperature of 165°F (74°C) using a different dry-heat cooking method such as sautéing, grilling, and baking. As a group, evaluate each finished product and record your observations on appearance, flavor, tenderness, and moisture. This experiment can be expanded to include other cooking methods.

Chef's E-portfolio
Cooking Method Handout

Ability to assess an audience and adjust your writing style for effective communication is an important workplace skill to master. Upload the handout from activity #15 to your e-portfolio. Ask your instructor where to save your file. This could be on the school's network or a flash drive of your own. Name your portfolio document *FirstnameLastname_Portfolio Ch#.docx* (i.e., JohnSmith_PortfolioCh18.docx).

Unit Three

Ingredients, Preparation, and Presentation

Marie C Fields/Shutterstock.com

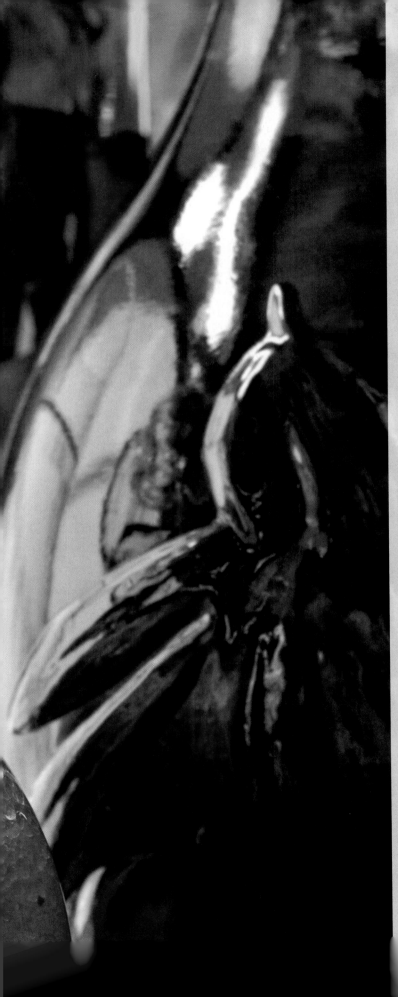

The Science of Consistency—
Suspensions, Emulsions, Foams

Consistency is largely the result of reducing the ability of water molecules to move freely in a food product. Chefs employ this strategy to thicken foods and create appealing mouthfeel. When food particles, oil droplets, or even air bubbles are introduced into a food, they restrict the water molecules' freedom. The water molecules are unable to flow very far before they bump into an obstacle (food particle, oil droplet, or bubble) and are slowed down.

When food particles are used to change a preparation's consistency, it is called a *suspension*. For instance, when cooked tomatoes are puréed to make sauce for spaghetti, this is an example of a suspension. When oil is the substance added, the thickened product is called an *emulsion*. An emulsion has a natural inclination to separate out to its original parts. This can be prevented by either rapid mixing or the addition of another ingredient called an *emulsifier*. Emulsifiers act to hold the emulsion together. A vinaigrette is a very visual example of an emulsion—you can see the science in action. Introduce gas bubbles to cream and a much-beloved *foam*—whipped cream—is created. Edible foams in food preparations can be created by adding air, steam, carbon dioxide, and even nitrous oxide.

1. List three additions that can be used to change the consistency of a food.

2. Differentiate between suspensions, emulsions, and foams.

While studying, look for the activity icon ⬈ to:

- Build vocabulary with e-flash cards and matching activities.
- Expand learning with video clips, photo identification activities, animations, and interactive activities.
- Review and assess what you learn by completing end-of-chapter questions.

Reading Prep

In preparation for reading the chapter, visit the USDA Fruit and Vegetable Market News Portal. Use the Retail report function to compare lettuce prices across a number of months. Does the price fluctuate much? As you read this chapter, consider how these prices fluctuations might affect a foodservice operation.

Culinary Terminology
Build Vocab

simple salad, p. 300
composed salad, p. 301
bound salad, p. 302
marinated salad, p. 302
mesclun, p. 305
vinaigrette, p. 308
pasteurize, p. 310
mayonnaise, p. 310

Academic Terminology
Build Vocab

palate, p. 308
emulsion, p. 308

Objectives

After studying this chapter, you will be able to

- recognize the different purposes salads serve on a menu.
- classify the different types of salads.
- recognize common salad greens.
- explain various factors involved when buying lettuce.

- execute the preparation of salad greens.
- compare and contrast the three salad dressings—simple vinaigrette, mayonnaise, and emulsified dressing.
- recall standard procedures that will ensure both sanitation and quality in salad preparation.

In a professional kitchen, salads and dressings represent a large part of the work assigned to the garde manger or cold station. This area may also be called the *pantry*. Salads take a starring role in the trend toward lighter eating. No longer just an appetizer, many salads can be served as main courses and sides. With a nearly limitless list of ingredients and dressings, salad possibilities can go as far as imagination and good taste will carry them.

Salads on the Menu

Salads are a popular part of the American diet and can serve a number of purposes on the menu.

Appetizer

Traditionally, salads appeared in the appetizer section of the menu. As an appetizer, the salad would be served before the main course of a meal. Salads are light and refreshing and therefore a good lead-in for the more substantial foods that follow. The quick preparation of salads also makes them an easy way to keep diners satisfied while their main courses are being prepared.

Main Course

Salads have gained an even more important purpose on the menu with the rising popularity of main course salads. Green salads paired with portions of cooked chicken, seafood, or meat are a great way for chefs to create lighter entrées, 19-1. Extremely popular on lunch menus, these main course salads may combine hot and cold elements on the same plate.

Salad Bars

Salads bars or buffets have become a fixture in American casual dining and fast-food restaurants. They are popular with diners because they offer variety, choice, and custom-salad creations. Restaurant operators find salad bars attractive because the ingredients are relatively low cost and the self-serve format saves labor costs.

The key to a successful salad bar is a large variety of attractively displayed ingredients, 19-2. Salad bars should be

Draz-Koetke/Goodheart-Willcox Publisher

19-2 An attractively displayed salad bar appeals to customers.

designed for easy access while still maintaining sanitary conditions. Maintaining the proper temperature of food on display is essential.

Types of Salads

Salads take on many different appearances. However, all salads can be categorized as one of three main types—simple, composed, or bound.

Simple

Simple salad is a term used to classify a salad of greens and various raw vegetables such as cucumbers, carrots, tomatoes, and others. A mixture of ingredients providing a variety of flavors, colors, and textures is desirable for simple salads.

Simple salads may be served with any type of dressing. The dressings can be either tossed with the salad or served on the side. Tossing simple salads with dressing too far in advance causes the salad, especially delicate

Getman/Shutterstock.com

19-1 A chicken Caesar salad is a popular main course salad.

Culture & Cuisine

Salad for Dessert

American diners are accustomed to eating their salad as an appetizer course, which is served before the main course of a meal. However, in Europe, it is typical to serve the salad after the main course. Historically, salad has played the role of aiding digestion and, therefore is served after the main course but before dessert.

greens, to wilt. For this reason, salads served at banquets are typically presented with the dressing on the side.

Composed

When salad ingredients are assembled in a particular arrangement, the finished salad is called a **composed salad**. Also known as *plated salads*, they are often made up of more than simply greens. These salads are popular as main courses, especially at lunch. Whatever the ingredients, composed salads usually include the following four parts:

- *Base.* Usually lettuce leaves or a bed of cut greens is used as the backdrop for the other ingredients.

- *Body.* The main ingredient of the salad might be greens, a marinated or bound salad, meat, fish, or poultry.

- *Dressing.* Any dressing that is compatible with the other ingredients may be used to add moisture and flavor to the salad.

- *Garnish.* Many different elements can be used to add color and texture to the finished presentation.

Bound

An almost endless list of cooked foods can be turned into salads. Salads provide a way for a creative chef to use up leftovers. These salads can be made of any complementary combination of vegetables, meats, poultry, seafood, cheese, potatoes, pasta, or grains.

When cooked items are mixed with mayonnaise, it is referred to as a **bound salad**. The thick, binding consistency of a proper mayonnaise acts to hold the salad together. Ingredients other than mayonnaise such as Greek yogurt can be used to bind the ingredients. When cooked foods are mixed with a vinaigrette, it is commonly called a **marinated salad**, 19-3.

Common Salad Greens

Salad greens come in a variety of shapes, colors, textures, and flavors. Chefs must be familiar with the various greens when planning menus and purchasing.

Draz-Koetke/Goodheart-Willcox Publisher

19-3 Marinated salads like this colorful pasta salad are dressed with vinaigrettes.

Salad Greens

Iceberg Lettuce

Iceberg lettuce is by far the most popular variety of lettuce in the United States. Its crisp leaves, round shape, and tightly packed head make it easy to pack and ship. These traits result in a relatively long shelf life. Most of the head is comprised of crisp pale green leaves with a mild, sweet, refreshing flavor.

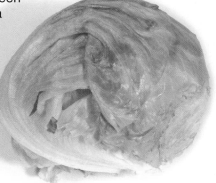

Romaine Lettuce (Cos)

Romaine has leaves with crisp ribs that make it sturdy and give this lettuce a distinctive crunch. The crisp ribs are surrounded by tender leaves which range in color from dark green outer leaves to pale yellow inner leaves. It has an elongated head with round-tipped leaves. Quality heads have tightly packed leaves with few or no blemishes on the tips or rust on the root end.

Escarole (Broad Leaf Endive)

Escarole is a loose, relatively crisp head with flat leaves that have curly tips or edges. Leaves are dark green at the tip to yellowish white at the base and in the core of the head. A lettuce with a slight bitter flavor, it is often prepared as a hot vegetable in Italian cookery.

Curly Endive (Curly Chicory)

Curly endive has crisp ribs that create narrow leaves with a curly edge. The outer leaves are deep green with a pale yellow core. This bitter green is usually served as part of a mixture to provide contrasting flavor and texture.

(Continued)

Salad Greens (Continued)

Belgian Endive (Witloof Chicory)

Belgian endive has a tightly packed, elongated head with a pointed tip. Heads are approximately five inches long. Leaves are white with yellow tips. Belgian endive has a bitter flavor with a slight sweetness. Individual leaves are often used as a garnish or filled and served as a cold appetizer.

Boston Lettuce (Butterhead)

The soft green leaves of this lettuce form a loose head with creamy-colored inner leaves. The leaves have a delicate texture and cupped shape that makes Boston lettuce popular as a salad base as well as in mixed salads.

Leaf Lettuce (Green Leaf Lettuce)

Large, tender, ruffled bunches of bright green color make leaf lettuce good in salads and as a liner for plates and platters. With a mild flavor, the supple leaves also work well for sandwiches.

Bibb Lettuce (Limestone Lettuce)

Bibb lettuce is a variety that was developed in Kentucky. It has a color and texture similar to Boston lettuce but forms a smaller head. Heads are elongated and small enough that one head is often served as a single portion.

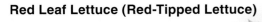

Red Leaf Lettuce (Red-Tipped Lettuce)

Red leaf lettuce has the same texture and flavor as green leaf lettuce but with reddish-brown color at the tip of the leaves. It is often added to salad mixes for contrasting color.

(Continued)

Salad Greens (Continued)

Spinach

The smaller, tender leaves of spinach are best for salads. Spinach can be purchased in bunches or cello pack. Cello pack means the spinach is packaged in plastic bags. In either form, fibrous stems should be removed and leaves should be washed several times to remove dirt and grit.

Watercress

Although watercress is the classic plate garnish for red meats, it is often used in salads. Prized for its peppery flavor, it has small round leaves attached to long stems. Thicker stems should be removed before serving.

Radicchio

A red lettuce with white stems and veins, radicchio is an Italian variety of chicory. It has a bitter flavor; so small amounts are added to mixed greens for a dramatic colorful accent.

Mesclun

Sometimes referred to as *spring mix* or *field greens*, **mesclun** is a mixture of baby lettuces. It is often purchased cut, washed, mixed, and ready to use. Mesclun should contain an attractive variety of textures, colors, and flavors.

Sprouts

Seeds or beans, which are soaked in water, begin to grow as sprouts. These tender little shoots of various plants are used as an ingredient in salads. The most popular sprouts are from alfalfa, bean (mung beans), radishes, and mustard. Unfortunately, sprouts are grown in a high moisture and high temperature environment which is perfect for bacterial growth. Therefore, great care should be taken when handling sprouts to reduce the risk of foodborne illness.

Buying Lettuce

Of all produce items, none is more subject to fluctuations in quality and price than lettuce. Factors such as growing conditions, weather, and market demand make buying lettuce a complicated matter. Produce wholesalers can choose from a wide range of quality and cost for the most popular lettuces. The lowest priced lettuce is not always the best buy, 19-4.

Most lettuce comes packed 24 heads to a case instead of by standard weight. It is important to determine how much product will be lost from trimming away wilted, bruised, or rusted leaves. The amount of waste affects the actual cost of the lettuce.

A reputable produce supplier will help you determine the product and price that is a value for your operation.

Ready-to-Eat Greens

One choice for chefs and restaurateurs that continues to grow in popularity is ready-to-eat greens. Sold prewashed and precut, these products are significantly more expensive than traditionally packed greens. The advantage of no prep time and no waste often makes up for the higher cost. Stock of prepared lettuce should be rotated and consumed quickly since cut and washed greens loose flavor, texture, and nutrients more rapidly than uncut.

Draz-Koetke/Goodheart-Willcox Publisher

19-4 Lettuce should be inspected for quality before accepting delivery.

SCIENCE & TECHNOLOGY

Hydroponic Greens

A viable option for commercially growing lettuce and herbs today is hydroponics. Hydroponics is the science of growing produce in a nutrient-rich water bath rather than in soil. Hydroponic produce is grown indoors, often under artificial light. Though hydroponic items have a milder flavor than field-grown products, they contain no dirt, insects, or pesticides. Hydroponic produce is also available year-round.

Preparing Salad Greens

If your operation does not purchase ready-to-eat greens, the greens must be prepared for salads before use. Each step is important in order to produce a quality salad.

Cutting

When lettuces and other greens are received in whole heads, the first step in preparation is trimming and cutting. This step is done first so that dirt or insects lodged in the core of the lettuce are more easily removed during the washing process.

Lettuce and greens should be trimmed of any whole or partial leaves that are wilted or discolored. Remove the cores on head lettuce, 19-5. The thick fibrous stems from leafy greens must also be removed.

Cut the lettuce into bite-size pieces. In most cases, the pieces should be small enough that the diner does not have to use a knife to cut his or her salad. Some cooks maintain the belief that salad greens should be torn by hand rather than cut. This belief probably originates in a time when all

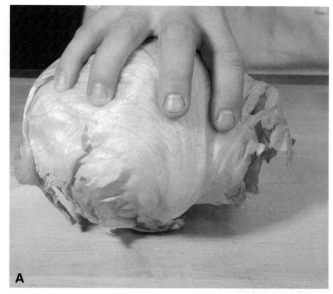

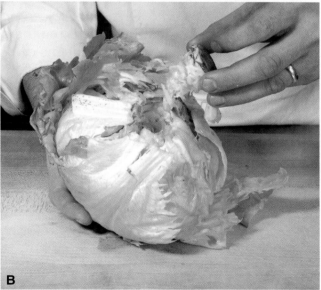

Draz-Koetke/Goodheart-Willcox Publisher

19-5 To core iceberg lettuce, (A) strike the core on a firm surface and (B) pull the core out of the head.

kitchen knives were made of carbon steel. Cutting leafy greens with a carbon steel knife causes them to oxidize or discolor and possibly take on a metallic taste. Today, most chefs use stainless steel or high carbon stainless steel knives and oxidation is not a problem. In high volume commercial kitchens, cutting lettuce with a knife is the most efficient way to cut large volumes of lettuce. In fine-dining restaurants, lettuce is still commonly torn.

Washing

At home, lettuce is often washed by running cold water over it. In a commercial kitchen, lettuce and other greens are washed by submersion. Cut greens are put into a sink or container of cold water that is deep enough for them to be fully covered and float freely. The product is stirred to help loosen dirt or sand that will sink to the bottom. The greens are lifted from the water and drained, leaving the dirt and sand in the sink.

Drying

After salad greens are washed, excess water must be drained off. Wet greens become soggy over time. Dressings placed on wet greens can become diluted, making them runny, bland, and unappetizing. Greens can be drained in a colander or perforated hotel pan. Paper towels can be used to remove excess water, but a salad spinner is the best option. A salad spinner uses centrifugal force to remove moisture. The greens are placed in the basket and then spun at a high rate of speed. The result is salad greens that are dry and uncrushed.

Nutrition Connection

Color your Salad with Nutrients

ChooseMyPlate.gov suggests that you include a green salad with your dinner every night. Use color as your guide when selecting ingredients for your salad. Red and dark green leafy vegetables are generally higher in antioxidants, vitamin B_6, and other nutrients than lighter colored greens. Remember this tip from ChooseMyPlate.gov: Make your garden salad glow with color. Brighten your salad by using colorful vegetables such as black beans, sliced red bell peppers, shredded radishes, chopped red cabbage, or watercress. Your salad will not only look good but taste good, too.

Salad Dressings

A salad dressing should enhance the flavor of the salad. Many different ingredients can be used to make dressings. However, dressings fit into one of three basic types—simple vinaigrette, mayonnaise, or emulsified dressing.

Simple Vinaigrettes

The French term *vinaigrette* tends to make something that is beautifully simple sound unnecessarily complex. In its most basic form, a **vinaigrette** is nothing more than a mixture of oil and vinegar. Oil is liquid at room temperature and provides the **palate**, or roof of the mouth, with a supple mouth-feel. It also acts as an excellent flavor carrier for other ingredients. The task of the acidic vinegar is to "cut" the fat, add another taste sensation, and stop the oil from coating the palate. In short, the only real secret to preparing a good vinaigrette is to achieve a balance in fat, acid, and other seasonings.

Proportion In most cases, the ratio of three parts oil to one part vinegar by volume achieves the desired balance for a vinaigrette. Sometimes, due to the characteristics of the vinegar, these proportions may need to be altered. When working with a stronger vinegar, most chefs choose to adjust the ratio and use four or five parts oil to one part vinegar, rather than dilute the vinegar.

Simple vinaigrette does not stay blended for long. The nature of vinegar and oil is to repel each other and separate. Therefore, it is important to stir simple vinaigrette immediately before serving.

Mayonnaise and Emulsified Dressings Animation

When simple vinaigrette is shaken or whipped, the oil and vinegar mix together in microscopic droplets creating an emulsion. An **emulsion** is a mixture of two liquids that

TECHNIQUE
Preparing Salad Greens

1. Remove any wilted outer leaves.
2. Cut away any rusted or discolored parts, especially on the leaf tips.
3. Remove the core or stem of the salad green.

4. Cut or tear the lettuce or greens into bite-size pieces.
5. Wash greens by submerging them in cold water.

6. Remove the greens by lifting them from the water with a spider.

7. Drain in a salad spinner.

do not naturally mix such as oil and vinegar. In an emulsion, tiny droplets of one ingredient are suspended in the other. A simple vinaigrette soon separates back to oil and vinegar because it is a temporary emulsion.

The culinary solution to prevent oil and vinegar from separating is to stabilize the emulsion with egg or egg yolks. Raw eggs are not recommended for this because they present a food safety concern. Instead, pasteurized eggs should be used. Eggs and other foods are **pasteurized** by heating at a temperature and for a period of time that destroys unsafe organisms, but does not cause major changes to the food itself.

Mayonnaise is a cold sauce that is an emulsion of oil and vinegar stabilized with egg yolk and mustard. To make mayonnaise, oil is formed into tiny droplets by gradually adding it to the other ingredients while whipping. These tiny droplets are suspended in the water contained in the vinegar and egg. Lecithin, cholesterol, and proteins found in egg yolks keep these suspended droplets of oil and water from separating. Mustard is another ingredient commonly used in mayonnaise and emulsified dressings. Compounds found in mustard also help prevent an emulsion from breaking or separating.

Mayonnaise is an important item in the cold kitchen because it is often used as a base in creating dressings or cold sauces. The quality of these preparations relies on the quality of the mayonnaise.

Mayonnaise Proportions   One key to successful mayonnaise is the right proportion of egg yolk to oil. The standard proportion for making mayonnaise is one egg yolk to one cup of oil. This ratio creates a proper emulsion.

Fluid, pasteurized egg products are commonly used in commercial kitchens. Since one yolk is roughly equivalent to one fluid ounce, the proportion is also expressed as one ounce pasteurized egg yolk to one cup oil.

Mix In Math

Using Ratios

Ratios tell how one number is related to another number. They can be used to describe relationships that are "part to whole," "part to part," or "whole to part." Ratios are often used in cooking. For example, vinaigrette is prepared using a ratio.

One cup of vinegar plus **three** cups of oil yields four cups of vinaigrette.

Ratios can be written in a number of different ways—1:4 or ¼ or one part to four parts or simply, one to four. Therefore, the ratio for vinaigrette can be written as 1:3.

Let's say you need 1 gallon (128 fl. oz.) of vinaigrette. How would you calculate the amounts of oil and vinegar you need? You already know that the ratio for vinaigrette is

1 part vinegar : 3 parts oil

1:3 means there are 4 equal parts

1 + 3 = 4

Divide 128 fluid ounces by 4 parts to find how many ounces each equal part is.

128 fluid ounces ÷ 4 parts = 32 fluid ounces/part

Now you know that each equal part is 32 fluid ounces. You can solve your problem now.

1 part vinegar × 32 fluid ounces/part = 32 fluid ounces of vinegar

3 parts oil × 32 fluid ounces/part = 96 fluid ounces oil

Double-check your work.

32 fluid ounces vinegar + 96 fluid ounces oil = 128 fluid ounces vinaigrette

Mustard and vinegar play a supporting role in creating an emulsion, therefore, measurement of them need not be exact. They are often added to taste.

Creating Emulsified Dressings with the Mayonnaise Technique

Once you have mastered the technique for making mayonnaise, you can apply this technique to create any emulsified dressing. Most recipes for emulsified dressings incorporate additional ingredients in the emulsion besides egg yolks and oil. Herbs, spices, and cheese are commonly included. The consistency of most emulsified dressings is thinner than mayonnaise, a result of added liquid or the use of whole eggs rather than just yolks.

Ingredients for Dressings

All dressings include oil, vinegar, and often mustard in their list of ingredients. However, each of these ingredients can be derived from a variety of different sources or methods of preparation. Each source or method lends a unique flavor or texture to that particular ingredient. This range of choices allows chefs to customize the dressing for a specific salad.

SANITATION & SAFETY
Pasteurized Egg Products

Traditionally, mayonnaise and salad dressings have been prepared with fresh shell eggs. However, the danger of salmonella bacteria that is found in eggs and poultry has made the use of raw eggs ill-advised and in most areas illegal. In most places, the sanitation codes prohibit foodservice operations from serving dressings made with raw eggs. Because of this, many varieties of pasteurized egg products have become available. Processed, refrigerated or frozen, whole eggs, yolks, or whites—these products should be used instead of raw eggs to ensure the safety and shelf life of the finished dressing.

TECHNIQUE
Preparing Mayonnaise

Preparation of mayonnaise and emulsified dressings can be done by hand, with an electric mixer, or in a food processor. However it is done, the same basic procedure is followed:

1. Place egg yolks, mustard, and vinegar in a bowl and whip to combine them well.

2. While constantly whipping the yolk mixture, add the oil in a thin stream.

3. Continue to whip and add oil simultaneously until all the oil is incorporated.

4. Adjust consistency by thinning with a small amount of water or lemon juice if needed.
5. Season with salt and pepper. Adjust acidity with additional vinegar or lemon juice if needed.
6. Refrigerate immediately.

Recipe No.	Name		Category
19.4	Mayonnaise		Dressings, emulsified
Yield	**Portion Size**		**No. Portions**
1½ pt. (720 mL)	1 fl. oz. (30 mL)		24

US Quantity	Metric Quanity	Ingredient	TCS
2 fl. oz.	60 mL	pasteurized egg yolks	●
2 Tbsp.	30 mL	vinegar	
1 tsp.	5 mL	dry mustard	
1 pt.	480 mL	salad oil	
to taste		salt	
to taste		white pepper	
to taste		lemon juice (optional)	
as needed		water	

Method	CCP
1. Combine yolks, vinegar, and mustard in a bowl.	
2. While constantly whipping the yolk mixture, add the oil in a thin stream.	
3. Continue to whip and add oil simultaneously until all the oil is incorporated.	
4. Adjust consistency by thinning with a small amount of water or lemon juice if needed.	
5. Season with salt and pepper. Adjust acidity with additional vinegar or lemon juice if needed.	
6. Cool to 41°F (5°C) or below within 4 hours and hold until service.	CCP

Portion (g)	Calories	Fat (g)	Protein (g)	Carbohydrate (g)	Cholesterol (mg)	Sodium (mg)	Fiber (g)
24	169	18.79	0.44	0.20	25.40	50.08	0.03

Oils   Oil makes up the bulk of most salad dressings; so good quality oil is essential for making a good vinaigrette, mayonnaise, or dressing. Oil is an excellent carrier for the flavors in the dressing and can also contribute its own flavor. Oils are classified as either neutral or flavored. Neutral oils are manufactured to be essentially flavorless and are interchangeable in recipes. The general term *salad oil* refers to neutral oils. Flavored oils are extracted from flavorful ingredients and have a unique flavor. Flavored oils contribute an additional flavor profile to a salad, 19-6.

Oils	
Neutral	**Flavored**
Soybean oil	Olive oil
Corn oil	Nut oils (such as walnut, hazelnut, macadamia)
Sunflower oil	
Safflower oil	Sesame oil
Peanut oil (hot pressed)	Peanut oil (roasted)
Canola	Infused oils (such as chile, herb)

19-6 There are a variety of oils to choose from when making salad dressings and vinaigrettes.

Vinegars The name *vinaigrette* is derived from "vinegar" which often gives this cold sauce its pronounced flavor and acidity. Vinegar was originally made from fermented barley juice, wine, or apple cider. Today, many varieties and flavors of vinegar are available. Some vinegars are made from specific varieties of wine or others are flavored with fruits or herbs. The acidity of commercially produced vinegars is diluted to consistently deliver a product with five percent acid. Natural fermentation of most wine vinegars produces vinegar with six to seven percent acid, 19-7.

In addition to vinegar, citrus juice such as lemon or lime can be used to provide acid for a vinaigrette.

Flavored Vinegars

Apple cider vinegar

Balsamic vinegar

Fruit vinegars (raspberry, apricot, blueberry, peach)

Infused vinegars (herbs, chiles, spices)

Malt vinegar

Rice vinegar

Wine vinegars (such as red wine, white wine, champagne, sherry)

19-7 Flavored vinegars add interest to vinaigrettes.

Recipe No.	Name		Category
19.5	Caesar Dressing		Dressings, emulsified
Yield	**Portion Size**		**No. Portions**
1 qt. (0.95 L)	1 fl. oz. (30 mL)		32
US Quantity	**Metric Quantity**	**Ingredient**	**TCS**
15 ea.		anchovy fillets	•
2 tsp.	10 mL	garlic, chopped	
2 fl. oz.	60 mL	fresh lemon juice	
2 fl. oz.	60 mL	red wine vinegar	
1 fl. oz.	30 mL	pasteurized egg yolks	•
2 tsp.	10 mL	Worcestershire sauce	
1 pt.	480 mL	salad oil	
4 fl. oz.	120 mL	extra virgin olive oil	
4 oz.	115 g	Parmesan cheese, grated	•
1 tsp.	5 mL	salt	
½ tsp.	3 mL	ground black pepper	
Method			**CCP**
1. Purée or finely chop anchovies and garlic.			
2. Place anchovies and garlic in a bowl with lemon juice, vinegar, and egg yolks.			
3. While constantly whipping, pour oil into purée in a thin stream to create an emulsion.			
4. Blend in remaining ingredients. Adjust seasoning.			
5. Cool to 41°F (5°C) or below within 4 hours and hold until service.			CCP

Portion (g)	Calories	Fat (g)	Protein (g)	Carbohydrate (g)	Cholesterol (mg)	Sodium (mg)	Fiber (g)
27	169	18.29	1.49	0.44	12.62	151.3	0.02

Extra Virgin Olive Oil

Leojones/Shutterstock.com

By far the most popular flavored oil is olive oil. Used in the Mediterranean for centuries, it has recently gained praise because of its health benefits in lowering cholesterol. To choose the best olive oil for salads and cold sauces, select an olive oil that is graded "extra virgin." Extra virgin olive oil is the first pressing of the olives and is done without heat. Extra virgin oils have a fruitier, mellower flavor because heat, which destroys the delicate flavor of olive oil, is not used. Less expensive pomice (nonvirgin) oil is more commonly used for cooking because the heat destroys the delicate flavors of extra virgin oil.

Mustard   Mustard adds a sharp flavor which helps counter the richness of the oil in vinaigrette. More importantly, mustard helps to emulsify mayonnaise and emulsified dressings. Dry mustard powder, Dijon-style mustard, or other prepared mustards can all be used in vinaigrettes. Since the flavor of these mustards is strong, they are used in small amounts.

Sanitation and Quality in Salad Preparation

As with many other areas of the professional kitchen, quality and sanitation go hand in hand. By following sanitary procedures, you are also ensuring the quality of the salads you serve, 19-8. The following standard procedures help ensure both quality and sanitation:

- Thoroughly wash all salad ingredients before using in a salad presentation.
- Keeping salad ingredients well chilled keeps them crisp and sanitary as well.
- Keep dressings containing egg or dairy products refrigerated at or below 41°F (5°C).
- Chill salad plates before plating to avoid wilting greens and other ingredients.
- Use gloves or utensils to handle salad ingredients because salads are ready-to-eat foods.
- Mix tossed salads with dressing as close to service as possible.
- Do not overdress salads. Use only enough dressing to lightly coat the greens.

19-8 Well-trained staff know that sanitation procedures must be followed when handling salad ingredients.

SUSTAINABLE CULINARY
Composting

Sharon Day/Shutterstock.com

What happens to lettuce trimmings or carrot peels once they go into the trash? Typically, they end up in a landfill where they will slowly decompose in an anaerobic environment (without oxygen). The nutrients contained in those food scraps could be used to help grow more vegetables, but instead are forever lost in the landfill. Additionally, as food in landfills slowly decomposes it creates methane gas. This gas is destructive to the atmosphere. Many restaurants are now separating their food waste so that it can be composted. The waste is picked up by licensed composting companies, which are growing in number. Composting has been practiced by people for centuries and by nature— always. When food is composted properly, it biodegrades into a very rich substance that is then used for fertilizer. Take some time and learn what composting possibilities are available in your community for homes and businesses. With some effort, you can even learn how to compost at your home!

Summary Points

- Salads have experienced a rise in popularity and serve a variety of purposes on the menu.
- There are three basic types of salads—simple, composed, and bound.
- Proper preparation of salad greens includes cutting or tearing, washing, and drying.
- The same basic ingredients are used in the three main categories of salad dressings.
- Proper sanitation in garde manger is necessary to produce a safe, quality salad.

In Review Assess

1. Explain why restaurant operators like salad bars.
2. List the four parts of a composed salad.
3. True or false. Bound salads can be a creative way to utilize leftovers.
4. Name each salad green described below.
   A. The most popular variety of lettuce in the United States with crisp leaves and round, tightly packed heads.
   B. Large, ruffled bunches of tender, bright green leaves used in salads and as plate liners.
   C. Mixture of baby lettuces sometimes referred to as spring mix or field greens.
   D. Tender shoots that are grown by soaking beans or seeds in water.
5. True or false. Chefs prefer ready-to-eat greens because they maintain their flavor, texture, and nutrients a long time.
6. Explain why salad greens are cut before they are washed.
7. The best method for drying lettuce is to use a _____.
8. The standard ratio for vinaigrette is _____ part(s) oil to _____ part(s) vinegar.
9. What are the ingredients in mayonnaise that act to stabilize the emulsion?
10. List the two classifications of oils used in salad dressings.

11. List five standard procedures to follow when making salads to ensure sanitation and food quality.

Core Skills

12. **Math.** Using the standard ratio discussed in this chapter, calculate how much oil and vinegar you would use to make one quart of simple vinaigrette.
13. **Writing.** Select your two favorite salads and write a one-page, summary on each. The paper should include the original recipe, the type of salad (simple, composed, or bound), and the role each ingredient plays. For instance, the lemon juice is the acidic ingredient that "cuts" the fat. Propose modifications to your original recipe with substitute ingredients. Explain your reason for the ingredients you selected. Consider preparing your recipe and including a photo in your paper.
14. **Reading.** Use print or digital sources to research when people first began preparing salads for their meals. What were common ingredients used? Compare these early salads to those found on menus today. Write one-page paper sharing your findings.
15. **Math.** Using the recipe for Caesar dressing in this chapter, scale the recipe to yield one gallon of dressing.
16. **CTE Career Readiness Practice.** Use reliable Internet or print resources to investigate the pros and cons of hydroponic crops. Read two or more articles and summarize your findings in writing. When evaluating the reliability of the information, remember the following:
   - *Identify author/writer credibility.* Who is the author or writer (well-known)? Is the author, writer, or publisher known for reliable fact-checking?
   - *Verify details.* Can you verify the facts in the article from other sources (government, medical, or educational institutions)? Is the information current? Is the copyright recent?

- *Identify bias.* Is the information presented from only one point of view? Is it from a scientific, medical, or well-known educational institution? Avoid articles that lack objectivity.

Critical Thinking

17. **Analyze.** Find a recipe for a salad dressing. Determine if it is a simple or emulsified dressing. Cite your reasoning.

18. **Compare.** Read the ingredients label on a bottle of prepared salad dressing and compare it to the recipe in activity #17. Are the lists of ingredients similar? If there are any ingredients you are unfamiliar with, research them to find out their role in the recipe.

19. **Debate.** Form small groups, debate the following topic: It is advantageous for a food-service operation to use convenience products such as ready-to-use dressings and precut greens on the salad station.

20. **Assess.** The kitchen is preparing an evening banquet for 500 people. The salad is greens dressed with vinaigrette. The garde manger wants to dress and plate up the greens early in the day so she can begin working on the appetizers for the event. Is this good planning? Explain your answer.

Technology

In recent years, there have been large outbreaks of foodborne illness traced back to salad greens. As a result, salad is now tracked from the field to the restaurant. Using the Internet, research how companies are tracking the movement of salad greens (and other products as well) as they make their journey from field to table. Record your findings and identify the technologies involved in this process.

Teamwork

Organize a small team and assign roles and responsibilities to complete the following lab. Take photos or video to illustrate your report. Create two preparations each consisting of 2 fl. oz. vinegar

Video Clip

Preparing Mayonnaise

Visit the G-W Learning Companion Website and view the bonus video clip "Preparing mayonnaise." After viewing the clip, answer the following questions:

1. List three ways mayonnaise can be prepared.
2. How can you prevent a bowl from slipping while preparing mayonnaise?
3. Why does mayonnaise require immediate refrigeration?

Video

and 6 fl. oz. salad oil. Note the separate layers of vinegar and oil. Add 1 teaspoon of dry mustard to one of the preparations. Place each preparation in a clear container with a lid. Shake the preparations simultaneously for 30 seconds. After 30 seconds of shaking, place both containers on the counter and begin timing. Record the time it took for each preparation to separate back out into the vinegar and oil layers. Record your observations. Did both preparations separate out at the same time? If not, which separated first? Why do you think that is? Consider replacing the dry mustard with other ingredients to further explore this concept. Prepare a report summarizing your findings.

Chef's E-portfolio
Emulsion Demonstration

Upload your report from the Teamwork activity to your e-portfolio. Ask your instructor where to save your file. This could be on the school's network or a flash drive of your own. Name your portfolio document *FirstnameLastname_Portfolio Ch#.docx* (i.e., JohnSmith_PortfolioCh19.docx).

While studying, look for the activity icon ↱ to:

- Build vocabulary with e-flash cards and matching activities.
- Expand learning with video clips, photo identification activities, animations, and interactive activities.
- Review and assess what you learn by completing end-of-chapter questions.

G-WLEARNING.com

grintan/Shutterstock.com

Fruit Identification 20

Reading Prep

In preparation for reading the chapter, visit the USDA Fruit and Vegetable Availability and Handling Charts. As you read about the different fruits in this chapter, identify countries that export these fruits to the United States. Consider how this might affect cost and freshness of the products.

Culinary Terminology

individually quick frozen (IQF), p. 339

Academic Terminology

grading, p. 319
United States Department of Agriculture (USDA), p. 319
hybrid, p. 321

Objectives

After studying this chapter, you will be able to

- recognize different containers and terms used for produce packaging.
- explain the grading process for fruits in the United States.
- identify the most common fresh fruits used in commercial foodservice.
- apply various quality factors when selecting fresh fruits.
- recall seasons for a variety of fresh fruits.
- explain methods used for processing fruits.

A successful chef is familiar with the many characteristics of fruits available on the market. This knowledge is helpful when making salads, garnishes, buffets, pastries, sauces, condiments, and desserts. The number of varieties available to chefs is continually expanding; heirloom varieties of fruits, hybrids, and new exotic and tropical fruits keep chefs on the lookout for products to add a new twist to recipes and menus. Processed fruits play a role in many commercial kitchens as well.

Packing Fresh Produce

Fresh produce is packed in containers of differing sizes and shapes. Each item is packed in a container that is suited to its size, shape, and texture. For the same fruit, different growers may use different size packages depending on their operation or local custom. A case for grapes, for instance, may hold 19 pounds or 22 pounds of product. It is important for a chef to know what size package he or she is buying when comparing prices. Individuals that are responsible for ordering, purchasing, or using produce must be familiar with the terms that are commonly used in packing fresh produce, 20-1.

Grading

Evaluating a food against a uniform set of quality standards is called grading. The United States Department of Agriculture (USDA) is the federal agency that imposes standards for the quality and safety of food products in the United States. The USDA develops grade standards and provides grading and inspection services throughout the country. Both fresh and processed fruits may be graded by the USDA, but grading of fruit is not mandatory. Grade categories for fresh fruits are different for each type of fruit. Grade categories used for canned or frozen fruits include the following:

- US Grade A or Fancy
- US Grade B or Choice
- US Grade C or Standard

Packing Terms for Fresh Produce	
Bushel	A volume measure of 35.24 liters or about 2200 cubic inches.
Case	A box or container of varying size. Cases for produce may be cardboard, wood, plastic, or foam.
Count	A specific number of pieces of uniform-sized produce in a case or container. For example, a case of 140-count lemons has 140 uniform-sized lemons in each case.
Crate	A wooden case.
Flat	A shallow single-layer case used for delicate products such as berries and figs.
Gross weight	The total weight of a container and the product.
Lug	A large bulk-packed case.
Net weight	The weight of the product without the package.
Peck	One-fourth bushel.
Tare weight	The weight of the package alone.

20-1 Foodservice professionals use common terminology for purchasing food.

SUSTAINABLE CULINARY

How Far Does Your Food Travel?

Walk through the produce section in the supermarket and consider where different fruits originate. If it is winter, some of the fruit may be coming from halfway around the world. Other fruits, such as tropical fruits, never grow in the United States. Transporting these fruits to your store is not just an issue of distance, but also of the amount of energy required to move them. Some restaurants and foodservice companies are seeking to change this food model by committing to only buy foods within a certain radius of their operations. Depending on the restaurant's location, the radius may be 150, 300, or 500 miles. Deciding not to purchase foods that must travel great distances helps support local economies, ideally lessens energy consumption, and forces the chef to be creative with the ingredients she has at her disposal.

Citrus Fruit

Whether it's for their flesh, juice, rind, or zest, citrus fruits have a wide variety of uses in the commercial kitchen. These tropical fruits are available nearly year-round. Most citrus comes packed for foodservice in a case size equivalent to four-fifths of a bushel, with a net weight of 38 to 40 pounds.

One of the key indicators of quality with all citrus fruits is weight. Heavier fruit generally has greater juice content and is more desirable.

Grapefruit

Once only a breakfast table staple, grapefruit has now become popular in salads, sauces, and desserts. Florida and Texas are the leading producers in the United States. Though they are available year-round, grapefruit are at their peak from September through June. Skin color is not a sign of ripeness since fully ripe fruit may have spots of green in their skin.

Grapefruit fall into one of two categories based on the color of their flesh—white or pink. The most popular white-fleshed grapefruit is the white Marsh seedless grapefruit. In the pink category, the ruby-red grapefruit is most in demand because of the deep reddish-pink color of the fruit.

White grapefruit

Pink grapefruit

Tangerines and Mandarins

Tangerines are a part of a larger category of citrus fruits known as *mandarins*. Mandarins are varieties of citrus fruits that have an easy-to-peel skin. The majority of US mandarins are grown in Florida and are available October through May. The height of the season is November through January.

Tangerine

Clementine is a popular variety imported from Spain. Mineolas and tangelos are hybrids of tangerine and grapefruit. A **hybrid** is the offspring of two different plant varieties. Often hybrids are bred to produce a new, exciting fruit or a more disease resistant plant. Temple oranges are an orange and tangerine hybrid.

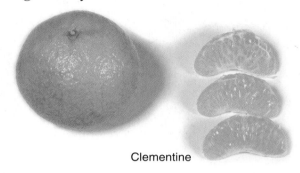

Clementine

Limes

Two main categories of lime are Tahiti and Mexican. The Tahiti lime is a larger, oval fruit with a thicker skin and dark-green color. It is the more commonly used lime in the United States. Within the category of Tahiti limes, the Persian lime is the most popular variety.

Mexican limes are smaller, lighter-colored fruit with thin skins. The Key lime, a variety cultivated in the Florida Keys, is probably the best-known variety of Mexican limes.

Persian lime

Key lime

Lemons

Though not usually eaten as a lone ingredient, lemons are a staple in most kitchens. They are prized for their acidic juice and use as a garnish. Look for lemons with fine-textured skin and relatively heavy weight for their size. Deep yellow color is a sign of maturity and less acid. California and Arizona are responsible for most of the US production of lemons year-round.

Oranges

Some variety of orange is available every month of the year in the United States. Florida is the nation's number one producer, followed by California and Arizona.

When choosing oranges do not be fooled by the color. Green streaks in the skin are not necessarily a sign of underripeness—sometimes it's just the opposite. Bumpy-skinned oranges are usually thick-skinned, easier to peel, and best for eating out of hand. Smooth-skinned oranges are usually harder to peel and are reserved for juicing. There are a few common varieties of oranges available for use in foodservice.

Varieties of Oranges

Valencia

Valencia oranges are the most important variety of orange and are grown in both Florida and California. They are in season from February through October.

Navel

Navel oranges are named for the navel-like protrusion near their stem and are grown primarily in California. They have slightly thicker skin, which makes them easier to peel. Navels are in season from November through May.

Blood

Blood oranges are named for the deep red color of their flesh. They are originally from the Mediterranean island of Malta and lend their name to sauce Maltaise, a hollandaise sauce flavored with their juice. Blood oranges are in season from March through May.

Apples and Pears

Apples and pears have been popular since ancient times. They grow abundantly in all regions of the world with a continental climate and store well without refrigeration. They are a great source of dietary fiber. Numerous varieties of apples and pears make these staples of the fruit group continually interesting.

Apples

Apples are by far the most popular and recognized fruit in the United States. They are grown in most parts of the country, but the production of fresh apples is led by Washington State.

The most common pack for foodservice is a 40-pound case (approximately one bushel). Apples are typically packed with a foam tray between each layer of apples to prevent bruising. Apples are sized for uniformity and range from 48 count for the largest to 216 count for the smallest. Apples may be sprayed with a food-grade wax for appearance and to prevent moisture loss.

When selecting apples, look for a bright fresh appearance with appropriate color according to variety. They should be firm to the touch and not mushy. The skins should be smooth and free of bruises.

The bulk of the commercial apple crop is harvested in late summer and autumn. Refrigerated and controlled atmosphere storage allows apples to stay at their peak for months. These storage methods make the most popular varieties of apples available year-round.

When choosing apples for a particular use, the texture and flavor of the variety of apple should be considered. Firmer, tart apples are better for cooking, baking, and applesauce. Sweeter, softer fleshed apples are better for eating fresh. Apples can be classified by their best use for cooking.

A SERVING OF HISTORY

Heirloom Apples

The first apple orchard planted in America was in Boston in 1625. Since that time, orchardists have strived to plant a wide variety of apples. Before the invention of refrigeration and modern storage techniques, it took a wide array of varieties to ensure that apples were available year-round. Early varieties ripen in mid-summer. Other varieties have a succession of ripening times lasting through late autumn. Some apples were prized for their ability to be stored through the winter months. Each variety had slightly different flavor and texture characteristics, some with flavors reminiscent of lemons or bananas. This extended availability helped to make apples a kitchen staple in this country.

Throughout the twentieth century, commercial orchards were propagated with only a handful of apple varieties. The few varieties with greatest appeal to the mass market were grown and hundreds of other varieties were all but forgotten. Fortunately today, some orchardists are working to plant, maintain, and reintroduce many of these "antique" or heirloom apples. So if someone offers you a "Roxbury Russet" or a "Peck's Pleasant," go ahead and take a bite of history.

Pears

Pears are a popular fruit because most pears can be stored for several months or longer under refrigeration. The pears are ripened at room temperature when needed. For this reason, chefs enjoy a steady supply of fresh pears for the better part of the year. Pears are commonly packed in a 45-pound case (approximately one bushel). They are often either packed in trays or individually wrapped in paper to prevent damage. Pears, like apples, are sorted by size. Case counts for pears range from 70 to 245 per case. The 110 to 135 counts are most common.

Apples

Eating Apples

Cortland

The Cortland variety is a red apple with fine-grained white flesh that resists browning. It is available from September through November.

Gala

The Gala apple is originally from New Zealand and has yellow-orange skin and crisp sweet mellow flavor. It is in season from August through March.

McIntosh

McIntosh apples are a medium-sized apple with red on green skin, fine-textured flesh, and a pleasant sweet-tart flavor. It is in season from September through June.

Red Delicious

Red Delicious is the most popular variety of apple in the United States due to its appearance. It is heart-shaped fruit with deep red skin and a crisp texture and sweet, mild flavor. This apple is available year-round.

Cooking and Baking Apples

Granny Smith

The Granny Smith apple variety originated in Australia and has become the favorite baking and cooking apple of chefs and pastry chefs. It has green skin, extremely crisp texture, and a robust tart flavor. Granny Smith apples are available year-round.

Newton Pippin

Newton Pippin is a green apple, sometimes streaked with yellow or red. It has a tart flavor and firm flesh. This apple is in season from September through June.

Northern Spy

Northern Spy apples have red striped skin with blushes of yellow, yellowish flesh, and a tart flavor. It is available from October through April.

(Continued)

Apples (Continued)

All-Purpose Apples

Braeburn

Braeburn apples are sweet-tart, crisp, and juicy with red blushes over a green skin or sometimes solid red. It is available from October through July.

Fuji

Originally grown in Japan, the Fuji apple is yellow with red streaks. It has a crisp texture and mild, sweet flavor and is available year-round.

Golden Delicious

Golden Delicious is a golden-skinned apple with a sweet, mellow flavor and moderately crisp texture. It is in season year-round.

Jonagold

Jonagold is a blend of Jonathan and Golden Delicious varieties. It has a yellow skin that is well streaked with red hues and a sweet-tart flavor and nice crisp texture. It is available from September through March.

Jonathon

A red apple often with yellow stripes, the Jonathan is slightly acidic with crisp flesh. It is available year-round.

Rome Beauty

The Rome Beauty is an attractive apple with a round fruit and bright red color. It has sweet, slightly juicy flesh and is a favorite for baked apples. It is in season from September through July.

Pear Varieties

Anjou

Anjou pears are light green with blushes of red and very flavorful. They are available from October through April.

Bosc

Bosc pears have yellow to golden-brown color with a distinctive slender neck and are quite juicy. This pear is in season from September through April.

Asian Pear (apple pear)

The Asian pear has a round shape with yellow to green color. They are sweet, firm, crisp, and fragrant.

Comice

A Comice pear is a light greenish-yellow pear with a soft texture and squat shape. It bruises easily. The season for Comice pears is from October through March.

Bartlett

The most popular pear is the Bartlett. It is an early variety and has yellow skin with red blush. A Red Bartlett with deep ruby skin is also available. It is in season from July through December.

Seckel

Seckel is the smallest variety of pear and is often quite sweet. It has green skin with a maroon blush. This pear is available from October through April.

Ripe pears should yield slightly to a gentle squeeze. Avoid pears that are scarred or have soft spots. Many chefs prefer to buy immature pears and ripen the pears themselves. If pears are allowed to ripen on the tree, they tend to have a gritty texture. Varieties of pears differ in size, shape, and their season.

Stone Fruits

Stone fruits are grouped together because of their pits or stones. They are often called *tree fruits* or *drupes*. They tend to be at the peak of their relatively short season during the summer months.

Apricots

Fresh apricots are fragrant with juicy, yellow fruit. The season for fresh apricots is rather short—June through July—therefore much of the apricot crop is canned, dried, or preserved. Since tree-ripened fruit has the best flavor and because the shelf life of fresh apricots is so short, selecting quality fruit is essential. Reject immature greenish or hard fruit, as well as, overly soft or bruised over-ripe fruit.

Peaches

The peach is called the "queen of fruits." When at the peak of ripeness, no other fruit has such a wonderful, juicy, fragrant flavor.

The season for fresh peaches is May to October. Fresh peaches fall into one of two categories—clingstone or freestone. The fruit of clingstone peaches is difficult to separate from the pit. These peaches are used primarily for canning. Freestone peaches, as their name implies, have pits that are easy to remove. Freestones are most popular for eating fresh. Of the hundreds of varieties of freestone peaches, the most popular varieties are Elberta and Red Haven.

Peaches are most commonly packed in a 20-pound case. Look for peaches that are slightly firm because they ripen quickly. Quality peaches should have a fragrant aroma. Avoid hard peaches with no give to their flesh, as well as, green color or fruit with bruised or broken skin.

Nectarines

Nectarines have a similar flavor and texture as peaches, yet they are a distinct type of stone fruit. Nectarines are not a peach without fuzz, or a cross between a peach and plum, as many people believe. Their deep red-on-orange color is not a sign of ripeness, so ripeness must be judged by texture. A ripe nectarine is firm with a slight give to pressure. Look for the same ripeness and qualities factors as with peaches.

Cherries

Cherries are classified into two main categories—sweet or sour. Sweet (dessert) cherries are best for eating fresh. Sour (pie) cherries are best for cooking, baking, or preserving. Select cherries with good color for their variety and that are firm and good-sized. The most important consideration is good flavor, so sample before accepting if possible. Sweet cherries are most commonly packed in an 18- or 20-pound case. Washington State and Oregon are leaders in the production of sweet cherries, while Michigan and Wisconsin are prime producers of sour cherries. The season for fresh cherries is June to August.

Plums

There are over 200 varieties of plums. All of them fall into one of two main classifications—

Japanese

European

Varieties of Cherries

Bing

Bing cherries have a mahogany-red color and sweet, rich flavor. They are in season from June through August.

Montmorency

Montmorency is the main variety of sour cherry grown commercially in the United States. It is notable for its bright red skin and juicy fruit. These cherries are available from June through August.

Rainier (Golden Bing)

Rainier cherries have a yellow color, sweet delicate flavor, and fine-textured flesh. They are available from June through August.

European plums or Japanese plums. European plums are oval in shape with a bluish-purple color. These plums are often referred to as prune plums because they can be used for making dried prunes. Japanese plums come in a variety of different colors—red, yellow, orange, green—but not purple.

Plums are traditionally available from May to October, but shipments of fruit from the Southern Hemisphere make certain varieties available during the winter months. Look for plums with good color for their variety and a firm texture that yields slightly to pressure.

Berries

Most of the fruits in the berry category have the following in common:
- They are some of the more expensive fruits used in commercial kitchens.
- They have a delicate texture and must be handled very carefully.
- Most have a relatively short shelf life and need to be used in a timely manner.

Despite these issues, berries are still some of the most popular fruits in the kitchen and bakeshop because of the intense flavor and bright colors.

Although the spring and summer months are the traditional season for most berries, demand for these "fruit jewels" has created a worldwide growing and distribution arrangement that provides berry fruits almost year-round. Off-season demand is met by imports from tropical regions and the Southern Hemisphere, especially Chile and New Zealand. Although they are available all months of the year, the imported berries are a great deal more expensive due to the cost of shipping.

Berry fruits are packed by volume rather than by weight. They are shipped in flats or single layer cases of dry pints or half pints. Berries should be firm, plump, bright colored, and free of dirt, insects, or mold. Watch for juice stains at the bottom of the containers as a sign of deterioration. Berries should be stored in the refrigerator at 33°F to 38°F (1°C to 3°C).

Grapes

The term *table grapes* is used for grapes that are eaten fresh rather than used for juice or raisins. Table grapes are a popular and versatile fruit used in salads, pastries, and fruit plates. The majority of table grapes consumed in the United States come from California. Eastern states produce a number of grapes, such as Concord, Catawba, and Delaware, that are native to America. These grapes are more often used in canning and preserving than for the table. The traditional season for table grapes is summer and fall. Though available domestically in winter months, there is an increasing quantity imported from the Southern Hemisphere.

Unlike some fruits, the flavor of grapes does not improve or ripen after they are picked, so choose grapes with a sweet flavor. Look for compact bunches with plump fruit and good color for their variety. The stem is a good indicator of freshness; reject grapes with dry, brittle or moldy stems or with a large number of empty spots on the clusters. Grapes are most often packed in 22-pound cases of bunches bundled in mesh bags.

Melons

Cantaloupe, honeydew, and watermelon are the melons commonly used in commercial kitchens. Some less notable varieties are quite delicious in season and can provide interest to the menu, fruit plates, and buffet presentations.

One of those less well-known melons is the crenshaw. Crenshaw (also cranshaw) is a large melon with striped, green skin and salmon-colored flesh. The casaba is a melon with a tough, wrinkled yellow skin and white flesh. Santa Claus or Christmas melon is a large, green oval melon with slightly netted skin and light-colored flesh. This melon earns its name because it is available through December.

Varieties of Berries

Blackberry

Blackberries are plump and shiny dark fruit with excellent juice content. They are less delicate than most other berries. They are in season from June through September.

Blueberry

Fresh blueberries have a patina or dull frosty appearance to their skin. Look for plump, firm berries without dimples, shriveled skin, or debris. The cultivated varieties of blueberry are a high bush type of blueberry. They are grown all over the United States and Canada and are available from June through September.

Cranberry

Cranberries are the fruit of an aquatic plant that grows in ponds. They have a good shelf life (2 to 3 months in refrigeration), freeze well, and are sturdy and easy to handle. Select cranberries with an even bright red color and a springy texture. Avoid dull looking, shriveled, or spotted berries. They are in season from September through January.

Currant

Currants have small round fruit and intense tart flavor. Red currants are more tart and bright red with a delicate texture. Black currants, sometimes referred to by their French name *cassis*, are more fragrant but less juicy. Currants are used for jellies, preserves, flavoring vinegars, liquors, and sauces and are available from June through August.

Raspberry

Red raspberries are prized for their slightly tart intense flavor. Golden raspberries are a specialty item gaining popularity. Black raspberries with a dark blue to purple color are less common. Raspberries are the most delicate-textured berry, and therefore, the hardest to handle. They are in season from May through August.

Strawberry

Strawberries have a distinctive heart shape, seeds on the outside, and are packed with their hull intact. Look for bright-colored berries with a shiny skin, a fragrant aroma, and sweet flavor. They are in season from May through July.

Grape Varieties

Concord

Concord grapes are round purple grapes with seeds and soft fruit. It is the most popular variety native to America and is often used for jelly and juice.

Corinth (Champagne)

The Corinth variety is identified by the tiny red seedless grapes that form in long clusters. This variety is often called *champagne grapes* probably because their small size brings to mind small champagne bubbles. This variety is *not* used to produce champagne.

Flame Seedless

Flame Seedless is a cross of Thompson Seedless and red varieties. It is a red seedless grape with sweet flavor.

Red Globe

Red Globe is a red grape with seeds and is noted for its large clusters of plump, large round fruit.

Ribier

The Ribier variety of grape is a black, large round fruit with seeds.

Thompson Seedless

Thompson Seedless is the most popular variety of table grape. It has green oblong fruit with a juicy mild flavor.

Cantaloupe

The term *cantaloupe* has become the name for all varieties of muskmelons. Muskmelons are characterized by the netted or lace pattern on their skin. Cantaloupe is recognizable because of its deep orange- or salmon-colored flesh and green inner rind. When ripe, it is juicy, fragrant, and very sweet.

Although the flesh of melons may soften if left at room temperature for a few days, they don't ripen or get any sweeter after they are picked. Cantaloupe is the only melon that gives an outward clue to its ripeness. Inspect the stem end of the cantaloupe. If there is an indentation where the stem was, the melon was ripe and pulled away from the vine easily. This state of ripeness is called *full slip*. If there is no indentation or a stem is intact, the melon was unripe when picked and will not improve in flavor.

Cantaloupe, as with all melons, should be served well chilled. June through August are prime months for US cantaloupe growers. Mexican and Central American producers supply much of the melons in other months. Cantaloupe is commonly packed in a 30-pound case and 18 count is the most requested size.

Honeydew

Ripe honeydew melons have a smooth, creamy white rind, and pale green to white flesh. They are noted for their sweetness.

Honeydew melons are often picked before they reach the full slip stage and ripened by the wholesaler. Unlike cantaloupe, honeydew will ripen at room temperature. When ripe, the blossom end becomes slightly soft. Avoid honeydew melons with dark green streaks. The streaks are a sign that the melon is too underripe. Honeydews are packed in a 20-pound case with 6 count and 8 count being the most common sizes. They can weigh as much as 7 pounds each. Honeydew melons are at their peak between May and November.

Watermelon

The iconic summertime fruit is the chilled wedge of watermelon. There are hundreds of varieties of watermelon grown throughout the United States. Shapes range from small round to oval to elongated. The flesh ranges from light pink, to deep

crimson, to golden yellow. The quantity, size, and color of the seeds also vary. Due to their size, watermelon is usually sold by weight. Many foodservice operators tend to prefer oblong-shaped melons that average 18 to 22 pounds.

Ideal storage temperature for watermelons is 55°F (13°C). It is important to avoid temperatures near freezing as they destroy the melon's texture. Regardless of the color of the outer rind, the best sign of ripeness is a pale yellow underside.

Tropical and Exotic Fruits

Many of the fruits used in commercial kitchens are grown in tropical climates, such as the Caribbean, South or Central America, the South Pacific, or Asia, and imported to this country. Bananas and pineapples are tropical fruits that are now considered kitchen staples. Others are less well-known and provide new, unfamiliar flavors for chefs and diners.

Bananas

Bananas are a staple item in most kitchens since they are available year-round. They are nutrient dense, providing substantial amounts of potassium and vitamins A and C.

Their fruit is actually the flower of a large tropical plant. The flower is made of 7 to 10 hands with each hand containing 5 to 30 fingers, or individual bananas. The United States imports most of its bananas from Central America, primarily from Costa Rica, Honduras, and Ecuador. Bananas are picked green then shipped and stored at 55°F (13°C). They are ripened at 59°F to 68°F (15°C to 20°C) until they reach the desired stage of ripeness. Stages of ripeness progress from green, to green tipped, to yellow, to yellow with brown speckles. Bananas are stored at room temperature to allow them to ripen. Placing bananas in the refrigerator stops the ripening process and does not hurt the quality of the fruit. However, the skin turns an unappealing dark brown color while in the refrigerator.

The Cavendish banana is the most common variety eaten in this country. However, there are also smaller, sweeter finger bananas available in yellow and red varieties. Plantains are a larger member of the banana family. They have a thick, fibrous green skin. Their fruit is very starchy. Plantains are fried, baked, or boiled but never eaten raw. They are often used as a starchy vegetable rather than a fruit.

Finger bananas

Cavendish bananas

Plantain

Dates

The fruit of certain varieties of palm trees, dates originated in the Middle East. Dates are an amber-colored, thumb-sized fruit with thin skin. Under the skin is an extremely sweet, sticky flesh. Although they are available fresh, dates are most often used in a dried or semidried form. In the United States, commercially produced dates are grown in the Coachella Valley of Southern California and in Arizona. Dried dates are available year-round.

Figs

Figs are one of the oldest cultivated fruits. Their sweetness has been enjoyed for centuries. There are hundreds of varieties of figs, but the most popular varieties are the Calimyrna, Mission type, and Kadota. The Calimyrna has a greenish-yellow skin. The Mission type fig has a deep purple to black color. The Kadota has a light green skin, which ripens to an amber color and contains few seeds. Another variety, the Adriatic fig, is used mostly for drying.

The season for fresh figs is May to October. Figs are tray packed in flats because of their delicate texture. Ripe figs also have a rather short shelf life, and can become over-ripe, mushy, and sour if not used promptly. Fresh figs can be eaten out of hand, and are sometimes lightly poached for use in desserts.

Kiwifruit

The kiwifruit—named for a New Zealand bird—was originally known as *Chinese gooseberry*. The name change occurred when other countries began to import it on a large scale from New Zealand. Kiwifruits are about the size of an egg and have distinct brown fuzzy skin, which is not edible. Their flesh is a deep green, highlighted with tiny black seeds. Kiwifruits are now grown in the United States and many other parts of the world. They have a rather soft texture and are tray packed in single layer, 8-pound cases. The most popular size is 36 count.

Mangoes

Mangoes are fragrant and juicy when ripe and have a distinctive large seed at their core. This fruit has long been a staple item in tropical climates. They have gained in popularity in the United States in recent years as more Americans discover the sensual pleasures of mangoes. Mangoes are grown throughout the tropical regions of the world and are available year-round. The most popular varieties are Atkins, Hayden, and Kent. Look for the green skin to turn yellow, red, or orange as a sign of ripeness. Underripe fruit can be ripened at room temperature.

Papayas

Papayas are grown throughout the tropical regions of the world, including Asia, South and Central America, and the Caribbean. The most common type used in the United States is the Hawaiian papaya. It is a pear-shaped fruit with sweet orange flesh and a central cluster of round black seeds. Look for papayas with skin that is at least half yellow as a sign of ripeness. Underripe fruit can be ripened at room temperature. The skin of papayas is tough and therefore seldom eaten. The seeds have a peppery flavor and are sometimes used as a garnish or flavoring. Papayas are available year-round and are packed in 10-pound cases of 9 to 12 count.

Pineapples

The pineapple has long been the symbol of hospitality. In the minds of most people, it is synonymous with the state of Hawaii, and for a good reason. Hawaii produces the vast majority of fresh pineapple consumed in the United States. Mexico and Caribbean countries are also producers.

Pineapples do not ripen after harvest and there is no sure way to determine ripeness without tasting them. Fruit left at room temperature may soften in texture, but will not gain any sweetness. Chefs must rely on the skill of grower and packer for getting the most flavorful product. Pineapples are most commonly packed in a 20-pound, single-layer case. The most popular size for pineapples is 6 count. Pineapples are available year-round.

Carambola (Star Fruit)

Carambola is an oval yellow fruit with five ribs that looks like a five-point star when sliced. It has a thin skin and crisp, sweet, slightly acidic flavor.

Cherimoya (Custard Apple)

Cherimoya is a fruit native to South and Central America that looks like a stout green pinecone with creamy white flesh. It has a sweet fragrant flavor and black seeds.

Guava

Guava is a golf ball-sized fruit with green skin and pink or yellow flesh. This fragrant fruit is desirable for its juice, which is used in tropical drinks, sauces, and preserves.

Kiwano (Horned Melon)

The kiwano is a spiked oval orange fruit with thick skin and a tart juicy interior.

Kumquat

The kumquat is a small thumb-sized citrus fruit with virtually no juice. The rind and flesh of this fruit are eaten and provide a fragrant and tart citrus flavor.

Lychee

Lychee is a small reddish-skinned fruit that has a white inner flesh with sweet, juicy, subtle flavor. Originally grown in China, it is popular in Asian cuisines.

Passion Fruit

Passion fruit is a small round fruit with a thick bumpy purple skin and an interior

of seeds covered with a golden pulp. It has a tart fragrant flavor with floral notes. Its pulp or juice is used in a wide variety of pastries and frozen desserts.

Persimmon

Persimmon looks a bit like an orange tomato and has tart and fragrant flesh when ripe. Its texture is rather soft when ripe, so it is often used as a purée and is especially popular in persimmon pudding.

Pomegranate

Pomegranate is a round fruit with a thick red skin. Its interior holds seeds surrounded by a layer of crimson fruit with a mild sweet flavor.

Prickly Pear (Cactus Pear)

Prickly pear is the fruit of a desert cactus that is about the size of an egg. It has a thick bumpy olive- to purple-colored skin and reddish-purple fruit with the texture

of watermelon. The flesh is abundant with small seeds and so it is commonly puréed.

SCIENCE & TECHNOLOGY

Controlled Atmosphere—To Ripen or Not to Ripen

Ripening changes fruit in many ways. During the ripening process, the fruit's texture softens and starches turn to sugar, which makes the fruit sweeter. It is important to know which fruits ripen after being picked and which do not. Fruits taste best when fully ripened.

A necessary part of the ripening process is respiration. During respiration, fruit takes in oxygen and gives off carbon dioxide and ethylene gas. Fruit packers and shippers can suspend the ripening process of fruits that ripen after harvest by storing them in a *controlled atmosphere*. A controlled atmosphere for produce is an environment with little or no oxygen. Refrigeration also retards ripening in some fruits; therefore packers are able to hold certain fruits in low temperature, low oxygen storerooms for months. Apples harvested underripe in autumn can be stored in controlled atmosphere and brought to market months later.

Processed Fruits

Fresh fruits are only fresh for a short time once they are harvested. In addition, the growing seasons of many fruits are quite short, which limits availability. Methods such as drying, canning, and freezing are used to preserve fruits that might otherwise go to waste. These methods also make it possible to enjoy these fruits year-round.

Dried

A large number of fruits can be preserved by drying. Raisins (dried grapes), sultanas (dried green grapes), prunes (dried plums), dried currants, dried apricots, and dried cherries are just a few of the dried fruits found in most commercial kitchens. Dried fruits are used for a variety of dishes including breads, pastries, sauces, salads, and breakfast items, 20-2.

Some dried fruits are treated with sulfur dioxide to preserve their color and stop spoilage. Keep dried fruits in a sealed container to preserve their flavor. Dried fruits are often rehydrated or moistened before using.

Canned

Canned fruits are a good option for many restaurants and institutions. Canned fruits are usually packed at the peak of ripeness, so their flavor is consistent all year long. They are often more economical than

Draz-Koetke/Goodheart-Willcox Publisher

20-2 People have been preserving food by drying it for over 14,000 years.

fresh fruits and require less labor. Commonly canned fruits include peaches, pears, and sour cherries.

When choosing canned fruit products, the main consideration is the liquid in which the canned fruits are packed. Most canned fruits come packed in water or various concentrations of sugar syrup. Fruit packed in water retains more of the natural flavors of the fruit and has fewer calories than syrup-packed fruits. On the other hand, fruits packed in syrup are always sweet and are less likely to be broken or crushed. Heavier syrups are used to preserve the shape of more delicate fruits.

The canning process preserves foods from spoilage. During processing, food is placed into a sterile can and all the air is removed to create a vacuum. The entire can and its contents are cooked to destroy any microorganisms present, 20-3. The contents of the can remain sterile until it is opened and the vacuum is broken.

Frozen

The canning process requires heat which cooks the fruit to some extent. For this reason, frozen fruit often has a flavor advantage over canned fruit because it retains more of the fresh fruit flavor. Not all frozen fruits are processed in the same way. Fruit or fruit pieces that are flash frozen before packing so that they retain their original shape are said to be **individually quick frozen (IQF)**, 20-4. IQF fruits are available packed in cases bulk or in 2- or 3-pound plastic bags. Some fruits are frozen in syrup or with added sugar. The added sugar adds flavor and keeps fruit from fully freezing, thus helping to preserve the shape and texture of the fruit. Fruit frozen in syrup is packed in buckets and a variety of can sizes.

© iStock/vladmir_n

20-4 These raspberries were flash frozen prior to being packaged.

zmkstudio/Shutterstock.com

20-3 During the canning process, fruit is heated to destroy microorganisms.

Summary Points

- Fresh fruits come packed in a variety of sizes, often sorted by count or uniform size.

- The USDA develops grade standards and provides grading services but it is not mandatory for fresh and processed fruits.

- Each classification of fruit has unique characteristics that determine quality and ripeness.

- The quality and availability of fresh fruit are greatly influenced by its growing season.

- Processing fruit is a way to ensure year-round availability.

In Review
Assess

1. True or false. A lug would be the best pack option for raspberries.

2. List the three grade categories used for canned or frozen fruits.

3. The key indicator of quality with all citrus fruit is _____.

4. Name the most popular variety for each of the following fruits:
   A. apple
   B. pear
   C. table grape

5. List five stone fruits.

6. True or false. Berries are some of the most expensive fruits used in commercial kitchens.

7. What are Concord grapes most likely to be used for?

8. If a cantaloupe is picked ripe, the stem end of the melon has a slight indentation. This state of ripeness is called _____.

9. Identify which of the following fruits ripen after being picked:
   A. honeydew
   B. pears
   C. pineapples
   D. cantaloupe
   E. bananas
   F. grapes

10. Name the fresh fruits that are used to make the following dried fruits:
    A. raisins
    B. sultanas
    C. prunes

11. What purpose does sugar syrup serve in canned and frozen fruits?

Core Skills

12. **Math.** A case of kiwifruit has a gross weight of 8.75 pounds. The weight of the empty case is 8 ounces. What is the tare weight of the case? What is the net weight of the fruit?

13. **Writing.** Using reliable sources, research to learn about the number of apple varieties that exist globally. Explain why so few of these varieties are seen in supermarkets. Write a two-page paper sharing the results of your research. Cite your sources.

14. **Speaking.** Choose a fruit and research to learn its history. From what part of the world does it originate? Has its appearance changed? How did it get its name? Prepare an electronic presentation to share your findings with the class. Make use of visual and interactive elements in your presentation to enhance understanding and add interest.

15. **Math.** A fresh grape weighs 5 grams, but only weighs 20 percent of its original weight when dried. How much does the raisin (dried grape) weigh? Calculate the amount of fresh grapes needed to produce 20 grams of raisins.

16. **Research and Speaking.** Imagine you have been assigned to select and prepare a fruit dish for the culinary department's graduation banquet. First, identify the time of year that the banquet takes place so you can consider what fruits are in season. Determine the preparation you will make and find a recipe if necessary. Research to learn which variety, grade, and/or form of the fruit is best suited to the dish. Identify the pack size and the state of ripeness you would order. How and where will the fruit be stored until you are

ready to prepare your dish? Give a digital presentation to the class sharing the steps in your decision-making process and the rationale for each decision. Consider preparing the dish and taking photos at various steps during the preparation or find images online. Use these to illustrate your presentation.

17. **CTE Career Readiness Practice.** Use academic and technical skills to research the following topic: Organic fruits are safer and more nutritious than nonorganic fruits. Provide evidence to support your position.

Critical Thinking

18. **Determine.** If you were presented with a fruit you have never used before, how might you determine its best use?

19. **Conclude.** How do special sales on fruit at your local supermarket relate to the peak season of fruits as noted in this chapter?

20. **Evaluate.** When and why might you substitute frozen or canned fruits for fresh? What adjustment might be needed when using processed fruits?

Technology

Ensuring traceability of produce is important for food safety reasons. Traceability provides the means to track a particular piece of fruit or case of fruit from the field to the restaurant or from the restaurant back to the field. Research the technology that makes this possible. Why is traceability important from a food safety perspective?

Teamwork

Working in small teams, perform the following evaluation of different grades of fruit. Obtain three grades—US Grade A (Fancy), B (Choice), and C (Standard)—of the same canned fruit. You could use a frozen fruit instead of canned. Either drain or thaw the fruits as appropriate for your selection. Place each grade in a separate dish. Assess the appearance of each grade and record your observations. Include photographs as needed to enhance your report. Taste each grade and record your evaluation of each grade's texture and flavor. Identify what would be an appropriate way to use each of the different grades.

Chef's E-portfolio
Identifying Fruit Grades

Upload your report from the Teamwork activity to your e-portfolio. Ask your instructor where to save your file. This could be on the school's network or a flash drive of your own. Name your portfolio document *FirstnameLastname_Portfolio Ch#.docx* (i.e., JohnSmith_PortfolioCh20.docx).

While studying, look for the activity icon ⬀ to:

- Build vocabulary with e-flash cards and matching activities.
- Expand learning with video clips, photo identification activities, animations, and interactive activities.
- Review and assess what you learn by completing end-of-chapter questions.

Margouillat/Shutterstock.com

Fruit Preparation 21

Reading Prep

In preparation for reading the chapter, observe and compare whole fruits versus prepared fruits in the supermarket, on a restaurant menu, or online. Consider the cost, appearance, and convenience of the various options.

Culinary Terminology Build Vocab

blanching, p. 345
zest, p. 347
pith, p. 347
suprême, p. 347
garnish, p. 349
plumping, p. 355

Academic Terminology Build Vocab

oxidation, p. 349
acidulation, p. 349

Objectives

After studying this chapter, you will be able to

- execute techniques used when preparing fruit for service and recipes.

- apply techniques for presenting fruit as garnishes on individual plates and buffet platters.

- recognize cooking methods for preparing fruits.

A wide variety of fruit is available to chefs year-round. Preparation of these fruits is an important task in the garde manger (cold station), pastry kitchen, and other stations. Whether as fruit plates, platters, or garnishes, fruit makes an appearance in all parts of the menu. Fruit is used at breakfast, for brunch, as an appetizer, for garnish in sauces, in main courses, and in desserts.

Basic Skills

Most fruit preparation is performed to make the item easier for the diner to eat. This is the reason for removing inedible skins, cores, stones, and membranes. There are a few basic skills that are needed for fruit preparation. Other techniques are designed to make the fruit more attractive in presentation.

Washing Fruits

A step that is often overlooked is properly washing fruits to remove dirt from the field, handling, and packing containers. Washing may also remove residual pesticides or wax coatings. Even if the fruit is to be peeled, it should be washed first. If it is not washed, contamination on the outside of the fruit is introduced to the interior flesh by the knife or peeler. In fact, some fruits are associated with foodborne illness outbreaks and are considered TCS food.

Washing fruits before preparation is not difficult. Gently rinse or submerge fruits in cold water, 21-1. Special care should be taken

TECHNIQUE
Coring Apples and Pears

Method 1

1. Using an apple corer, insert the corer into the apple or pear following the stem.
2. Push corer through to the bottom of the apple or pear.
3. Pull out the corer and the core together.

Method 2

1. Using a knife, cut the apple or pear in quarters through the stem.
2. Cut out the core and seeds with a knife.

3. Continue to cut into smaller pieces if desired.

Draz-Koetke/Goodheart-Willcox Publisher

21-1 Place fruit in a colander and wash under running water.

with delicate fruits such as berries. Berries should be gently submerged in cold water and allowed to drain to avoid crushing or bruising their delicate texture. Wash berries as close to time of service as possible so they do not get mushy.

Coring Apples and Pears

Removing the cores from apples and pears is a task that can be accomplished in one of two ways. Which method you select depends on the tools available and the desired shape of the finished product. The first technique is used when whole fruit or round slices is the desired result. The second technique is quicker and easier, but can only be used when fruit quarters or smaller pieces are needed.

Pitting Stone Fruits

Peaches, nectarines, and plums are often presented in halves without their pits. Use a paring knife and cut through the skin and flesh to the pit. Cut to the pit a full 360 degrees. Gently twist the two halves of the fruit in opposite directions until they separate. Remove the pit from the fruit with the tip of the paring knife.

Cherries are pitted using a special tool that pushes the pit through the flesh while leaving the fruit uncrushed.

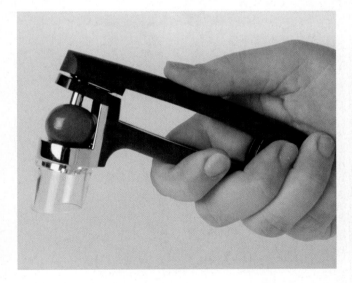

Peeling Fruits

A number of methods can be used to peel fruits. Select the method that works best for the type of fruit to be peeled.

Using a Knife Thick-skinned fruits are peeled with a knife. A utility knife or flexible boning knife is best because it forms more easily to the contour of the fruit. This flexibility results in cutting less of the flesh and preserving

the natural shape of the fruit. Smaller fruits such as lemons or kiwifruits are peeled more easily with a paring knife. One indicator of proper peeling skill is a peeling with little flesh attached. Fruits should also retain their rounded shape. This technique is used on melons, pineapples, citrus fruits, and kiwis.

Blanching Peaches and nectarines have thin skin and relatively soft flesh when ripe. These two factors can make peeling a peach or nectarine with a knife or peeler difficult. An easier method is to remove the skin by blanching. **Blanching** is briefly cooking an item in boiling water. Peaches are dropped into rapidly boiling water for a few moments to allow the skins to release from the fruit. The cooking time varies depending on the fruit's ripeness. The fruit is then placed in ice water to cool it down, 21-2. This keeps the fruit from becoming overcooked and makes it easier to handle.

Draz-Koetke/Goodheart-Willcox Publisher

21-2 Once peaches are blanched and cooled, the skin can be removed easily.

TECHNIQUE
Peeling and Seeding Melons

1. Using a flexible knife, cut the top and bottom off the melon.

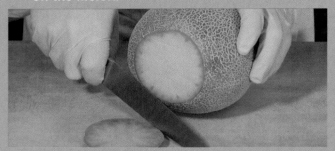

2. With a slicing motion, trim the skin following the rounded contour of the melon from top to bottom.

3. Continue trimming around the melon until all the skin and rind is removed.

4. Cut the peeled melon in half.

5. Scrape out the seeds with a spoon.

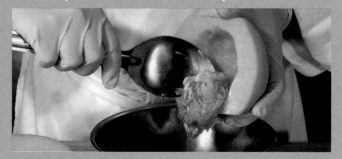

TECHNIQUE
Peeling and Coring Pineapples

1. Using a rigid knife, cut the top and bottom off the pineapple.

2. With a slicing motion, trim the skin following the contour of the pineapple from top to bottom.

3. Continue working around the pineapple until the skin is removed. Shave enough off of the pineapple to remove all the "eyes."

4. Cut the pineapple in quarters lengthwise.

5. Cut away the fibrous core.

Using a Peeler   Most firm, thin-skinned fruits can be peeled with a stationary or swivel peeler. Peelers work well on apples, pears, mangoes, and papayas.

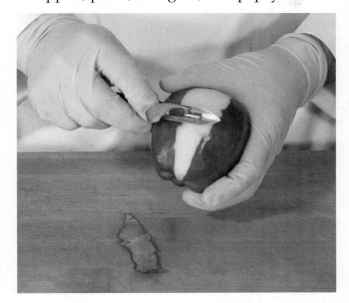

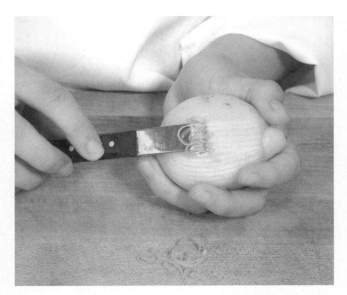

Zesting Citrus Fruits

The zest of citrus fruits is the colorful, outermost part of the skin. This part of the skin contains highly flavorful and aromatic oils. The **zest** is used to add citrus flavor to a dish when the acid from a citrus juice is not desirable. It is important that the zest does not contain any pith. The **pith** is the white, spongy inner part of citrus skin that tastes bitter.

A special tool called a *zester* is used to remove the zest in fine julienne strips and leave the pith behind. If a zester is not available, the zest can be removed with a peeler and then cut into julienne. It can also be removed using a grater. The fine teeth of a box or rasp grater make citrus zest into fine particles, 21-3.

Citrus Suprêmes

In the professional kitchen, the term suprême is used to designate the best, edible part of certain food products. A **suprême** of any citrus fruit is an individual segment

Draz-Koetke/Goodheart-Willcox Publisher

21-3 There are a variety of ways to zest citrus fruits.

TECHNIQUE
Preparing Orange Suprêmes

1. Using a flexible knife, cut the top and bottom off the orange.

2. With a slicing motion, trim the skin following the contour of the orange from top to bottom.

3. Continue working around the orange to remove all skin. Be careful to remove all the pith as well.

4. Hold the orange in the palm of your hand. Cut close to the membrane that separates the segments and slice to the center of the orange.

5. Make another cut just inside the membrane on the other side of the same segment, and slice to the center.

6. Use the knife to lift the suprême out once the second cut is made and the segment is freed from the membrane.

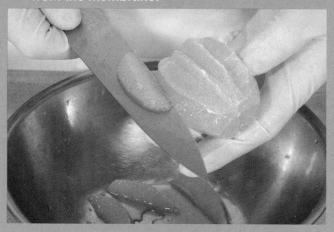

7. Continue making V-cuts on the remaining segments to release them all from the membrane.

8. Squeeze any remaining juice from the membrane and use it to keep the suprêmes moist. Remove any visible seeds from the suprêmes with the tip of a knife.

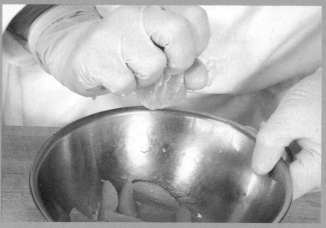

without skin, pith, seeds, or membrane. The technique for making orange suprêmes shown can also be performed on grapefruit, lemons, limes, and mandarins.

Acidulating Fruits

Many fruits brown once they are cut and exposed to the air; this reaction is known as **oxidation**. These fruits include apples, pears, bananas, and avocados. This browning is a reaction by enzymes found in the fruit and is not a sign of contamination. Nevertheless, it does detract from the appearance of cut or portioned fresh fruits.

Acidulation is the process of adding acid to an item. To keep cut fruits looking fresh, chefs dip or brush them with acidulated water. The most common acid used for fresh fruits is the citric acid found in lemon juice. The addition of one tablespoon of lemon juice to one quart of water works well to preserve the color of most items that oxidize, 21-4. If the solution is too strong, the fruit will have a strong lemon flavor. Fruits should be dipped

Draz-Koetke/Goodheart-Willcox Publisher
21-4 Dipping apple slices in acidulated water delays the fruit from browning.

rather than soaked to keep them from becoming waterlogged or mushy.

Fruit Presentation

Fruits come in a wide variety of colors, textures, and shapes. This variety makes creating interesting and appealing fruit presentations easy and fun. Some of the many ways that fresh fruits can be utilized for their eye appeal are discussed in this section.

Fruit Garnishes

A **garnish** is a decoration added to a dish to make it attractive. Garnishes should be edible and suitable for the dish they are decorating. Fruit is often used as a garnish in both sweet and savory dishes. Examples of simple garnishes prepared with fresh fruit include citrus slices, crowns, parisiennes, and fans.

Citrus Slices Slices of citrus fruits are often used to adorn savory dishes, desserts, and even beverages. Slices can be made more interesting with the help of a channel knife.

Hints from the Chef
Garnishing Fruit

Garnishes need to be appropriate for the foods that they decorate. Many garnishes that are appropriate for savory dishes are unsuitable for fresh fruits. Tradition and taste dictate which items should be used when garnishing fruit plates and platters, and which are out of place.

Use	Avoid
Mint leaves	Parsley
Citrus leaves	Lettuce
Grape leaves	Watercress

Cut channels perpendicular to the direction the slices will be cut. This exposes alternating stripes of white pith and colorful zest. Cut the citrus fruit into thin slices, 21-5.

A

B

Draz-Koetke/Goodheart-Willcox Publisher

21-5 Two easy steps create a citrus garnish that is visually interesting and attractive.

Citrus slices can easily be turned into twists by cutting the slice through the flesh and rind from the center to the outer edge. When the two halves are bent in opposite directions the twist will stand up on a plate, 21-6.

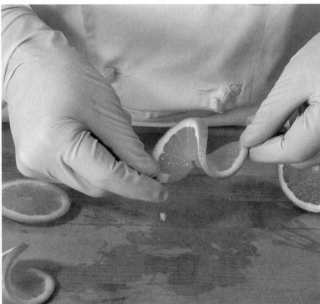

Draz-Koetke/Goodheart-Willcox Publisher

21-6 Citrus slices can be quickly turned into garnish twists that add dimension to the plate.

Crowns   Almost any round fruit can be cut into a crown. Smaller crowns may be used to garnish individual plates and larger crowns of melons are used as serving containers or to garnish large platters.

Crowns can also be made using a U-shaped or V-shaped garnishing knife. Change the length and angle of the cuts for different effects.

TECHNIQUE
Preparing Fruit Crowns

1. Grip a paring knife on the blade at a point that is about the length of the radius of the piece of fruit.

2. At the middle of the fruit hold the knife at a 45° angle to an imaginary line around the middle of the fruit. Insert the tip of the knife into the fruit and push in until it reaches the center.

3. Hold the knife at an opposing 45° angle and make a cut adjacent to the first one. Be sure that the two cuts overlap slightly.

4. Continue these overlapping, zigzag cuts around the center of the fruit until you reach the starting point. Be sure that each cut slightly intersects its adjacent cuts.

5. Grasp the two opposing halves of the fruit and pull apart revealing two crowns.

6. Oranges, lemons, and limes can be used to create fruit crowns of varying sizes and colors.

7. A U-shaped garnishing tool can be used to create an interesting variation to the fruit crown.

Parisiennes   Parisiennes are small balls cut from fruits— most often melon. Many

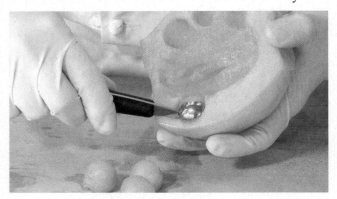

call the tool used to make them a *melon baller* rather than a parisienne scoop. When making parisiennes or balls, press the parisienne scoop well into the fruit before turning it to make a perfectly round sphere. Be sure to make one scoop close to the next to minimize waste.

Fans   Fruit halves, wedges, or whole pieces can be made into an attractive fan garnish. With a little practice you can master this technique. The key to this technique is a sharp knife with a thin blade.

TECHNIQUE
Preparing Fruit Fans

1. Cut a flat side on the bottom of a piece of fruit so that it is stable.

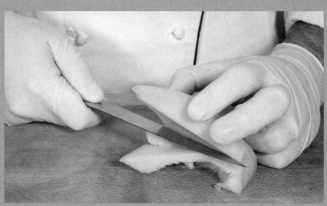

2. Make a slice at a 45° angle to the cutting board. Cut through all but a small portion of the fruit near the tip of the knife

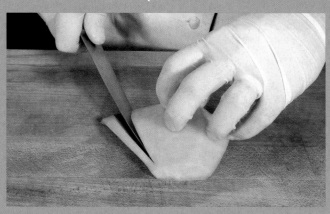

3. Make additional slices parallel to the first slice across the piece of fruit. Be sure to leave each slice partially attached to a small portion near the tip of the knife.

4. Press on the piece of fruit in the same direction as the slices to open the fan.

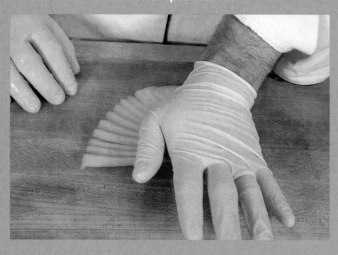

Fruit Plates

Fruit plates are served as a breakfast item, appetizer, main course (often with other ingredients such as cheese or cottage cheese), and healthy dessert option. When creating fruit plates keep in mind that the plate should offer a variety of textures, shapes, colors, and flavors. The fruits should also be ripe for maximum flavor. The fruits should be presented in a way that makes them easy for the customer to eat. This may include peeling, removing seeds, and cutting the fruit. Fruit plates often include a garnish, 21-7. No matter how many fruit plates are being made, it is important that they are all uniform. Each plate should be portioned and presented exactly the same as the others.

Fruit Platters

Presenting a variety of textures, shapes, colors, and flavors is as important when creating fruit platters as it is for fruit plates. When chefs plan buffet platters, service is an additional concern.

Draz-Koetke/Goodheart-Willcox Publisher

21-7 The simple garnish on this plate contributes to the variety of textures, colors, shapes, and sizes used to construct this fruit plate.

Nutrition Connection

Phytonutrients

Fruits, vegetables, grains, herbs, and spices contain compounds called *phytochemicals*—often called *phytonutrients*. Plants naturally contain these compounds to help protect themselves from insects, disease, and extreme temperatures. There are thousands of phytochemicals and many appear to have potential health benefits. These compounds also give foods their flavors and colors. The amounts of phytochemicals increase as food colors intensify. For instance, spinach, watercress, and collard greens contain more phytochemicals than iceberg lettuce. Foods highest in phytochemicals include broccoli, dark green leafy vegetables, red and purple grapes, onions, garlic, chives, and tomatoes. Consider phytochemicals when creating your next fruit salad.

Pieces of fruit must be easy to pick up because customers serve themselves from the buffet platters, 21-8. The size of the fruit pieces must also be able to fit neatly on the plate.

A fruit platter's appearance is greatly enhanced by a larger garnish that creates an attractive focal point. Uniform-sized fruit pieces are also a critical part of the overall appearance because a platter has a greater quantity of fruit than a fruit plate does.

Fruit Salads and Cups

Combinations of fruits are often served as a breakfast item, an appetizer course, side dish, or salad. Fruit salads and cups are a great way to utilize fruit trimmings and extras left from other preparations. To keep flavor and texture at their best, serve fresh fruit well chilled and on chilled plates, cups, or glasses.

Draz-Koetke/Goodheart-Willcox Publisher

21-8 This platter attractively displays fruit pieces in a neat arrangement so customers can serve themselves with ease.

Cooking Fruits

Fruits can be cooked using any cooking method—sautéed, fried, baked, grilled, steamed, poached, or stewed. However, some cooking methods are better than others for specific types of fruits. The cooking process breaks down the fruit's rigid cell structure to make it tender. For this reason, care should be taken to avoid overcooking fruits to the point where they become mushy and lose their shape.

Determining cooking time and doneness varies from fruit to fruit. The degree of ripeness also affects the cook time. In general, cooked fruits should be tender when pierced with a fork or tip of a knife. Fresh fruits contain enough moisture to eliminate the concern of drying the product out during cooking.

Plumping Dried Fruits

Dried fruits are often plumped before use in a dish. **Plumping** reconstitutes or returns some of the liquid removed from the fruit during the drying process. When dried fruits are not plumped, their chewy texture can detract from the dish in which they are used.

Plumping is done by soaking the dried fruits in hot liquid or simmering them in liquid. The liquid used to plump fruits may be water or a flavored liquid that enhances the dish. Some moist recipes, such as muffins or breads, plump dried ingredients during the cooking process.

Recipe No.	Name			Category	
21.7	Poached Pears			Fruit	
Yield	**Portion Size**			**No. Portions**	
10 servings	1 pear			10	
US Quantity	**Metric Quantity**	**Ingredient**		**TCS**	
10 ea.		pears			
2 qt.	1.9 L	water			
1 lb.	450 g	sugar			
2 ea.		lemons, cut in half, juice and rind			
1 tsp.	5 mL	whole black peppercorns			
1 piece		fresh ginger (1 inch)			
1 ea.		cinnamon stick			
Method				**CCP**	
1. Peel and core pears. Cut in even halves.					
2. Combine the remaining ingredients in a pot and bring to a boil.					
3. Add pears and simmer until tender.					
4. Allow pears to cool in the syrup.					
5. Drain pears and serve.					

Portion (g)	Calories	Fat (g)	Protein (g)	Carbohydrate (g)	Cholesterol (mg)	Sodium (mg)	Fiber (g)
173	119	0.20	0.64	31.46	0	1.68	5.15

Summary Points

- Fruits need to be prepared so they are easy for diners to eat.
- All fruits must be washed before preparation begins, even if the fruit is to be peeled.
- Fruits make interesting presentations because of their wide variety of colors, textures, and shapes.
- Fruits can be cooked using most cooking methods.

In Review
Assess

1. True or false. Fruits that are going to be peeled do not need to be washed first.
2. List three ways to remove skin from fruits.
3. True or false. Zest is the white spongy part of citrus skin.
4. What is the name for citrus segments without seeds or membrane?
5. List four fruits that can be dipped in an acid solution to prevent browning.
6. To make acidulated water for fruits add _____ of lemon juice to _____ of water.
7. Name four garnishes made from fresh fruits.
8. List two considerations when making a fruit platter for a buffet.
9. True or false. Cooking breaks down a fruit's rigid cell structure and makes it tender.
10. Before using dried cherries in a recipe, they should be _____.
    A. washed
    B. peeled
    C. plumped
    D. acidulated

Core Skills

11. **Math.** The chef has asked you to prepare 12½ pounds of fresh fruit salad made with strawberries, pineapple, and cantaloupe. He would like the salad to be approximately one-fifth strawberries, two-fifths pineapple, and two-fifths cantaloupe. How many pounds of each fruit do you need to prepare?

12. **Writing.** Research different ways that fruits are cooked. Write a 2-page informative paper describing a minimum of four different cooking methods used to cook fruits. Discuss which cooking methods might be best suited to different fruits. Include at least one recipe for each cooking method.

13. **Reading.** Many food items often referred to as vegetables are technically fruits. Read a botany text or other reliable source to understand why tomatoes, avocados, and cucumbers are fruits. Write a brief summary of your findings.

14. **Math.** A chef purchases 12 pounds of grapefruit to prepare suprêmes. She pays $1.99 per pound. After preparation, the chef determines the suprêmes weigh 124 ounces. What is the price per pound of the suprêmes?

15. **Speaking.** Select two fruit preparations discussed in this chapter. Imagine you are a culinary instructor and prepare a demonstration of the two preparations to present to your classmates who are your "students." Adjust your rate of speech, vocabulary, and delivery of content to fit your audience. Be sure to make eye contact to assess the audience's understanding.

16. **Listening and Writing.** As each classmate delivers his or her presentation in activity #15, listen and observe carefully. Take notes on important points and write down any questions or critiques that occur to you. After the presentation, ask questions to obtain additional information or clarification. Write a brief evaluation of each "instructor's" technique as well as demonstration skills. Be sure to provide constructive criticism, noting both strengths and weaknesses.

17. **CTE Career Readiness Practice.** Problems such as last minute requests or failing to receive ordered food products are common in commercial kitchens. Chefs must be able to respond quickly to problems and determine solutions. Imagine you are a chef that just received a last minute request for a fruit salad. Using ingredients you find either in your home kitchen or the lab kitchen, write a recipe for a fruit salad. Prepare the salad, take a photo, and evaluate it for flavor and creativity.

Critical Thinking

18. **Compare.** What are the advantages and disadvantages of using fresh fruit rather than fruit that has been processed?

19. **Assess.** Which fruit would take longer to cook—an apple or a peach? Why?

20. **Conclude.** Suppose a chef serves fruit plates for a banquet of 100 guests and each fruit plate is different. How do you think the diners might react? What problems could this cause in the kitchen?

Technology

Some countries have fruit and vegetable carving traditions that are centuries old. Use the Internet to research fruit carving techniques in countries such as Thailand, Taiwan, or China. Prepare an electronic presentation describing the history behind the traditions. Include photos or video to enhance understanding and add interest. Present to the class.

Teamwork

Form small teams and assign each member a role. Obtain two oranges. Weigh and record the weight of each orange. Give two team members each one orange from which to prepare suprêmes. Weigh and record the weight of the suprêmes from each orange separately. Calculate the yield percentage of the orange by dividing the weight of the suprêmes by the weight of the whole orange and multiplying by 100. This is the usable or edible percent of the orange. Perform a visual evaluation of the suprêmes and record your observations. Compare the two sets of results and discuss why the edible percents may be different. Which result is ideal and why? Take a photo and attach it to the report.

Chef's E-portfolio
Fruit Salad Solution

Upload your recipe and photo of the salad you created for the CTE Career Readiness Practice activity to your e-portfolio. Ask your instructor where to save your file. This could be on the school's network or a flash drive of your own. Name your portfolio document *FirstnameLastname_ Portfolio Ch#.docx* (i.e., JohnSmith_PortfolioCh21.docx).

While studying, look for the activity icon ⤴ to:
- Build vocabulary with e-flash cards and matching activities.
- Expand learning with video clips, photo identification activities, animations, and interactive activities.
- Review and assess what you learn by completing end-of-chapter questions.

G-WLEARNING.com

Cold Sandwiches 22

Reading Prep

In preparation for reading the chapter, review a variety of restaurant menus for the types and numbers of sandwiches offered. Identify the different ingredients being used. Compare your findings to the chapter as you read.

Culinary Terminology Build Vocab

sandwich, p. 359
wrap, p. 360
canapé, p. 360
finger sandwich, p. 360
tea sandwich, p. 360
Danish sandwich, p. 361
Pullman loaf, p. 362
baguette, p. 362
à la carte, p. 366

Academic Terminology Build Vocab

pungent, p. 364

Objectives

After studying this chapter, you will be able to

- list different types of sandwiches.
- recognize the attributes of successful sandwiches.
- explain the role of different sandwich ingredients.
- compare sandwich assembly methods.

Sandwiches are an important part of America's eating habits. Many foodservice concepts are centered around the idea of serving sandwiches. They are eaten at school, home, and work every day. Sandwiches are convenient because you do not need flatware to eat them. Their portability makes them perfect for busy lifestyles. In fact, many are eaten in cars. From fast food to fine dining, foodservice employees prepare many different types of sandwiches at all times of the day, from breakfast to late at night.

Types of Sandwiches

At its most basic, a **sandwich** consists of a number of ingredients placed on, in, or between bread. Beyond that simple definition is an endless variety of sandwiches. They can be as simple as peanut butter and jelly on white bread or as imaginative as herb bread topped with grilled marinated chicken, sprouts, avocado, and chipotle mayonnaise.

Closed Sandwiches

Closed sandwiches consist of ingredients placed between two pieces of bread. Closed sandwiches may have more than two pieces of bread as well as numerous layers of fillings. These sandwiches are referred to as multidecker sandwiches. One famous example of a multidecker is the club sandwich that uses three pieces of toasted bread per sandwich.

Open-Faced Sandwiches

Open-faced sandwiches are made using only one piece of bread. The sandwich's fillings are placed attractively on top of the bread.

Rolled Sandwiches

Rolled sandwiches are made using flatbreads such as tortillas or flattened white bread. The most common rolled sandwich today is the wrap. Wraps consist of various ingredients rolled in a tortilla. Classical rolled sandwiches, which are less common today, are made using soft white bread that has been flattened with a rolling pin. Ingredients are then rolled tightly in the flattened bread.

Canapés

A canapé (kan ah PAY) is a small, bite-sized hors d'oeuvre that resembles an open-faced sandwich and is well garnished and attractive. Canapés are bite-sized so guests can eat them with their fingers without making a mess. Canapés are served before a meal or as part of a reception. At formal receptions, waiters offer them neatly arranged on trays, 22-1. The term *canapé* can also refer to many different preparations in addition to small open-faced sandwiches. Canapés can include anything from small filled cucumber cups to minitarts.

Finger Sandwiches

Finger sandwich is a category of sandwiches that are attractive and slightly larger than canapés. Finger sandwiches include tea sandwiches and Danish sandwiches.

Tea Sandwiches   A tea sandwich is a small, neatly made sandwich that is served during afternoon tea. Afternoon tea is a British custom that began in the late 1800s.

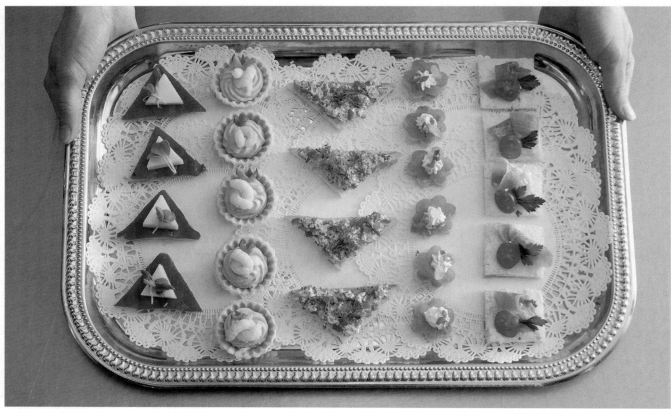

Draz-Koetke/Goodheart-Willcox Publisher

22-1 Canapés are often presented to guests during a formal reception.

Afternoon tea is a small meal designed to provide a midday snack. In addition to tea sandwiches and hot tea, other foods such as scones, cookies, and small cakes are served. Tea sandwiches are small, closed sandwiches made with crustless bread and trimmed to neat shapes, 22-2. They are typically made using delicately flavored ingredients. Classic tea sandwiches include watercress, egg, and cucumber.

Draz-Koetke/Goodheart-Willcox Publisher

22-2 A selection of tea sandwiches are often served for afternoon tea.

Danish Sandwiches A Danish sandwich is a neat, open-faced sandwich that often includes strongly flavored foods. Some common ingredients are pickled herring, smoked salmon, blue cheese, and salami.

Sandwich Attributes

Sandwiches can be complex creations of different flavors, colors, and textures. Combining different elements to produce satisfying sandwiches requires practice and skill. Successful and delicious sandwiches should have the following attributes.

- *Easy to eat.* Sandwiches should be neatly made so the ingredients do not fall out of the sandwich when eaten.
- *Appearance.* Fresh food that is arranged attractively excites the appetite. Bright colors are especially appealing.
- *Texture.* Using a wide variety of textures, such as crunchy, chewy, soft, or smooth creates interesting sandwiches.
- *Moisture.* Both moist and high-fat ingredients are essential to counter dry bread. Dry sandwiches have little appeal.
- *Flavor.* Sandwiches must be made of flavorful ingredients. Strongly flavored condiments, ripe vegetables, smoked meats, and cheese increase the sandwich's flavor profile.

Sandwich Ingredients

Sandwiches generally consist of four parts—bread, spread, filling, and garnish. Each part of the sandwich is important to the overall success of the sandwich.

Bread

All sandwiches include some type of bread. The choice of bread contributes to the overall character of the sandwich. Fortunately, there are an increasing number of different breads available to the foodservice market. Certain types of sandwiches even require specific breads.

When choosing a bread, consider how sturdy or tender it is. Sturdy, country-style loaves support wet ingredients and add a chewy texture. Tender breads are ideal for delicate sandwiches such as tea sandwiches and some canapés.

While many sandwiches simply call for sliced bread, others require bread that is manipulated in some way. For instance, the crusts may be cut from the slices of bread. For other sandwiches, breads may be warmed, grilled, or toasted prior to assembly. Grilling or toasting adds crunch and increased flavor to the finished sandwich.

Pullman Loaf   Pullman loaf is a finely textured bread that cuts into perfectly square slices. The slices are square because the loaves are baked inside a mold with a cover. Originally, Pullman loaves were named after the famous Pullman railroad dining cars. Their square shape made them easy to stack; therefore, they took up less room in the train's cramped quarters.

Italian and French Bread   These are long, thin breads with a crunchy crust and airy, white interiors. A baguette (bah GEHT) is the name for a long, thin French bread.

Whole-Grain Bread   A wide variety of whole-grain breads are readily available. The texture of these breads can vary enormously. Some of these breads incorporate whole seeds such as sesame and sunflower seeds, or grains such as millet, barley, and oats. Whole seeds and grains contribute a chewy or crunchy texture.

Focaccia (foh KAH chee ah)   This flat Italian bread is typically cut into square pieces. It is often flavored with olive oil, garlic, tomato, and assorted herbs.

Pita Bread   This round flatbread originates in the Middle East. Pita bread is most often served cut in half. The cut half opens easily to form a pocket, which can be filled with either hot or cold ingredients.

Tortillas (tor TEE yahs)   These thin Mexican flatbreads are often used to make wraps or rolled sandwiches. They are made from wheat flour or cornmeal.

Croissants (kwah SOHN)   These light flaky crescent-shaped rolls were originally French breakfast rolls. Today, croissants are used increasingly for sandwiches.

Rolls   Rolls comprise a large category of small yeast doughs. Rolls come in a wide variety of shapes, sizes, and textures. These bread products make excellent sandwiches.

Naan   This leavened flatbread from India is made from wheat flour and yogurt. The bread is baked in a clay oven (tandoor) which imparts a unique flavor, 22-3.

Chapati   An unleavened flatbread made from finely milled whole-wheat flour, it is cooked on a curved griddle. This bread is popular throughout India and Pakistan where it is used for scooping up food or dunking in soups.

Lavash   This thin, crisp leavened bread made from wheat flour is widely baked and consumed throughout Iran, Armenia, and Afghanistan. In some areas, it is rolled so thin that you can almost see through it.

Joe Gough/Shutterstock.com

22-3 Flatbreads such as naan bread can be substituted for traditional breads in sandwiches.

Spreads

Spreads are thick, paste-like ingredients that are applied to the bread. They are often rich in fat and for that reason should be used sparingly. Spreads include softened butter or margarine, cream cheese, mayonnaise, and vegetable or dried bean purées. Bound salad sandwiches such as egg or chicken salad do not need a spread since bound salads already contain ingredients such as mayonnaise.

Many spreads are rich in fat, and therefore, prevent wet fillings from soaking into the bread. At the same time, the fat-rich spreads contribute moisture and considerable flavor to the finished sandwich. Some creatively flavored spreads include herb butters, roasted garlic mayonnaise, sun-dried tomato cream cheese, and garbanzo purée (also called *hummus*). Aside from moisture and flavor, spreads help hold the sandwich together. Most spreads are thick and creamy and act as a binding agent for the bread and other ingredients.

Sandwich Fillings

The sandwich's fillings make up the bulk of any sandwich. In fact, a sandwich is often named after the fillings—peanut butter and jelly, ham and cheese, corned beef. Many fillings are high-protein ingredients. For this reason, proper sanitation practices must be rigorously followed when preparing sandwiches, 22-4.

The number of possible sandwich fillings is almost endless. Some of the more common fillings include the following:

- *Meat, poultry, and seafood.* These are among the most common sandwich ingredients. Within this category, there are a wide variety of options including grilled chicken breast, deep-fried oysters, shrimp, sautéed steak, bacon, hard-boiled eggs, smoked sausages, ham, and smoked salmon.
- *Cheeses.* Well suited for sandwich making, cheeses contribute flavor and texture. Those with high moisture content such as

Hints from the Chef

Sandwich Portion Amounts

Correct portioning can be the difference between a profitable and an unprofitable sandwich. The following portions are suggested amounts. Chefs might set specific standards according to individual operations or recipes. Amounts of the following ingredients also depend on the other ingredients of a particular sandwich.

Ingredient	Suggested Portion per Sandwich
Bacon	3 strips, cooked [about 2 oz. (58 g) raw bacon]
Cheese slices	3 oz. (85 g)
Cooked meat (ham, turkey, beef, other)	3 oz. (85 g)
Hard sausage, salami	3 oz. (85 g)
Proscuitto	2 oz. (58 g)
Bound salad	1 cup (240 mL)
Smooth peanut butter	2 Tablespoons (30 mL)
Butter	1 Tablespoon (15 mL)
Cream cheese	1 Tablespoon (15 mL)
Mayonnaise	1 Tablespoon (15 mL)

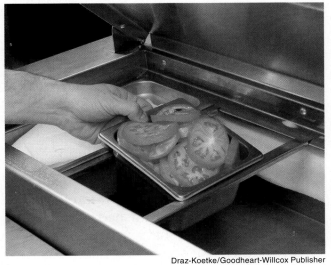

Draz-Koetke/Goodheart-Willcox Publisher

22-4 Use of refrigerated wells on sandwich stations helps maintain ingredients at safe temperatures.

Recipe No.	Name		Category
22.4	Vegetarian Focaccia Sandwich		Sandwiches, cold
Yield	**Portion Size**		**No. Portions**
10 sandwiches	1 sandwich		10

US Quantity	Metric Quantity	Ingredient	TCS
10 pc.		focaccia bread, 4"×4" (10 × 10 cm)	
2 Tbsp.	30 mL	sun-dried tomatoes, finely chopped*	
5 ea.		large portobello mushroom caps, rinsed and dried	
2 Tbsp.	30 mL	extra virgin olive oil	
4 Tbsp.	60 mL	fresh basil, chiffonade	
4 fl. oz.	120 mL	mayonnaise	•
1 ea.		small red onion, thinly sliced	
15 oz.	420 g	marinated canned artichoke hearts, cut into quarters	
20 oz.	560 g	roasted red pepper	
20 oz.	560 g	Provolone cheese, sliced	•

Method	CCP
1. Soften sun-dried tomatoes in hot water (about 30 minutes). Drain water and squeeze tomatoes to expel excess water.	
2. Rub the portobello caps with olive oil. Season the caps with salt and black pepper. Place on a sheet tray, gill side up.	
3. Bake mushrooms in a 400°F (204°C) oven for 4 minutes. Turn mushrooms and cook until they soften (about 5 minutes).	
4. Slice cooled mushrooms into ¼-inch slices. Season with salt and black pepper if necessary.	
5. Cut the focaccia pieces in half horizontally.	
6. Mix sun-dried tomato, basil, and mayonnaise together. Spread on the cut surfaces of both pieces of the focaccia.	
7. Layer sandwich with portobello, red onion, artichoke, red pepper, and Provolone cheese.	
8. Top sandwich with other piece of focaccia, wrap, and refrigerate at or below 41°F (5°C) until service.	CCP

Portion (g)	Calories	Fat (g)	Protein (g)	Carbohydrate (g)	Cholesterol (mg)	Sodium (mg)	Fiber (g)
359	739	36.05	27.51	75.74	44.00	1723.55	4.82

*If sun-dried tomatoes are not available, 3 Tbsp. (45 mL) well-cooked tomato concassé can be substituted. It is not necessary to soak the tomato concassé.

cream cheese and fresh mozzarella also add moisture to the finished sandwich. More **pungent**, or sharp, varieties of cheese provide a flavor boost.

- *Vegetables.* Vegetables can also be considered sandwich fillings when they become the focal point of the sandwich. This is especially true of vegetarian sandwiches. The number of vegetable-based sandwiches is endless because of the great variety of vegetables. They can be used raw, grilled, sautéed, roasted, or marinated.

- *Nut butter.* Sandwiches made with this filling are especially popular in the United States. Certainly, the most common nut butter used in America is peanut butter. Other nut butters, such as cashew or almond butter, can also make interesting sandwiches. Often, nut butters are paired with sweet ingredients such as jelly or sliced fruit.
- *Bound salads.* These fillings include protein-based salads such as ham or tuna salad. Bound salads consist of a finely chopped main ingredient mixed with a thick dressing—often mayonnaise—and various flavorings.

Garnishes

Many sandwiches consist of more than bread, a filling, and a spread. Garnishes make the finished sandwich more attractive and flavorful. Garnishes are ingredients that are often added in small amounts and are not the biggest attention-getter. There are many ingredients that could be used as sandwich garnishes, however, it is important to choose a garnish that complements the flavors of the sandwich. Some common garnishes include the following:

- *Fresh vegetables* add color, flavor, crunch, pungency, or moisture. Some examples include tomatoes, lettuce, onions, and sprouts.
- *Pickled vegetables* add acidity, crunch, and sometimes sweetness. Examples include sweet or dill pickles, pickled onions, and sauerkraut.
- *Cooked vegetables* increase flavor and may add sweetness. Examples include roasted portobello mushrooms, grilled eggplant, sautéed zucchini, and caramelized onions.

Some open-faced sandwiches, such as canapés, require detailed garnishes to make them as visually appealing as possible, 22-5. Before applying such garnishes, make sure the canapé has been neatly arranged. Garnishes will not hide a poorly made sandwich. Some canapé garnishes include

Draz-Koetke/Goodheart-Willcox Publisher

22-5 Special attention is paid to garnishing canapés to ensure an attractive presentation.

- fresh herbs like chives, parsley, or basil
- sliced olives
- diced or julienned red or yellow pepper
- diced or julienned tomato
- cream cheese or butter decoratively piped through a fine-tipped pastry bag

Sandwich Assembly

There are three basic assembly strategies restaurants use when making sandwiches

- sandwiches made to order or à la carte
- self-serve sandwich bars
- sandwich assembly lines

In each of these three strategies, the physical sandwich assembling area and workflow must be well designed. This ensures an efficient and speedy operation.

À la Carte

Preparing food à la carte (ah lah KAHRT) refers to a system in which food is prepared only when an order is received from the service staff, 22-6. In an à la carte setting, speed is important to ensure that the time it takes for the food to be served to the customer is minimized. If the wait is too long, the customer becomes impatient, which detracts from the dining experience.

À la carte sandwich stations are designed with speed in mind. Consider the following when setting up an à la carte sandwich station:

- All sandwich ingredients should be within easy reach.
- Sandwich stations should have a consistent linear workflow. This means the different sandwich components should

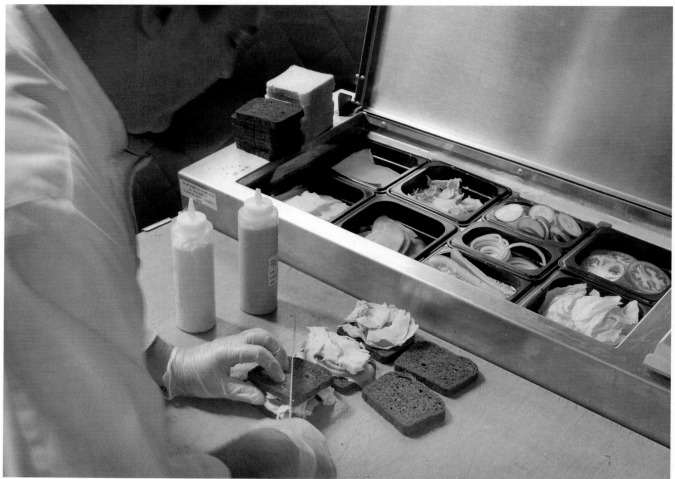

Draz-Koetke/Goodheart-Willcox Publisher

22-6 Making sandwiches to order ensures a fresh sandwich is served to the customer.

be arranged in a line from left to right or vice versa, 22-7.

- Make sure that all spreads have accompanying small spatulas.
- A cutting board should be within easy reach of the ingredients. The cutting board should be large enough so that several sandwiches could be assembled at the same time.
- A serrated knife should be easily accessible to cut sandwiches.
- Disposable gloves and a garbage can are also part of the mise en place.
- Preportioned ingredients such as meats and cheeses save valuable time during service.

Refrigerated wells are ideal for sandwich production. These refrigerated systems keep ingredients out of the temperature danger zone while keeping them readily accessible. Some units even blow a curtain of cold air over the top of the wells to keep the food cold. No matter which refrigerated-well unit is used, temperatures must be checked periodically to be sure that the food is at or below 41°F (5°C). Take the temperature of the ingredients near the top of the well where food may be warmest. Covering refrigerated units when not in use helps keep the food cold.

Sandwich Bar

Sandwich bars have become increasingly popular lunch options. Sandwich bars are a type of buffet because the customers are serving themselves. As with all buffets, they should be attractively presented. Perishable sandwich ingredients must be kept cold by placing them on ice or in a well-style refrigeration unit.

Arrange the sandwich bar in a logical manner, beginning with plates and bread and ending with various supporting ingredients. In many states, sneeze guards are not only recommended, but mandated by law, 22-8. Sneeze guards are panes of tempered glass or Plexiglas® positioned above a salad bar to shield the food in the event a customer sneezes or coughs.

Sandwich Station Mise en Place	
Workflow Order	**Ingredients**
1st-Breads	White bread, Pullman Whole wheat, Pullman Light rye Dark rye 7-Seed bread Baguettes Croissants
2nd-Spreads	Mayonnaise Soft butter Cream cheese Chive cream cheese Hummus

3rd-Fillings	Slice cheeses:
	    American
	    Swiss
	    Cheddar
	    Provolone
	    mozzarella
	    brie
	Proteins:
	    Turkey*
	    Ham*
	    Roast beef*
	    Corned beef*
	    Assorted sausages*
	    Bacon
	    Smoked salmon
	    Chicken salad
	    Egg salad
	    Tuna salad
	*sliced and preportioned in 3 oz. amounts

4th-Supporting Ingredients	Leaf lettuce, washed and dried Sliced tomatoes Sliced onions Dill pickles Roasted red peppers Mustard (prepared and Dijon) Salsa Prepared horseradish Sliced black olives Coleslaw in portion cups
Last-Nonfood	Toothpicks with colored frills Wax paper Plate or basket

Draz-Koetke/Goodheart-Willcox Publisher

22-7 Every sandwich station has a unique mise en place based on the sandwiches on the menu.

During service, sandwich bars should be kept clean, stocked, and organized. Replenish as necessary to keep them from looking sparse. Sandwich bars that look dirty, are improperly stocked, and disorganized detract from the diner's eating experience.

Assembly Line
Animation

In many foodservice operations, sandwiches are made in large numbers and well in advance of service. The assembly line technique is the fastest way to make large

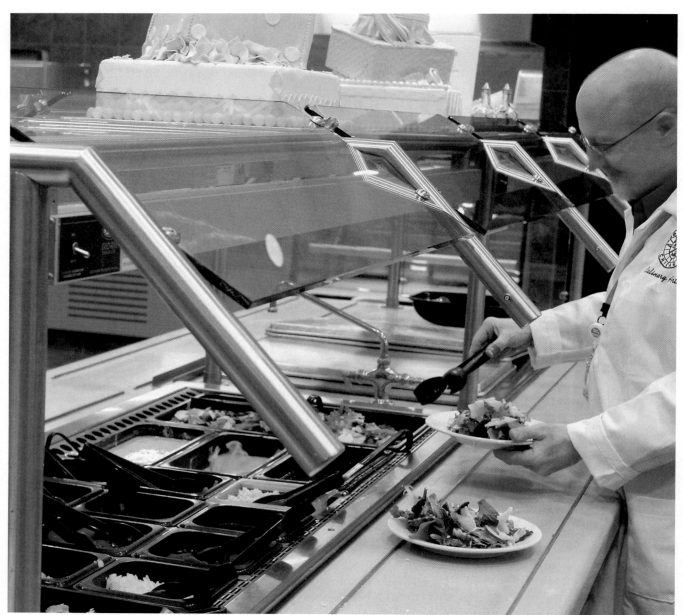

Draz-Koetke/Goodheart-Willcox Publisher

22-8 Sneeze guards are often required by law at self-serve areas such as salad or sandwich bars.

numbers of sandwiches. With this strategy, each person performs only a limited number of repetitive jobs. If each sandwich was individually assembled by individual cooks—as in à la carte production—sandwich production would be much slower.

To form an assembly line, cooks line up on one or both sides of a worktable. Each person is assigned a limited number of operations to perform. As the sandwiches are passed along the assembly line, each cook adds one or two ingredients. By the end of the assembly line, the sandwich is completely constructed.

For instance, to make a ham and cheese sandwich, an assembly line strategy might resemble the following:

- First cook spreads mayonnaise on one piece of bread.
- Second cook places preportioned ham on the mayonnaise.
- Third cook places preportioned cheese on the ham, 22-9.
- Fourth cook spreads mustard on the top piece of bread, which is then placed on the ham.
- Fifth cook wraps or packages finished sandwiches.

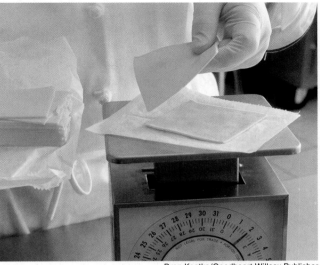

Draz-Koetke/Goodheart-Willcox Publisher

22-9 Preportioning ingredients before service increases speed during service.

If not served immediately, sandwiches containing perishable ingredients must be refrigerated until needed. Sandwiches must also be protected from drying out. Wrap sandwiches in plastic wrap before refrigerating. Some sandwiches, such as tea sandwiches made from Pullman loaves, are particularly prone to drying out.

Summary Points

- An endless selection of sandwiches are possible through combinations of ingredients and different sandwich types.
- Successful sandwiches usually have certain attributes in common.
- Sandwiches typically consist of four parts—bread, spread, filling, and garnish. For each of these parts, there are many different options from which to choose.
- Sandwiches can be prepared when ordered, by the customer, or in large quantities on assembly lines.

In Review
Assess

1. List five types of sandwiches and give an example of each.
2. True or false. A wrap is a type of open-faced sandwich.
3. Why should canapés be small?
4. _____ and _____ are two types of finger sandwiches.
5. List five attributes of a successful sandwich.
6. True or false. Crusty, rustic bread is ideal for sandwiches made from wet ingredients.
7. The role of a _____ is to add moisture and flavor, and to help to hold the sandwich together.
8. Why is speed crucial in à la carte sandwich production?
9. True or false. Sandwich bar ingredients should be allowed to run out if most of the customers have been served.
10. Why is assembly line sandwich production faster than à la carte sandwich production when making large numbers of sandwiches?

Core Skills

11. **Math.** The chef has asked you to prepare 75 closed sandwiches for an event. You are to use a variety of fillings and garnishes on white bread. Each 1½ pound Pullman loaf yields 24 usable slices. How many loaves will you need to make the sandwiches? (Round up to whole loaves.)
12. **Writing.** Sandwiches are increasingly consumed at all times of the day and designed to reflect local tastes and culinary traditions. Design a different sandwich for breakfast, lunch, midday snack, dinner, and late night that reflects local ingredients, tastes, or culinary traditions in your part of the country. Be sure to describe the sandwich in detail and how it relates to your part of the country.
13. **Speaking.** Read history textbooks or other reliable sources to learn the history of the sandwich and how it got its name. Present your findings to the class.
14. **Math.** The chef has asked you to slice a two-pound sausage into thin slices for a sandwich. The sliced sausage is to be preportioned into three-ounce portions. Assuming that five percent of the sausage is lost to end trimmings and mistakes, how many three-ounce portions should the sausage yield? (Round down to the nearest whole number.)
15. **Speaking.** Imagine you are a culinary instructor giving your "students" a demonstration on how to prepare a sandwich. Select a sandwich and plan your presentation. As you practice giving the presentation, consider your audience and adjust your rate of speech, vocabulary, and delivery of content as needed. Be sure to make eye contact to gauge the audience's understanding.
16. **Listening and Writing.** As each classmate delivers his or her presentation in activity #15, listen and observe carefully. Take notes on

important points and write down any questions or critiques that occur to you. After the presentation, ask questions to obtain additional information or clarification. Write a brief evaluation of each "instructor's" technique as well as demonstration skills. Be sure to provide constructive criticism noting both strengths and weaknesses.

17. **CTE Career Readiness Practice.** Use your text and the Internet to design and equip a new à la carte sandwich assembling area. Locate equipment that enhances productivity and workflow. List the prices of all items necessary to fully equip the sandwich station. Create an electronic spreadsheet to compare the cost data for the equipment from the two vendors. Which vendor offers the best quality products for prices that meet your budget?

Critical Thinking

18. **Assess.** Select your favorite sandwich and write a paragraph describing the attributes that make it successful for you.

19. **Apply.** Identify two specialty breads that you are unfamiliar with and select appropriate spreads, fillings, and garnishes to make a quality sandwich. Explain your reasoning behind your selections.

20. **Consider.** List the pros and cons of sandwich bars and à la carte sandwiches. Which method would you select to serve your customers sandwiches?

Technology

Research the Internet for different sandwich concept restaurants. Compare how these restaurant concepts are different from one another. Find out potential startup costs for these restaurants. Compare startup costs to those for other (not just sandwich) concept restaurants. Based on your findings, recommend and make a case for the best restaurant concept for a new, young entrepreneur to take on. Prepare an electronic presentation of your findings.

Teamwork

Working in small teams, assemble all the ingredients for one well-known closed sandwich as well as some additional garnish ingredients. Convert this sandwich into as many different canapés as possible. Remember that canapés are bite-sized, finger foods that can be hot or cold. Be as creative as possible. Write a recipe for each canapé and attach a photo. Have other teams taste them and evaluate the results.

Chef's E-portfolio
Designing a Sandwich Station

Upload your report from the CTE Career Readiness Practice activity to your e-portfolio. Ask your instructor where to save your file. This could be on the school's network or a flash drive of your own. Name your portfolio document *FirstnameLastname_Portfolio Ch#.docx* (i.e., JohnSmith_PortfolioCh22.docx).

While studying, look for the activity icon ↱ to:

- Build vocabulary with e-flash cards and matching activities.
- Expand learning with video clips, photo identification activities, animations, and interactive activities.
- Review and assess what you learn by completing end-of-chapter questions.

G-WLEARNING.com

Stocks

Reading Prep

In preparation for reading the chapter, find a container of prepared stock at a supermarket. Make a copy of the ingredients list. Compare this list of ingredients to those discussed in the chapter. Consider how the flavor of the two stocks might compare based on your findings.

Culinary Terminology Build Vocab

stock, p. 373
fumet, p. 374
gelatin, p. 374
mouthfeel, p. 374
collagen, p. 374
reduce, p. 375
sachet, p. 375
bouquet garni, p. 375
white stock, p. 377
brown stock, p. 377
blanching, p. 379
deglaze, p. 380
bouillon, p. 382
broth, p. 382
base, p. 382

Academic Terminology Build Vocab

principal, p. 374

Objectives

After studying this chapter, you will be able to

- summarize the role of various ingredients in the production of stock.
- recall the attributes of a well-made stock.
- execute the basic stock-making procedure.
- understand bouillons and broths and their uses.
- explain how vegetable stocks are made and how they differ from classic meat-based stocks.
- compare bases and stocks.

Chances are good that you have eaten stock recently. You will probably never see stock featured on a menu, but it plays a crucial, supporting role in cooking.

Stock is a highly flavored liquid made by simmering bones with vegetables, herbs, and spices. Many recipes are made with water in home cooking. In the professional kitchen, stock is often used instead of water. Stock adds depth of flavor and color to a wide range of dishes.

Stock plays an important role in the preparation of many dishes. Without well-made stocks, it is difficult to produce high-quality cuisine. Some of the dishes in which stock is used include the following:

- soups
- sauces
- gravies
- braised meat and vegetable preparations
- rice, grain, and potato preparations

Stock is part of so many culinary preparations that it is considered one of the main building blocks of cooking. Learning to make stocks correctly is an essential part of your training in the culinary arts. A well-made stock is an asset in the kitchen. However, an improperly made stock can ruin the preparations it is intended to improve.

Basic Stock Ingredients

Stock is composed of three types of ingredients—nutritive, aromatic, and liquid.

Nutritive Ingredients

Bones are the **principal**, or most important, nutritive ingredient. Bones are also the stock's key ingredient. Stocks are named after their nutritive ingredient(s). Therefore, game bones are used to make game stock and chicken bones to make chicken stock. Fish stock is commonly referred to by its French name, **fumet** (foo MAY).

Nutritive ingredients contribute the predominant flavor to stocks. Meat may also be added along with bones to add flavor to the stock. The more meat added to a stock, the better the stock's flavor intensity. In many foodservice operations, little or no meat is added to stocks because meat is more expensive than bones. If meat is added, the toughest cuts are used since they are inexpensive and provide the best flavor.

Bones also add body to the stock. Bones produce gelatin. **Gelatin** is an animal protein that when dissolved in a hot liquid adds to a rich mouthfeel. **Mouthfeel** is the sensation created in the mouth by the body, texture, and temperature of a food as it is eaten. Stocks that are low in gelatin are thin like water and not satisfying. For this reason, gelatin levels are also important when making sauces and braised items. In addition, high levels of gelatin cause liquids to solidify into a wiggly mass when cooled, 23-1.

Gelatin is not present in bones. Rather, it is derived from another protein found in bones called **collagen**. When collagen is simmered in liquid for long periods of time, it turns into gelatin. Gelatin dissolves into the surrounding simmering liquid.

Different types of bones have varying levels of collagen. Bones from younger

Draz-Koetke/Goodheart-Willcox Publisher

23-1 Stocks that are rich in gelatin may solidify when chilled.

animals contain higher levels of collagen. As animals age, their bones become harder and collagen levels drop. A stock made from veal bones has greater gelatin content than an identical stock made from beef bones. Collagen levels also vary from one part of the animal to another. In addition, certain parts of the animal, such as joints, feet, and skin, have higher levels of collagen than other parts of the animal.

The time it takes to extract the gelatin from the bones depends on the size of the bones and the age of the animal. Larger bones and bones from older animals require longer cooking times than smaller bones and bones from younger animals, 23-2. For this reason, chefs often cut the bones into smaller pieces to extract gelatin faster. In general, the smaller the pieces are cut, the faster the stock cooks and the richer the flavor.

Aromatic Ingredients

Aromatic ingredients include the vegetables, herbs, and spices added to a stock to improve its flavor. These ingredients improve overall flavor by adding background flavors to the main meaty flavor. Without aromatic ingredients, stocks taste unsatisfactorily one-dimensional.

One ingredient that is not added to stock is salt. The reason for this is that stock is the

Cooking Times for Stocks	
Type of Stock	**Cooking Time**
Fumet (fish stock)	30 to 45 minutes
Chicken stock	3 to 5 hours
Veal stock	8 to 12 hours
Beef stock	10 to 15 hours

23-2 The amount of time it takes to extract gelatin from the bones determines how long the stock must cook.

foundation of many preparations. If stocks were salted, they could not be used for such a wide range of preparations. For instance, in many preparations stocks are reduced to improve and strengthen their flavor. To **reduce** a stock, you heat it to a rapid boil so that water evaporates. The result is a thicker, more concentrated liquid. If stocks were salted, they would become overly salty if allowed to reduce.

Vegetables   The universal vegetable flavoring in stock is mirepoix. Mirepoix is a combination of vegetables. Both regular mirepoix (two parts onion, one part celery, one part carrot) and white mirepoix (two parts onion, one part celery, one part leek)

are used to make stocks. Mirepoix is cut to different sizes depending on the length of the stock's cooking time. The longer a stock cooks, the larger the mirepoix can be. In general, one pound of mirepoix is added for every 10 pounds of bones.

In addition to mirepoix, other vegetables are sometimes added to stock, 23-3. Mushrooms—either cooked or raw—can improve a stock's color and flavor. Tomato is frequently added to stocks to add flavor and acidity and deepen color. Raw tomatoes, tomato sauce, puréed tomatoes, and tomato paste can all be used in stock production.

Herbs and Spices   Most stocks are flavored with three herbs (thyme, bay leaf, and parsley), and one spice (whole black peppercorns). Herbs and spices are added to a stock in the form of a sachet or bouquet garni.

A **sachet** (sa SHAY) is a small cheesecloth bag containing herbs and spices. While sachets can be made with fresh herbs, sachets are ideal for finely chopped dried herbs.

A **bouquet garni** (boo KAY gar NEE) is a bundle of fresh herbs tied to a piece of celery, leek, or carrot. It does not incorporate spices or chopped dried herbs. When using a bouquet garni, a small sachet is also needed to hold the peppercorns.

TECHNIQUE 🔄 Animation
Preparing a Sachet

1. **Cut an eight-inch square of cheesecloth. Lay it flat on a table.**
2. **Position the herbs and spices in the center of the cheesecloth.**
3. **Draw the four corners of the cheesecloth off the board until they are all touching.**
4. **Holding the four corners in one hand and the filled center of the cheesecloth in the other hand, twist to form a ball.**
5. **Tie the sachet with a piece of kitchen twine to keep it from opening.**

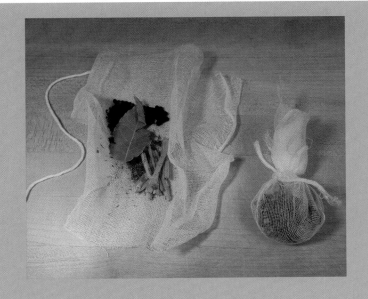

TECHNIQUE
Preparing a Bouquet Garni

Animation

1. **Cut a three-inch piece of celery.**
2. **Position the thyme and parsley inside the celery. Place a bay leaf on top of the herbs.**
3. **Tie tightly with a piece of kitchen twine.**

Vegetables' Contributions to Stock Flavor	
Vegetable	**Flavor**
Onion, raw	Strong pungent flavor, especially if the stock is not simmered for a long time
Onion, sautéed, roasted, or caramelized	Sweetness
Leek	Same as onion
Carrot	Sweetness and a touch of earthiness, also adds an orange hue to the stock
Tomato, fresh	Acidity and fresh tomato flavor
Tomato, cooked, canned, or paste	Acidity and a deep tomato sauce flavor, as well as, adding a red color to the stock
Fennel	Anise flavor, touch of sweetness
Mushrooms, raw	Delicate flavor
Mushrooms, sautéed or roasted	Intense meaty flavor and deepens the color of the stock
Parsnip	Fresh carrotlike flavor
Beets	Earthy and somewhat sweet flavor, deepens the color of the stock, especially if the stock is slightly acidic
Green cabbage, raw	Bitterness
Green cabbage, sautéed	Touch of sweetness
Turnips	An assertive flavor that can sometimes be bitter
Celery/celery root	Freshness

23-3 Vegetables can be used to create different flavor profiles in stock.

Liquid

Most stocks are made by simmering the nutritive and aromatic ingredients in water. Sometimes, a small amount of wine is also added to the water. For instance, fumet is made with water and white wine. Wine adds acidity to the stock. This acidity brightens the stock's flavor and improves overall clarity.

How much liquid is added to a stock depends on the amount of bones. The rule of thumb is that bones should be covered by one or two inches of water. Covering the meat and bones with too much water yields a weak flavored stock. If the bones are not completely covered with water, they cannot add flavor to the stock. In general, one pound (454 g) of bones yields one pound (454 g) or two cups (480 mL) of finished stock.

Attributes of a Well-Made Stock

All well-made stocks share four attributes.
- *Color.* Different ingredients yield different colored stocks. Fish stocks are valued for their light, almost transparent color. Chicken stock often has a rich golden hue. Most beef or veal stocks are characterized by a brown color.
- *Clarity.* A good stock should be clear. Clarity means the stock is not cloudy, murky, or muddy.
- *Flavor.* Quality stock has an intense flavor that mirrors the nutritive and aromatic ingredients used to make the stock.
- *Body.* This refers to the amount of gelatin in a stock. Stocks have varying levels of gelatin depending on the type of nutritive ingredient and length of cooking. In general, stocks should be as gelatin-rich as possible depending on the type of stock. Many well-made stocks partially solidify when cooled.

Stock Preparation

Stocks are categorized as either brown or white, 23-4. **White stock** is made from raw or slightly cooked bones and white mirepoix. White stocks can have a light pale to deep golden color. **Brown stock** is made from roasted bones and roasted or sautéed mirepoix. Brown stocks are noted for their rich roasted flavor and caramel color.

White Stock

The most common white stocks are made using poultry (usually chicken), fish, or veal bones. As these bones are different in size and composition, they are prepared differently prior to making stock.
- Chicken bones are rinsed in cold water to remove excess blood.
- Fish bones are coarsely chopped and then rinsed in cold water to remove excess blood. Gills are removed from fish heads. If the heads are large, they are cut into three-inch pieces and rinsed well in cold water.
- Large bones, such as veal bones, are cut into two- to three-inch-long pieces.

Draz-Koetke/Goodheart-Willcox Publisher

23-4 White and brown stocks differ in appearance as well as flavor.

TECHNIQUE
Preparing White Stock

1. Place bones in a stockpot and cover with about two inches of cold water.

2. Heat the stock over medium heat. Once the stock comes to a slow boil, reduce heat to a bare simmer. Slow heating improves the stock's clarity by allowing impurities, in the form of proteins, to coagulate and rise to the surface.

3. Using a ladle, skim the top of the stock in order to remove scum (foamy coagulated proteins) and grease. If the stock is not skimmed thoroughly just after the stock comes to a boil, clarity will suffer. When skimming, lower the bottom of the ladle into the stock so as to only remove scum and grease. Do not simply scoop with the ladle, as this will remove stock in addition to the grease and scum. Empty the ladle's contents into a pan near the stove.

4. Add aromatic ingredients. Adding the aromatic ingredients after the initial skimming allows for a more complete removal of all scum and grease.

5. Allow the stock to simmer for the appropriate amount of time. Skim as needed. Maintain the level of the liquid. For stocks that cook many hours, it is necessary to add water occasionally.

6. When the stock is done, it must be strained. A stock can simply be poured through a china cap or chinois and into a proper container. If the stock is too heavy to pour safely, scoop out the stock using a large ladle or small pot. Once the stockpot can be handled safely, strain the remaining stock.

7. If the stock is not to be used immediately, cool according to local health codes. Chilling stock in an ice water bath is the most efficient way to chill large quantities of stock. Cover with plastic wrap, label, and store in cooler until needed.

8. When the stock has chilled, remove any solidified fat that has risen to the surface of the stock.

Some chefs blanch bones before using them to prepare a white stock. When preparing a stock, **blanching** refers to the process of placing bones in cold water, bringing the water to a boil, and then discarding water. (This blanching technique differs from blanching done in vegetable cookery.) Blanching produces clear stocks since most of the bone's impurities are discarded with the blanching water. Blanching also removes some of the bone's

Recipe No.	Name		Category
23.3	Brown Stock		Stocks
Yield	**Portion Size**		**No. Portions**
5 qt. (4.75 L)	8 fl. oz. (240 mL)		20
US Quantity	**Metric Quantity**	**Ingredient**	**TCS**
10 lb.	4.54 kg	veal or beef bones, cut into 2-3 inch pieces	•
5 qt.	4.75 L	cold water (or enough to cover bones)	
1 lb.	450 g	mirepoix, cut into 1-inch (2.54 cm) pieces	
3 Tbsp.	45 mL	vegetable oil	
3 Tbsp.	45 mL	tomato paste	
1 ea.		sachet:	
20 ea.		black peppercorns	
2 tsp.	10 mL	dried thyme leaf	
1 ea.		bay leaf	
6 ea.		parsley stems	

Method	CCP
1. Place bones in a lightly oiled roasting pan. Roast in a 350°F (177°C) oven until bones are well browned (about 1 hour), stirring occasionally.	
2. Place bones in a stockpot and discard any grease left in roasting pan.	
3. Place the pan over a medium heat and cover bottom of pan with ½ inch of water to deglaze. Bring the water to a boil while scraping the bottom of the pan with a wooden spoon. When all the browned bits on the pan have been loosened, pour the contents into the stockpot with the bones. (Taste the deglazing water before adding to the bones. If it is bitter, do not use it.)	
4. Sauté mirepoix in 3 Tbsp. oil over medium heat until softened and lightly browned.	
5. Add tomato paste to mirepoix and cook for 5 more minutes or until the tomato paste has turned a dark red. Stir often to prevent burning.	
6. Cover bones with water and bring to a simmer over medium heat.	
7. Skim stock using a ladle to remove all scum and grease.	
8. Tie peppercorns, thyme, parsley, and bay leaf into a sachet. Add sachet along with mirepoix to the stock.	
9. Simmer for 9–12 hours. As the water level reduces below the bones, add more cold water to cover bones again. Skim the stock periodically.	
10. Strain the stock and cool below 70°F (21°C) in two hours or less, and below 41°F (5°C) in less than a total of six hours.	CCP

Portion (g)	Calories	Fat (g)	Protein (g)	Carbohydrate (g)	Cholesterol (mg)	Sodium (mg)	Fiber (g)
225	29	0.20	4.43	2.70	0	445.50	0

Note: Using veal bones results in a more gelatinous stock and is preferable.

flavor. For this reason, larger bones such as veal bones can be blanched while fish bones are never blanched.

Brown Stock

Brown stock can be made from all bones except fish bones. Brown stocks differ from white stock in that brown stocks are made from well-roasted nutritive ingredients and vegetables. Roasting turns these ingredients brown. While the stock simmers, these roasted ingredients release their brown color and roasted flavor into the stock. The roasted bones leave some of their flavor behind in the pan. To capture this flavor, the roasting pan is deglazed. To **deglaze**, liquid is added to a roasting pan to dissolve the browned bits off the bottom and the liquid is then added to the stock. Deglazing greatly improves the flavor and color of a stock, as these browned bits are very flavorful. If the bottom of the roasting pan burns (turns black) during roasting, the pan should not be deglazed. Deglazing a burned pan deepens the color of the stock, but also makes the stock bitter.

Another difference between white and brown stocks is that a cooked tomato product is added to brown stocks. The tomato product is often tomato paste. It contributes color and depth of flavor to the stock.

Unlike white stocks, chefs never blanch bones for brown stocks. Blanching is not necessary since the proteins that could cloud a white stock are coagulated during the roasting process.

Storing Stocks

Once stocks are chilled and out of the temperature danger zone, they must be stored correctly until needed for service. Properly chilled stocks have a shelf life of about five days. Be sure the refrigerator temperature remains at or below 41°F (5°C) and that the stock is well covered. If stocks need to be stored for longer periods of time, they can be frozen successfully.

Checking Quality

Stock is high in protein, low in salt, high in moisture, and close to a pH of 7. These qualities make stock a perfect medium in which microorganisms can flourish. Always inspect a stock's appearance and odor before using it, 23-5. Signs that a stock has "turned," or spoiled, include the following:

- offensive smell
- cloudy appearance
- ropy or stringy texture
- bubbles rising to the surface of the stock

Stock Errors	
Symptom	**Cause**
Cloudy stock	Stock improperly or never skimmed
	Stock boiled instead of simmered
	Nutritive ingredients were first covered with hot water instead of cold water
	Bones not blanched for a white stock
No flavor	Stock not cooked long enough
	Too much water added to the stock ingredients
Little body	Too much water added to the stock ingredients
	Stock not cooked long enough
	Bones with little collagen were used
Pale-colored brown stock	Nutritive ingredients not roasted enough
	Too much water was added to the stock ingredients
Stock has spoiled	Stock was not chilled properly
	Stock stored in cooler too long

23-5 It is important to diagnosis problems with stocks and make necessary corrections.

TECHNIQUE
Preparing a Brown Stock

1. Spread bones in a single layer across the bottom of a lightly oiled roasting pan.

2. Roast the bones uncovered, in a 350°F–400°F (177°C–204°C) oven until they have turned a rich brown color. Stir the bones every 20 to 30 minutes to ensure even browning.

3. Remove pan from oven. Using tongs, remove bones from the pan and place them in a stockpot. Carefully pour the hot grease left in the roasting pan into a separate container. (Discard grease once cooled.)

4. Place the empty roasting pan on a medium-high burner on the stove. Add enough water to just cover the bottom of the pan. When the water comes to a boil, scrape the bottom of the roasting pan with a wooden spoon or heat resistant silicone spatula. Pour the deglazing liquid into the stockpot with the bones.

5. In a separate pan, sauté mirepoix in a small amount of oil until golden brown. Add a small amount of tomato paste, reduce heat, and continue cooking until the tomato paste turns a dark red color. Stir the mirepoix and tomato paste mixture often as the tomato paste burns easily. Cooking the tomato paste removes some of the acidity from the tomatoes and helps deepen the color of the finished stock. Reserve until needed. (Some chefs prefer to cook the mirepoix and tomato product with the bones.)

6. The brown stock now follows steps 1 through 8 of the white stock technique.

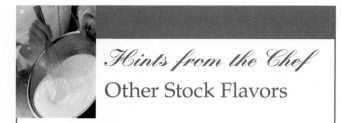

Hints from the Chef
Other Stock Flavors

While most all stocks are seasoned with thyme, bay leaf, parsley, and black peppercorn, there can be exceptions. Some chefs vary the herbs and spices to achieve different flavor profiles. These individualized stocks often have specific purposes. For instance, flavoring a lamb stock with sachet that includes rosemary and oregano would give the stock a decidedly Mediterranean character.

Bouillons and Broths

Bouillon and broth are two names for the same preparation. **Bouillon** (BOOL yohn) and **broth** are stock-like preparations that are made with a larger proportion of meat than bone and a greater variety of vegetables than stocks. Bouillons and broths are clear and contain less gelatin than stocks due to the lack of bones. Classically, broths and bouillons are reserved for soup production. However, many restaurants make soup using stock because bouillon or broth is more expensive than stock.

Bouillons and broths can be made from many different types of meat. Vegetables, such as turnips and parsnips, can be added along with a classical mirepoix. Both brown and white bouillons and broths can be prepared using a procedure that mirrors the basic stock procedure.

Vegetable Stock

Technically, vegetable stocks are not true stocks since they are not made from bones. Nonetheless, vegetable stocks are prepared in many professional kitchens. While these stocks are essential to vegetarian cooking, they are also used in a wide variety of nonvegetarian cuisine.

The variety of vegetable stocks that can be prepared is endless because there are so many different types of vegetables. Both white and brown vegetable stocks can be made. For white vegetable stocks, vegetables are raw or lightly sautéed. For brown vegetable stocks, vegetables are browned in the oven or on the stove.

Vegetable stocks differ from meat-based stocks in one important way—vegetable stocks contain no gelatin, 23-6. Gelatin is derived from the collagen in bones and no bones are used when preparing vegetable stocks. As a result, vegetable stocks lack the mouthfeel of meat-based stocks and do not solidify when chilled.

Bases

A **base** is a concentrated instant powder or paste that dissolves in hot water to make a stock-like liquid. Bases are available in a range of different flavors.

Bases are advantageous for several reasons. Bases save valuable stove space since they only require the addition of boiling water. Compare this to stock production, which occupies stove space for hours. Since bases take much less time to make than stocks, they have a lower labor cost and free cooks up to do other tasks. Also, many bases are less expensive than stocks made from scratch.

There are also disadvantages to using bases. Bases do not have the same taste as a stock made from scratch. In addition, most bases contain salt, which limits their use in sauce making.

Bases can vary considerably in quality. Those that require refrigeration after opening and list meat or meat juices as their first ingredient tend be the highest quality. Bases that list salt, sugar, and fat as their main ingredients are lower quality.

Comparison of Stocks

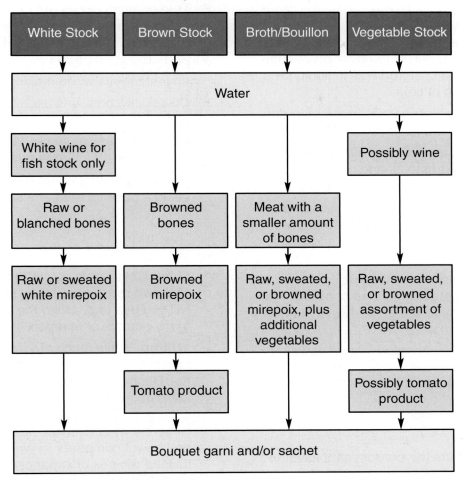

23-6 Chefs choose from a variety of stocks in their dishes.

Summary Points

- Stock is a clear, highly flavored liquid that is made by simmering a combination of nutritive and aromatic ingredients in liquid for a specific length of time.

- Well-made stocks share four common attributes—color, clarity, flavor, and body.

- Stocks are categorized as either white or brown. The ingredients and method of preparation determine the color of the stock.

- Bouillons and broths are stock-like preparations that are made with a greater proportion of meat than bone and contain additional varieties of vegetables.

- Vegetable stocks are made using a wide variety of vegetables instead of bones. For this reason, there are an endless variety of vegetable stocks.

- A base is a concentrated instant powder or paste that dissolves in boiling water to make a stock-like liquid.

In Review
Assess

1. _____ contribute the predominant flavor to stocks.
   - A. Aromatic ingredients
   - B. Gelatins
   - C. Nutritive ingredients
   - D. Sachets

2. What is the source of gelatin in stock and how does it affect the stock?

3. True or false. The time it takes to extract the gelatin from bones depends on the size of the bones and the age of the animal.

4. What is the difference between a sachet and a bouquet garni?

5. Which attribute of a well-made stock refers to the amount of gelatin in the stock?
   - A. fumet
   - B. body
   - C. clarity
   - D. color

6. True or false. Bones are blanched before using them for white stock preparation because it adds more flavor to the stock.

7. Describe the deglazing process and why it is advantageous when making a brown stock.

8. Classically, bouillons and broths were used to make _____.

9. Why do vegetable stocks lack the body of stocks made from large quantities of bones?

10. List one advantage and one disadvantage to using a base instead of a stock.

Core Skills

11. **Math.** Chef wants you to prepare 5 gallons of brown stock. How many pounds of bones will you use to produce the stock? How many pounds of mirepoix?

12. **Writing.** While much of Western cuisine is based on stocks, other global cuisines are not. Research print or Internet sources to learn about Japanese dashi. Write a two-page paper comparing it to Western stocks. Describe what dashi is, how it is prepared, and how it compares to Western stocks. Include recipes of Japanese dishes that use dashi. Cite your sources.

13. **Speaking and Writing.** Select a type of stock and create an in-service explaining how it is prepared. Make use of visual and interactive elements in your in-service to enhance understanding and add interest. Have a classmate video your presentation. Review the video and write a critique of your performance. Note ways you could improve your presentation skills in the future.

14. **Math.** You are responsible for preparing the stocks for use in a hotel kitchen. Various workstation chefs have ordered the following amounts: 24 ounces, 6 gallons, 11 cups, and 16 quarts. How many total ounces of stock do you need to prepare?

15. **Writing.** Develop your own stock recipe. Provide a brief description of the stock product you are trying to create and its intended use. Begin by deciding whether it will be an animal-based stock or vegetable

stock. Will it be a white stock or a brown stock? Write the list of ingredients you would include in your stock. Next to each ingredient, state your reason for selecting that ingredient and the contribution it will make to the stock flavor. Be sure to note if the ingredient requires any preparation in advance of being added to the stock such as blanching or browning. Prepare your stock and taste it. Write a brief summary describing your results. Were you satisfied with your final product? Would you make any changes to the recipe? What changes would you make and why?

16. **CTE Career Readiness Practice.** Create a flowchart that could be used to troubleshoot quality issues with a stock.

Critical Thinking

17. **Analyze.** Your coworker has prepared a classic white stock that is weak flavored and has little or no body. He or she asks for your opinion about how they could improve their product next time. What suggestions would you give?

18. **Compare.** Locate three different bases either in your food lab, grocery store, or online. Make a chart that shows the name of each base, their ingredient list, and price. Do you see a correlation between the ingredients and price?

19. **Evaluate.** The chef has asked you to observe a new cook as she prepares a fumet for the first time. The cook begins to blanch the fish bones in preparation for making the fumet. What feedback would you give the cook?

Technology

Use the Internet to find 20 recipes that use stock as an ingredient. List the recipe name, type of stock used, and the function the stock performs in the recipe. Create a table using either word processing or spreadsheet software to organize your information.

Teamwork

Working as a team, perform a comparison of a base with a stock prepared from scratch. Prepare a base according to directions. Reheat some homemade stock. Perform a side-by-side comparison of the two preparations based on the attributes of a well-made stock—color, clarity, and body. Have each team member participate in a blind taste test to evaluate the fourth attribute—flavor. Record your observations and conclusion.

Chef's E-portfolio
Stock Preparation In-Service

Upload the in-service you created for activity #13 to your e-portfolio. Ask your instructor where to save your file. This could be on the school's network or a flash drive of your own. Name your portfolio document *FirstnameLastname_Portfolio Ch#.docx* (i.e., JohnSmith_PortfolioCh23.docx).

While studying, look for the activity icon ➦ **to:**

- Build vocabulary with e-flash cards and matching activities.
- Expand learning with video clips, photo identification activities, animations, and interactive activities.
- Review and assess what you learn by completing end-of-chapter questions.

G-WLEARNING.COM

Sauces

24

Reading Prep

In preparation for reading the chapter, read an article or book about the history of sauces. As you read, consider how sauces might change in the future.

Culinary Terminology Build Vocab

Academic Terminology Build Vocab

Objectives

After studying this chapter, you will be able to

- explain the role of sauces.
- compare thickening agents and how to use them.
- understand the classic system of mother sauces and derivative sauces.
- recall several nontraditional sauces.

Along with stocks, sauces are considered one of the building blocks of the culinary arts. **Sauces** are thickened liquids that complement other foods. There are literally thousands of sauces, and even more ways they can be paired with different foods. Many chefs consider sauce making to be among the most challenging skills to master in the kitchen. For that reason, chefs dedicate years of their professional careers to learning how to make exceptional sauces.

The Role of Sauces

Sauces are not recent inventions. They can be traced back at least 2,000 years to the Roman Empire, and possibly even before this. At that time, sauces were not like the sauces you know today. Recipes from that time period suggest that their sauces were intensely flavored, like a condiment. Roman sauces were often flavored with numerous spices and a fermented fish liquid called *garum*. During the Middle Ages, sauces were not only strongly flavored, but also often heavily thickened with ingredients such as bread crumbs. As sauces continued to evolve, they gradually became thinner and more subtly flavored. Today, sauces are designed not to overpower, but to complement by adding complexity and balance to different dishes.

Through the centuries, thousands of different types of sauces have been created. New types of sauces continue to be developed today. Despite this large number of sauces, all sauces perform one of the following roles:

- Improve the appearance of food by adding color and shine.
- Contribute flavors that complement or accent the flavors of a particular dish.
- Add moisture to keep the dish from tasting dry and unappetizing.
- Add richness, especially if the sauce is high in fat.
- Add visual appeal to a simple center of the plate item and command a higher value on the menu.

Thickening Sauces

Nearly all sauces are thickened liquids. This is one of the ways stocks differ from sauces. Sauces are traditionally thickened to nappé (na PAY) consistency. **Nappé** means that a sauce is thick enough to coat the back of a spoon, 24-1.

There are several ways to thicken liquids when making a sauce. Each thickening method has its advantages and disadvantages and produces different results. Starches can be used in the form of a roux, slurry, or beurre manié (ber manYAY). Sauces can also be thickened by reduction, puréeing, addition of egg yolks, or emulsion.

Starch

Starch is a category of carbohydrates. Starches commonly used to thicken sauces include flour, cornstarch, and arrowroot. When starches are combined with hot liquid, they absorb liquid in a process called *gelatinization*. This process explains how starches thicken liquids. As more starch is added to a hot liquid, the thicker the liquid becomes.

When using a starch to thicken liquid, the liquid must come to a full boil. If the liquid does not boil, the starch's full thickening potential is not attained. If the liquid does not boil, the temptation is to add more and more starch to the liquid. Unfortunately, when the liquid eventually does come to a boil, the liquid will overthicken as the starch's thickening power is realized.

Roux   The classic starch-based thickener is roux (ROO). **Roux** is a mixture of equal parts flour and fat by weight that is cooked to varying degrees of doneness and used to thicken liquids. Cooking the starch and fat coats the individual starch granules with fat. The fat-coated starch then distributes evenly in the hot liquid, which prevents lumps of starch in the finished sauce. From a flavor standpoint, the cooking process accomplishes two objectives. It removes the taste of raw starch from the flour and can add additional flavors depending on how long the roux is cooked.

There are three different types of roux—white, blond, and brown, 24-2. Each roux is made from the same proportions of fat and flour. While any fat can technically be used to make a roux, chefs generally use butter for its superior flavor. Often, chefs use clarified butter as it burns less easily than whole

Draz-Koetke/Goodheart-Willcox Publisher

24-1 Nappé refers to the thickness of a sauce when it is thick enough to lightly coat the back of a spoon.

Draz-Koetke/Goodheart-Willcox Publisher

24-2 White, blond, and brown roux only differ in how long they are cooked.

butter. The difference between each type of roux is the length of time it is cooked.

- White roux is cooked until the raw flour taste disappears (3 to 5 minutes). The color of the white roux should not darken during cooking.
- Blond roux is cooked until the color turns an even straw color (10 minutes).
- Brown roux is cooked until the color turns brown (20 to 30 minutes). Some chefs make a brown roux in a 300°F (149°C) oven to keep the roux from scorching. In some cuisines of the American south, a roux may be cooked until it is very dark.

When using a roux to make a sauce, cool roux is added to hot liquid. This reduces the possibility of lumps. In the professional kitchen, large batches of roux are often prepared in advance. The amount of roux added to a liquid depends on the desired consistency of the finished sauce:

Light = 1 gal. liquid + 8–10 oz. roux
Medium = 1 gal. liquid + 12–16 oz. roux
Thick = 1 gal. liquid + 18–20 oz. roux

Slurry A slurry is a mixture of cold liquid and starch. Slurries must be mixed well so the starch is evenly distributed in the liquid to avoid lumps. To thicken, the slurry is slowly poured into a boiling liquid while whisking constantly. Slurries thicken liquids very quickly. Liquids must be stirred as the slurry is added to avoid lumps of starch from forming. Such lumps are not only unsightly, but are also unable to thicken the sauce.

There are a few starches that are commonly used to make slurries.

- *Cornstarch.* Consisting entirely of starch derived from corn, cornstarch is inexpensive and produces a glossy sauce. Sauces thickened with cornstarch gradually become thinner the longer they are held hot.
- *Arrowroot.* Another pure starch similar to cornstarch, arrowroot is derived from a tropical root. It is expensive and produces

TECHNIQUE
Preparing Roux

1. **Melt fat over low heat and add flour.**

2. **Stir until the flour is evenly distributed and a paste forms.**

3. **Stirring frequently, cook the roux over low heat until the desired doneness.**
4. **Transfer roux to another pan and let it cool.**

a glossy sauce. Unlike cornstarch, arrow-root will not lose its thickening ability if held hot. Arrowroot is also the best choice if a thickened product is to be frozen for later use.

- *Flour.* Unlike cornstarch and arrowroot, flour is not a pure starch. As a result, it does not produce the same glossy trans-parent appearance as sauces thickened with pure starches. A slurry made with flour is called a **whitewash**. Whitewashes are often used when making American-style gravy, 24-3.

Beurre Manié Beurre manié (BEHR man yay) is a mixture of softened whole butter and flour. It is occasionally used to thicken sauces and stews at the last minute. Unlike a roux, the longer it is in the liquid, the more pronounced the flavor of raw flour will be. For this reason, roux is most often preferred over beurre manié.

Draz-Koetke/Goodheart-Willcox Publisher

24-3 Boiling liquids thicken very quickly when slurry is added.

Reduction
Animation

Reducing a sauce is not only a way to concentrate flavor, but also a way to thicken some liquids. Reduction is accomplished by boiling a sauce to evaporate some of the water. As the water evaporates, other components in the liquid become increas-ingly concentrated. Some of these substances, such as gelatin, gradually thicken the sauce. Reduction-based sauces are expensive to make since they cook for long periods of time and the volume is greatly reduced.

When making reduction-based sauces, chefs often speak of reducing a liquid by a certain fraction or percentage. For instance, if one gallon of sauce is reduced by three-fourths, there will be one quart of sauce left after the reduction.

Purée

Another way of thickening liquids is to add finely ground solids to them. Many different puréed fruits, vegetables, seeds, and nuts can be used to thicken sauces. A sauce made from puréed fruits or vegetables is called a **coulis** (coo LEE). For instance, a red pepper coulis is made by puréeing roasted red peppers with a flavorful liquid. The purée technique is also used to thicken sauces such as Mexican moles or pipíans.

Egg Yolk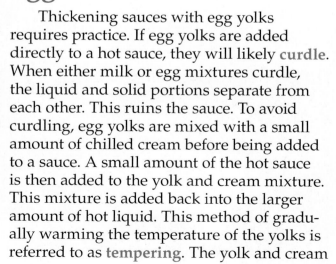
Animation

Thickening sauces with egg yolks requires practice. If egg yolks are added directly to a hot sauce, they will likely **curdle**. When either milk or egg mixtures curdle, the liquid and solid portions separate from each other. This ruins the sauce. To avoid curdling, egg yolks are mixed with a small amount of chilled cream before being added to a sauce. A small amount of the hot sauce is then added to the yolk and cream mixture. This mixture is added back into the larger amount of hot liquid. This method of gradu-ally warming the temperature of the yolks is referred to as **tempering**. The yolk and cream

mixture that is used to thicken liquids is called a liaison (lee AY zun).

Once the yolk mixture is added to the liquid, the sauce is slowly cooked while stirring constantly. The sauce will thicken between 160°F and 179°F (71°C and 82°C). If it is heated much above 180°F (82°C), the egg yolks curdle and the sauce thins out. The only time an egg yolk thickened sauce can be heated above 180°F (82°C) without curdling is if the sauce has previously been thickened with a starch.

Emulsion

An emulsion is a mixture of fat and water that is homogeneous, or uniform throughout. Normally, fat and water do not remain mixed, but rather separate back into fat and water. Properly made emulsions will thicken a sauce. Making hot, emulsion-based sauces requires practice. To successfully thicken a sauce using an emulsion, it is important to pay close attention to the following:
- Maintain the recommended temperature ranges.
- Use natural emulsifiers such as those found in egg yolks or mustard to create and hold the emulsion together.
- Add the fat portion slowly to the water portion of the emulsion while stirring constantly.

Bread

Bread is one of the oldest and most rustic ingredients used to thicken sauces. Toasted or untoasted bread crumbs can be added to a sauce. Bread crumbs are rarely used today because they produce a somewhat pasty texture.

Mother Sauces and Derivative Sauces

As the number of sauces increased through the centuries, a method to classify and streamline sauce preparation became necessary. In the early 1900s, French chefs created a system of sauces. As a result, many of the sauces have French names that are universally recognized by professional chefs.

The French sauce system consists of five mother sauces from which a large number of derivative sauces are produced. Mother sauces are the base sauces from which other sauces can quickly be made. A derivative sauce is a sauce that is made from a mother sauce. Some chefs refer to derivative sauces as *compound* or *small sauces*.

The system of mother and derivative sauces was developed to save time. When large batches of mother sauces are made in advance, the chef can quickly make many derivative sauces as needed.

The classical French system includes the following mother sauces, 24-4:

- white sauce (béchamel sauce)
- velouté sauce
- brown sauce (demi-glace sauce)
- tomato sauce
- hollandaise sauce

White Sauce

White sauce consists of milk thickened with a white roux and flavored with onion, bay leaf, and a small amount of nutmeg. Classically, this mother sauce is called **béchamel** (bay shah MEHL) **sauce**. In order to easily find and retrieve the bay leaf, it is speared to the onion with whole cloves. This is called an **onion piqué** (pee KAY).

Derivative Sauces The white sauce is a mother sauce from which numerous derivative sauces can be made. The derivative sauces are made by adding various ingredients to the existing mother sauce. These sauces are routinely served with vegetables, poultry, veal, and fish dishes. Some of the more prominent derivative sauces and their added ingredients include the following:

- Cheddar sauce–addition of aged cheddar cheese
- Crème (KREHM) sauce–addition of reduced cream and a small amount of lemon juice
- Soubise (soo BEEZ) sauce–cooked with generous amounts of sweated onions
- Mornay (mohr NAY) sauce–addition of Gruyère and Parmesan cheeses

In addition to accompanying different dishes, white sauce is used as an ingredient in certain preparations. For instance, a thick white sauce may be used to bind the ingredients of a casserole. White sauces enriched with egg yolks or cheese can be poured over preparations and then browned in a hot broiler or salamander.

Velouté

The French term *velouté* (vehl oo TAY) means "velvety." **Velouté sauce** is a mother sauce made by thickening a white stock with a blond roux. The finished sauce should have an attractive beige appearance. Since it is the principal ingredient of velouté sauce, the

White

Velouté

Brown

Tomato

Hollandaise

24-4 The mother sauces are often made in advance to save chefs time at service.

stock must be well flavored and free from any defects.

Derivative Sauces   As with white sauce, velouté sauce has many derivative sauces. Aside from complementing a variety of dishes, velouté-based derivatives are also instrumental in the preparation of certain soups. Two of the most well-known derivative sauces and their added ingredients include the following:

- Allemande (ahl MAHND) sauce–addition of mushroom cooking liquid, lemon juice, egg yolks, and butter
- Suprême (soo PREHM) sauce–addition of cream and butter

TECHNIQUE
Preparing White Sauce

1. Using clarified butter as the fat portion, cook and cool white roux.
2. Add an onion piqué to milk and bring to a boil.

3. Remove the onion piqué temporarily. Add appropriate amount of roux to the milk. Whisk immediately so the roux dissolves completely. Replace the onion piqué in the sauce.
4. Bring milk back to a boil. Add nutmeg, reduce heat, and simmer over very low heat for 20 to 30 minutes. There should be no flavor of raw flour in the finished sauce. Stir the sauce periodically so that it does not scorch on the bottom of the pan.
5. Strain the sauce through a chinois. Cover the surface of the sauce with plastic wrap and chill the sauce according to local health codes. (Covering the sauce with plastic wrap prevents a skin from forming as the sauce cools.)

TECHNIQUE
Preparing Velouté

1. Cook and cool blond roux made with clarified butter as the fat portion.
2. Bring white stock to a boil.
3. Add appropriate amount of roux to the stock. Whisk immediately so the roux dissolves completely.
4. Bring stock back to a boil and simmer over very low heat for 20 to 30 minutes. There should be no flavor of raw flour in the finished sauce. Be sure to stir the sauce periodically so that it does not scorch on the bottom of the pan. Skim the sauce as scum rises to the surface.

5. Strain the sauce through a chinois. Cover the surface of the sauce with plastic wrap and chill the sauce according to local health codes. (Covering the sauce with plastic wrap prevents a skin from forming as it cools.)

Recipe No.	Name			Category
24.1	White Sauce (Béchamel)			Sauces, mother sauces
Yield	**Portion Size**			**No. Portions**
1 gal. (3.8 L)	2 fl. oz. (60 mL)			20
US Quantity	**Metric Quantity**	**Ingredient**		**TCS**
8 fl. oz.	240 mL	clarified butter		•
8 oz.	225 g	all-purpose flour		
1 gal.	3.8 L	milk		•
1 ea.		small onion, peeled		
2 ea.		whole cloves		
1 ea.		bay leaf		
pinch		nutmeg, grated		

Method	CCP

1. Prepare a white roux:
  a. Place clarified butter in a small pan.
  b. Add flour and cook over low heat for 5–10 minutes or until the raw flour taste is cooked out of the roux. Stir the roux so the color does not deepen.
  c. Remove roux from pan and let cool.	

2. Prepare an onion piqué by spearing the bay leaf to the onion with the 2 cloves.	
3. Add onion piqué to milk and bring to a boil.	
4. Remove onion piqué and reserve.	
5. Add the cool roux to the milk and stir with whisk to dissolve the roux.	
6. Add the onion piqué back to the sauce.	
7. Bring sauce back to a boil, reduce heat to very low and simmer for 20–30 minutes. Stir often so sauce does not stick to the bottom of the pan and burn. (A heavy bottomed pot lessens the chance of burning.)	
8. Remove onion piqué and strain sauce through a chinois. Season with nutmeg. If the sauce is not being turned into a derivative sauce, add salt and white pepper to taste.	
9. Cover the surface of the sauce with plastic wrap to prevent a skin from forming. Cool below 70°F (21°C) in two hours or less, and below 41°F (5°C) in less than a total of six hours.	CCP

Portion (g)	Calories	Fat (g)	Protein (g)	Carbohydrate (g)	Cholesterol (mg)	Sodium (mg)	Fiber (g)
68	81	5.54	2.34	5.46	15.17	24.54	0.10

Brown Sauce

At its most basic, brown sauce is a thickened brown stock. There are three principal ways to make this mother sauce. The fastest type of brown sauce to make is **jus lié** (JOO lee AY). Jus lié is the name for a reduced brown stock that is thickened with a cornstarch or arrowroot slurry. This stock does not require hours of simmering. For this reason, the stock used must be flavorful or the resulting sauce will lack depth of flavor.

Another brown sauce that is used for making derivative brown sauces is espagnole (ehs pan YOHL). **Espagnole sauce** is made by slowly reducing brown stock, a small amount of tomato product, mirepoix, and brown roux for hours. Gradually, the sauce develops the proper consistency, flavor, and brilliant appearance.

Recipe No.	Name		Category
24.6	Jus Lié		Sauces
Yield	**Portion Size**		**No. Portions**
1 qt. (0.95 L)	2 fl. oz. (60 mL)		16
US Quantity	**Metric Quantity**	**Ingredient**	**TCS**
1 gal.	3.8 L	brown veal or beef stock	•
1 oz.	30 g	arrowroot	
4 fl. oz.	120 mL	cold water	
Method			**CCP**
1. Over high heat, reduce the stock to 1 quart. Skim the stock as scum rises to the surface as it reduces.			
2. Stir the arrowroot in water until it is well dissolved.			
3. Add slurry to the reduced stock while stirring constantly with a whisk. Bring back to a boil. If additional thickening is necessary, add small amounts of slurry and bring back to a boil after each addition.			
4. Remove from heat and strain through a chinois.			
5. Cool below 70°F (21°C) in two hours or less, and below 41°F (5°C) in less than a total of six hours.			CCP

Portion (g)	Calories	Fat (g)	Protein (g)	Carbohydrate (g)	Cholesterol (mg)	Sodium (mg)	Fiber (g)
62	9	0.05	1.18	1.11	0	118.85	0.02

The most time-consuming brown sauce to prepare is demi-glace (DEH mee glahs). **Demi-glace sauce** is classically made by reducing espagnole sauce to proper nappé consistency. A recent trend in sauce making has been to thicken sauces with something other than starch. Some chefs make brown sauces that are thickened by a combination of a reduction of brown stock and an emulsion of butter. To make this type of brown sauce, stock is reduced until it takes on a sauce-like consistency due to the increased concentration of gelatin. The stock has an intense flavor because it is reduced by as much as one-tenth its original volume. To prevent the sauce from becoming too intense and to round out the mouthfeel, butter is stirred into the sauce just before it is served.

Derivative Sauces Brown sauces have the largest family of derivative sauces, 24-5. Often, these sauces are made by combining an acidic ingredient—wine, vinegar, or fruit juice—with other flavors. Some of the most common derivative sauces and their added ingredients include

- Bordelaise (bor deh LAYZ) sauce–addition of red wine, shallots, black pepper, and bone marrow (optional)
- Charcutière (shahr koo TEEYHR) sauce–addition of julienne of cornichon (kor nee SHOHN), a small acidic pickle, to Robert sauce
- Chasseur (shah SUR) sauce–addition of mushrooms, shallot, white wine, and tomatoes
- Madère (mah DUR) sauce–addition of Madeira wine
- Robert (roh BEHR) sauce–addition of onion, dry or Dijon mustard, and white wine
- Bercy (bair-SEE) sauce–addition of shallots, white wine, and chopped parsley

Tomato Sauce

Tomato sauce is an example of a purée-thickened sauce (although some recipes also

Family Tree of the Classical Brown Sauce

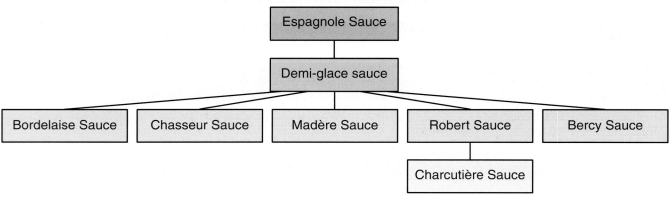

24-5 The French system of sauces is similar to the concept of a family tree.

include a small amount of flour). There are many ways to make tomato sauce. A basic tomato sauce consists of tomatoes cooked with flavoring elements such as vegetables, herbs, and even pieces of raw or cured meats.

Derivative Sauces   Of all the mother sauces, tomato sauce has perhaps the fewest derivative sauces. Despite this, tomato sauce can be varied in multiple ways. Some possible variations include the addition of the following:
- paprika and cream
- fresh herbs such as basil, parsley, and chervil
- puréed roasted garlic
- sweet red peppers and chiles

Hollandaise Sauce

Hollandaise (hahl an DAYZ) **sauce** is a hot emulsified sauce that combines egg yolks and warm clarified butter. Hot emulsified sauces take practice to master. To produce a stable emulsion, the sauce must be prepared with extreme care. If the sauce is prepared improperly, the emulsion will break. An emulsion breaks when the egg yolk and clarified butter separate. Broken sauces are not servable, 24-6.

TECHNIQUE
Preparing Tomato Sauce

1. Sweat vegetable flavorings in fat. The fat can be either olive or vegetable oil and rendered animal fat such as salt pork or bacon. Vegetables commonly used to flavor tomato sauce are onions, garlic, carrot, and celery.
2. Add herbs and seeded, coarsely chopped tomatoes. (The riper the tomatoes, the better the sauce will be.) Traditionally, a meaty pork bone may also be added at this point.
3. The sauce is simmered until it attains proper consistency. Stir often to avoid scorching.
4. Grind the sauce using a ricer, food processor, or blender.

5. Chill the sauce according to local health codes.

Draz-Koetke/Goodheart-Willcox Publisher

24-6 The broken hollandaise on the left has separated. The properly prepared hollandaise on the right is smooth and creamy.

Derivative Sauces   The most famous hollandaise derivative sauce is béarnaise (behrn AYZ) sauce. It has its own small family of derivative sauces. Some hollandaise derivative sauces and their added ingredients include

- Béarnaise sauce–addition of a vinegar, shallot, parsley, and tarragon reduction
- Chantilly (shahn tee EE) sauce–addition of unsweetened whipped cream
- Choron (shohr ON) sauce–addition of cooked, diced tomato or tomato purée to béarnaise sauce
- Maltaise (mahl TAYZ) sauce–addition of blood orange juice and zest.

Causes and Remedies for Broken Hollandaise   When first learning to make a hot emulsified sauce, it is not unusual to break a sauce or two. When a hot emulsified sauce begins to break, small droplets of fat separate from the yolk mixture. When the sauce is completely broken, droplets of egg yolk float in a pool of clarified butter.

Hot emulsion sauces break for several reasons. Perhaps the butter was added too quickly. The egg yolks may not have been cooked enough. Perhaps the butter was too cool or the egg yolks were overcooked. The

TECHNIQUE
Preparing Hollandaise

1. Egg yolks are mixed in a stainless steel bowl with water and lemon juice. Some chefs add reduced vinegar instead of lemon juice.
2. The bowl is placed over boiling water. The egg yolk mixture is whisked constantly. Gradually, the yolk mixture will thicken and become foamy. When the mixture is steaming and has a thick ribbon-like consistency, remove the bowl from the boiling water.
3. Gradually drizzle warm clarified butter (about 110°F or 43°C) into the yolk mixture while whisking constantly. As the clarified butter is emulsified into the yolk mixture, the remaining clarified butter can be added more quickly.

4. Once all the butter has been incorporated, season the sauce with salt and a pinch of cayenne.
5. Strain the sauce through cheesecloth.
6. Hold the sauce according to local health codes.

remedy you choose to fix the broken sauce depends on the state of the hollandaise.

- If the sauce is too cold, warm gradually over boiling water or add a small amount of hot water. If the sauce refuses to reemulsify or breaks completely, proceed to the third bullet point.
- If the sauce is too hot, add a small amount of cold water or crushed ice. If the sauce refuses to reemulsify or breaks completely, proceed to the third bullet point.
- If the sauce is completely broken, begin a fresh batch of hollandaise. Once the egg yolks, water, and lemon juice are hot enough, remove from heat and whisk in the warm broken sauce instead of clarified butter.

Safety Concerns with Hollandaise Sauce There has been much debate over the safety of serving hollandaise sauce since the eggs—a potentially hazardous food—are never fully cooked. Hollandaise has been the source of salmonella outbreaks. For this reason, you should consult with your local health department to develop a procedure for safe preparation and holding of hollandaise sauce. Additionally, it should be made using pasteurized eggs only.

Nontraditional Sauces

There are many other sauces that do not fit into the French system of mother sauces and their derivative sauces. Chefs are continually experimenting with new flavors and sauce-making techniques. The butter sauces, salsas, relishes, and chutneys are just a few examples of these nontraditional sauces.

Butter Sauces

Beurre blanc (BUHR BLAHN) is the name of a delicate emulsified sauce that is composed almost entirely of butter. Despite the large amount of butter, the sauce gives the impression of lightness. It is a versatile

sauce that can be flavored many different ways. As with other hot emulsion sauces, beurre blanc requires practice and exact attention to procedure.

In addition to emulsified butter sauces, there are several other broken butter sauces. Broken butter sauces are basically melted butter. The most well-known broken butter sauce is beurre noisette (BUHR nwah ZEHT). Beurre noisette is the French name for browned butter finished with lemon juice. It is served with fish dishes and some vegetables, 24-7.

To make beurre noisette, simply place whole butter over medium heat and cook it until the milk solids turn a light brown color. Immediately pour the butter from the pan. If it is not removed quickly, the heat of the pan will burn the butter. Add lemon juice to the butter.

Other Nontraditional Sauces

Increasingly, chefs are experimenting with different types of sauces to provide new textures and flavors. The textures of

24-7 Making beurre noisette requires close attention to ensure the butter does not burn.

salsas, relishes, moles, pipíans, Asian dipping sauces, chutneys, and curries range from thin to nappé to thick and chunky, 24-8. These sauces originate from different parts of the world and incorporate a wide range of flavors.

- *Salsas.* Salsas are less acidic than relishes. While salsas vary considerably, they originate in Latin America and tend to be spicy hot due to chiles. They can be made from either cooked or uncooked chopped or puréed ingredients. Sometimes the ingredients are first charred on a grill or in a heavy pan before being chopped or puréed.
- *Relishes.* Relishes are typically a combination of coarsely chopped vegetables and fruits marinated with a large amount of vinegar. Many relishes are also noticeably sweet.
- *Moles.* Moles originate from Mexico and are very complex sauces that rely on puréeing for their texture. There are nine basic styles of moles that vary in color from white, yellow, red, or black depending on their ingredients. Despite the use of chiles, they range in spiciness from mild to hot.
- *Pipíans.* Historically, pipíans are the precursor to moles. They are made throughout Mexico and are generally easier to prepare than moles as they contain less ingredients. They come in a number of different styles and colors and are thickened by puréeing different ingredients including sesame seeds, pine nuts, pumpkin seeds, and peanuts.
- *Asian dipping sauces.* These sauces tend to be very thin and are used principally as a condiment for different dishes. They often rely on soy-based sauces and are flavored with ingredients as varied as mirin (sweetened rice wine), lime juice, rice wine vinegar, sugar, chiles,

Draz-Koetke/Goodheart-Willcox Publisher

24-8 Nontraditional sauces offer a variety of flavors and textures.

fermented fish sauces, garlic, scallion, and a wide variety of spices. They also vary in character depending on the country and region from which they originate.
- *Chutney.* Chutneys originate in India. They are similar to relishes, but use different spices. Chutneys range from spicy hot or mild. Some chutneys are cooked while others are simply a mixture of raw ingredients.
- *Curry.* Curry is a broad category of sauces that are popular in India and Southeast Asia. Curries are typically complex sauces that bring together a wide range of flavors into one cohesive sauce. Some can be quite spicy while others can be mild. Curries also vary greatly based on the region from which they originate.

Summary Points

- Sauces have been refined over many centuries, but their role in cooking has not changed.
- Sauces consist of thickened liquids. There are several techniques that are used to thicken liquids.
- The French system of sauces consists of five mother sauces from which many derivative sauces can be made.
- Some nontraditional sauces fall outside of the traditional French system of sauces.

In Review
Assess

1. True or false. Most chefs consider sauce making to be one of the greatest challenges to master in the kitchen.
2. List four roles that sauces perform.
3. A roux consists of _____ parts flour and fat by weight.
4. Explain the difference between a white, blond, and brown roux.
5. List three starches commonly used in slurries.
6. A chef uses a process called _____ to avoid curdling egg yolks when adding them to a hot sauce.
7. What are the liquid and thickener used to make a white sauce?
8. True or false. A jus lié sauce requires more total preparation time than a demi-glace.
9. What is the principal method used to thicken tomato sauce?
10. List four types of nontraditional sauces.

Core Skills

11. **Math.** The chef asks you to prepare enough roux to thicken two gallons of liquid to a thick level of consistency. How much butter and flour would you need?

12. **Writing.** Choose one of the following sauces: curry, mole, pipían, or salsa and write an informative two-page paper. Identify different variations of the sauce, what part of the world it comes from, how it is made, a list of ingredients, and how it is traditionally served. Include as much history about the sauce as possible.

13. **Speaking.** Prepare a short speech to either support or refute the following statement: The role of sauce on a plate is to make the plate presentation look as attractive as possible. Give your speech in class.

14. **Math.** Suppose the cost of 1 gallon of prepared brown stock is $22.00. The stock is reduced to 1/10th its original volume and then 2 ounces of butter are added to finish the sauce. The butter costs $3.00 per pound. Calculate the cost for a one-ounce portion of the sauce.

15. **CTE Career Readiness Practice.** Emulsions are critical to sauce making. Emulsifiers are specific chemical compounds that perform an important role in attaining an emulsion. Presume you are an executive research chef working on a new sauce formulation. Locate three reliable sources of the latest information on emulsifiers used in food preparation. Read and interpret the information and write a report summarizing your findings.

Critical Thinking

16. **Distinguish.** How would sauce making be different if the system of mother sauces and derivative sauces had not been developed?

17. **Critique.** A coworker is trying a new sauce recipe that uses egg yolks as a thickening agent. Your coworker is having a problem with the egg yolks curdling every time she adds them to the hot sauce. What advice would you give?

18. **Consider.** What factors should a chef take into account when choosing a thickening method for a preparation?

Technology

Find an example of how the technology used in molecular gastronomy was used to prepare a sauce in an unconventional manner. Prepare an electronic presentation of your findings to share with the class.

Teamwork

Working as a team, prepare three white sauces. Use a roux to thicken the first sauce, slurry to thicken the second, and a beurre manié to thicken the third. Observe and taste all three sauces. Record your observations about the appearance, flavor, and ease of preparation for each sauce in a chart.

Chef's E-portfolio
Nontraditional Sauce Preparation

Prepare the sauce you wrote about in activity #12 and upload a photo of it to your e-portfolio. Ask your instructor where to save your file. This could be on the school's network or a flash drive of your own. Name your portfolio document *FirstnameLastname_Portfolio Ch#.docx* (i.e., JohnSmith_PortfolioCh24.docx).

Video Clip

Preparing Roux

Visit the G-W Learning Companion Website and view the bonus video clip "Preparing roux." After viewing the clip, answer the following questions:

1. List two fats other than clarified butter that can be used to make roux.

2. True or false. Cooking roux in the oven requires constant stirring.

3. To make a sauce, what temperature should the roux be? the liquid?

Video

While studying, look for the activity icon to:

- Build vocabulary with e-flash cards and matching activities.
- Expand learning with video clips, photo identification activities, animations, and interactive activities.
- Review and assess what you learn by completing end-of-chapter questions.

G-WLEARNING.com

yamix/Shutterstock.com

Soups

25

Reading Prep

In preparation for reading the chapter, review a number of restaurants' menus for their soup offerings. As you read, identify what type each soup is. Are there any that do not fit into a category described in this chapter?

Culinary Terminology Build Vocab

consommé, p. 405
clearmeat, p. 406
raft, p. 407
purée soup, p. 407
cream soup, p. 407
bisque, p. 408
chowder, p. 408

Academic Terminology Build Vocab

epitome, p. 403

Objectives

After studying this chapter, you will be able to

- differentiate between the two types of clear soups.

- compare the different types of thick soups.

- recognize the types of soups in the specialty soups category.

- understand the role of soup garnishes.

- execute proper techniques for serving hot and cold soup.

Chefs know that first impressions are important and can make or break a great meal. Many times, soup is the first course in a menu. Knowing how to prepare and serve top-shelf soups is, therefore, an important part of the culinary arts.

Today, soups are an increasingly significant part of the menu. Soups are no longer reserved for the beginning of a meal. Instead, soups are routinely served as an entire lunch or as part of a main course. Many quick-serve restaurants feature soup and sandwich specials for lunch and dinner. Some restaurants even include a sweet soup on their dessert menu.

Soup is popular in many different cuisines. The sheer variety of soups worldwide is astonishing. Soups can be made from meats, seafood, fruits, vegetables, pastas, and even seaweed. Some soups are served hot while others are served cold. Some are thick and hearty, while others are thin and delicate. Some soups are chunky while others are perfectly smooth. Some are exotic while others are the epitome, or ideal example, of comfort food. Due to the large variety, chefs categorize soups to make them easier to understand, produce, and remember. Soups are grouped into one of three categories—clear, thick, or specialty.

Clear Soups

From the most rustic to the finest restaurant, clear soups are served in all types of restaurants, 25-1. Clear soups are easily recognized for their thin consistency and generally transparent appearance. Often, chopped vegetables, various starches, and

Draz-Koetke/Goodheart-Willcox Publisher

25-1 Soups are often the first dish served to a customer.

pieces of meat are served floating in the soup. Clear soups are further divided into broth soups and consommés.

Broth Soups

When preparing broth soups, different vegetables, starches, and meats are cooked in a flavorful broth or stock. Some of the most common soups such as minestrone, vegetable, and chicken noodle soup are broth soups. Traditionally, broth (and sometimes

TECHNIQUE
Preparing Broth Soups

1. Sweat or sauté meats and vegetables. Depending on the ingredients, cooking times will vary. (Some broth-based soups omit this step or only sweat some of a soup's ingredients.)

2. Cover the ingredients with broth or stock. Bring the liquid to a boil, and then reduce to a simmer.

3. If other ingredients are added to the soup, they may be added at different times during soup preparation. For instance, if diced carrots, zucchini, and tomatoes were among the ingredients for a soup, they should be added at different times. The carrots would be simmered for 20 minutes before the zucchini is added. The zucchini would then be simmered for 5 minutes before the tomato is added. Besides vegetables, other ingredients may include herbs and spices, and starches such as pasta, rice, or barley.

   (Due to the variety of starches, cooking times will vary.)

4. Serve soup once the ingredients are tender and the soup has developed enough flavor.

Recipe No.	Name		Category
25.3	**Beef and Barley Soup**		Soup
Yield	**Portion Size**		**No. Portions**
1 gal. (3.8 L)	8 oz. (240 mL)		16

US Quantity	Metric Quantity	Ingredient	TCS
2 Tbsp.	30 mL	vegetable oil	
8 oz.	225 g	carrot, small dice	
8 oz.	225 g	celery, small dice	
12 oz.	340 g	mushrooms, sliced	
12 oz.	340 g	onions, small dice	
½ tsp.	3 mL	garlic, minced	
1 gal.	3.8 L	beef broth or stock	•
8 oz.	225 g	tomatoes, concassé	•
1 ea.		bay leaf	
8 oz.	225 g	frozen peas	
1 lb.	450 g	cooked beef, diced	•
1 lb.	450 g	cooked barley*	
To taste		salt and black pepper	

Method	CCP
1. Brown the celery, carrots, mushrooms, and onions in oil over high heat in a large saucepan. Stir often.	
2. When the vegetables are browned and softened, add the garlic. Cook for 1 more minute.	
3. Add the tomatoes, broth or stock, and bay leaf. Bring to a boil. Reduce heat to a simmer and cook for 45 minutes.	CCP
4. Remove bay leaf. Add peas, cooked beef, and barley. Continue simmering until these ingredients reach 165°F (74°C).	CCP
5. Season soup with salt and black pepper. Serve when hot.	
* To cook barley, place 8 oz. (225 g) of barley in 3 c. (720 mL) lightly salted water. Bring to a boil and simmer until the barley is tender (about 40 minutes). Drain barley and cool.	

Portion (g)	Calories	Fat (g)	Protein (g)	Carbohydrate (g)	Cholesterol (mg)	Sodium (mg)	Fiber (g)
225	114	4.66	8.18	10.28	14.07	800.14	1.64

water) is used to make these soups. In today's foodservice, stock has largely replaced broths or bouillons. As a result, these soups are most commonly made from stock. Whether using stock or broth, the quality of the stock or broth is critical to the quality of the soup. Stock or broth should be free of fat, clear, and flavorful. Poor quality stock or broth ruins a soup.

The procedure for preparing most broth soups follows the same general technique. However, there are so many different soups in this category that procedures may vary slightly. For instance, different vegetables and meats have different cooking times. Also, the size of the ingredients affects how the soup is prepared. Despite these variations, broth-based soups follow the same basic steps.

Consommé

Many people believe that consommé is the finest clear soup. **Consommé** is a perfectly transparent and intensely flavored soup that is made by clarifying a stock. It is routinely served in fine-dining restaurants. Consommé is expensive since it is time-consuming to make. It also requires practice to prepare correctly.

Consommé is unique from other soups because it involves removing all impurities from the stock. To do this, a mixture of ground meat, vegetables, and egg whites is added to the stock. This mixture is called **clearmeat**. As the stock simmers, the albumin from the egg white and the protein in the meat begins to coagulate the clearmeat. As it coagulates, it traps impurities and rises to the top of the stock. The coagulated clearmeat that is now

TECHNIQUE
Preparing Consommé

1. Prepare the clearmeat by mixing lean ground meat, finely chopped vegetables, and egg white either by hand or in a food processor.

2. Add the clearmeat to a pot containing cold, defatted stock. Stir the clearmeat and stock until they are well combined.

3. Place the pot over low-medium heat. As the stock heats up, gently scrape the bottom of the pot periodically with a wooden spoon. Do not stir the mixture, only carefully scrape the bottom of the pot so that the clearmeat does not stick to the bottom of the pot. If the clearmeat sticks, it will burn and ruin the consommé.

4. Stop scraping the bottom of the pot once the consommé becomes warm. The clearmeat will then coagulate and slowly rise to the surface as the consommé heats up.

5. Reduce the heat to a slow simmer as soon as the consommé comes to a boil. As the clearmeat coagulates and forms the raft, it rises and traps impurities. If the consommé boils rapidly at any point, the raft can break apart and turn the consommé cloudy.

6. Simmer the consommé for 1 to 3 hours. During this time, the consommé will deepen in color and increase in flavor. Both of these are hallmarks of a fine consommé.

7. Strain the consommé through a chinois lined with a large coffee filter or several layers of cheesecloth. Do not pour the consommé from the pot, this could break the raft and ruin the consommé. Instead, delicately ladle it into the chinois.

8. Chill consommé according to your local health department's guidelines. Once the consommé is cold, remove any fat that solidifies on top.

floating on top of the consommé is called a **raft**. Once the consommé is carefully removed from the raft and filtered, a perfectly transparent consommé results. The other ingredients in the clearmeat—ground meat and vegetables—act to add flavor to the consommé.

Thick Soups

Thick soups are filling due to their dense consistency. Because these soups are thickened, they are not transparent and have a round mouthfeel. Soups are thickened using a purée, starch-based thickener, or combination of both. Thick soups are further divided into purée soups, cream soups, and bisques and chowders.

Purée Soups

A **purée soup** is thickened using a purée of well-cooked ingredients. Typically, starchy foods such as legumes, potatoes, winter squashes, or rice are among the ingredients of a purée soup. When these starchy ingredients are cooked until soft and blended into the soup, they add thickening power.

Cream Soups

A **cream soup** consists of milk or stock, thickened with both flour and puréed

TECHNIQUE
Preparing Purée Soups

1. Simmer all ingredients—starchy ones as well—in a flavorful stock until they are soft and easily crushed. Some of the ingredients may be sweated first.

2. Purée the soup using a blender, food processor, immersion blender, or food mill. Certain types of purée soups may be passed through a strainer.

3. Adjust the thickness of the finished soup. If the soup is too thin, additional cooked ingredients may be puréed into the soup. If this is not possible, the soup could be thickened with a starch such as arrowroot or a roux. If the soup is too thick, add additional stock.

ingredients, and often finished with cream. Some chefs may even swirl whole butter into these soups just prior to serving them. Cream soups tend to be the richest and silkiest due to the addition of cream and butter.

A blender is a powerful piece of equipment that can produce a smooth soup in a short period of time. Its power also makes it dangerous. For instance, if the blender is turned on at high speed and without proper caution, it may propel hot soup out the top of the blender. To safely blend soups, follow these precautions.

- Do not fill the blender more than halfway.

- Do not turn the blender on if it is set on high speed.

- Hold the top of the blender on using a thick towel. If hot soup does come out of the blender, it will be caught in the towel.

- Do not blend piping hot soups, but rather let them cool slightly before blending.

TECHNIQUE
Preparing Cream Soups

1. Sweat the solid ingredients in whole butter.
2. Add flour to the vegetables and butter, and cook until the flour taste has disappeared. (This is actually similar to making a roux.) This will take several minutes.
3. Add milk or stock to the cooked vegetables. Bring to a boil and reduce heat to a simmer.
4. Simmer the vegetables until they are soft.
5. Purée the vegetables. The soup may need to be passed through a strainer.
6. Place the soup in a clean pot and bring to a boil. Hot cream and possibly butter may then be added.

Bisques and Chowders

Bisques and chowders represent a smaller category of soups compared to the many cream and purée soups. A **bisque** is a seafood-based soup that is thickened traditionally with rice, although modern methods use a roux. Bisques are often considered luxury soups and require considerable skill to make. They are often flavored with sherry and brandy, tinted red from the addition of tomato product, and fortified with cream. Shrimp, lobster, and crayfish bisques are examples of this category.

Chowder is an American seafood-based soup that is flavored with dairy product, bacon, and potato; and thickened with flour. Some chowders are also made with large amounts of tomato. Chowders tend to be filling soups that were traditionally made and consumed by fishermen. The most well-known chowder is clam chowder. Clam chowder is made from large clams that are finely chopped after cooking to tenderize them.

Specialty Soups

During your career in the culinary arts, you will certainly observe chefs making soups that do not fit perfectly into the categories just listed. For instance, chefs sometimes make cream or purée soups that do not exactly follow the classic procedure. A chef may make a traditional purée soup, but decide to finish it with cream or a drizzle of spicy olive oil. Another chef may make a classical purée soup using a small amount of flour to help thicken the soup.

In the same way, there are numerous soups that cannot be classified as either clear or thick soups. These soups were classically grouped under the heading of specialty soups. Many of these soups were regional or national specialties. Cold soups fit under the heading of specialty soups.

Cold Soups

While most soups are served hot, cold soups are traditionally served chilled. These soups are refreshing and are especially appreciated in hot weather. Some of the most popular cold soups include

- Gazpacho (gahz PAH choh)–a Spanish soup of puréed tomatoes, red peppers, garlic, and cucumber

Hints from the Chef
Salty Soup

Many soups are heated before service and held hot in a steam table. If a soup is held for long periods of time in a hot steam table or is reboiled a few times, it may reduce. When this happens, the soup may become salty. To minimize the chance of this happening, keep soups covered in a steam table, and taste them periodically.

- Vichyssoise (vee shee SWAHZ)–a cold cream of potato and leek soup
- Borscht (BOHRSHT)–a beet and red cabbage soup

Garnishing Soups

Any piece of food floating in a soup is considered a garnish. Garnishes add visual appearance, texture, and flavor to finished soups. Garnishes are varied and can be as simple or elaborate as desired, 25-2. For example, vegetables, noodles, and pieces of chicken meat would garnish a basic chicken noodle soup. At the other end of the spectrum, small pastries stuffed with ground chicken, brunoise of carrot, and julienne of mushroom may be used to garnish a flavorful consommé.

Use the following guidelines when preparing soup garnishes:
- *Garnishes should be bite-sized pieces or smaller.* Excessively large garnishes are difficult to eat easily.
- *Garnishes should be tender.* Crunchy garnishes are unpleasant in most soups.

Draz-Koetke/Goodheart-Willcox Publisher

25-2 A well-garnished soup improves the appearance and texture of the finished soup.

Recipe No.	Name		Category
25.9	Gazpacho		Soup
Yield	**Portion Size**		**No. Portions**
1 gal. (3.8 L)	8 fl. oz. (240 mL)		16

US Quantity	Metric Quantity	Ingredient	TCS
2 ea.		cucumber, peeled and seeded	
3 lb.	1360 g	ripe tomato, seeded	•
4 Tbsp.	60 mL	onion, diced	
4 ea.		red peppers, seeded	
1 tsp.	5 mL	garlic, minced	
4 fl. oz.	120 mL	extra virgin olive oil	
4 oz.	115 g	bread crumbs	
8 fl. oz.	240 mL	tomato juice	
2 fl. oz.	60 mL	sherry vinegar or red wine vinegar	
as needed		water	
to taste		salt and white pepper	
as needed		garnishes*	

Method			CCP
1. Grind all ingredients in a blender or food processor. Do not allow the ingredients to become completely smooth.			
2. Taste for seasoning and cool to 41°F (5°C) or less within four hours.			CCP
3. Serve the garnishes on top of individual cups of soup or serve them separately on the side of the soup.			

*Appropriate garnishes for gazpacho include diced or Parisienne scoop cucumber, brunoise red pepper, croutons sautéed in butter, diced tomato, and minced parsley.

Portion (g)	Calories	Fat (g)	Protein (g)	Carbohydrate (g)	Cholesterol (mg)	Sodium (mg)	Fiber (g)
225	91.79	5.44	1.56	7.46	0	482.82	1.81

- *Garnishes for hot soups should be served hot and served cold for cold soups.*
- *Fatty or oily garnishes must be avoided for consommés.* Nothing should be added to the finished consommé that could cloud it or produce a layer of fat floating on the top.
- *Garnishes should complement the soup in flavor and style.*

Serving Soups

Preparing a soup is only part of the story. Serving soup properly is just as important as making the soup. More specifically, the temperature of the soup when served determines whether the soup is a success. For instance, a lukewarm cream of mushroom soup is not as enticing as the same soup served piping hot. The rule of thumb is that hot soups must be served very hot while cold soups are served very cold. To ensure proper serving temperatures, consider the following:

- *Temperature of the soup.* Hot soups are frequently heated in advance of service and held hot in a steam table. Be sure the soup is boiled before placing it in the steam table. Also, be certain the steam table is hot enough to keep the soup very hot. Cold soups should be stored in a refrigerator and perhaps even on ice to ensure they stay very cold.

- *Serving container temperature.* Hot soups should be ladled into hot soup bowls or soup plates. If hot soup is ladled into lukewarm or cool containers, the soup invariably cools off. Cold soups should be served in chilled containers in order to keep the soup as cold as possible.

- *Soup plate versus soup bowl.* Soup can be served in soup bowls or plates. Soup plates can make a beautiful presentation.

Unfortunately, there are two drawbacks to using soup plates. Soup cools off faster in a soup plate compared to a soup bowl. Also, soup plates can be difficult to serve since the soup tends to slosh out or onto the sides of the plate, 25-3.

- *Immediate service.* As soon as a soup is portioned, it must be served. Any delay in service can ruin a soup. In some restaurants, soup is ladled into a hot container directly in front of the customer. This is time-consuming, but ensures the soup is served hot.

Draz-Koetke/Goodheart-Willcox Publisher

25-3 Although the presentation is attractive, soup cools off more quickly when served in a soup plate because more surface area is exposed.

Summary Points

- Clear soups are divided into broth soups and consommés. Broth soups contain a variety of vegetables and starches that are cooked in broth. Consommés are a clear soup that is often garnished with various vegetables, proteins, and starches before serving.

- Thick soups are divided into purée soups, cream soups, and bisques and chowders. These soups vary in the method used to thicken them.

- Soups that do not fit into the clear or thick soups categories are considered specialty soups. Cold soups are in this category.

- Soups can be garnished in a number of different ways. Garnishes add visual appeal as well as flavor and texture.

- When serving soup, it is crucial that the soup be served hot or cold depending on the type of soup. In addition, the serving container should be appropriately hot or cold. Once soup is portioned, it needs to be served immediately.

In Review Assess

1. List three categories into which soups are divided.
2. Broth soups and consommés are examples of _____ soups.
3. True or false. The added vegetables and meat determine the quality of the soup.
4. List two functions the clearmeat performs in consommé preparation.
5. Explain the difference between a purée and a cream soup.
6. A traditional bisque is thickened with _____.
7. List three cold soups.
8. True or false. Soup garnishes should be bite-sized or smaller.

9. What is the most important factor to consider when serving soup?
10. Soup served in a soup _____ cools off more quickly and spills more readily.

Core Skills

11. **Math.** Gazpacho soup is on the menu for a dinner. Chef has told you to prepare for 200 orders. Your restaurant serves an 8-ounce soup portion. How many gallons of gazpacho should you make?

12. **Speaking.** Research to learn what scientific concept contributes to faster heat loss when soup is served in a soup plate compared to a soup bowl. Give a demonstration to illustrate this concept to the class.

13. **Writing.** Use digital or print sources to research the history of soup kitchens. Write a two-page informative paper sharing what you learn.

14. **Math.** The restaurant where you work uses the metric system for measuring. The restaurant serves 250-mL portions of soup. You are told to make enough soup to serve 34 people. How many liters of soup should you make?

15. **Research and Writing.** Perform research to learn popular soup trends over the past century. Select one of these soups and write an informative paper. The paper should describe the soup and how it reflected the time period. Your research should include the popular culture of the time, economy, and current events. Gather appropriate sources and cite them in your paper. Be sure to edit and revise your paper to refine your thoughts and communicate them clearly.

16. **CTE Career Readiness Practice.** Suppose your work supervisor gave you the following problem to solve: customers are complaining that the soup is not hot enough. Your first effort to creatively solving the problem is to ask questions. Create a mind map like the following to dig deeper into the problem.

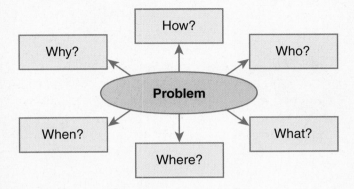

Critical Thinking

17. **Consider.** Discuss the advantages of serving a clear soup versus a thick soup. Are there instances when it would be better to serve one instead of the other?

18. **Predict Outcome.** A soup recipe is prepared and divided into two identical pots to cook. One pot is cooked with the lid on while the other pot remains uncovered. Predict the possible impact this might have on the final products. How might the soups be the same? different?

19. **Compile.** Search the Internet, culinary magazines, and restaurant menus for soup garnish ideas. Create a reference of soup garnish ideas for your future use in the industry. Include your own ideas or expand the reference to include ideas for other types of garnishes.

Technology

Research soups from other ethnic cuisines. Select one and prepare an electronic presentation describing the culture of the region from which the soup originates. Be sure to explain any unique ingredients and preparation methods that are used in the making of the soup. Prepare the recipe and serve with your presentation to the class.

Teamwork

Working as a team, organize a taste test to evaluate the effect of a soup's appearance and temperature on customer satisfaction. For instance, measure the effect adding two tablespoons of oil to consommé has on satisfaction. Measure the effect of temperature by serving the same soup both lukewarm and very hot. Devise your own rating scale and have other classmates take your taste test. Calculate the mean, mode, and median ratings. Prepare a summary of your findings and share with the class.

Chef's E-portfolio
The World of Soups

Upload your presentation from the Technology activity to your e-portfolio. Be sure to include a photo of your soup preparation. Ask your instructor where to save your file. This could be on the school's network or a flash drive of your own. Name your portfolio document *FirstnameLastname_Portfolio Ch#.docx* (i.e., JohnSmith_PortfolioCh25.docx).

While studying, look for the activity icon ↗ **to:**

- Build vocabulary with e-flash cards and matching activities.
- Expand learning with video clips, photo identification activities, animations, and interactive activities.
- Review and assess what you learn by completing end-of-chapter questions.

G-WLEARNING.COM

Tischenko Irina/Shutterstock.com

Vegetable Identification

26

Reading Prep

In preparation for reading the chapter, visit the USDA Fruit and Vegetable Availability and Handling Charts. As you read about the different vegetables in this chapter, compare the "Handling and Storage" and "Quality and Receiving" recommendations for each vegetable. Consider how this affects the complexity of ordering, receiving, and storing vegetables.

Culinary Terminology Build Vocab

Scoville heat units (SHU), p. 433
legumes, p. 433

Academic Terminology Build Vocab

aromatic, p. 416
foraged, p. 439

Objectives

After studying this chapter, you will be able to

- recognize the most common fresh vegetables used in commercial foodservice.

- apply quality factors when selecting vegetables.

- recall growing seasons related to fresh vegetables.

- recognize purchase forms of vegetables.

- compare different methods for processing vegetables.

- explain how vegetables are graded.

A chef's ability to properly select and prepare vegetables continues to grow in importance. Vegetables have always been used in cooking to add flavor to dishes. They also played a supporting role to the protein on the plate. This is no longer the case. In modern entrées, vegetables are taking center stage, having gained equal importance to meat, fish, or poultry. Vegetables are rising to stardom in vegetarian main dishes.

Chefs have an ever-expanding array of fresh produce available to them. Keeping informed about new items entering the market, and how to select and handle these new items is a constant concern. Effective communication with produce suppliers is important to most chefs. The best chefs seek out specialty sources for key items to ensure the highest level of freshness.

One of the differences between a good restaurant and a great restaurant is the chef's ability to get great ingredients. How the chef handles and cooks these ingredients is equally important. This most certainly applies to vegetables. This chapter describes vegetables commonly used in foodservice, their uses, and how to recognize and purchase quality produce.

Onion Family

You may not know that all members of the onion group are part of the lily family. Like lilies, they grow from underground bulbs. Onions are some of the most widely used products in the kitchen.

Onions

Onions are a staple in every kitchen. Their **aromatic** or distinctive smell and quality is a common element in most savory dishes. Most chefs categorize onions by their color.

- *Yellow onions* are also called "Spanish onions." They are the most commonly used onion in commercial kitchens. "Summer sweet onions" are a subcategory of yellow onions and are prized for their mild sweet flavor. The best known summer sweets are Vidalia onions from Georgia, Walla Walla onions from Washington State, Maui onions from Hawaii, and Texas Sweets.
- *Red onions* stand out with their purple color and are a favorite in salads, sandwiches, and other cold items.
- *White onions* are preferred in traditional Mexican cuisine and in preparations where a very white onion is desired.

Jumbo onions (3- to 4-inch diameter) are the size typically used in commercial kitchens because they offer a better yield than smaller sizes. Pearl onions (½- to ¾-inch diameter), can be yellow, white, or red. They are used for pickling, vegetable medleys, and garnishing stews.

Dry onions are packed in 50-pound (22 kg) mesh sacks or cardboard cases, or 25-pound (11 kg) sacks. Select hard onions with dry crackly skins and no sprouts. Refrigeration of dry onions is not necessary. Instead, store them in a dry, well-ventilated area. Dry onions keep for several months under proper conditions and are available year-round.

Garlic

Pound for pound, garlic is the most aromatic vegetable in the kitchen. A little garlic goes a long way.

A head of garlic is comprised of 12 to 16 cloves, each wrapped in skin. White garlic is the most commonly used variety. Less common in commercial kitchens is pink garlic with a rosy-hued skin or elephant garlic with extremely large cloves. Choose garlic with plump, firm, compact heads. If properly stored, garlic can have a long shelf life—two months at 50°F to 60°F (10°C to 15°C) and six to eight months at 33°F to 38°F (1°C to 3°C). Garlic may be packed in a variety of ways

- 3- to 6-pound (1 to 3 kg) braids
- 10-pound (4½ kg) cases
- 30-pound (14 kg) cases

One of the most common convenience products in commercial kitchens is processed garlic. Garlic can be purchased chopped, crushed, or as peeled cloves. Chopped or crushed garlic may be packed in water or vegetable oil. Though processed garlic saves labor, some chefs maintain that it has less flavor than fresh garlic.

Shallots

Shallots have an onion flavor but grow in clusters much like garlic. This may explain why some people mistakenly call them a cross between onions and garlic. Shallots are smaller than onions with a stronger, more

complex flavor. They are especially useful in sauce making. Shallots are most commonly packed in 5-pound (2 kg) mesh bags.

Scallions

Scallions, or green onions, are young onions of any color that are picked early for their small bulb and green leaves. Spring onions, or bulb onions, are slightly more mature than scallions. They have bulbs that range from about 1- to 1½-inch (3 to 4 cm) diameter. Both scallions and spring onions have a milder flavor than fully mature onions. Their green tops are often used in salads and for garnishing.

Leeks

Leeks may look like overgrown scallions, but they are different. Leeks have a more fibrous texture. Their multiple layers of leaves often harbor dirt and sand. Leeks

are called a winter vegetable because they can be harvested late in the growing season. The white and light green part of the leek is preferred for most dishes. Leeks are prized for the mellow aromatic quality they give to soups and stews. They can also be served as a vegetable.

Leeks often come bundled in bunches of two to four leeks depending on size.

Root Vegetables

The roots of plants draw water and nutrients from the ground and help support the plant while it grows. Roots also store plant nutrients, which makes them some of the most nutritious of all vegetables.

Roots are hardy and store well. For centuries, they have been a winter staple in cold climates. Most root vegetables are available year-round, but their peak season is in the fall and winter months.

Carrots

Carrots are the most popular root vegetable in commercial kitchens. Carrots are valued for their aromatic flavor in many savory dishes. They are also served as a vegetable. Carrots are popular for their bright orange color and sweet flavor. Large carrots

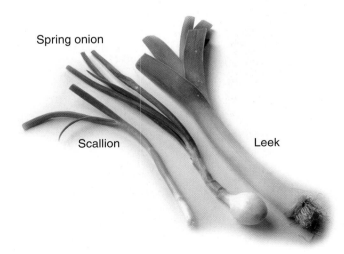

Spring onion

Scallion

Leek

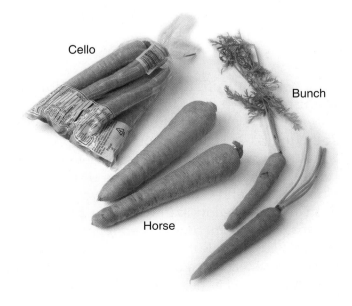

Cello

Bunch

Horse

without tops are called *horse carrots*. They are preferred in most commercial kitchens due to their better yield after peeling and trimming. Some chefs prefer either carrot bunches with tops still intact or *cello carrots*, which are packed in plastic bags. Both are smaller carrots.

A steady supply of carrots is available year-round because they are so popular. Look for carrots with a crisp texture. They should break with a sharp snap when bent. Avoid carrots with a limp texture or green shoulders. These are signs of age or poor storage. The green tops of bunch carrots also give a good indication of freshness.

Turnips

Turnips are a root vegetable of European origins. Turnips are related to cabbages. The most popular variety of turnip is the purple-topped globe turnip. It has an even, round shape and white flesh. Its skin is white except for the top one-third, which has an attractive purple color.

Turnips

Rutabaga

Look for turnips that are firm and without blemishes. Avoid those with soft, spongy roots. Turnips are most often purchased in 25-pound (11 kg) bags without tops.

Rutabagas are a large dense variety of turnip grown in Northern regions of the United States and Canada. They have yellow flesh and pale yellow skin with a purple top. Rutabagas are sometimes called *yellow turnips* or *Swedish turnips*. Rutabagas come packed in 50-pound (22 kg) bags or cases. They are often coated with wax to help retain moisture.

Parsnips

Parsnips look like beige-colored carrots with noticeably more tapered roots. They are related to carrots, but have a sweeter flavor.

Parsnips are packed in 25-pound (11 kg) bags. Avoid extremely large parsnips since they tend to have woody cores.

Beets

Beets, or beetroots, are spherical roots with deep red color. They were first cultivated in central Europe during the Middle Ages. Beets are served hot as a vegetable or marinated in salads. The green tops can be prepared like spinach. Other varieties of beets, not used for the table, are grown for sugar production or animal feed.

Beets may be purchased with or without green tops attached. Choose beets with a nice globe shape, smooth surface, and deeper red color. Beets without tops are often packed in 25-pound (11 kg) bags. Increasingly, other

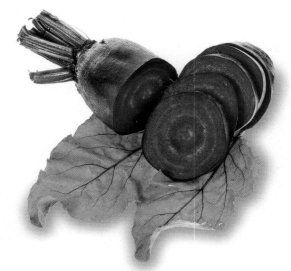

varieties of beets including white beets, golden, and candy striped beets (concentric white and pink layers) are common in food-service operations.

Celery Root

Celery root, or celeriac, is a plant related to the common green-stalked Pascal variety of celery. Celery root is cultivated for its root rather than its stems and leaves. It has a flavor like celery but with greater intensity of flavor and aroma. It can be used as an aromatic vegetable just like celery. It is also used in salads.

Celery roots have a rough tan-colored exterior. They should be scrubbed thoroughly because they often harbor dirt or sand. The inside of the celery root is a creamy white color and may darken slightly when exposed to air. Choose heavy, firm celery roots.

Jicama

Jicama (HEE cah mah) is a round root grown originally in Latin America.

It has a thin light brown skin and white flesh. Jicama's high moisture content and crisp texture make it refreshing. It is most commonly served raw.

Radishes

There are numerous varieties of radishes of varying shapes, sizes, and colors. Most are eaten raw as an appetizer or in salads. The most common variety of radish in the United States is the small round red-skinned variety sometimes called *button radishes*. Red radishes range between 1 to 2 inches (2 to 4 cm) in diameter. They are available in bunches either with their tops or cello-packed in 8-ounce (225 g) plastic bags.

Horseradish

Daikon

Button radishes

Other varieties of radishes commonly used in foodservice are horseradish and daikon. Horseradish is a strong-flavored radish. It is grated and used as a condiment for its hot flavor. Daikon is a long white Asian radish that is often used as a garnish for cold dishes.

Cabbages and Greens

Cabbages and greens have long been important vegetables in the kitchen. They provide an abundance of vitamins, minerals, and dietary fiber. Many members of this vegetable group have an undeserved reputation for being coarse, bitter, and unappetizing. If properly cooked, all of these vegetables can be tender and delicious.

Cabbages

Cabbages are of European origin and have been a part of most European cuisines for centuries. They are dense, sturdy, and keep well during winter months. Sauerkraut, a preserved form of cabbage, is a staple item in many European cuisines. Cabbage is inexpensive and versatile. It can be used as a vegetable, wrapper, or even in a salad such as coleslaw.

Cabbages are available year-round. They are packed for foodservice in 50- to 55-pound (22 to 25 kg) cases or in 50-pound (22 kg) mesh bags. Choose cabbages with firm, tightly packed heads and crisp leaves. Cabbages should be free of blemishes or spots.

Cabbage

Green Cabbage

Green cabbage is the most widely used cabbage. Its waxy leaves form a dense head with darker green leaves on the outside and pale green to white leaves near the core.

Savoy Cabbage

Savoy cabbage is a popular European variety of cabbage that is easily identified by its crinkled leaves and deep green color. Heads of savoy cabbage are looser than most other varieties.

Napa Cabbage

Napa cabbage, or Chinese cabbage, has an elongated head with wide white ribs and light green leaves. It has a mild flavor and is used in many Asian cuisines.

Red Cabbage

Red Cabbage has tightly packed, deep purple-red leaves and white core. It is valued for its unique color. It is often shredded and added to mixed greens.

Broccoli

A flowering member of the cabbage family, broccoli originated in Italy and is known to be cultivated as far back as the sixteenth century. It is one of the most popular members of the cabbage family. The majority of fresh broccoli produced in the United States comes from California.

Broccoli does not store as well as most other members of the cabbage family. It tends to lose its moisture and becomes limp. For this reason, broccoli is often packed in crushed ice. Broccoli is packed in 22-pound (10 kg) cases with 14 to 18 bunches per case. Choose broccoli with tight heads and dark green flowers. Look for broccoli with slender moist stalks. There is a steady supply of broccoli all year.

Cauliflower

Cauliflower is another flowering member of the cabbage family, its name means "cabbage flower." It is denser and hardier than broccoli but served in similar ways.

The snowy white heads come packed in 25-pound (11 kg) flat cartons with 9, 12, or 16 heads in each. The green leaves at the base of the head are a good indicator of freshness. The heads should be white, firm, and compact. The size of the head has no effect on its quality. Avoid spotted or bruised heads. Cauliflower is available year-round.

Brussels Sprouts

Brussels sprouts are the buds of an unusually tall member of the cabbage family. These miniature cabbages get their name from the Belgian city of Brussels, where they have been cultivated since Roman times.

Since brussels sprouts do best with a long cool growing season, they are at their peak between October and March. Look for brussels sprouts with firm compact heads, good green color, and few or no yellow leaves.

Broccoli Rabe (Rapini)

This vegetable is known for its pronounced flavor that many consider bitter.

It consists of stems, dark green leaves, and small semi-formed heads of broccoli. It is used in various international cuisines in soups, stir-fries, and as a vegetable.

Greens

Many greens, such as kale and turnip, are members of the cabbage family. When choosing greens, look for crisp leaves with solid green color and no yellow or brown spots. Crisp stems are also a good indicator of freshness.

Spinach   The most popular of all greens is spinach. It differs from most of the other greens because of its mild flavor and delicate texture. It cooks quickly and is even tender enough to be used raw in salad greens.

Flowering kale

Kale

Bunch   Cello

There are two distinct varieties of spinach—curly leaf (savoy) and flat leaf (broad leaf). The curly leaf is most often used for cello-pack spinach, which is prewashed and packed into plastic bags. The flat leaf type is most often sold bundled in bunches.

Bunched spinach comes in 20- to 22-pound (9 to 10 kg) wooden crates containing 24 bunches. Cello spinach comes in 5-pound (2.3 kg) cases containing eight 10-ounce (280 g) bags.

Kale   Kale is a curly green member of the cabbage family. Its bluish green leaves have curly edges and wrinkles across the surface. Kale is hardy and requires sufficient cooking to make it tender.

Flowering kale, or ornamental kale, has the same shaped leaves but with colorful centers and either white or purple stems. It is used mostly for garnishing and displays.

Kale is packed in 20- to 25-pound (9 to 11 kg) cases containing 24 bunches per case.

Collard Greens   Collards are a close relative of kale. They have large, flat waxy leaves

with medium green color and thick round stems. They are largely popular in southern cooking and are often stewed with flavorful pork products.

Turnip Greens   The leafy tops of turnip roots are also eaten as a green vegetable.

They have a sharp flavor. Turnip greens are recognizable by their long slender stems and finely wrinkled dark green leaves.

Mustard Greens   Mustard greens are the curly-edged leaves of the mustard plant. They have a unique peppery flavor and are usually

served cooked. Tender, young mustard greens are sometimes used in salads.

Swiss Chard   A variety of beet grown for its leaves, Swiss chard has broad white stems

and large tender crinkled leaves. Red chard is a variety with red stems. Chard is used much like spinach. It can be boiled or sautéed and tender, young leaves can be used in salads.

Stalks and Shoots

This group of vegetables is raised for their stalks or shoots. They tend to be fibrous,

a factor which should be considered when choosing and preparing these vegetables.

Artichokes

Artichokes are actually thistles. They are sometimes referred to as *globe artichokes* to distinguish them from Jerusalem artichokes, which are roots related to the sunflower. Artichokes are Mediterranean in origin. Today, the commercial artichoke crop in the United States is grown in California.

Artichokes can be cooked whole. They are eaten by pulling off each leaf and eating only the small amount of the flesh at the base of the leaf. All the leaves are removed until the bottom of the artichoke is uncovered. The bottom is totally edible with the exception of the fuzzy central core called the *choke*. Artichokes are also prepared by trimming away the outer leaves before cooking to reveal the bottom or the heart. Artichoke bottoms and hearts are also available canned.

Artichokes are available year-round but are best in late spring and summer months. Look for tightly closed leaves and a lack of brown leaves. Artichokes come packed in 20-pound (9 kg) cases packed by size.

Asparagus

Asparagus plants grow largely underground, but produce edible shoots that thrust

up through the soil surface. Green asparagus is typically picked when the shoots are 6 to 8 inches (15 to 20 cm) above ground. White asparagus is grown with limited exposure to the sun so green chlorophyll does not develop.

For many diners, the appearance of fresh asparagus signals the arrival of spring. Though asparagus is available year-round, the majority of it is produced from mid-February to July. The peak of the season is April to June.

Quality asparagus should have tight tips, straight stalks, and no more than one inch of woody base at the bottom of the stalk. They should break with a crisp snap when bent.

Asparagus is packed in crates of 15 or 30 pounds (7 or 14 kg). Asparagus is sized for consistent product. Sizes range from very small—less than 5⁄16-inch (0.8 cm) diameter at the base, to colossal—7⁄8-inch (2.22 cm) diameter at the base.

Celery

Celery, often referred to as Pascal celery to distinguish it from celery root, is a staple in kitchens around the world. Its aromatic flavor contributes to a multitude of savory dishes. Celery can also be served as a vegetable course or as the main ingredient in a salad. The pale center stalks are called the *heart*.

Choose celery with straight stalks and crisp texture. The inside of the stems or ribs should be smooth. Check the hearts for full formation and the absence of rot or decay. The most popular celery pack size is a 50- to 60-pound (22 to 27 kg) case containing 18, 24, or 30 bunches. Large bunches of celery typically offer a better yield.

Fennel

Fennel, also called *anise*, has a squat round base, long stalks, and feathery leaves. The white base or bulb is the most used part of the plant. It has a texture similar to celery and a light licorice flavor.

Fennel bulb is used in stews and broths for its aromatic qualities. It is also braised and served as a vegetable. The seeds of fennel are used as a spice in a number of dishes.

Cardoons

Cardoon looks like an oversized pale bunch of celery. It is quite fibrous and must

be cooked. Cardoon can be boiled, baked, fried, or braised.

Cardoons are more popular in Europe, especially France and Italy, than in the United States. They are a winter vegetable that comes into season in late autumn and winter months.

Squashes

All squashes originated in the Western Hemisphere. Squashes were unknown to Europeans before Columbus' journeys to the New World. Today, squash varieties are found in all parts of the globe.

Summer and Winter Squashes

There are hundreds of varieties of squashes. Squashes can be divided into two main groups—summer and winter. Summer squashes have thin skins and soft flesh. They begin to spoil if not used within a few days of harvest. Winter squashes have thick skins and dense flesh. They can be stored for several months in a cool dry place.

Other Members of the Squash Family

Some members of the squash family, such as cucumbers and chayotes, are not usually recognized as squashes though they are closely related botanically. They are often overlooked as members of this vegetable group because

Summer Squash

Zucchini

Zucchini, sometimes called *Italian squash*, is a popular variety of summer squash. It has shiny green skin and a delicate flavor.

Yellow Squash

Yellow squash has yellow skin and white flesh. Yellow squash comes in a straight neck variety, which is preferred for foodservice, and a crookneck variety with an irregular curved neck.

Pattypan

Pattypan or scallop squash is a flat disk with scalloped edges. It may be white, pale green, or yellow.

cucumbers are used for salads and pickling, and chayote looks different from most squash.

Cucumbers There are three main types of cucumbers used in foodservice—standard, pickling, and European.

Standard cucumbers are field grown. They are often coated with edible wax to slow moisture loss after picking.

Pickling cucumbers are varieties raised especially for making pickles. They are smaller in size than standard cucumbers and

European

Standard

Pickle

Winter Squash

Pumpkins

Pumpkins, an important member of the squash family, are well-known for their round shape and orange skin. Though many think of the classic jack-o'-lantern, the yellow flesh of pumpkins can be used for pies, breads, custards, and soups.

Butternut Squash

Butternut squash has a spherical bottom and a long wide cylindrical neck. Its skin is beige and its flesh is a bright orange color. It is the sweetest of the winter squashes.

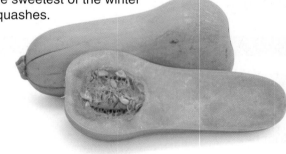

Spaghetti Squash

Spaghetti squash is a large, pale yellow oval squash. When cooked and removed from its shell, its flesh divides into strands that resemble spaghetti.

Acorn Squash

Acorn squash has a round shape with a pointed tip much like an acorn. It has a dark green skin and yellowish orange flesh.

have fewer seeds. Pickling cucumbers are not waxed.

European cucumbers, also called *English* or *seedless cucumbers*, are hothouse grown. They have an even shape and size. They are longer than standard cucumbers, ranging between 12 and 20 inches (30 and 50 cm) in length. European cucumbers are shrink-wrapped in plastic to deter moisture loss.

Select cucumbers with good green color, firm texture, and no soft spots. Overmature cucumbers, noted by large size and yellow color, tend to have large woody seeds.

Standard cucumbers are packed in 50- to 55-pound (22 to 25 kg) bushel cartons or smaller 24-count baskets.

Chayote   The chayote is a light green pear-shaped member of the squash family. It is closely related to the cucumber. Chayote goes by many other names including vegetable pear, mirliton, and christophene. It is a popular vegetable in Latin America.

Chayotes have a flat seed in their middle that is removed along with the skin. They are usually cooked before serving because of their firm starchy texture. Chayotes have a delicate flavor similar to summer squashes.

Fruit Vegetables

This group of vegetables has the same botanical characteristics as fruits. However, they are commonly prepared and served as vegetables.

Avocados

The avocado is a fruit with origins in Central America. The majority of avocados consumed in the United States are of the Hass variety. Hass avocados have rough, green- to black-colored skin. Their skins darken as they ripen. Other varieties have shiny green skins that do not change color when ripe.

The avocado's high fat content accounts for its rich buttery texture. Avocados must be used at the proper stage of ripeness. They are ripe when they yield slightly to light pressure. Avocados will ripen at room temperature.

California avocados come packed in 22- to 25-pound (10 to 11 kg) cases with counts ranging from 36 to 84 per case. Frozen or canned avocado purée is an option used by many foodservice operations.

Tomatoes

Tomatoes are one of the most popular vegetables. There are hundreds of tomato varieties. Chefs can create an array of dishes featuring specialty and heirloom varieties of tomatoes. Their colors are as varied as green, yellow, orange, and purple. Tomatoes range in shape from "ox heart" to "miniature tear-drop." Most of these unique tomatoes are specialty items with limited availability. In foodservice, there are a few types of tomatoes that are used most often, 26-1.

Regular Tomatoes   Regular tomatoes, sometimes called *salad tomatoes,* are what most people think of when tomatoes are mentioned. They are an even round shape and ripen to a red color. Round tomatoes come sorted by size and are usually packed in a two layer, 20-pound (9 kg) case.

Plum Tomatoes   Plum tomatoes are smaller than regular tomatoes and oval shaped like a plum. Plum tomatoes have fewer seeds and less water than regular tomatoes. This makes them the preferred choice for sauces and purées. Plum tomatoes come packed in a 25-pound (11 kg) bulk case.

Cherry Tomatoes   Cherry tomatoes are smaller than plum tomatoes and round in shape. They are a favorite for salads and vegetable trays since they can be served whole. Cherry tomatoes are packed in flats of 12 dry pints.

Tomatoes are a delicate product when ripe. Commercially packed tomatoes are picked underripe and allowed to ripen after packing to minimize damage. Most tomatoes are picked in the mature green stage. Vine-ripened tomatoes

Hints from the Chef

Tomato Sizes

A size designation of "6 by 6" refers to how many tomatoes are packed in a single layer. A case of 6 by 6 tomatoes has two layers of 36 tomatoes per layer, or 72 tomatoes per case.

In 1991, the USDA instituted new size standards. Many chefs, produce suppliers, and packers still use the old designations.

are picked as they start to turn pink. To ensure even ripening and full development of flavor, tomatoes should not be refrigerated until they are fully ripe.

Tomatillos

A tomatillo (TOH mah tee oh) is a member of the tomato family that grows on creeping vines. They are covered by a papery husk. Underneath the husk, a tomatillo resembles a small green tomato. They have a

Draz-Koetke/Goodheart-Willcox Publisher

26-1 Different varieties of tomatoes have different uses.

slightly tart flavor, which makes them good in salsas and relishes.

Peppers

All peppers are members of the *Capsicum* genus. There are hundreds of varieties of peppers. Some varieties of peppers are known by several different names. This makes the topic of peppers quite complicated. To make this topic less confusing, peppers are divided into two categories—sweet and chile.

Sweet Peppers Sweet peppers are those peppers that have a sweet fresh flavor rather than a hot burning flavor. The most common and least expensive variety of sweet peppers is the green bell pepper. It is a large round, slightly heart-shaped pepper with a deep, dark green color.

Most green peppers, if allowed to ripen on the vine, will turn red. Special varieties turn yellow, orange, or even purple. Once a specialty item, colored bell peppers have become an important ingredient in commercial

SANITATION & SAFETY
Handling Chiles

The hot taste of chile peppers is really a chemical irritation caused by capsaicin. When cutting chile peppers and exposing the capsaicin, gloves should be worn. Some people can handle even the most intense chiles bare-handed, while others are irritated by even mild peppers. Whatever your tolerance is, wash your hands well after working with chiles and never rub your eyes!

Culinary Trends

Value Added Produce

One trend that continues to gain popularity in foodservice is ready-to-use fresh produce. There is a wide range of prewashed, peeled, and precut fresh vegetables available to chefs. Though they cost more than traditionally packed produce, they offer many advantages. The most important advantage is reduced labor cost in the kitchen. Additionally, ready-to-use products reduce waste and storage space, and provide consistent yield and uniformity. One downside to these vegetables is they have a tendency to lose some flavor and nutrients.

Common Chile Peppers

Ancho

The ancho is a dried pepper with deep red-colored, wrinkled skin and is about 4½ in. (11.5 cm) long and 3 in. (7.5 cm) wide at the stem. It has a relatively mild fruity and slightly acidic flavor. It rates 1,000–2,000 SHU.

Bird's Eye

Also known as *chile tepín*, this pepper is less than ¼ in. (0.5 cm) round. The bird's eye is popular in African and Caribbean cuisines. It rates 100,000–225,000 SHU.

Anaheim

A mild green chile with medium green color, the Anaheim chile ranges in size from 6 to 10 in. (15 to 25 cm) long and 1–2 in. (2.5–5 cm) around. It rates 500–2,500 SHU.

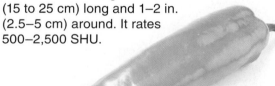

Cascabel

The cascabel is a small, round, reddish brown dried chile with a 1–1¼ in. (2.5–3 cm) diameter. It rates 1,000–2,000 SHU.

Arbol

Arbol is a thin smooth-skinned red chile that is thin fleshed and very hot. It is approximately 3 in. (7.5 cm) long. It rates 15,000–30,000 SHU.

Cayenne

A bright red, fairly hot red pepper that is usually ground and used as a condiment. Cayennes are typically 5 in. (13 cm) long and 1 in. (2.5 cm) wide. It rates 30,000–50,000 SHU.

(Continued)

Common Chile Peppers (Continued)

Cherry

The cherry pepper is a mild red or green fresh pepper with a 1–1¼ in. (2.5–3 cm) diameter. It rates 0-500 SHU.

Habañero

Also known as *Scotch bonnets*, habañero are small fresh, yellow- to orange-colored bell-shaped peppers. They are about 1¼ in. (3 cm) in diameter and extremely hot with a 100,000–325,000 SHU rating.

Chipotle

The chipotle is a fully ripened, smoke-dried jalapeño. It is brown with wrinkled flesh and measures 2½ in. (6.5 cm) long and 1 in. (2.5 cm) wide. It is sold dried or canned in sauce. It rates 5,000–8,000 SHU.

Hungarian Wax

This pale yellow, medium hot pepper measures 6 in. (15 cm) long and is 1½ in. (3.8 cm) wide. It rates 5,000–10,000 SHU.

Jalapeño

One of the most common green chiles, the jalapeño measures 2½ in. (6.5 cm) long and 1 in. (2.5 cm) wide. It rates 2,500–8,000 SHU.

Guajillo

The guajillo is a deep red, smooth-skinned, dried chile pod measuring about 5 in. (13 cm) long and 1¼ in. (3 cm) wide. It gives moderate heat and rates 2,500–5,000 SHU.

Mulato

The mulato is a dried, deep brown, broad triangular pepper with an average size of 5 in. (13 cm) long and 3½ in. (9 cm) wide. It rates 1,000–2,000 SHU.

(Continued)

Common Chile Peppers (Continued)

New Mexico

Also known as *Big Jim* and *chile Colorado*, this large pepper measures 5 in. (13 cm) long and 3 in. (7.5 cm) wide. It is a dried, red, mild-flavored chile with smooth skin and rates 500–2,500 SHU.

Poblano

Deep, dark green chiles often used for stuffing or salsas, poblanos measure 4–5 in. (11–13 cm) in length and 2 to 3 in. (5–7 cm) wide at the shoulder. The poblano rates 1,000–2,000 SHU.

Pasilla

Pasilla, also known as *chile negro*, is a dried chile with dark brown, almost black color. It's long and narrow measuring 6 in. (15 cm) long and about 1 in. (2.5 cm) wide. It rates 1,000–2,000 SHU.

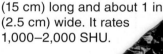

Serrano

The Serrano is a small green, bullet-shaped chile measuring 2 in. (5 cm) long and less than ½ in. (1.5 cm) wide. It rates 8,000–22,000 SHU.

Pequín

These tiny, fresh chile pods measure ½ in. (1.5 cm) in length or less and range from dark green to bright red. They are very hot and rate 40,000–58,000 SHU.

Thai

These small red chiles measure about ½ in. (1.5 cm) in length. Asian cuisine uses Thai chiles in both fresh and dried forms. It rates 50,000–100,000 SHU.

foodservice. Red and yellow peppers are especially valuable to chefs for the bright color that they add to a dish. Bell peppers are available year-round. Whether green, red, or yellow, choose peppers that are plump, firm, and have shiny skins.

Chile Peppers   Chile peppers are used for their spicy flavor. Like bell peppers, chile peppers start out green and can be picked at the green stage. If allowed to ripen, most will turn some shade of red. Red chiles can be used fresh or may be dried. Dried chile peppers are available as whole chile peppers or ground into a powder. Ground dried chiles are considered a spice.

The heat of these peppers comes from a chemical called *capsaicin* found in the veins and seeds. This chemical is measured in Scoville heat units. **Scoville heat units (SHU)** are a measure of the heat of chile peppers. Since the heat intensity of peppers of the same variety varies, the Scoville scale is only a guideline. To know exactly how hot a pepper is, it must be tasted with caution.

Eggplant

Eggplant is a member of the nightshade family. It is believed to have originated in India and derives its name from the egg-like shape of some varieties. While there are white varieties, the purple eggplant is most common. It has a purplish-black color and is typically 4 inches (10 cm) in diameter and 8 to 10 inches (20 to 25 cm) long. Japanese eggplants, used in Asian cuisines, have a light purple color and are smaller in size. They are typically 1 to 2 inches (3 to 5 cm) in diameter and 6 to 7 inches (15 to 18 cm) long. Select eggplants with soft texture and shiny skin that is free from blemishes. Avoid wilting or shriveling eggplants.

Legumes and Seeds

Legumes are a group of vegetables that includes beans, peas, and lentils. This family of vegetables has met the needs of human nutrition for centuries. They are relatively easy to grow and a good source of protein. Legumes store well since they can be preserved indefinitely by drying.

String Beans

String beans are beans with small seeds and edible pods. They are picked immature before the seeds harden and the shells get tough. Most string beans marketed today are stringless, which means they do not have a fibrous string that runs down the length of the pod. The most commonly used string beans in commercial foodservice include

- *Green beans.* Round pods with a length of about 4 inches (10 cm)
- *Wax beans.* Yellow string beans with round pods and a length of about 4 inches (10 cm)
- *French beans.* Thin, delicate green beans picked very immature at approximately 3 inches (7.5 cm) in length, the French call them *haricorts verts* (ar ee KOH VAIR)

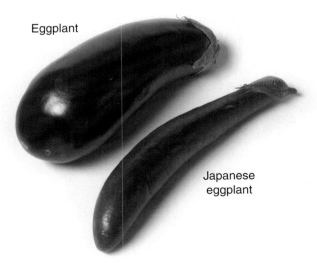
Eggplant

Japanese eggplant

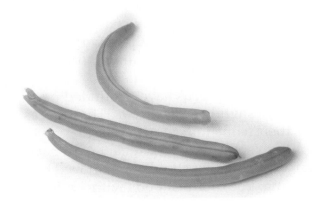

Look for crisp straight beans with good color and no signs of decay or excessive rust spots. String beans are packed in bushel crates or cartons with a net weight of 28 to 30 pounds (12 to 14 kg). French beans are packed in 5-pound (2 kg) cases. Green beans and French beans are available year-round. Wax beans and Italian beans are available during summer months.

Shell Beans

Shell beans are beans with large seeds and an inedible pod. Shell bean is the term many chefs use for legumes in their fresh form. Relatively few shell beans are sold fresh, while more are available frozen. The vast majority of these legumes are dried.

Peas

Peas are a popular member of the legume family. Young peas are tender and have a considerable amount of natural sugar, which gives them a sweet flavor. As young peas are picked, the sugars start to turn into starches. Mature peas have lost most of their sugar. For this reason, chefs prize young fresh peas. Many prefer frozen peas that were quickly picked and processed, thus preserving their sweet flavor. Dried peas are a staple item in many kitchens and are mostly used for soups.

Pea Pods   Some varieties of peas have edible pods. These peas are picked immature before the peas inside have fully developed. They also retain a great deal of sugar. The two most common varieties of pea pods are snow peas and sugar snap peas.
- Snow peas have a flat pod with very small seeds. They are an important ingredient in Asian cuisines.
- Sugar snap peas have a rounded pod with slightly larger seeds. They are, as their name indicates, very sweet.

Both snow peas and sugar snaps have a fibrous string that should be removed before cooking. Look for pea pods with a bright

green color and crisp texture. Pea pods are packed in 10-pound (4.5 kg) cases.

Lentils

Lentils are a small, flat, round legume. They are always dried. Varieties of lentils are easily identified by color. Brown lentils

are the most commonly used variety. Green lentils are popular in French cuisine. Red lentils are used widely in Middle Eastern cuisines.

Okra

Okra pods are also called *gumbos* or *lady fingers*. These round, ridged pods are 3 to 4 inches (7 to 10 cm) in length and taper to a point. The pod contains small tender, edible

Common Shell Beans

Black Beans

Also called *turtle beans*, black beans are a medium-sized bean with a jet-black skin. They are popular in Caribbean cuisines as well as other cuisines throughout Latin America.

Black-Eyed Peas

Black-eyed peas are a tan-colored bean with a black spot. They are an important ingredient in Southern cuisine.

Fava Beans

Fava beans are mostly sold fresh in their pods. They are shelled to reveal a flat green seed with a delicate texture. Fava beans are popular in Mediterranean cuisines.

Great Northern Beans

Great Northern beans are medium-sized, oval-shaped, white beans.

Lima Beans

Lima beans are large pale green beans. They have a flat shape and starchy texture. They are most often sold frozen and fresh. Butter beans are a dried white lima bean.

Navy Beans

Sometimes called *pea beans*, navy beans are a small white oval bean. They are an important ingredient in the cuisine of New England.

(Continued)

Common Shell Beans (Continued)

Pinto Beans

Pinto beans are medium-sized oval beans. They have a pinkish-tan color with dark speckles. Pinto beans are an important staple in the cuisine of Mexico and the American Southwest.

Red Kidney Beans

Red kidney beans are a large reddish-pink bean with a kidney shape. They are associated with the cuisines of Louisiana.

Soybeans

Soybeans are tan or black in color. They are available dried or canned. Edamame is a unique variety of soybeans that is picked slightly immature. These

spring green-colored beans are sold most often frozen either in the pod or shelled.

seeds and starch. Cooked okra often has a slimy appearance due to this starch.

Okra is used in Indian, Middle Eastern, and African cuisines. It is also important in the cuisine of the South, especially Creole cuisine. It is commonly stewed or used in soups.

Corn

Corn, sometimes called *maize,* is a grain rather than a legume. The majority of corn grown in the United States is feed corn for livestock. Sweet corn, on the other hand, is grown for its sweet flavor. The most important consideration in choosing sweet corn

is freshness. Once corn is picked, its sugar begins to convert into starch. Old corn will have a bland, starchy flavor. Once corn is picked, it should be iced or refrigerated to preserve its sweetness. Various varieties of sweet corn produce ears with yellow, white, or bicolor kernels.

When choosing corn, look for good-sized kernels that are closely packed. The husk should be a nice green color and the silk should be moist. Check for signs of decay or rot. Sweet corn is commonly sold in 42-pound (19 kg) crates with counts ranging between 48 and 60 ears. Summer is the peak season for sweet corn.

Mushrooms

Mushrooms are one of the most flavorful vegetables. They add a rich satisfying character to dishes that contain them. Mushrooms are a fungus, which is a plant that does not

Wild Mushrooms

Morel (mawr EHL) Mushrooms

Morels range in color from tan to dark brown. Their distinctive cone-shaped cap with honeycomb pattern sits on top of a tube-like stem. Morels are available fresh in spring and dried the rest of the year.

Chanterelle (shohn tur EHL) Mushrooms

Chanterelle mushrooms have a bright golden color and somewhat flat cap that curls under around its edges. They are available fresh in summer and autumn, and canned the rest of the year.

Cèpe (SEHP)

Cèpe is the French term for "bolete mushrooms," also known by their Italian name *porcini*. These mushrooms are fleshy with a large head and wide stem. They are hunted in the summer and often purchased in their dried form.

Truffles

An underground fungus, truffles come in two varieties: white and black. The black ones are sometimes referred to as "black pearls of gastronomy." They are prized for their intense flavor and are the most expensive mushrooms available. Harvested in winter, fresh truffles commonly sell for hundreds and sometimes thousands of dollars per pound. Canned or frozen truffles are often less expensive and available year-round. France produces black truffles and Italy produces both black and white truffles.

Cultivated Mushrooms

Button Mushrooms

Button mushrooms are the most common type of cultivated mushroom. They have the creamy white color, round cap, and stem that people have come to identify with the mushrooms. Button mushrooms are the type most often used in the professional kitchen, they can be used raw in salads, sautéed, grilled, or poached. Look for mushrooms with clean firm white caps that are free of spots. Caps should be tight and closed showing none of the dark gills underneath. Button mushrooms are sold in 10-pound (4.5 kg) baskets.

Crimini Mushrooms

Crimini are brown-colored, button shaped mushrooms that originated in Italy.

Enoki (Enokidake) Mushrooms

Enoki are white, Japanese mushrooms with long stems about the thickness of a matchstick topped with a small round cap.

Oyster (Pleurote) Mushrooms

Oyster mushrooms are beige- to tan-colored mushrooms with a flat shape that grows in clusters.

Portobello Mushrooms

Portobellos are crimini mushrooms that have matured to the stage where their caps open. Portobellos are quite large reaching 6 in. (15 cm) in diameter.

Shiitake Mushrooms

Shiitake mushrooms are brown-capped mushrooms of Japanese origin. They are sometimes called "golden oak mushrooms" because in the wild they grow on decaying oaks. These mushrooms have a robust flavor and their fibrous stems should be removed before cooking.

SUSTAINABLE CULINARY

Organic Produce— What Is It?

One of the most visible signs that sustainability is gaining increased attention is the increasing market for organic produce. This is apparent in the expanding display space dedicated to organic products at supermarkets. The term organic is a legal term that is defined by the United States Department of Agriculture (USDA). For a product to be labeled *organic*, growers must meet all the criteria stated in the Organic Foods Production Act. This act spells out how food is grown, handled, and processed. It also lists which pesticides, fungicides, and herbicides may be used.

produce chlorophyll or flowers. Mushrooms are used in cuisines all around the world.

Mushrooms were originally wild fungi. In 1678, the first mushrooms were cultivated under controlled conditions. This gave way to mushrooms being available year-round. Still, some of the most prized members of the mushroom family are wild mushrooms. Wild mushrooms vary widely in availability and price due to seasonality and the weather. They are especially precious because they are foraged, or searched for and gathered by hand.

Many varieties of mushrooms have been domesticated and chefs today have ready access to a number of flavorful fungi. There are hundreds of different edible wild mushrooms. In some countries, mushroom hunting is a popular hobby. Gathering wild mushrooms should be left to the experts because there are a number of poisonous wild mushrooms that look similar to some of their edible counterparts. Always buy wild mushrooms from a reputable purveyor.

Never cook, taste, or serve any mushroom that may be suspect.

Processed Vegetables

Processed vegetables include canned and frozen vegetables. Canned vegetables are utilized by many foodservice operations because they require less labor and cost less to store. Canned vegetables also offer a more consistent quality and yield.

When choosing between fresh and canned vegetables, remember that the canning process essentially cooks the vegetable in the can. Therefore, canned vegetables often have a slightly different flavor and appearance than their fresh counterparts. Green vegetables in particular lose their bright green color in the canning process.

Frozen vegetables are usually slightly more expensive than their canned counterparts. They are also more expensive to store. Compared to canned vegetables, frozen vegetables are much closer in flavor and appearance to fresh. Remember that frozen vegetables are always parcooked before being frozen. As a result, their cooking time is often less than that for fresh vegetables.

Grading

Just as with fruits, the USDA has a voluntary grading system for both fresh and processed vegetables. Each type of vegetable has its own quality characteristics and grades. For most fresh vegetables, the top grade is either No. 1 or Fancy. For canned or frozen vegetables, the grades are

US Grade A or Fancy
US Grade B or Extra Standard
US Grade C or Standard

When grading processed vegetables, the product is scored on its color, uniformity of size, absence of defects, and character.

Summary Points

- Each vegetable has unique characteristics that determine their quality and uses.
- The quality, availability, and price of some vegetables are greatly influenced by their growing season, while certain common items are available year-round.
- Vegetables are packed in a variety of sizes, often sorted by count or uniform size.
- Vegetables can be stored either canned or frozen for availability year-round.
- The USDA develops grade standards and provides grading services, but grading is not mandatory for fresh and processed vegetables.

In Review

Assess

1. Name the variety of each of the following vegetables that is most often used in commercial kitchens:
   A. onion
   B. carrots
   C. mushroom
2. True or false. Shallots are used mainly for sauce making.
3. Celeriac is cultivated for its _____ and Pascal celery is grown for its _____.
4. List four members of the cabbage family.
5. Explain how white asparagus gets its unique color.
6. True or false. Summer squash store better and longer than winter squash.
7. The _____ is a fruit vegetable with a high fat content, which gives it a rich, buttery texture.
8. What part(s) of the pepper contain the chemical that gives the chile pepper its heat?
9. Why is freshness so important when choosing sweet corn?
10. List four factors used by the USDA to grade vegetables.

Core Skills

11. **Math.** Select two vegetables that are sold fresh, frozen, and canned. Create a chart that compares the price per ounce for fresh versus processed options.
12. **Writing.** Use reliable Internet or print resources to research six edible wild mushrooms. Identify the characteristics of each. Find several examples showing how different restaurants use each of these mushrooms in menu items and describe how they are used. If possible, provide the cost of the menu items. Write a paper summarizing your findings.
13. **Speaking.** The names of different chiles can be confusing because the names typically change depending whether the chiles are fresh or dried. Make a list of 10 fresh chiles. Use presentation software to give an illustrated report showing and naming the 10 fresh chiles and their dried counterparts. Also, describe the SHU for each of the chiles and their flavor profiles.
14. **Reading.** Use reliable Internet or print resources (such as the Smithsonion website or Mark Kurlansky's *Birdseye: The Adventures of a Curious Man*) to read about the history of Clarence Birdseye, the person who commercialized frozen vegetables in the United States. Write a brief report about Birdseye and his invention.
15. **Math.** Suppose you want to use haricot verts as a menu item. Haricot verts come packed in 5-pound cases. A case typically costs $25.00. After cleaning the case, 4 oz. of haricots verts is discarded. If 2 oz. of haricots verts is the portion size, how many portions remain in the case? What is the cost of each portion?
16. **CTE Career Readiness Practice.** Use the text and the USDA website (click on the Agricultural Marketing Service—AMS link) to write a paper on the USDA voluntary grading system for fresh and processed vegetables. Identify the quality characteristics for each grade. Summarize the differences in grading

systems for fresh and processed (canned or frozen) vegetables.

Critical Thinking

17. **Analyze.** Different vegetables are often served together as a part of a medley. What factors are important when creating a medley? What medleys do you find most appetizing?

18. **Propose.** Research the Internet or other sources to find a vegetable not discussed in this chapter. Write a brief description of the vegetable including the type of vegetable it is, its season, where it is commonly grown, and nutrient content. Propose how you would prepare the vegetable and what you would serve with it.

19. **Debate.** Debate the following topic: Chefs should use only seasonal and local vegetables on their menus.

20. **Evaluate.** Halfway through dinner service, you run out of fresh green beans for the steamed vegetable side dish. You have both canned green beans and frozen green beans available. Evaluate which you would choose as a replacement for the fresh green beans. Explain your answer.

Technology

Canning is a process by which vegetables are preserved through cooking. One reason for this is to eliminate the spores of anaerobic bacteria such as *clostridium botulinum* (the cause of botulism disease). Investigate the commercial canning process that creates temperatures high enough to destroy these potentially very harmful spores. Explain the process and how it creates such temperatures.

Teamwork

Working in small teams, peel and seed 1 lb. (454 g) each of regular tomatoes and plum tomatoes. Place the waste (skin, seeds, juice) for each type of tomato in one container and the usable tomato flesh for each type in another. Assign one team member to weigh and record the amount of

- waste for each type of tomato
- usable tomato flesh for each type of tomato

Which type of tomato yielded a higher amount of usable flesh? Write a team report of the findings.

Chef's E-portfolio
Calculating Waste

Upload your report from the Teamwork activity to your e-portfolio. Ask your instructor where to save your file. This could be on the school's network or a flash drive of your own. Name your portfolio document *FirstnameLastname_Portfolio Ch#.docx* (i.e., JohnSmith_PortfolioCh26.docx).

While studying, look for the activity icon ↗ **to:**

- Build vocabulary with e-flash cards and matching activities.
- Expand learning with video clips, photo identification activities, animations, and interactive activities.
- Review and assess what you learn by completing end-of-chapter questions.

G-WLEARNING.com

Vegetable Cookery 27

Reading Prep

In preparation for reading the chapter, review a variety of restaurant menus for vegetable dishes offered. Read the descriptions of the dishes to determine the type of cooking methods used. Compare your findings to the chapter as you read.

Culinary Terminology Build Vocab

al dente, p. 444
blanching, p. 447
shocking, p. 447
glaze, p. 448

Academic Terminology Build Vocab

cellulose, p. 444
chlorophyll, p. 445

Objectives

After studying this chapter, you will be able to

- recall factors that affect the flavor, texture, color, and retention of nutrients of cooked vegetables.

- execute the parcooking of vegetables.

- explain ways blanched vegetables can be finished.

- recognize various moist-heat and dry-heat methods used to cook vegetables.

Vegetables are a key component to any meal. For the chef, they are sometimes the most difficult element. Any chef must be able to present properly cooked vegetables for his or her diners. The importance of properly cooking vegetables should not be underestimated. The wide variety of flavors, colors, and textures in the produce market makes this skill even more challenging.

Principles of Vegetable Cookery

To choose the cooking method that is best for any vegetable, the chef must consider several factors including flavor, texture, color, and nutrition.

Pleasing Flavor

Cooking can change the flavor of vegetables in a number of ways. During cooking, the natural sugars present in the vegetables may be caramelized, which contributes a pleasing flavor. Additionally, various compounds from the vegetable's structure are released and mix together, altering the flavor. Many vegetables taste better after cooking because cooking can remove bitter or unpleasant flavor compounds. This is especially true for members of the cabbage and onion families, which diners sometimes avoid ordering. If cooked properly, these vegetables are quite enjoyable. For instance, some people dislike brussels sprouts because of their bitter flavor. With the right preparation, a pleasing—almost sweet—flavor

SUSTAINABLE CULINARY

Resources to Raise and Grow

You have been hearing the message since you were young—"Eat your vegetables!" Indeed, a diet that is high in fruits, vegetables, and grains, and lower in animal protein does have health benefits. But did you know that eating more fruits, vegetables, and grains is also easier on the planet? It takes far more resources—water, energy, and food—to grow animal protein than to grow fruits, vegetables, or grains. Research the amount of water, food, and energy it takes to produce one pound of your favorite animal protein. Compare this to the resources used to grow one pound of your favorite fruit, vegetable, or grain.

can be achieved. Taste is the most important consideration in choosing a cooking method and determining proper doneness of vegetables.

Appealing Texture

The rigid tissue of plants is composed mainly of microscopic fibers called **cellulose**. The human digestive system is unable to break down cellulose. When vegetables are cooked, this fibrous structure breaks down. This makes vegetables easier to digest and better tasting. Therefore, chefs determine what cooking method to use and length of cooking time based on the amount of cellulose in the vegetable.

Judging Doneness When describing the proper degree of doneness for vegetables, chefs often use the Italian term *al dente*. **Al dente** (ahl DEN tay), which literally means "to the tooth," is a way to describe a product being fully cooked but not soft or mushy. In other words, the food gives some slight resistance to the tooth when you bite into it. Properly cooked vegetables should be neither mushy nor crunchy.

Finding the proper point where vegetables are tender yet still firm enough to hold their shape is a challenge. Since vegetables vary a great deal in their raw textures, chefs cannot rely solely on cooking time to determine doneness. Doneness should always be tested by piercing the vegetable with the tip of a knife or by biting a piece of the cooked product. Test vegetables at the thickest or most fibrous part.

Color Retention

No other food category offers more color to a meal than vegetables. Preserving natural colors in vegetables is essential to their presentation. The old adage "People eat first with their eyes" is most appropriate when talking about vegetables. Before ever tasting vegetables, the visual signs of proper or improper cooking can be seen in their color and appearance.

Vegetables are classified by color—green, white, red, or yellow-orange. Though vegetables in the same color class may have different textures, their color pigments come from the same compounds. The acidity or alkalinity (pH) of the liquid used to cook vegetables affects their resulting color and appearance. Values on the pH scale between 0 and 7 are considered acidic, a pH value of 7 is neutral, and a pH between 7 and 14 is alkaline. The pigments of yellow-orange vegetables are least affected by the cooking liquid, but green vegetables can easily lose their bright green color. The pH of the cooking liquid has a great impact on color retention, 27-1.

pH of Common Cooking Liquids
Vinegar   2.0–3.5
Lemon juice   2.2
Wine   3.0–3.8
Milk   6.3–6.5
Salt water   7.6–8.4

27-1 Compare these pH values of cooking liquids to distilled water with a neutral pH of 7.0.

The Effects of Acid Solutions on Color   When cooked in an acidic solution, white vegetables such as cauliflower and turnips become a bright white color. Red vegetables, such as beets and red cabbage, turn a pleasing reddish-purple hue. Green vegetables should not be cooked in an acidic solution because their green pigments turn brown.

Many ingredients can be added to the cooking liquid to make it more acidic. Vinegar, lemon juice, and milk are commonly used to increase the acidity of cooking liquids for vegetables.

Many chefs believe that another way to create an acidic cooking environment is to cook vegetables in a covered pot. Most vegetables are naturally a bit acidic and release some of those acids during cooking. Normally, the acid would evaporate with the steam of the boiling liquid, but in a covered pot, the steam and acid are trapped. Covering the pot for cooking vegetables that require acid is a good way to speed up the cooking process. Green vegetables, which require alkali conditions, are always cooked uncovered.

Alkaline Solutions' Effect on Color   The chemical that gives green vegetables their color is chlorophyll. Chlorophyll is easily destroyed by acid. Since vegetables give off acids during cooking, chefs counteract these acids by cooking green vegetables in a slightly alkaline solution. Salt is the chosen alkali. Not only does salt provide the right degree of alkalinity, it also adds seasoning to vegetables.

Some cooks use stronger alkalis such as baking soda to season the water for green vegetables. Although these strong alkalis preserve the green color, they also destroy the vegetable's texture and nutrients and, therefore, should not be used.

Red and white vegetables may be cooked with salt for seasoning, but the liquid should also include an acid. Red vegetables cooked in a strictly alkaline liquid have a dull bluish appearance. White vegetables cooked in an alkaline liquid have a yellowed or ivory color, 27-2.

Nutrition Connection

Which Is Best: Fresh, Frozen or Canned?

From the moment of harvest, food begins to lose some of its nutrient value. For this reason, food producers typically transport and process items immediately after harvest. If handled properly, processed foods experience very little nutrient losses. Research proves that frozen and canned ingredients are comparable in nutrition to their fresh equivalents. Freezing helps retain the quality and nutrition of foods longer than the fresh version. Heat during canning makes some nutrients, such as beta carotene, folate, thiamin, niacin, and vitamin B_6 more easily absorbed by the body. When choosing frozen, pay close attention to shelf life and cooking instructions. When choosing canned vegetables, select varieties that contain less sodium or that have no added salt. In addition, opt for canned fruits packed in natural juice rather than in heavy syrup.

Nutrient Retention

A less obvious aspect of vegetable cookery is nutrient retention. You can see the color that results from cooking a vegetable and you can taste the flavor and texture, but you cannot see or taste the nutrients. However, retaining nutrients during vegetable preparation is important. Vegetables are a major source of many nutrients essential for good health such as minerals, vitamins A and C, and the B vitamins. Proper cooking technique and handling of vegetables produce not only the best looking and tasting product, but also the most nutritious.

Different nutrients are affected by different factors. Nutrients may be destroyed by exposure to air, light, heat, or become dissolved in the cooking water. The chef's strategy for retaining nutrients is to expose vegetables to these conditions for the shortest time needed to get a properly cooked

Effect of pH on Vegetables

Color of Vegetable	pH of Cooking Solution	Effect on Color	
White vegetables	Acidic (left)	Turns vegetables bright white color	
	Alkaline (right)	Turns vegetables yellowish or ivory color	
Red vegetables	Acidic (left)	Turns vegetables reddish-purple color	
	Alkaline (right)	Turns vegetables dull blue	
Green vegetables	Acidic (left)	Turns vegetables brownish-green color	
	Alkaline (right)	Turns vegetables bright green	

Draz-Koetke/Goodheart-Willcox Publisher

27-2 The colors of white, red, and green vegetables are affected by the pH of the cooking liquid.

product. The following are steps chefs can take to help preserve nutrients in the vegetables they serve:

- Use vegetables that are as fresh as possible.
- Store vegetables in a cool place with minimum exposure to light.
- Wash vegetables before cutting as close to cooking time as possible.
- Peel and cut vegetables as close to cooking time as possible.
- Cook vegetables as quickly as possible.

- Drain vegetables when cooked. Avoid storing vegetables in liquid.
- Serve as soon as possible.

Parcooking Vegetables

Part of the standard mise en place, or preparation, of most commercial kitchens is partial cooking, or parcooking. Vegetables to be used in the day's meal service are routinely parcooked. This is an important difference between the procedures used in the home and the professional kitchen.

Blanching

The process of partially cooking an item in rapidly boiling water is called blanching. There are a number of reasons why professionals choose to blanch vegetables in preparation for the meal service.

- Gives better control over the cooking process and degree of doneness.
- Saves time during busy service periods.
- Allows vegetables to be finished in a variety of ways.
- Allows vegetables with different textures and colors to be properly cooked when served together.

The blanching process is done as quickly as possible to help preserve color, nutrients, and texture. Therefore, the water should be at a rapid boil before the vegetables are added. If you begin the blanching process in cold water, the vegetables will be overcooked and unappealing.

Shocking

Once the vegetables being blanched reach the correct doneness, it is important that the cooking process stop. Simply removing the vegetables from the cooking liquid is not enough to stop the cooking process. The vegetables contain a lot of heat energy and continue to cook for some time after they are removed from the heat source. To quickly stop the cooking process, the blanched vegetables are plunged into ice water. Chefs call this process shocking, or "refreshing." After vegetables are shocked, they are drained so they do not sit in water any longer than necessary.

Finishing Techniques

The blanching and shocking process does not yield the chef a finished product

TECHNIQUE
Parcooking Vegetables

1. **Bring a large amount of water to a boil. The amount of water should be enough to allow vegetables to circulate freely during the cooking process.**
2. **Add salt or an acid according to the color of the vegetables being cooked.**
3. **Place the vegetables in the water and cook over high heat. Different types or sizes of vegetables should be cooked in separate batches.**

4. **Test the doneness of the vegetables to determine if they are properly cooked.**

5. **Remove the vegetables from the boiling water and shock.**

6. **When fully cooled, drain the vegetables and reserve for service.**

ready for serving. Vegetables are rarely served plain and may be finished by a number of methods. Parcooked vegetables are typically reheated (usually in boiling water), and then finished by either sautéing, glazing, or coating them with a sauce. These techniques also work well for canned or frozen vegetables. Canned and frozen vegetables are cooked or partially cooked during the canning or freezing process.

Sautéing

To sauté vegetables, first reheat them in boiling water and drain them. Place the vegetables in a sauteuse (a sauté pan with sloped sides), and toss over moderate heat with whole butter, salt, and pepper, 27-3. This process should be quick—just long enough to melt the butter and coat the vegetables. In some instances, smaller vegetables may not require reheating in boiling water and can simply be reheated in a sauté pan with butter.

Glazing

In cooking, when you **glaze** something it means to give it a shiny coating. The simplest form of glazing vegetables is similar to sautéing. Vegetables are tossed with butter plus a sweet syrupy ingredient that adds both flavor and a glossy shine. This method works best with vegetables that are complemented by a sweet flavoring, such as root vegetables. Examples may include honey-glazed carrots, orange-glazed beets, or brown sugar-glazed yams. In some recipes, vegetables become glazed with their own natural sugars.

Vegetables can also be glazed or finished with a sauce or reduced stock. The gelatin of the stock or the sheen of a rich sauce gives the vegetables a rich, glossy appearance.

Gratiner

Gratinéed vegetables make a beautiful presentation. This browning process can be used to finish parcooked vegetables.

Draz-Koetke/Goodheart-Willcox Publisher

27-3 Vegetables that are parcooked can be sautéed quickly for service.

Béchamel-based sauces, cheese, or bread crumbs are often used to create a browned surface on vegetable dishes, 27-4. These ingredients brown easily when placed under a broiler or salamander, or when cooked in a hot oven.

Draz-Koetke/Goodheart-Willcox Publisher

27-4 The browned surface on a gratinéed vegetable dish creates a pleasing contrast in color and texture.

Moist-Heat Cooking Methods

Moist-heat cooking methods are often used on vegetables and do not require parcooking. These methods are especially effective on hard-textured vegetables.

Steaming

Steaming is an excellent cooking method for some vegetables. The high temperature of steam is effective for breaking down the cellulose in fibrous vegetables such as root vegetables. Steamed vegetables retain more of their nutrients and natural flavors because

Recipe No.	Name		Category
27.4	Braised Red Cabbage (sweet and sour)		Vegetables
Yield	**Portion Size**		**No. Portions**
2 qt. (1.9 L)	½ c. (120 mL)		16
US Quantity	**Metric Quantity**	**Ingredient**	**TCS**
2 oz.	60 g	butter	•
4 oz.	115 g	onions, julienne	
8 oz.	225 g	cooking apples, cored and diced	
2½ lb.	1.2 kg	red cabbage, shredded	
6 fl. oz.	180 mL	cider or wine vinegar	
8 fl. oz.	240 mL	water	
2 fl. oz.	60 mL	honey	
4 oz.	115 g	sugar	
1 ea.		sachet:	
1 ea.		cinnamon stick	
2 ea.		cloves	
2 ea.		whole allspice berry	
1 ea.		bay leaf	
to taste		salt and white pepper	
1 Tbsp.	15 mL	cornstarch (optional)	
2 fl. oz.	60 mL	water (optional)	
Method			**CCP**
1. Sweat onions and apples in the butter in a heavy saucepot.			
2. Add cabbage, vinegar, and 8 fl. oz. water to saucepot and bring to a boil.			
3. Tie the spices and bay leaf in a sachet and add to the cabbage.			
4. Cover the pot and place in a 350°F (177°C) oven for 45 minutes. Stir the mixture occasionally during the cooking time.			CCP
5. Remove the pot from the oven and adjust the seasoning. Remove the sachet.			
6. If desired, thicken the cabbage mixture by adding cornstarch dissolved in water and returning to a simmer.			

Portion (g)	Calories	Fat (g)	Protein (g)	Carbohydrate (g)	Cholesterol (mg)	Sodium (mg)	Fiber (g)
118	97	2.91	1.12	18.30	7.59	237.62	1.86

cooking is quicker and there is limited exposure to liquid.

Steaming is not appropriate for green vegetables because the high temperature destroys the green color. Delicate vegetables such as spinach or pea pods are easy to overcook when steaming. For these reasons, steaming is not recommended for cooking green or delicate vegetables.

Braising and Stewing

The braising of meat dishes is a combination process that involves first browning or searing the meat. When vegetables are braised, it usually does not include browning or searing. Vegetables are braised by partially covering them with a flavored liquid and then simmering. This simmering process is excellent for tenderizing dense or fibrous vegetables such as root vegetables, cabbages, and stalks. This typically longer cooking process is also useful to cook away bitter flavors found in many greens and cabbages.

Vegetables can be braised on the stovetop, but braising is often done in the oven to maintain even heat. Braised vegetables are often whole or in large pieces as in the case of artichokes or endive. Stewing vegetables uses the same cooking process as braised vegetable dishes, except the vegetables are chopped, diced, or shredded.

Simmering

This technique is commonly used for dried beans and lentils that require long simmering to make them tender. Dried beans should first be soaked overnight in cold water. This soaking step is necessary to speed up the cooking time. Once the beans have soaked, the water is discarded. They are then covered with water which is brought to a boil and then reduced to a simmer. Different beans require different cooking times depending on the variety and size of the dried bean. It is also important that the beans are not cooked with salt

or acidic ingredients such as tomato. These ingredients prevent the beans from becoming tender. Salt and acidic ingredients should be added near the end of the cooking time. Other aromatic ingredients can be added to the simmering water during the cooking process.

Lentils are also simmered, but they are not soaked first due to their smaller size. Lentils are simply covered in cold water which is brought to a boil, and then reduced to a simmer. Salt and acidic ingredients should not be added to the liquid, although other aromatic ingredients can be added for increased flavor. As with beans, salt and acidic ingredients should be added near the end of the cooking time.

Dry-Heat Cooking Methods

Dry-heat cooking methods give vegetables a crisp or caramelized appearance. Sometimes, harder vegetables are first blanched and then finished with a dry-heat method.

Stir-Frying

Stir-frying, an Asian cooking method, cooks food in a wok with a small amount of fat, 27-5. The high heat and short cooking time help to retain the nutrients, texture, and flavor of vegetables. Vegetables to be stir-fried should be cut in small, uniform-sized pieces for proper cooking. Hard or dense vegetables may be parcooked before stir-frying. Although the wok is the traditional cooking pan for stir-frying, this technique is easily done in a sauteuse.

Deep Frying

Deep-fried vegetables are popular with American diners. Vegetables to be deep-fried are coated with a breading or batter before being fried. This helps to seal in the

Draz-Koetke/Goodheart-Willcox Publisher

27-5 Vegetables that are more dense should be parcooked before stir-frying.

moisture of the vegetables and keeps them from becoming too greasy. Soft-textured vegetables, such as mushrooms and summer squash, can be deep-fried from a raw state; however most other vegetables are parcooked before being coated and deep-fried. Deep-fried vegetables are a popular appetizer, but their crisp texture and golden color can also add interest to main courses.

Baking and Roasting

Vegetables cooked in the oven can be considered baked or roasted. Baking vegetables requires a small amount of moisture in the cooking process. The liquid may be a sauce, or even the vegetable's own moisture. Vegetable dishes are often baked covered to keep the vegetable's own moisture. Roasted vegetables are cooked without moisture and uncovered to create a caramelized finished product. Baking and roasting are often done with whole vegetables or large pieces as in

the case of yams, winter squash, fennel, or root vegetables. Smaller pieces of vegetables are often baked in a casserole mixed with sauce.

Grilling

The smoky flavor of grilling is an excellent complement to many vegetables. Vegetables are often grilled from the raw state, 27-6. Vegetables should be cut thick enough so they do not dry out during cooking and large enough so they do not fall through the grill rack. Smaller pieces of vegetables can be skewered. Before grilling, vegetables are brushed with oil to keep them from sticking to the grill.

Draz-Koetke/Goodheart-Willcox Publisher

27-6 Grilling gives vegetables an appealing appearance and flavor.

Summary Points

- When choosing which method to use for cooking vegetables, chefs must consider the flavor, texture, color, and nutrition of the finished product.

- In the professional kitchen, vegetables are often blanched, shocked, and then finished just before serving.

- Parcooked vegetables must be reheated before they can be finished. There are a variety of methods used to finish vegetables.

- All moist- and dry-heat cooking methods can be applied to vegetables.

In Review
Assess

1. The amount of _____ in a vegetable determines the appropriate cooking method to use and the length of cooking time.

2. True or false. Proper cooking removes the bitterness of vegetables such as cabbages and onions.

3. True or false. Vegetables cooked al dente should have a crisp, crunchy texture.

4. Describe how to check the doneness of cooked vegetables.

5. Cooking vegetables in a covered pot with water and lemon juice creates a(n) _____ cooking environment.

6. Why are vegetables shocked after blanching?

7. True or false. Blanched vegetables should be stored in water to keep them moist.

8. Blanched vegetables should be sautéed in _____ butter over _____ heat.

9. How does steaming destroy the color of green vegetables?

10. How do braised vegetables differ from stewed vegetables?

11. Why should salt and acidic ingredients be added to dried beans at the end of the cooking time?

12. List four dry-heat cooking methods used for vegetables.

Core Skills

13. **Math.** A fresh head of broccoli weighs one pound. After trimming and cleaning it for dinner service, you find the usable product weighs 10 ounces. What is the percent of waste from the head of broccoli?

14. **Writing.** Different cuisines around the world often share similar ingredients. Choose one vegetable and research how it is prepared in the cuisines of four different countries. Compare and contrast the techniques and flavoring elements with how it is prepared in your country. Write a summary of your findings.

15. **Speaking.** Choose a vegetable you want to parcook and finish per the text explanation. Use additional online or print resources if necessary. Create an illustrated speech showing how to parcook this vegetable and then finish it with the technique of your choice. Give your speech to the class.

16. **Speaking.** Choose a vegetable to prepare. Then choose one moist-heat method and one dry-heat method by which to cook this vegetable. Demonstrate your cooking techniques for the class.

17. **Reading.** Use online or print resources to read further about the gratiner finishing technique. What is the meaning of the term? In what country and when did it originate? Write a paragraph of your findings.

18. **Math.** A case of asparagus costs $25.00. It takes a cook 45 minutes to prepare and grill the asparagus for a party. Typically, the chef will get 20 portions from the case of asparagus. If the cook is making $12.00 per hour, how much will each portion cost considering the food and labor cost?

19. **CTE Career Readiness Practice.** Suppose you are a legumier who works in the restaurant of a high-end hotel. The executive chef has just hired two new staff members to work with you in the kitchen. What would you teach your new staff members about the restaurant's expectations for vegetable preparation including

- pleasing flavor
- appealing texture
- judging doneness

- retaining color and nutrition
- preparation techniques to use

Critical Thinking

20. **Predict.** What are the consequences of failing to cut vegetables in a uniform size before cooking? How might the vegetables look and taste?

21. **Infer.** Food styling photos in magazines and cookbooks often show cooked asparagus topped with slices of lemon for garnish. Is this a practical garnish? Why?

22. **Cause and effect.** Suppose a cook who works for you created a new gratinéed broccoli side dish and wants you to taste it. The broccoli is a pleasant, vibrant green and the gratiner finish is nicely browned. When you take a bite of the broccoli, it is mushy and has a slightly bitter taste despite the flavorful finishing technique. You proceed to talk with the cook about the method of preparation. What was the likely cause of the mushy texture and bitter flavor? How would you suggest the cook improve the side dish?

23. **Assess.** When assessing menu items, you notice the vegetable blend (cauliflower, broccoli, and carrot) is frequently ordered but not eaten by customers. You think the appearance needs improvement (although the carrots are cooked properly, the broccoli is mushy and brownish, and the cauliflower is yellow). What assessments can you make about cooking method to improve the appearance of this menu item?

Technology

Sous vide cooking has become very popular in some restaurants. Using the Internet, research sous vide technology and find examples showing how vegetables could be prepared using this cooking method. Share your findings in an oral report in class. Discuss the advantages of cooking vegetables using this method.

Teamwork

Working in small teams, each team member should obtain the same size and type of vegetable. The team members should decide on a method of cooking, for example steaming. Each team member should cook his or her vegetable until it is al dente and record the length of cooking time. Members should evaluate each cooked vegetable for al dente texture. Record all the members' names and cooking times in a chart. Select the vegetable the team believes to be prepared best and identify why. As a team, write a brief summary of the team's findings.

Chef's E-portfolio
Parcooking and Finishing Vegetables

Create a blog entry of your illustrated speech in activity #15 using school-approved web-based application and upload to your e-portfolio. Ask your instructor where to save your file. This could be on the school's network or a flash drive of your own. Name your portfolio document *FirstnameLastname_ Portfolio Ch#.docx* (i.e., JohnSmith_PortfolioCh27.docx).

Video Clip

Parcooking Vegetables

Visit the G-W Learning Companion Website and view the bonus video clip "Parcooking vegetables." After viewing the clip, answer the following questions:

1. True or false. In the professional kitchen, vegetables are parcooked when a customer orders his or her meal.

2. True or false. A vegetable is done parcooking once it is tender but gives slight resistance when pierced with a knife.

3. Why is it important to parcook different types and sizes of vegetables in separate batches?

Video

Jose Gil/Shutterstock.com

Starch Identification 28

Reading Prep

Before reading, review the objectives for this chapter. As you read, focus on how the chapter is structured. Does this structure make points clear, convincing, and engaging?

Culinary Terminology

mealy potatoes, p. 455
waxy potatoes, p. 457
new potato, p. 457
bran, p. 459
endosperm, p. 459
germ, p. 459
brown rice, p. 463
white rice, p. 463
converted rice, p. 463
instant rice, p. 463
semolina, p. 466

Academic Terminology

tuber, p. 455
New World, p. 457

Objectives

After studying this chapter, you will be able to

- compare different potato varieties for use in common foodservice applications.
- summarize factors related to grading, purchasing, and storing potatoes.
- recall common convenience potato products.
- summarize the variety of grain products common for foodservice applications.

- analyze common grain products for level of processing.
- compare different pastas and noodles for content and shape.
- summarize receiving and storage practices for grains and grain products.

Potatoes and grains are the main source of starch in people's diets. A number of starches, such as flour, cornstarch, and bread crumbs serve as staple ingredients in commercial kitchens. Potatoes, grains, and pasta are starches that form the foundation of every cuisine. You must be familiar with a wide selection of these products because they are used in almost every course of a meal.

Potatoes

The potato is a starchy vegetable that originated in the Andes Mountains in South America. Most of the potatoes grown in the United States come from the Northwest. Idaho is where many potatoes are grown. However, Maine and Washington also have a large potato growing industry.

Types of Potatoes

The part of the potato plant that is eaten is the **tuber** or the enlarged part of the underground root. The most important thing to consider when choosing a potato is its starch content. Potatoes that are high in starch are referred to as **mealy potatoes** and are commonly called *baking potatoes*. These potatoes tend to be long with coarse, thick skin.

Potato Varieties

Russet Burbank

This mealy potato, commonly known as the *Idaho*, is the most widely used potato in the United States. Most russets are grown in the Northwest and are available year-round. Their skin is brown and the flesh is white.

Round Red

These waxy potatoes are most often used for preparations using moist heat. They have rose-colored skin and white flesh. Round Red potatoes are in season from late summer to early fall but are often sold at the immature stage as new potatoes.

Long White

These all-purpose potatoes are oval shaped and grown primarily in California. They have light tan skin and white flesh and are in season from late spring to early fall.

Round White

The Round White is an all-purpose potato grown and used mainly in the northeastern United States. It has light tan skin and white flesh. This year-round variety is creamy when cooked and can be used in most preparations.

Yukon Gold

Yukon Gold is an all-purpose potato that is becoming more popular in the United States. They have a yellowish skin, yellow flesh, and a slightly flattened oval shape. These potatoes retain their yellow color when cooked and are in season from late summer to fall.

Peruvian Blue

These specialty potatoes are popular in South American and Caribbean dishes. They usually have blue or purple skin with flesh that can range in color from dark blue and lavender to mostly white. Some of these potatoes lose their bright color when cooked.

Fingerling

This specialty potato is a type of heirloom potato that is generally small and finger shaped. These potatoes tend to be low in starch and have a nutty flavor. They can be roasted or used in potato salads.

They have a dry, mealy texture because they are high in starch. When cooked, these potatoes become light and fluffy. They are ideal for baking and frying.

Potatoes that are relatively low in starch are called **waxy potatoes**, or boiling potatoes. These potatoes come in a variety of shapes and have thin, smooth skin. Waxy potatoes have a high level of moisture and sugar. These potatoes work well in applications such as soups, casseroles, and potato salads because they hold their shape after being cooked.

Some potato varieties fall in the middle of the starch content range. These potatoes are referred to as *all-purpose*. All-purpose potatoes tend to have more moisture than baking potatoes and retain their shape when cooked with moist heat. All-purpose potatoes can be baked, mashed, and fried. However, a mealy potato produces a superior finished product.

There are a number of specialty potatoes that are also popular. For instance, Peruvian Blue originated in South America, but is now grown in the United States. Restaurants serving Latin cuisine, as well as other trendy restaurants, feature these potatoes on their menus. The fingerling potato is an heirloom potato that is popular with many chefs. As the name implies, fingerling potatoes are small and slender. Increasingly, chefs are seeking out heirloom varieties to add interest to their menus.

A **new potato** is not a variety of potato, but rather an immature potato of any variety. Round Red may be the most common variety sold as a new potato. However, any variety of immature potatoes can be sold as a new potato. Round White and Yukon Gold are often sold at the immature stage.

Sweet Potatoes and Yams

Sweet potatoes and yams are botanically different from potatoes and each other. Sweet potatoes are roots originating in the **New World**, or the continental landmass of the Americas. One type of sweet potato is the boniato or Cuban sweet potato. It has a light yellow flesh, light-colored skin, and somewhat dry, mealy texture when cooked. The most commonly used sweet potato in the United States is the red sweet potato. A large percentage of these sweet potatoes used in the United States is grown in North Carolina. They are characterized by a reddish-brown skin, orange flesh, and somewhat sweet taste. Sweet potatoes are typically boiled, baked, mashed, or puréed.

Sweet potato

Yam

People often confuse yams and sweet potatoes because sweet potatoes are called yams in some areas of the United States. However, yams are a type of tuber that is different from both potatoes and sweet potatoes. Yams originated in West Africa or Asia rather than the New World. They have rough, scaly skin and flesh that ranges in color from almost white to deep red. The yam is drier and contains more starch than sweet potatoes. Sweet potatoes contain more moisture and taste sweeter. Yams are low in vitamin A and sweet potatoes are a good source of beta-carotene (vitamin A). Yams and sweet potatoes are often prepared in the same ways.

SUSTAINABLE CULINARY

Preserving Global Diversity

Globally, the number of plant varieties used to produce food is in decline. This is due to large numbers of growers that grow the same crop varieties. In the short term, this may be a good strategy to increase yields, but it is also creating a fragile ecosystem. For instance, if weather patterns change, the varieties that have worked in the past may no longer be suited for the changed environment. To avoid permanent loss of plant varieties, scientists across the world are striving to create seed banks where the genetics of many different plant varieties are saved for future use. In the case of rice, which is a staple crop for almost half of the world's population, there are well over 100,000 different varieties of cultivated and wild rices that are preserved just in case they are needed in the future.

Grading, Purchasing, and Storing Potatoes

Potatoes are subject to the same voluntary USDA grading system as vegetables. Most potatoes sold in foodservice are graded *US Number 1.*

When grading processed vegetables, the product is scored on its color, uniformity of size, absence of defects, and character.

The primary consideration when purchasing potatoes is determining the culinary use. A mealy potato should be selected if you want baked potatoes. Waxy potatoes would be a better choice if you want boiled potatoes or potato salad. Sometimes an all-purpose potato serves both purposes. You can purchase the best type of potato for the menu when you understand each variety's characteristics.

Potatoes are typically packed and shipped in 50-pound cases or bags. The potatoes are also sorted for sale by size or count. Eighty-, ninety-, and one hundred-count potatoes are common sizes used in foodservice. It is important to make sure the count received matches the count ordered.

Check for the following when you receive potatoes:
- uniform size
- unblemished skin with no deep cracks or black decay spots
- absence of insects or other pests

Potatoes should be stored away from light. Light causes a chemical reaction in the potato skin that produces a green tint. Potatoes with green skin can taste bitter. Green skin may also contain a harmful substance that causes illness if eaten in large quantities. Large eyes or sprouts can also form when potatoes are exposed to light.

Ideal storage for potatoes is a cool, dry, dark location. The best temperature for potato storage is 50°F (10°C). If stored in a refrigerator under 41°F (5°C), the starch turns to sugar and the potatoes taste too sweet.

Convenience Potato Products

There are a number of convenience potato products available to purchase. These products are usually purchased to reduce labor costs associated with potato preparation. The most common convenience items are precut fresh potatoes, frozen potato products, and dehydrated potatoes.

Refrigerated Fresh Potatoes

Fresh potatoes can be purchased in varying degrees of processing to reduce labor costs. For instance, potatoes can be purchased washed, peeled, wedged, sliced, cubed, tournéed, or shredded for hash browns. Partially cooked potatoes can also be purchased in a variety of forms.

Frozen Potatoes

Many forms of potatoes are available frozen. The most common type of frozen potato is the French fry. Diced, hash browns, potato pancakes, wedges, cottage fries, and mashed potatoes can also be purchased frozen.

Dehydrated Potatoes

There are a number of dehydrated potato products available such as mashed, scalloped, au gratin, and hash brown.

Grains

Grains and foods made from grains are an important part of most diets around the world. Grains supply about one-fourth of the energy provided by foods eaten in the United States. Breads, cereals, and pasta are examples of popular grain-based foods.

Grains usually come from plants that produce edible seeds. The most common grains used in the United States are corn, rice, and wheat.

Anatomy of a Grain

Grains are seeds produced by grass or similar plants. Different parts of the grain serve different purposes and contain different nutrients, 28-1.

An outer cover called the *hull* or *husk* protects most grain kernels. Once the hull is removed, the first part of the kernel—the **bran** layer—is exposed. The bran layer is rich in fiber. The largest part of a grain kernel is called the **endosperm**. The endosperm is a good source of carbohydrate (starch) and plant protein. The smallest part of the grain is the **germ**. The germ is a good source of protein, vitamins, minerals, and oils.

Processing Grains

People have been eating grains for thousands of years. Early humans probably gathered grains and possibly toasted or boiled

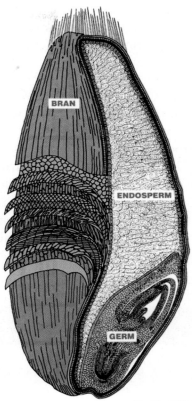

Courtesy of Wheat Foods Council

28-1 Grains have kernels with similar structures but may differ in size and shape.

Culture & Cuisine

Mano and Matate

The mano and matate is used to grind corn in many areas of Mexico and Central America. The matate is a large stone on which the grain is placed. The mano, a smaller stone tool, is used to roll over the matate and grain to grind the grain into powder. The hand-ground corn is used to make many traditional dishes.

them to make them easier to eat. Many methods have been developed to process grains to make them easier to cook and eat.

Milling Grains Milling is a process used to grind grains into usable forms. Milling was originally done by hand and still is in some parts of the world.

Machines do most of the milling around the world. However, animals or running water may power the machines in underdeveloped countries. Large industrial machines do most of the milling in modern countries.

Grains can be milled in a number of ways. There are four common processes.

One or more may be used when processing a grain.
- *Cracking.* Breaking open the hull of the grain.
- *Hulling.* Removing the hull from the rest of the grain.
- *Pearling.* Removing all or just part of the hull, bran, and germ from the grain.
- *Grinding.* Reducing the grain to a meal or powder. The finished product can range from a coarse texture to a fine powder.

Lime (Lye) Processing of Corn Corn is sometimes processed in a highly alkaline mineral lime (lye) solution to make a variety

Lime (Lye) Processed Corn Products

Hominy

Hominy is also called *posole*. It is whole kernels of corn that have been treated with lye. After being treated and rinsed, the kernels are dried, canned, or frozen. Hominy can be served as a side dish or an ingredient in soups and stews.

Grits

Grits are coarsely ground hominy. This product is commonly cooked as a hot cereal and is often served with breakfast in the southern United States. Flavorings such as butter and cheese are common additions.

Masa Harina

Masa harina is finely milled flour made from hominy. This flour is used to make the outside coating for tamales. It is also used to make tortillas, baked goods, and other Mexican and southwestern dishes.

of products. This process causes the endosperm of the corn to swell and the bran to release. The resulting product has improved nutrient availability.

Corn

Corn is the only grain native to the Americas. It is a giant grass plant with no known wild form still in existence. Corn is second only to rice in the tons produced worldwide. Fresh corn, called *sweet corn*, is often categorized as a vegetable. Corn is the only grain that is eaten as a fresh vegetable in the United States.

Sweet corn used as a vegetable is usually not dried. Corn that is ground to make cornmeal or other products is a different variety. There are hundreds of varieties of corn grown around the world. Dent corn, also called *field corn*, is the most important dried corn produced in the United States. Corn is processed to produce a number of common kitchen products.

Common Corn Products

Cornmeal

Cornmeal is made by milling a special type of corn into different size grinds ranging from coarse to very fine. It is used for coating fried products, in breads, and as a cooked cereal called *mush*.

Cornstarch

Cornstarch is a finely milled corn flour used as a coating or thickening agent for hot liquids. It is made from waxy corn originally developed in China.

Polenta

Polenta is the Italian version of cornmeal which is considered to be higher quality than cornmeal and costs more. It is used to prepare an Italian side dish or entrée usually flavored and served with a sauce.

A SERVING OF HISTORY

Corn and Lye

Native Americans taught European settlers how to treat corn with lye. This process was thought to make corn more digestible. It did release the niacin that is normally not digestible. Release of niacin helps prevent a vitamin deficiency disease called *pellagra*. This disease was common in the southeastern United States in the 1800s. Corn in that area was not treated with lye. Pellagra was not common in the southwestern United States because corn was treated with lye in that area.

Rice

Rice is the seed of a grass plant that is grown in flooded fields called *paddies*. Many areas where rice is grown are flat. Rice is also grown in hilly areas where farmers have constructed rice paddies. These areas have been leveled in stages up the sides of hills and in plains areas. Small dams hold the water and separate the paddies.

Rice was an important food in Asia as early as 2500 BC. It has spread around the world to become one of the world's most important food crops. There are thousands of varieties of rice grown around the world but only a few are grown commercially in the United States. Today, rice is grown on each of the seven continents except Antarctica.

Rice is usually identified by the length of the grain. Rice is classified as either short, medium, or long grain, 28-2. The classification is based on either the length of rice grain, the grain's length to width ratio, or a combination of both. Each type of rice is preferred for different applications.

Long-grain rice is the most common type used around the world. The grains are three to four times as long as they are round. When cooked, the grains are separate and firm in texture. This dry, fluffy product is used for steamed rice, pilafs, casseroles, and salads. Basmati and white long grain are examples of long-grain rice.

Short-grain rice has short, rounded grains that contain more starch than long-grain rice. When cooked, these short grains are softer and stickier than long-grain rice. You can use short-grain rice in an application where a moist product is needed such as pudding type desserts, pancakes, risotto, and paella. Arborio used for risotto and sushi rice are examples of short-grain rice.

Medium-grain rice falls between the other two in length and starch content. These grains tend to be separate when hot but

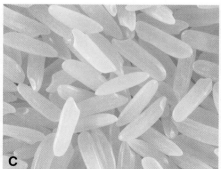

Optimarc/Shutterstock.com, marekuliasz/Shutterstock.com, amenic181/Shutterstock.com

28-2 Rice is classified as (A) short, (B) medium, or (C) long grain.

become sticky when cool. Medium-grain rice can be used for many dishes and recipes that call for short-grain rice. It is commonly used to make dishes such as paella, Asian dishes requiring stickier rice, and rice pudding.

Whole-grain rice or rice sold with the bran layer left attached is called brown rice. However, other colors of rice can also be whole grain as long as the bran layer is left intact, 28-3. The bran layer can be pearled during the milling process to produce white rice.

Converted rice is another product that you may use in the kitchen. Converted rice has been parboiled to remove surface starch. Converted rice cooks up fluffier and is less sticky. This process also transfers some of the nutrients from the outer bran layer to the grain's interior. As a result, white converted rice usually contains more nutrients than regular white milled rice.

Instant rice is a common convenience product. Instant rice is rice that has been fully cooked and then freeze-dried. The rice loses some flavor and nutrients but cooks much faster than regular rice.

Wild rice is not true rice but the seed from a water plant that grows in the upper United States. This seed was an important source of food for Sioux and Chippewa Indians around the Great Lakes. It has a nutty flavor when cooked. Cooking time for wild rice is much longer than regular rice.

Wheat

Five grains—wheat, barley, millet, oats, and rye—have fed Western civilization for the last 12,000 years. Wheat is the most important of these five.

Wheat is sold in the whole-grain form as wheat berries that can also be processed and dried to produce bulgur. Most wheat is milled and further processed into flour that is used to make many more products. Important wheat products made with flour are couscous and pasta.

AlenKadr/Shutterstock.com

28-3 Whole-grain rice can provide interesting color for a meal.

Common Wheat Products

Wheat Berries

Wheat berries are whole-wheat kernels without the hull. They are dense, remain firm even after long cooking, and are a good source of dietary fiber.

Bulgur

Bulgur is made by first removing the bran layer from wheat, and then steaming and drying the product. It can be ground into different textures and soaked in water to be eaten raw or cooked.

Couscous

Couscous is a fine pasta-like product made from hard durum wheat. It can be steamed or cooked in a liquid and is traditionally served in North Africa with stews.

Other Grains

Other grains have played important roles in feeding people over the course of history. Some may be less popular today but no less nutritious. As people consider ways to increase whole grains in their eating patterns, these other grains may see a rise in popularity. Today, chefs are turning to old grains for new inspiration.

Pasta and Noodles—Grain-Based Products

The origin of pasta—Italy or China—has been argued a long time. Both regions have long histories of preparing and eating pasta or noodle products. It may never be known where pasta was actually first made. It is possible that it was

Other Grains

Amaranth

This ancient grain of Mexico is very small, but a good source of protein. It is used in a wide variety of recipes.

Barley

Barley is one of the oldest grains eaten by humans. Today, most barley is used to make beer or animal feed. Pearled barley is used in soups and stews.

Millet

Millet was a staple of the Chinese diet before rice and of poor people in Europe during the Middle Ages. It is typically boiled to make porridge. Today millet is most often used as an animal feed.

Oats

Oats are the most widely consumed grains in the United States after wheat, corn, and rice. They are most often cooked in liquid and eaten as hot oatmeal. Oats are also added to whole-grain breads and used as a bread topping. Rolled oats are a common breakfast food and cook quickly due to their flattened shape. Steel cut oats are oat grains that are chopped instead of rolled and require longer cooking time. They can be used as a breakfast food or in savory recipes.

Quinoa

Quinoa (KEEN wah) is a small grain that originated thousands of years ago in the Andean region of South America. It is a source of high quality protein, which is unique for grains and makes it beneficial for vegetarian diets. Rinse quinoa before cooking to remove the bitter substance that often coats the grain.

Rye

Rye has been grown since ancient times. It was, and still is, primarily used as a flavoring in fermented beverages and bread products.

Common Pasta Shapes

Angel Hair

Angel hair is long, thin, delicate pasta. It is also called *fidelini*.

Fusilli

Fusilli has a long twisted shape. It is served with a sauce, broken and added to soup, or in pasta salad.

Fettucini

Fettucini is long, flat pasta about ¼ inch (1 cm) wide. It is served with a variety of sauces.

Lasagna

Lasagna is long, flat pasta that is typically used in casseroles.

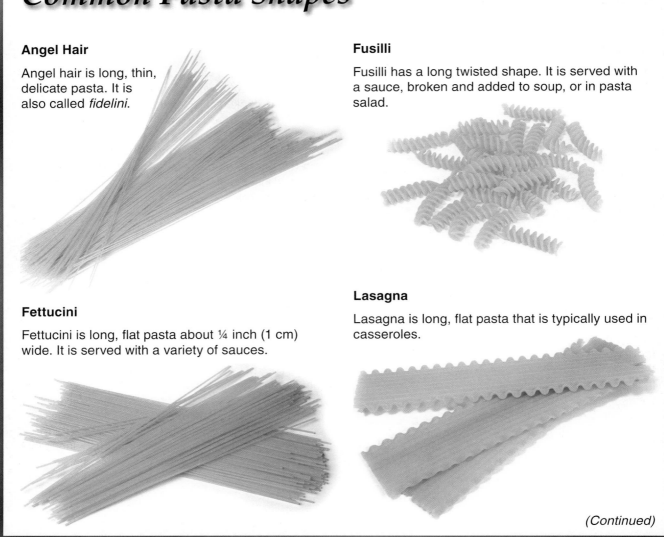

(Continued)

developed and produced in different regions independently.

Western-style pasta is made from wheat flour and liquid. Other ingredients may be added such as egg, salt, and flavorings. This type of pasta is the Italian variety. Most pasta is made with semolina flour. **Semolina** is milled from a hard variety of wheat and is favored as a pasta ingredient because its texture allows pasta to stay firmer longer.

There are at least 200 shapes of Italian-style pasta. The shapes can generally be described as
- ribbons such as lasagna and spaghetti

Common Pasta Shapes (Continued)

Linguine

Linguine is long pasta about ¾₁₆ inch (0.5 cm) wide. It is served with a variety of sauces.

Spaghetti

Spaghetti is the favorite pasta in the United States. It is long and round and can be served with almost any sauce and topping.

Manicotti

Manicotti is a medium-sized round tube that can be served with a sauce plus a variety of toppings. It is also served stuffed, baked, and topped with sauce.

Ziti

Ziti is small, tube pasta often used for baked dishes and pasta salads.

Rotelle

Rotelle is shaped like a wagon wheel. It is added to soup, made into pasta salad, or served topped with sauce.

Common Types of Asian Noodles

Buckwheat Noodles

The buckwheat noodle, also called *soba*, is popular in Japan. It is cooked and served hot in soup or cold with a dipping sauce.

Rice Noodles

Rice noodles are sold in a variety of shapes and sizes. They are typically soaked in water before serving. Very fine rice noodles are deep-fried and used as a base for a number of dishes or as a garnish.

Wheat (Egg) Noodles

Wheat or egg noodles are the most popular Asian noodles. They are typically served in soups, dressed with a sauce, or fried until crisp and served as a pancake or used to garnish.

Bean Starch Noodles

These noodles are made from bean starch and prepared in ways similar to rice noodles.

- tubes such as manicotti and ziti
- shapes such as fusilli and rotelle

Both fresh and dry pasta must be cooked before being eaten. Dried pasta takes longer to cook than fresh pasta.

Asian noodles are not made in as many shapes as pasta. Most Asian noodles are made into long lengths of varying diameters. They may be made from wheat, rice, beans, or other grains. Some Asian noodles do not need to be cooked and can be eaten after they are soaked in water.

Receiving and Storing Grains and Grain Products

Packages should be inspected to make sure they were not damaged or punctured during shipping. All products should be stored off the floor in a clean, dry area, 28-4. When opened, products should be placed in airtight containers and used as soon as possible. Some products that contain natural oils, such as brown rice and wheat germ, should be refrigerated to maintain freshness.

©iStock.com/Baloncici

28-4 Grain products are stored and delivered on pallets to keep them off the floor away from possible contamination and pests.

Summary Points

- Potatoes are selected based on their starch content. The level of starch content determines the use for which the potato is best suited.

- Potatoes, sweet potatoes, and yams are all botanically different from each other.

- There are many different types of grains that people eat. These grains are used in a variety of forms for cooking.

- Grains can be processed in a number of ways to make them easier to cook and eat.

- Wheat is the most important grain and is processed further into many products.

In Review Assess

1. The enlarged, edible portion of a potato plant root is called the _____.

2. Contrast mealy potatoes with waxy potatoes.

3. What is a new potato?

4. True or false. Sweet potatoes have more moisture, taste sweeter, and are a better source of vitamin A than yams.

5. When receiving potatoes for the commercial kitchen, for what should you check?

6. Grains are the edible _____ produced by grass or similar plants.

7. List the three parts of a kernel of grain and the nutrient each part contributes.

8. List the four common processes used to mill grains.

9. Name the only grain that is native to America.

10. List three lime-processed corn products and a use for each.

11. In the commercial kitchen, which length of rice grain would you use to make pilaf? Why?

12. Name four grains other than wheat and rice.

13. Pastas are often made with _____ flour because it helps the pasta to stay firmer.

14. How should grains and grain products be stored in the commercial kitchen?

Core Skills

15. **Math.** You are planning a meal for 500 people. Baked potatoes are on the menu. How many cases of 90-count russet potatoes do you need to order to have enough for service?

16. **Writing.** Rice is an unusual plant. Use Internet and print resources to research how rice is planted, where and how it grows, what varieties grow in various geographical areas, and how it is harvested. Then write a paper detailing this agricultural information about rice.

17. **Speaking.** Quinoa is considered an ancient grain. Use reliable Internet and print resources to research the history of this grain and why it was so nutritionally important. In contrast, why is it an important, nutritional grain today? What are its uses in the commercial kitchen? Use presentation software to prepare an illustrated oral report for the class.

18. **Reading.** Use reliable Internet and print resources to research the process of nixtamalization in relationship to lime (lye) processed corn products. What is the history of this process? How is it done? What similar process is used today? Why is it important? How did failure to pass along the nixtamalization process impact Europe when corn was introduced and became a staple food? Report your findings to the class.

19. **Math.** It takes about 45 minutes for steel cut oats to cook. Rolled oats take 5 minutes to cook. How much longer does it take to cook steel cut oats compared to rolled oats?

20. **CTE Career Readiness Practice.** Imagine you are the chef of a trend-setting restaurant in your area. The restaurant manager has taken customers' interests in more unique foods to heart and is developing a new menu. The manager has asked you to choose three different varieties of potatoes or potato products and three new varieties of grains or grain products to use with the new menu. What items would you recommend? Why? What process would you use to come to your conclusions?

Critical Thinking

21. **Analyze.** You assigned a new cook to make potato salad. The cook brings the salad to you to find out what went wrong—the salad looks like a pile of mashed potatoes mixed with mayonnaise. What question(s) would you ask the cook to determine what went wrong?

22. **Consider.** Your kitchen is short staffed due to illness and vacations. You are considering using convenience potato products to help you during the labor crunch but do not want your customers to be disappointed with quality. In which menu items could you use convenience potatoes to replace fresh potatoes with the least impact?

23. **Evaluate.** Why would you choose cornmeal for coating deep-fried catfish and not polenta?

24. **Analyze.** Suppose you want to make rice pudding for dessert as a special menu item. Which type of rice would you choose? Why? How would your rice pudding be affected if you chose another type of rice?

Technology

Use reliable Internet resources to research the history of the potato from its origins to its common usage throughout the world today. Trace its journey to different parts of the world and how it came to be planted in states like Idaho. Then use a school-approved Web-based application to create an interactive report of your findings to put on the class website. Collaborate with your classmates about their findings in real time.

Teamwork

Divide the class into five teams. Each team should select one of the following groups of grain or grain products: corn products, rice, wheat products, other grains, or pasta and noodles. Each team should

- gather as many items from their grain group as possible
- place approximately ⅛ cup of each product in its own dish and assign it a number
- write the name of each product and its number on a note card and place it face down in front of the sample

Each team should visit the grain displays of the other four teams and try to identify the products on display. Students should write their answers on a sheet of paper using the numbers on the dishes to indicate the product they are identifying. After everyone has finished, the teams should turn the cards over in front of each dish so that the other teams can check their answers.

Chef's E-portfolio
Creative Grains on the Menu

Upload your report from the CTE Career Readiness Practice activity to your e-portfolio. Ask your instructor where to save your file. This could be on the school's network or a flash drive of your own. Name your portfolio document *FirstnameLastname_Portfolio Ch#.docx* (i.e., JohnSmith_PortfolioCh28.docx).

While studying, look for the activity icon to:

- Build vocabulary with e-flash cards and matching activities.
- Expand learning with video clips, photo identification activities, animations, and interactive activities.
- Review and assess what you learn by completing end-of-chapter questions.

Matteo Cozzi/Shutterstock.com

Starch Cookery

Reading Prep

In preparation for reading the chapter, review a variety of restaurant menus for starch dishes offered. Read the descriptions of the dishes to determine the type of cooking methods used. Compare your findings to the chapter as you read.

Culinary Terminology
Build Vocab

gaufrette, p. 474
pilaf, p. 478
risotto, p. 478
al dente, p. 482

Academic Terminology
Build Vocab

Persia, p. 478
rehydrate, p. 481

Objectives

After studying this chapter, you will be able to

- implement common cooking methods for the two types of potato.
- execute the most common cooking methods used to prepare grains in foodservice.
- implement the appropriate cooking method for preparing both fresh and dry pasta.
- explain proper handling of cooked starches.

Starches such as potatoes, grains, and pastas are staples that form the foundation of every cuisine. A chef must be able to properly cook these products because they play a role in almost every meal.

Potatoes

Potatoes are a starchy vegetable that can be prepared in a variety of ways. Potatoes are generally classified as mealy or waxy. Each type of potato is more successfully prepared in different ways.

Baked or Roasted Potatoes

Mealy potatoes, commonly called *baking potatoes*, are relatively high in starch. They have a dry texture and become light and fluffy when cooked. These potatoes are ideal for baking and frying.

One of the most popular potato items in foodservice is the baked potato. It is also one of the easiest to prepare. Baked potatoes can be prepared whole with their skin, or cut into chunks or wedges before roasting.

Baked potatoes can be served and eaten plain. Whole baked potatoes are most often eaten with one or more garnishes such as butter, sour cream, chives, grated cheese, bacon bits, or chopped green onions. Baked potatoes can be served as a side dish or garnished and served as an entrée. When baked whole, they can be used in other recipes such as twice-baked potatoes.

Boiled Potatoes

Potatoes that are relatively low in starch are called *waxy potatoes*, or boiling potatoes. The most common method used to prepare these potatoes is the boiling method. Boiled potatoes can be mashed or used as ingredients in a variety of recipes.

TECHNIQUE
Baking Potatoes

1. Wash the needed number of potatoes well with clean water.
2. Arrange potatoes on a clean sheet pan.
3. Rub potatoes lightly with vegetable oil or spray with vegetable spray.

4. Season potatoes with salt.
5. Bake potatoes in a 350°F–400°F (177°C–204°C) oven approximately one hour or until done. A paring knife should easily pierce a baked potato that is done.

TECHNIQUE
Boiling Potatoes

1. Peel the needed number of potatoes and wash them with clean water.
2. Cut the potatoes into uniform-sized pieces to ensure they cook at the same rate. If potatoes are to be used as an ingredient in a recipe, make sure the pieces are an appropriate size.
3. Place the potatoes in a pot and cover with cool water to several inches above the potatoes. Add salt to water if recipe calls for it.
4. Bring water to a boil, then reduce heat and simmer. Cook the potatoes until they reach desired doneness. Test doneness using a paring knife.
5. Drain potatoes in a colander or perforated pan, or add directly to recipe.

Sautéed and Panfried Potatoes

Another common method used to prepare potatoes is sautéing or panfrying. Many times potatoes are cut into shapes and parboiled or completely cooked before being cooked in fat. Any fat used for sautéing such as clarified butter, vegetable oil, or bacon or duck fat can be used to finish cooking potatoes.

Deep-Fried Potatoes

Deep-fried potatoes are the most popular way to serve potatoes with many American diners. French fries are on menus everywhere from fast food to fine dining. Mealy potatoes are best for deep frying.

Deep-fried potatoes are classified by their size and shape. Some of the most popular deep-fried potatoes are

- Cottage fries—Cut in rondelles ¼ inch (6.4 mm) thick
- French fries—Cut into sticks measuring ⅜ × ⅜ × 3 inch (9.5 × 9.5 × 76 mm)
- Gaufrette (goh-FRET)—Waffle shaped, cut on a mandoline
- Shoestring—Cut into juliennes
- Steak fries—Potatoes cut into large wedges

TECHNIQUE
Sautéing Potatoes

1. Peel and wash the number of potatoes needed in clean water.
2. Cut potatoes into desired size and cook in water according to the recipe.
3. Drain water from potatoes.
4. Heat a sauté or frying pan and add enough fat to prevent potatoes from sticking to the pan.
5. Toss potatoes or stir to allow even cooking. Cook potatoes until well browned and crispy.

6. Add any garnish and seasonings according to the recipe.

TECHNIQUE
Cutting Gaufrette Potatoes

1. Set the wavy blade on a mandoline to a thickness of about ⅛ inch.
2. Pass a potato over the wavy blade to remove a slice. Discard the first slice.
3. Turn the potato 90° so that the cut grooves on the potato are perpendicular to the blade. Cut another slice.

4. Adjust thickness if necessary to achieve a "basket weave" appearance.
5. Continue cutting slices being sure to rotate the potato 90° after each slice.

Potatoes present unique problems as compared to other fried foods. Thicker cuts of potatoes become too dark if cooked directly in oil at the customary temperature for deep frying. Therefore, most deep-fried potatoes need to be parcooked in oil at a lower temperature, and later finished at a higher temperature to achieve a crisp golden brown exterior. Thin cut potatoes such as potato chips and shoestrings can be cooked directly in hot oil without parcooking.

Sweet Potatoes and Yams

Sweet potatoes and yams are often prepared in much the same way as potatoes—mashed, puréed, baked, or roasted.

Grains

Grains and foods made from grains are an important part of most diets in the world. Many of the grain products prepared in a foodservice kitchen are boiled, simmered, or prepared using either the pilaf or risotto cooking methods. Even though the methods differ in some respects, all employ cooking the product in a liquid.

A wide variety of grains are used in soups, salads, entrées, and even desserts.

TECHNIQUE
Deep-Frying Potatoes

1. Cut potatoes into desired shape in the needed quantity (potatoes may or may not be peeled depending on usage).
2. Heat oil to 250°F (120°C) and add potatoes in batches being careful not to cause the temperature to fall. Deep-fry for 2–3 minutes until potatoes are partially cooked and start to turn brown at the edges. (This step is omitted for frozen potatoes because they are precooked.)

3. Remove potatoes from oil, drain, and set aside.
4. For service, deep-fry potatoes in 350°F (180°C) oil until golden brown and cooked internally.
5. Drain and season with salt to serve.

Grains commonly used include corn, rice, wheat, barley, buckwheat, and oats.

There are many different methods employed to cook grains. Behind these methods and recipes are thousands of years of trial and error from different cultures worldwide. It is important to master many different methods for cooking each grain in order to provide variety on menus. When choosing a cooking method, many factors should be considered including the following:

- the type of grain
- desired taste and look for the end product
- cooking equipment available
- amount of time available

No matter what factors are involved, the first decision to be made when cooking any grain is the proportion of liquid to grain that is required.

Proportion of Liquid

Most methods of grain cookery require a fixed ratio of liquid to grain. This ratio ensures a properly cooked product. The general rule for rice, for example, is two parts liquid to one part rice by volume. However, different types of rice may require slightly more or less liquid.

Depending on the product and how fresh it is, the ratio of liquid to product as well as the cooking time will vary, 29-1. It is best to check the product label to verify the proper ratio of liquid to product and cooking time.

Boiling Method

The boiling method for preparing grains is the least complicated and easiest to carry out. Some chefs refer to this method as the "pasta method" because the product is cooked in the same manner as dried pasta. A large amount of lightly salted water is brought to a boil and the product is added. The product is boiled until done and then drained of excess water.

Rice to Liquid Ratios		
Rice Type	**Parts Liquid to 1 Part Rice (by volume)**	**Cooking Time**
Arborio	3	20–30 minutes
Basmati	1½ to 2	20–25 minutes
Brown, long-grain	2½ to 3	40–45 minutes
Converted	1¾ to 2	25–30 minutes
White, long-grain	1½ to 2	18–20 minutes
White, medium-grain	1½ to 1¾	20–30 minutes
White, short-grain	1½ to 1¾	20–30 minutes

29-1 Cooking times may differ depending on the freshness of the grain.

TECHNIQUE
Boiling Rice

1. Determine the amount of rice to be cooked.
2. Bring one gallon (3.8 L) of water to a boil for each pound of rice to be cooked. Season each gallon of water with one ounce (28 g) salt.
3. Add rice to boiling water. Stir occasionally and boil for 18 minutes.
4. Drain rice. Rinse in cold water to cool. Properly store and reheat for service.

TECHNIQUE
Simmering Rice

1. Combine rice, water, and salt in a heavy pot.
2. Bring ingredients to a boil.
3. Reduce heat to a simmer. Cover the pot and continue to cook at a simmer over low heat for the appropriate time for the type of rice being cooked.
4. When the rice is tender, remove the pot from the heat and fluff the rice with a fork.

Although this method is easy to execute, it is not appropriate for all grains and nutrients are lost in the cooking water. Barley and rice are examples of grains that could be cooked with the boiling method.

Simmering Method

Unlike the boiling method, simmering uses a measured amount of liquid to ensure that the finished texture of the product is correct. The gentler, less agitating heat of simmering releases less starch from the grain. Fewer water-soluble nutrients are lost than in boiling.

This method yields a product that is tender and not sticky. For this reason, simmered rice works well as a starch to accompany stews and other entrées. Short-grain rice, such as sushi rice, cooked by this method is tender with unbroken grains.

Pilaf Method

Pilaf (also spelled "pilaw" or "pilau") can be traced back to ancient **Persia**, an ancient kingdom within Iran. **Pilaf** is a cooking method that sautés the grain in hot fat, then hot liquid is added, and the grain is simmered without stirring. This method is similar to simmering because a measured amount of liquid is used to make the pilaf. As with simmering, this precise measurement ensures proper doneness of the finished product. Flavorful liquid is used (usually a stock) and aromatic ingredients are added to the grain as well. The pilaf method is different from simmering because the aromatic ingredients are first sweated in a fat before the grain is added. The grain is then mixed in so it is coated in the same fat, which helps to keep the grains from sticking together in the finished product.

Other products such as barley and bulgur wheat can be cooked by the pilaf method, as well as small pasta products such as orzo.

Risotto Method

Risotto is both the name of a traditional Italian rice dish and the cooking method employed to create the dish. **Risotto** is rice grains that are cooked at an active simmer while being stirred. Hot seasoned liquid is continually added in small amounts until the rice is cooked to a point where it gives slight resistance when eaten. This cooking method produces a hearty dish in which the grain is bound in a rich sauce thickened by starch from the grain. In contrast, both the simmering and pilaf methods create a product with rice grains that are fluffy and separated.

Risotto made from short-grain rice has become very popular in the United States. Grains such as barley and steel-cut oats can also be cooked by this method. However, short-grain rice is the most typical grain used when preparing risotto.

TECHNIQUE
Preparing Pilaf

1. Heat a small amount of fat in a heavy saucepan and sweat the appropriate aromatic ingredients.

2. Add the measured amount of rice and stir to coat grains with the fat.

3. Add the measured amount of seasoned liquid to the rice and bring to a boil.

4. Cover saucepan with a tight fitting lid and place in a 350°F (180°C) oven for the correct cooking time. Large batches can be cooked in the oven in a covered hotel pan.

5. When all of the liquid has been absorbed, remove the rice from the oven, uncover and fluff with a fork.

Recipe No.	Name			Category
29.5	Rice Pilaf			Starches
Yield	Portion Size			No. Portions
3 pt. (1.44 L)	½ c. (120 mL)			12
US Quantity	Metric Quantity	Ingredient		TCS
2 oz.	60 g	butter		•
2 oz.	60 g	onion, small dice		
1 pt.	480 mL	long-grain white rice		
1 qt.	0.95 L	chicken stock		•
1 ea.		bay leaf		
1 ea.		parsley sprig		
to taste		salt and white pepper		
Method				CCP
1. Sweat the onion in the butter.				
2. Add rice and stir to coat with the butter.				
3. Add the stock, bay leaf, and parsley sprig. Season to taste.				
4. Bring the ingredients to a simmer. Cover tightly and place in a 350°F (177°C) oven for 18–20 minutes or until all the liquid is absorbed.				CCP
5. Remove from the oven, uncover, and fluff with a fork.				

Portion (g)	Calories	Fat (g)	Protein (g)	Carbohydrate (g)	Cholesterol (mg)	Sodium (mg)	Fiber (g)
185	188	4.94	4.62	30.08	12.52	406.18	0.46

Traditionally, risotto is served immediately because it does not hold well. Holding risotto tends to overcook the rice and produce a product with a soft, pasty, unappealing consistency. Some chefs partially prepare risotto and complete the cooking when needed. Other chefs maintain that risotto cannot be fully appreciated unless served immediately after cooking.

Risotto Variations Risotto is a versatile dish. It may be served as an appetizer, a main course, or as a side dish. Risotto can also be enhanced with a wide variety of ingredients and flavors. Proteins such as ham, shrimp, shellfish, and chicken can be added to the dish. In addition, mushrooms, various cheeses, herbs, spices, and vegetables can be added. Chefs have created many other variations of risotto as well, 29-2.

Risotto Variations

Risotto con funghi—Sweat 6 to 8 oz. (170 to 225 g) of domestic or wild sliced mushrooms with the onion and proceed with the basic recipe.

Risotto alla Milanese—Add ½ tsp. (3 mL) saffron threads to the chicken stock and allow to steep before using the stock in the risotto recipe.

Risotto con zucca—Sweat 10 oz. (280 g) small diced pumpkin or butternut squash with the onions in the basic risotto recipe.

29-2 Many variations of risotto are possible.

TECHNIQUE
Preparing Risotto

1. Bring the seasoned cooking liquid to a simmer.
2. In a heavy saucepot, heat a small amount of fat. Sweat the appropriate aromatic ingredients in the fat.

3. Add the rice and stir to coat with the fat.

4. Add a portion (⅓ or less) of the seasoned cooking liquid while continuing to stir and cook over moderate heat. Cook until the liquid is absorbed.

5. Continue to add portions of the cooking liquid and continue to stir over heat. Repeat the process until the rice is tender.
6. Finish the risotto with whole butter and grated cheese. If appropriate, add other finishing ingredients.

Pasta and Noodles

Pasta and noodles are important foods in both Eastern and Western cuisine. In Italian cuisine, pasta is typically served as a course before the fish and meat during a traditional meal. In America, pasta has become a popular entrée item. The same holds true in Asia where noodles can be the main part of a meal.

Pasta and noodles are found in a variety of sizes and shapes. Typically, commercial products are made from ground grains such as wheat, rice, and buckwheat. The ground grain, or flour, is mixed with water and pressed or passed through a form to create various shapes. Additional flavorings or coloring ingredients can be added for variety such as spinach, saffron, or ground chiles. Egg products can be added to produce egg noodles.

Pasta and noodles are sold commercially fresh, frozen, or dried. Many of these products can be made easily from scratch with a few common ingredients. The most common product made from scratch is sheet pasta. This is a thin, flat sheet of dough that can be used as lasagna or cut into various shapes such as ribbons, circles, and squares.

Pasta Dough

Pasta dough is one of the simplest products to make. Basically, pasta dough consists of flour and liquid. The most common pasta in Western cuisine is made from wheat flour. To create a finished cooked product that stays firmer for a longer time, many chefs prefer to use semolina for some or all of the flour content. Liquid for pasta dough is usually water or egg products, 29-3. The texture of the dough is quite firm, which makes it easier to roll out and cut than a softer, sticky dough.

Small batches of pasta dough can be mixed and kneaded by hand. Larger batches are best done in an electric mixer with a dough hook attachment. Regardless of how it is done, the dough should be mixed until it is smooth, without lumps or dry spots.

After the dough has been kneaded, it will be elastic and hard to work with. Allow at least 30 minutes for the dough to relax and become manageable before rolling and cutting.

Shaping Fresh Pasta

Fresh pasta is quick and easy to make using a few kitchen staples. Simple, flat pasta such as fettuccini or the wider version called *tagliatelle* can be made with a rolling pin and knife. Other shapes such as lasagna and ravioli can also be made in this manner by first creating sheets of fresh pasta.

Draz-Koetke/Goodheart-Willcox Publisher

29-3 A trough is formed in the flour to contain the eggs before mixing pasta dough.

Although fresh pasta can be produced by hand using common kitchen tools, the most common method for producing pasta sheets is with a pasta machine. While some machines are electric and may also mix the dough, most machines are manual. The manual machines have two rollers that both knead the dough and form the pasta sheets. In addition, pasta machines have attachments that cut the sheets into various widths such as angel hair and fettuccine.

In addition to cutting pasta sheets into ribbons of various widths, pasta sheets can be used for lasagna and an assortment of filled pasta shapes.

Perhaps the most common filled pasta is the ravioli. Ravioli can be made from two similar-sized sheets of fresh pasta. One sheet is placed flat on a lightly floured work surface. A piping bag with a straight tip, a portion scoop, or small spoon is used to place the portions of filling on the pasta sheet at equal intervals. The desired dimension of the finished product determines the distance between each portion of filling. The second sheet of pasta is placed over the first. The two sheets of pasta must be sealed around each mound of filling to remove air pockets and hold the product together. Desired shapes are then cut out with a knife, pastry wheel, or shaped cutter, 29-4. Ravioli can be cooked and served immediately or covered and held for later use.

Cooking Pasta

The boiling method for preparing pasta or noodles is referred to by some chefs as the "pasta method." A large amount of slightly salted water is brought to a boil and the product is added. The product is boiled until done and then drained of excess water. The best method for determining if pasta is done is to carefully remove one piece and taste. Dry, fresh, and fresh frozen pasta are cooked by this method. Dry pasta is cooked longer because cooking also serves to rehydrate the pasta. **Rehydrate** means to add water back to a product.

Draz-Koetke/Goodheart-Willcox Publisher

29-4 To make ravioli, (A) space filling at equal intervals, (B) place pasta sheet on top, seal, and (C) cut into desired shape.

Italian pasta is considered done when **al dente**, or fully cooked but not soft or mushy. However, Asian noodles are typically cooked until soft or stir-fried until crisp.

Dry Pasta   Dry pasta needs a longer cooking time because cooking also rehydrates the product. One pound of dry pasta produces from two to three pounds of cooked product. Two ounces of dry pasta is considered an average entrée portion when cooked.

Fresh Pasta   Fresh pasta is delicate and requires a short cooking time because no

TECHNIQUE

Animation

Cutting Noodles by Hand

1. Start with a manageable amount of pasta dough.
2. Dust a work surface with flour and flatten the dough with the heel of your hand.

3. Roll out the dough with a rolling pin making sure to sprinkle with flour to prevent the dough from sticking to the pin or work surface.
4. Continue to roll the dough into a thin rectangular sheet approximately ⅛-inch thick.

5. Beginning at one end of the rectangle, loosely roll the dough up.

6. Use a sharp knife to make ¼- to ½-inch thick slices in the roll, forming individual spirals.

7. Unwind spirals to form noodles and place on a sheet pan.
8. Cover and hold for service or cook immediately.

rehydration is required. Fresh frozen pasta also needs a short cook time.

Reheating Pasta Reheat pasta by placing it in a strainer and submerging the product in boiling water. Sautéing is not recommended as a typical method for reheating pasta. In some cases, chefs sauté pasta shapes to produce a somewhat dry, crisp product.

Handling Cooked Starches

Cooked starches require time and temperature control for safety and must be handled properly to avoid spoilage or illness caused by pathogens. After preparation, starches should either be served immediately or held at or above 135°F (57°C). Unused cooked starches should be refrigerated as soon as possible. As

with any other food product, starches can be reheated on top of the stove, in a steamer, or in an oven. Some preparations may require the addition of more liquid. All reheated foods must be heated to an internal temperature of at least 165°F (74°C).

TECHNIQUE
Boiling Pasta

1. Bring one gallon (3.8 L) of slightly salted water (2 to 3 Tbsp.) per pound of pasta to a boil.
2. Add pasta and stir to separate the pieces.
3. Cook pasta at a rolling boil until al dente.
4. Drain pasta immediately and serve. Pasta can be shocked in ice water to stop cooking, coated with a little olive oil, and reheated for later service.

TECHNIQUE
Using a Manual Pasta Machine

1. Start with a manageable amount of pasta dough.
2. Open the rollers of the pasta machine to the widest possible setting.
3. Flatten the dough with the heel of your hand so it will fit between the rollers of the pasta machine. Dust the dough and the rollers lightly with flour.
4. Run the dough through the pasta machine holding one end of the dough with one hand while holding up the dough as it comes out of the machine.

5. Fold the dough into thirds so the sheet of dough is in three layers.
6. Run the dough through the machine three or four more times to knead the dough until it is smooth.
7. When the dough is smooth, move the rollers together one or two notches and pass the dough through without folding.
8. Continue moving the rollers together and passing the dough through the machine until the dough is at the desired thickness—usually ⅛ inch.
9. Cut the sheet with the cutting attachment to create the width of pasta ribbons desired or use the pasta sheet for another recipe such as filled pasta.

Summary Points

- The most common methods for cooking potatoes are baking, boiling, and frying.
- Grains can be cooked by a variety of methods. The method is selected based on many factors such as characteristics of the grain, desired end product, and equipment and time available.
- An important factor in cooking grains is to determine the ratio of liquid to grain.
- Pasta and noodles are easy to make and are usually cooked using the boiling method.
- Cooked starches require proper handling to avoid spoilage or illness caused by pathogens.

In Review
Assess

1. Mealy potatoes are ideal for what cooking methods?
2. Many times potatoes are cut into shapes and _____ or completely cooked before sautéing or panfrying.
3. True or false. Thicker cuts of potatoes often need to be boiled in water before being deep-fried at a higher temperature to achieve a crisp golden brown exterior.
4. List four methods used for cooking grains.
5. Which cooking method for grains results in the greatest loss of water-soluble nutrients?
6. How much of the liquid is added in the pilaf method after the grain and aromatics are sweated?
7. How much of the liquid is added in the risotto method after the grain and aromatics are sweated?
8. True or false. Cooked starches can be held at room temperature safely.
9. After dough is kneaded, you must allow at least _____ minutes for the dough to relax before you begin rolling and cutting it.
10. Why does fresh pasta cook more rapidly than dry pasta?

Core Skills

11. **Math.** The chef tells you to prepare enough pasta for a luncheon serving 150 people. The menu features a spaghetti entrée. How many pounds of dry pasta would you obtain from the storeroom?
12. **Speaking and Listening.** In teams, choose one of the following preparation techniques for potatoes: boiling, sautéing, or deep-frying. Gather enough potatoes to prepare four portions. With your team members, prepare your potatoes according to text directions. Plate your cooked potatoes to share with the class. Discuss your potato preparation technique and any challenges you faced. Team members should taste and evaluate the flavor and appearance of one another's potatoes.
13. **Speaking.** Discuss the pro's and con's of preparing your own french fries from scratch versus purchasing prepared french fries that only require a quick deep-fry before serving. Then demonstrate the preparation of french fries from scratch and prepared french fries that require a quick deep-fry. Describe the process as you complete each step. Have the class time your preparations and taste-test the finished product for flavor and appearance.
14. **Writing.** Use cookbooks and the Internet to research information about rice pilaf. Gather information about the history of this dish and the different variations. Write a summary of your findings.
15. **Speaking and Listening.** In teams, choose one of the following preparation techniques for rice and grains: boiling, simmering, pilaf, or risotto. Prepare four portions according to text directions. Plate your cooked grains to share with the class. Discuss your grain preparation technique and any challenges you faced. Team members should taste and evaluate the flavor and appearance of one another's grain dishes.
16. **CTE Career Readiness Practice.** Presume you are the chef at a local Italian restaurant. Part of your job is to train new cooks to make pasta. Create a plan outlining how you will

proceed in training the new cooks in making pasta. Execute the plan with your new cooks (several class members).

Critical Thinking

17. **Identify evidence.** Use reliable Internet or print resources to research and write a short paper identifying how potato chips were invented. Based on your research, what evidence can you give about the invention of potato chips and the impact on foodservice?

18. **Assess.** Find a risotto recipe online or in a cookbook and personalize it by adding or changing ingredients to create your own risotto recipe. Suggest what else you might serve with your risotto. Then prepare the risotto and assess the outcome. Evaluate the appearance, flavor, and texture of the risotto. How did the added ingredients impact the recipe and the finished product?

19. **Generate.** You have been given an assignment to plan, prepare, and serve a meal for your chef instructor and class. You want to make a good impression and select an impressive entrée but it is very labor intensive. You want an equally impressive starch to accompany your entrée but you will have little time to prepare it. What starch dish would you select? Why?

Technology

Create a spreadsheet listing the basic ingredients for rice pilaf as listed in this text. Then develop a formula by which the recipe can be increased 2 times and then 3 times. Use formulas in the cells to allow you to easily change the recipe amounts.

Teamwork

Gather a team of four students. Two team members will
- use the basic pasta dough recipe
- prepare fresh fettuccini pasta and cook it
- carefully record its beginning weight, how long it took to cook, and its ending weight

The other two team members will cook dried, store-bought fettuccini, also keeping track of cooking times, beginning and ending weights. Once the pastas are cooked, the groups will evaluate the different fettuccines to compare how much their weight changed between before and after cooking, how long each one took to cook, and the pasta's appearance, texture, and flavor. Write a brief summary of your observations.

Chef's E-portfolio
Rice Preparation

Select and prepare one of the rice preparation techniques discussed in this chapter. Have a friend or family member video you as you work or take photos of various stages during the process. Upload your video or photos to your e-portfolio. Ask your instructor where to save your file. This could be on the school's network or a flash drive of your own. Name your portfolio document FirstnameLastname_Portfolio Ch#.docx (i.e., JohnSmith_PortfolioCh29.docx).

Video Clip

Preparing Risotto

Visit the G-W Learning Companion Website and view the bonus video clip "Preparing risotto." After viewing the clip, answer the following questions:

1. The cooking process releases the rice's _____, which produces a creamy texture.
2. What portion of the seasoned cooking liquid is added to the rice first?
3. True or false. The risotto is cooked until the rice is fluffy.

Video

While studying, look for the activity icon to:

- Build vocabulary with e-flash cards and matching activities.
- Expand learning with video clips, photo identification activities, animations, and interactive activities.
- Review and assess what you learn by completing end-of-chapter questions.

G-WLEARNING.com

Nana77777/Shutterstock.com

Reading Prep

In preparation for the chapter, read the Institutional Meat Purchase Specifications for Fresh Beef (or other type of meat such as pork) published by the Agricultural Marketing Service (AMS). As you read this chapter, use the AMS publication to verify and expand on the chapter content.

Culinary Terminology Build Vocab

shrinkage, p. 488
connective tissue, p. 488
elastin, p. 488
collagen, p. 488
marbling, p. 489
aging, p. 489
rigor mortis, p. 490
inspection, p. 491
quality grade, p. 492
yield grade, p. 492
primal cuts, p. 492
render, p. 505
offal, p. 505
giblets, p. 506

Academic Terminology Build Vocab

constitute, p. 487
enzyme, p. 489

Objectives

After studying this chapter, you will be able to

- understand the elements that compose meats and how they impact the texture of the meats.

- summarize how aging affects the texture of meat.

- explain the factors to consider when selecting the best cooking method for a cut of meat.

- summarize how meats and poultry are inspected and graded in the United States.

- understand how meat carcasses are cut and identified for foodservice use.

- recognize subprimal cuts of meat and the appropriate cooking methods for each.

- recognize poultry items commonly used in commercial kitchens and the appropriate cooking methods for each.

- summarize what offal is and its common sources.

Meat is traditionally considered the center of the plate, or the focus of the meal. The chef's ability to choose quality meat and poultry is crucial. Equally as important to selecting quality ingredients is the ability to choose the proper method of preparation and cooking for a specific raw product. In this chapter, you will discover how to identify quality meat and poultry and select appropriate cooking methods.

Meat Composition

Cuts of meat and poultry are a combination of muscle, connective tissue, fat, and sometimes bone.

Muscle

Muscle tissue constitutes, or makes up, the most important part of meat. Most meat cuts are skeletal muscle. Skeletal muscle is connected to bone and provides the animal structure and movement. Water is the main ingredient in this muscle tissue, comprising up to 75 percent. The loss of water during the cooking process is called **shrinkage**. Excessive shrinkage can cause a meat or poultry dish to be dry and tough. Protein is the second most abundant element in muscle tissue. Proteins give cooked meats much of their texture, nutrients, and flavor.

The structure of meat is made up of bundles of muscle fibers that contract to create movement. These muscles are made up of long thread-like cells. Groups of muscle cells are held together by connective tissue. **Connective tissue** is protein that bundles muscle tissue together and connects muscle to bones, joints, and skin. These bundles form strands of muscle tissue, which make up a particular muscle. Strands of muscle tissue tend to run in the same direction giving each muscle a *grain*, 30-1. The grain of a muscle is an important consideration when cutting raw meat or carving cooked meat. Cutting perpendicular to the grain shortens the muscle strands and creates a tender finished product.

Connective Tissue

The amount of connective tissue in a particular cut of meat is the most important factor in determining how tough that cut is. Active muscles have the most connective tissue. The age of an animal also influences the tenderness of a meat because older animals have more developed connective tissue than younger animals.

There are two types of connective tissue that are important to chefs—elastin and collagen. **Elastin** is a flexible but tough connective tissue found in ligaments and tendons. It is sometimes referred to as *silver skin*. Elastin should be removed from meat during the cutting and trimming process. Cuts of meat with large amounts of elastin are often tenderized by cutting, cubing, or grinding.

Collagen is the most prevalent connective tissue in meats. When collagen is cooked with moisture, it breaks down into tender, rich gelatin. It does not need to be removed if the proper cooking method is utilized.

Fat

Fat provides moisture, tenderness, and flavor to meats. There are two different types

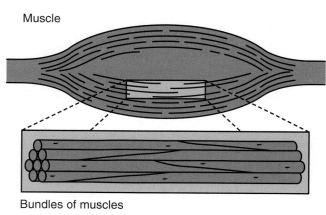

A

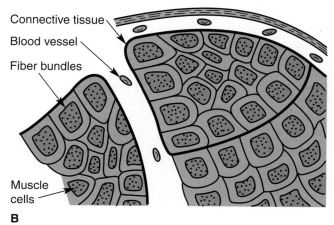

B

30-1 (A) Strands of muscle tissue running in the same direction create the grain of a muscle. (B) Cutting across a muscle perpendicularly reveals the grain.

of fat to be considered when evaluating meat—the fatty tissue that forms around the outside of muscles called *subcutaneous fat*

Hints from the Chef
Tenderizers

The connective tissue in a cut of meat greatly affects its tenderness. Through the years, chefs and butchers have come up with a number of ways to diminish the effects of connective tissue and create a tender finished product. Aside from the cooking process, two strategies are employed on raw meat—mechanical and chemical tenderizers. Mechanical tenderizers act to break connective tissue into small pieces. Chemical tenderizers dissolve the tissue.

Mechanical Tenderizers

Pounding—Cutlets are often pounded with a mallet to not only flatten them for even cooking, but also to break up connective tissue.

Dicing—Tougher meats for stews are cut into small pieces to break up the connective tissue and shorten the cooking time.

Grinding—Tough cuts are often ground and used in meat loaf, patties, or sausage.

Cubing—A cuber is a machine that flattens and cuts small incisions in a piece of meat to tenderize it.

Jaccard—This tenderizing device inserts a series of thin needle-like knives into the meat to sever connective tissue without destroying the shape of a piece of meat. This device is named for its inventor, a Swiss butcher named Jaccard. This process of tenderizing is also known as *pinning* or *needling*.

Chemical Tenderizers

Acidic marinades—Marinating tough cuts of meats in vinegar or citrus juices helps to break down collagen in the cooking process.

Bromelain—An enzyme derived from raw pineapple used to break down connective tissue in meats.

Papain—An enzyme extracted from papaya used to dissolve connective tissue in meats.

and fat that is distributed within the muscle tissue called *intramuscular fat*.

Layers of fat that form around a muscle are often left intact by chefs and butchers. A moderate layer of fat can protect meat from drying out. During roasting and grilling the fat melts, essentially basting the meat as it cooks.

Well-fed animals also develop streaks of fat within a muscle. This intramuscular fat is called **marbling**, 30-2. Marbling is a key factor in meat grading. In general, the more marbling a carcass has, the better its grade. Marbling makes certain cuts more tender, juicy, and flavorful.

Aging

The texture of meat is greatly influenced by aging. **Aging** is the time meat is allowed to rest after slaughter. **Enzymes** are complex proteins produced by living cells that bring about many different reactions in the body. Enzymes in meat cause muscle tissues to relax and even break down connective tissue. Reputable meat processors and purveyors always age meats under the proper temperature conditions to avoid the development of foodborne pathogens.

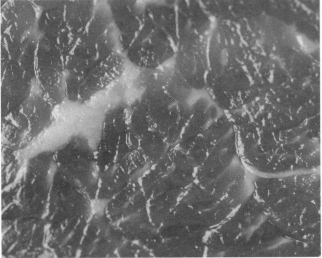

Draz-Koetke/Goodheart-Willcox Publisher

30-2 This marbling results in a more tender, juicy meat product.

Rigor Mortis

Shortly after death, all carcasses pass through a state called *rigor mortis*. **Rigor mortis** is when muscle tissue temporarily becomes extremely hard and stiff. While meat is in this state, it is difficult to cut and extremely tough to eat. As time passes, the muscle tissue begins to relax and becomes usable. The length of time required for a carcass to soften depends on the size of the animal and a number of other factors. The process can take as long as 48 hours. All carcasses must be hung long enough to pass through rigor mortis before being cooked.

Besides aging to eliminate rigor mortis, some meats are aged to improve flavor and tenderness. Beef, lamb, and certain game meats benefit from aging. Pork, veal, and most poultry do not improve from aging and should be used as fresh as possible. Aging for tenderness relies on the natural enzymes in the meat to break down protein and connective tissue.

Dry Aging

The traditional method for aging meat is done by hanging a carcass or large cut of meat in a low humidity refrigerator for as long as six weeks. During this time, the surface of the meat being aged becomes dry or moldy. When ready to use, the surface is trimmed of the unusable parts. The interior muscle is left tender and flavorful.

Wet Aging

The disadvantage of the traditional dry aging method is the amount of loss from trimming and shrinkage. This loss can be as much as 20 percent. A large portion of meat packed today is packaged in vacuum-sealed plastic bags. Aging meat while still in these vacuum bags is known as *wet aging*. Today, most meat is wet aged. This process has none of the loss associated with dry aging and is therefore more cost effective.

Meat and the Cooking Process

Being able to identify various cuts of meat and which part of the animal they come from is important for determining how to prepare and cook them. The most important consideration when trying to match the best cooking method to a cut of meat is the amount of connective tissue the cut contains. Cuts of meat and poultry can be categorized as tough or tender. Tough cuts have more connective tissue than tender cuts. Collagen, the primary connective tissue in meat, is broken down by heat and moisture. Tough cuts are, therefore, best cooked by a moist method to achieve tenderness and the best flavor. Tender cuts, which do not need tenderizing are best cooked by dry methods. The emphasis in cooking tender cuts is not to dry them out.

As mentioned earlier, connective tissue is more abundant and developed in the muscles that are most active. Active muscles

SUSTAINABLE CULINARY

Heritage Livestock

More restaurant menus are including the actual breed of animal in the menu descriptions. For instance, you might find a restaurant featuring Roasted Berkshire Pork Loin. Over the years, the number of breeds used for the commercial production of meat, dairy, poultry, and eggs has decreased dramatically. As a result, there is renewed interest in heritage animal breeds. Heritage breeds are old varieties of animals that have specific genetic traits developed for specific reasons. These unique genetic traits can give the animals different survival skills in different environments, produce unusual appearances, and result in different flavor experiences.

are those that support the animal's weight and are responsible for mobility. Therefore, active muscles are found in the front legs and shoulders of any four-legged animal or the legs and thighs of poultry. It makes sense then that muscles along the backs of four-legged animals and the breasts of farm-raised poultry are less active, contain less connective tissue, and are considered tender.

Cuts of meat from the shoulder section of an animal are best simmered, braised, or stewed. A moist-heat cooking method not only tenderizes these cuts, but also breaks down the collagen to produce gelatin. The gelatin gives these dishes added richness and flavor. Cuts from along the back of an animal such as the pork loin, beef rib or loins, and lamb or veal rack are best when roasted, grilled, or sautéed, 30-3.

Inspection and Grading

The inspection and grading of meat and poultry are two separate functions performed by the United States Department

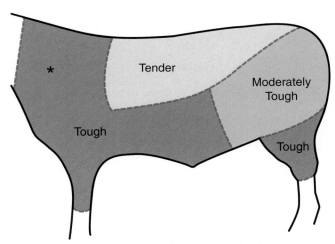

* Some muscles in the shoulder are more tender
30-3 Tough cuts of meat generally come from those muscles which are most active.

of Agriculture (USDA). Inspection is mandatory and grading is voluntary, 30-4.

Inspection

All meat sold in the United States must be inspected. The USDA Food Safety and Inspection Service (FSIS) is responsible for ensuring the safety of much of the meat sold in the United States. It is important to note that **inspection** is strictly an assurance of safety and wholesomeness and not an indication of quality. In states that have their own meat inspection programs, standards must meet or exceed those of the USDA.

USDA inspectors work in meatpacking plants to ensure the safety of meats and poultry. They perform inspections on live animals before slaughter and examine the

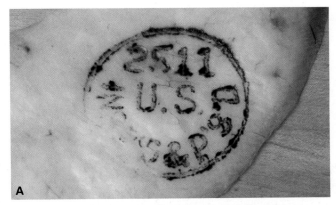

Draz-Koetke/Goodheart-Willcox Publisher

30-4 These stamps indicate the meat has been (A) inspected and (B) graded.

animals' organs after slaughter to ensure that the animals are not ill or diseased. Inspectors also ensure that meat is handled, processed, and stored under sanitary conditions. Any product not meeting the USDA standards is rejected for human consumption.

Grading

The USDA's Agricultural Marketing Service (AMS) grades meats and poultry. There are two types of grades—quality and yield. A meat is assigned a **quality grade** based on an evaluation of traits related to tenderness, juiciness, and flavor. These traits include marbling, maturity, and muscle conformation. For poultry, a quality grade evaluates the bird for normal shape that is fully fleshed and meaty, and free of defects. Each classification of meat and poultry has its own set of quality grades and criteria for grading, 30-5. Grading is voluntary and helps meatpackers market their products. Packers pay the USDA for the service.

Beef and lamb may also undergo another form of grading—the yield grade. **Yield grade** is an evaluation of the amount of lean, closely trimmed boneless cuts a carcass will produce. Yield grades for beef and lamb are rated on a scale of 1 through 5. *Yield grade 1* is leanest, providing the most lean, boneless product. *Yield grade 5* has the most fat and waste.

Foodservice Cuts

After slaughter, meat carcasses are cut into large sections. These major divisions of the carcass are called **primal cuts**. Primal cuts are broken down further into *subprimal cuts*, or foodservice cuts. There are many different ways to cut subprimals depending on their final use. Foodservice operations commonly use similar subprimal cuts and most chefs are familiar with them. Foodservice subprimals are often different from retail cuts sold in supermarkets and butcher shops.

USDA Quality Grades	
Beef	Prime*
	Choice*
	Select*
	Standard
	Commercial
	Utility
	Cutter
	Canner
Veal	Prime
	Choice
	Good
	Standard
	Utility
Lamb	Prime
	Choice
	Good
	Utility
Pork	No. 1
	No. 2
	No. 3
	No. 4
	Utility
Poultry	Grade A
	Grade B
	Grade C
*Grades most commonly used in foodservice	

30-5 These quality grades are listed in descending order.

There are many different ways to cut and trim subprimals and these variations can have a great effect on the quality of the final product and its cost. The USDA and the North American Meat Processors Association (NAMP) established an identification system for meat and poultry products called the *Institutional Meat Purchasing Specifications (IMPS)*. In this system, most variations on cutting and trimming subprimals are specifically described and assigned a number. Chefs and foodservice purchasers typically use this numbering system to specify meat items when ordering from a purveyor. This chapter identifies some of the most popular foodservice cuts of meat and poultry, and their IMPS numbers.

Chef Speak

Butchery Glossary

The following are terms used by chefs, butchers, and meat purveyors:

BRT—Boned, rolled, and tied.

Chain—The side muscle of a tenderloin.

Chine bone—The backbone or vertebrae.

Cryovac®—Vacuum packaging.

French—To clean bone ends of all meat and fat.

Pump—To inject with liquid such as a marinade or brine.

PC—Portion control.

RTC—Ready to cook.

Trimmed—Exterior fat and connective tissue removed.

WOG—Poultry packed without giblets.

Beef

The bovine subfamily of animals includes cattle. The most commonly used cattle for beef production are steers (males castrated at a young age) and heifers (females that have not borne a calf). Primal cuts of beef include the chuck, rib, loin, round, brisket, plate, and flank, 30-6. Common foodservice cuts are created from these primal cuts.

Chuck

The front shoulder of a beef carcass is known as the chuck. It is one of the most active muscles in the animal and therefore

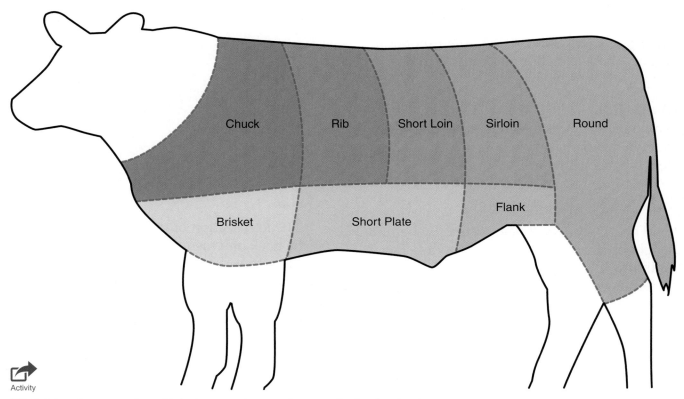

30-6 A beef carcass is cut into large, primary pieces called *primal cuts*.

rather tough. Chuck cuts are often braised, stewed, or utilized for ground beef.

Square Cut Chuck, IMPS# 113   Square cut chuck is an untrimmed, primal cut of the chuck. It is typically braised, stewed, or used for ground beef.

Square Cut Chuck

Shoulder Clod, IMPS# 114   The shoulder clod is a boneless shoulder muscle that is usually braised or roasted.

Chuck Roll, IMPS# 116A   The chuck roll is a boneless cut of the chuck that does not include the arm portion. It is sold rolled and tied. It is typically braised or roasted.

Rib

The rib section of beef is directly behind the chuck. It contains seven rib bones. The main muscle is called the *rib eye*. The rib section is very tender and is utilized for steaks and roasting.

Rib, roast ready, IMPS# 109   Rib roast is trimmed and tied and ready to roast.

Rib, roast ready

Rib Eye, IMPS# 112   The rib eye roast is the boneless version of the rib roast (IMPS# 109).

Rib Steak, boneless, IMPS# 1103A   The rib steak is a portion cut from the rib eye roast. This steak is usually grilled or broiled.

Rib Eye Roll Steak, boneless, IMPS# 1112 The rib eye roll steak is the portion cut from the rib eye roast with the lip portion removed. This cut is grilled or broiled.

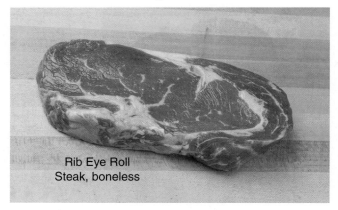

Rib Eye Roll Steak, boneless

Loin

The loin section of the carcass is found on the back between the rib section and the hind leg (round). Like the rib, it is a tender cut and is used for roasts and steaks. The tenderloin runs most of the length of the loin section. Since the loin is a rather long primal cut, it is often separated into two main sections—short loin and sirloin.

Beef Loin Foodservice Cuts

Strip Loin, boneless, IMPS# 180

The strip loin is a boneless cut. When used whole, it is typically roasted. It is more commonly fabricated into steaks.

Tenderloin, peeled, side muscle on (PSMO), IMPS# 189A

Tenderloin PSMO has had the fat layer peeled off. This boneless cut is typically roasted.

Porterhouse Steak, IMPS# 1173

The porterhouse steak, similar to the T-bone steak, contains the strip loin and a section of the tenderloin. It is served grilled or broiled.

Strip Loin Steak, boneless, IMPS# 1180

The strip loin steak is also known as the *New York strip steak*. This cut is commonly grilled or broiled.

Tenderloin Steak, IMPS# 1190

The tenderloin steak is also known as *filet mignon*. It is typically grilled or broiled.

Bottom Sirloin Butt Steak, IMPS# 1185B

The bottom sirloin butt steak is a boneless steak cut from the ball tip. It is served grilled or broiled.

Sirloin Butt Tri-Tip, IMPS# 185D

The sirloin butt tri-tip is a tender, flat muscle that is typically roasted, grilled, or broiled.

Short Loin The short loin is the section of the loin adjacent to the rib. Its two main muscles are the strip loin and the tenderloin. It is one of the most prized cuts of beef.

Sirloin The sirloin is the rear section of the loin, adjacent to the round. The sirloin is often cut into top and bottom sections. Boneless sirloin with the tenderloin is often referred to as *sirloin butt*.

Round

The hind leg of beef is known as the *round*. The texture of the round is a combination of tough and tender cuts. How it is trimmed determines whether it should be cooked by dry or moist methods. However, most round cuts are suitable for roasting.

Round Foodservice Cuts

Round, IMPS# 166B

A trimmed round of beef is suitable for buffet presentation. It is also called *steamship round* or *baron of beef*. This cut is roasted.

Top Round (Inside), IMPS# 169

The top round of beef is also known as the *inside round*. This cut is served roasted.

Top Round Steak, IMPS# 1169

The top round steak is a boneless round steak. It can be served grilled, broiled, panfried, sautéed, or braised.

Bottom Round (Gooseneck), IMPS# 170A

The bottom round is comprised of the bottom (outside) round and the eye of the round. It is often roasted or braised.

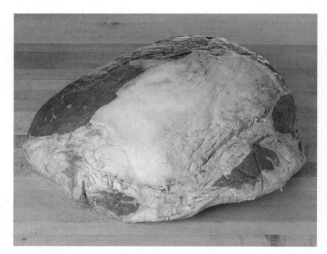

Brisket, Plate, and Flank

The lower portion of the animal is cut into three separate primal cuts. From front to back, they are the brisket, plate, and flank. Compared to other primal cuts, these muscles are smaller and generally flatter. The forward section—the brisket—has a significant amount of connective tissue. Cuts from the flank and plate can be quite tender if properly trimmed and prepared.

Brisket, deckle-off, boneless, IMPS# 120
The brisket is a boneless cut from the breast muscle. It is often simmered or braised.

Brisket, deckle-off

Plate, inside skirt, IMPS# 121D   The plate is a cut from the diaphragm muscle. It is typically grilled or broiled.

Veal

Veal is the term used for immature bovines. Most veal comes from male calves of dairy breeds. Many chefs prefer "special-fed" veal. Special-fed veal has light color and smooth velvety texture. Special-fed veal is produced from animals between 18 and 20 weeks old that are fed milk or a milk-based formula. Primal cuts of veal include the shoulder, rack, loin, leg, and shank/breast, 30-7. Common foodservice cuts are created from these primal cuts.

Shoulder

In veal, the shoulder is the foremost primal cut on the upper part of the carcass.

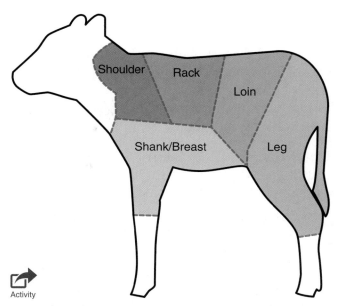

Activity

30-7 A veal carcass is cut into primal cuts from which the subprimal cuts are portioned.

It includes the neck, shoulder muscles, and front part of the rib section. Like the shoulder section of most animals, it contains active muscles and connective tissue. The connective tissue is less developed because veal is a young animal.

Chuck, square cut, boneless, IMPS# 309D
The chuck is the boneless shoulder of the veal without the neck portion. It is often braised or stewed.

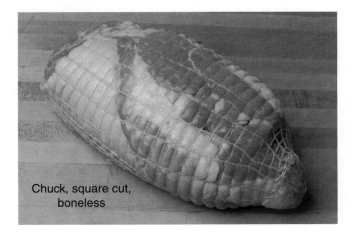

Chuck, square cut, boneless

Shoulder Clod, IMPS# 310B   The shoulder clod is the boneless shoulder that has been rolled and tied. It is served braised or roasted.

Rack

Found directly behind the shoulder, the rack is the center of the rib section. It contains the backbone and seven rib bones. It is very tender and used for roasting and other dry-heat cooking methods.

Hotel Rack, IMPS# 306A A hotel rack is a split veal rack containing the last six ribs. This cut is served as a roast.

Hotel Rack

Rib Chops, IMPS# 1306E Rib chops are cut into individual chops from the rack. The tips of the rib bones are cleaned of skin or meat. Chops can be grilled, broiled, or sautéed.

Rib Chops

Rib Eye, boneless, IMPS# 307 The boneless rib eye is from the rib muscle that has been trimmed of most fat. This cut is typically roasted.

Loin

The loin section is located between the rack and the leg. It contains the backbones and one rib. It is a tender and highly valued cut.

Loin, trimmed, IMPS# 332 The veal loin is split and trimmed of excess fat and flank. This cut is roasted.

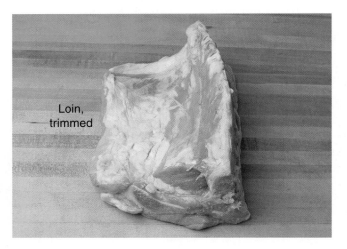

Loin, trimmed

Loin Chops, IMPS# 1332 Loin chops are cut from the split loin with the bone in. They are typically grilled or sautéed.

Strip Loin, boneless, IMPS# 344 The strip loin is the boneless trimmed loin. The strip loin is roasted.

Butt Tenderloin, defatted, IMPS# 346 The butt tenderloin is the widest portion of the tenderloin. It is commonly roasted or broiled.

Leg

In veal, *leg* refers to the rear leg of the animal. It is the largest of the primal cuts of veal and has a wide range of uses.

Leg, IMPS# 334 The leg is the entire cut untrimmed. The leg is served as roast.

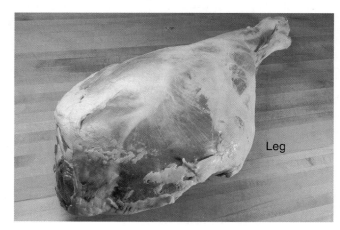

Leg

Leg, shank off, boneless, IMPS# 336 The boneless leg is trimmed and tied. It is typically roasted.

Cutlets, boneless, IMPS# 1336 The cutlets are sliced from the boneless leg. Cutlets are often sautéed.

Hind Shank, IMPS# 337 The hind shank is the portion between the veal's knee and ankle. The shank is frequently braised or simmered.

Top Round, IMPS# 349A The top, or inside, round is trimmed and typically roasted.

Top, Bottom, and Sirloin (TBS), IMPS# 363A The top, bottom, and sirloin cuts are the boneless leg which has been separated into its three largest muscles. These cuts are roasted or prepared as cutlets.

Shank and Breast

The shank and breast cut includes the lower portion of the front leg along with the lower portion of the rib cage. It produces tough cuts that should be braised, stewed, or simmered.

Foreshank, IMPS# 312 The foreshank is the lower portion of the front leg. This cut is best braised or simmered.

Osso Buco, IMPS# 1312 The osso buco is the crosscut sections of the foreshank. Osso buco should be braised or simmered.

Osso Buco

Lamb

Sheep under one year of age are categorized as lamb. The meat of fully mature sheep is called *mutton*. Mutton is darker, fattier, and has stronger flavor than lamb. The use of mutton in the United States is very limited. Primal cuts of lamb include the shoulder, rack, loin, leg, and shank/breast, 30-8. Common foodservice cuts are created from these primal cuts.

Shoulder

The shoulder is the upper, foremost primal cut on the lamb. It includes the neck, shoulder muscles, and front part of the rib section. This cut contains active muscles and connective tissue. However, like veal, lamb is a young animal with less developed connective tissue.

Shoulder, square cut, boneless, IMPS# 208 This cut consists of the entire boneless shoulder that has been rolled and tied. Shoulder is typically braised or roasted.

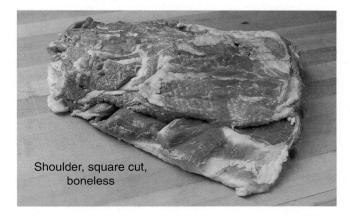

Shoulder, square cut, boneless

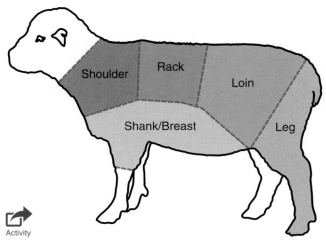

Activity

30-8 A lamb carcass is cut into primal cuts from which the subprimal cuts are portioned.

Shoulder Chops, IMPS# 1207 Shoulder chops are bone-in chops that are cut from the shoulder. The chops can be braised, sautéed, or broiled.

Rack

The rack is the most prized primal cut of lamb. It contains the backbone and eight rib bones. It may be roasted whole or cut into chops to be grilled or sautéed.

Rack, frenched, IMPS# 204C A frenched rack is a rack that has been split, backbone removed, and the ends of the rib bones cleaned. This cut is served roasted.

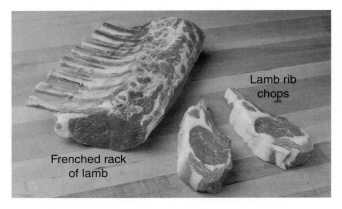
Lamb rib chops
Frenched rack of lamb

Rib Chops, IMPS# 1204D Rib chops are cut from a rack that has had the blade bone

removed. The ends of the rib bones are cleaned. This cut is grilled, broiled, or sautéed.

Loin

The loin is the section of the lamb at the rear part of the back located between the rack and leg. Its meat is found mostly in the two loin muscles on either side of the backbone. It is a tender and expensive cut.

Loin, trimmed, split, IMPS# 232 The loin is a bone-in cut that is typically roasted.

Loin, trimmed, split

Loin Chops, IMPS# 1232 Loin chops are bone-in chops cut from the loin. This cut is grilled, broiled, or sautéed.

Leg

In lamb, as with veal, the leg refers to the rear leg of the animal. Lamb leg is most commonly used for roasting.

Leg, IMPS# 233E The leg cut is the leg that has had the shank, pelvic bones, and sirloin removed. The leg is commonly roasted.

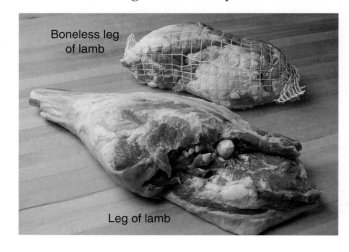
Boneless leg of lamb
Leg of lamb

Leg, boneless, IMPS# 234   This cut is the leg cut with the bones removed, then rolled and tied. Boneless leg is served roasted.

Shank and Breast

The shank and breast are the lower portion of the front and the lower portion of the rib cage. These active muscles contain noticeable amounts of connective tissue and should be braised, stewed, or simmered.

Foreshank, IMPS# 210   The foreshank is the lower portion of the front leg. This cut is typically braised.

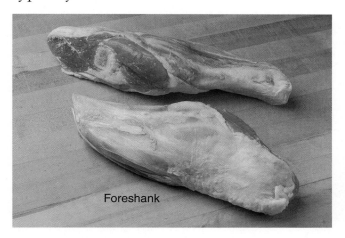

Foreshank

Ribs, IMPS# 209A   This cut is the lower portion of the ribs with breast meat. Also known as *Denver ribs*, this cut is barbecued, grilled, roasted, or braised.

Pork

Pork processed in the United States comes mostly from animals that are 7 to 12 months old. At this age, there is no discernible difference between the meat of male or female pigs. Unlike other meats, pork is often cut and sold with the skin. Primal cuts of pork include the shoulder butt, picnic shoulder, loin, ham, and belly, 30-9. Common foodservice cuts are created from these primal cuts.

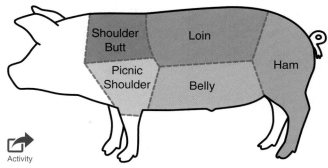

Activity

30-9 A pork carcass is cut into primal cuts from which the subprimal cuts are portioned.

Shoulder Butt

The upper part of the pork shoulder is called the *butt* or *Boston butt*. It contains the bones of the neck and shoulder blade. It contains a good deal of connective tissue and fat.

Boston Butt, bone-in, IMPS# 406   The bone-in Boston butt is an untrimmed primal cut. This cut should be braised or simmered.

Boston Butt, bone-in

Boston Butt, boneless, IMPS# 406A   The boneless Boston butt has had the neck and blade bones removed. It is typically braised, simmered, stewed, or ground.

Boston Butt Steak, IMPS# 1406   The Boston butt steak is a bone-in cut that is usually braised.

Butt, cellar trimmed, IMPS# 407 This cut is boneless butt with the surface fat removed. It is typically braised, simmered, stewed, or ground.

Picnic Shoulder

The picnic section is the lower part of the shoulder. It includes the arm bones. Like the butt, it contains a substantial amount of fat and connective tissue.

Shoulder Hocks, IMPS# 417 The shoulder hocks are the lower portion of the arms above the foot. This cut is braised or simmered.

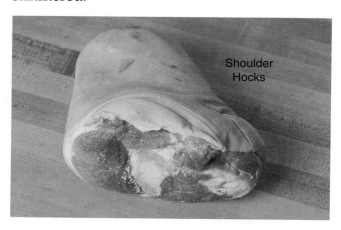

Shoulder Hocks

Belly

The belly is the primal cut that is found directly below the loin. It is a flat, fatty cut. It is best known as the cut used to make bacon.

Pork Belly, IMPS# 408 Pork belly is also known as *fresh bacon*. It can be panfried or simmered.

Pork Belly

Spare Ribs, IMPS# 416 Spare ribs are the ribs from the belly section. They are braised, simmered, roasted, or barbecued.

Spare Ribs, St. Louis style, IMPS# 416A St. Louis-style ribs are spare ribs with the ends and breastbone removed. This cut is braised, simmered, roasted, or barbecued.

Spare Ribs, St. Louis style

Ham

The hind leg of a pig or hog is called the *ham*. It contains large muscles that are moderately tender. The ham can be cooked by either moist- or dry-heat methods.

Fresh Ham, IMPS# 402A Fresh ham is a primal cut that is typically roasted, baked, braised, or simmered.

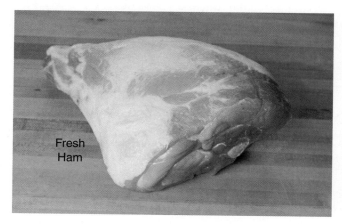

Fresh Ham

Fresh Ham, boneless, IMPS# 402B This cut is the fresh ham that has had the bone removed and is rolled and tied. It is roasted, baked, braised, or simmered.

Loin

The back section of pork is cut as one continuous primal. It is not divided into rib (rack) and loin sections as are beef, veal, and

Pork Loin Foodservice Cuts

Loin, bone-in, IMPS# 410

The bone-in loin is an untrimmed primal cut that is typically roasted.

Loin Chops, center cut, IMPS# 1412

The center cut loin chops are cut from the center cut, bone-in loin roast (IMPS# 412). This cut can be grilled, broiled, baked, or panfried.

Loin Chops, center cut, boneless, IMPS# 1412B

Center cut, boneless loin chops are cut from the boneless loin without the blade or sirloin. This cut can be grilled, broiled, baked, or panfried.

Loin, bone-in, center cut, IMPS# 412

The center cut, bone-in loin has had the blade and sirloin removed. This cut is usually served roasted.

Loin, boneless, roast, IMPS# 413A

The boneless loin roast is a boneless loin that is rolled and tied. This cut is usually roasted.

Loin, Canadian back, IMPS# 414

The Canadian back loin is the center cut boneless loin. This cut is usually roasted.

Tenderloin, IMPS# 415

The tenderloin is trimmed of extra fat. This cut is served roasted, grilled, or sautéed.

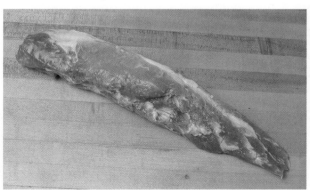

Back Ribs, IMPS# 422

The back ribs are the rib bones from the loin. Back ribs are typically barbecued or grilled.

lamb. The loin contains both the ribs and the backbone, as well as parts of the shoulder blade and pelvis. It is the best primal cut of pork since its main muscles—the loin and tenderloin—are lean and tender.

Poultry

Domesticated birds, especially the chicken, have been a part of man's diet since before recorded history. Poultry enjoys near universal popularity and can be found in just about every cuisine on the globe. Poultry is versatile. It can be prepared using all cooking methods and is compatible with a wide range of ingredients and cooking styles, 30-10.

All poultry used in foodservice are farm-raised birds, including the items referred to as game birds. All birds share the common characteristics of relatively tender breast muscles and tougher legs and thighs.

Chicken

Undeniably the most popular bird world-wide, chicken is relatively inexpensive and

Description of Poultry Classes				
Type of Poultry	**Class**	**Weight Range**	**Description**	**Cooking Methods**
Chicken	Poussin	16–18 oz. (454–510 g)	Very small, immature birds	Grill, broil, roast, sauté
	Cornish game hen	18–24 oz. (510–680 g)	Cornish breed of chicken, small plump bird	Grill, broil, roast, sauté
	Broiler/fryer	1.5–3.5 lb. (680–1590 g)	Most common class size	All
	Roaster	3.5–5 lb. (1.6–2.3 kg)	Larger bird with tender meat	All
	Fowl	3.5–6 lb. (1.6–2.7 kg)	Mature female, flavorful but tough	Simmer, braise
	Capons	5–8 lb. (2.3–3.6 kg)	Castrated male, tender	Roast, poach
Turkey	Hen	8–16 lb. (3.6–7.3 kg)	Young bird with tender flesh	All
	Tom	16 lb. (7.3 kg) or larger	Mature bird, fairly tender	Roast
Duck	Duckling (broiler/fryer)	3–6 lb. (1.4–2.7 kg)	Young tender duck most popular form for foodservice	All
	Roaster	4–7 lb. (1.8–3.2 kg)	Larger bird under 16 weeks old	Roast, braise
	Mature	4–10 lb. (1.8–4.5 kg)	Tough, older bird	Processed foods
Goose	Young	6–10 lb. (2.7–4.5 kg)	Young, tender bird	Roast
	Mature	10–16 lb. (4.5–7.3 kg)	Tougher fleshed bird	Braise or stew

30-10 Classes of poultry vary in size and preferred cooking method.

nutritious. Its mild flavor and low fat content make it a popular choice on all menus.

Broiler/Fryer   Roaster   Capon

Turkey

Turkey is a bird native to North America. Its size makes it suitable for roasting and it is a fixture on holiday menus. Creative chefs can utilize turkey in a variety of menu preparations from BBQ turkey legs to turkey breast scaloppine.

Duck

Both the breast and legs of duck are dark meat. The duck's skin contains a large amount of fat. Cooking methods such as slow roasting help **render**, or extract by melting, most of this fat from the skin. Duck traditionally has a lower proportion of meat per bird than other forms of poultry. Recently, duck has gained in popularity due to advances

Duck   Goose   Turkey

in breeding. Today, ducks are raised to have greater amounts of breast meat.

Goose

Goose shares several similarities with duck. Both birds are waterfowl, yield only dark meat, and have thick fatty skin. Goose is larger than duck. Goose is popular in the cuisines of northern Europe but is less popular in the United States than duck. Goose is a large bird and often the centerpiece of holiday meals.

Game Birds

Many poultry varieties in this category are hunted in the wild. Game birds used in foodservice, however, are domesticated farm-raised birds. These items add an exotic touch

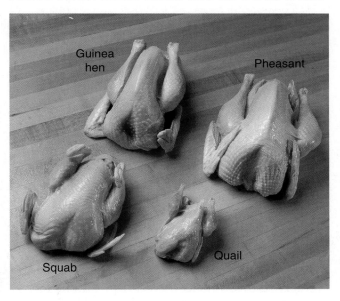

Guinea hen   Pheasant   Squab   Quail

to menus, 30-11. All have a stronger, richer flavor than chicken.

Offal Meats

Offal, also called *variety meat*, is the term given to the internal organs and extremities that are removed before an animal or bird is butchered. Many people consider these items to be inferior to muscle tissue, which constitutes the majority of meat items. However,

Varieties of Game Birds			
Variety	Weight Range	Description	Cooking Methods
Guinea	12–24 oz. (340–680 g)	African bird related to pheasant, lean meat, both dark and light meat	All
Squab	Under 1 lb. (454 g)	Young pigeon, rich flavored, all dark meat	Roast, grill, sauté
Pigeon	1–2 lb. (454–908 g)	Mature bird with stronger flavor, all dark meat	All
Partridge	12–24 oz. (340–680 g)	Bird of European and Asian origin with light and dark meat, mild flavor	All
Pheasant	1.75–4 lb. (0.8–1.8 kg)	A long-tailed game bird originally from Asia, lean with delicate breast meat and darker, sinewy legs	All
Quail	3–7 oz. (85–200 g)	A very small migratory bird originally from Europe, delicate flesh, usually served in pairs	Roast, grill, sauté

30-11 A variety of game birds are used in foodservice.

as with any food product the key to a delicious dish is proper preparation. These items represent a challenge of skill and creativity to chefs. In many cases, these secondary products have become true delicacies, 30-12.

The offal meats that are commonly obtained from poultry are called **giblets**. Dressed birds are often sold with the giblets packed in the cavity. Giblets consist of four items—the neck, gizzard, heart, and liver. Necks are often used for poultry stock. The other organs should be cooked separately from the bird itself because they have a stronger flavor.

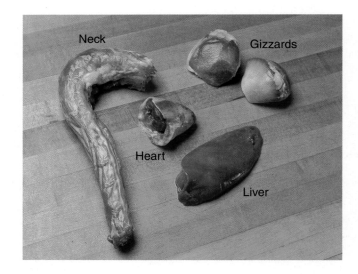

Common Offal Meats		
Item	**Sources**	**Preparation**
Brains	Beef, veal	Sauté
Ears	Pork	Simmer, fry
Feet (trotters)	Pork	Simmer, braise
	Veal	Used to add gelatin to stocks, sauces, and meat dishes
Gizzards	Poultry	Simmer, stew
Hearts	Beef	Simmer, braise
	Chicken	Simmer, stew
Intestines	Beef, pork, lamb	Used for sausage casings
	Pork chitterlings	Stew, fry
Kidneys	Beef, veal, lamb	Stew, sauté
Liver	Beef, veal	Sauté, grill
	Pork	Ground (for sausages and pâtés)
Marrow	Beef	Garnish for sauces, main courses, and vegetables
Stomach	Beef (tripe)	Simmer, stew
Sweet breads (thymus gland and pancreas)	Veal, lamb	Simmer, braise, sauté
Tails	Beef (oxtail), pork	Simmer, braise, stew

30-12 Chefs prepare offal meats that come from a variety of sources.

Summary Points

- Meat is composed of muscle, bone, fat, and connective tissue. Muscle tissue contains a high percentage of water.

- Aging gives muscle tissue time to relax and some connective tissue may break down during this time.

- Tougher cuts with a great deal of connective tissue are best cooked by moist-heat cooking methods. Tender cuts with little connective tissue are best cooked by dry-heat cooking methods.

- All meat sold in the United States must be inspected in compliance with USDA standards. Grading meat is a measure of its quality characteristics and is voluntary.

- Meat carcasses are broken down into standard primal cuts. For standardization, an IMPS number is used to identify subprimal cuts in detail.

- Poultry is classified by type of bird, its size, and the age of the bird. Younger and smaller birds are best prepared by dry cooking methods. Older larger birds are best prepared by moist methods.

- Offal meats are organs and extremities of meat and poultry that can be utilized in a variety of preparations.

In Review
Assess

1. Water can comprise up to _____ percent of muscle tissue.
   A. 25
   B. 33
   C. 50
   D. 75

2. The amount of _____ _____ is the most important factor in determining the toughness of a cut of meat.

3. True or false. The layer of fat that forms around the outside of a muscle is called marbling.

4. How do enzymes impact the aging of meat?

5. List three types of meats that improve in flavor and tenderness by aging.

6. In four-legged animals, where are the most active muscles typically located? in poultry?

7. What is the purpose of the USDA meat inspection?

8. Contrast a *quality grade* with a *yield grade*.

9. True or false. Meat carcasses are cut into large sections called subprimal cuts.

10. List the top three grades for the following:
    A. beef
    B. pork
    C. poultry

11. List the primal cuts of veal.

12. Arrange the following poultry in order from smallest to largest: tom turkey, poussin, roaster chicken, quail.

13. What does *render* mean?

14. List the four items that make up the giblets of a bird.

Core Skills

15. **Math.** You are planning a menu that serves a four-ounce cooked portion of beef roast. From past experience, you know that this roast has 20 percent loss from shrinkage when cooked properly. How many four ounce cooked portions will you get from a raw, 12-pound, boneless, trimmed roast?

16. **Reading.** Read the book *The Jungle* by Upton Sinclair. When was it written? What was its subject matter? What changes did it effect? How do these changes influence foodservice today? Write a short book report.

17. **Writing.** Create a T-chart on a sheet of paper. At the top of the left column write *Types of Meat* and at the top of the right column write *Preferred Cooking Methods*. Then list the types of meat and two subprimal cuts for each in the left column. Identify the preferred cooking methods (moist heat or dry heat) in the right column for each subprimal cut. When finished, do the same for *Types of Poultry* and *Preferred Cooking Methods*.

18. **Writing.** Choose a primal cut of beef, pork, or lamb. Use reliable Internet and print resources to research the bone shapes for the primal cut. Then create a chart and sketch the bone shapes in that primal and label the bones/shapes. Write a summary about how knowing the various bone shapes can help you as a chef.

19. **Math.** Suppose a butcher breaks down a 78 lb., 2 oz. beef round into the following:
    - 19 lb., 3 oz. top round
    - 26 lb., 8 oz. bottom round
    - 6 lb. 6 oz. eye of round
    - 9 lb., 12 oz. knuckle
    - 2 lb., 2 oz usable trim
    - 10 lb., 5 oz. bone
    - 3 lb., 14 oz. fat

    What are the percentages of the primal round for each of the following: top round, bottom round, eye round, knuckle, trim, bone, and fat? Create a chart or use spreadsheet software to show your work. Label the columns: Product, lbs., oz., Total oz., and % Primal. (Hint: to calculate percentage, divide the part by the whole and multiply by 100). Write the column totals at the bottom of the chart.

20. **CTE Career Readiness Practice.** Use reliable print or online resources to investigate the uses for offal products in various international cuisines. In addition, identify cultural and economic factors that influence the use of offal products. How is offal used in the United States by comparison? Discuss your findings.

Critical Thinking

21. **Draw conclusions.** Use both a chemistry textbook and a biology textbook to investigate the definitions of *Fat* (Fatty Acid, Triglyceride) and *Muscle* (protein, skeletal muscle). Write the definitions on a sheet of paper. Draw conclusions about how these definitions help you, as a chef, understand the nature of meats

22. **Differentiate.** Chefs have the option of buying meat as primal cuts or as portion control products. For example, chefs have the option of buying a rough beef rib or portioned rib eye steaks. Differentiate between the advantages and disadvantages of each.

23. **Identify evidence.** What evidence can you identify about how the different sizes of poultry items affect the portion size, tenderness, and cost of a finished dish? Give examples to support your evidence.

24. **Analyze.** Presume you have recently started using a new meat supplier. You are having some problems getting the exact cuts of meat that you need for your operation. Analyze possible reasons for this problem and identify one or more ways to solve it. Discuss your solutions.

Technology

Choose a particular primal or subprimal cut. Watch an Internet video that demonstrates how to fabricate that cut. How was the demonstration similar or different from what you learned about that cut in this chapter? For further reading on this topic, check out the *Bovine Myology & Muscle Profiling* link on the University of Nebraska, Lincoln website.

Teamwork

Working in a small group, choose four different foodservice meat cuts. Create one lunch and one dinner menu item using each of the four cuts. Include portion size, cooking method, ingredients in each dish, and garnish. Present your menu items to the class.

Chef's E-portfolio
What the Bones Tell You

Upload your summary and images from activity #18 to your e-portfolio. Ask your instructor where to save your file. This could be on the school's network or a flash drive of your own. Name your portfolio document *FirstnameLastname_Portfolio Ch#.docx* (i.e., JohnSmith_PortfolioCh30.docx).

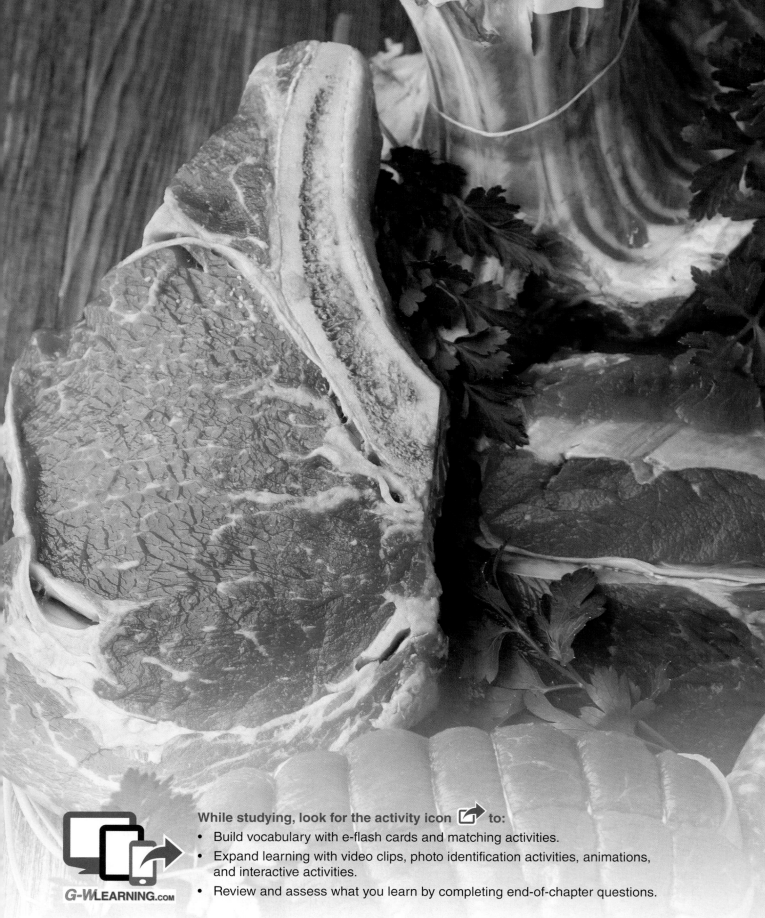

While studying, look for the activity icon to:
- Build vocabulary with e-flash cards and matching activities.
- Expand learning with video clips, photo identification activities, animations, and interactive activities.
- Review and assess what you learn by completing end-of-chapter questions.

margouillat photo/Shutterstock.com

Basic Meat and Poultry Preparation

31

Reading Prep

Imagine you are an executive chef of a large restaurant kitchen. As you read the chapter, think about what you would like your employees to know. When you finish reading, write an in-service for your employees and include key information from the chapter.

Culinary Terminology
Build Vocab

fabrication, p. 512
airline breast, p. 512
trussing, p. 517
steak, p. 517
chop, p. 517
cutlet, p. 518
barding, p. 518

Academic Terminology
Build Vocab

alternative, p. 519

Objectives

After studying this chapter, you will be able to

- recall proper handling and storage methods for meat and poultry.
- execute poultry fabrication techniques.
- recognize common portions into which meats are cut.
- summarize the importance of uniform portioning.

Years ago, most hotels, clubs, and large restaurants had butchers on staff to cut all the meat items used in the operation. Today, butchery is a dying art. Fewer and fewer culinarians are able to cut an entire animal carcass into the many cuts that are used in the professional kitchen. While a full knowledge of meat cutting is not necessary for most chefs, they still need to master some basic skills. Performing some basic meat and poultry cutting tasks allows chefs to control the quality of their raw ingredients and to customize certain cuts.

Handling and Storing Meat and Poultry

Meats and poultry have two qualities, which make proper handling and storage important—both are expensive and highly perishable.

Fresh meat and poultry should be stored in the coldest part of the refrigerator at 30°F to 35°F (−1°C to 2°C). Many operations have a separate refrigerator designated for storing only meat and poultry.

Film-wrapped, vacuum-packed meats have a refrigerated shelf life of several weeks in their sealed bags. These items should be left in their packages until ready for use. Other meats and poultry items should be stored wrapped to prevent them from drying out.

A conscious effort must be made to prevent cross-contamination when handling and storing meats and poultry. Following a few simple procedures helps keep all foods safe in storage.

- Store meats and poultry on a tray or sheet pan to prevent them from dripping onto other items.
- Never store raw meat or poultry above cooked or ready-to-eat foods in the refrigerator.
- Sanitize all food-contact surfaces when storing meats and poultry including pans, utensils, and refrigerators.

Poultry Fabrication

Chefs routinely cut whole raw chickens or other poultry into serving portions. This, or any other meat or poultry cutting, is called **fabrication**. When working with poultry,

those portions may be halves, quarters, or "eight-cut"—also called *disjointed*. Eight-cut poultry yields two wings, two thighs, two breasts, and two legs, 31-1.

A chef's knife should be used when cutting bone-in poultry. The heavier blade is necessary for cutting thin bones and joints.

Boneless Breasts

Boneless chicken breasts are perhaps the most popular cut of poultry. Once you are proficient, or skilled, at removing the breasts of a chicken, it is easy to prepare any other bird using the same technique. In fine dining, it is often common to present each lobe of the breast with the first joint of the wing still attached. This fabrication is commonly called an **airline breast**.

Draz-Koetke/Goodheart-Willcox Publisher

31-1 The eight-cut chicken yields fabrications that are easily prepared using most cooking methods.

CHEF'S ETHICS
How Animals Are Raised

Increasingly, chefs and consumers are asking how the animals they are preparing and eating were raised. These questions result from reports of some animals being raised in conditions in which they are deprived of space, given antibiotics when not sick, administered growth hormones, and generally mistreated. More chefs are becoming concerned about the conditions in which livestock are raised and advancing the cause for humane and ethical stewardship. Issues such as access to proper food common to the animal's digestive system, antibiotic use only when an animal is sick, banning of growth hormones, and sufficient space for healthy activity are being promoted. Additionally, animals that have been raised in healthy environments produce a better product and taste better.

To fabricate airline breasts, you should use the boning knife. Its thin blade makes separating the meat and bone easier and more accurate. The process yields two airline breast halves, two legs, and a meatless carcass that can be used for stock, 31-2.

Draz-Koetke/Goodheart-Willcox Publisher

31-2 This bird has been fabricated to yield airline breasts.

TECHNIQUE
Fabricating Poultry
Splitting Poultry in Half

Fabricating poultry begins with cutting the bird in half.

1. Place the bird on the cutting board with the back toward you and the tail up. Hold the bird by the tail. Place the tip of the knife slightly to the outside of the tail and slice downward. Cut through the thigh, then the rib bones, and then through the wing until the knife exits near the bird's neck.

2. Spread the bird open and split it in half by cutting through the center of the breast.

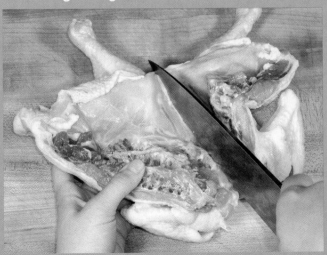

(Continued)

TECHNIQUE
Fabricating Poultry (Continued)

3. Create two equal-sized portions by removing the backbone from the half to which it is still attached. This can be done either by holding the bird by the neck with the backbone vertical, or by placing the bird flat on the cutting board. Cut through the ribs and hip bone just off the center of the spine as in step 1.

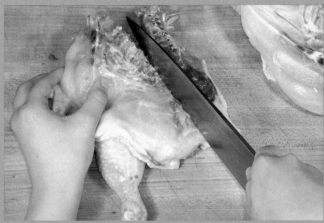

Quartering Poultry

Once the bird is in halves, it can be cut into quarters.

1. Find the natural separation between the breast and thigh. The separation runs diagonally to the line of the backbone.
2. Cut through the skin to separate the half into two quarters—one consisting of breast and wing and the other, leg and thigh.

Preparing Eight-Cut Poultry

The quarters are further fabricated to disjoint or eight-cut the bird as follows:

1. Locate the knee joint on a leg and thigh quarter. It can be found just below the streak of fat that is visible near the knee on the inside of the leg.
2. Slice through the joint connecting the thigh and drumstick. If you encounter much resistance, reposition the knife slightly to find the joint.

3. On the breast and wing quarter, separate the breast and wing by slicing through the joint at the base of the wing.

TECHNIQUE
Preparing Airline Breasts

1. Place a whole bird, breast side up on the cutting board. Cut the skin between the thigh and breast.

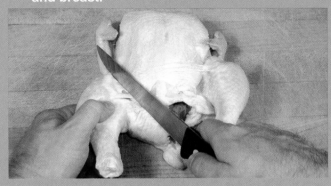

2. Pull the leg and thigh down toward the backbone until the thigh bone pops out of the hip socket.

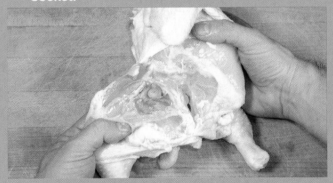

3. Cut through the meat of the thigh close to the backbone to remove the leg and thigh from the carcass.

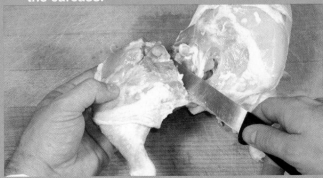

4. Turn the carcass 180° and repeat steps 1 through 3 on the opposite leg.

5. Locate the keel bone, which separates the breast into two halves. It protrudes above the breast meat near the cavity. Slice through the skin over the keel bone. Make shallow cuts with the tip of the boning knife on one side of the keel bone, separating the breast meat from the keel bone.

6. Continue making short shallow cuts and scraping the breast meat away from the ribs, working toward the wing joint.

7. At this point, the breast should be attached to the carcass by only the wing joint. From the underside of the breast, cut the tendons of the joint where the wing is attached to the carcass. This releases the breast and wing together.

8. Sever the wing at the "elbow" or first joint below the breast to make an airline breast.

9. Turn the carcass 180° and repeat steps 4–7 on the other half of the breast.

TECHNIQUE
Trussing Poultry

1. Cut a piece of butcher's twine about 2 feet (60 cm) long. At the midpoint of the string, tie it around the tail.

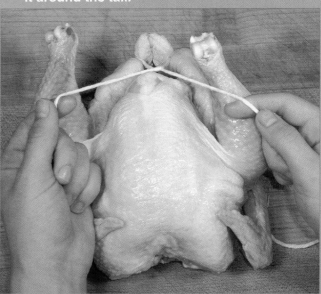

2. Bring the ends of the string over the drumsticks and tie a simple overhand knot. Draw the knot closed pulling the ends of the drumsticks tight to the tail.

3. Lay the ends of the strings along the crease between the breast and legs, and over the wings to hold them close to the breast.

4. Turn the bird over and draw the strings tight over the wing joint and tie them together between the neck and the neck cavity. The bird should be tied tightly as it will shrink during cooking.

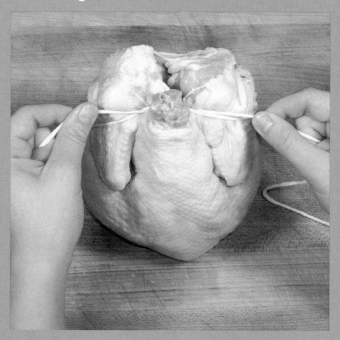

Trussing Birds

Birds that are to be roasted whole are often tied or trussed. **Trussing** is tying a bird in order to give the cooked product a pleasing appearance and to ensure even cooking, 31-3. There are many ways to truss birds. Some methods even employ needles to sew the bird to create the desired form. The technique described in this chapter is one of the easiest to master.

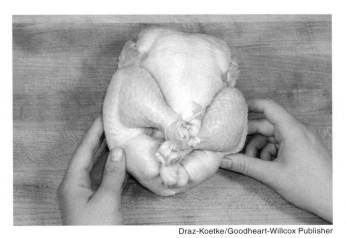

Draz-Koetke/Goodheart-Willcox Publisher

31-3 A trussed bird will cook more evenly.

Meat Fabrication

A **steak** is a portion-sized piece of meat that is cut from a larger muscle or group of muscles. A steak may or may not have a bone; however, a **chop** is a steak that always contains a bone. When cutting steaks or chops, it is important to determine what the grain of the meat is. The grain is the direction that the muscle fibers run. Steaks should always be cut across the grain of the meat. This ensures that the muscle fibers will be short, which makes the steak tender. The knife used to cut steaks or chops should be longer than the width of the muscle being cut. Many chefs use a scimitar or chef's knife for this task, 31-4.

Draz-Koetke/Goodheart-Willcox Publisher

31-4 Steaks must be cut across the grain of the muscle.

A **cutlet** is a thin, boneless steak. Cutlets are prepared by cutting thin slices of a boneless muscle. They are often pounded to an even thickness with a meat mallet. Pounding tenderizes the meat and creates an even, thin product that cooks quickly, 31-5.

Tough cuts of meat may be pounded with a textured mallet to further tenderize them. To avoid tearing more delicately textured meats, they are often placed between sheets of plastic wrap or waxed paper before pounding. Cutlets are most commonly sautéed or breaded and panfried.

Tying Roasts

Just as birds are trussed to retain their shape when roasted, large pieces of meat are tied for uniform shape and even cooking. Large cuts of meat to be roasted are often tied with butcher's twine so they have a rounder shape and cook more evenly. Occasionally, roasts are tied in order to hold in a stuffing.

An alternative to tying a roast is an elastic net. Many meat processors place roasts in a special ovenproof net instead of tying them. The net saves time and effort for the butcher.

Draz-Koetke/Goodheart-Willcox Publisher

31-5 Cutlets are ideal for sautéing and panfrying because they are thin.

One reason for tying a large cut to be roasted is to bard it, 31-6. **Barding** is the process of covering an item with a thin sheet of fat. A thin layer of fat placed on a lean piece of meat keeps it moist during the cooking process. The fat insulates the meat somewhat. As the item cooks, the fat melts and bastes the meat.

Portioning

It is important to maintain uniform portion sizes when cutting meat or poultry in a commercial kitchen. Uniformity in portions is not measured by appearance, but rather by weight. The portion scale is the most important tool in this process. It is essential to weigh every portion cut. For most chefs, a variance in portion size of more than

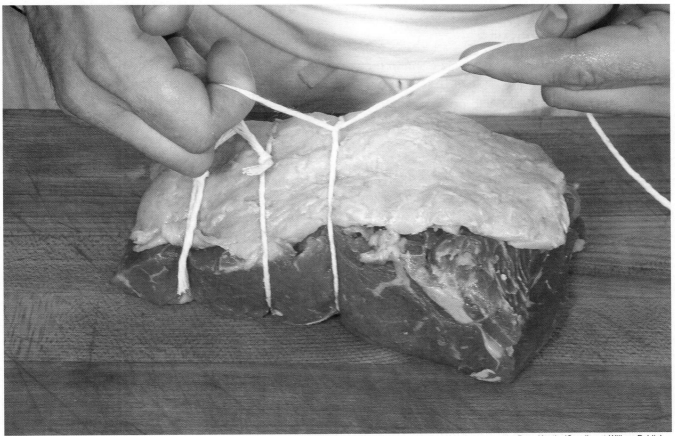

Draz-Koetke/Goodheart-Willcox Publisher

31-6 The layer of fat being tied onto this roast will melt and baste the meat as it cooks.

one ounce (28 g) is unacceptable. Weighing ensures that each diner receives an equal portion each and every time.

Along with customer satisfaction, maintaining consistency in product cost is essential to profitability. Since meat and poultry are some of the most expensive items in the kitchen, even small inconsistencies in portion size can add up to a large amount of money.

Many kitchens deal with the challenge of portioning by buying portion-cut meats and poultry. These portion-controlled products are often vacuum-packed in individual portions. This packaging extends the shelf life of fresh meats considerably. Portion-controlled meats provide a consistent product cost, eliminate in-house labor, and reduce waste. However, they are significantly more expensive. A chef must carefully calculate whether purchasing portion-controlled meats or cutting meats in house is the best **alternative**, or option, for his or her operation.

Summary Points

- A limited amount of butchery is done in most professional kitchens.
- Chefs should know how to portion poultry into halves, quarters, eight-cut, and boneless breasts.
- Whole birds are often trussed to give them a uniform shape and promote even cooking.
- Steaks, chops, and cutlets are portion-sized pieces of meat cut from a larger muscle or group of muscles.
- Uniform meat and poultry portions are achieved by weighing every portion.

In Review
Assess

1. True or false. It is unnecessary for chefs to master basic meat-cutting skills.
2. List three actions that can be taken to prevent cross-contamination during storage of meats and poultry.
3. List the eight pieces of an "eight-cut" chicken.
4. True or false. Airline breasts are a common way to present chicken in fine-dining restaurants.
5. Birds that are to be roasted whole are often tied or _____.
6. True or false. Steaks and chops that are cut across the grain will be tough.
7. Contrast a chop with a cutlet.
8. Why are cutlets pounded with a mallet?
9. What is barding and why is it important?
10. What is the most important tool in portion control?

Core Skills

11. **Math.** Visit the supermarket and record the price for an average-size, whole chicken. Next, find a package of chicken breasts and note the package price and the number of breasts in the package. Do the same for each of the following cuts: wings, thighs, and legs. Calculate the average cost to purchase each cut (breast, wing, thigh, leg) already fabricated. Estimate the cost of a "whole" chicken purchased precut by adding the cost of two breasts, two wings, two thighs, and two legs. Compare the cost of a whole chicken to the equivalent amount of chicken purchased precut. Which is the better price? Show your work.

12. **Reading.** Research the trend of "Nose to Tail" dining and restaurants. Read a cookbook, blog, or article about a chef who runs a "Nose to Tail" restaurant. Report to the class and explain this trend. Discuss the importance of this trend and the butchery skills chefs need to follow the trend.

13. **Speaking.** Divide a group of four classmates into teams of two. Assign a position to each team to be either pro or con the following statement: "It is advantageous for a food-service operation to use in-house butchery." Formulate arguments to support your position. Present your case to the class in a two minute presentation.

14. **Math.** An inaccurate portion scale in the butchery of a commercial kitchen is resulting in strip steaks that weigh 0.6 oz. more than specified. The butchery portions 220 strip steaks over the course of a week. If strip loins cost $7.84 per lb., calculate the cost of this weighing error for the week.

15. **CTE Career Readiness Practice.** The executive chef for the restaurant at which you are a butcher informed you that she needs 350 airline breasts of chicken for a banquet at the end of the week. Since you have several new staff members, you decide to demonstrate the procedure (page 515) for preparing airline breasts for your staff. As you prepare your demonstration, think about the following:

- ways to save time in fabricating airline breasts
- ways to utilize other parts of the chicken carcass for restaurant use
- reminders of how to keep poultry safe during fabrication

Critical Thinking

16. **Critique Outcomes.** Obtain a boneless pork loin roast. Cut as many 5-ounce boneless, center cut loin chops as you can from the roast. Weigh each chop and record. How many chops weighed 5 ounces? How many more fell in the range of one ounce greater or less than 5 ounces? As a customer, would these be acceptable to you if they were served to you? How many more chops were either less than 4 ounces or greater than 6 ounces? Would this be acceptable to the chef? Write a summary.

17. **Create.** Visit a butcher or conduct online research to find out what equipment is needed to equip a butcher station. Then create a layout diagram and equipment list for a butcher station for a hotel that wants to fabricate some or all of its meat and poultry.

Technology

Use Internet resources to research automated meat and poultry portioning technology used in the meat and poultry processing industry. What role do lasers and high-pressure water jets play in this technology? What products are most commonly portioned using automated technology? Predict whether these technologies will ever be found in a commercial kitchen. Explain your rationale to the class.

Teamwork

With a partner, create a rubric of evaluation criteria for the flavor, texture, and moisture of roast beef. Then, prepare two small roasts from the same piece of beef top or bottom round. Bard and tie one roast with a layer of fat as shown in 31-6. Season and roast both pieces in the same manner. After cooking, untie the barded roast. Slice and serve both products in a blind tasting to your classmates and have them evaluate the flavor, texture, and moisture of both roasts. Analyze the results of the blind tasting. Based on the results, is the technique of barding a beef roast worthwhile?

Chef's E-portfolio
Eight-Cut Poultry

Fabricate a whole chicken into eight-cut. Document your process by video or taking digital photos at various stages of completion. Upload your images to your e-portfolio. Ask your instructor where to save your file. This could be on the school's network or a flash drive of your own. Name your portfolio document *FirstnameLastname_Portfolio Ch#.docx* (i.e., JohnSmith_PortfolioCh31.docx).

Video Clip

Poultry Splitting, Quartering, and Eight-Cut

Visit the G-W Learning Companion Website and view the bonus video clip "Poultry splitting, quartering, and eight-cut." After viewing the clip, answer the following questions:

1. Why is the chef's knife preferred for cutting bone-in poultry?

2. The natural separation between the breast and thigh runs _____ to the line of the backbone.

3. True or false. You should encounter significant resistance when cutting the joint connecting the thigh and drumstick.

Video

While studying, look for the activity icon → to:
- Build vocabulary with e-flash cards and matching activities.
- Expand learning with video clips, photo identification activities, animations, and interactive activities.
- Review and assess what you learn by completing end-of-chapter questions.

Neveshkin Nikolay/Shutterstock.com

Dry-Heat Cooking Methods for Meat and Poultry

32

Reading Prep

In preparation for reading the chapter, review a variety of restaurant menus for meat and poultry entrées. Read the descriptions of the entrées to determine the type of cooking methods used. Compare your findings to the chapter as you read.

Culinary Terminology
Build Vocab

searing, p. 523
dredging, p. 523
carryover cooking, p. 528
jus, p. 529
gravy, p. 529

Academic Terminology
Build Vocab

compensate, p. 529

Objectives

After studying this chapter, you will be able to

- execute proper sauté method and pan sauce preparation.
- summarize how meats and poultry are grilled and broiled to desired doneness.
- compare the two approaches used for roasting meats and poultry.

All the cooking methods in this chapter are considered dry-heat cooking methods. Even though some of these methods use hot fat, hot air or radiant heat waves actually cook the food product. These methods use no moisture. Dry-heat cooking methods should only be used for cuts of meat that do not require moisture and long cooking times to make them tender.

All these methods, if properly carried out, sear the product. **Searing** is the process of browning meat to form an even crust, which produces an appealing brown color and a richer flavor.

Sautéing

Sautéing meat is a quick cooking process done over high heat. Only enough fat to coat the bottom of the pan is used. The pan and the fat are preheated before the meat or poultry is added. A properly sautéed item is evenly seared.

To make the searing process easier, some items are dusted with a light coating of flour before being sautéed. The process of coating foods with flour is often referred to as **dredging**. To dredge, the food is dragged through a pan of flour, 32-1. Any excess flour should be shaken from the product. The flour used for dredging is often mixed with seasoning such as salt and pepper. In this way, the product is both coated and seasoned in one step. White meats such as poultry and veal should be dredged to help properly brown them. Red meats such as beef and lamb are seared without being dredged.

Draz-Koetke/Goodheart-Willcox Publisher

32-1 After dredging, shake meat to remove excess flour.

Fats for Sautéing

When sautéing meats or poultry, the choice of fat makes a difference. Choose a fat that does not smoke or burn at the high temperatures needed to properly sear. Clarified butter is the classic choice. Most liquid oils such as vegetable oil or olive oil also do well. Whole butter, although it is excellent for sautéing vegetables, burns at the high temperatures used to sauté meat items.

Keys to Proper Searing

The process of searing a piece of meat or poultry sounds simple, yet it is one of the hardest tasks for inexperienced cooks. Often, sautéed items end up pale, dry, and chewy.

When searing meat or poultry, it is critical that the pan and fat are preheated before any product is added. The key is to get the fat as hot as possible without burning it. Many chefs preheat the pan until the fat begins to emit the first signs of smoke. Others place a tiny drop of liquid in the fat. If the liquid splatters, then the cooking surface is sufficiently heated. Whichever method is used, close attention should be paid so that the product can be added as soon as the fat has reached its peak temperature.

The number one reason that meats or poultry do not sear properly is overloading the sauté pan. When too much product is placed into a preheated pan, the pan cools quickly and does not recover fast enough to brown the product. Instead, the moderate heat causes the meat juices to come out of the item and the product simmers in its own juices. When sautéing, never add more than a single layer of product to the pan. If a large amount of product needs to be sautéed, cook multiple smaller batches.

Pan Sauces

Many average cooks do not realize what all chefs know well—the drippings left in a sauté pan after cooking meat or poultry are the essence of an excellent sauce. They may look like crusty browned bits, but drippings are flavorful concentrated meat juices. Traditionally, sauces for sautéed meat and poultry items are created from these drippings.

To create a sauce from the pan drippings of a sautéed item, remove the sautéed meat from the pan and then add liquid. The liquid is brought to a simmer to dissolve the drippings in a process called *deglazing*. The liquid used for deglazing may be water, stock, wine or a sauce. The deglazing liquid may be reduced, mixed with a sauce, or thickened to create a sauce.

Be sure to remove the meat from the pan before deglazing. The boiling needed for deglazing has a negative effect on the meat. If left in the pan and boiled, the meat's crust dissolves and the meat loses its juices. If boiled long enough, the meat may become tough.

Grilling and Broiling

Grilling and broiling share many similarities with sautéing. All three methods use intense heat to sear a piece of meat and seal in its juices.

In broiling, the heat source is located above the meat. For grilling, the searing is done with radiant heat located below the product. In both methods, the food is cooked on a grill or rack, so that excess fat drips away from the meat. On the grill, these drippings create smoke that adds flavor during the cooking process. Since drippings are lost in both grilling and broiling, they cannot be used to create a sauce. Sauces for grilled or broiled items are often flavored butters, butter sauces, tomato sauces, hollandaise derivatives, or others that do not require pan drippings.

The intense heat of the grill or broiler sears the surface of the meat or poultry being cooked. For this reason, it is important that the grill or broiler be preheated. A cool grill or broiler causes the meat to stick or tear. To know whether a grill is hot enough to cook on, test by holding your hand a few inches over the grill. If you can keep it there for more than four or five seconds, the grill is not hot enough for searing.

Another key to good grilling or broiling is a clean cooking surface. Most kitchens keep a wire brush near the grill to scrub off burnt food residue. A clean grill is essential for keeping foods from sticking. For added assurance, some cooks also like to brush some oil on the grill rods.

Once the grill or broiler is ready, the meat or poultry to be grilled should be brushed with a light coating of oil or clarified butter. Season the product with a sprinkling of salt and pepper.

The product is now ready to be placed on the grill. Allow some time for the meat to become seared. Trying to move it too soon may cause it to stick or tear. When handling meats on the grill, use tongs that will not pierce or tear the seared surface of the meat causing the loss of juices.

Cross markings are a traditional sign of properly grilled meat. Once the meat starts to sear, rotate it 90 degrees so that the grill rods create cross markings. When the first side is fully seared, turn the piece of meat or poultry and repeat the searing and cross marking process on the second side. When grilling or broiling thick pieces or those that need to be cooked well done, the intense heat used to

TECHNIQUE
Sautéing Meats and Poultry

1. Use only tender cuts of meat in small or thin pieces such as dice, cutlets, or medallions.
2. Use only enough fat to coat the bottom of the pan.
3. Preheat the fat and pan as hot as possible without burning the fat.
4. Remove excess moisture on red meats with a paper towel. Dredge white meats.
5. Place the meat in sauté pan no more than a single layer deep. Brown it on all sides.

6. Remove the meat from the pan.
7. Pour off any excess grease and deglaze the pan.

8. Incorporate the deglazed drippings into a sauce.
9. Meat may be tossed in the sauce to coat and reheat, but should not be boiled in the sauce.

sear the item is very hot. If left on this same heat to cook all the way through, the item will burn. Once seared, thicker pieces of meat or poultry should be finished on a lower heat. They may also be finished in the oven to keep them from becoming excessively charred or burned.

Determining Doneness

The ability to determine the doneness of grilled meats is the product of repeated experience. Piercing the seared crust of a grilled piece of red meat causes it to bleed and lose its juices. Therefore, probing a grilled steak or chop with a thermometer, skewer, or paring knife is poor technique. Chefs learn through repeated experience to judge the doneness of cooked meats by touch. By pressing gently on a piece of cooked meat, an experienced cook senses the firmness of the product. The firmer the meat is, the more well done it will be.

It is customary for diners to order red meats, such as beef and lamb, by degree of doneness, especially when grilled, 32-2.

Roasting

Roasting seeks to achieve the same browned exterior and juicy interior of meat or poultry as do sautéing and grilling. The process, however, uses a much less intense heat and a longer cooking time. Roasting originated from cooking meat on a spit over a flame. Today, this method of roasting is often referred to as *rotisserie cooking* and is much closer to broiling than modern roasting. Since most roasting today is done in the oven, hot air—not radiant heat—does the cooking.

There are two different approaches employed in roasting, the searing method and the constant-heat method. The searing method starts the roasting process in a hot

TECHNIQUE
Grilling Meats and Poultry

1. Preheat the grill.
2. Clean the grill with a wire brush.

3. Brush the item to be grilled with oil or clarified butter. Season the product.
4. Place the item on a hot area of the grill. Allow grill marks to form.
5. Turn the product 90° and allow cross marks to form.

6. Flip the product and finish cooking over moderate heat. After searing the second side, larger or well-done pieces may be finished in the oven.

Degrees of Doneness for Grilled Items

Term	Appearance	Final Temperature
Blue (extra rare)	Center is red and cool to touch	Less than 140°F (60°C)
Rare	Center is red and warm to touch	140°F (60°C)
Medium rare	Center is red to pink and hot to touch	150°F (66°C)
Medium	Center is pink and hot to touch	155°F–160°F (68°C–71°C)
Medium well	Center is slightly pink and hot to touch	165°F (74°C)
Well-done	Center is brown/grey and hot to touch	170°F (77°C)

32-2 Chefs must be able to prepare meats to various degrees of doneness.

Recipe No.	Name		Category
32.8	Roast Cornish Hens with Pan Gravy		Roasting
Yield	Portion Size		No. Portions
10 servings	1 hen		10
US Quantity	Metric Quantity	Ingredient	TCS
10 ea.		Cornish hens	•
to taste		salt and white pepper	
as needed		clarified or melted butter	•
8 oz.	225 g	mirepoix, medium dice	
3 oz.	85 g	blond roux	
1 qt.	0.95 L	chicken stock	•

Method	CCP
1. Remove the giblets from the hens and reserve the necks. Season cavities with salt and pepper.	
2. Truss the hens (optional), brush them with butter, and season the outsides.	
3. Place the mirepoix and necks in the roasting pan, and place the hens on top.	
4. Place the roasting pan in a preheated 375°F (190°C) oven. Roast for about 45 minutes until the bird reaches 165°F (74°C). Test doneness by piercing the thickest part of the thigh. If juices run clear, the birds are done.	CCP
5. Remove the hens from the pan and hold at 135°F (57°C) or above.	CCP
6. Pour or skim any excessive grease from the roasting pan.	
7. Add the stock to the pan. Place the pan over a medium heat and simmer to dissolve the drippings.	
8. Transfer liquid from the roast pan to a saucepot. Stir in the roux and simmer for 15–20 minutes to extract flavor from the mirepoix and thicken the gravy.	
9. Strain the gravy and adjust the seasoning.	

Portion (g)	Calories	Fat (g)	Protein (g)	Carbohydrate (g)	Cholesterol (mg)	Sodium (mg)	Fiber (g)
422	970	71.02	71.06	6.72	440.03	798.59	0.15

oven or on the cooktop to create browning. The product then finishes cooking at a lower temperature. This method is useful for items that may not ordinarily brown in a relatively short cooking time. The disadvantage is that more of the natural juices are lost as compared to the constant-heat method.

When lower temperatures and longer times are used for roasting, the amount of moisture loss in the meat product is minimized. The constant-heat method is based on this fact. Products are cooked in an oven at one temperature throughout the cooking process. This method produces a moister product but may not create an appealing browned surface on some meats and poultry.

Equipment for Roasting

One important consideration when roasting is the use of a rack. Placing an item on a rack allows fat to drip away from the meat or bird. It also promotes even cooking. When roasting fatty meats or birds without a rack, the bottom of the roast may dry out or burn and possibly stick to the roasting pan, 32-3.

The choice of roasting pan is also important. As you will see, in order to create a pan sauce from the drippings of the roast, the roasting pan needs to be placed on the range top. A thick-gauge roasting pan is preferable.

Hotel pans are a poor choice due to their thin gauge. Sheet pans are also not effective because of their low sides.

Determining Doneness

The best method for determining the doneness of roasted meats and poultry is the thermometer. Since roasts are much larger than most grilled meats, the loss of a small amount of moisture caused by piercing the crust is insignificant. When using a thermometer to check doneness, be sure the tip of the probe is at the center of the piece being tested.

Along with the thermometer, chefs have other indicators of doneness. The color of the juices that runs from the roast is a good sign of doneness, 32-4. The redder the juices are, the rarer the roast is. Looking for clear juices running from the thigh—the part that takes longest to cook—is the traditional method for telling that poultry is fully cooked. With experience, chefs can also check doneness by touch, the same as with grilled meats.

Large roasts, near the end of their cooking time, contain a good deal of heat energy and continue to cook after being removed from the oven. This effect is known as **carryover cooking**. In large roasts, carryover cooking can account for an increase of 10°F to 15°F (6°C to 8°C). Cooks

Draz-Koetke/Goodheart-Willcox Publisher

32-3 Using the proper equipment for roasting promotes even cooking.

Roast Temperatures		
Term	**Appearance**	**Final Temperature**
Rare	Center is red and warm to touch	140°F (60°C)
Medium	Center is pink and hot to touch	155°F–160°F (68°C–71°C)
Well-done	Center is brown and hot to touch	170°F (77°C)

32-4 Chefs use a combination of indicators to determine when a roast should be removed from the oven.

should anticipate this rise in temperature and remove roasts from the oven below the desired finished temperature. The roast should then be allowed to finish cooking outside the oven. The process usually takes about 15 minutes. During this time, the muscle fibers relax and the juices move from being concentrated in the center to being evenly distributed throughout the roast. Carving a roast before it is allowed to relax results in a loss of juices and a drier finished product.

Roasts are typically cooked either rare, medium, or well-done. No matter what degree of doneness you are cooking the roast to, you must **compensate**, or make up for, carryover cooking and remove the roast in advance of the final desired temperature.

Pan Sauces and Gravy

When the roasting process is finished, the bottom of the roasting pan is covered with richly flavored drippings. Mirepoix is often added to the roast to give the drippings added flavor and color. Just as with sautéed items, the drippings are degreased, deglazed, and incorporated into a sauce. The liquid used for deglazing is typically a stock. In order to efficiently deglaze a roasting pan, it should be simmered on the stove, 32-5.

The deglazed drippings of a roast that are strained and seasoned are called a **jus** (zhoo), which is French for "juice," 32-6. The menu term *au jus* describes a roasted item served with its natural juices.

Gravy is the jus from a roast that has been thickened. The thickening agent for a gravy may be roux or slurry. Traditionally, gravies for white meats utilized white stock and blond roux or a slurry. Gravies for red meats are made with brown stock and brown roux. As with all good sauces, gravies should be strained and seasoned before serving.

32-6 The deglazed juices are poured into a saucepan for further seasoning.

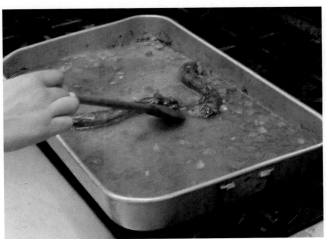

32-5 Once the roast is removed, the roasting pan is placed on the stovetop for deglazing.

Summary Points

- Tender cuts are seared to produce a complex flavor and pleasing brown color.
- Sautéing uses a small amount of fat for searing meat and poultry.
- Drippings from sautéed and roasted items are used to create sauces.
- Grilling and broiling use intense radiant heat to sear and cook meats.
- Roasting at lower temperatures for longer times produces juicier finished products.

In Review Assess

1. When done properly, dry-heat cooking methods _____ the meat to produce an appealing brown crust.
2. Which types of meat and poultry are most often dredged before sautéing?
3. True or false. Whole butter is an excellent choice of fat for sautéing meat items.
4. What happens to meat if it remains in the pan during deglazing?
5. True or false. Meat and poultry items should be cut in small or thin pieces to be suitable for sautéing.
6. What steps should be taken to prepare a grill for cooking meat or poultry?
7. Which of the following cooking methods will result in a juicier finished roast?
   A. Cook roast at 425°F (218°C) for 1 hour.
   B. Cook roast at 300°F (149°C) for 2 hours.
8. Cooks should compensate for _____ _____ by removing the roast from the oven before it reaches the desired finished temperature.
9. Explain the difference between jus and gravy.

Core Skills

10. **Math.** Your assignment is to roast a large, 15-pound inside round of beef. The chef told you he would like it cooked to medium doneness. What temperature should the roast be when you remove it from the oven to achieve the chef's desired finished temperature?

11. **Writing.** As a marketing tool, the restaurant at which you are a chef has started a business blog to reach out to current and potential customers. *Ask the Chef* is part of the blog. This week one of your customers writes in and asks "What is the secret for grilling a flavorful, juicy steak?" Your job is to write creative tips for grilling meats and testing them for perfect doneness. Write your blog and share it with your customers (the class).

12. **Speaking and Listening.** Select either grilling or broiling technique to demonstrate for the class. Use a boneless, skinless chicken breast or another cut as provided by your instructor. Follow the text directions for grilling or broiling. As you cook, describe the process as you complete each step. Plate your grilled or broiled chicken breast to show the class. Discuss your demonstration technique and any challenges you faced. Have several classmates evaluate your chicken breast for proper grill marks, flavor, and appropriate doneness.

13. **Reading.** Read reliable Internet or print resources to research historical information on rotisserie cooking. Write an illustrated report that explains what types of equipment was used. What heat source was used? What foods were roasted? How were they served? Use a school-approved Web-based application to post your report to the class website.

14. **Speaking and Listening.** Demonstrate the technique of *sautéing* for the class. Use a boneless, skinless chicken breast or another cut as provided by your instructor. Follow the text directions for sautéing. As you cook, describe the process as you complete each step. Plate your sautéed chicken breast to show the class. Discuss your demonstration technique and any challenges you faced.

Have several classmates evaluate your chicken breast for proper searing (dredging as needed), flavor, and appropriate doneness.

15. **Writing.** Sautéing is a cooking method that utilizes conduction. Use reliable Internet or print resources to research and define *thermal conductivity* as it relates to cooking and cooking equipment. Then compare the conductivity of the sauté pan and the meat in this cooking process. Write a summary of your findings.

16. **Writing.** Since you are the grill cook, the chef has asked you to develop a training program for apprentices on determining doneness of grilled meat and poultry items. Write a detailed outline of information you would present to the apprentices.

17. **CTE Career Readiness Practice.** Use Internet or print resources to read three or more restaurant reviews (from reliable sources) of establishments that specialize in foods cooked by dry-heat methods. Summarize the key details about cooking methods reviewed in writing. When evaluating the information, remember to:

- *Identify writer credibility.*
- *Verify details.*
- *Identify bias.*

Critical Thinking

18. **Identify evidence.** Make a list of meat and poultry items that might be sautéed or roasted. For each item on the list, make an accompanying list of liquids that could be used as a deglazing liquid for each meat or poultry item. Next to each liquid, give evidence to support your reason for selecting that liquid.

19. **Analyze variables.** This is your first day on the job as saucier and sautéed chicken is on the menu. Your first attempt resulted in chicken that was pale, dry, and chewy. Identify all the steps in the process that if performed incorrectly could result in this unsatisfactory product. Then analyze and

identify how you would correct each possible error.

20. **Recognize alternatives.** Use an equipment catalog or search online for information (specifications) sheets on charbroilers (grills) and broilers. Which equipment would you choose for your restaurant kitchen? What factors would influence your decision? Write a summary identifying the alternatives and evidence supporting your choice.

Technology

Combination convection-microwave ovens are gaining popularity in the foodservice kitchen. Use reliable Internet or print resources to obtain information about convection-microwave technology used in commercial foodservice. How do these ovens work? What products can be cooked in them? Are they appropriate for roasting meat and poultry? Prepare an illustrated digital report to share with the class.

Teamwork

Obtain a large meat roast or chicken as provided by your instructor and roast it to medium doneness. Remove the roast from the oven and insert a thermometer into its center immediately. Record the initial temperature when you removed it from the oven and continue recording temperatures every minute for 15 minutes. How much carryover cooking occurred? Had the temperature stopped rising after 15 minutes? Discuss your findings with other teams in class.

Chef's E-portfolio
Sauté Technique

Upload a video of your presentation from activity #14 to your e-portfolio. Ask your instructor where to save your file. This could be on the school's network or a flash drive of your own. Name your portfolio document *FirstnameLastname_Portfolio Ch#.docx* (i.e., JohnSmith_PortfolioCh32.docx).

While studying, look for the activity icon  to:

- Build vocabulary with e-flash cards and matching activities.
- Expand learning with video clips, photo identification activities, animations, and interactive activities.
- Review and assess what you learn by completing end-of-chapter questions.

Moist-Heat and Combination Cooking Methods for Meat and Poultry

Reading Prep

In preparation for this chapter, review a variety of restaurant menus for braised or stewed meat and poultry entrées. Compare the prices for these entrées to those of entrées prepared by dry-heat cooking methods. As you read the chapter, consider how menu price might be related to the type of cooking method used.

Culinary Terminology Build Vocab

poaching, p. 533
simmering, p. 535
fork-tender, p. 537
braising, p. 537
stewing, p. 539

Academic Terminology Build Vocab

abundant, p. 535

Objectives

After studying this chapter, you will be able to

- recognize when poaching is an appropriate cooking method to use.

- execute simmering meat and poultry to proper doneness.

- apply braising technique to meat and poultry.

- explain the cooking methods used to make stews.

Moisture is an effective cooking medium. Moist heat is able to cook foods more effectively at lower temperatures than dry heat. Nowhere is the use of moist heat more important than in meat cookery. The role of liquid in the cooking process is twofold. First, it tenderizes tough cuts of meat and poultry. Second, the cooking liquid adds flavor to the finished dish. The stock and other cooking liquids blend with meat juices in the cooking process. This combination is the foundation for creating rich and flavorful meat and poultry entrées.

Poaching

Poaching, though very important in fish cookery, has a somewhat limited role with meats and poultry. **Poaching** cooks foods in liquids at relatively low temperatures, usually between 160°F and 180°F (71°C and 82°C). This temperature range is too low to break down connective tissue in meat. For this reason, poaching is reserved for extremely tender cuts with delicate texture. Typically, poaching is limited to tender cuts of young poultry such as the breast. Poaching may also be used for sausages since they may burst or become dry if cooked at temperatures that are too high.

While poaching has little tenderizing effect, one of its main benefits is the infusion of flavor to the product being cooked. Stock is a common poaching liquid. Another option is water flavored with aromatic herbs and mire-poix, known as a *court bouillon*. The poaching liquid is often used to create a sauce or may simply be served as a broth along with the poached item.

Recipe No.	Name		Category
33.1	Poached Chicken Breast "Fines Herbes"		Moist-heat method, poaching
Yield	**Portion Size**		**No. Portions**
10 servings	1 breast		10
US Quantity	**Metric Quantity**	**Ingredient**	**TCS**
10 ea.		chicken breast, boneless, skinless, 6 oz. (170 g)	•
to taste		salt	
to taste		white pepper	
1 Tbsp.	15 mL	butter	•
2 Tbsp.	30 mL	shallots	
1 pt.	480 mL	chicken stock	•
8 fl. oz.	240 mL	heavy cream	•
2 tsp.	10 mL	parsley, chopped	
2 tsp.	10 mL	fresh chervil, chopped	
2 tsp.	10 mL	chives, chopped	
2 tsp.	10 mL	fresh tarragon, chopped	

Method	**CCP**
1. Preheat an oven to 350°F (177°C).	
2. Season the breasts with salt and pepper.	
3. Butter the bottom of a sauté pan suitable to hold the chicken breasts. Sprinkle the shallots on the bottom of the pan.	
4. Place the breast on top of the shallots.	
5. Add the stock.	
6. Cover the pan with a buttered piece of parchment paper.	
7. Bring the pan to a simmer on the stovetop and place in the oven.	
8. Allow the breasts to poach for 15 minutes to 165°F (74°C).	CCP
9. Remove the breasts from the pan. Cover and hold at or above 135°F (57°C).	CCP
10. Add the cream to the pan and reduce the liquid on the stovetop until it is thick enough to coat the back of a spoon.	
11. Add the fresh herbs and return to a simmer.	
12. Adjust seasoning with salt and white pepper. Serve the poached breasts coated with the sauce.	

Portion (g)	Calories	Fat (g)	Protein (g)	Carbohydrate (g)	Cholesterol (mg)	Sodium (mg)	Fiber (g)
270	314	12.60	41.05	5.54	135.70	565.15	0.04

Simmering

Often, meat dishes on menus and in recipes are referred to as "boiled"—boiled ham, boiled short ribs, or boiled brisket. Even though meat and poultry dishes are called *boiled*, they are actually simmered. **Simmering** cooks foods in liquid at temperatures between 185°F and 205°F (85°C and 96°C). Meat and poultry should never be cooked at a boil because extended exposure to the higher temperature (212°F, 100°C) causes the proteins to toughen. Simmering is hot enough to break down meat's connective tissue, but not so hot as to toughen it.

Simmering is the most effective way to break down the connective tissue known as *collagen*. Collagen is **abundant**, or plentiful, in

TECHNIQUE
Simmering Meats and Poultry

1. **Place the meat or poultry item, any aromatic vegetables, herbs or spices, in a suitably sized pot. Cover with cold water.**

2. **Bring the pot to a full boil and then reduce the heat to a gentle simmer.**

3. **Skim any scum that rises to the top of the pot.**
4. **Keep the item at a simmer throughout the cooking process. Add more liquid to keep the item covered if necessary.**
5. **Test doneness with a long fork.**

6. **Save the cooking liquid to serve with the meat or poultry or for another use.**

tough cuts of meat and poultry. Cuts from the forequarter of animals and mature poultry are best cooked by this method.

As you learned in stock making, connective tissue breaks down during moist cooking and turns to gelatin. The result is that the simmering process also produces a rich broth. This broth is often served with the simmered meat or poultry. To produce a clear broth, the simmering process always starts with cold liquid.

Determining Doneness

Determining the proper doneness of a tough cut of meat or poultry is essential for serving a quality product. A simple time measure is not sufficient because of natural variance in size, shape, and the amount of

Recipe No.	Name		Category
33.2	Simmered Beef Short Ribs		Moist-heat method, simmering
Yield	**Portion Size**		**No. Portions**
4½ lb. (2 kg)	7 oz. (200 g)		10
US Quantity	**Metric Quantity**	**Ingredient**	**TCS**
4½ lb.	2 kg	beef short ribs	•
4½ qt.	4.25 L	cold water	
2 Tbsp.	30 mL	salt	
1 ea.		sachet	
1 ea.		onion piqué	
6 oz.	170 g	turnips, peeled and cut into wedges	
6 oz.	170 g	carrots, peeled, quartered lengthwise (3 in. lengths)	
6 oz.	170 g	celery stalks, cut in 3 in. lengths	
3 ea.		leeks, white, quartered lengthwise (3 in. lengths)	
2 Tbsp.	30 mL	parsley, chopped	
Method			**CCP**
1. Place the meat, water, and salt into a large pot. Bring to a rapid boil and lower heat to a simmer. Skim any scum that rises to the surface.			
2. Add the sachet and onion piqué. Allow the meat to simmer 1 hour. Cook to an internal temperature of 145°F (63°C) or above.			CCP
3. Add the carrots and simmer 10 minutes.			
4. Add the remaining vegetables and simmer for an additional 20 minutes. Check to see if meat is fork-tender. If not, continue to simmer until done.			
5. Discard the sachet and onion piqué.			
6. Adjust the seasoning of the broth with salt and pepper if needed.			
7. Serve the short ribs and broth in a soup plate garnished with the vegetables.			
8. Sprinkle each portion with chopped parsley.			

Portion (g)	Calories	Fat (g)	Protein (g)	Carbohydrate (g)	Cholesterol (mg)	Sodium (mg)	Fiber (g)
180	494	41.54	22.07	6.78	92.63	1478.25	1.61

connective tissue in cuts of meat and poultry. Judging doneness by internal temperature is not accurate since a piece of meat may have reached a designated temperature, but may not have been at that temperature long enough to be tenderized.

Larger cuts of meat and poultry cooked by simmering or braising are judged done when they are fork-tender. **Fork-tender** is determined when a long-tined fork or skewer is inserted into a cut of cooked meat and the meat easily slides off the fork. If the meat

Chef Speak

A Glossary of Classical Stews

Many stews are well-known in the world of cuisine. These are some of the classics.

Blanquette (blahn KET)—White stew made by the simmering technique finished with cream.

Cassoulet (kas oh LAY)—Stew from southwest France combining white beans with lamb, goose, and sausage.

Curry (KUR ee)—White stew flavored with curry spice.

Daube (DOHB)—Brown beef stew from the south of France, cooked slowly in an earthenware casserole.

Estouffade (es too FAHD)—Rich brown beef stew made by braising.

Fricassée (frik ah SEE)—Stew made with white meats such as chicken or rabbit. The meat is lightly browned, cooked with white stock, and finished with cream.

Goulash (GOO lahsh)—Brown Hungarian beef stew flavored with paprika.

Irish stew—White lamb stew with potatoes and onions made by the simmering method.

Navarin (naV ah RAHN)—Brown stew traditionally made with lamb using the braising method.

Ragout (rah GOO)—Brown stew made by the braising method.

clings to the fork, it is a sign that the connective tissues that bundle the muscles are still elastic and the item needs more cooking.

Braising

Braising is a combination of dry- and moist-heat cooking methods. **Braising** employs the techniques of first searing and then simmering meat.

Braising, like simmering, is used for tough cuts of meat and poultry to make them tender. The braising method first sears the product to brown it on all sides. This creates a dish with deeper color and richer flavor.

The braising process starts with browning the meat or poultry in a small amount of hot fat on top of the stove. Often mirepoix and tomato product are added and caramelized. Liquid is then added to the pan to create a moist cooking environment. The amount of liquid added is less than the amount used for simmered dishes. The amount of liquid is determined by how much sauce will be needed for the finished dish. Usually, the amount of liquid is enough to cover the item half way.

Once the liquid is added, all the ingredients are brought to a boil. The heat is lowered and cooking continues at a simmer. The product is cooked covered because there is less liquid than in simmered or boiled dishes. Braised dishes are more easily simmered in the oven than on the stovetop. Cooking in a covered pan in the oven allows the item to cook at a steady simmer without the risk of scorching.

As with simmered dishes, braised meats are done when they are fork-tender. The braising process produces a tender piece of meat and a cooking liquid that is rich with the concentrated flavors of the braised ingredients. Especially important to the flavor and richness of braised dishes is the gelatin contained in the cooking liquid. This gelatin comes from the meat's connective tissue that was softened and dissolved during the cooking process. It is most appropriate for

TECHNIQUE
Braising Meats and Poultry

1. Sear meat over high heat in a small amount of fat on the stovetop.

2. Add mirepoix to the pan and sweat for white meats and poultry (light-colored sauce) or caramelize for red meats (brown sauce).

3. Tomato product is added for red meats (brown sauce).

4. Add appropriate liquid: stock, marinade, sauce, or water. The amount of liquid is determined by the amount of sauce needed.

5. Add herbs, spices, and seasoning and bring all ingredients to a simmer.

6. Cover and place in a preheated oven.

7. Turn and baste meat occasionally during the cooking process.

8. Test for fork-tender doneness.

9. Remove the meat and prepare a sauce with the braising liquid. Either serve sauce as is, reduce to nappé consistency, or thicken with roux or slurry.

this liquid to be served with the braised meat or poultry. The cooking liquid may be served as is, reduced to a sauce consistency, or thickened with roux or slurry.

Stewing

Simmering and braising are cooking methods that can be carried out on large or small pieces of meat or poultry. When these methods are applied to bite-sized pieces of meat or poultry, the method is called **stewing**. A stew can contain any combination of meat, poultry, fish, seafood, vegetables, and starches. In all stews, whether simmered or braised, enough liquid to fully cover the ingredients is used. The liquid used for cooking may be thickened or left thin depending on the recipe.

Stews made by the simmering method are simple in their preparation, yet they become rich from the blending of flavors of many ingredients. Stews made by the braising technique are most often prepared with red meats, which benefit from the browning process. In both simmered and braised stews, the finished dish is rich from the gelatin extracted from the meat.

Since stews often contain not only meat or poultry, but also vegetables, some consideration should be given to the vegetables. Most vegetables require a much shorter time to cook than the tough cuts of meat used in stews. Aromatic vegetables are often added at the beginning of the cooking process. These are often removed before serving since most of the flavor and texture is lost in the long simmering time. Vegetables to be left in the finished dish for garnish should be added to the stew in accordance with their cooking time. Otherwise, vegetable garnishes may be cooked separately and added to the dish before service. Either way, the finished stew will contain tender, properly cooked meat with properly cooked vegetables.

Summary Points

- Poaching is a way to cook tender items such as breasts of young poultry in a flavored liquid.

- Simmering is an effective way to tenderize tough cuts of meat.

- Braising employs the same moist-heat cooking process as simmering, but the item is first seared to develop color and flavor.

- Meats that have been simmered or braised are done when they are fork-tender.

- Stewing uses either simmering or braising method.

In Review
Assess

1. What two roles do liquids serve in moist-heat cooking methods?

2. True or false. Poaching has little tenderizing effect.

3. The moist-heat cooking method that takes place between 185°F and 205°F (85°C and 96°C) is which of the following?
   A. Poaching
   B. Simmering
   C. Boiling
   D. Steaming

4. Why are simmered dishes started in cold water?

5. How do you test cuts of meat and poultry that have been simmered or braised for doneness?

6. When meat and poultry are _____, their proteins begin to toughen.

7. What is the advantage of searing meats and poultry for braising?

8. How does the process of making a braised dish with a brown sauce differ from making a braised dish with a light-colored sauce?

9. Compare the amount of liquid used when simmering meat or poultry to that used for braising.

10. What is the advantage of cooking braised items in the oven?

11. List three ways cooking liquid from a braised item can be made into a sauce.

12. True or false. Vegetables to be left in a stew as garnish are always added at the beginning of the cooking process.

Core Skills

13. **Math.** You are responsible for preparing a beef stew for 36 people for a luncheon. Your recipe yields 8 servings and calls for 2 pounds of stew meat. How many pounds of stew meat will you need in order to produce 36 servings?

14. **Reading.** Read about the French dish *Pot au Feu* from at least three different sources. What are the origins of the dish? Describe the ingredients and cooking method. How is it served? Create an illustrated digital report of your findings to share with the class.

15. **Speaking and Listening.** In teams, practice your *poaching* skills by preparing the chapter recipe, *Poached Chicken Breast "Fines Herbes."* Follow the recipe and text guidelines for preparing the poached chicken breasts. Then taste-test the chicken breast and evaluate the final product for appropriate cooking technique, flavor, tenderness, and appearance. Discuss your results in class.

16. **Speaking and Listening.** Demonstrate the simmering technique for the class. Use a cut of meat or poultry as provided by your instructor. Follow the text directions for simmering. As you cook, describe the process as you complete each step. Plate your simmered item to show the class. Discuss your demonstration technique and any challenges you faced. Have several classmates evaluate your simmered item for flavor, tenderness, and appropriate doneness.

17. **Speaking and Listening.** Demonstrate the braising technique for the class. Use a cut of meat or poultry as provided by your instructor. Follow the text directions for braising. As you cook, describe the process as you complete each step. Plate your braised item to show the class. Discuss your demonstration technique and any challenges you faced. Have several classmates evaluate your braised item for flavor, appearance, tenderness, and appropriate doneness.

18. **CTE Career Readiness Practice.** Obtain a copy of Escoffier's *Le Guide Culinaire* from the library and examine his description of the braising process for red meats. Then discuss the following questions regarding information this author presented:

    ● What is the method Escoffier proposes?

    ● How is the method described in this chapter similar to or different from Escoffier's classic method?

    ● Are the differences in preparation and technique still valid today? Why or why not?

Critical Thinking

19. **Distinguish.** Suppose you are a chef training a new cook in the braising/stewing technique. You tell the trainee to check the braised item for doneness and turn to answer a question from the restaurant manager. When you return, you see the trainee is attempting to check doneness with a thermometer. How would you explain why using a thermometer is not accurate for determining doneness of braised or stewed items as it is with roasted items?

20. **Infer.** When serving braised or simmered dishes in an à la carte restaurant, infer how they can be held for service. Discuss your conclusions in class.

21. **Recognize alternatives.** Search online or in cookbooks for a recipe for a braised or simmered meat, fish, or poultry dish. Create a T-chart. Label the top of the left column *Alternatives for Recipe Cooking Liquid*, and label the right column *Changes the Alternatives May Have on the Recipe*. List the alternatives for the cooking liquid in the left column. In the right column, propose how these liquids might change the flavor, texture, tenderness of the meat, fish, or poultry. Discuss your alternatives with the class.

Technology

Locate a recipe for a meat item cooked sous vide style. What temperature is the item cooked at and for what length of time? Is this a moist-heat cooking method? Do you think the time and temperature is sufficient to tenderize a tough cut of meat? Why or why not? Then investigate new technology related to cooking equipment for cooking in the sous vide style. What options are available to chefs for making this method more convenient? Share your findings with the class.

Teamwork

Work with a partner and obtain a piece of beef chuck or brisket as provided by your instructor. Cut the beef in half and give one half to your partner. Weigh the pieces and record the weight. Use separate suitably sized pans to sear each piece and then cover each with cold water and your choice of herbs and spices. Have one partner simmer one piece and the other boil the other piece of beef. Cook both pieces of beef until the simmered one is fork-tender and then remove both from the heat. Weigh each piece after cooking. Taste both pieces of beef. Write an evaluation comparing the flavor, texture, and tenderness of each piece of beef. Draw conclusions about how the cooking method impacted the meat and share your conclusions with the class.

Chef's E-portfolio
Moist-Heat Cooking Method Demo

Have a classmate or your instructor video or take photos of your demonstration of poaching, simmering, or braising from the Core Skills activities. Upload your video or photos to your e-portfolio. Ask your instructor where to save your file. This could be on the school's network or a flash drive of your own. Name your portfolio document *FirstnameLastname_Portfolio Ch#.docx* (i.e., JohnSmith_PortfolioCh33.docx).

While studying, look for the activity icon to:
- Build vocabulary with e-flash cards and matching activities.
- Expand learning with video clips, photo identification activities, animations, and interactive activities.
- Review and assess what you learn by completing end-of-chapter questions.

Fish and Shellfish Identification

Reading Prep

In preparation for this chapter, locate the FDA's Regulatory Fish Encyclopedia (RFE) online. As you read, use this resource to verify and extend identification of fish and shellfish.

Culinary Terminology
Build Vocab

finfish, p. 544
shellfish, p. 544
round fish, p. 544
flatfish, p. 544
crustacean, p. 551
mollusk, p. 551
univalves, p. 551
bivalves, p. 551
cephalopods, p. 553
shucked, p. 554
aquaculture, p. 555

Academic Terminology
Build Vocab

confer, p. 555

Objectives

After studying this chapter, you will be able to

- recognize different types of fresh finfish and shellfish used in foodservice.
- interpret various indicators of freshness and quality for finfish and shellfish.
- recall various ways fish are processed for sale.
- summarize the role of aquaculture in the fish industry.

- explain how fish and seafood are regulated and inspected in the United States.

Fish is a popular foodservice menu item. For years, certain items such as lobster, scallops, and shrimp were considered luxury products. As fish gained recognition for its role in a healthy diet, consumers' demand for it increased. Some fish are particularly rich in omega-3 fatty acids and unsaturated fats, which makes them a healthy source of protein. As consumer demand increased, advances in transportation made quality fresh fish available in virtually all major markets in the United States. In feeding the growing appetite for fish, many waters throughout the world have become overfished. To meet the growing demand for fish, farm-raised fish have become increasingly common. The fish supply, whether wild or farm-raised, continues to be a serious concern for the future.

Nutrition Connection

Omega-3's in Fish

Scientists are continually learning more about the health benefits of consuming omega-3 fatty acids. High levels of this fatty acid appear to lower the risk of heart disease and stroke. Current recommendations suggest eating two or more servings of fish per week. Some fish contain more omega-3 fatty acids than others. Salmon, tuna, and herring are high in these beneficial fatty acids. In general, saltwater fish are better sources than freshwater fish.

There are thousands of edible varieties of fish. Becoming familiar with the many different types of fish available to foodservice takes considerable effort. Learning about the different types of fish is only the first step. Chefs must then understand how to cook each type of fish. There are two main categories of fish—finfish and shellfish. **Finfish** are all species of fish that have an internal skeleton and swim in water. **Shellfish** are those water creatures that have no bones, but their bodies are covered by hard external surfaces such as the bony body of a lobster or the hard shell of a clam. Finfish and shellfish are further subdivided into smaller categories.

Finfish

A finfish is most commonly referred to simply as a fish. Finfish are further divided into two categories—saltwater and freshwater fish.

Saltwater Finfish

Within the saltwater finfish category is an astonishing number of edible species. Saltwater finfish are caught in the saltwater of the world's oceans. Saltwater species vary widely in size, texture, and flavor. To better understand the diversity of this category, it is helpful to further divide saltwater finfish into round and flatfish, 34-1.

Round Fish   Round fish have one eye on each side of their head and swim through the water with their dorsal fin upright. There are many common species of saltwater round fish used in foodservice.

Flatfish   Flatfish have two eyes on one side of their head and none on the other side. They typically swim or lay on the ocean bottom. Flatfish have dark-colored skin on the side with two eyes and light-colored skin on the side with no eyes.

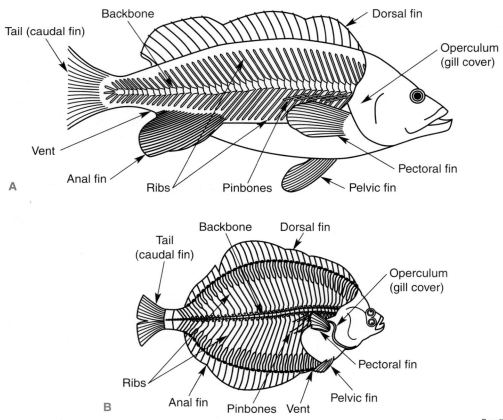

34-1 When selecting and preparing (A) round fish and (B) flatfish, it is necessary to know their anatomy.

Round Saltwater Finfish

Sea Bass

Striped sea bass range from 15 to 20 pounds and black sea bass from 2 to 5 pounds. These fish have medium flake, moderate flavor, and white color. They are typically fished from the mid-Atlantic Ocean.

Cod

Cod has very flaky flesh with mild taste, white to opaque color, and ranges from 3 to 7 pounds. Pacific cod are found near Alaska and Atlantic cod are from the northern Atlantic Ocean.

Grouper

There are two types of grouper—red or black. Typically found in the Caribbean Sea, Gulf of Mexico, or southern Atlantic Ocean, grouper range from 3 to 15 pounds with large flakes, firm texture, moderate flavor, and rosy-white color.

Haddock

Haddock are found in the northern Atlantic Ocean and range from 3 to 6 pounds. They have very flaky flesh with mild taste and white to opaque color.

Herring

Herring ranges from 4 to 6 ounces and is fished from the northern Atlantic and Pacific oceans. It has soft oily flesh and is usually sold pickled or smoked.

Mackerel

Mackerel is found in the mid-northern Atlantic Ocean and ranges from 1½ to 3 pounds. It has high oil content, strong flavor, and dark-colored flesh with firm flaky texture. It is often sold smoked.

Mahi-Mahi

Mahi-mahi, known in some places as *dorado*, ranges from 5 to 20 pounds and is found in warm oceans. Its flesh has firm flaky texture, beige color, and moderate flavor.

Marlin

Marlin are large-billed fish. Types include blue, striped, and black ranging from 20 to 200 pounds. They are found worldwide and have dense, meaty flesh that is white with an occasional pink hue.

(Continued)

Round Saltwater Finfish (Continued)

Monkfish

Monkfish range from 2 to 4 pounds with their head off and are fished from the deep waters of the mid-north Atlantic Ocean. Their flesh is white with sweet moderate flavor and firm, nonflaky texture.

Orange Roughy

Orange roughy ranges from 3 to 5 pounds. Its flesh is white with moderately flaky texture and mild flavor.

Salmon (Atlantic)

Atlantic salmon range from 4 to 15 pounds. They are fished from the northern Atlantic Ocean or many are farm raised. They have pink flesh that is moderately flaky and oily with a somewhat strong flavor.

Salmon (Pacific)

Types of Pacific salmon include chinook (king), chum, coho, pink, and sockeye that range in weight from 4 to 15 pounds. They are found in the northern Pacific Ocean and have pink flesh that is moderately flaky and oily with a slightly strong flavor.

Shark

Shark should range between 15 and 50 pounds and are found worldwide. Black tip, thresher, and mako sharks are common types. They have dense, meaty flesh that should be light in color.

Snapper

The most popular types of snapper include American red and yellowtail that weigh between 3 and 10 pounds. They are fished from the mid-southern Atlantic Ocean, Gulf of Mexico, and Caribbean Sea. They have white, moderately flaky flesh with sweet flavor.

Swordfish

Swordfish range from 50 to 150 pounds and are found worldwide. They have dense, chewy, white to rosy flesh with moderate oil content and sweet flavor.

Tuna

Types of tuna include bluefin, yellowfin, and albacore that can range from 5 to 200 pounds. They are fished worldwide and have dense, chewy flesh with white to dark red color. Tuna have moderate flavor and oil content.

Flat Saltwater Finfish

Dover Sole

Dover sole are fished from the European Atlantic Ocean and Mediterranean Sea, and range in weight from 1 to 2 pounds. They have moderate to firm texture with mild flavor and white flesh. Many chefs consider them the finest flatfish.

Halibut

Types of halibut include Atlantic and Pacific that can range in weight from 10 to 50 pounds. They are fished from the northern Pacific and Atlantic oceans. Halibut flesh is white with moderately toothy texture and mild flavor.

Flounder

Types of flounder include fluke, blackback, gray sole, and rex sole that range in weight from 1 to 5 pounds. Found in the mid-northern Atlantic Ocean and Pacific Ocean, they have white flesh with flaky texture and mild flavor.

Turbot

Turbot can range from 2 to 20 pounds and are found in the North Atlantic Ocean. Their meat is prized for its white color and delicate texture.

Freshwater Fish

Freshwater fish live in salt-free bodies of water such as lakes, rivers, and ponds. There are fewer species of freshwater fish used in foodservice than saltwater fish. Freshwater fish typically have a milder flavor than saltwater fish.

Judging the Quality of Fresh Fish

As with all products used in the professional kitchen, it is important to know how to judge the quality of a product before purchasing or cooking a given item. For

Freshwater Fish

Catfish

Catfish are fished from the bottoms of rivers and lakes or many are farm raised. They range from 1 to 4 pounds and have white, dense textured flesh. Farm-raised catfish have mild flavor but wild catfish can have a muddy flavor.

Hybrid Striped Bass

Hybrid striped bass are a farm-raised fish that range from 1 to 3 pounds. They have white, flaky flesh with mild flavor. They are the result of cross-breeding ocean striped bass with white bass.

Lake Perch

Lake perch are fished from lakes with weights ranging from ½ and 1 pound. They supply small tender cuts with a translucent white color and very mild flavor.

Lake Trout

Types of lake trout include steelhead and brown trouts that range from 2 to 10 pounds. They are found in the Great Lakes and other lakes in Canada and the northern United States. Trout have soft, orange flesh with mild flavor.

Sturgeon

The common type of sturgeon is the white sturgeon. These fish range between 10 and 30 pounds and are found in the Pacific Northwest. Sturgeon flesh has high oil content, firm texture, and mild flavor.

Tilapia

Tilapia sold in the United States are farm raised and range from 1 to 2 pounds. They have somewhat firm texture and mild flavor.

Trout

Common types of trout include brook and rainbow that range in size from ½ to 2 pounds. They are fished from lakes, rivers, or are farm raised. Trout have translucent white to rose-colored flesh with tender flake and mild flavor.

Walleyed Pike

Walleyed pike range in size from 1 to 3 pounds and are found in lakes in the northern United States and Canada. They have moderately firm, translucent flesh with a mild flavor.

Whitefish

Whitefish are found in the Great Lakes and western US lakes. They range in size from 1 to 6 pounds. Whitefish have a very tender flake, translucent white flesh, and very mild flavor.

finfish, this is particularly important as these products spoil easily and can be expensive. When assessing the quality of a whole fish, inspect the following:

- *Eyes.* The eyes should be bulging and clear. Dried out, cloudy, or sunken eyes indicate old fish.
- *Gills.* The gills should be a bright rosy color. The gills of older fish turn gray or brown. If the gills are red on one side and gray on the other, this could indicate the fish was lying in water. Water will turn the gills gray, so this may not always be a reliable indicator of freshness, 34-2.
- *Scales.* If the fish has not had the scales removed, look for scales that are firmly attached to the skin.
- *Smell.* Smell the fish around the gills and gut, as these two areas will spoil first. A fresh saltwater fish should have a pleasant ocean-like aroma. Freshwater fish should smell mild. Spoiling fish develop pungent aromas.
- *Texture.* Fresh fish should feel firm and not flabby. Pressure applied should not leave an indentation.

When assessing the quality of fish that have been further processed into smaller cuts, inspect the following:

Draz-Koetke/Goodheart-Willcox Publisher

34-2 Inspecting the freshness of fish is crucial because fish are very perishable.

SCIENCE & TECHNOLOGY
Fish with No Bones

There are a few odd species of fish that have no bones. Instead of bones, these fish have skeletons made of cartilage. Some common examples include skate, shark, and sturgeon. Skate, also called a *ray*, is especially uncommon as only the wings are eaten.

- *Smell.* Cuts from saltwater fish should have the same pleasant ocean-like aroma as a whole fish. Freshwater fish should smell mild. Overly strong or pungent aromas should be a warning.
- *Texture.* The fish should be firm and not mushy. If a boneless cut is gently folded in half and then unfolded, no line should appear where it was creased. (Do not fold delicate cuts such as salmon.)

Shellfish

The second main category of fish—shellfish—is divided into crustaceans and mollusks.

Chef Speak
Anadromous Fish

There are some species of fish that spend part of their life in freshwater and part of their life in saltwater. These types of fish are referred to as anadromous (ah nah DROH muhs) fish. For instance, salmon are born in freshwater, journey to the ocean, and return to freshwater to reproduce and die. Sturgeon is another common anadromous fish.

Crustaceans

Crab

Common types of crab are blue, Dungeness, king, Jonah, and snow which can range from 6 ounces to 15 pounds. Depending on the variety, they may be found in the warm or cold waters of the Pacific and Atlantic oceans. Crab in the shell is most often sold frozen, though some varieties such as blue crabs are sold live. Crab meat is white and tender with a slightly sweet flavor. It can be sold cleaned and cooked or pasteurized and canned.

Crayfish

Crayfish are found in bodies of freshwater worldwide or may be farm raised. They range in size from 3 to 6 inches and offer small amounts of sweet, reddish white meat found in the tail and claws. Meat is also sold cleaned and cooked.

Maine Lobster

Maine lobsters are found in the northern Atlantic Ocean and range from 1 to 10 pounds. The meat is sweet with a firm texture and white color when cooked. Once the lobster is dead, the flesh deteriorates quickly and must be either cooked or frozen.

Rock (Spiny) Lobster

Rock lobsters range from 1 to 10 pounds and are found in warm ocean waters. Their meat is sweet with firm texture and white color. Once the lobster is dead, the flesh deteriorates quickly and must be either cooked or frozen. These lobsters have no claws.

Shrimp

Common types of shrimp include brown, pink, tiger, and white that range in size from ¼ to 4 ounces each. They are harvested throughout the world depending on the variety. Fresh shrimp is very perishable so most are sold cooked or frozen. They have firm, white to pink flesh with a salty sweet flavor.

Crustaceans

A **crustacean** (kruhs TAY shuhn) is an aquatic species that has a hard and segmented exoskeleton, or shell. Crustaceans are among the most prized shellfish. The meat found inside crustaceans is noted for its richness and sweet flavor. While not strictly edible, the shells of many crustaceans are used to make bisques and seafood sauces.

Mollusks

The **mollusk** (MOHL uhsk) family consists of univalves, bivalves, and cephalopods. **Univalves** are shellfish that have only one shell. While there are some edible univalves such as conch, they are not common in commercial foodservice. **Bivalves** are shellfish that have two shells. The two shells clamp shut tightly to protect the tender interior flesh. Bivalves filter water and in doing so gather nutrients necessary to live. For this reason, the flavor of bivalves is dependent on the waters they inhabit. If harvested from dirty waters, the bivalves will also absorb any pollutants and harmful viruses in the water. For that reason, it is important to buy bivalves from reputable suppliers.

Bivalves are sold with seafood tags stating where the bivalves were harvested, 34-3. The foodservice establishment must keep these tags for 90 days so that if customers become ill from eating bivalves, the authorities can trace the source.

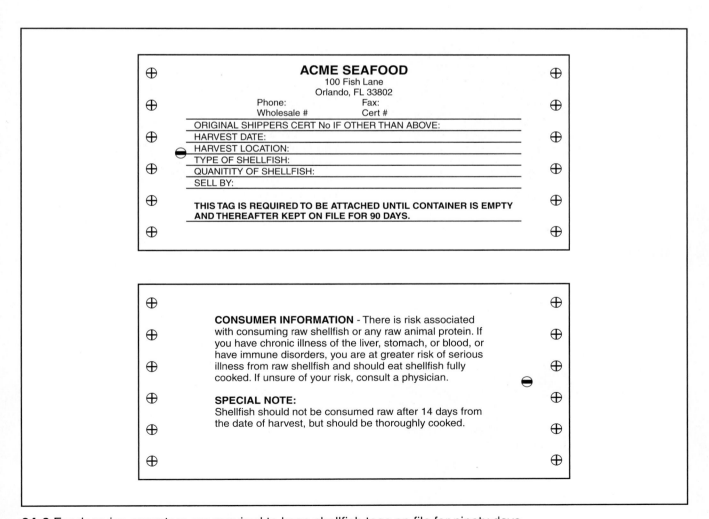

ACME SEAFOOD
100 Fish Lane
Orlando, FL 33802
Phone: Fax:
Wholesale #   Cert #

ORIGINAL SHIPPERS CERT No IF OTHER THAN ABOVE:

HARVEST DATE:

HARVEST LOCATION:

TYPE OF SHELLFISH:

QUANITY OF SHELLFISH:

SELL BY:

THIS TAG IS REQUIRED TO BE ATTACHED UNTIL CONTAINER IS EMPTY AND THEREAFTER KEPT ON FILE FOR 90 DAYS.

CONSUMER INFORMATION - There is risk associated with consuming raw shellfish or any raw animal protein. If you have chronic illness of the liver, stomach, or blood, or have immune disorders, you are at greater risk of serious illness from raw shellfish and should eat shellfish fully cooked. If unsure of your risk, consult a physician.

SPECIAL NOTE:
Shellfish should not be consumed raw after 14 days from the date of harvest, but should be thoroughly cooked.

34-3 Foodservice operators are required to keep shellfish tags on file for ninety days.

Bivalves

Hard-Shell Clams

Common hard-shell clams include cherry, stone, top neck, and little neck. They can range from ½ to 4 inches and are found in the northern Atlantic Ocean. Clams are most tender when small and become tougher as they get larger. They have a briny flavor and some varieties can be served raw.

Soft-Shell Clams

Types of soft-shell clams include razor and steamers. They are irregular in size and sold by bushel or weight. These clams can be sandy and are not eaten raw.

Mussels

Common mussel types include black or green lip and range from 1 to 4 inches. They are found in northern Atlantic and Pacific oceans and other locations worldwide. Most mussels are farm raised. They have black shells with tender, yellow-orange flesh inside that has a sweet briny flavor.

Oysters

Oysters are commonly named for their place of origin and can range from 2 to 4 inches. They are found in the Atlantic, Pacific, and other oceans around the world. Their flavor and salt content vary depending on their place of origin. Oysters taste either rich and fatty or have a briny, mineral flavor. They can be served raw.

Scallops

Common types of scallops are sea or bay and have a weight of from ½ to 3 ounces without the shell. Unlike other bivalves, only the adductor muscle that holds the shell closed is eaten. The flesh has a firm texture and sweet, succulent flavor. They are served cooked.

Bay scallops

Sea scallops

Cephalopods

Octopus

Octopuses are typically named for the area of harvest and range from ½ to 3 pounds. They are found worldwide and have very firm, white flesh with a sweet succulent flavor.

Squid (Calamari)

Squid are often named for the area of harvest and range from 3 to 10 inches long. They are found worldwide and have very firm, white flesh with a sweet succulent flavor.

The last member of the mollusk family that has culinary importance is the cephalopod (SEHF ah low pahd). **Cephalopods** are a category of mollusks that are known for their long arms that are covered with suckers, well-developed eyes, and sac which holds and ejects ink. Of the types of cephalopods, only two have culinary significance—octopus and squid. Both octopus and squid are prized for their flavor and texture. Both the head, which must be carefully cleaned, and the tentacles are edible. Black squid ink is a specialty item that is added to many preparations.

Judging the Quality of Fresh Shellfish

Crustaceans, such as Maine lobsters and soft-shell crabs, are often sold live because they deteriorate quickly once they die. Live crustaceans should respond vigorously when touched. Crustacean meat, such as lobster tail, can be purchased frozen. When thawed, it should have a firm texture and mild aroma. Crabmeat is always sold precooked and should have a clean, ocean-like aroma. If crabmeat or lobster smells like ammonia, it is not fresh and should not be used.

For bivalves purchased in the shell, the basic rule is to be sure the shell is firmly closed. As long as the shell is closed, the bivalve is still alive. When a bivalve dies, its shell automatically opens and remains open. In such cases, the dead bivalve is discarded. There is an exception to this rule. Sometimes a live bivalve will open its shell for a period of time. If you see an open shell, gently tap the bivalve on a counter, 34-4. A live bivalve

Draz-Koetke/Goodheart-Willcox Publisher

34-4 Tap an open bivalve on a hard surface to test if it is dead or alive.

will immediately close its shell, which indicates that it is ready to be used. A dead bivalve is unable to close its shell.

Some bivalves are sold **shucked**, which means that the contents of the bivalve are separated from the shell. For many bivalves such as oysters and clams, the entire contents inside the shell are consumed. For scallops, only the muscle inside the shell is eaten. The best test for shucked bivalves is to smell them to be sure they smell fresh and briny. Beware of scallops that are floating in large amounts of milky liquid as this denotes a lower quality scallop.

Both squid and octopus are judged similarly. To determine the quality of squid and octopus, inspect the following:

- *Smell.* Neither octopus nor squid should have a particularly strong smell.
- *Texture.* Squid and octopus should be firm and slightly elastic. They should not be mushy.
- *Color.* Any dark discoloration, especially on the body of the octopus or wings of the squid, indicates mishandling or old product.

Processed Fish Products

Not all fish and seafood is sold fresh. Much of the world's supply of fish and shellfish

products is processed in some fashion. Processing seafood increases shelf life and adds to the flavor and texture of the finished product. Processed fish products are sold in the following forms:

- *Frozen.* There are two important distinctions when purchasing frozen seafood. IQF (Individually Quick Frozen) describes products that are individually frozen and then packaged. For instance, it is possible to thaw individual pieces of IQF shrimp. Block frozen items are packaged and then frozen into a solid mass of frozen food. In the shrimp example, it would be necessary to thaw the entire block of frozen shrimp at once.
- *Salted and Dried.* Traditionally, some fish were preserved for long periods of time simply by heavily salting them. The large amount of salt caused the moisture to leave the fish, which made bacterial growth impossible. Three common examples of salted and dried seafood are salted shrimp, some varieties of herring, and salt cod.
- *Marinated.* Occasionally, seafood products are preserved using a flavorful acidic liquid. Marinated herring is a good example of a marinated product that must still be refrigerated.
- *Smoked.* This is one of the oldest preservation techniques. Seafood to be smoked is generally salted first. Smoking adds flavor, color, and texture to the finished product. Most smoked seafood products must still be refrigerated. Smoked salmon, mussels, and trout are used often in foodservice.
- *Canned.* Crabmeat, clams, clam juice, tuna, salmon, and anchovies are among the most common canned seafood products. Canned products are fully cooked, shelf stable, and often less expensive than the fresh equivalent.

Aquaculture

A chapter on finfish and shellfish identification would not be complete without

Chef Speak

Roe and Caviar

Caviar is considered one of the world's great luxury foods. Strictly speaking, caviar is the lightly salted eggs of a sturgeon from the Caspian Sea. True caviar is exceptional, very expensive, and currently endangered. Other fish eggs harvested from other waters are prepared similarly to caviar. While these eggs are sometimes called caviar, they are technically considered salted roe (ROH). Salted roe is made from fish such as lake trout, salmon, and whitefish.

SUSTAINABLE CULINARY

How Fish Are Harvested and Raised—It Matters!

Restaurants used to purchase and receive fish with little concern for how they were harvested or raised. As fish populations face unprecedented challenges around the world, there is a greater need for responsible fishing. Harvesting wild fish commercially is done using different fishing techniques such as purse seining, gillnetting, longlining, dredging, trolling, and so on. Some of these methods can have detrimental effects on ocean habitats and in the form of bycatch. Bycatch refers to the catching of different species of fish and marine mammals besides the intended catch.

There are also different methods of fish farming or aquaculture. Some of these can have detrimental effects on the environment while others can have little impact.

As part of sustainable kitchen practices, always inquire how your fish was harvested or raised before buying it. To learn more about wild fish harvesting techniques and aquaculture methods, go to the Monterey Bay Aquarium Seafood Watch website.

discussing one of the most important trends in seafood. **Aquaculture** is the farming of fish and shellfish. Aquaculture takes place in the wild (oceans, rivers, lakes) or within man-made, self-contained structures. Finfish or shellfish that are farm raised in the wild are still contained to a specific space. They are fed, monitored, and eventually harvested when they have reached the appropriate size. Some of the most common aquaculture products include salmon, hybrid bass, catfish, oysters, mussels, trout, and shrimp.

Aquaculture is growing rapidly and foodservice is increasingly using these products. People have conflicting views of

aquaculture. For instance, since aquaculture products are raised in a controlled environment, they are usually available year-round. They also have a consistent price and quality level. Some people also believe that aquaculture has the potential of supplying large amounts of food to a growing population. Other people argue that aquaculture damages the environment due to large concentrations of fish and other detrimental processes. Some chefs also believe that aquaculture products lack the flavor of wild fish. When making decisions about which fish products to use, it is important to be informed as to how they were raised and the impact on the environment.

Inspection and Regulations

Inspection and grading of fish and seafood products are voluntary and provided by the National Oceanic and Atmospheric Administration (NOAA) Seafood Inspection Program for the US Department of Commerce (USDC). The USDC **confers**, or grants, inspection and grade marks, 34-5. The USDC also inspects and certifies fish and seafood processing facilities also on a voluntary basis.

The US Food and Drug Administration establishes and enforces regulations for processing and importing fish and fishery products. The FDA also maintains a list of acceptable market names for specific fish and seafood species.

34-5 USDC marks denote (A) grading and (B) inspection of fish and seafood products.

Summary Points

- Finfish are divided into saltwater and fresh-water fish. Saltwater fish are further categorized as either round fish or flatfish.

- Shellfish have no bones but have hard, external surfaces. Shellfish are categorized as either crustaceans or mollusks.

- Chefs must be able to judge the quality of finfish and shellfish before purchasing or preparing it. These products spoil easily.

- Proper storage and handling is important with finfish and shellfish because these products are some of the most perishable items in the kitchen.

- Much of the world's supply of finfish and shellfish is processed in some way.

- Aquaculture is the farming of finfish and shellfish.

- Inspection and grading of fish and seafood products are voluntary.

In Review Assess

1. Finfish are species of fish with a(n) _____ skeleton and shellfish have bodies that are covered by hard _____ surfaces.

2. True or false. Freshwater fish typically have a less pronounced fishy flavor than saltwater fish.

3. Describe the difference between a round and flat finfish.

4. A fresh fish should have _____ colored gills and an older fish will have _____ colored gills.

5. List four types of crustaceans commonly used in foodservice.

6. List the three subgroups of the mollusk family.

7. Unlike other bivalves, only the adductor muscle of the _____ is eaten.

8. True or false. Maine lobsters and soft-shell crabs are often sold live because they deteriorate quickly once they die.

9. List four methods used to process fish products.

10. True or false. Aquaculture takes place only in man-made structures.

Core Skills

11. **Math.** Select one type of fish that is sold fresh. Research online or go to a grocery store to find three ways the same fish is processed and sold. Create a chart comparing the price per ounce for each of the three forms of the fish. Share your findings with the class.

12. **Reading.** Read *Cod: A Biography of the Fish that Changed the World*, by Mark Kurlansky, © 1997. What impact did cod fishing have on history? What nations and cultures where influenced by the search for cod? Write a book report summarizing the author's key points about cod fishing and its impact on the world.

13. **Speaking.** Choose an edible bivalve and create a digital diagram of its anatomy. Use presentation software to show your diagram to the class. Discuss the names of each part and their biological functions. Highlight the part of the bivalve that is commonly eaten. How can understanding bivalve structure better help you make good purchases for the commercial kitchen?

14. **Math.** A bushel of live crabs costs $125.50. After cooking and separating meat from the shells, the poissonier is left with 7½ pounds cooked crab meat. What is the per-pound cost of the cleaned crab meat? What is the cost of a 2½ ounce portion?

15. **CTE Career Readiness Practice.** As the poissonier at a fine-dining restaurant, part of your responsibility is to teach and train the other cooks on your staff. Your menu items are based on market availability and price. Today you will be addressing how to recognize the characteristics and judge the quality of three types of finfish (your choice), and one type of each shellfish (your choice)—

crustacean and mollusk. Think about the following as you prepare and give your illustrated presentation:

- individual characteristics of the finfish in regard to origin, size, and flesh texture
- quality characteristics of the finfish
- individual characteristic of the shellfish in regard to origin, size, shell type, and texture
- quality characteristics of the shellfish

Critical Thinking

16. **Recognize suitability.** The Food and Drug Administration has categorized fish and shellfish based on their mercury content levels. Use reliable Internet or print resources to learn about the mercury content of various fish and shellfish. As a chef writing a menu, would this information impact your menu offerings? Explain.

17. **Recognize alternatives.** Presume you are the chef at a restaurant located in the Midwest. The owner has asked you to add a seasonal fresh fish entrée to the menu. What are your alternatives? What type of fish would you choose and why?

18. **Analyze evidence.** You are going to cook an order of mussels when you notice that some of the shells are open. What should you do?

19. **Infer points of view.** The text states that people have conflicting points of view regarding aquaculture. Use the text and other reliable Internet or print resources to further investigate these various conflicting views. Examine the validity of these concerns. Write a summary of your findings and indicate your views on aquaculture.

Technology

Use reliable Internet or print resources to research current methods of raising fish and shellfish through aquaculture including open-net pens, ponds, raceways, and recirculating systems. What are the advantages and disadvantages of each? Use a school-approved web-based application to create an illustrated report of your findings. Share your report in class or post it to the class web page.

Teamwork

Tour a fish market with a group of classmates. Take notes on what you observe as the three items you see that are of the best quality and record their price. After your tour, compare notes with others in your group. As a group, create a menu of five dishes based on the fish or shellfish you saw on the tour. Describe the cooking process, other ingredients, plate presentation, and a selling price based on each item's cost.

Chef's E-portfolio
Anatomy of a Bivalve

Upload your digital presentation from activity #13 to your e-portfolio. Ask your instructor where to save your file. This could be on the school's network or a flash drive of your own. Name your portfolio document *FirstnameLastname_Portfolio Ch#.docx* (i.e., JohnSmith_PortfolioCh34.docx).

While studying, look for the activity icon 📲 to:

- Build vocabulary with e-flash cards and matching activities.
- Expand learning with video clips, photo identification activities, animations, and interactive activities.
- Review and assess what you learn by completing end-of-chapter questions.

G-WLEARNING.com

Fish and Shellfish Preparation and Cookery

35

Reading Prep

Before reading this chapter, look at the illustrations in the chapter to preview the content that will be presented. Illustrations help describe the content in an easy-to-understand manner.

Culinary Terminology Build Vocab

pin bones, p. 560
beurre noisette, p. 566
court bouillon, p. 570

Academic Terminology Build Vocab

entrails, p. 559

Objectives

After studying this chapter, you will be able to

- recognize the basic fabrication forms of finfish.
- apply preparation techniques for a variety of shellfish.
- explain how to store fresh finfish and shellfish.
- execute various dry-heat and moist-heat cooking methods for fish and shellfish.

American diners are eating more fish and shellfish than ever before. Many establishments buy fish and shellfish already fabricated or prepared. However, it is still important to know how to fabricate fish and seafood items since a large number of operations continue to receive their fish uncut. Whole fish and shellfish have the advantage of being easier to judge for freshness.

Fabrication Forms of Finfish

Chefs have a number of options when selecting what form of fresh fish to purchase, 35-1. These choices are influenced by the intended use for the product, the skill level and availability of kitchen labor, and the desired food cost. As with most food products, the more the fish is fabricated, the more its cost increases.

- *Whole.* This form describes the entire fish as it was when it was caught. It is an uncommon way to buy fish. The first part of the fish to begin to deteriorate is the **entrails**, or guts. Most commercial fishing operations gut fish as soon as they are caught to guard the quality and freshness of the product.
- *Drawn.* Fish that have been slit on the belly and had their internal organs removed are sold as drawn or gutted. Gutting fish improves their shelf life. Many chefs prefer this form because they can inspect the eyes and gills, which are good indicators of freshness.
- *Dressed.* A dressed fish is first drawn and then the head and collar are removed,

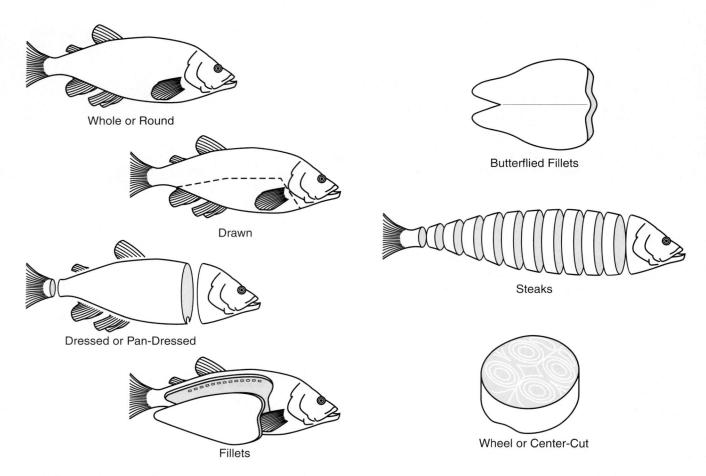

Whole or Round

Drawn

Dressed or Pan-Dressed

Fillets

Butterflied Fillets

Steaks

Wheel or Center-Cut

35-1 Chefs must consider what fabrication form will work best for their operation when purchasing fish.

and the tail and fins are trimmed. Trout and other small fish that will be panfried, baked, or grilled are commonly sold in this form.

- *Fillet.* Fillet is the muscle that has been removed from the carcass of the fish. Fillets may be "sides," butterfly fillets (two sides attached), or "suprêmes" (half sides cut from flatfish).
- *Skinless fillets.* Removing the skin from boneless fillets provides a totally edible product.
- *Steaks.* Steaks are crosscut individual portions. They often include the backbone and skin. Salmon, halibut, swordfish, and tuna are often cut into steaks.
- *Center cut.* Large round fish are often cut into steaks. In order to get uniform-sized portions, these items can be purchased without the head, collar, or narrow tail section.

Filleting Round Fish

Round fish swim vertically and have an eye on each side of their head. These fish have rib bones and pin bones that make the filleting process more difficult than flatfish. **Pin bones** are small bones that are imbedded in the fillet and must be removed with pliers or tweezers.

Filleting Flatfish

Flatfish are fish that swim with their body horizontal to the ocean bottom, 35-2. They have eyes on the top side of their head. They are dark on top and have a white or light-colored underside. They have a simple bone structure, which makes them easier to fillet than round fish.

TECHNIQUE
Filleting Round Fish

1. **Start with a drawn fish. Cut the fish behind the head and gills, or remove the head entirely.**

2. **Make a shallow cut along the back close to the back fin.**

3. **Start along the back using short smooth strokes with the tip of the knife to separate the flesh from the backbone. Work over the rib bones and detach the fillet from the bone all the way from the back fin to the belly.**

4. **Place the fillet knife perpendicular to the backbone behind the rib bones. With the blade angled toward the backbone, use a sawing motion and cut the fillet from the backbone. Continue this motion all the way through the tail to fully free the fillet from the carcass.**

5. **Turn the fish over and repeat this process to remove the fillet from the other side of the fish.**

6. **Use a pair of pliers to remove the small pin bones found in the fillet where the rib bones were connected with the backbone.**

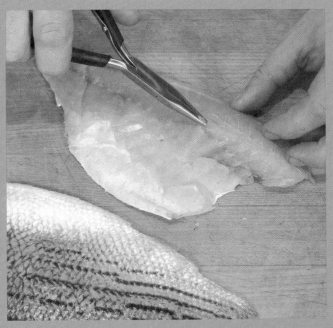

Common Flatfish	
• Flounder	• Plaice
• Fluke	• Sole
• Halibut	• Turbot

35-2 The typically sedentary existence of these flatfish contributes to a relatively mild flavor making them popular on foodservice menus.

Skinning Fillets

With some practice, removing the skin from a fillet is an easy task. Remember to use a knife with a blade that is longer than the widest part of the fillet you are trying to skin. A knife with a thin, flexible blade works best. The technique for removing the skin from fillets is the same for both round and flatfish.

TECHNIQUE
Filleting Flatfish

1. Place the fish on the cutting board with its dark side up. Using a flexible boning or fillet knife, cut through the skin in a line down the middle of the fish from behind the head to the center of the tail.

2. Start at the slit in the skin near the head. Using short smooth strokes with the tip of the knife separate the flesh from the backbone. Work from the center of the fish toward the outer edge, putting moderate pressure on the knife to keep the blade close to the bones.

3. When all the muscle of the fillet is detached from the bone, cut through the skin around the outer edge of the fish to release the fillet from the fish.

4. Repeat this process with the other fillet on the dark side of the fish.

5. Turn the fish over and repeat the filleting procedure on the two fillets on the light side of the fish.

Shellfish Preparation

Each variety of shellfish has its own method of preparation. Most dishes made with shrimp require the shrimp to be peeled and deveined. Peeling and deveining, which removes the shell and the digestive tract, is a simple process. Mussels have become a popular seafood product, especially since

TECHNIQUE
Peeling and Deveining Shrimp

1. On the underside of the shrimp, pinch the shell between your thumb and forefinger. Peel back to remove the shell. The last section of the shell and the tail may be left on for presentation. Peel off any remaining shell and legs with your fingers.

2. Use a paring knife to make a shallow slit down the back of the shrimp.

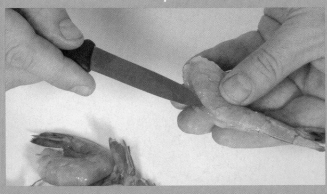

3. Spread the slit area open and remove the dark vein from the shrimp. Rinse with cold water if necessary to remove all parts of the vein.

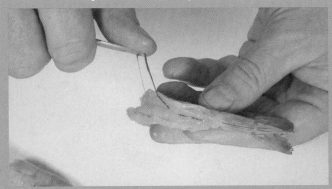

TECHNIQUE
Skinning Fillets

1. Place the fillet, skin side down and grab the skin of the fish at the end of the tail.

2. Cut between the skin and the fillet.
3. Hold the skin taut. Angle the knife blade down and use a sawing motion to remove the skin.

they have become available farm raised. Checking to be sure that none of the mussels are dead or spoiled is a critical part of the cleaning procedure. Any mussels that do not close are dead and must be discarded. Hard shell clams are often served with the flesh presented in the natural cup formed by the lower half of the clam's shell. This presentation is called *on the half shell.* Hot or cold clam dishes often call for clams to be opened before being cooked or served raw. A special clam knife is used to open the clams. As with clams, oysters are often served on the half shell or shucked. An oyster knife is designed

TECHNIQUE
Opening Clams

1. **Wash and scrub clams to remove any sand or mud from the outside of their shells. Discard any clams that are open.**
2. **Using a towel or protective glove to protect your hand, hold the clam in your palm.**
3. **Place the blade of the clam knife on the outer edge of the clam where the top and bottom shells meet.**
4. **Place the fingers of the hand holding the clam on the back edge of the clam knife.**

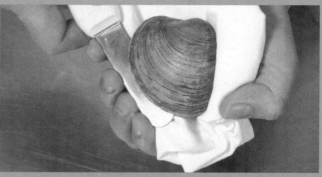

5. **Squeeze the knife into the clam and sever the muscles that attach the clam to the shell.**

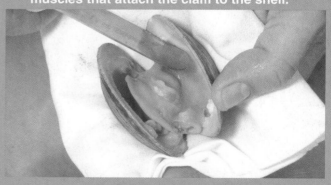

6. **Detach the clam meat from both the top and bottom shell with the clam knife. Remove the top shell.**

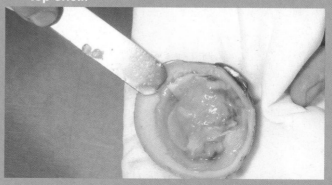

TECHNIQUE
Cleaning Mussels

1. **Submerge the mussels in cold water to wash off any mud or silt.**
2. **Check each mussel individually by pressing on the shell. Any mussels that are not closed or do not close when squeezed should be discarded.**

3. **Scrub shell to remove any barnacles or other foreign matter on their surface.**
4. **Debeard the mussels by pulling off the fibers that stick out of the shell, also known as the beard.**

especially for this task. Rather than using the knife as a wedge to open the lip of the shell as with clams, oysters are opened by prying on the hinge.

Storage and Handling of Fish and Shellfish

Fish and shellfish are the most perishable items in commercial kitchens. Proper handling is essential for serving a safe and quality product. Fish should be stored between 30°F and 34°F (–1°C and 1°C). Since most commercial refrigeration is designed to hold foods at 40°F (4°C), fresh fish must be stored on crushed ice.

Proper care must be taken when storing fish on ice in order not to destroy its flavor and delicate texture. When fish is stored on ice, there must be a way for the water from the melting ice to drain away. Without drainage, the flesh of the fish becomes waterlogged, destroying its texture and diluting its flavor.

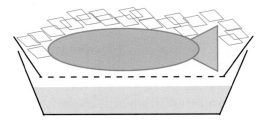

Place whole or drawn fish directly on the ice, 35-3. Completely cover the fish with additional ice. Storing whole or drawn fish directly on ice is acceptable because the fish's skin protects the flesh. Fillets, on the other hand, should not come in direct contact with ice or they may become "ice burned" and mushy. Fillets should be wrapped and covered with butcher's paper or plastic before being iced.

TECHNIQUE
Opening Oysters

1. **Wash and scrub oysters to remove any sand or mud from the shells. Discard any oysters that are open.**
2. **Using a towel or use a protective glove, hold the oyster on the work surface with the cupped part of the shell on the bottom.**
3. **Place the tip of the oyster knife between the upper and lower shells at the hinge (where the shell tapers to a point opposite the rounded edge).**

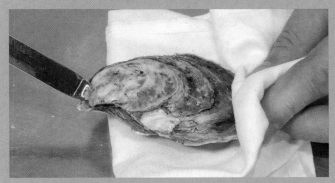

4. **Use the knife like a lever to pry the upper shell until it pops open.**

5. **Use the blade of the knife to detach the oyster from the top and bottom shells. Take care to leave the oyster whole and uncut.**

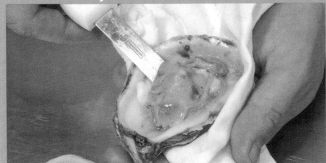

Draz-Koetke/Goodheart-Willcox Publisher

35-3 Fish with skin on can be placed directly on ice for storage.

Mollusks such as clams, oysters, and mussels, should be stored at 40°F (4°C). Since they are alive, storing them at lower temperatures or on ice may cause them to freeze and die. Store mollusks in the container in which they were received and in the coldest part of the refrigerator. Cephalopods should be stored in the same manner as fillets.

Cooking Fish and Shellfish

Most of the principles of cooking vegetables, grains, meat, and poultry hold true for fish and seafood items. The most important distinction to keep in mind when dealing with seafood cookery is that fish and seafood items are far more delicate than meat, poultry, vegetable, or grains. Fish and shellfish have little connective tissue so there is no need to tenderize them through the cooking process. Fish and seafood are also high in moisture.

Since fish and seafood items are delicate and tender, the cooking process should be quick. Probably the most common mistake in seafood cookery is overcooking. Overcooked fish and seafood become dry and have a mealy or rubbery texture.

Determining Doneness

Cooking fish to the proper doneness is key for producing a quality product. Fish should be cooked to the point where its protein is fully coagulated and no more. Any further cooking only serves to dry out the product.

The appearance of the interior of the flesh is important when determining doneness. Underdone fish is translucent and fleshy. Fully cooked fish has flesh that is opaque and flaky. In many cases, it may be necessary to "peek" at the interior of the flesh to judge its doneness. Experienced cooks can do this by bending the fillet or delicately poking into the interior of the flesh without damaging the appearance of the product. Unlike meats, fish do not lose moisture if they are probed.

Dry-Heat Methods

The dry-heat methods used for cooking fish and shellfish are sautéing, panfrying, deep frying, grilling, broiling, and baking. These methods are appropriate because the flesh of most fish and shellfish is naturally tender.

Sautéing   The process of sautéing fish is similar to sautéing white meats such as chicken or veal. To help seal in the moisture, fish and fish fillets are usually dredged before being sautéed. Dredging also helps to create the golden-brown color desired in most sautéed fish and seafood items.

Many chefs prefer clarified butter for sautéing fish or seafood because of its rich flavor. The smoking point of butter is sufficient to create a golden-brown finished product.

Whole butter is often used to create a sort of sauce for sautéed fish. After the item is sautéed, a small amount of whole butter is added to the hot pan and allowed to brown. Browned butter is a classical preparation called **beurre noisette** (BEHR nwah zhet). The browned butter is poured over the fish with a few drops of lemon juice and some

TECHNIQUE
Sautéing Fish

1. Choose fillets or pieces of uniform thickness.
2. Use only enough clarified butter to coat the bottom of the pan.
3. Preheat the butter as hot as possible without burning the fat.
4. Dredge fish and shake off any excess flour.
5. Add no more than a single layer of fish pieces into pan.

6. Brown on both sides. Remove the fish from the pan. Thick pieces may be finished in the oven.

7. Add whole butter to the pan and allow it to brown.*

8. Add lemon juice, chopped parsley, and almonds (if desired) to the butter. Pour over fish.*

9. Serve immediately.

*note: Steps 7–8 are classical techniques not required in all recipes

chopped parsley. The nutty flavor of the browned butter is an excellent complement to most sautéed fish and seafood items. The basic browned butter can be modified with the addition of almonds, capers, or other ingredients.

Panfrying Another popular dry-heat method for preparing fish is panfrying. This method is very similar to sautéing. The main difference between the two methods is that panfrying requires more fat. Fish is always dredged in breading or batter before panfrying. It is important that the fat is hot before the fish is added to the pan.

Deep Frying Deep frying uses enough fat to completely submerge the fish. As with panfrying, the fish is usually breaded or battered before cooking. The fat should be preheated before adding the fish. Fish is usually cooked until the coating is golden brown and the flesh is opaque.

Grilling The most important consideration for grilling fish is the choice of fish, 35-4. Not all varieties work equally well for grilling. Intense heat of the grill and the ability to handle the fish during the grilling process without it breaking requires a firm-fleshed fish. Some oil content also helps to keep the

Recipe No.	Name		Category
35.1	Fillet of Sole Amandine		Fish, sautéing
Yield	**Portion Size**		**No. Portions**
4 servings	1 fillet		4
US Quantity	**Metric Quantity**	**Ingredient**	**TCS**
4 ea.		sole fillets, 4-5 oz. each	•
8 oz.	225 g	flour	
1 Tbsp.	15 mL	salt	
¼ tsp.	1 mL	ground white pepper	
2 fl. oz.	60 mL	clarified butter	•
2 oz.	60 g	whole butter	•
2 oz.	60 g	sliced almonds, toasted	
1 Tbsp.	15 mL	parsley, chopped	
2 tsp.	10 mL	lemon juice	
Method			**CCP**
1. Combine the flour, salt, and white pepper. Dredge fillets in flour and shake off excess.			
2. Heat clarified butter in a suitably sized sauté pan to the smoking point.			
3. Add fillets and cook until golden brown on the first side.			
4. Turn the fillets and cook until golden brown on the second side.			
5. Remove the fillets from the pan and place on serving plates and sprinkle them with the parsley and lemon juice. Hold at 135°F (57°C) or warmer.			CCP
6. Place the whole butter and almonds in the pan and cook the butter until it becomes brown and bubbly and the almonds are lightly browned.			
7. Spoon the butter and almonds over the fish fillets and serve immediately.			

Portion (g)	Calories	Fat (g)	Protein (g)	Carbohydrate (g)	Cholesterol (mg)	Sodium (mg)	Fiber (g)
188	454.37	29.98	27.58	17.72	127.89	802.30	1.33

Fish on the Grill	
Most Suitable for Grilling	**Least Suitable for Grilling**
Catfish	Cod
Grouper	Flounder
Halibut	Haddock
Mahi-mahi	Pollack
Salmon	Sole
Swordfish	Whitefish
Tuna	

35-4 Not all types of fish hold up well during grilling.

fish moist during the cooking process. The cut of fish is also important. Thick fillets or steaks work best since they are easy to handle on the grill and are less likely to become overcooked.

Even with firm-fleshed fish cut to an appropriate size, fish is much more difficult to grill than meat. It must be handled with care so that it does not stick to the grill or break. Fish can also char or dry out more easily than meat.

Broiling   Broiling is an easy way to cook most any variety of fish or seafood. It is an excellent alternative method for varieties that will not stand up to grilling.

Broiling is done on a metal plate or platter that many chefs refer to as a *sizzle plate*. The item to be broiled is placed on a buttered or oiled sizzle plate. It is seasoned and brushed or coated with more butter or oil. The plate is placed under the broiler to cook the item, 35-5. The heat of the broiler cooks and browns the fish.

Baking   Baking uses a gentler heat than broiling. For delicately textured fish and seafood items, this lessens the chance of overcooking. Additionally, the process of baking fish usually involves adding a small amount of liquid or butter, which aids in

Hints from the Chef
Fish in a Bag

An interesting variation on baking fish is to bake fillets or smaller pieces of fish in a sealed package with other flavorful ingredients. Often the fish is cooked in a bag or envelope made of parchment paper. This method is done in many different cuisines. In French, this method is referred to as *en papillote*, and in Italian it is called *in cartoccio*. Both terms mean "in paper."

This method of cooking is a cross between baking and steaming. Although the item is cooked in the oven, as it cooks the moisture of the fish creates steam. This steam cooks the fish and other ingredients blending their flavors. The steam also causes the parchment package to puff up like a balloon. It is traditional for the parchment envelope to be opened at the table where the steam releases the aromas of all the ingredients in the bag to the pleasure of the diners.

Draz-Koetke/Goodheart-Willcox Publisher

35-5 Fish are placed on an oiled metal plate for broiling.

TECHNIQUE
Grilling Fish

1. Preheat the grill.
2. Clean the grill with a wire brush.
3. Brush item to be grilled with oil or clarified butter. Season the product.

4. Place the item on a hot area of the grill. Allow grill marks to form.
5. Turn the product 90° and allow cross marks to form.

6. Flip the fish and finish cooking the other side of the fillet or steak on the grill. More delicate items may be finished in the oven.

keeping the product moist. Many times fish are baked as whole dressed fish. These dishes have the beautiful presentation of a whole fish combined with the moist texture produced by baking.

Moist-Heat Methods

Since most fish and shellfish are naturally tender, moisture is not used to tenderize fish. Rather, the moisture used in cooking fish is intended to add flavor. Poaching cooks fish in a flavored liquid with gentle heat. Poaching is ideal for many types of fish because it does not destroy the fish's delicate texture. It can be done in two different ways. Deep poaching is a method where the item is fully covered with liquid. Shallow poaching uses a small amount of liquid so the product is only partially covered.

Deep Poaching Deep poaching is best used for large whole dressed fish or large pieces. The gentle cooking temperature keeps the fish from disintegrating and preserves its natural shape. The fish cooks evenly and does not dry out during the cooking process because the fish is fully submerged in the cooking liquid.

The liquid used to deep poach a fish adds flavor to the finished product. Since acid helps to coagulate the proteins found in fish, an acidic ingredient is added to the poaching liquid to prevent the fish from breaking up or falling apart. This acidic ingredient might be vinegar or lemon juice.

Court bouillon is the preferred liquid for deep poaching. **Court bouillon** (kohr BOO yohn) is made by simmering aromatic vegetables, herbs, and spices—such as mirepoix and a sachet—in water with an acid. The term *court bouillon* means "short broth" because the liquid needs to be simmered only long enough to extract flavor from the aromatic ingredients. The acid ingredient in a court bouillon can be vinegar or lemon juice. Salt is also added to a court bouillon to add flavor to the poached item.

TECHNIQUE
Deep Poaching Fish

1. Make a court bouillon by simmering mirepoix and sachet in water. Season with salt and an acid such as vinegar or lemon juice.

2. Strain and cool the court bouillon. Small pieces of fish are often started in hot liquid.

3. Place the item to be poached in a suitably sized pan and cover with the court bouillon. If the product floats, it may need to be weighed down with a rack to keep it submerged.

4. Place the pan on the range and heat the liquid until small bubbles begin to break the surface. Proper temperature of the poaching liquid, 160°F–180°F (71°C–82°C), can be verified with a thermometer.

5. Allow the product to poach, taking care to maintain proper temperature. Some chefs find placing the pan, uncovered, in a moderate 350°F (176°C) oven is a good way to maintain the proper poaching temperature.

6. Test doneness by checking the texture of the flesh near the center of the piece. For large pieces, doneness can also be tested with a thermometer. Fish are fully cooked when an internal temperature of 145°F (63°C) is reached.

Chef Speak

Classic Sautéed Fish Preparations

Fish sautéed in butter and finished with beurre noisette has long been a favorite with diners. Many classic variations on this technique have become well-known. Here are some of the most popular variations familiar to both chefs and diners.

À la Meunière (ah lah MOON yehr)—Sautéed, finished with beurre noisette, chopped parsley, and lemon juice.

Amandine (ah MAHN deen)—Sautéed and finished with beurre noisette, toasted almonds, parsley, and lemon.

Doria (DOR ee ah)—Prepared the same as à la meunière with the addition of cucumbers.

Grenobloise (grehn OH blaws)—Sautéed and garnished with capers, lemon suprêmes, buerre noisette, and chopped parsley. The term means "in the style of Grenoble," a town in the French Alps.

Shallow Poaching As with deep poaching, shallow poaching uses gentle heat and a flavored liquid. The difference is that shallow poaching uses considerably less liquid. The liquid does not fully cover the product being poached. After poaching is complete, the flavorful cooking liquid is used to create a sauce. The amount of liquid used in shallow poaching depends on the amount of sauce needed for the finished dish.

Shallow poaching is done with small fillets. It is a quick process that is often used for cooking fish in restaurants as they are ordered. As with other moist-heat cooking methods, shallow poaching is often started on the stovetop and finished in the oven. It is customary to loosely cover the items being poached with a buttered piece of parchment paper or foil. This keeps the fish from drying out. A tightly sealed cover would seal in steam making

TECHNIQUE
Shallow Poaching Fish

1. Butter a sauteuse and add aromatic ingredients according to recipe.
2. Add fish fillets and cooking liquid to the pan.

3. Bring to a simmer on top of the stove.
4. Cover with buttered parchment and finish poaching in the oven.

5. When done, remove fish from the pan and reduce cooking liquid.
6. Add additional ingredients to create a sauce.

7. Serve fish with the sauce.

the cooking temperature too high for the delicate texture of most fish.

After the fish is cooked, it is removed from the pan and kept warm while a sauce is prepared from the richly flavored cooking liquid. To create a sauce, the cooking liquid may be reduced or beurre manié may be added to thicken it. The poaching liquid may also be enriched with cream or butter.

Steaming Steaming is a cooking method best used on shellfish and crustaceans that are protected by a thick outer shell. The shell protects the flesh from the intense heat of steaming. Steaming is a good method for cooking lobsters, crabs, mussels, and clams, 35-6. Steaming is not recommended for finfish and fillets. Since the flesh of most fish is delicate, the high heat of steaming makes the flesh tough or rubbery.

Steaming shellfish is often done on the range in a pot. A small amount of rapidly boiling liquid at the bottom of a pot with a tight fitting cover creates the steam needed for cooking shellfish such as clams and mussels. The juice released from these items is often served with the steamed shellfish. Steaming may also be done in a steamer or steam oven. If steamed shellfish are not to be served immediately, they should be shocked in cold water to prevent overcooking.

Draz-Koetke/Goodheart-Willcox Publisher

35-6 Mussels can be steamed because their shells protect them from the intense heat of the steam.

Summary Points

- Fish can be purchased in a number of different market forms. The more processed the product is, the greater the cost.

- Fish can be categorized as either flatfish or round fish. Each type of fish requires a different technique for filleting.

- Various types of shellfish require different preparations before cooking.

- Proper storage and handling is important with finfish and shellfish because these products are some of the most perishable items in the kitchen. Storage guidelines vary depending on the type of fish and the fabrication.

- The delicate nature of fish and seafood requires great care to avoid overcooking.

- Fish should be cooked only long enough to allow the protein to fully coagulate.

- Dry-heat or moist-heat cooking methods can be used on most fish and shellfish because they are tender by nature and have high moisture content.

- Choosing firm fleshed varieties of fish is key to a good grilled product.

- Steaming is best used on shellfish and crustaceans that are protected by an outer shell.

In Review

Assess

1. A fish that has been drawn or gutted has had its _____ _____ removed.

2. True or false. Flatfish are easier to fillet than round fish.

3. What type of fish has pin bones and how are they removed?

4. What has been removed from a shrimp that has been peeled and deveined?

5. How does the technique for opening clams differ from that for opening oysters?

6. Describe how fish fillets should be stored on ice.

7. Fish and shellfish have much less _____ _____ than meat and poultry so there is no need to tenderize them through the cooking process.

8. Describe the appearance of a fully cooked fillet of fish.

9. What is often done to a fillet of fish before it is sautéed?

10. List the key ingredients in a court bouillon.

Core Skills

11. **Math.** Visit a grocery store or use online resources to find the price per pound for whole salmon, salmon fillets, and salmon steaks. Calculate the percent price difference for these various fabrications.

12. **Writing.** Obtain a menu for a seafood restaurant or find one online. Write an inventory list of all the seafood products needed to execute the menu. Decide how you, as chef, would purchase each of the items by listing its fabrication form and whether it is fresh or frozen.

13. **Reading.** Use Internet or print resources to read about the cooking process for the traditional *New England clambake*. What ingredients are used? What is unique about the cooking process? How would you create a clambake in a professional kitchen? Use presentation software to create an illustrated report of your findings.

14. **Speaking.** Use reliable resources to identify the process for drawing and dressing a whole fish. Demonstrate for the class how to draw and dress a whole fish. During your demonstration, describe each of the steps of the technique as you do them. Discuss the importance of properly removing the entrails.

15. **Math.** The poissonier receives 30 lb., 4 oz. of dressed mahi-mahi. After filleting and skinning, 13 lb., 12 oz. of fillets were produced. What is the yield percentage of the fillets? If the whole dressed mahi-mahi was purchased for $5.85/lb., what is the per pound cost of the fillets?

16. **Speaking.** Using a type of shellfish as assigned by your instructor, demonstrate how to steam the shellfish using the text technique. During your demonstration, describe the process and the desired outcome for the finished product. Plate the product when done. Have the class evaluate the appearance, flavor, and texture. Discuss any challenges you faced during preparation.

17. **CTE Career Readiness Practice.** Suppose you work as a poissonier at a fine-dining restaurant. The restaurant manager tells you he wants to add locally sourced fish dishes to the menu but is unsure about the availability and cost. The manager asks you to do some research. Your first effort to creatively solve the problem is to ask questions. Create a mind map like the following to dig deeper into the problem.

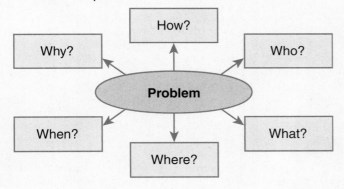

Critical Thinking

18. **Analyze criteria.** Under what circumstances would a chef choose to fillet fish in the kitchen rather than purchase it already filleted from a purveyor? What criteria might the chef use for making this decision?

19. **Analyze criteria.** Visit a restaurant that specializes in seafood or research online to find out what types of equipment and procedures are used to store fish in professional kitchens. What factors would you consider when choosing which seafood storage equipment for a new commercial kitchen?

20. **Draw conclusions.** How will the way in which a fish is fabricated (dressed, steaks, fillets) affect a chef's choice of cooking method?

Technology

Use Internet resources to research recipes for fish or shellfish cooked using the *sous vide* method. What temperature is indicated for the cooking process? How does that temperature compare to poaching or steaming? What special equipment is needed to cook fish or shellfish by the *sous vide* method? Create a digital report to share your findings with the class.

Teamwork

In teams, prepare the *Fillet of Sole Amandine* recipe found in this chapter or another fish or shellfish recipe as assigned by your instructor. Assign specific tasks of the preparation method to each team member following the recipe and text instructions. Plate the finished dish. As a team, evaluate the final dish for appearance, flavor, and appropriate doneness. Prepare a report that includes a summary of your findings, a photo of the final dish, and the recipe used.

Chef's E-portfolio
Fish Preparation

Upload your report from the Teamwork activity to your e-portfolio. Ask your instructor where to save your file. This could be on the school's network or a flash drive of your own. Name your portfolio document *FirstnameLastname_Portfolio Ch#.docx* (i.e., JohnSmith_PortfolioCh35.docx).

Video Clip

Deep Poaching Fish

Visit the G-W Learning Companion Website and view the bonus video clip "Deep poaching fish." After viewing the clip, answer the following questions:

1. What is the role of the liquid when deep poaching fish or shellfish?

2. How could you tell if poaching liquid has reached proper temperature if you do not have a thermometer?

3. True or false. To test for doneness, test the flesh at the center of the fish.

Video

While studying, look for the activity icon ⤴ to:

- Build vocabulary with e-flash cards and matching activities.
- Expand learning with video clips, photo identification activities, animations, and interactive activities.
- Review and assess what you learn by completing end-of-chapter questions.

G-W LEARNING.com

Hot Sandwiches and Pizza

36

Reading Prep

In preparation for reading the chapter, review a variety of restaurant menus for the types and numbers of hot sandwiches offered. Identify the different ingredients being used. Compare your findings to the chapter as you read.

Culinary Terminology Build Vocab

clamshell griddle, p. 581
panini grill, p. 581
pizza, p. 585
pizza peel, p. 586

Academic Terminology Build Vocab

perforated, p. 586

Objectives

After studying this chapter, you will be able to

- recognize various types of hot sandwiches and the ingredients used to make them.
- explain how to make thin crust and deep dish pizzas.

Think of all the hamburgers, grilled cheese, and pizza served every day in cafeterias, diners, and fast-food restaurants. Hot sandwiches and pizza are among the most popular items in foodservice today. For many people, hot sandwiches and pizza represent comfort food. For others, hot sandwiches and pizza slices "to go" are ideal for fast-paced lifestyles.

Hot Sandwiches

Unlike a cold sandwich, either part or the entire hot sandwich is hot when served. Aside from this difference, many of the same considerations are given to hot sandwiches as to cold sandwiches. For instance, hot sandwiches must create a perfect combination of bread, main ingredients, and condiments. Hot sandwiches must also have an appealing appearance. Hot sandwiches can be divided into two categories—sandwiches made using hot fillings and whole cooked sandwiches, 36-1.

Sandwiches with Hot Fillings

Many hot sandwiches contain only one or two hot fillings. The rest of the ingredients in the sandwich are cool or cold. This combination of ingredients and their temperature differences is very satisfying. Popular hot sandwiches include hamburgers, Italian beef, and corned beef. Some common hot sandwich ingredients are
- chicken breast
- lunch meats

Draz-Koetke/Goodheart-Willcox Publisher

36-1 Sandwiches with hot fillings are among the most popular items in foodservice.

- ham
- fish
- sliced beef
- sausages
- caramelized onions
- grilled peppers
- sautéed portobello mushrooms

Hints from the Chef
Reheating Refresher

Reheating cooked meat products should be done carefully and slowly. If a cold cooked piece of meat is reheated at high temperatures, it will toughen and dry out. Be sure that a precooked piece of meat is reheated to 165°F (74°C) within 2 hours.

To serve these sandwiches successfully, the hot components must be hot and the other components must remain cool. If improperly prepared, the entire sandwich becomes unpleasantly lukewarm. To prevent this from happening, these sandwiches are assembled only as needed. This does not necessarily mean that the hot ingredients need be cooked at the last moment. In fact, some foodservice operations cook the hot ingredients in advance and hold them in a warmer until needed. When the sandwich is ordered, it is simply assembled using the precooked items.

Sautéed or Griddled Ingredients Many of the most common hot sandwiches contain sautéed or griddled ingredients. Hamburgers, chicken breasts, eggs, and pork chops are frequently served as a sautéed or griddled sandwich item, 36-2.

Draz-Koetke/Goodheart-Willcox Publisher

36-2 Special thermometers are used to accurately measure the temperature of thin items such as hamburgers.

Photo courtesy of Eric Futran/chefShots

One of America's greatest food traditions is barbecue. Barbecue is not grilling. Barbecuing uses a smoker to slow-cook the food. Some barbecue favorites may take 10 to 14 hours to cook. Specialties such as pulled pork and beef brisket make delicious sandwiches. To make the sandwiches, place the hot barbecued meat on a bun or between slices of bread. Top with barbecue sauce and serve additional sauce on the side.

When cooking raw meats and fish for a sandwich, it is important to cook the item to a safe degree of doneness. Checking the finished cooked product with an instant-read thermometer is essential. Special thermometers have been developed to accurately measure the temperature of a thin item such as a hamburger patty. Refer to the local health code to determine the safe degree of doneness for different proteins.

Hamburger in particular has been the source of some deadly outbreaks of *E. coli* contamination. Steaks can be cooked to a lesser degree than hamburger meat because *E. coli* is located on the surface of a solid piece of meat. When a steak is cooked, the *E. coli* is subjected to high temperatures and is killed. When a steak is ground into hamburger, the *E. coli* bacteria is distributed throughout the meat. As a result, hamburger must be cooked to a minimum of 155°F (68°C) to ensure that any *E. coli* in the meat is killed.

Deep-Fried Ingredients   Sandwiches featuring deep-fried ingredients are popular menu items. Deep-fried ingredients have the advantage of adding crunch to a sandwich. Unfortunately, deep-fried ingredients can become soggy if they are not served shortly

after deep-frying. For this reason, sandwiches made from deep-fried ingredients are best prepared at the last moment possible. If it is necessary to hold the cooked product, hold it uncovered in a warmer. If it is covered, the enclosed steam from the product will make it soggy. Sandwiches with deep-fried ingredients have a higher fat content and therefore, benefit from spicy, acidic, and fresh condiments. Some common deep-fried ingredients for sandwiches include the following:

- mild, flaky fish such as cod or haddock
- catfish
- oysters
- chicken breast
- falafel (deep-fried patties made from ground garbanzo beans)

Grilled Ingredients   With the increase in healthy eating trends and bold flavors, grilling has become a popular cooking method. As with sautéed or griddled ingredients, grilled ingredients must be cooked to an internal temperature that makes them safe to eat. Grilling is also a good technique for cooking vegetables and warming sandwich buns and bread. Hamburgers, chicken breasts, fish, and vegetables are commonly grilled for sandwiches, 36-3.

Poached Ingredients Poaching is rarely used to cook or heat hot sandwich ingredients. The most common examples of poached sandwich ingredients are sausages—especially hot dogs. Poaching a raw or cooked sausage allows the meat to heat with minimal shrinkage. Boiling sausages at high temperatures will cause the sausage to shrink, dry out, and split. Most sausages are simply cooked or heated in poaching water. Sometimes, sausages are poached in a flavorful liquid. Bratwurst poached in beer and onions is a common example.

Whole Cooked Sandwiches

A whole cooked sandwich differs from a sandwich with hot filling because the entire sandwich is cooked and served hot. These sandwiches often have an appealing crunchy exterior because they are cooked after being assembled. Like sandwiches with a hot filling, they can be prepared using numerous cooking methods.

Sautéed or Griddled Whole Cooked Sandwiches Sautéed or griddled sandwiches are made in two steps—assembling and cooking. The first step is to assemble

Draz-Koetke/Goodheart-Willcox Publisher

36-3 While hot sandwich items may be prepared in advance, it is best to assemble the sandwiches at the last moment.

the sandwich between two pieces of bread. The exterior surfaces of the bread are then lightly coated with butter or oil. The second step is to cook the assembled sandwich on a griddle or in a sauté pan. Halfway through the cooking process, the sandwich must be flipped. A properly cooked sautéed or griddled sandwich should be crisp on the outside and hot on the inside.

For large volume or fast-paced operations, these sandwiches should be assembled in advance and held in the cooler until needed. When an order is received, the assembled sandwich is sautéed or griddled. Despite its name, the familiar grilled cheese sandwich is actually a sautéed or griddled sandwich, 36-4.

A variation of sautéed or griddled sandwiches is sandwiches that are cooked in a clamshell griddle or panini grill. A **clamshell griddle** consists of two hot, smooth surfaces that close on the top and bottom of the sand-

Draz-Koetke/Goodheart-Willcox Publisher

36-4 These sautéed or griddled sandwiches have an appealing golden brown finish.

wich, thus cooking both sides at once. A **panini grill** is similar to a clamshell griddle except the hot surfaces have ridges that leave grill marks on the cooked sandwich, 36-5.

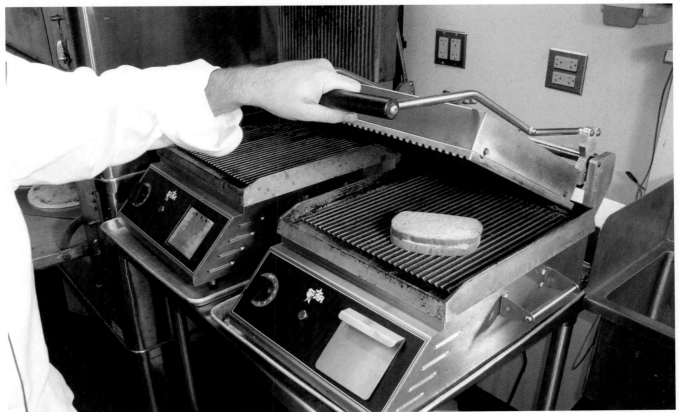

Draz-Koetke/Goodheart-Willcox Publisher

36-5 Panini machines grill both sides of the sandwich at once.

Chef Speak

Hot Sandwich Specialties

Beer Brats—A specialty of Wisconsin, this sandwich features bratwurst simmered in beer and onions. The brat is served on a bun with German-style mustard.

Burrito—A Southwestern specialty that includes assorted ingredients such as grilled or braised meats, cheese, refried beans, tomatoes, and salsa wrapped in a large tortilla.

Chimichanga—This Southwestern specialty is a deep-fried burrito.

Crab Cake Sandwich—Crab cakes are made from a mixture of crabmeat, bread crumbs, and mayonnaise that is deep fried or sautéed. The crab cake is served on a bun with spicy mayonnaise. This is a specialty of the Atlantic states.

Cuban Sandwich—This baked or pressed sandwich is made of pork, ham, Swiss cheese, pickles, and mustard on crusty French bread. Served on softer bread it is often called a *media noche*.

Egg and Pepper—This sandwich was created as a nonmeat sandwich option. It consists of scrambled eggs cooked with grilled green peppers and served on a bun.

Gyros—This Greek and Middle Eastern specialty is thinly sliced rotisserie lamb or lamb loaf that is stuffed inside a pita bread. It is served with tomato, lettuce, and cucumber yogurt sauce.

Italian Beef—This sandwich is thin slices of beef simmered in a flavorful liquid and served on an Italian bun. It is accompanied by plenty of the simmering liquid and grilled green peppers.

Kentucky Hot Brown—Toast triangles are topped with turkey and cheese sauce and then browned. It is served with bacon and tomato.

Maxwell Street Pork Chop Sandwich—A specialty of Chicago, this sandwich is a cooked, bone-in pork chop served on a hamburger bun with grilled onions and mustard.

Meatball Grinder—Meatballs cooked in tomato sauce and served on a bun.

Patty Melt—A hamburger topped with melted cheese and served with grilled onions on rye bread.

Philly Cheese Steak—This specialty of Philadelphia is thinly sliced beef steak griddled with onions, topped with melted cheese, and served on a French or Italian roll.

Po' Boy—Deep-fried oysters, catfish, or shrimp served on French bread with spicy mayonnaise, lettuce, and tomato is a specialty sandwich of Louisiana.

Pulled Pork—This Southern barbecue tradition is made from pork butts that have been slowly smoked for 8 to 10 hours. The pork is then torn or chopped, mixed with a tart spicy sauce, and served on a bun.

Reuben—This sandwich was invented in Omaha, Nebraska. It consists of hot corned beef, Thousand Island dressing, sauerkraut, and Swiss cheese on rye bread.

Sloppy Joe—A thick mixture of cooked ground beef and slightly sweet tomato sauce served on a hamburger bun.

As with the sautéed or griddled sandwiches, grilled sandwiches start with an assembled sandwich. They are then cooked in a clamshell griddle or panini grill until the bread is crispy and the interior is hot.

Deep-Fried Whole Cooked Sandwiches   A limited number of sandwiches are deep fried, 36-6. These sandwiches are assembled then dipped in a batter or coated with egg and breadcrumbs. These

Draz-Koetke/Goodheart-Willcox Publisher

36-6 The Monte Cristo is dipped in beaten eggs and then deep-fried.

sandwiches are cooked immediately and served so they do not become soggy. Some chefs may choose to sauté or griddle these sandwiches instead of deep-frying them. The most well-known example of a deep-fried sandwich is the Monte Cristo.

Baked Whole Cooked Sandwiches Baked sandwiches can be wrapped in aluminum foil or simply placed on a sheet pan before being baked in the oven, 36-7. Sandwiches that are wrapped before cooking produce a flavorful sandwich because all the flavors remain concentrated within the wrapping. A firm bread such as French or Italian bread is most often used to prepare these sandwiches. Once they are cooked, wrapped sandwiches maintain their heat for long periods of time.

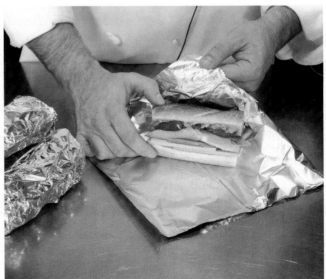

Draz-Koetke/Goodheart-Willcox Publisher

36-7 Sandwiches baked in aluminum foil concentrate flavor and hold well in a warmer.

Recipe No.	Name		Category
36.6	Monte Cristo		Sandwiches, hot
Yield	Portion Size		No. Portions
10 servings	1 sandwich		10

US Quantity	Metric Quantity	Ingredient	TCS
20 pieces		white bread, sliced	
20 oz.	560 g	cooked turkey breast, thinly sliced	•
12 oz.	340 g	ham, thinly sliced	•
12 oz.	340 g	Swiss cheese, sliced	•
4 ea.		eggs, beaten	•
12 fl. oz.	360 mL	milk	•
As needed		clarified butter	•

Method	CCP
1. Lay out 10 slices of bread on a work surface. Put a slice of cheese on each piece of bread. Reserve half of the cheese.	
2. Top the cheese with 1¼ oz. (35 g) of ham and 2 oz. (60 g) of turkey. Top with remaining cheese and then the remaining bread slice.	
3. Mix the eggs and milk together until homogenous.	
4. Dip the prepared sandwiches briefly in the egg and milk mixture.	
5. Immediately cook the sandwiches on a well-greased (preferably with clarified butter) griddle or sauté pan.	
6. Once the first side is browned, turn the sandwich over and continue cooking. Do not allow the outside of the sandwich to brown too much before the inside of the sandwich is heated through.	
7. It is traditional to serve a side of strawberry jam with the Monte Cristo.	

Alternative Monte Cristo:

Traditionally, the Monte Cristo is a deep-fried sandwich. While it is easier to prepare the Monte Cristo as a griddled/sautéed sandwich, it is possible to also prepare it as a deep-fried sandwich. To deep-fry the sandwich, prepare as follows:	
1. Heat the deep-fryer baskets in hot oil for at least 5 minutes so they are very hot.	
2. Once the sandwiches are dipped in the milk and egg mixture, place them in the hot deep-fryer baskets (which have been removed from the oil at this point).	
3. Immediately drop the baskets in the deep fryer. Shake the baskets if the sandwiches appear to be sticking to the bottom of the baskets.	
4. Once the sandwiches are nicely browned, remove them from the fryer. Drain the sandwiches and serve as indicated in the above recipe.	

Portion (g)	Calories	Fat (g)	Protein (g)	Carbohydrate (g)	Cholesterol (mg)	Sodium (mg)	Fiber (g)
238	500	27.07	34.71	29.28	187.61	1446.19	1.00

Recipe courtesy of chef Mike Artlip CEC, CCE

Baked sandwiches that are simply baked on a sheet tray are often open-faced. This method heats the sandwich and often browns the surface of the sandwich. Tuna melts and grilled cheese can be made this way.

Pizza

Without a doubt, pizza is one of the most popular foods in America. **Pizza** is a flat-bread that is cooked in a hot oven with an assortment of toppings. While pizza origi-nated in Italy, it is now an internationally appreciated food. Unlike sandwiches, pizzas are made from raw dough instead of bread.

Pizza begins with yeast dough that is similar to bread dough, 36-8. Two types of pizza can be made with this dough—thin crust and deep-dish. For thin crust pizza, the dough is rolled into a thin circle. The dough is then topped with tomato sauce, assorted toppings, and grated mozzarella cheese. Once assembled, the thin crust pizza is slid

Culinary Trends

New Pizza

Recently, chefs have introduced pizza into bistros and even high-end menus. But these chefs are not making the usual cheese and sausage. Instead, these are creative interpretations of pizza. The following are a sampling of some of these pizzas creations:

- Cornmeal crust topped with roasted red pepper, smoked turkey, mozzarella, and jalapeño jack cheese.

- Thin-crusted pizza with smoked salmon, shrimp, chives, ricotta, and crème fraîche.

- Whole-wheat crust topped with blue cheese, fresh figs, and prosciutto.

- Black pepper crust topped with venison sausage, dried sour cherries, aged cheddar, and seared spinach.

A

B

C

D

Draz-Koetke/Goodheart-Willcox Publisher

36-8 To prepare a pizza, (A) roll out the dough and (B) spread the sauce on top. (C) Ingredients are placed on top of sauce and (D) pizza is placed on a pizza peel.

onto a pizza peel. A **pizza peel** is the name for a long-handled, large spatula that is used to slide the pizza in and out of the oven. With one quick motion the peel is slid under the pizza and, in a similar motion, the pizza slides off the peel and onto the floor of a hot pizza oven, 36-9. The pizza develops a crisp dough because it cooks in direct contact with the oven floor.

It is also possible to cook thin crust pizza on sheet trays or on special perforated pans designed for pizza. If the pizza is baked on a sheet tray, the sheet tray should first be sprinkled with cornmeal to prevent the pizza from sticking. When cooked on a sheet tray, the dough tends to steam and lose some crispness. Cooking on a pan that has been **perforated**, or had holes punched in it, reduces the steam and produces a crispy crust.

Deep-dish pizza also begins with a rolled out circle of pizza dough. The dough is rolled thicker than the dough for a thin crust pizza and several inches larger than the size of the deep dish pizza pan. Deep-dish pizza pans have sides that are two inches high. To place the dough in the metal deep-dish pan, first place it in the bottom of the pan, and then slightly press the dough up the sides of the pan. The bottom of the dough is coated with tomato sauce, assorted toppings, and grated mozzarella cheese. Deep-dish pizza is baked in the pan in a hot oven.

Mozzarella is the cheese of choice for pizza as it becomes pleasantly stretchy when hot. Other cheeses such as cheddar, Fontina, provolone, or Parmesan are sometimes combined

Hints from the Chef
Other Pizza Crusts

Throughout the years, people have made pizzas without actual pizza crusts. For instance, English muffins and slices of French bread are fast pizza crust substitutes.

Draz-Koetke/Goodheart-Willcox Publisher

36-9 A pizza peel is used to move pizzas in and out of a hot oven.

with mozzarella for added flavor. A list of some common pizza toppings includes

- cooked sausage
- pepperoni
- green pepper
- ham
- bacon
- Canadian bacon
- onions
- mushrooms
- spinach
- olives
- pineapple
- anchovies

Since preparing pizza dough requires time and the proper facilities, many food-service operations choose not to make their own pizza dough. Some operations purchase frozen circles of raw dough. This reduces the time it takes to make pizza. Still other operations choose to buy precooked pizza crusts. Using precooked crusts is the fastest way to make pizzas since the crust is already cooked. Care must be taken not to burn the bottom when cooking precooked crusts.

Besides pizza, there are other pizza-type products that begin with raw dough. While less common than pizza, these products are still popular among diners. Three pizza-type products are

- *Calzone* (kal ZOHN). A sheet of pizza-style dough that is filled with various ingredients, folded in half, and baked, 36-10. Calzones originated in Italy.
- *Stromboli* (strohm BOH lee). Originating in Philadelphia, a stromboli is a large rolled or stuffed bread that is baked and then sliced to order. It is filled with ingredients such as mozzarella, lunch meats, and spinach.
- *Panzerotti* (pahn zah RO tee) are smaller versions of calzone often deep fried, though sometimes baked. They are often served as an appetizer.

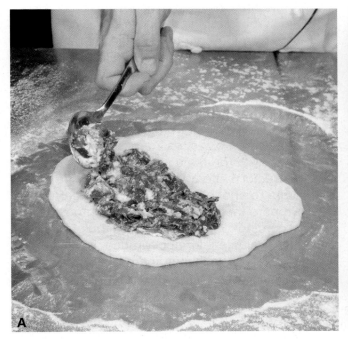

Draz-Koetke/Goodheart-Willcox Publisher

36-10 To prepare a calzone, (A) place ingredients on one-half of the crust. Then (B) fold the crust over and seal the edges.

Summary Points

- Hot sandwiches are a very popular category in foodservice.

- Sandwiches with hot fillings often consist of a hot ingredient that is placed on a bun or between slices of bread. This hot ingredient is most often sautéed or griddled, deep fried, or grilled.

- Another category of hot sandwiches is whole cooked sandwiches. Whole cooked sandwiches can be sautéed or griddled, deep fried, or baked.

- Pizza is a flatbread that is cooked in a hot oven with an assortment of toppings. It is among the most popular items in foodservice.

In Review Assess

1. List three examples of sandwiches with hot fillings.

2. True or false. Hamburger must be cooked to 155°F (68°C) to kill the E. coli that may be distributed throughout the meat.

3. Why is it advisable to hold deep-fried items in the warmer in an uncovered container?

4. How is a whole cooked sandwich different from a sandwich with hot filling?

5. A _____ _____ consists of two hot surfaces with ridges that close on a sandwich cooking both sides at once and creating grill marks.

6. True or false. Wrapping a sandwich in aluminum foil before baking produces a flavorful sandwich because it helps to concentrate the flavors.

7. What role does a pizza peel have in the preparation of pizza?

8. Cooking pizza on a _____ pan reduces the steam and produces a crispy crust.

9. In addition to cheese, name four common pizza toppings.

10. List three pizza-type products that begin with raw dough.

Core Skills

11. **Math.** The chef is adding a six-ounce, hand-pattied burger to the menu and is forecasting sales of 50 burgers per day. You are responsible for prepping the patties. How many pounds of ground beef will you need to prepare burgers for one day?

12. **Writing.** Use Internet or print resources to research various cultural uses of hot sandwiches. How do hot sandwiches vary around the world? What ingredients are commonly used? What time of the day are they served? Choose three sandwiches from other cultures you discover and describe them. Write a summary of your findings.

13. **Reading.** Pizza originated in Naples, Italy. Use Internet or print resources to read about Naples, its geography, economy, cuisine, and authentic Neapolitan pizza. Use presentation software to give an illustrated oral presentation to the class on your findings.

14. **Math.** Suppose your team must prepare 18 *Monte Cristo* sandwiches for a faculty luncheon. Change the yield of the *Monte Cristo* sandwich recipe in this chapter to meet your luncheon needs. (Remember to use the following formulas: new yield ÷ old yield = conversion factor and old quantity × conversion factor = new quantity.)

15. **Speaking and Listening.** In teams, locate a recipe for pizza, calzone, stromboli, or panzerotti (or use a recipe supplied by your instructor). Alter the yield of the recipe to prepare enough portions for your team. Prepare the pizza or pizza-type product according to the recipe. Plate the product and evaluate it for appearance, flavor, and texture. Discuss your findings in class, including any challenges your team faced during preparation.

16. **CTE Career Readiness Practice.** Write a sandwich menu for a new restaurant offering a selection of three hot sandwiches. Include a summary explaining your menu choices and discuss why these choices are appropriate for your market area.

Critical Thinking

17. **Recognize trends.** Why do you think pizza and hot sandwiches were destined to become popularized by fast-food restaurants? What trends support your thinking?

18. **Analyze variables.** Suppose you are considering serving pizza in your restaurant. What factors would you consider when deciding whether to make your own pizza dough; buy frozen, raw pizza dough; or purchase precooked crusts?

19. **Analyze cause and effect.** The manager is receiving complaints from customers that the fried-fish sandwich is soggy. As the chef, what steps would you take to correct the problem?

Technology

Many quick-service restaurants bake sandwiches in a turbo oven which combines high-velocity convection and microwaves. Use reliable Internet or print resources to investigate the capabilities and cost of a turbo oven. What is the energy usage of the ovens? How important is speed to profitability? Make a case either for or against a restaurant incorporating a turbo oven into its operation.

Teamwork

Divide into four teams. Each team will pick one of the following service situations: off-site catered event; buffet serving 200 people; large volume, fast-paced sandwich shop; cook-to-order restaurant. Each team will then select an appropriate sandwich for their service setting and prepare it. The teams will present their sandwich and explain their choice based on their particular service setting. The teams should then evaluate all of the sandwiches for taste, appearance, and appropriateness for service setting.

Chef's E-portfolio
Assessing the Sandwich Market

Upload your menu and summary from the CTE Career Readiness Practice activity to your e-portfolio. Ask your instructor where to save your file. This could be on the school's network or a flash drive of your own. Name your portfolio document *FirstnameLastname_Portfolio Ch#.docx* (i.e., JohnSmith_PortfolioCh36.docx).

While studying, look for the activity icon ⬈ **to:**

- Build vocabulary with e-flash cards and matching activities.
- Expand learning with video clips, photo identification activities, animations, and interactive activities.
- Review and assess what you learn by completing end-of-chapter questions.

Pinkcandy/Shutterstock.com

Dairy and Egg Identification

37

Reading Prep

Skim the review questions at the end of the chapter first. Use them to help you focus on the most important concepts as you read the chapter.

Culinary Terminology

Build Vocab

lactose, p. 591
ultra high temperature (UHT) pasteurization, p. 592
homogenization, p. 592
churning, p. 593
curds, p. 597
whey, p. 597
flats, p. 602

Academic Terminology

Build Vocab

concentration, p. 593
coagulant, p. 595

Objectives

After studying this chapter, you will be able to

- understand the composition of milk.
- compare the three most common concentrated milk products used in foodservice.
- summarize how butter is made and packaged.
- explain how cultured dairy products are made.
- compare the different categories of cheeses and how they are made.
- recognize the different parts of the egg and various purchase forms.
- recall important considerations for storing dairy and egg products.

Eggs and dairy products are among the most important ingredients in the kitchen. There is a good chance that every day you eat some form of egg or dairy product. Dairy and egg products are added to many different sweet and savory preparations. These products are important in many recipes because they add richness, emulsify, thicken, and lighten. Both eggs and dairy products are also excellent sources of many nutrients and calories. Understanding the structures and types of different dairy and egg products is crucial to understanding how to cook with them.

Fresh Dairy Products

Worldwide, milk is collected from animals such as cows, goats, sheep, yaks, and water buffalo. The US dairy industry focuses primarily on the milk produced by millions of cows, 37-1.

Milk

Milk is the basic building block for all dairy products. Milk is composed of

- *Water (87.7%)*. Human beings, as with all animals, require more water than any other nutrient.
- *Lactose (4.7%)*. **Lactose** is the main carbohydrate in milk, also called a sugar though it is not sweet to taste. It can cause digestive problems for some people.

- *Butterfat (3.7%).* Butterfat is the fat portion of the milk. The more butterfat in the milk, the richer it tastes.
- *Protein (3.2%).* Milk proteins are crucial for making cultured dairy products and cheese.

©2008 Wisconsin Milk Marketing Board, Inc.

37-1 The morning milking is the first step in the production of dairy products.

SUSTAINABLE CULINARY

Organic Dairy Products

Organic produce has become commonplace on menus and in supermarkets. Similarly, organic dairy products have become increasingly common on menus across the United States. US organic products are regulated by the United States Department of Agriculture (USDA). To qualify as an organic dairy product, the dairy animal which produced the milk must
- be fed only 100 percent organic feed
- have access to the outdoors at all times
- be allowed to graze on pasture during the grazing season (at least 120 days), and
- be given no growth hormones or antibiotics

- *Minerals (0.7%).* Milk is an excellent source of minerals needed for growth such as calcium and phosphorus.

Aside from making milk taste rich, butterfat is the most coveted part of the milk. Dairy products are largely defined by the amount of butterfat they contain, 37-2. A centrifuge is used to adjust the levels of butterfat in milk. The centrifuge spins the milk at high speeds, separating the butterfat from the rest of the milk.

Once the fat levels in the milk are adjusted, the milk is pasteurized. The process of *pasteurization* heats the milk to a specific temperature for a specific length of time to kill pathogens. For instance, milk can be pasteurized by heating it to 161°F (72°C) for 15 seconds or 275°F (135°C) for 2 to 4 seconds. Another type of pasteurization is called ultra high temperature. **Ultra high temperature (UHT) pasteurization** heats milk to 280°F (138°C) for 2 to 6 seconds, and then it is sealed in sterilized containers. As a result, UHT dairy products do not need refrigeration until they are opened.

In addition to pasteurization, milk is commonly homogenized. **Homogenization** permanently and evenly distributes the butterfat in the milk. Milk that has not been homogenized has a greenish tint and easily separates into a cream layer that floats to the top of a thin watery portion. During the homogenization process, the butterfat

Milk Products' Required Butterfat Content	
Type of Milk	**Butterfat Content**
Whole milk	Minimum of 3.5 percent
2% milk (reduced fat)	2 to 2.5 percent
1% milk (low fat)	1 to 1.5 percent
Skim milk (nonfat)	Less than 0.5 percent

37-2 The percent butterfat content in various milk products influences their taste and texture.

is broken into very small droplets. These droplets are so small that they are no longer able to join together and rise to the surface of the milk. Another result of homogenization is that the color of the milk becomes bright white.

High Butterfat Products

The butterfat removed during centrifuging is used to create high butterfat dairy products. Like milk, high butterfat products are defined by their levels of butterfat content, 37-3.

As with other dairy products, higher levels of butterfat result in higher prices. Products rich in butterfat are valued for their ability to add texture and flavor to beverages and sauces. With the exception of half-and-half, these products are also valued for their ability to produce the foam that is commonly known as *whipped cream*.

Concentrated Milk Products

The composition of milk can also be changed by **concentration**, or the removal of water to make a liquid less dilute. As water is removed from the milk, the levels of proteins, sugars, and butterfat increase. The three most common concentrated milk products include the following:

- *Evaporated milk.* This milk has had 60 percent of the water removed, which yields a thick, rich product. It is sold canned.
- *Sweetened condensed milk.* This milk has had 60 percent of the water removed and a large amount of sugar added. Sweetened condensed milk is thick, rich, and very sweet. It is sold canned and is commonly used in baked products.
- *Dried milk powder.* This product is skim milk that has had nearly all of the water removed during the drying process. The resulting white powder does not require refrigeration and has a long shelf life.

High Butterfat Dairy Products' Butterfat Requirement	
Product	**Butterfat Content**
Half-and-Half	10 to 18 percent
Light Cream	18 to 30 percent
Light Whipping Cream	30 to 36 percent
Heavy Cream	Minimum of 36 percent

37-3 High butterfat products are often used to add richness to sauces and desserts.

Nutrition Connection

Lactose Intolerance

Lactose, the sugar found in milk, is not digestible by all people. In fact, large segments of the world's populations cannot digest lactose. This condition is called *lactose intolerance.* Lactose intolerance arises when the human body no longer produces enough of the enzyme called *lactase.* Lactase is needed to break down lactose during digestion. Without lactase, the lactose is not digested and leads to digestive discomfort. Historically, lactose intolerant populations did not drink milk after infancy. Some lactose intolerant populations did eat cultured dairy products and cheese. This was possible since the bacteria in these products eliminate much of the lactose.

Butter

Butter is the dairy product with the highest percentage of butterfat. Churning cream makes butter. **Churning** is another word for rapid mixing. As the cream is churned, lumps of butterfat emerge and begin to stick together to form larger and larger pieces of butter. Eventually, a large mass of butter is produced along with a small amount of watery liquid. This watery liquid is referred to as *buttermilk*. If salt is added to the butter, it is labeled as salted butter. Salt is added to butter to improve its shelf life. Unsalted butter does not have any added salt.

Butter is packaged and sold in a number of different forms, 37-4. The most common purchase forms include

- *Individually wrapped, one-pound pieces* of butter typically called *butter prints.* Packed 36 pounds to a case, this pack is popular with foodservice.
- *Individually wrapped, quarter-pound sticks.* Packed four sticks to a box and 36 boxes to a case, this pack is commonly sold in grocery stores.
- *Individual portions, such as cardboard backed patties, foil wrapped chips, and cups.*
- *Whipped.* Whipped butter has been mixed with a gas such as nitrogen. The added gas makes the butter soft and fluffy.

Cultured Dairy Products

Cultured dairy products have been made for thousands of years and remain popular today. They are easily recognized for their sour taste and moderately thick texture. What separates fresh dairy products from cultured dairy products is the addition of "friendly" bacteria. Not all bacteria are dangerous to humans. Indeed, some bacteria are beneficial to humans and can produce tasty food products such as cultured dairy products.

To make cultured dairy products, fresh milk is first pasteurized to kill any harmful bacteria. Next, specific strains of bacteria are added to the warm milk. Milk is nutrient rich, high in moisture, and has a neutral pH, which makes it a perfect environment for bacterial growth. As the bacteria reproduce, they consume the lactose and produce lactic acid. During this time, the dairy product becomes less sweet and noticeably more acidic. The increase in acid also thickens the dairy product, 37-5.

Once the cultured dairy product reaches the desired stage of thickness and acidity, it is refrigerated. The colder temperature stops bacterial growth, but does not kill the bacteria. In fact, the labels of many cultured dairy products indicate that the cultures are live.

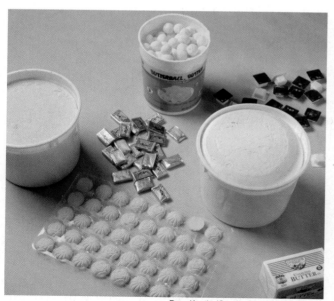

Draz-Koetke/Goodheart-Willcox Publisher

37-4 The purchase form of butter is dependent on the intended use.

Draz-Koetke/Goodheart-Willcox Publisher

37-5 Friendly bacteria are added to milk to produce cultured dairy products.

Buttermilk

The name *buttermilk* originally referred to the watery liquid that remained after churning butter. The liquid was traditionally slightly sour since the cream used to make butter was also slightly sour. The buttermilk would also have picked up a mild butter flavor. Today, buttermilk is made commercially by adding strains of bacteria to skim milk. These strains not only thicken the milk and increase its acidity, but also add the characteristic butter flavor. Buttermilk is used in baked products and salad dressings.

Yogurt

Yogurt is a centuries-old product. It is made by adding several types of bacteria to warm milk. Yogurts have varying degrees of fat depending on the fat level of the milk used to make the yogurt. Once the bacteria have changed the flavor, texture, and acidity level of the milk, it is often sweetened and flavored before being sold. Adding thickeners such as gelatin or pectin to the yogurt produces some thick varieties of yogurt.

Sour Cream

Sour cream is a common product in baked goods and is served as a condiment for savory dishes. Unlike buttermilk and yogurt, sour cream starts with a high-fat dairy product—light cream. Finished sour cream must have a minimum butterfat content of 18 percent.

Cheese

Worldwide, there are literally thousands of varieties of cheese, 37-6. Cheese varies dramatically in shape, color, and flavor. What distinguishes cheese from cultured dairy products is the amount of moisture in the finished product. Cultured dairy products such as yogurt and sour cream have the

Culture & Cuisine

Greek Yogurt

In the eastern Mediterranean, the yogurt that is made is a thicker and more versatile product than typical yogurt. The process begins by making normal yogurt. The yogurt is then placed in a large piece of fabric. The four corners of the fabric are drawn together and hung up. As the yogurt hangs, whey drips from it. After several hours, the resulting yogurt has the consistency of thick sour cream. It is marketed as Greek or Lebanese yogurt, and is certainly worth trying. In countries such as Greece, Turkey, and Lebanon, this yogurt is often used for savory preparations.

same amount of moisture as milk. Cheeses have lower amounts of moisture than milk. Reduced moisture levels decrease the likelihood the cheese will spoil. The more moisture removed from the cheese, the longer it will last. In fact, a very dry cheese can last for years without spoiling.

Every cheese begins as milk. In the United States, most cheese is made from cow's milk; although goat's milk and sheep's milk cheeses are gaining popularity. Before the cheese-making process begins, the levels of cream in the milk are adjusted. If a higher fat cheese is desired, butterfat is added to the milk. If a low-fat cheese is desired, butterfat is removed from the milk.

As with cultured dairy products, bacteria are added to the milk to make cheese. The bacteria increase the acidity, change the flavor, and thicken the milk. However, bacteria alone are not enough to produce cheese. A small amount of a **coagulant**, or thickening agent, is added to the milk. The coagulant causes the milk to thicken dramatically. The coagulant that is traditionally added to produce cheese is called *rennet*.

Common Cheeses			
Cheese	**Category**	**Country of Origin**	**Additional Information**
Brie	Soft	France	The soft white exterior is an edible mold.
Camembert	Soft	France	The soft white exterior is an edible mold. Flavor is stronger than Brie.
Cheddar	Hard	England	All Cheddars are not orange. The orange color comes from the annatto seed.
Colby	Medium firm	United States	The orange color comes from the annatto seed.
Cottage Cheese	Fresh	United States	Very fresh curds mixed with a milk and cream mixture.
Cream Cheese	Fresh	United States	Traditionally made from fat enriched milk.
Emmental	Hard	Switzerland	The original Swiss cheese. When made in America, it is called *Swiss cheese*.
Feta	Fresh, but aged in a salty brine	Greek	Feta is also now made in other countries like the U.S. Traditionally made from sheep's milk.
Fontina	Medium firm	Italy	Made in the Italian Alps.
Gorgonzola	Blue	Italy	This medium firm cheese has a creamy texture.
Gruyère	Hard	Switzerland	A full-flavored cheese.
Manchego	Hard	Spain	Full flavored, can have some grits of protein, which is expected when well aged. Made from sheep's milk.
Mascarpone	Fresh	Italy	Made from cream although not a true cheese because it is thickened only with the addition of acid.
Monterey Jack	Medium firm	United States	A mild and elastic cheese that is often flavored with ingredients such as chile.
Mozzarella	Stretched cheese	Italy	Made with varying levels of butterfat. Traditionally, it was (and still is in parts of Italy) made from water buffalo's milk.
Munster	Medium firm	United States	The traditional Munster is a very strong, soft cheese from France. The American version is very mild.
Parmesan	Hard	Italy	This is a grating cheese.
Provolone	Stretched cheese	Italy	This is an aged mozzarella with a medium firm texture.
Ricotta	Fresh	Italy	A unique cheese because it is made from whey and not milk.
Roquefort	Blue	France	Medium firm cheese with a strong, salty flavor, and made from sheep's milk.
Stilton	Blue	England	Creamy medium firm cheese.

37-6 In many instances, cheeses are now made in countries other than the country of origin. For instance, while Brie originated in France, Brie-style cheeses are also made in the United States. Other cheeses now made in large amounts in the U.S. include Cheddar, Emmental, feta, mozzarella, Parmesan, provolone, and ricotta.

The addition of bacteria and rennet turns the milk into a semisolid mass. The thickened milk is then cut into cubes. These cubes, which contain the casein proteins (one of the two types of protein found in milk) are called **curds**. As the curds are drained, mixed, and sometimes heated, they shrink and whey is expelled. **Whey** is the watery portion of the milk that contains the whey proteins (the other type of milk protein). The more whey that is removed from the curds, the firmer the cheese will be. Salt is also added to the curds to remove even more moisture. The curds are then placed in a mold and perhaps pressed. As this mass of curds ages, it knits together to form cheese, 37-7.

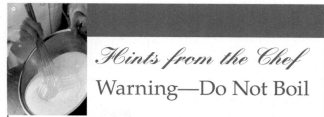

Hints from the Chef
Warning—Do Not Boil

Anyone who has tried to add cultured dairy products to hot liquids may have encountered a separation problem. During the culturing process, the milk proteins become unstable in the presence of the increased acidity. If a cultured dairy product is brought to a boil, it will separate into unsightly white specks. Nonetheless, cultured dairy products are sometimes added to hot preparations. The key is that they should only be added to a hot liquid at the last moment and not allowed to boil.

The Cheese Making Process

Milk

↓

Adjust butterfat levels in milk

↓

Add culture

↓

Add rennet and cut curds

Soft Cheese:
- cut large curd
- do not press
- do not heat curds

Medium Firm Cheese:
- cut medium curd
- press moderately
- may heat curds minimally

Firm Cheese:
- cut small curd
- press hard
- heat curd

↓

Processed Cheese:
- melt and add emulsifier to make a paste

Blue Cheese:
- add special mold to curds

String Cheese:
- stretch hot curd

Animation

37-7 Though all cheeses begin with milk, the finished products can be quite different.

Fresh Cheese

Fresh cheeses are high moisture cheeses that are barely aged at all. Examples of fresh cheeses include cream cheese, cottage cheese, and ricotta. Fresh cheeses are slightly sweet and milky flavored. Since fresh cheeses are high moisture, they spoil more easily than other cheeses. As a result, they should be used shortly after purchase and kept refrigerated at all times.

Ricotta

Cottage cheese

Cream cheese

Soft Cheese

Soft cheese has elastic or creamy texture. When some of these cheeses are well aged, they can even become runny. Soft cheeses have limited amounts of moisture removed from the curd. When making soft cheeses, the curds are cut into large cubes so they do not lose too much whey. After the curds are

SCIENCE & TECHNOLOGY

Aromatic Cheeses

Some of the world's greatest cheeses are often strongly aromatic. To cheese connoisseurs, these intense aromas are desirable. To others, the same aromas are offensive. These "barnyard" aromas come from an assortment of bacteria, yeasts, and molds that are added to some cheeses. Many times these microorganisms are repeatedly smeared on the surface of the cheese as it ages. This produces a very strong smelling type of cheese called a *washed rind cheese.*

placed into molds, they are either pressed lightly or not at all. The lack of any significant pressing ensures that the cheese keeps a high level of moisture. Examples of soft cheeses include Brie (BREE), Camembert (cahm ehm BEHR), and lightly aged goat cheeses also known as *chevre* (SHEHVR).

Medium Firm Cheese

Medium firm cheese has a drier and firmer texture than soft cheese. It also has a longer shelf life than soft cheese. Medium firm cheeses are made with curds that are cut smaller than the curds used to make

soft cheeses. The curds are sometimes lightly cooked, which causes more whey to be expelled. The curds are then placed in a mold and pressed to remove additional whey. Medium firm cheeses are aged for at least a month before being sold. They feel firm, but still elastic. Examples of medium firm cheeses include Morbier (mohr bee AY), Monterey Jack, Fontina (FOHN teen ah), and Colby.

Hard Cheese

Hard cheeses are the driest cheeses and, therefore have very long shelf lives. The curd is cut into small pieces, cooked at high temperatures, and firmly pressed to make

hard cheeses. These cheeses are then aged for a period of months or even years. When these cheeses become very hard, they are referred to as *grating cheeses*. Examples of hard cheeses include Parmesan, Cheddar, Swiss cheese, Manchego (mahn CHAY goh), Gruyère (grwee AIR), and Romano.

Blue Cheese

While there are many unique cheeses in the world, blue cheeses are among the most unique. The blue color in blue cheese is actually a type of edible mold. The mold that grows inside the cheese intensifies the flavor of the cheese. Not all blue cheeses are blue. The mold in different blue cheeses can have varying shades of green, grey, and blue. Blue cheeses may be soft or medium firm. Examples of blue cheeses include Roquefort (rohk FOHR), Stilton (STIHL tohn), Gorgonzola (GOHR gohn zoh lah), Maytag Blue, and Danish Blue.

Stretched Cheese

While there are not many individual cheeses in this category, stretched cheeses are among the most popular. This category of cheese is also called *pasta filata*. To make stretched cheeses, hot curds are repeatedly stretched to produce strands of cheese. Stretch cheeses are generally eaten with little aging and have an elastic, medium

SCIENCE & TECHNOLOGY

Hole-y Cheese!

Ever wonder where the holes come from in cheeses such as Swiss cheese? These holes are the result of a specific strain of bacteria that are added to these cheeses. As the cheese ages, the bacteria produce carbon dioxide gas which is trapped within the cheese. The result is the characteristic holes—called *eyes*—distributed throughout the cheese.

firm texture. Examples include mozzarella (MOHTZ ahr rehl ah), string cheese, and Provolone (PROH voh lohn).

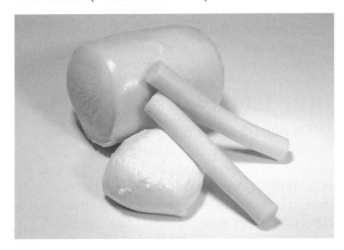

Processed Cheese

Vast quantities of processed cheese are eaten daily in America. Perhaps the most famous member of this family is American cheese. Processed cheese begins with medium firm or hard cheeses that are grated and melted. As the cheese melts, it is mixed with an emulsifier, water, and possibly additional fat. The emulsifier keeps the fat from separating from the cheese. The resulting hot cheese paste is then rolled into singles, formed into blocks, or squirted into jars.

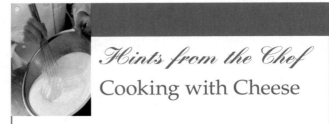

Hints from the Chef
Cooking with Cheese

Cheese is an important ingredient in many recipes. However, different cheeses may behave differently when heated. The following are a few guidelines to follow when cooking with cheese:

- The higher the fat percentage in the cheese, the more the cheese will run when heated.
- The longer a cheese is aged, the less likely it is to form tough elastic strands when heated.
- String cheeses retain their chewy stringiness when heated.
- Very hard cheese will not melt much when heated.

Eggs

Along with dairy products, eggs are among the most versatile and common ingredients in the kitchen. In the United States, chicken hens are the most common source of eggs. Other eggs, such as duck and quail eggs, are also eaten occasionally. Nutritionally, eggs are a rich source of high quality protein, vitamins, and minerals.

The outside of an egg is covered with a protective shell. Shells are either white or brown. The color of the shell is not an indicator of quality, but rather related to the breed of hen. Shells are porous, which means that moisture and aromas can travel through the shell. For this reason, eggs should never be stored near foods that have strong aromas. Eggs are perishable and should be refrigerated in a covered container until needed. They should be used within a few weeks.

Just underneath the shell is the egg white. The egg white contains large amounts of water and an important protein called *albumin* (ahl BYOO mehn). The egg white of a fresh egg is thick, while the egg white of an old egg is thin and runny. Within the egg white is a twisted white cord called the *chalaza* (keh LAY zeh). The chalaza connects the yolk to the shell so that the yolk is always in the center of the egg. The chalaza is sometimes visible inside the white of a cracked egg and is edible, 37-8.

At one end of the egg between the shell and the egg white is a small air pocket. As eggs get older, the air pocket gets larger because moisture is lost through the porous shell into the environment.

The egg yolk, or the yellow sphere within the egg, contains most of the nutrients and fat in the egg. The yolk also has a distinctive flavor. The shade of yellow of the yolk is not a quality indicator, but rather reflects the hen's diet. The occasional spot of blood on the yolk is not dangerous, and is the result of a broken blood vessel on the egg yolk. The blood spot may be removed before cooking, but this is not essential for health reasons.

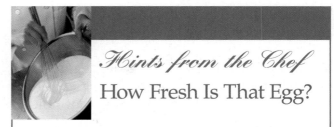

Hints from the Chef
How Fresh Is That Egg?

The freshness of an egg has perhaps the largest effect on its quality. A common test traditionally used to judge the freshness of an egg is to float the egg in a saltwater solution. As an egg ages, the air gap between the shell and the white grows. The air gap acts as a flotation device. Therefore, the higher the egg floats in the saltwater solution, the older the egg.

Purchase Forms, Grades, and Sizes

Eggs play an important part in many recipes, so it is easy to understand why there are so many different ways to purchase egg

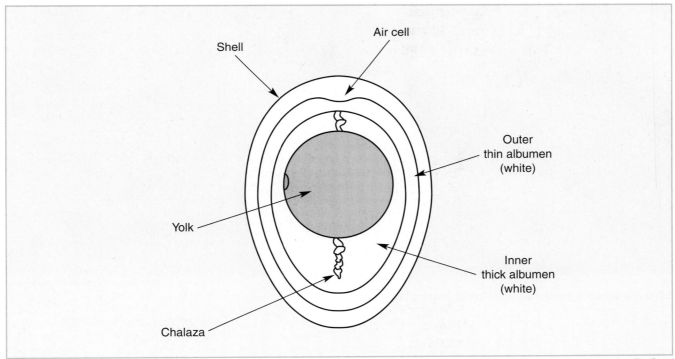

American Egg Board

37-8 Many aspects of an egg's composition are not readily visible.

products, 37-9. The following is a list of the most common forms in which eggs can be purchased:

- *In the shell*. In grocery stores, eggs are sold by the dozen. In foodservice, eggs are packed in trays, or **flats**, that hold 30 eggs. These flats are packed into cases that hold either 15 or 30 dozen eggs.
- *Pasteurized*. Many restaurants buy pasteurized eggs to reduce the risk of foodborne illness. Pasteurized eggs

have been heated to kill pathogens. Pasteurized eggs are sold as a liquid or occasionally in the shell.

- *Blends*. There are many specialized blends of egg products available. For instance, it is possible to buy whites or yolks separately. Some egg blends already have specific amounts of salt or sugar added to them.
- *Dried*. Similar to dried milk, dried egg products have enough water removed to make them shelf stable. They are often

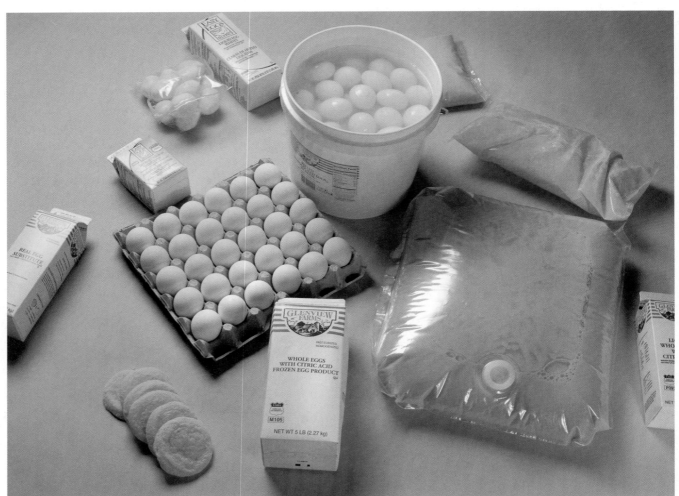

Draz-Koetke/Goodheart-Willcox Publisher

37-9 Eggs can be purchased in almost any stage of preparation.

used in baked products or in instances where it is difficult to get regular shipments of fresh eggs.

- *Hard-cooked.* Eggs can also be purchased already hard-cooked. This is especially attractive for high volume restaurants.

Eggs are graded by the USDA. They receive either a AA, A, or B grade. Grade AA eggs are the highest quality, although grade A eggs can also be successfully used in egg preparations. During the grading process, inspectors look for firm whites and yolks, a small air gap, and shells that are free from defects.

Eggs are also sold by their size, which can differ considerably, 37-10. This explains why in many professional recipes, eggs are listed by weight and not by count.

Storing Dairy and Egg Products

Egg and dairy products are potentially hazardous foods. This means that they are susceptible to spoilage. As a result, all fresh dairy and egg products must be held at or below 41°F (5°C). Dairy products are stamped with a "use by" date. Dairy products should be discarded if not used by this date. Both eggs and dairy products readily absorb flavors and should never be stored near strong smelling items such as onions and garlic. Eggs that have cracks in the shell should not be used.

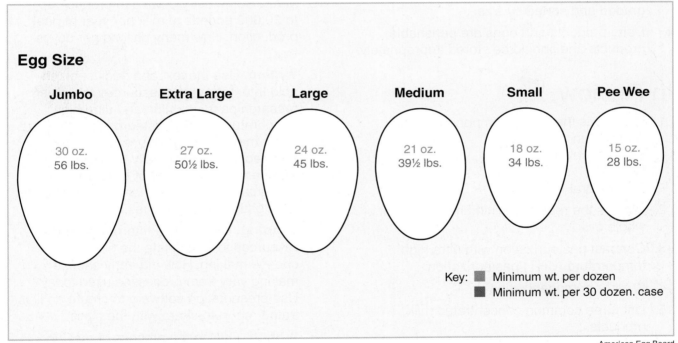

Egg Size

Jumbo	Extra Large	Large	Medium	Small	Pee Wee
30 oz. 56 lbs.	27 oz. 50½ lbs.	24 oz. 45 lbs.	21 oz. 39½ lbs.	18 oz. 34 lbs.	15 oz. 28 lbs.

Key: ■ Minimum wt. per dozen
■ Minimum wt. per 30 dozen. case

American Egg Board

37-10 Standard egg sizes are determined by the weight per dozen eggs rather than the weight of an individual egg.

Summary Points

- Fresh dairy products are pasteurized, homogenized, and defined by the amount of butterfat they contain.

- Concentrated milk products are made by removing various amounts of water from milk.

- Butter is made by churning cream.

- Cultured dairy products are made by adding "friendly" bacteria to milk.

- Cheese is made by adding culture and a coagulant to milk so that it separates into curds and whey. Cheeses can be divided into fresh, soft, medium firm, hard, blue, stretched, and processed categories.

- Eggs are a rich source of high quality protein, vitamins, and minerals. They are graded and sorted by size.

- Dairy products and eggs are perishable products and should be stored appropriately.

In Review
Assess

1. Lactose is the _____ component in milk.
   A. protein
   B. carbohydrate
   C. fat
   D. mineral

2. What is the required minimum fat content of whole milk?

3. Contrast pasteurization with ultra high temperature (UHT) pasteurization.

4. What is homogenization?

5. List three common concentrated milk products.

6. What dairy product has the highest percentage of butterfat?

7. List the forms in which butter is packaged.

8. Cultured dairy products are acidic and thick because the bacteria that is added to the milk produces _____ _____.

9. What is the coagulant that is added to milk when making cheese?
   A. Lactose
   B. Curds
   C. Albumin
   D. Rennet

10. True or false. The more whey that is removed from the curds, the firmer the cheese will be.

11. What are the parts of an egg?

12. Compare the look of a fresh, raw egg white with an egg white from an old egg.

13. Name the five purchase forms of eggs.

14. List four guidelines for storing dairy and egg products.

Core Skills

15. **Math.** Some dairy cows can produce up to 30,000 pounds of milk per year at peak production. How many gallons per day is that?

16. **Writing.** Use the text and additional reliable Internet or print resources to further research pasteurization and ultra high temperature (UHT) pasteurization. Why are these methods of pasteurization beneficial and necessary, especially for foodservice? What are the concerns of using raw milk products? Write a summary of your findings highlighting the key issues.

17. **Reading.** Use reliable Internet and print resources to investigate the history of cheese making. How did early cheese making vary from processes used today? Use presentation software to create an illustrated report to share with the class.

18. **Writing.** Outline the process of making cultured dairy products. Include any health benefits of cultured dairy products. Write a report of your findings. Use the text and reliable Internet resources as necessary to complete your report.

19. **Math.** Suppose you are preparing French toast for a weekend buffet service. Your recipe calls for two quarts of beaten eggs. The foodservice operation for which you

work purchases large eggs which are typically 24 ounces per dozen. How many eggs do you need for two quarts of beaten eggs?

20. **CTE Career Readiness Practice.** Effective communication is a vital workplace skill. In the past, you have demonstrated your skill in creating menu items and descriptions that capture customer interest. The manager of the fine-dining restaurant at which you work wants to add a cheese course to the menu that utilizes a selection of soft, medium firm, hard, and blue cheeses. As the head chef, it is your responsibility to choose five varieties of cheeses for the cheese course and write their descriptions for the menu. Make your selections and write appealing descriptions. Use additional references as needed for your descriptions.

Critical Thinking

21. **Draw conclusions.** Some restaurants or hotels prefer to purchase UHT dairy products. Draw conclusions about the reasons for these preferences.

22. **Analyze evidence.** Traditionally, cheese was a way of preserving milk since milk spoils easily. Provide evidence that shows why cheese is more resistant to spoilage than milk.

23. **Judge worth.** You are the chef of a restaurant and have the option to purchase either hard-cooked eggs or fresh shell eggs that your staff must cook. What factors would influence your purchase decision? What is the worth, or value, of purchasing one product over the other?

24. **Generate a plan.** Your guests are complaining that your milk has an "off" flavor. Generate a plan describing the steps you will take to resolve this problem. Share your plan with employees (the class).

Technology

Choose a category of cheese (soft, medium firm, hard, blue, stretched, or processed) and create an illustrated blog about how cheeses in the category are made and used. Be sure to include images of various cheeses in your chosen category. Use a school-approved web-based application to create your blog. Then post your blog to the class website for peer review.

Teamwork

In teams, observe and taste an assortment of cheeses gathered by your instructor. Create a three-column chart on which to record your responses. Label the columns: Cheese Name, Type of Cheese, and Taste Description. Identify each of the following types of cheese: fresh, soft, medium firm, hard, stretched, and processed. Then taste each cheese and record your flavor descriptions. Be sure to take a drink of water between tasting various cheeses. Compare and discuss your results with the class.

Chef's E-portfolio
Menu Descriptions

Potential employers are interested in your ability to use written communication effectively. Upload your cheese menu descriptions from the CTE Career Readiness Practice activity to your e-portfolio. Ask your instructor where to save your file. This could be on the school's network or a flash drive of your own. Name your portfolio document *FirstnameLastname_Portfolio Ch#. docx* (i.e., JohnSmith_PortfolioCh37.docx).

While studying, look for the activity icon to:

- Build vocabulary with e-flash cards and matching activities.
- Expand learning with video clips, photo identification activities, animations, and interactive activities.
- Review and assess what you learn by completing end-of-chapter questions.

Breakfast Cookery 38

Reading Prep

Before reading this chapter, go to the In Review section at the end of the chapter and read the questions. This will prepare you for the content that will be presented. Review questions at the end of the chapter serve as a self-assessment to help you evaluate your comprehension of the material.

Culinary Terminology Build Vocab

coddled eggs, p. 607
poached eggs, p. 609
omelet, p. 610
frittata, p. 611
sunny-side up eggs, p. 613
basted eggs, p. 613
eggs over, p. 613
French toast, p. 615

Academic Terminology Build Vocab

cohesive, p. 612

Objectives

After studying this chapter, you will be able to

- implement basic egg preparation methods.
- summarize how various breakfast meats are cooked.
- compare breakfast batters and their uses.
- explain how to properly prepare common hot cereals.

For many people, breakfast is the most important meal of the day. Diners are often particular about how they like their favorite breakfast dishes prepared. The foods prepared at breakfast are different from other meals and require some unique skills. Being a good breakfast cook requires speed, timing, and attention to detail.

Preparing Eggs

Eggs are at the center of the plate of most breakfasts. Perhaps no other food is as versatile. Eggs can be prepared in so many ways that folklore maintains the number of pleats in a chef's toque represents the number of ways a chef can prepare eggs. The basic methods to be described here include simmered, poached, scrambled, omelets, and fried eggs.

Simmered

Although these preparations are typically called *boiled eggs*, to prepare them properly they should be simmered—not boiled. Eggs cooked at a full boil tend to become tough or rubbery and may have a green ring surrounding the yolk. Lower-temperature cooking methods, such as simmering and poaching, produce a tender, evenly cooked egg with a bright yellow yolk.

Cooked in the Shell   Coddled, soft-cooked, and hard-cooked eggs are all simmered in their shells. **Coddled eggs** are eggs cooked in their shells for one to three minutes.

SANITATION & SAFETY
Egg Safety

- Shell eggs should be clean and uncracked.
- Wash, rinse, and sanitize utensils, equipment, and work surfaces after preparing eggs or egg-containing foods.
- Raw shell eggs that are intended for immediate preparation and service should be cooked until they reach a temperature of 145°F (63°C) for at least 15 seconds. All parts of the egg must reach that temperature.
- Foods prepared with raw shell eggs should be cooked immediately for service and all parts

of the food must reach a temperature of 155°F (68°C) for at least 15 seconds.

- If cooked eggs and egg-containing foods are held in hot-holding equipment, they should be held at a temperature of 135°F (57°C) or above.
- As a general rule, treated eggs or pasteurized egg products should be used in any recipe that calls for combining more than one egg ("pooling") and for any recipe, preparation, or serving procedure that involves holding eggs or egg-containing foods before or after cooking.

SUSTAINABLE CULINARY
Local Eggs

Perhaps you have eaten at a restaurant that features locally raised eggs on its menu. Sometimes, the menu may even name the local farm that supplies the eggs. One of the advantages of buying eggs locally is that chefs develop relationships with the farmers and better understand the product. Another advantage is that the eggs are extremely fresh and flavorful. Local farmers are more likely to raise unique breeds such as the Araucana chicken, which lays beautiful blue eggs. By supporting the local farmers, species diversity is also being promoted.

There are no visual clues to tell the doneness of eggs in their shells, therefore time is the key, 38-1. Cooking time is also the way some diners describe their preferences. For instance, they might request a "three-minute egg" or a "seven-minute egg."

Cooking Times for Eggs in the Shell	
Doneness	**Cooking Time (simmering)**
Coddled	1 to 3 minutes
Soft-cooked	3 to 5 minutes
Medium-cooked	5 to 7 minutes
Hard-cooked	12 to 15 minutes

38-1 The initial temperature of an egg affects the length of time required to cook it.

TECHNIQUE
Cooking Eggs in the Shell

1. Place enough water in a pan to cover eggs and bring to a simmer [185°F–205°F (85°C–96°C)].
2. Gently lower egg(s) into the water.
3. After the water returns to a simmer, time the cooking according to desired doneness.
4. Remove the egg(s) from the water and serve immediately. Eggs should be served in an egg cup or bouillon cup. Hard-cooked eggs should be cooled in cold water before peeling.

TECHNIQUE
Poaching Eggs

1. Fill a pot with enough water to fully cover eggs and bring to a boil. Lower heat to poaching temperature [165°F–180°F (74°C–82°C)] and add 1 ounce vinegar for every quart of water (30 mL per liter).
2. Crack an egg into a small bowl or cup. Lower the egg to the water and turn it out of the bowl.

3. Using a slotted spoon, gently turn or swirl the egg to form a round shape with the white enveloping the yolk.

4. Poach the egg for about 3 minutes. When properly cooked, the egg can be easily handled. Check doneness by removing the egg from the water with a slotted spoon and gently pressing on the egg with your finger. The egg should be soft to indicate that the yolk is still liquid.
5. After the poached egg is removed with a slotted spoon, shock it in ice water or pat dry on a clean towel for immediate service.

Poached

Poached eggs are eggs removed from the shell and cooked in liquid. Since there is no shell to protect them, they must be cooked at a lower temperature than simmered eggs. Poaching provides gentle heat to prevent the eggs from breaking up or becoming rubbery and overcooked.

When poaching eggs, add a small amount of vinegar to the water. The acid in the vinegar aids in coagulating the egg white, which makes for a better formed poached egg. A properly poached egg should be somewhat spherical in shape, not flat. The white should evenly cover the yolk at the center. To achieve this, when the egg is lowered into the water, it should be gently turned or swirled. Using fresh eggs also helps produce a well-formed poached egg.

In large production situations, eggs are often poached and then shocked in ice water. They are held submerged in water until ready to use. At time of service, they are reheated in water at poaching temperature.

TECHNIQUE
Scrambling Eggs

1. Break eggs into a mixing bowl and add 2 tsp. (10 mL) of water or milk for each egg. Beat the mixture well using a whisk. The egg mixture may be seasoned with salt and pepper if desired.

2. Heat enough butter to coat the bottom of a seasoned or nonstick pan until it begins to bubble. Pour eggs into pan.

3. Stir continuously while cooking over moderate heat.

4. Cook until eggs are set but still moist. Serve immediately.

Scrambled Eggs

Scrambled eggs are beaten before being cooked. Beat the eggs with a whip until there are no streaks of egg white visible in the mixture. A small amount of liquid, usually water or milk, is often added to the eggs. This liquid creates steam when the eggs are cooked, making the scrambled eggs fluffier.

Scrambled eggs are stirred while cooking to help create fluffy light eggs. The heat should be moderate so that the eggs don't become dry, rubbery, brown, or curdled.

Omelets

Omelets are an extension of scrambled eggs. An **omelet** is a fluffy sheet of scrambled eggs served folded or rolled. The process for making an omelet begins the same as for scrambled eggs—the beaten eggs are cooked in a small amount of fat. The eggs are stirred while cooking but once the eggs begin to coagulate, stirring stops. The eggs are allowed to form into a single mass. The finished omelet should be light, fluffy, and moist.

In addition to the eggs, omelets often include other ingredients. Cheese, mushrooms, herbs, meat, and vegetables are all popular ingredients for omelets. How the other ingredients are incorporated into the omelet is one of the distinctions between American-style and French-style omelets. An American-style omelet starts by placing the additional ingredients into the pan at the same time as the eggs. These ingredients become bound up in the eggs when they cook. When preparing a French-style omelet, only the eggs are placed in the pan at the beginning of the process. The eggs are scrambled and only after they begin to coagulate are additional ingredients added. These ingredients become a filling that is enveloped by the omelet.

American-style omelets are cooked until the outer surface of the eggs is lightly

Chef Speak

Omelet Glossary

Most kitchens that prepare omelets to order will prepare mise en place of common omelet fillings including onions, peppers, tomatoes, spinach, mushrooms, Cheddar or American cheese, Swiss cheese, and diced ham and sausage.

Some commonly requested types of omelets include

Denver—Diced onions, bell peppers, and ham.

Greek—Spinach and feta cheese.

Spanish—Tomato sauce, peppers, and onions.

Tortilla Espagnole—Frittata with sautéed onions and potatoes.

Western—Diced onions, bell peppers, and sausage.

TECHNIQUE Animation
Preparing American-Style Omelets

1. Heat a small amount of clarified butter in a small nonstick sauteuse.
2. Sauté any ingredients that need to be cooked in the butter.
3. Pour in beaten eggs and cook while stirring.
4. When the eggs begin to coagulate, stop stirring and allow the eggs to form into a single sheet. Cook until lightly brown.
5. Fold the omelet in half and slide onto the serving plate.

browned. The omelet is removed from the pan and folded in half to form a half circle on the serving plate. French-style omelets should have a smooth, unbrowned surface. French omelets are folded three times or rolled when placed on the serving plate, 38-2.

Frittata A *frittata*, or Italian-style omelet, is cooked on both sides and served open rather than folded or rolled, 38-3. Cooking of a frittata begins the same as an American-style omelet. The eggs and ingredients are placed into the preheated pan at the same time. The

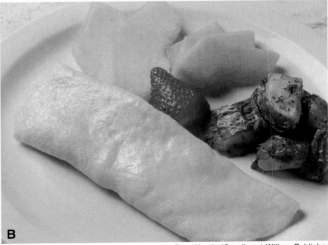

Draz-Koetke/Goodheart-Willcox Publisher

38-2 The (A) American-style omelet is browned and folded in half. The (B) French-style omelet is folded in thirds.

Draz-Koetke/Goodheart-Willcox Publisher

38-3 Frittatas are served open face.

omelet is allowed to brown lightly once the eggs form a **cohesive**, or unified, mass. The omelet is then flipped and the other side is allowed to brown. Frittatas are often thicker than other omelets because they are served open-faced.

Fried Eggs

Fried eggs may be cooked in a small sauteuse or on a griddle. Whole eggs are cracked and placed directly into a preheated pan with fat. Clarified butter is preferred by many chefs because its flavor is complementary to eggs and it does not burn as readily as whole butter.

Most diners when ordering fried eggs request that they be cooked to a certain doneness. Eggs cooked

- *easy* are cooked enough to fully coagulate the whites, but the yolks are left liquid and runny.
- *medium* have yolks that are thick and sticky but still liquid.
- *hard* have yolks that are fully coagulated and dry.

Hints from the Chef

Egg Pans

Perhaps the most important factor for preparing properly cooked fried eggs and omelets is a good egg pan. Most breakfast cooks guard and maintain their egg pans with great care. The ability to flip eggs and slide them easily out of the pan requires a good nonstick surface. In addition to a nicely formed product, nonstick pans require less fat to properly cook the product. Two different types of egg pans are used in professional kitchens for cooking eggs—Teflon® and black steel.

Teflon

Teflon is a plastic polymer that is used as a coating or is embedded in the surface of cookware to make it nonstick. Teflon pans are excellent for allowing eggs to release easily, provided that the surface is unscratched. In order to keep the Teflon coating from being scratched, most cooks only stir or move foods being cooked with a silicone spatula. Be certain that the spatula used for cooking is heat resistant and will not melt into the food.

Black Steel

Pans made of black steel are the more traditional option for egg cookery. In order to create a nonstick surface in a steel pan, it must be "seasoned." A pan is seasoned by heating it with oil or fat for an extended period of time. When the metal is heated, pores in the surface of the metal expand and absorb some of the oil or fat. This creates a nonstick surface. As with other nonstick pans, it is important not to scratch the cooking surface.

Once a pan is seasoned, it is wiped clean after every use. It is not washed. Washing may rinse away the surface coating and also cause the pan to rust. Although seasoned pans are not washed, they are considered sanitary because they are dry heated to a high temperature each time they are used.

Experience is necessary to tell the doneness of eggs without breaking into the yolk. Experienced cooks can tell how done eggs are by gently pressing on the yolks to tell how firm they are.

The simplest fried eggs to prepare are sunny-side up eggs, or "eggs up." **Sunny-side up eggs** are fried eggs that are not flipped over during cooking. When they reach the desired degree of doneness, they are gently slipped out of the pan and onto the plate with the yolks facing up.

Basted eggs are fried in butter while the hot fat in the pan is spooned over the top and lightly cooks the yolks. Basted eggs are not flipped. The eggs should be basted with enough butter to make the surface of the yolks slightly opaque. Some chefs achieve this appearance by placing the eggs under a salamander or broiler for a short time.

After frying on one side, **eggs over** are flipped so that they can continue cooking on the other side. Eggs over should be flipped without breaking the egg yolks. Great skill and much practice are required to master the technique of flipping eggs without a spatula.

Breakfast Meats

Meats complement eggs in the traditional American breakfast. The rich and highly seasoned flavors of bacon and sausage are popular with diners. Home cooks often panfry breakfast meats. Professional cooks frequently cook bacon, sausage, and ham in the oven for a more evenly cooked and less greasy product.

Bacon

The crisp texture and smoky rich flavor of bacon is an all-time favorite on American breakfast tables. In most commercial kitchens, bacon is cooked in the oven. Baking sliced bacon in the oven offers the advantage of even cooking, nicely shaped bacon strips and, most importantly, the ability to cook more bacon at one time with less effort.

TECHNIQUE
Frying Eggs

1. Heat enough butter to coat the bottom of a seasoned or nonstick pan until it begins to spatter when a drop of water is added.
2. Crack the desired number of eggs directly into the pan and cook over moderate heat according to the desired method:

Sunny-side up–cook eggs to desired doneness.

Basted–spoon hot fat from the pan over the eggs while cooking them to the desired doneness.

Eggs over–cook the eggs long enough to fully coagulate the whites. Gently flip the eggs and continue to cook to the desired doneness.

3. Slide the eggs out of the pan onto a serving plate. Serve immediately.

To cook bacon in the oven, lay out the strips of bacon in a single layer on a sheet pan, 38-4. Many kitchens purchase bacon that is already laid out on ovenproof parchment paper. Bacon is baked in a moderate oven. The degree of doneness is a matter of personal preference. Bacon should always be cooked at least until white fat is no longer visible.

Ham and Canadian Bacon

Ham slices or steaks are often served as an accompaniment to eggs. Ham is best quickly panfried or grilled to keep it moist and tender. Canadian bacon is a boneless pork loin cured and smoked the same as ham. It is cooked in the same manner as ham.

Sausage

Breakfast sausage comes in two forms—links and patties, 38-5. Sausage links are made by stuffing fresh ground pork, turkey, or chicken into casings. Sausage patties consist of ground meat formed into small disks without casings. Breakfast sausages

Draz-Koetke/Goodheart-Willcox Publisher

38-4 Cooking bacon laid out on sheet pans allows cooks to prepare large quantities of bacon more efficiently.

Draz-Koetke/Goodheart-Willcox Publisher

38-5 Individuals often prefer one form of breakfast sausage over another.

Nutrition Connection

Boosting Fruits and Vegetables at Breakfast

Many consumers do not eat enough fruit and vegetable servings as part of their daily meal plan. Chefs can add these nutrient-rich foods to breakfast items by creating

- omelets and frittatas with extra veggies
- egg dishes topped with various salsas, including fruit salsa
- veggie breakfast burritos
- yogurt and hot cereal options made with berries, dried fruit, apples, or bananas
- pumpkin, carrot, or sweet potato pancakes
- a berry compote or fresh fruit slices to top pancakes and waffles

Chefs create many tasty breakfast dishes by adding fruits and vegetables.

are panfried or grilled until well-done. Like bacon, professional kitchens often prepare breakfast sausage by baking it on a sheet pan.

Breakfast Batters

French toast, pancakes, and waffles are popular breakfast foods. They all involve the use of a batter containing eggs.

French Toast

French toast is a simple preparation, which has become a breakfast favorite. **French toast** is made from bread soaked in a milk and egg mixture. It probably originated as a way to utilize stale bread. The batter that is used for French toast could be described as a custard, or *royale*. It is used to soak slices of bread. Once the bread has absorbed the batter, it is fried on a griddle or a nonstick pan to create a golden brown exterior with a moist, rich inside. Many variations on basic French toast can be made by using different

Hints from the Chef
Griddle Care

Griddles are an efficient way to cook many breakfast items such as eggs, omelets, French toast, and pancakes. An effective griddle is similar to a well-seasoned sauté pan. It requires some special care to work effectively and maintain its nonstick surface.

- Before cooking on a griddle, allow it sufficient time to preheat. Check the thermostat to be sure it is at the proper temperature for the items you wish to cook.
- Do not scratch the surface by chopping or cutting on the griddle.
- Regularly empty the grease tray.
- Clean the griddle daily with a griddle brick. Griddles are cleaned with an abrasive stone that removes food residue and buffs the cooking surface to keep its smooth and nonstick surface.

types of breads and by adding various flavorings to the batter.

Pancakes

Pancakes, also called *hot cakes*, are a form of quick bread that is cooked in a pan or griddle. Like all quick breads, pancakes are leavened with baking soda or baking powder. Their preparation is rather simple and straightforward but the following will ensure a good product:

- Avoid overmixing the batter or finished pancakes may become dense or tough.
- Preheat the pan or griddle to the proper temperature to ensure that the pancakes become golden brown with a fluffy inside.
- Turn the pancakes when bubbles appear on the surface and the bottom is golden brown, 38-6. Turn only once.

- Serve pancakes as soon as possible because they may become dry or flat if held too long.

Variations on basic pancakes are numerous. The use of flavorings and adding fruits or nuts to the basic pancake batter are popular options.

Waffles

Waffles are also a quick bread, but the batter is thicker and contains more fat than pancake batter. This difference creates a crisp exterior in the finished waffle. Waffles are cooked on a special waffle iron, which forms its grid-like pattern, 38-7. It is important that the nonstick surface of the waffle iron be maintained and kept seasoned. Waffle irons should be preheated before making waffles to ensure that they are crisp and do not stick.

Draz-Koetke/Goodheart-Willcox Publisher

38-6 The bubbles on the surface indicate these pancakes are ready to be turned.

Draz-Koetke/Goodheart-Willcox Publisher

38-7 Waffles can be made in a variety of shapes and sizes depending on the waffle iron.

Hot Cereals

Hot cereals are a nutritious source of B vitamins and fiber. They are a hearty and satisfying part of many traditional breakfasts.

To ensure the correct consistency, the proper ratio of liquid to cereal is essential, so measure carefully. The ratio of liquid to cereal and the cooking time vary depending on the type of grain and how it was processed. Follow package directions for the best results. Cook the cereal until it is smooth and moist, with no lumps. Hot cereals continue to thicken when held in a steam table. After a period of time in the steam table, their consistency may need to be adjusted by adding more liquid.

Some of the more popular hot cereals include:

- *Farina*–a cereal made of processed and ground wheat.
- *Grits*–cereal made from coarsely ground hominy corn.
- *Rice*–starchy varieties of rice that are cracked and cooked to a smooth consistency.
- *Cornmeal mush*–coarsely ground dried corn cooked as a porridge.
- *Oatmeal*–the most popular hot cereal, comes in two different styles—rolled oats and steel cut. The more popular rolled oats are smoother and quicker cooking. Steel cut oatmeal (also known as Irish or Scotch oatmeal) has a coarse texture and requires a longer cooking time.

Summary Points

- Simmered eggs are cooked in the shell.
- Poached eggs are removed from the shell and gently cooked in acidulated water.
- Scrambled eggs are beaten and cooked in a small amount of fat while being stirred to create a fluffy finished product.
- Omelets are scrambled eggs that are cooked to form a sheet. Omelets can be prepared in the French-style, American-style, or as a frittata.
- The doneness of fried eggs is determined by the consistency of the yolk.
- There are three principle ways to cook fried eggs and to different degrees of doneness.
- Breakfast meats are usually rich and highly seasoned, and complement eggs well.
- Pancakes, waffles, and French toast are popular American breakfast items. Proper consistency of the batter and proper cooking temperature are keys to quality.
- Preparing hot cereals is a responsibility of breakfast cooks. Smooth, lump-free cereals are a result of properly measuring cereals and liquid.

In Review Assess

1. True or false. Higher temperature cooking methods for eggs cooked in the shell produce a tender, evenly cooked egg.
2. How does a chef determine doneness for eggs cooked in their shell?
3. List two things you should do to produce a well-formed poached egg.
4. Which omelet is prepared by placing the ingredients in the pan at the same time as the eggs, lightly browning the eggs, and folding in half to serve?
   A. Frittata
   B. French-style omelet
   C. American-style omelet
5. What type of pan is best for preparing fried eggs and omelets?
6. True or false. Basted eggs are fried in butter and the yolk is lightly cooked by spooning the hot fat from the pan over the top of the egg.
7. List three benefits of baking bacon in the oven.
8. What is done to bread to make French toast?
9. What ingredient(s) is used to leaven pancakes and waffles?
10. What happens to hot cereals while they are held in a steam table?

Core Skills

11. **Math.** Visit the supermarket or contact a foodservice supplier to obtain the prices per dozen for the various size (jumbo, extra large, large, and so on) eggs. Create a chart comparing prices per ounce. Which egg size is the best buy?

12. **Speaking and Listening.** Prepare and demonstrate how to perfectly cook coddled, soft-cooked, and hard-cooked eggs for the class. Follow the text technique for cooking eggs in the shell. When all the eggs are done, display them in egg or bouillon cups and have your classmates evaluate the appearance. Discuss any challenges in preparing eggs by this method.

13. **Reading.** Use Internet or print resources to research the history of the breakfast favorite, French toast. What are the origins of French toast? How did early versions compare to the French toast today? Write a short report of your findings. To extend this activity, locate a recipe for an early version of French toast and prepare it for the class to sample. How does it compare to today's favorite?

14. **Speaking and Listening.** Divide into five teams. Each team should prepare one of the following hot cereals according to package directions (enough for a taste by each class-mate): farina, grits, rice, cornmeal mush, and oatmeal (either rolled oats or steel cut). When cereals are cooked, serve a taste in a small bowl or prep dish for each person.

Teams should taste and evaluate the cereals for proper consistency and doneness. Discuss the products and any challenges the teams faced during preparation. What accompaniments could be served with each of the cereals during breakfast service?

15. **CTE Career Readiness Practice.** Teaching and mentoring others is an ability that employers value. With a classmate, practice your teaching and mentoring skills for the class. One person should take the role of "chef" and the other as the "cook-trainee." The chef should teach the new cook how to prepare an *American-Style Omelet* using the text technique. After completing the technique, reverse roles and repeat the process. Have the class evaluate the teaching/mentoring methods along with evaluating the finished egg product. What challenges can you face when teaching a skill to others? Why is it important to be affirming as you teach your craft?

Video Clip

Poaching Eggs

Visit the G-W Learning Companion Website and view the bonus video clip "Poaching eggs." After viewing the clip, answer the following questions:

1. Why are poached eggs cooked at a lower temperature than simmered eggs?
2. How much vinegar is added to water for poaching eggs?
3. True or false. Water for poaching eggs should be salted.

Video

Critical Thinking

16. **Draw conclusions.** Why might a chef choose to cook fried eggs and omelets on a griddle rather than in pans? Draw conclusions about how the results might differ.
17. **Generate.** In teams, brainstorm a list of possible ingredients that can be added to basic French toast, pancakes, and waffles to add variety to breakfast menus. Generate a T-chart showing which ingredients are appropriate for each item.
18. **Infer.** What egg items would you serve at meals other than breakfast? How would you change their preparation and presentation?
19. **Analyze cause and effect.** The new cook's poached eggs are rubbery, flat, and the yolk is off center. What actions could have caused these problems? What steps would you suggest to correct these problems?

Technology

With a teammate, create a video demonstrating how to properly poach eggs. Follow the text technique for poaching eggs and plate immediately for service. Show a close-up of the properly poached egg. Discuss any challenges with using this poaching technique. Use a school-approved web-based application to upload your video to the school/class website for class evaluation.

Teamwork

Divide into five teams. Each team will prepare one of the following types of fried egg: easy, medium, hard, basted, eggs over. Display the eggs for comparison. Evaluate each egg for appearance and texture. Discuss any challenges the teams faced with their egg preparation method.

Chef's E-portfolio
Poaching Eggs

Upload your video from the Technology activity to your e-portfolio. Ask your instructor where to save your file. This could be on the school's network or a flash drive of your own. Name your portfolio document *FirstnameLastname_Portfolio Ch#.docx* (i.e., JohnSmith_PortfolioCh38.docx).

While studying, look for the activity icon to:

- Build vocabulary with e-flash cards and matching activities.
- Expand learning with video clips, photo identification activities, animations, and interactive activities.
- Review and assess what you learn by completing end-of-chapter questions.

Food Presentation 39

Reading Prep

Before reading this chapter, look at the illustrations in the chapter to preview the content that will be presented. Illustrations help describe the content in an easy-to-understand manner.

Culinary Terminology
Build Vocab

chafing dish, p. 627
garnish, p. 628

Academic Terminology
Build Vocab

detract, p. 622
focal point, p. 623
symmetry, p. 626
asymmetry, p. 626

Objectives

After studying this chapter, you will be able to

- apply plating principles to design an attractive plate presentation.
- explain principles that guide platter and buffet presentation.
- compare various garnishing techniques.

It's going to be another busy Saturday and the chef is designing a new special for the night menu. The chef wants to feature pork tenderloin, as there is an extra case in the refrigerator. She first considers how to cook the tenderloin. She decides to roast it and serve it with an apple cider sauce made with demi-glace. Immediately, the chef realizes that she has a color problem since the pork and the sauce are both brown.

Looking around the kitchen, the chef spots a case of sweet potatoes. Sweet potato would add orange to the plate and complement the apple and pork flavors. She decides to make a sweet potato dauphinoise. This sweet potato preparation consists of layers of sliced sweet potato, cheese, eggs, and cream baked in a large pan. Instead of scooping the cooked sweet potato dauphinoise from its baking container, the chef decides to use a round cutter to cut the sweet potato into cylinders. The chef also decides to put buttered green beans on the plate. The bright green color adds another vibrant color. The beans are prepared simply in contrast to the more complex sweet potato dish.

There are still more decisions the chef must make before the dish is done. The chef considers how the tenderloin is to be presented. She decides to serve it sliced. The sweet potato cylinder is first placed in the center of the plate. Keeping the slices in the order they were sliced, the chef shingles the meat around the sweet potato. The beans are arranged leaning on the sweet potato. Remembering that sauces are not put on top of roasted meat, the sauce is spooned onto the plate next to pork. The chef decides the plate lacks height. To solve this, she prepares deep-fried sweet potato chips and a batonnet of apple tossed in a vinaigrette. These are arranged on top of the sweet potato, 39-1.

Lastly, the chef considers how long it will take to assemble the dish and whether the

Draz-Koetke/Goodheart-Willcox Publisher

39-1 The final presentation of the pork tenderloin special is a result of many decisions made by the chef.

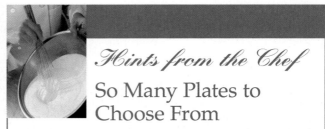

Hints from the Chef

So Many Plates to Choose From

Many restaurants have plates with bold patterns and bright colors on a white background. Sometimes, they may be entirely green, red, black, or blue. When plating food on these plates, the color of the plate must be considered along with the color the food being served. In general, arranging food on predominantly white plates is the simplest. White provides a neutral background, which focuses the diner's attention on the food itself.

plate lids will fit on top of such a preparation. Failure in either of these areas will cause the chef to redesign the dish.

Many times a day, chefs need to create attractive and balanced menu items. How a plate looks is the customer's first impression of the food. If it is arranged attractively, the guest will want to eat it. If the dish is unattractive, the customer will start to form a negative opinion of the dish and the restaurant as a whole.

Arranging food on plates and platters, or assembling an entire buffet requires practice and creativity. Chefs are continually thinking of innovative new ways to attractively present food. Presentation must never be placed above flavor and proper cooking of a dish. While appearance is the first impression, it is taste that is the last impression.

Plating Principles

Most of the food served in restaurants is served on plates. Being able to present attractively plated food is part of the chef's art.

When considering how to arrange food on a plate, the cook needs to consider color, height, focal point, proportion, variety, and temperature. Neglecting any of these areas can **detract** from, or diminish the effectiveness of, an otherwise successful presentation.

Color

The skilled use of color on a plate adds to the eye appeal of a dish. When thinking about pairing items on a plate, consider how the colors relate. Vibrant contrasting colors make food look appetizing. Plates that have similar colors should be avoided. For instance, in the plate at the beginning of this chapter, it would be a mistake to replace the green beans with carrots, since both the carrots and sweet potatoes are orange, 39-2. Instead the plate is composed of green, orange, brown, and white.

Vibrant colors often result from properly cooked products. For example, the green beans are bright green since they were correctly blanched in boiling salted water and shocked in ice water. If these beans were not blanched in boiling salted water or not shocked in ice water, they would have had

39-2 This pork tenderloin plate was arranged without proper thought to color.

a dull olive green color. Similarly, correctly roasting the pork tenderloin produces an appetizing caramelized crust. If it is improperly roasted, it might look gray or even black. The color of food should always be natural. Adding food coloring to food produces colors that are too intense and unappetizing.

Many times, chefs add garnishes to plates or platters to improve the color. For instance, tomato roses or fanned strawberries contribute an intense red hue. A sprig of parsley or other herb adds a splash of bright fresh green. However, remember that garnishes should reflect the dish being garnished. Putting fanned strawberries on the chef's new special plate would be a mistake since they do not complement the flavors of the dish.

Height

Food is three-dimensional. It not only covers part of the plate surface, but also rises above the plate. Chefs consider how high they want their food to be. Plates with too little height lack dramatic presentation and seem flat. The other extreme is also problematic. Overly tall food may look comical. Tall and unsteady presentations are challenging to serve and difficult to eat. It is also impossible to cover tall, hot presentations with a plate cover. This can result in cold food, 39-3.

Focal Point

A **focal point** is the location or item to which the eye is first drawn when looking at a plate presentation. The focal point is most often the highest, biggest, or most colorful item on the plate. It is usually the main item on the plate, like the pork tenderloin in the example. Plate designs with a definite focal point create a satisfying sense of order.

Proportion

Proportion refers to the relationship between the amounts of the different

39-3 A presentation that is too tall is unstable and difficult to serve and eat.

food items on a plate. Proper amounts of different components of a particular dish create good proportion. For instance, if the amount of pork tenderloin was reduced by half and the amounts of vegetables were doubled, the pork tenderloin plate would no longer be in proportion. Also, if a half cup of sauce were spooned onto each plate, the excess sauce would look odd. At the same time, placing several small drizzles of sauce is no better, 39-4.

Proportion also refers to the relationship between the size of the actual plate and the amount of food arranged on it. The amount of food placed on a plate should be in proportion to the size of the plate. Putting too much food on a small plate is not attractive. Similarly, arranging too little food on a large plate requires practice to avoid making the portion look small and the plate look empty.

Variety of Shapes, Sizes, and Textures

Creating variety on a plate improves the overall appeal of a dish. Foods come in a variety of shapes. Avoid repeating the same shapes on the plate. In terms of appearance, different knife cuts can create a variety of shapes. In the chef's special example, the sweet potato dauphinoise was cut out in a circle and the apple cut into a batonnet to improve the variety of shapes.

While the shape of food is important, the size of food also needs to be considered. Attractively designed plates combine foods of different sizes. For instance, it is unattractive to have a plate composed of many small pieces of food. Instead, a large piece of food complemented with smaller pieces is more appealing.

Variety can also refer to differences of texture. Common food textures are hard, chewy, soft, crisp, smooth, sticky, dry, gritty, and tough. A plate should include a variety of these textures—neither all soft nor all

39-4 This plate is not in proportion because it contains too much food and the vegetables are overwhelming the pork tenderloin.

SUSTAINABLE CULINARY

Portion Sizes

Nutrition-related health issues such as obesity and diabetes are growing health concerns. As a result, there is also a growing emphasis on healthful eating. One area where sustainability and nutrition intersect is portion size. Excessive portions result in over-consumption of calories which can lead to many health issues. At the same time, producing food uses precious resources including energy and water. In restaurants where portions are very large, patrons often do not eat everything on the plate. This means the resources used to produce the food were basically squandered. In addition, the food waste often goes into a landfill which then contributes to further environmental issues. Reducing portion sizes could improve health outcomes and reduce waste!

crunchy. Adding a crunchy sweet potato chip contributes to the textural variety in the chef's new special.

Temperature

Serving food at its optimal temperature is part of plate presentation. When plating food, care must be taken to ensure hot food stays hot and cold food stays cold. Proper serving temperature begins with the plate itself. Cold food is served on a chilled plate. Hot food is presented on a preheated plate. Using the wrong temperature plates either cools hot food or warms cold food. For instance, a salad wilts when placed on a warm plate and ice cream melts if served in a warm bowl.

To be sure that hot food remains hot, the plating process must happen rapidly. Taking too much time to arrange hot food reduces the temperature of the food. As a result, the plate may be visually attractive at the expense of the overall enjoyment of the dish. Once the plate of hot food is arranged, it should be covered with a plate cover, 39-5. Plate covers help keep the food hot while it is delivered to the dining room.

Hints from the Chef
Plating Pitfalls

Attractive plate presentations rely on the artistic creativity of the chef. While creativity is necessary, it should be within certain boundaries. The following points provide guidance on what *not* to do when plating:

- *Avoid placing food on the rim of the plate.* While there are chefs that do this, it is not advisable as it makes serving the food difficult. View the rim as the frame around a picture. Always be sure that the rim is free of stray food and fingerprints.

- *Avoid overly tall or unstable plating designs.* Tall or unstable food is difficult to serve and difficult to eat. It is also difficult to cover with a plate cover, which may then result in cold food.

- *Avoid overfilling a plate.* Proper portion sizes should always be maintained.

- *Avoid overly complicated dishes and garnishes.* Knowing when to stop or hold back comes with experience. Understated simplicity is often best.

- *Avoid the use of nonedibles on the plate.* Plates should only contain edible product.

Draz-Koetke/Goodheart-Willcox Publisher

39-5 Plate covers should be removed by the waitstaff just before serving the customer to keep the food as hot as possible.

Platter Presentation

At one time or another in the course of a culinary career, all cooks will be required to present food on a platter. Many of the same considerations that are given to the color, height, proportion, and variety of plate presentation also apply to arranging a platter.

On a platter, the focal point is often a centerpiece. Platter centerpieces are often not designed to be eaten and offer a chance for the chef to express his or her artistic creativity. Such centerpieces should be positioned so they are not damaged as food is removed from the platter.

The principal difference between a platter and a plate presentation is size. Plates are designed to feed one, while platters may serve 50 people or more. Because of the increased amount of food being presented, the chef also needs to consider lines and flow. Generally, different food items are arranged in lines on a platter. This creates flow, or a sense of movement, as the eye follows the lines of food. Flow can be straight or curved, 39-6.

While arranging these lines of food on a platter, always consider the amount of empty space. Empty space is also called *negative space*. Negative space is any part of the platter not covered with food. Platters without enough negative space are crowded, while those with too much negative space appear empty.

When planning how to arrange a balanced platter, chefs consider symmetry. **Symmetry** refers to a balanced arrangement that is identical on opposite sides of a center point. Symmetry produces an orderly and predictable pattern. With **asymmetry**, a sense of balance is achieved by artistically arranging items without creating two identical sides of a center point. Asymmetrical designs are more difficult to arrange successfully and require much practice. Asymmetrical designs, when well executed, can be very exciting and creative, 39-7.

Platters need to be functional so customers can easily serve themselves or be served by a cook or server. Customers should be able to reach all the food on a platter. The size and shape of the portions must be easy

Draz-Koetke/Goodheart-Willcox Publisher

39-6 Flow on a platter results from lines of precisely arranged food items.

A

B

Draz-Koetke/Goodheart-Willcox Publisher

39-7 Do you find the (A) symmetrical platter or the (B) asymmetrical design more pleasing?

to handle. Additionally, platters must be easy to replenish during a busy service, 39-8.

Buffet Presentation

Designing an entire buffet table requires considerable experience. Buffet setups are designed much like an individual platter. The same considerations that pertain to platter presentation also pertain to an entire buffet. When setting up a buffet, there are many factors to consider.

- *Color.* Buffets should make wise use of different colors and pleasing color schemes.

39-8 The garnish on this (A) serving bowl will not be disturbed as customers serve themselves. As the first customers serve themselves, (B) this garnish will be destroyed.

- *Height.* Buffets are three-dimensional. Various serving containers should be placed at different heights on the table.
- *Focal point/centerpiece.* Buffet centerpieces are similar to platter centerpieces but much larger. They perform the same function. Buffet centerpieces are often the customer's first impression. Thus, dramatic ice carvings or floral arrangements attract the customer's attention and can reflect the theme of the buffet.
- *Balance and proportion.* The items on the table should be precisely displayed, varied, and create a sense of balance.
- *Variety.* Buffets should consist of a variety of dishes presented in different ways.
- *Temperature.* Buffets need to keep hot items hot and cold items cold. **Chafing dishes** are decorative covered stands that keep food hot. Chafing dishes come in a variety of different sizes, 39-9. Cold food items are often placed on crushed ice.
- *Symmetry or asymmetry.* Buffets are arranged symmetrically or asymmetrically.
- *Negative space.* Buffet tables should not have too many nor too few items.

Draz-Koetke/Goodheart-Willcox Publisher

39-9 A chafing dish is used to keep food hot on a buffet.

- *Functionality.* Buffets are designed to feed many people. Servers and cooks should be able to easily keep the buffet clean and well stocked with food.
- *Serving utensils.* When arranging a buffet, it is important to place the proper serving utensils next to each item on the buffet.

Garnishes

The modern definition of garnishing refers to the chef's ability to improve the appearance of a dish by adding various decorative touches. Edible decorative additions or accompaniments are called **garnishes**. Through years of kitchen experience, professional chefs develop a repertoire of garnishing techniques.

When deciding which garnish to make, remember that garnishes should coordinate with the flavors and temperature of the dish they garnish. Garnishes should never overshadow or detract from the main dish. Garnishes should be used sparingly and only when functional. Nonfunctional garnishes are those that do nothing but provide a visual stimulus. The following examples demonstrate situations where garnishes are used improperly:

- *Deep-fried tortilla strips garnishing a plate of traditional German cuisine.* Adding a Mexican touch to an otherwise traditional German dish is out of place.
- *Lettuce garnishing a hot entrée or appetizer.* The heat wilts the lettuce quickly.
- *Raw carrot flowers placed on top of beef stew.* The texture of the raw carrot is unappealing when combined with very tender elements of beef stew.

Simple Garnishes

Garnishing need not involve complicated techniques. In fact, simplicity is often best. Chefs often use fresh herbs to decorate platters and individual plates, 39-10. Parsley is traditionally one of the most common herbs used for garnishing. Increasingly, chefs are

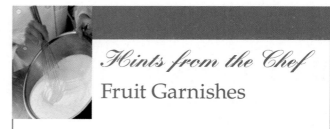

Hints from the Chef

Fruit Garnishes

Fruits can also be cut or carved into interesting shapes. Fruits are often used to garnish breakfast and pastry items. Popular fruit garnishes include strawberry fans, melon baskets, and apple swans.

Draz-Koetke/Goodheart-Willcox Publisher

39-10 Fresh herbs and neatly cut vegetables can improve the appearance of a dish.

using other herbs such as thyme and rosemary to complement a dish. Some herbs such as cilantro, chervil, and basil are less suitable for garnishing hot food as they wilt rapidly under heat.

Chefs can also use vegetables as a simple garnish. Vegetables can be minced or cut into exact traditional knife cuts such as brunoise or julienne. Vegetables contribute not only bursts of color, but additional flavors as well.

Crispy Garnishes

A recent trend in food presentation is the use of crispy foods as garnishes. Crispy items add height and a sense of sculpture to the plate, 39-11. They also contribute a crunch to the eating experience. Some examples of crispy garnishes include
- thinly sliced croutons
- deep-fried root vegetables such as sweet potato, beet, and potato
- baked or deep-fried wonton wrappers
- deep-fried raviolis
- thin, artistically shaped baked flatbreads or crackers
- fleurons, which are crescents of baked puff pastry
- various cookies and sugar garnishes for pastry presentations

Sprinkles

Sprinkling very small pieces of food or powders on plates of prepared food has become a popular garnishing technique. Savory sprinkles include minced herbs, nuts, and mild spices. Sweet sprinkles include chocolate shavings, nuts, cocoa powder, powdered sugar, and finely chopped fruits.

Vegetables

Vegetable carving requires more practice than sprinkling food on a plate. Depending on the design, vegetable carvings can be simple or extremely complicated. When executed well, vegetable garnishes certainly impress the customer. Simpler vegetable garnishes are a good place to start.

Vegetable cutouts, scallion flowers, and radish roses are classic garnishes that are simple to prepare. The tomato rose is a little more difficult to master, but also more elegant.

Draz-Koetke/Goodheart-Willcox Publisher

39-11 Deep-fried root vegetables arranged on top of a filet mignon add texture, color, shape, and height.

TECHNIQUE ⟳ Animation
Making Vegetable Cutouts

1. Begin with a room temperature vegetable. Root vegetables such as turnips, large carrots, beets, and rutabagas work well. If the vegetable is too cold, it is difficult to cut and tends to break.
2. Peel the vegetable. Slice a ¼-inch thick piece of the vegetable.
3. Place the slice on a cutting board. Cut out the shape using a cookie cutter.
4. Place the cutouts in ice water until needed. The water prevents the cutouts from drying out and looking old.

TECHNIQUE
Making Scallion Flowers

1. Cut the bottom 2½ inches from the scallion. Save the top green portion for another use.
2. Trim the roots from the scallion. Only trim what is necessary to remove just the root.
3. Starting ¼ inch from the root end, make as many lengthwise cuts down the scallion as possible. Be sure the knife does not cut all the way through the root end of the scallion.

4. Roll the scallion 90°.
5. Cut a new series of slices lengthwise down the scallion as in step three. Be sure that the knife does not cut all the way through the root end of the scallion.
6. Place the scallion in ice water for at least 30 minutes. During this time, the scallion will curl and fan out. If the scallion does not open satisfactorily, the scallion was not cut close enough to the root end.

TECHNIQUE
Making a Radish Rose

1. Choose large radishes that are free of blemishes. Carve radishes that are at room temperature. Cold radishes are hard to carve because they are brittle and tend to break.
2. Trim both ends of the radish using a paring knife. Trim away as little radish as possible.
3. Starting at the top of the radish, cut petals down the sides of the radish. Each petal should be about ⅛-inch thick and should be left attached at the bottom of the radish.

4. If desired, the center of the radish can be removed using a small knife or Parisienne scoop.
5. Place the radish roses in ice water until needed to allow them to open.

TECHNIQUE
Making a Tomato Rose

1. Starting at the bottom (opposite the stem end) of the tomato, slice almost the entire bottom off. Be sure to leave the bottom attached to the rest of the tomato by about one inch. The bottom of the tomato will be the bottom of the finished rose.

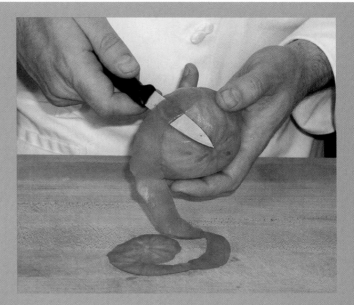

2. At the point where the bottom is attached to the rest of the tomato, begin to slice one long continuous spiral of tomato skin. The piece of skin is about ⅛ inch thick and one inch wide. Turn the tomato while slicing off the skin. It is important to remove the skin with a slicing motion. Simply pushing the knife through the tomato produces a poor piece of jagged skin.

3. By the time you reach the stem end of the tomato, there should be little skin attached to the tomato. Cut the long piece of skin from the rest of the tomato.

4. Roll the skin tightly, starting at the stem end of the peel. Be sure that the shiny side of the peel is facing outward. Continue rolling the peel until it reaches the attached piece of the tomato bottom. At this point, place the rolled tomato skin naturally on the tomato bottom.

5. If necessary, store the tomato rose covered in plastic wrap in the refrigerator. It is best to make the tomato rose as close to service as possible.

Summary Points

- The appearance of a dish is important because it is the customer's first impression of a dish.

- When arranging food on a plate, the color, height, shape, focal point, proportion, and temperature of the food should be considered.

- Preparing attractive platters requires many of the same considerations as arranging food on an individual plate.

- Designing an entire buffet follows many of the same considerations of a platter, such as color, height, shape, centerpiece, proportion, temperature, symmetry, negative space, and functionality.

- Garnishes are designed to improve the visual appearance of food. It is important that the garnish coordinate with the dish.

In Review
Assess

1. True or false. When arranging a plate of food, chefs often assemble foods of similar colors.

2. List two disadvantages of overly tall plate presentations.

3. _____ refers to the relationship between the amounts of different food items on a plate.

4. List three ways to create variety when selecting foods for a plate presentation.

5. True or false. A centerpiece is often the focal point of a platter presentation.

6. _____ _____ is any part of a platter that is not covered with food.

7. Contrast symmetry with asymmetry in conjunction with platter presentation.

8. If a chef is evaluating his buffet presentation for functionality, which of the following is he considering?
   A. Servers and cooks can keep the buffet clean.
   B. Servers and cooks can restock the food easily.
   C. Buffet can easily feed the number of people attending.
   D. All of the above.

9. Name three crispy garnishes.

10. List two reasons many vegetable carvings are placed in ice water for several hours before being used.

Core Skills

11. **Math.** The chef assigned you to make fresh fruit platters for a buffet serving 600 people. If each fruit platter serves approximately 50 people, how many platters will you need to make?

12. **Speaking.** Choose an entrée from a restaurant menu. Consider various ways to plate that menu item for the greatest visual appeal following text guidelines. Discuss your thoughts with the class. To extend this activity, locate digital photos that display your ideas and share them with the class or post them to the class blog for discussion.

13. **Writing.** Use reliable Internet or print resources to research garnishes for at least six different cultural cuisines. Write an illustrated report of your findings.

14. **Speaking and Listening.** Prepare each one of the vegetable garnishes covered in this chapter—vegetable cutouts, scallion flower, radish rose, and tomato rose. Present your garnishes for evaluation. Discuss one another's garnishes for appearance and technique. What challenges did classmates have in creating vegetable garnishes?

15. **Reading.** Read additional information on garnishes in one or more culinary books such as those recommended by the *American Culinary Federation (ACF)*. How does this information support the guidelines in this text? What further information did you find about types of garnishes and methods to produce them? Write a summary of your findings.

16. **CTE Career Readiness Practice.** The ability to teach others is a valuable skill in the culinary kitchen. Suppose you are preparing to set up a buffet presentation for 500 guests. You have new kitchen staff members with little background in platter and buffet presentation. You have decided to have a training session for your new staff. Prepare the script for your lesson on platter and buffet presentation. Give your presentation to the staff (your class).

Critical Thinking

17. **Make inferences.** From an appearance standpoint, what is wrong with a plate of poached boneless, skinless chicken breast served with a béchamel sauce and mashed potatoes? How would you improve this plate presentation?

18. **Recognize relationships.** What are the similarities between how a plate, platter, and buffet are arranged? How can understanding and executing plating principles benefit a chef with platter and buffet arrangement?

19. **Analyze consequences.** A cook arranges very hot food on a plate. The plate is then immediately brought to the table and served to the customer. The customer complains that the food is not hot. What are some possible explanations for why the food is not hot? As the chef de cuisine, you are responsible for the quality of the food. What would you teach the cook to eliminate this problem?

20. **Create.** Obtain a menu from a restaurant or online. Select and record five entrées. For each entrée, propose an appropriate garnish and record it next to the entrée. Discuss your reasoning for selecting each garnish.

Technology

Use the Internet to research images of various plating techniques that you find of interest and that follow text guidelines for appropriate presentation techniques. Create a digital resource book of ideas for future reference. Be sure to note the source of each idea with each image in your resource book.

Teamwork

As foodservice director for a multinational corporation, it has come to your attention that foods served in the company cafeteria are not meeting cultural and presentation needs of all employees. Most offices in the United States have many employees from Asian and Middle Eastern cultures. You and your culinary team need to make changes in some types of foods served and the way they are presented, but require more information. With your team members, create a plan to gather and analyze the information you need with culture in mind. List culturally sensitive questions you should ask about food needs and potential sources of reliable information.

Chef's E-portfolio
Plating Resource

Upload your digital resource book from the Technology activity to your e-portfolio. Ask your instructor where to save your file. This could be on the school's network or a flash drive of your own. Name your portfolio document *FirstnameLastname_Portfolio Ch#.docx* (i.e., JohnSmith_PortfolioCh39.docx).

Unit Four
In the Bakeshop

HLPhoto/Shutterstock.com

The Science of Volume—Leavening

Breads and cakes baked without leavening are flat, dense, and tough. Humans figured out 6,000 years ago that leavening made their bread better. These early cooks had discovered how to use a leavening agent called *yeast* to add volume and lightness to their bread. These helpful microscopic, single-celled fungi feed on the flour and release gas and other by-products. The gas is trapped in the dough, which adds volume. Cutting a loaf of bread reveals the pockets where gas bubbles formed to make a lighter, less dense product.

Yeast is not the only leavening agent used to add volume to baked goods. Chemical leaveners such as baking soda and baking powder produce gas much more quickly than yeast. While food leavened with yeast harnesses the work of tiny fungi, chemical leaveners rely on the work of chemicals such as sodium bicarbonate as it reacts with an acid. The acid may be an ingredient in the recipe, such as milk or molasses, or may be part of the chemical leavener. And, although the chemical leaveners act more quickly, they produce the same gas—carbon dioxide—that yeast produces.

Different leaveners are better suited to some dishes than others. For example, yeast is preferred for many breads, while chemical leaveners are used in cakes and quick breads more often.

1. Briefly describe how yeast adds volume to bread.

2. What gas is produced by yeast? by chemical leaveners?

While studying, look for the activity icon  **to:**

- Build vocabulary with e-flash cards and matching activities.

- Expand learning with video clips, photo identification activities, animations, and interactive activities.

- Review and assess what you learn by completing end-of-chapter questions.

Introduction to the Bakeshop

40

Reading Prep

Skim the review questions at the end of the chapter first. Use them to help you focus on the most important concepts as you read the chapter.

Culinary Terminology
Build Vocab

pastry chef, p. 638
pastry cook, p. 638
baker, p. 638
gluten, p. 638
simple syrup, p. 640
shortening, p. 640
leavening, p. 640
baking soda, p. 641
baking powder, p. 641
fermentation, p. 641
blooming, p. 643
extract, p. 646

Academic Terminology
Build Vocab

potential, p. 638

Objectives

After studying this chapter, you will be able to

- explain various jobs in the bakeshop.
- recognize baking ingredients and understand their functions in baked goods.
- recognize smallwares, hand tools, and large equipment used in the bakeshop.

Professional cookery is separated into two main areas of work—cooking and baking. Cooking involves preparing savory hot and cold dishes. Baking includes preparing breads, pastries, and sweets. In this chapter, you will learn about the jobs, ingredients, tools, and equipment that are found in the bakeshop.

Working in the Bakeshop

The skills needed in baking are rather different from those needed in other parts of the kitchen. Exactness of measurement and strict adherence to recipe directions are essential. Once an item is removed from the oven, there is no chance to correct any errors. Even slight variations in ingredients, quantities, or process can ruin bread and pastry items.

Foodservice operations that prepare their own baked goods and pastries have a specific work area set aside for their preparation. This area may be called the *bakeshop, bakery,* or *pastry kitchen.* The work schedule of the bakeshop is often very different from the rest of the kitchen. Preparation of breads and pastries needed for breakfast often starts in the late hours of the previous night. Much of the work for pastries needed for dinner is done in the morning and early afternoon.

The set of skills applied in baking and pastry work is different from those used in cooking. For this reason, some food professionals find themselves better suited for work in the bakeshop or pastry kitchen and make career choices to specialize in baking and pastry. The head of the bakeshop is the

SUSTAINABLE CULINARY

Fair Trade

In many countries, the people who grow the world's food are often paid very little and even mistreated. In response to this, many organizations have been created such as Fair Trade to empower those who produce food and provide for them a fair, living wage. Products that conform to the standards of Fair Trade are labeled as such so that consumers and chefs can make a choice to support them. Many times, Fair Trade and other similar organizations not only provide a living wage, but also create additional funds for education, healthcare, and infrastructure through their pricing strategies. In some instances, growers have formed cooperatives. As a cooperative member, the growers are part owners of the company and have more control over pricing and other aspects of the business. Fair Trade also encourages sustainable farming techniques. There are many products that are certified Fair Trade such as coffee, tea, honey, chocolate, and fruits.

pastry chef who is responsible for supervising the preparation of all breads, cakes, pies, pastries, ice creams, and candies. Under the supervision of the pastry chef, the **pastry cooks** are responsible for preparing sweet dessert items. A **baker** works preparing and baking breads. Large pastry kitchens may have staff that specialize in particular tasks such as creating decorations and showpieces, working only with ice creams and frozen desserts, or concentrating solely on candies. Despite this great degree of specialization, it is necessary for all professional culinarians to have basic skills in baking and pastry techniques.

Bakeshop Ingredients

The amount and type of ingredient is more important in baking and pastry work than other areas of the kitchen. Even minor variations in ingredients can create noticeable differences in the finished product, therefore choosing the right ingredient for a recipe is critical. The accuracy of the measurement is also important.

Flour

Flour is finely milled wheat. Most bakeshops have several large bins of different types of wheat flours. To the untrained eye, these flours look identical but they give very distinct qualities to the breads and pastries in which they are used. The main difference between these flours is the protein content of the wheat from which they are made, 40-1.

When flour is mixed with water, the protein in the flour produces gluten. **Gluten** is a rubbery substance that is responsible for giving baked goods structure. Strands of gluten stretch and trap gases that create the spongy texture of breads and cakes.

The wheat flours used in professional bakeshops are categorized by their **potential**, or capability, to produce gluten. Harder wheat kernels produce flours with higher protein content, often referred to as *hard flours*. Softer wheat kernels produce flours with lower protein content. These are often called *soft flours*. The amount of protein is directly related to gluten content.

Sweeteners

The primary sweetener used in baking and pastries is sugar. Sugar can be refined from the sugarcane plant or from sugar beets. Cane and beet sugar are used interchangeably, except when creating sugar sculptures and candies. Cane sugar is preferred for work involving sculptures and candies.

In addition to adding a sweet taste, sugar performs other important functions in pastries and baked goods. Sugar helps maintain moistness in cakes. It assists with the leavening process in breads. Sugar can also be used to achieve crispness in cookies and pastries and, it is key to browning and caramelization.

Flours Commonly Found in the Bakeshop

- *High-gluten flour* has high protein (14 to 15 percent) and low starch content. It is used primarily for specialty breads or mixed with low-protein flours to create stronger dough.

- *Bread flour* is a blend of hard, high-protein wheat that is milled primarily for commercial bakers. It is used for breads because of the texture and structure it provides. Its protein content ranges from 12 to 14 percent.

- *All-purpose flour* is a blend of hard and soft wheat. It is applicable for many kinds of products, including some yeast breads, quick breads, cakes, cookies, and pastries. Its protein content varies between 8 to 11 percent.

- *Pastry flour* is milled from soft wheat. It is used for pastry making, as well as for cookies, cakes, crackers, biscuits, and similar products. It differs from hard wheat flour in that it has a finer texture and lighter consistency. Protein content ranges from 8 to 9 percent.

- *Cake flour* is fine-textured, silky flour milled from soft wheat with low protein content. It is used to make cakes, cookies, crackers, quick breads, and some types of pastry. Cake flour has a greater percentage of starch and less protein, which keeps cakes and pastries tender and delicate. Protein varies from 7 to 9 percent.

- *Whole wheat flour*, sometimes called *graham flour*, is made by either grinding the whole-wheat kernel or recombining the white flour, germ, and bran that have been separated during milling. Its fiber content is higher than that of white flours.

- *Self-rising flour* is a convenience product made by adding salt and chemical leavening to all-purpose flour.

- *Rye flour* is milled from the grain of the cereal grass rye. It is darker, more flavorful, and has less gluten than wheat flours. It comes in dark and light forms and is used primarily for bread making. Pumpernickel flour is coarsely ground dark rye flour.

- *Multigrain flours* are mixtures of various grains used to produce specialty breads. Oat, millet, barley, and corn are popular ingredients in multigrain mixtures.

40-1 The choice of flour used for a preparation affects the final product.

SCIENCE & TECHNOLOGY

The Milling Process

To begin the milling process, incoming wheat is weighed, sampled, and analyzed. It is sorted according to protein content.

Cleaners remove weed seeds, dirt, and other foreign matter. Specialized cleaning equipment scours the surface of the kernel, removing contaminants and the outermost layers of the bran. Water is then added to the wheat kernels making the outer bran layer easier to remove in the milling process.

Milling is essentially a process of grinding and separating. Break rolls crush the kernels making separation of the bran and endosperm possible. Corrugated sizing rolls reduce the size of the particles of grain. Then, a series of reduction rolls reduces the endosperm into flour and allows removal of the bran.

Bolting is the separation of the different-sized flour particles, which is done using machines called *sifters* and *purifiers*.

Flours can be made of a blend of different wheats mixed before milling. Alternately, they may be mixed after milling.

After milling, it is common to further process flour. Some of the most common flour products that have had further treatment include

- *Enriched flour* has iron and B vitamins (thiamin, niacin, riboflavin, and folic acid) added to it. It may also be supplemented with calcium. There is no change in taste, color, texture, baking quality, or caloric value.

- *Bleached flour* has been chemically whitened to improve its appearance and baking qualities. No change occurs in the nutritional value of the flour and no harmful chemical residues remain.

- *Unbleached flour* is bleached naturally by oxygen in the air. It has a slightly golden color. It is generally more expensive than bleached flour and may have different baking characteristics.

The main distinction between the different types of white sugar found in the bakeshop is how finely the crystals are ground.

Another sweetener that is often made in large batches in a pastry shop is *simple syrup*. **Simple syrup** is equal parts of water and sugar by weight that is brought to a boil and simmered just until the sugar dissolves in the water. It has many uses including moistening cakes and poaching fruits, 40-2. Other sweeteners used in the bakeshop include molasses, honey, and corn syrup.

Sweeteners Commonly Used for Baking

- *Granulated sugar* is the most common form of sugar in the kitchen and bakeshop. It has fine uniform crystals.

- *Powdered sugar*, also called *confectioner's sugar*, is granulated sugar that is ground to a fine powder. It is available in 6X and 10X grades, meaning it is 6 or 10 times finer than granulated sugar. Powdered sugar often has a small amount of cornstarch or other additives to prevent caking.

- *Superfine sugar*, sometimes called *castor sugar*, is an extremely fine, granulated sugar with no additives. It dissolves easily without clouding.

- *Brown sugar* is granulated sugar with added molasses. Light or golden-brown sugar has less molasses than dark brown sugar.

- *Sanding sugar* has larger crystals than granulated sugar. It is used for dusting, topping, and decorating cookies and pastries. It is often colored for added eye appeal.

- *Molasses* is the liquid that remains after refined sugar is extracted from sugarcane juice. It is less sweet than sugar.

- *Honey* is formed from flower nectars gathered by bees. The type of flowers from which the nectar is gathered affects the honey's flavor.

- *Corn syrup* is extracted from the starchy part of corn. Many foodservice professionals refer to it as *glucose*.

40-2 Bakers and pastry chefs have a variety of sweeteners to consider when preparing a recipe.

Shortenings

Fats used in the bakeshop are often referred to as **shortening**. The term *shortening* comes from the fact that fat shortens strands of gluten in dough, making the finished product more tender and less elastic or chewy. Shortenings also add flavor, color, moisture, and richness to baked products. Some fats add flakiness to products and assist with leavening.

Shortenings come in both solid and liquid forms. The source for shortenings can be either animal or vegetable. Animal shortenings include butter, lard, and blends which use rendered beef fat. These fats are solid at room temperature.

Vegetable-based shortenings are made from soybean, corn, coconut, and other refined vegetable oils. They may be solid or liquid. The choice of which shortening to use for a given application is based on its melting point and nutritional content.

Vegetable shortenings are made from vegetable oils, which are normally liquid at room temperature. A process called *hydrogenation* incorporates hydrogen into the oil making them solid. This process is important because it creates solid fats from vegetable sources. Hydrogenated vegetable shortenings are useful in making pies, cakes, and cookies. They also have a longer shelf life because of the hydrogenation process.

Margarine is a hydrogenated vegetable shortening that is flavored to serve as a substitute for butter. Along with butter flavoring, some margarines have a small amount of dairy product incorporated to achieve a more authentic butter flavor. Though margarine looks and tastes like butter, it has a slightly higher melting point that may change the quality of the finished product when substituted for butter.

Leavening Agents

Leavening is the process in which gases are trapped in dough creating small bubbles that give baked goods a light and airy texture.

In order for this process to happen, some ingredient in the dough must cause a reaction, which creates the gas. That ingredient is called a *leavening agent*. There are two types of leavening agents—chemical leaveners and yeasts.

Chemical Leaveners   **Baking soda**, also known as sodium bicarbonate, is an alkaline powder. When it is mixed with moisture and acid, it releases carbon dioxide gas. This gas becomes trapped in the dough. When the dough is heated during the baking process, the carbon dioxide gas expands, causing the dough to rise. Many ingredients used in baked goods can provide the acid needed for this reaction such as milk, buttermilk, cocoa, molasses, and cream of tartar.

Baking powder is baking soda that is premixed with an acid chemical. Single-acting baking powder requires only the moisture in the dough to produce carbon dioxide gas. Double-acting baking powder requires both moisture and heat to produce carbon dioxide.

Yeast Animation Yeast is a living microscopic plant. In a warm moist environment, yeast feeds on any carbohydrates that are present and produces carbon dioxide and alcohol. The carbon dioxide and alcohol act to leaven baked goods. This process is known as **fermentation**. Fermentation happens most quickly at temperatures between 90°F and 110°F (32°C and 43°C). Eventually the higher temperatures during baking kill the yeast.

Yeast comes in two forms in the bakeshop—compressed and dry. Compressed yeast is a fresh product with a limited shelf life. It should be refrigerated to maintain freshness. It is creamy white with a clay-like texture and mixes easily into liquids used in dough. Dry yeast is labeled either *active dry yeast* or *instant dry yeast*. Active dry yeast requires no refrigeration. It comes in powdered or granular form. It must be dissolved in lukewarm liquid before being mixed into dough. Instant dry yeast does not need to be dissolved. It can be mixed directly into the dry ingredients in a recipe.

SCIENCE & TECHNOLOGY

Chocolate Manufacturing

Cocoa or "cacao" trees grow in tropical rainforests near the equator. The world's leading cocoa producers are Ivory Coast, Ghana, Indonesia, Cameroon, and Brazil. Cocoa trees sprout blossoms on their trunks. Only one blossom in 300 becomes a pod that contains cocoa beans.

Cocoa pods are harvested by hand—a labor-intensive process. Beans are removed from the pod by cutting the pod open with a machete.

The beans are piled up and covered with banana leaves and allowed to ferment. Pulp on the outside of the beans changes from white to brown and creates the distinctive chocolate flavor. The fermented beans are dried. This is best done in the sun, but some farms utilize fans and heaters to speed the process. The dried beans are sorted, graded by size, and shipped to the factory.

At the factory, the cocoa beans are cleaned, weighed, and blended to create a particular formula. Some chocolates may contain as many as 12 different varieties of beans.

Beans are then roasted to develop flavor and to make removal of their husks easier. The roasted beans are cooled, crushed, and the husks are removed. The resulting pieces are called *nibs*. The nibs contain 53 percent cocoa butter and 47 percent cocoa solids.

The nibs are ground into a paste, which is the chocolate liquor. Sugar and possibly milk or vanilla may be added at this stage.

Next, the gritty chocolate is finely ground, kneaded, and aerated with heat. This process, called *conching*, lasts as long as four days and gives the finished chocolate a silky texture while removing acid and water.

The chocolate is then removed from the conch machine and cooled. It is poured into molds and cooled further to create shiny blocks that can be easily unmolded.

Chocolate

No ingredient causes such a passionate response from diners as chocolate. The expertise needed to make chocolate creations involves such skill and knowledge that some pastry chefs, known as *chocolatiers*, specialize almost entirely in working with chocolate.

Most bakeshops have many different types of chocolate on hand, 40-3. Each type has specific qualities and uses. The quality of chocolate products is measured by their flavor, smell, appearance, texture, and melting point. Both the quality of the raw cocoa used and the manufacturing process contribute to the quality of chocolates. Within categories of chocolate there is a wide range of costs and qualities, so many pastry chefs have a strong preference for particular brands of chocolate.

Chocolate products are categorized and rated by the amount of chocolate liquor they contain, 40-4. Chocolate liquor is the name given to pure roasted and ground cocoa beans. Chocolate liquor (nonalcoholic) is composed of cocoa solids and fat called *cocoa butter*. Other ingredients commonly added to chocolate products are sugar, vanilla, milk solids, and other flavorings.

Chocolate should be stored covered or wrapped, in a cool dry place. When stored in conditions of fluctuating temperature or humidity, chocolate can develop a white film on its surface. This condition discolors the

Draz-Koetke/Goodheart-Willcox Publisher

40-3 Many different forms of chocolate are found in the bakeshop.

chocolate and can give the chocolate a gritty texture. To avoid this condition, never store chocolate in the refrigerator.

Chocolate Products Commonly Found in Pastry Kitchens

- *Cocoa powder* is a dry powdered form of chocolate liquor with most of its fat (cocoa butter) removed. It mixes easily with dry ingredients in recipes.

- *Cocoa butter* is the fat extracted from chocolate liquor. It is solid at room temperature and melts at 95°F (35°C). Cocoa butter is one of the keys to fine quality chocolates. Cheaper chocolate products substitute less expensive fats for cocoa butter.

- *Unsweetened chocolate*, also called *bitter chocolate* or *baking chocolate*, is pure chocolate liquor with no added sugar.

- *Semisweet chocolate* or bittersweet chocolate contains a minimum of 35 percent chocolate liquor with the remainder being mostly sugar.

- *Sweet chocolate* contains at least 15 percent chocolate liquor with the remainder being mostly sugar.

- *Dark chocolate* is chocolate made without milk. Only vanilla and sugar are added to the chocolate liquor.

- *Milk chocolate* is a lighter colored and milder flavored chocolate containing at least 15 percent dried milk and milk fat combined with at least 10 percent chocolate liquor.

- *White chocolate* is not technically chocolate because it contains no cocoa solids. It is composed of cocoa butter, sugar, milk products, and vanilla flavoring.

- *Chocolate coating* is used for dipping and coating. The high cocoa butter content causes it to harden at room temperature.

- *Compound chocolate* is a less expensive form of chocolate, sometimes called *summer chocolate*. The cocoa butter is replaced with other fat that has a higher melting point.

40-4 Other ingredients may be added to change the flavor or performance of a chocolate product.

Gelatin

There are two types of gelatin that pastry chefs use—sheet and powdered. Most pastry chefs prefer sheet gelatin as it is easier to use. Gelatin is used to thicken various sweet and savory preparations.

Using gelatin is a two step process. The first step is called **blooming**, which means that the gelatin is softened in cold water. To bloom sheet gelatin, cover the sheets in cold water until they become soft. Then, remove them from the water and squeeze them to remove excess water. To bloom powdered gelatin, mix with roughly four times its weight in cold water. Let this mixture sit until the gelatin loses its white, granular appearance and the water is absorbed. The bloomed gelatin then must be melted or dissolved in a small amount of liquid. It is then carefully added to a particular recipe. Extreme care must be taken if adding the melted gelatin to a cool or cold mixture. If the melted gelatin is not vigorously stirred into the other mixture, it may solidify prematurely and form inedible lumps.

Nuts and Seeds

Nuts are used in the kitchen, but nowhere are they used in greater quantities than the bakeshop. Nuts are one of the most expensive products in the kitchen. By weight, many nuts are more expensive than most meat items. Care should be taken when storing nuts because they are expensive. Store nuts in tightly sealed containers in a cool dark place. Nuts may be frozen for long-term storage.

Nuts come in many forms. They can be purchased whole in the shell, shelled whole nuts, halves, pieces, chopped, or ground. Their form reflects their cost. Generally, the larger the nut pieces, the more expensive they are. For instance, walnut pieces are less expensive than walnut halves, and chopped walnuts are even less expensive. Nuts can be purchased raw, roasted, blanched, or roasted and salted.

Common Nuts

Almonds

Almonds originally came from the Mediterranean region, however, California is now an important source. The nutmeat may be purchased with its brown skin or without (blanched). Almonds are commonly used in sliced or slivered form.

Cashews

Cashews are a crescent-shaped nut that originated in South America and is always sold shelled. They are relatively expensive and prized for their rich flavor.

Chestnuts

France and Italy are key producers of chestnuts. They have a slightly sweet flavor and starchy texture with little oil. Chestnuts are often used with savory dishes and treated like a vegetable.

Coconuts

Coconuts can be loosely defined as the large nuts of tropical palms, but is botanically classified as a drupe. Their flesh is often processed into chips or shredded coconut. The liquid found inside the nut is called *coconut water*. Coconut milk is made by extracting the oils and flavor from the flesh of the nut.

Hazelnuts (Filberts)

Hazelnuts are small round nuts with a rich flavor when toasted. Cultivated hazelnuts are called *filberts*. They are extremely popular in pastries. Like almonds, they may be used with or without the brown skin.

(Continued)

Common Nuts (Continued)

Macadamia Nuts

Native to Australia and now widely grown in Hawaii, the macadamia is one of the most expensive nuts. This round nut has a high oil content and a rich flavor.

Peanuts

Peanuts are not technically nuts, they are legumes related to peas and beans. They grow underground and are sometimes called *ground nuts*. They are an important ingredient in American, Asian, and African cuisines. They are relatively inexpensive and are the source for peanut oil and peanut butter.

Pecans

Pecans are native to the American South. Pecan halves are the largest form of the nut and are always used with their brown skin intact. They are widely used in desserts and candies.

Pine Nuts

Pine nuts are the small light-colored kernels of the pinion pine tree. Pine nuts are rich with a subtle flavor. They are popular in Mediterranean cuisines.

Pistachios

A major nut crop of California, the pistachio has a naturally light-colored oval shell. It is unique for the green color and sweet nutty flavor of its nutmeat. Pistachios are popular as a snack food and in ice creams.

Walnuts

Walnuts are one of the most popular nuts in commercial foodservice with a wide variety of uses. English walnuts, the most commonly used variety, have light-colored flesh with a mild flavor. Black walnuts, a variety native to America, are darker and have an intense flavor.

Common Seeds

Poppy

The small round seeds of the poppy flower are popular as a decoration for bread and as a filling for sweet pastries.

Sunflower

The meat of the seeds found at the center of the sunflower is used to add texture and richness to savory breads. These seeds are also a popular snack food and a source of refined oil.

Pumpkin

The shelled kernels from pumpkins and winter squash are used in breads and candies. In the kitchen, they are used as a garnish and in sauces. They are a popular ingredient in Mexican cuisine where they are called *pepitas*.

Sesame

The tiny white teardrop-shaped seeds are a common decoration for breads. A black variety of sesame seed is also available. A sesame seed paste called *tahini* is a popular Middle Eastern ingredient. Sesame seed oil is a common Asian ingredient.

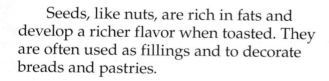

Seeds, like nuts, are rich in fats and develop a richer flavor when toasted. They are often used as fillings and to decorate breads and pastries.

Flavorings and Extracts

Concentrated flavorings derived from spices, nuts, fruits, or liquors are widely used in the bakeshop. Alcohol-based flavorings are called **extracts**. Other flavorings may be referred to as *concentrates* or *compounds* and may be in either liquid or paste form. When working with these ingredients, follow recipe quantities closely and measure carefully. Since their flavor is strong, an incorrect amount can ruin a recipe.

Vanilla   The most widely used flavor ingredient in the bakeshop is vanilla. Vanilla's subtle aromatic flavor is an excellent complement to fruits, nuts, chocolate, and dairy products. Vanilla is the bean of a tropical plant which is a member of the orchid family.

When recipes call for vanilla beans, the whole bean is typically simmered in a liquid to extract its flavor. Many times, vanilla beans are split lengthwise before being simmered. This releases the tiny black seeds that are often left in the finished dish to indicate the use of this expensive spice, 40-5.

Vanilla is more commonly used in extract form. Since vanilla and pure vanilla extracts are expensive, some kitchens may use artificial vanilla extract. Artificial vanilla is made from a synthetic compound called *vanillin*.

Convenience Products

Ideally, baked goods and pastries would be made in-house from scratch. The reality is most operations utilize some sort of convenience or labor-saving products to produce baked goods. Convenience products may be used to save labor, but they also offer product consistency. Lack of proper bakeshop equipment or space can also be a reason these products are used. Bakeshop convenience products commonly used include:

- dry mixes for cakes, breads, and pastries
- frozen or refrigerated "scoop-and-bake" doughs
- frozen portioned raw dough products
- frozen par-baked products
- fully baked frozen cakes, breads, and pastries
- ready-to-use icings
- ready-to-use fruit and cream fillings
- pre-made pastry decorations

Draz-Koetke/Goodheart-Willcox Publisher

40-5 Vanilla extract is a common ingredient in baked goods.

Chef Speak

Mix It Up!

Chefs use a variety of methods for mixing ingredients. They select the method based on the nature of the ingredients and the desired final product.

Beat—To combine a number of ingredients with brisk stirring.

Blend—To mix a number of ingredients together until evenly distributed throughout the final product.

Creaming—Mixing room temperature butter or shortening with sugar until smooth and light with a texture similar to cream.

Cut in—To combine solid shortening with dry ingredients until pieces of a particular size are formed.

Fold—To gently combine ingredients so that incorporated air is not lost or delicate ingredients damaged.

Kneading—Repeated folding and pressing of dough after it is mixed to develop gluten.

Whipping—Rapid mixing of ingredients with a whisk in order to add in air and produce a frothy product.

Bakeshop Equipment

There are many pieces of equipment that are unique to the bakeshop or pastry kitchen. Becoming familiar with them will make producing baked goods and pastries easier and more efficient.

Smallwares and Hand Tools

A variety of smallwares and hand tools should be available for use in the bakeshop. These include the balance scale, rolling pin, palette knife, turntable, pastry comb, pastry bag, and various types of pans.

Balance Scale　When measuring quantities of ingredients used in large-scale recipes, most bakers and pastry cooks use a balance

scale. The scale consists of two platforms, an ingredient scoop, and a counterweight to balance the scoop. Individual free weights equal to the quantity desired are placed on the platform opposite the scoop. A horizontal beam on the scale allows weight to be added in small increments. The scoop is filled with ingredients until its platform balances with the weighted one. The scoop can be removed from the scale to easily carry ingredients.

Rolling Pin   The rolling pin is used to roll pieces of dough into thin sheets. There are several styles of rolling pins used by bakers and pastry chefs. They may be a single piece that is either cylindrical or thin with tapered ends. Another popular style consists of a cylindrical pin connected to two handles by

ball bearings. They usually are made from hardwood. The choice of which type rolling pin to use is strictly a matter of personal preference.

Palette Knife   Palette knives have thin flexible blades. They are made in a variety of

lengths and widths. Palette knives are used to spread icings and coatings on pastries. They are also used like a spatula to pick up or turn items.

Turntable   Decorating round cakes and pastries is made easier when they are decorated on a turntable. The turntable allows the pastry chef to work on all sides of a cake or pastry without having to change position. Icings and coatings can be evenly spread over the surface of a cake by holding a palette knife stationary and spinning the cake on the turntable.

Pastry Comb   A pastry comb is a simple piece of metal or plastic with a zigzag edge that is used to put a decorative texture on

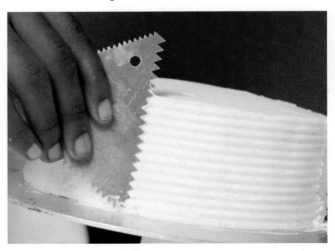

a pastry's coating or icing. The comb is dragged through an icing or coating to create a grooved pattern on the surface.

Pastry Bag A pastry bag is a cone-shaped bag made of cloth or plastic. It has a small opening at the point of the cone into which

a metal tip is placed. The shape of the tip determines the shape of the product piped from the bag. The bag is filled with product that is squeezed through the tip to create a decorative effect. The pastry bag is also useful for portioning semiliquid ingredients such as batters and foams. Pastry bags come in a range of sizes for holding different quantities of product. There is a wide range of sizes and shapes of tips available for decorative work with the pastry bag.

Baker's Peel A baker's peel is a large paddle used as a spatula. It has a long handle and is used for sliding baked goods in and out of deep ovens.

Pans A number of different-sized and -shaped pans are used for baking breads and pastries. The following are some of the most common pans used in the bakeshop:

- *Loaf pans* are rectangular pans used for baking bread.
- *Sheet pans* are also referred to as baking sheets. The standard size is 18 × 24 inches (45 × 60 cm). The sheet pan is shallow so bakers often use a 3-inch frame called a *sheet pan extender* to create higher sides on the pan. A half-size sheet pan, 18 × 12 inches (45 × 30 cm) is also common.
- *Pie pans* are round pans with tapered sides used to make pies. They may be made of lightweight disposable aluminum or reusable heavier gauge aluminum.
- *Cake pans* are round pans with straight sides used for baking cakes.
- *Springform pans* are deep cake pans with sides made of a flexible band of metal, which is closed and held to the round bottom with a hinged fastener. These pans are used for cakes and pastries that might be hard to remove from a standard cake pan.
- *Tart pans* are shallow round pans, most with removable bottoms. The traditionally shaped tart pan has fluted sides.
- *Muffin pans* are a set of small round pans pressed into a single sheet of metal. They are used for easier handling of individual muffins or cupcakes.

Large Equipment

Appliances in the professional bakeshop can be distinguished by their large capacity. These pieces of equipment can produce large quantities of product efficiently. They are also highly adjustable to give bakers and pastry chefs the ability to create a large variety of products with the same equipment.

Mixers Large batches of dough and batter are mixed easily with electric mixers. Mixers used in pastry kitchens and bakeries range in size from tabletop models that hold 5 quarts (5 L) to floor models that can hold as much as 140 quarts (140 L).

There are three basic attachments for an electric mixer, each with its own special functions.

- *Dough hook* is used for mixing and kneading thick dough mixtures.
- *Paddle* is used for beating thick batters and light dough mixtures.
- *Whip* is used for mixing and whipping air into liquids and mixtures with light consistency.

Deck Ovens   To meet the need for high-volume baking capacity, bakeshops

SANITATION & SAFETY
Mixer Safety

Electric mixers are some of the most effective pieces of equipment in the bakeshop. They are also potentially some of the most dangerous. Care should always be exercised when using this equipment to avoid accidents and serious injuries.

- Do not attempt to operate a mixer until you have been trained to do so.
- Locate the emergency shut off for the mixer before using.
- Some mixers are equipped with bowl guards. Do not attempt to operate these machines without the guards in place.
- Do not wear dangling jewelry or loose clothing when using a mixer.
- Be sure the attachments and bowl are the correct size and are properly attached.
- Be sure the bowl is raised before starting the machine.
- Shut off the power supply before disassembling or cleaning the mixer.

utilize different oven configurations than commercial kitchens. One of the most popular oven types in the bakeshop is the deck oven. A deck oven has a deep wide cavity with a height of about 10 inches. Each oven is capable of holding several sheet pans. Most deck ovens consist of three or more stacked oven compartments. Most models allow the baker to control heat from the bottom, top, and sides for different baking effects. Steam injection on deck ovens allows bakers to create breads with a crisp crust.

Revolving Ovens   Revolving or rotary ovens have a series of trays set up in a Ferris wheel-like configuration. As items are baking, the trays holding the food product

revolve inside the oven. This revolving allows a large number of items to bake evenly.

Rack Ovens Rack ovens, sometimes called *roll-in ovens*, are large enough to hold an entire

sheet pan rack. The rack, which is on wheels, is loaded with items to be baked and then rolled into the oven and baked on the rack.

Proofers Baked goods made with yeast require time in a warm moist environment to allow the yeast to leaven the product.

A proofer is a cabinet that holds dough products at a warm temperature so they will rise. Most proofers allow the baker to control both the heat and humidity in order to create proper leavening conditions.

Dough Sheeter A dough sheeter is a mechanized rolling pin. Dough is placed on a belt and fed through a set of rollers. The thickness of the rollers can be adjusted. With

a sheeter, large amounts of dough can easily and quickly be rolled into thin sheets.

Dough Divider   A dough divider is a press that evenly divides a preweighed amount of dough into many smaller portions. It makes the job of evenly portioning dough for individual rolls or buns more efficient.

Ice-Cream Machines   Ice-cream machines are common in many pastry shops because many pastry chefs make their own ice cream. An ice-cream machine is essentially a refrigerated drum with a blade or paddle that spins inside it. Liquid ice-cream mixture is poured in and slowly frozen while the paddles stir the mixture.

Summary Points

- The bakeshop, or pastry kitchen, is a separate department in most large foodservice operations. The pastry chef supervises the work in this department.

- Ingredients in baked goods perform different functions. Gluten in flour provides structure. Shortenings give baked goods a soft texture and richness. Leavening agents make baked goods light and airy.

- The bakeshop utilizes an array of tools and equipment not found in the kitchen. Being familiar with these items makes work in the bakeshop easier and more efficient.

In Review
Assess

1. Indicate if a baker or a pastry cook would be more likely to prepare each of the following items in a large bakeshop:
   A. Croissants
   B. Dinner rolls
   C. Fresh fruit tart
   D. Chocolate cake
   E. Rye bread

2. True or false. When assembling ingredients for a baked product, it is normal to estimate amounts rather than measure them.

3. Flours with higher _____ content will contain more gluten.

4. When would you use cane sugar over beet sugar?

5. Other than sugar, what sweeteners are used in the bakeshop?

6. True or false. Most animal shortenings are liquid at room temperature.

7. Name two different types of leavening agents.

8. Contrast baking soda and baking powder.

9. Chocolate liquor is composed of cocoa solids and _____ _____.

10. List five chocolate products commonly found in professional pastry kitchens.

11. What is blooming?

12. Generally, larger pieces of nuts are _____ expensive than smaller pieces.

13. True or false. Vanilla is the bean of a tropical plant.

14. Name two reasons why a bakeshop might use convenience products.

15. What is the purpose of the metal tip used with a pastry bag?

16. The cabinet that bakers use to hold dough products at a warm temperature so they will rise is called a _____.
   A. rack oven
   B. proofer
   C. sheeter
   D. peel

Core Skills

17. **Math.** Visit the supermarket or use online resources to price pure vanilla extract and imitation vanilla extract. Calculate the percent price difference.

18. **Writing.** Place a teaspoon each of baking powder and baking soda in separate dishes. Add one-fourth cup water to each dish. Record your observations. Now add a few drops of lemon juice or vinegar. Record your observations. How can understanding the effects of an acid on chemical leaveners lead to better baked products? Write a summary about the reactions you observed.

19. **Reading.** Use reliable Internet and print resources to research the history of sugarcane cultivation. Write a report on the effects of sugarcane cultivation on trade, politics, and social issues.

20. **CTE Career Readiness Practice.** Presume the owner of the sandwich shop you work for wants to sell chocolate chip cookies as a dessert option. Your owner needs to decide whether it is cost effective to purchase ready-made "scoop-and-bake" cookie dough or to make the dough at the shop. As the pastry cook, the owner asks for your help. Use a vendor supply catalog to compare the costs of the scoop-and-bake dough to

the cost of ingredients to make the owner's favorite chocolate chip cookie recipe. How long will it take to make each? Predict the economic impact each might have on the business. Write a summary of your findings and identify the most cost-effective option.

Critical Thinking

21. **Analyze criteria.** Many kitchens buy some or all of their baked goods rather than produce them in house. Analyze what factors should be taken into consideration when making this decision. What evidence supports this decision? Discuss your thoughts in class.

22. **Recognize suitability.** Would using only all-purpose flour in a bakery or pastry shop be possible? Explain your answer.

23. **Identify consequences.** What chocolate products would you choose for baking? What qualities would each choice give to finished baked goods.

24. **Differentiate.** Suppose your bakery is going to begin making banana nut bread. What form of walnuts would you purchase for this recipe? Explain your answer.

Technology

Silicone bakeware is a popular option in commercial bakeshops. Use Internet or print resources to research these products and their uses in the bakeshop. Give an illustrated oral presentation on what silicone is, types of bakeware are available in silicone, and the advantages and disadvantages of using silicone bakeware.

Teamwork

In teams, use the text and Internet information to create an identification game for bakeshop equipment. Equipment identification should include uses for the equipment. Take turns playing each team's game until all class members know and understand the use of each piece of equipment.

Chef's E-portfolio
Buy or Make Decision

Employers value employees with good decision-making skills. Upload your summary from the CTE Career Readiness Practice activity to your e-portfolio. Ask your instructor where to save your file. This could be on the school's network or a flash drive of your own. Name your portfolio document *FirstnameLastname_Portfolio Ch#.docx* (i.e., JohnSmith_PortfolioCh40.docx).

While studying, look for the activity icon → **to:**

- Build vocabulary with e-flash cards and matching activities.
- Expand learning with video clips, photo identification activities, animations, and interactive activities.
- Review and assess what you learn by completing end-of-chapter questions.

G-WLEARNING.com

Marie C. Fields/Shutterstock.com

Copyright Goodheart-Willcox Co., Inc.

Quick Breads and Batters

Reading Prep

In preparation for reading the chapter, review a variety of bakery or restaurant menus. Read the descriptions of the dishes to identify the preparation techniques used. Compare your findings to the chapter as you read.

Culinary Terminology

Build Vocab

quick bread, p. 657
dough, p. 657
batter, p. 657
biscuit method, p. 658
fritter, p. 661
crêpe, p. 661
pâte à choux, p. 662

Academic Terminology

Build Vocab

expedite, p. 657

Objectives

After studying this chapter, you will be able to

- explain how ingredients and preparation procedures affect the quality of quick breads and batters.

- execute different techniques for making common quick breads.

- compare other batter-based products and their preparation.

Most baked products are leavened using either yeast or chemical leaveners. Yeast requires time to ferment. Chemical leaveners, such as baking powder or baking soda, expedite, or speed up the leavening process so preparation time for these products is shorter.

Quick Bread and Batter Basics

Baked products that are leavened chemically are called quick breads. Quick breads may begin in the form of either a dough or batter. A dough is a mixture of flour, liquid, and other ingredients that is stiff enough to form into shapes for baking. Quick breads that begin as dough include biscuits and scones. A batter is also a mixture of flour and liquid, but the proportion of liquid is greater which makes it pourable. Muffins, pancakes, waffles, crêpes, and cream puffs all begin as batters. Batters for coating or binding fried desserts are another common form of quick bread. However, not all batters are quick breads.

One characteristic all quick breads share is soft texture. Quality quick breads are light and tender. Ingredients used in quick bread recipes contribute to this delicate texture. Quick bread dough has high moisture content. These products are often made with low gluten flours such as cake and pastry flours. Many quick breads contain a good amount of shortening, which also helps create a tender product.

The manner in which the dough is prepared is also important in trying to achieve a soft tender texture. Most quick breads are mixed only to the point necessary to properly combine ingredients. Mixing develops gluten in the dough's flour. Overmixing results in too much gluten making the finished product tough or chewy. Products that are overmixed are also likely to form holes or tunnels inside and be poorly shaped.

Types of Quick Breads

There are many different types of quick breads with various methods of preparation. Some common quick breads include biscuits, muffins, fritters, and scones.

Biscuits

Biscuits are a savory quick bread and can be served at any meal. Biscuits are a perfect example of how the right choice of ingredients and proper preparation of the dough can produce a light and flaky quick bread.

Many bakers demand that special biscuit flours be used to prepare their biscuit recipes. These flours are prepared from soft wheat, which has little gluten and high starch content. This helps produce a light flaky biscuit. Some biscuit recipes call for self-rising flour. Self-rising flour is a ready-made mixture of flour and baking powder.

The method for mixing biscuit dough is fairly consistent regardless of the ingredients used in the recipe. The **biscuit method** combines dry ingredients first, and then solid shortening is "cut in," or mixed with the dry ingredients until it breaks into small pieces. Finally, the liquid ingredients are added and mixed just long enough to combine with the other ingredients. During this last step, the gluten develops and the leavening agent reacts.

Once biscuit dough is made, there are two different ways of portioning biscuits. The dough may be rolled out to an even thickness and then cut into individual biscuits using a round pastry cutter. Alternately, the dough may be portioned with a scoop into loosely formed biscuits known as *drop biscuits*. Drop biscuit recipes contain a higher proportion of liquid than rolled biscuit recipes.

Nutrition Connection

Alternative Flours

Supermarkets and ethnic food stores sell unique flours that add distinctive flavors to many culinary dishes. Chefs produce sauces and baked goods with almond, peanut, rice, potato, spelt, sorghum, corn, oat, and rye flours. Some alternative flours allow chefs to create substitute dishes for people who are allergic to traditional wheat flours. Chefs focused on a more ethnic fare use flours ground from ingredients found around the world. These include cassava, chickpea, chapatti, kamut, and teff flours. Alternative flours have unique cooking qualities to consider and offer specific nutrient profiles.

Culture & Cuisine

Biscuits with a British Accent

The scone is a close cousin to the American biscuit. Like biscuits, they are a quick bread leavened with baking powder or baking soda. Scones are believed to have originated in Scotland. Their original form was a round griddlecake divided into four or six wedges. Today, scones are commonly cut into their familiar triangle shape before baking.

Scones are popular throughout Great Britain as a pastry served with afternoon tea. They are often served with jams, fruit preserves, or thickened cream. Many different ingredients can be incorporated into scone dough to create a variety of flavors. Spices, dried fruits, and nuts are popular flavorings for scones.

Recipe No.	Name			Category
41.1	Biscuits			Quick breads
Yield	**Portion Size**			**No. Portions**
2½ lb. (1.14 kg)	1½ oz. (45 g)			2 dz.
US Quantity	**Metric Quantity**	**Ingredient**		**TCS**
1¼ lb.	560 g	all-purpose or pastry flour		
½ oz.	15 g	salt		
1 oz.	30 g	sugar		
1 oz.	30 g	baking powder		
7 oz.	200 g	solid shortening		
12 oz.	360 g	milk		•
Method				**CCP**
1.	Sift the dry ingredients together.			
2.	Using a mixer with a paddle attachment or by hand, cut the shortening into the dry ingredients until it resembles a coarse meal.			
3.	Add the milk and mix briefly to create dough.			
4.	On a floured surface, roll the dough into an even sheet 1 in. (2.5 cm) thick.			
5.	Cut with a round pastry cutter about 2 in. diameter.			
6.	Leftover dough can be rolled out to cut more biscuits. Take care not to overwork the dough or the biscuits will be tough.			
7.	Place the biscuits on a sheet pan lined with parchment.			
8.	Bake 425°F (220°C) for 15–20 minutes.			
9.	When removed from the oven, biscuits may be brushed with melted butter for a richer moister product.			

Variations:

Buttermilk biscuits—replace the milk in the above recipe with buttermilk.

Cheese biscuits—add 6 oz. grated cheese (Cheddar, Parmesan, etc.) to the above recipe.

Drop biscuits—rather than rolling and cutting, form the biscuits with a #20 scoop and drop directly on the baking sheet.

Portion (g)	Calories	Fat (g)	Protein (g)	Carbohydrate (g)	Cholesterol (mg)	Sodium (mg)	Fiber (g)
49	175	8.96	2.90	19.85	1.42	353.17	0.64

Muffins

Muffins are individual pastries similar to cupcakes. They are often baked in a muffin pan, which has a series of individual baking cups for producing multiple muffins in a single batch. Muffin batters can also be baked in a loaf pan. Muffins often include additional ingredients, such as fruits and nuts.

In preparing the batter for muffins, there is one distinct difference from the preparation of biscuits—the fat used to prepare muffins is usually liquid. Either liquid shortening is used or solid shortenings, such as butter, are melted before being incorporated.

As with biscuits, once the liquid is added to the dry ingredients, the mixing time should be kept to a minimum. This ensures a light and tender finished product.

TECHNIQUE
Preparing Biscuits

1. Weigh all ingredients carefully.
2. Sift dry ingredients together.
3. Cut the shortening into the dry ingredients until it resembles a coarse meal using either the paddle attachment on an electric mixer or a pastry blender.
4. Add the liquid ingredients and mix only long enough to incorporate them evenly. Overmixing creates tough, chewy biscuits.
5. Portion the dough into individual biscuits using a scoop or by rolling the dough into an even sheet and cutting with a pastry cutter.

6. Place biscuits on a greased or parchment-lined sheet pan.
7. Bake according to recipe instructions. When done baking, biscuits should be nearly double in height and have a pleasing golden-brown finish.

TECHNIQUE
Preparing Muffins

1. Weigh all ingredients carefully.
2. Sift dry ingredients together.
3. Combine liquid ingredients including the shortening.
4. Add liquid ingredients to dry ingredients and mix until all ingredients are combined. Do not overmix.
5. If fruits or nuts are to be added, fold them in with a spatula.

6. Portion the batter into greased pans or paper liners.

7. Bake according to recipe instructions. Finished muffins have an appealing golden-brown color with rounded tops and are free of tunnels and peaks.

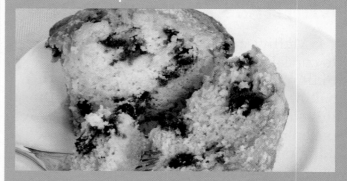

Cornbread Cornbread is essentially a muffin batter that uses cornmeal as a main ingredient. Since cornmeal contains no gluten, it must be combined with wheat flour to create a dough or batter. A fifty-fifty mixture of cornmeal and wheat flour is typical for cornbreads. As with muffin batter, cornbread can be baked in muffin tins, loaf pans, or shallow baking dishes.

Fritters

Fritters are small individual fried pastries. In classical cuisine, fritters may be called *beignets* (BEHN yeahs). Some fritters are formed from a dough that may be a quick bread or yeast raised. Other fritters are made from a batter that acts as a binder to hold chopped or small pieces of ingredients into a ball or other shape. Fritter batters can also be used as a coating for larger pieces of fruit. A wide variety of fruits can be used to make fritters. After frying, fritters are often dusted with powdered sugar, 41-1. They are always served piping hot.

Other Products Made from Batters

A wide variety of products other than quick breads begin as batters. Crêpes and pâte à choux are two very different products that both begin as batters.

Crêpes

A crêpe (KRAYP) is a very thin pancake. It can be used as a savory item, dessert item, or at breakfast. Crêpes are often filled with fruit or pastry cream. Crêpes made without sugar can be filled with many different savory ingredients for a lunch or dinner item. Popular savory crêpe fillings include seafood and chicken in cream sauce.

Crêpes require no leavening agent because they are paper-thin. The batter for crêpes is simple to make. Cooking crêpes requires a nonstick pan and a little bit of practice.

Draz-Koetke/Goodheart-Willcox Publisher

41-1 Fritter batter either acts to (A) bind small ingredients together or (B) to coat larger ingredients. (C) Fritters are then deep-fried, dusted with powdered sugar, and served hot.

TECHNIQUE
Preparing Crêpes

1. **Measure ingredients for the batter.**
2. **Combine dry ingredients.**
3. **Beat in eggs.**
4. **Add liquid gradually to make a thin batter. Strain to remove any lumps.**
5. **Heat a nonstick pan and coat it with a thin film of clarified butter.**
6. **Pour a small amount of batter into the pan and tip the pan to coat the entire surface of the pan.**

7. **Pour off any excess batter.**
8. **Cook crêpe over moderate heat until nicely browned.**
9. **Turn the crêpe and brown the other side.**

10. **Remove the crêpe from the pan and allow it to fully cool before stacking.**

Pâte à Choux

Pâte à choux (POHT ah shoo) is the paste or thick batter used to make cream puffs and éclairs. In French, its name means "cabbage paste" because the cream puffs it is used to create resemble small cabbages. It is a staple of the bakeshop because, in addition to cream puffs, éclairs, and cakes, it can be used as a base for doughnuts and popovers or as a binder in savory dishes.

Pâte à choux is one of the few pastry preparations that is made on the stovetop. The paste or batter needs to be thin enough to be piped from a pastry bag. It is batter that is leavened by the steam created when it bakes. When it bakes, the batter rises slightly, its center becomes hollow, and the outside becomes crisp. Once the baked pastries cool, they can be filled with a number of different options including whipped cream, pastry cream, and fruit or nut purées.

Chef Speak

Classic Pâte à Choux Preparations

Cream Puffs—Individual pâte à choux balls filled with whipped cream and dusted with powdered sugar.

Croquembouche (KROHK em boosh)—Cream puffs are fused together with cooked sugar to form a large cone or pyramid. This is a traditional French wedding cake.

Éclairs—Individual pâte à choux pastries piped in a line, baked, and filled with pastry cream and glazed with chocolate.

Paris-Brest (pahr EE brest)—Pâte à choux piped into a large ring that is sprinkled with almonds before baking. It is then split and filled with almond-flavored pastry cream.

Profiteroles (proh FEE teh rohls)—Individual pâte à choux balls filled with pastry cream or ice cream and glazed with chocolate. They can also be used as canapés when filled with savory fillings.

Saint-Honoré (sahnt OHN eray)—A circular base of pâte à choux is baked. Carmel-dipped cream puffs are placed to create a border on the outer edge. The center is filled with pastry cream.

TECHNIQUE
Preparing Pâte à Choux

1. Measure all ingredients and sift flour to remove lumps.
2. Combine liquid, fat, sugar, and salt in a saucepot and bring them to a boil.

3. Add flour all at once and stir immediately.

4. Cook over moderate heat while stirring until the batter forms a ball and pulls away from the sides of the pot.

5. Transfer the thick batter to the bowl of a mixer.

6. Use the paddle attachment. With the mixer at medium speed, add one egg. When the egg is fully incorporated, add another. Continue to add the eggs in this manner until all the eggs are incorporated into the batter.

7. Allow the batter to cool, place into a pastry bag, and pipe into desired shape.

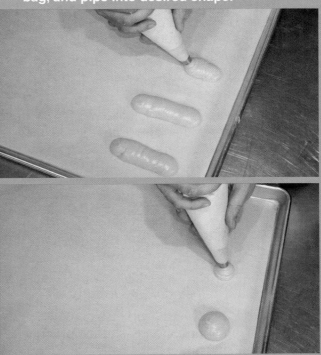

8. Bake until pastry is evenly brown with a rigid, hollow structure.

Summary Points

- Quick breads use chemical leaveners which act more quickly than the yeast used to leaven other baked products.

- Quick breads may begin as either a dough or batter.

- The biscuit method should be used when combining ingredients for biscuits. Care must be taken not to overwork the dough.

- Muffins and cornbread are quick breads that use a liquid shortening or melted solid shortening.

- Fritters are small fried pastries that are made with a batter or dough. Other ingredients are often added to the batter.

- Crêpes and pâte à choux are products that begin as batters but are not quick breads.

- Crêpes are very thin pancakes that can be used for dessert, breakfast, and savory dishes.

- Pâte à choux is the thick batter used to make cream puffs and éclairs. Pâte à choux is a unique batter because it is cooked on the stovetop.

In Review

Assess

1. What is the difference between dough and batter?
2. List the ingredients in quick breads that contribute to their delicate texture.
3. True or false. Overmixing quick bread dough results in a tough, poorly shaped product that contains air tunnels.
4. Self-rising flour is a ready-made mixture of flour and _____ _____.
5. List the seven steps in the biscuit method.
6. True or false. Rolled biscuits contain a higher proportion of liquid than drop biscuits.
7. What type of fat or shortening is used in muffins?
8. Describe a perfectly baked muffin.
9. Cornmeal has no _____ so it must be combined with flour to make cornbread.

10. In classical cuisine, _____ are called beignets.
11. True or false. Pâte à choux preparation begins on the stovetop.
12. As pâte à choux bakes, the center becomes _____ and the outside becomes _____.

Core Skills

13. **Math.** You are using a cornbread recipe that calls for a total of three cups of starch ingredients. How much cornmeal will you need? How much wheat flour will you need?

14. **Speaking and Listening.** In four teams, prepare the *Biscuits* recipe in this chapter. Team 1 will prepare the basic recipe, Team 2 will prepare the cheese variation, Team 3 will prepare the buttermilk variation, and Team 4 will prepare the drop biscuits. Prepare the biscuits according to the text/recipe directions. Plate your completed biscuits for class evaluation. Each team should discuss their biscuits and any challenges they had with the recipe. Teams will evaluate one another's biscuits for appearance, flavor, texture, and tenderness. Discuss the similarities and differences.

15. **Writing.** Use Internet or print resources to research the history of *beignets*. What is the origin of beignets? What ingredients were used? How do ingredients differ today? How and when are beignets used today? How do the preparation techniques impact the quality of beignets? Write an illustrated report of your findings to share with the class.

16. **Math.** Suppose you need 60 portions of *Biscuits* (recipe in this chapter, Cheddar cheese variation) and your recipe yield is 24 portions. You will need to change the yield of your recipe. After using the conversion method, how much will you need of each ingredient?

17. **Speaking and Listening.** In teams, prepare a batch of muffins. Either research your own recipe or use a recipe provided by your

instructor. Depending on the recipe yield, complete a recipe conversion to yield one or two muffins per class member. Then prepare the muffins using text/recipe instructions and bake accordingly. Plate your team's muffins when completed. Discuss the challenges or successes you experienced with the recipe. Teams should then evaluate one another's muffins for appearance, flavor, texture, and tenderness. Discuss the evaluations.

18. **Writing.** Suppose you are blogging about what you learn in culinary class. Today's class was all about using pâte à choux for making cream puffs. Many of the people who read your blog are inexperienced with baking. In writing today's blog, explain how to make delicious cream puffs with pâte à choux. Consider adding an image to your blog.

19. **CTE Career Readiness Practice.** The ability to speak clearly or interpret information for others is an important workplace skill. To practice your skills, demonstrate how to prepare crêpes for the class. Presume no one in the class knows how to prepare crêpes. Locate a recipe. If the recipe makes a large amount, change the yield of the recipe to produce a portion for each member of the class. Follow the text/recipe directions for your demonstration. Prepare your explanation of each step for the demonstration. Complete the demonstration and have the class evaluate your crêpes.

Critical Thinking

20. **Draw conclusions.** What scenarios or situations might make biscuits a better option than leavened breads? Draw conclusions about the possibilities.

21. **Analyze cause and effect.** Make a list of different flavorings and additional ingredients you could add to a plain muffin batter to create a variety of interesting muffins. Then analyze the impact these ingredients might have on the batter.

22. **Predict consequences.** While mixing your muffin batter in the mixer, a coworker requested your help. You remembered to turn off the mixer ten minutes later. Would you use this batter? Predict what kind of product you think it would produce.

Technology

Use reliable Internet resources to identify how to convert baking time and temperature for a conventional oven to baking time and temperature for a convection oven. In two teams, prepare two batches of a plain muffin recipe as provided by your instructor (or one your team locates). Bake one batch in the conventional oven and the other batch in the convection oven. Record the beginning and ending baking times for each—conventional and convection. When the muffins have finished baking, compare the two batches for baking time. Then evaluate the muffins. How were they similar or different in appearance, flavor, moistness, texture, and tenderness? Based on your team's experience, which oven would you purchase if you were opening a new bakery? Why?

Teamwork

Divide into four teams. Each team will prepare the same muffin recipe. Team 1 will mix the ingredients just long enough to combine them all. Team 2 will mix an additional one minute. Team 3 will mix the ingredients an additional 2 minutes. Team 4 will mix the ingredients an additional 3 minutes after the ingredients are combined. Once the muffins have been baked and cooled, the teams will evaluate them for appearance, texture, and flavor. Record observations.

Chef's E-portfolio
Pâte à Choux Blog

Upload your blog from activity #18 to your e-portfolio. Ask your instructor where to save your file. This could be on the school's network or a flash drive of your own. Name your portfolio document *FirstnameLastname_Portfolio Ch#.docx* (i.e., JohnSmith_PortfolioCh41.docx).

While studying, look for the activity icon to:
- Build vocabulary with e-flash cards and matching activities.
- Expand learning with video clips, photo identification activities, animations, and interactive activities.
- Review and assess what you learn by completing end-of-chapter questions.

Cookies

42

Reading Prep

In preparation for reading the chapter, think about what qualities make a cookie successful for you. Visit a bakery and analyze its products to identify the qualities that contribute to a successful cookie. How would you measure a cookie's quality? As you read, consider how the information in this chapter supports or contradicts your answers to this question.

Culinary Terminology Build Vocab

Academic Terminology Build Vocab

Objectives

After studying this chapter, you will be able to

- summarize factors that contribute to cookie quality.
- explain the two most common methods for mixing cookie dough.
- recall common methods for forming cookies.

The popularity of cookies is no mystery. American consumers love these sweet little baked goods that come in many different shapes, sizes, and flavors. Shapes and sizes range from small cookies served with tea to oversized cookies that are a dessert all by themselves. They also come in a variety of flavors and textures. Some are sweet and crisp while others may be buttery with a soft chewy texture. There are so many varieties that there is no one definitive flavor or texture. However, knowing how various ingredients and methods influence the characteristics of a cookie is important when trying to achieve a particular finished product. It is also key to troubleshooting problems with finished cookies.

Cookies are popular with foodservice operation because they are easy to prepare, bake quickly, and store well.

What Makes a Cookie Good?

All good cookies share certain attributes, or characteristics. When analyzing the quality of a cookie, a chef evaluates its flavor, texture, and appearance.

Flavor

The flavor of cookies is primarily determined by the quality of the ingredients that make up the dough. Choosing high-quality ingredients that are as fresh as possible is the start to good quality finished products. Proper proportion of ingredients also contributes to the flavor of the product. Therefore, follow recipes carefully and measure ingredients exactly, 42-1.

tacar/Shutterstock.com

42-1 Quality ingredients in the proper amounts are necessary to produce a cookie with superior flavor.

Texture

The most important factor in achieving a particular texture in cookies is the ingredients. Choosing high-gluten flour can make cookies tough. Generally, crisper cookies have a larger proportion of sugar. Softer cookies contain more fat and moisture. Chewy cookies get their texture from a higher amount of sugar combined with moisture, as well as more eggs.

Mixing and baking procedures also affect a cookie's texture. Overmixing the dough will develop too much gluten creating a tough finished product. Baking too long or at a temperature that is too high usually results in a dry, hard cookie.

Appearance

Visual appeal is always important for a food product. Shaping raw dough so the end product has a pleasing, attractive appearance is an important step for creating a quality cookie. In addition, ensuring that the shape is uniform for all the cookies is key. Portioning the dough must be consistent so the cookies are the same size.

Baking at the proper temperature and for the proper length of time is essential for proper color. This also ensures that the dough spreads properly, 42-2. Remove cookies from the oven when the bottoms and edges turn golden brown. Allow them to firm up slightly before removing them from the pan to avoid tearing or breaking the cookies.

Decorating techniques such as applying icing, nuts, sanding sugar, or confections contribute greatly to the appearance of the finished cookies. Since cookies are often displayed in batches, decorating cookies uniformly is important to creating an attractive product.

Mixing Methods

How easy cookies are to make becomes clear when you learn the methods for mixing cookie dough. There are two common methods for making cookie dough—the one-stage method and creaming method. Both methods are done with an electric mixer using the paddle attachment.

One-Stage Method

The one-stage method is the simplest way to make cookie dough. Place all the ingredients into the bowl and mix. When using an electric mixer, the paddle is the best attachment for this task. Allow two to three minutes at moderate speed to fully blend all the ingredients. Avoid overmixing which can result in tough dough.

Problem-Solving Cookie Faults									
	Undermixed	Overmixed	Too much sugar	Lack of sugar	Too much fat	Lack of fat	Too much liquid	Lack of liquid	Baking temperature too high	Baking temperature too low
Spreads too much	●		●							●
Spreads too little		●		●					●	
Too soft	●				●		●			
Tough/hard		●	●	●		●		●		
Crumbles	●		●		●					
Pale color				●						●
Dark color					●				●	

42-2 Many factors influence the quality of a cookie.

Creaming Method

The first step in the **creaming method** is to mix the butter or shortening with the sugar and spices until smooth. Next, eggs and liquids are added and mixed until incorporated. Finally, the flour and leavening agent are added and blended. Since the flour is added last, gluten is less likely to overdevelop using this method.

Forming Methods

Cookies can be classified by the method used to form the cookie. Each technique creates a uniquely shaped cookie.

Drop Cookies

Drop cookies are the easiest and most common method of forming cookies. **Drop cookies** are made by placing (or dropping) small amounts of dough onto a sheet pan. A portion scoop is a good tool for creating equal-sized cookies, 42-3. During baking,

the small mounds of dough spread into flat cookies. When portioning drop cookies, allow enough space between the mounds of dough to allow the cookies to spread during baking. Chocolate chip and oatmeal cookies are often made using the drop method.

Draz-Koetke/Goodheart-Willcox Publisher

42-3 Customers expect cookies to be a consistent size.

Rolled Cookies

To make **rolled cookies**, cookie dough is spread out into a thin sheet and a cutter is used to cut cookies into the desired shape. The cut cookies are transferred to a sheet pan and baked. The sugar cookie is a popular rolled cookie.

Rolled cookies are especially popular for holidays and special occasions. Cookies can be shaped as people, animals, geometric shapes, holiday shapes, and more. A wide variety of cookie cutter shapes are available, 42-4. After cutting, these cookies are often decorated with sanding sugar and confections before baking. For added effect, after

Draz-Koetke/Goodheart-Willcox Publisher

42-4 Rolled cookies are easily customized for special events or holidays.

Recipe No.	Name		Category
42.4	Sugar Cookies		Cookies
Yield	**Portion Size**		**No. Portions**
2½ lb. (1.14 kg)	1½ oz. (45 g)		2 dz.
US Quantity	**Metric Quantity**	**Ingredient**	**TCS**
8 oz.	225 g	butter or shortening	•
10 oz.	280 g	sugar	
1 tsp.	5 mL	salt	
2 oz.	60 g	eggs (about 1 large)	•
2 oz.	60 g	milk	•
1 tsp.	5 mL	vanilla extract	
1¼ lb.	560 g	all-purpose or pastry flour	
½ oz.	15 g	baking powder	
Method			**CCP**
1. Cream the shortening, sugar, and salt until smooth.			
2. Incorporate the egg, milk, and vanilla.			
3. Sift the flour and baking powder and add to the other ingredients.			
4. Roll out on a floured surface to about ¼ inch (0.5 cm), cut, and decorate as desired.			
5. Place on a sheet pan lined with parchment.			
6. Bake 375°F (190°C) for approximately 15 minutes.			
Variation:			
Chocolate sugar cookies—replace 2 oz. flour with cocoa powder			

Portion (g)	Calories	Fat (g)	Protein (g)	Carbohydrate (g)	Cholesterol (mg)	Sodium (mg)	Fiber (g)
50	204	7.94	2.78	29.98	29.30	61.13	0.64

baking they may be decorated with fondant or other icings. Creativity with rolled cookies is only limited by the imagination of the baker.

Spritz (Pressed) Cookies

Spritz cookies are made from a soft cookie dough that is forced through a pastry bag to form shapes such as rosettes, shells, and scrolls, 42-5. Some bakeshops use a special cookie press to make these cookies. The dough is pressed through a specially shaped die to create specific shapes.

Sheet Cookies

Sheet cookies are made by evenly spreading dough or batter onto a sheet pan. The entire sheet pan is baked and later the sheet is cut into individual cookies. Brownies are popular sheet cookies, 42-6. This method of forming cookies has the advantage of saving labor. It is also possible to create multilayered cookies using this method.

42-6 Care must be taken to cut sheet cookies in consistent sizes.

42-5 Various shaped tips can be used with pastry bags to create cookies with interesting shapes.

Chef Speak

Cookie Glossary

Biscotto—Italian bar cookie that is baked a second time after being cut to give it a hard texture.

Fortune Cookie—Chinese-American, wafer-type cookie that is folded and filled with a strip of paper containing a proverb or "fortune."

Florentine—Lacy crisp wafer based on caramelized sugar often with nuts or dried fruit.

Macaroon—Round, soft-textured cookies typically made of almond paste and egg whites.

Madeleine—Small light-textured cookie that is baked in a scallop shell mold.

Pfeffernüesse (Peppernut)—Small spice-flavored, ball-shaped German cookie that is finished with a dusting of powdered sugar.

Shortbread—Scottish cookie, particularly rich in shortening or butter, giving it a delicate texture.

Snickerdoodle—Rich cookie flavored with cinnamon.

Toll House—Another name for a chocolate chip cookie with nuts. It is named for the Toll House Inn in Whitman, Massachusetts where the recipe originated.

Tuile—Very thin crisp wafer cookie.

Icebox Cookies

Icebox cookies are made by forming cookie dough into a log, square, triangle, or other shape while the dough is still soft. The shaped dough is wrapped in plastic wrap or parchment paper and refrigerated. When fully chilled, the dough is firm and can be sliced into individual cookies. Each slice of dough is laid out on a sheet pan and baked to create individual cookies, 42-7.

Draz-Koetke/Goodheart-Willcox Publisher

42-7 Icebox cookie dough must be fully chilled for the dough to maintain its shape during cutting.

This technique makes it possible to create effects such as checkerboard or pinwheels by forming logs using different colored dough.

Bar Cookies

Bar cookies are made by portioning and forming cookie dough into approximate one-pound (454 g) logs about the length of a sheet pan. The log is flattened and baked. Once the log has cooked and while it is still warm, it is sliced into one-inch (2 cm) segments to form cookies. These cookies are baked a second time to create a hard texture, 42-8. Biscotti are an example of a popular bar cookie.

Draz-Koetke/Goodheart-Willcox Publisher

42-8 These bar cookies will go back in the oven for further baking.

Summary Points

- Cookies are popular and profitable items in bakery production.
- Good cookies share certain attributes.
- Cookie dough can be mixed by either the one-stage or creaming method.
- Cookies can be shaped by drop, rolled, spritz, sheet, icebox, or bar methods.

In Review
Assess

1. What ingredient contributes most to the texture of a crisp cookie?
2. Cookies that have a higher proportion of shortening and moisture will have a _____ texture.
3. List four factors that contribute to the appearance of a quality cookie.
4. True or false. The one-stage method for mixing cookies has a greater chance of over-developing gluten and producing a tough cookie than the creaming method.
5. List the ingredients that are mixed to a smooth paste in the creaming method of mixing cookies.
6. What utensil is best for forming drop cookies?
7. A pastry bag is used to shape _____ cookies into a variety of forms.
8. True or false. Icebox cookies do not require baking.
9. Name two factors that affect how cookies spread during baking.
10. True or false. Sheet cookies are portioned before they are baked.

Core Skills

11. **Math.** You have been told to make 144 two-ounce chocolate chip cookies for a banquet. The recipe yields three pounds of cookies. By what factor would you need to increase the recipe?

12. **Writing.** Imagine that you are a pastry chef who also has a weekly column in the local newspaper. The title of this week's column is *Chef Secrets for Quality Cookies*. When writing your column, address all the factors that contribute to cookie quality. Use Internet resources to locate photos of each form of cookie to add interest to your article.

13. **Reading.** Use Internet and print resources to investigate the history of cookies. When were the first cookies invented and why? How did the term "cookie" come about? What early forms of cookies were most popular? How do cookies vary among cultures and countries? Through your reading, locate an early cookie recipe. Prepare a batch of these cookies to share during an oral report of your findings to the class.

14. **Speaking and Listening.** Divide into two teams and obtain a drop cookie recipe from your instructor. Team 1 should prepare the recipe using the *One-Stage Method* and Team 2 should prepare the recipe with the *Creaming Method*. Bake the cookies according to the recipe instructions. When done, plate the cookies for evaluation. Compare the outcome of the two mixing methods for appearance, flavor, and texture. What are the similarities and differences? Discuss your findings.

15. **Math.** Suppose your class has been asked to prepare 15 dozen *Sugar Cookies* (see the recipe in this chapter) for a school banquet. The original recipe yields 2 dozen cookies. What conversion factor will you use to create the needed cookies? How much will you need of each ingredient?

16. **CTE Career Readiness Practice.** Suppose you are a pastry chef for a large hotel that serves a weekend buffet brunch. The executive chef has come to you and asked you to develop two new cookie recipes to add to

the menu next month. The chef anticipates that these cookies will become a *signature item* for the brunch. The cookies must be bite-sized and highly decorated. Use your creativity and innovation, along with reliable Internet and print resources, to research and develop the new cookie recipes. Prepare yourself with the following as you develop your new recipes:

- What information do you need about cookie-recipe formulation?
- What ingredient proportions will you need?
- What flavor options might be most appealing for the menu?
- How will you decorate the cookies?

Then develop your recipes. Photograph your cookie creation and attach it to the recipe. Bake a sample to serve to the executive chef (your instructor/class) for evaluation. Do your new cookies have good flavor, texture, and appearance? Why or why not?

Critical Thinking

17. **Analyze variables.** The general manager wants you to cut expenses in the bakeshop. He is suggesting using less expensive ingredients for your popular cookies which are widely recognized as a quality product. You sell a high volume of these cookies daily. After analyzing all the variables, what would you tell him? How might this change eventually impact profitability of the bakeshop?

18. **Draw conclusions.** You are developing a new cookie recipe and believe the cookies are rather dry and hard. What steps could you take to improve this recipe?

19. **Identify evidence.** Not all bakeshops make cookie dough from scratch. Use reliable Internet or print resources to research what convenience products are available for pastry chefs to produce fresh-baked cookies. What are the benefits of using convenience products? What are the drawbacks? How does use of convenience products in the bakeshop impact profitability? Write a summary of your findings.

Technology

As a pastry chef, you are always looking for ways to save time when baking cookies. You have typically used parchment paper for lining pans; however, you notice some new options are available in your supplier's product catalog. You decide to investigate disposable, treated-parchment liners and reusable food-grade silicone liners. What are the pros and cons of each liner—parchment versus treated-parchment and silicone? How does each option impact the flavor, texture, and appearance of cookies? What are other pastry chefs recommending? Create a chart to track the features of the various options. Which do you think may be most cost effective? the least cost effective?

Teamwork

Divide the class into four teams. Each team will prepare a variation on the sugar cookie recipe from this chapter. Team 1 will prepare the recipe using butter. Team 2 will prepare the recipe using shortening. Team 3 will prepare the recipe using two ounces less sugar. Team 4 will prepare the recipe using brown sugar. Evaluate the final product from each version of the recipe for appearance, texture, and flavor. Record your observations.

Chef's E-portfolio
Cookie Creativity

Upload your recipe, photo, and instructor evaluation from the CTE Career Readiness Practice activity to your e-portfolio. Ask your instructor where to save your file. This could be on the school's network or a flash drive of your own. Name your portfolio document *FirstnameLastname_Portfolio Ch#.docx* (i.e., JohnSmith_PortfolioCh42.docx).

While studying, look for the activity icon  to:

- Build vocabulary with e-flash cards and matching activities.
- Expand learning with video clips, photo identification activities, animations, and interactive activities.
- Review and assess what you learn by completing end-of-chapter questions.

G-WLEARNING.com

Tischenko Irina/Shutterstock.com

Yeast-Raised Products

43

Reading Prep

Before reading the chapter, skim the photos and their captions. As you are reading, determine how these concepts contribute to the ideas presented in the text.

Culinary Terminology
Build Vocab

kneading, p. 678
fermentation, p. 678
punching, p. 679
scaling, p. 679
proofing, p. 679
wash, p. 680
docking, p. 680

Academic Terminology
Build Vocab

craft, p. 677

Objectives

After studying this chapter, you will be able to

- explain how dough for yeast-raised products is prepared.
- recall the basic forms into which yeast breads are shaped.
- summarize what happens to yeast-raised products during the proofing and baking stages of preparation.

Yeast is a microscopic plant that acts as a leavening agent in baked goods. Under the right conditions, it creates tiny pockets of carbon dioxide gas that make dough rise. In turn, these gases expand during baking and create a light and airy texture in the finished baked good.

Dough Preparation

Preparing dough for a yeast-raised bakery product is not as simple as preparing quick bread dough or batter. Yeasts require specific conditions in order to be effective leavening agents. The success of the dough depends on how the yeast performs. Understanding that yeast is a living organism and knowing how it reacts to various conditions and ingredients is essential to the baker's **craft**, or occupation.

Using Yeast

Both compressed fresh yeast and granulated dried yeast need to be mixed with the liquid ingredients in a dough recipe before adding the dry ingredients. Mixing the yeast with liquid hydrates dried yeasts. Dissolving either type of yeast allows it to be evenly mixed into the dough, 43-1.

The optimal temperature for yeast is between 100°F and 105°F (38°C and 41°C), so lukewarm liquid is typically used for dissolving yeast. Liquids at temperatures over 138°F (59°C) may kill the yeast organism rendering it ineffective. Bakers often calculate the temperature of the flour, the room temperature, and the heat created by the friction of mixing to determine their effect on fermentation. Proper conditions for fermentation are achieved by adjusting the temperature of the liquid to account for these effects.

A

B

kuvona/Shutterstock.com, jeehyun/Shutterstock.com

43-1 Both (A) fresh and (B) dried yeasts should be dissolved in liquid before adding to dry ingredients.

SCIENCE & TECHNOLOGY

Sourdough

Commercially produced yeasts are used for many breads because of the consistency and speed with which they ferment. Before these consistently performing yeasts were available, bakers used natural yeast found in the air to leaven their breads. The acidic flavor that these "wild" yeasts imparted on their baked goods, resulted in them being called *sourdough*.

The process of harnessing "wild" yeasts is simple. Some flour and water—often water that has been used to boil potatoes—are mixed into a thin paste and allowed to sit out at room temperature for several days or more. During this time, the mixture becomes bubbly and sour, and acquires a yeasty aroma. This simple paste is called a *starter*. A small amount of the starter is added to dough to ferment. Fermentation of sourdough typically takes longer than commercial yeast.

The remainder of the starter can be kept indefinitely as long as some new flour and liquid are added periodically to feed the yeasts. Starters have been perpetuated for decades.

Mixing and Kneading Dough

Mixing combines ingredients into a smooth mass with no dry spots or lumps. Kneading, or repeatedly folding and pressing the dough after it is mixed, is done to develop gluten. Small quantities of dough can be kneaded by hand, 43-2. Larger quantities are usually kneaded on the mixer with the dough hook.

Gluten is the protein that gives dough its structure and elasticity. The more the dough is kneaded, the more gluten is developed. Recipe directions for how long and at what speed dough should be kneaded must be followed to create a finished product with the correct texture.

Fermentation

Yeast is a living organism that consumes carbohydrates found in flour, sugar, and other dough ingredients. When carbohydrates are consumed by yeast, alcohol and carbon dioxide are released. This process is called fermentation.

After kneading, yeast dough is allowed to ferment. This process can take as long as two and a half hours, depending on the recipe and quantity of dough. Fermentation is best done in a warm place with no drafts. The dough is loosely covered. Many bakers place the dough in an oiled container and brush oil on the surface of the dough so that a dry crust does not form. Fermentation is generally considered complete when the dough doubles in size.

Julija Sapic/Shutterstock.com

43-2 Gluten development is easy to detect when kneading by hand, as the dough becomes smooth and elastic.

When fermentation is complete and the dough has risen, it is punched. **Punching**, or folding, the dough allows carbon dioxide gas to be released. It also allows the yeast to come in contact with more "food" for the second fermentation in the proofing process. Some doughs only need to rise one time. The dough does not literally need to be punched, but rather pressed or folded. It should not be kneaded or worked at this stage.

Hints from the Chef
Sponges

Rather than mixing yeast directly into the other dough ingredients, some bakers use what is called a *sponge* or *preferment*. Yeast is mixed with liquid and some flour from the recipe, and allowed to ferment for several hours—usually overnight. The fermented sponge is then mixed into the balance of the dough ingredients and the dough is fermented.

There are several advantages to adding this extra step to the baking process. A sponge used in a dough speeds up the fermentation process, thus saving time and space with large batches. Sponges also create unique flavor in bread, as with a sourdough sponge. They can also improve the leavened texture of a bread and extend its shelf life.

Shaping

After fermentation and punching, dough is portioned by weight to create loaves or individual rolls of a uniform size. This process of portioning dough by weight is called **scaling**. For efficiently scaling large quantities of individual rolls, a dough divider is used. When using a dough divider, a large amount of dough is placed into a pan. The machine then presses and cuts the dough into even portions, usually three dozen at one time.

Most dough portions are first formed into balls. In this process, the surface of the dough is stretched to create a tight smooth surface on the topside of the ball. This helps the dough to rise evenly and retain its shape during proofing and baking. Often, dough is allowed to rest for a short time at this stage to make further shaping easier.

A large number of breads and rolls are left in the form of a ball. Others are cut, flattened, rolled into long loaves, tied into knots, braided, or sculpted to create a particular shape. Dough is often placed into a pan to give a desired shape to the finished product. The number of ways to shape yeast dough are seemingly endless. Some shapes are classics and are widely recognized, 43-3.

Proofing

Yeast dough is allowed to rise after it is shaped and before it is baked. This process is called **proofing** the dough. This step is important in creating the volume and texture of the finished bread.

Most bakeshops use a proof box for this step. The temperature in the proof box is typically around 100°F (38°C), which speeds up proofing. The steam or humidity in the proof box prevents a dry crust from forming on the dough, which would prevent it from rising. Breads can also be proofed in a warm place covered with a clean cloth. Proofing is complete when the dough doubles in size.

Chart of Dough Shapes	
Individual Rolls	**Loaves**
• Round	• Baguette
• Cloverleaf	• Boule
• Knot–single, double, figure eight	• Pan loaf
	• Pullman
• Rings	• Rye
• Crescent	
• Club roll	
• Kaiser	
• Bagel	

43-3 Dough can be formed into a variety of interesting shapes before baking.

Draz-Koetke/Goodheart-Willcox Publisher

43-4 Dough can be docked using different patterns.

When proofing is complete, the risen dough may be coated with a liquid such as beaten eggs, milk, or water. This liquid, called a **wash**, gives the dough a particular color or creates a textured crust. The most common wash is beaten eggs, which gives the finished bread a deep brown color and glossy finish. Egg wash is also used to apply a coating of sesame, poppy, or other seeds to breads or rolls.

Another technique used for some types of breads and rolls is docking. **Docking** is the act of cutting small slashes in the surface of the risen dough, 43-4. For bread with a hard crust, the slits allow gases to escape during the baking process. The slashes also create a decorative pattern on the surface of the finished loaf.

Baking

Breads are baked at varying temperatures and for various times depending on their size and the desired crispness of the finished product. At the beginning of the baking process the dough rises due to the expansion of the gases present in the dough. Yeast is killed, moisture evaporates, and the starches and gluten in the dough become

firm. Lastly, the dough browns creating a crust, 43-5.

One distinct variation on the baking process is the addition of steam to the oven. Often, crusty French and Italian breads get their crisp crust because steam is injected into the oven during the baking process.

Chef Speak

Danish and Croissants

Danish and croissant doughs are two similar yet unique types of yeast dough. They are both laminated or roll-in doughs that result in a flaky, buttery final product much like puff pastry. A roll-in dough is a yeast dough that is rolled out and a layer of butter or shortening is spread on it. The dough is folded back over the butter layer and then rolled out and folded a number of times. This rolling creates many very thin layers of fat in the dough, which give it a flaky texture when baked.

Croissant dough is used to produce the traditional crescent-shaped French breakfast bread. Danish has more butter and sugar than croissant dough and is used for individual pastries and coffee cakes.

Aleph Studio/Shutterstock.com

43-5 Good heat circulation in the oven contributes to even browning of the crust.

Some models of ovens come with a steam injection mechanism.

When baking is complete, breads should be allowed to cool to room temperature before being sliced or served. Most bread is best stored at room temperature. Crusty breads lose their crispness if stored in the refrigerator. Refrigeration will also cause bread to become stale more quickly. Baked breads can be frozen for long-term storage.

Recipe No.	Name		Category
43.2	**Hard Rolls/French Bread**		Yeast-raised products
Yield	**Portion Size**		**No. Portions**
2¼ lb. (1 kg)	1½ oz. (45 g) roll or 1 lb.(450 g) loaf		2 dz. rolls or 2 loaves
US Quantity	**Metric Quantity**	**Ingredient**	**TCS**
1½ lb.	680 g	bread flour	
½ oz.	15 g	salt	
12 oz.	360 g	water	
½ oz.	15 g	active dry yeast	
Method			**CCP**
1.	Combine flour and salt in the bowl of the electric mixer.		
2.	Dissolve the yeast in the water and mix into the dry ingredients.		
3.	Mix at medium speed for 12 minutes. The dough should be smooth and elastic.		
4.	Place dough in a lightly oiled bowl and loosely cover. Allow the dough to ferment in a warm place approximately 1 hour, until it has doubled in size.		
5.	Punch the dough and scale according to use. Shape into rolls and place on a sheet pan lined with parchment paper. If loaves are made, place in lightly greased loaf pan.		
6.	Proof dough in a warm place until dough has doubled in size.		
7.	Bake at 400°F (204°C). If using an oven equipped with steam, inject steam for the first 10 minutes. Bake rolls 15–20 minutes, loaves 30–40 minutes.		

Portion (g)	Calories	Fat (g)	Protein (g)	Carbohydrate (g)	Cholesterol (mg)	Sodium (mg)	Fiber (g)
44	93	0.02	3.89	20.39	0	229.96	0.87

Note: French bread gets its crisp crust from steam injected into the oven during the first stage of baking. If you are working with an oven that doesn't have injected steam, place a sheet pan in the bottom of the oven when preheating the oven. Pour 1 c. (240 mL) hot water onto the sheet pan at the beginning of the baking process.

TECHNIQUE
Preparing Yeast Breads

1. Weigh all ingredients carefully.
2. Dissolve compressed or dry active yeast in the liquid ingredients and mix with dry ingredients until fully incorporated. Instant yeast can be mixed directly into dry ingredients.

3. Knead the dough for the prescribed amount of time either by hand or on the mixer using the dough hook.

4. Allow the dough to ferment until it has doubled in size.

5. Punch the dough.

6. Scale the dough into uniform portions.

7. Shape the dough into the desired form.

8. Proof the dough until it doubles in size.
9. Bake according to recipe instructions. Bread should have a well-browned crust when done.

10. Allow bread to cool to room temperature before serving.

Summary Points

- Mixing dough is done to evenly combine ingredients, while kneading is done to develop dough's structure and elasticity.

- When yeast ferments in a dough, it gives off carbon dioxide gas that causes the dough to rise.

- Dough is portioned by weight and can be formed into many different shapes.

- After portioning, dough is allowed to rise a second time. This is known as proofing.

- Baking causes dough to rise further, after which the dough structure is solidified and a browned crust forms.

In Review

Assess

1. True or false. Yeast is mixed first with the dry ingredients so that it is distributed evenly.

2. Dough is kneaded to develop _____, which gives bread its structure and texture.

3. Why is the speed and length of time that dough is kneaded important?

4. During fermentation, yeast consumes carbohydrates and releases which of the following?
   A. Gases and protein
   B. Alcohol and carbon dioxide
   C. Gluten and protein
   D. Carbon dioxide and gluten

5. List two reasons why dough is punched after it has fermented and risen.

6. To create finished products of a uniform size, dough should be portioned by _____.
   A. volume   C. weight
   B. docking   D. sight

7. True or false. Steam or humidity is important when proofing dough to prevent a dry crust from forming on the dough.

8. Proofing is complete when the dough _____ in size.
   A. doubles   C. shrinks
   B. triples   D. quadruples

9. List two reasons why bread and roll doughs are docked.

10. List four things that happen to dough when it is baked.

Core Skills

11. **Math.** You have been asked to use the dough divider to portion enough dough for 900 dinner rolls. The dough divider cuts dough into three dozen portions at a time. How many times will you need to process dough through the dough divider?

12. **Speaking and Listening.** Demonstrate how to prepare yeast-raised dough. Use the recipe for *Hard Rolls/French Bread* in this chapter or another recipe of your choice. Prepare the script for your demonstration. Place special emphasis on properly dissolving the yeast along with mixing and kneading. What will you say as you prepare the dough? Use the text guidelines as you prepare. Arrange for someone to video you and give your demonstration to the class. As an alternative, use a school-approved web-based application to create a movie of your demonstration to post to the class website.

13. **Writing.** Use Internet or print resources to investigate how to create various shapes with yeast dough. Then write an illustrated report on how to create at least three roll shapes and two loaf shapes.

14. **Reading.** When did yeast as a leavener become an option for creating leavened bread products? Use reliable Internet or print resources to read about the history of yeast in bread making. Prior to yeast development, how were leavened bread products made? Give an oral report to share your findings.

15. **Math.** Locate a yeast roll or bread recipe that makes at least 20 portions. Suppose you need to create enough dough to make 75 portions. What is the conversion factor? How do ingredient amounts change? Use the formulas for changing recipe yield and calculating new ingredient amounts (new yield ÷ old yield = conversion factor *and* old quantity × conversion factor = new quantity).

16. **CTE Career Readiness Practice.** Imagine that you are the pastry chef for a major chain of supermarkets. Along with your bakeshop responsibilities, you also are responsible for speaking to customers about products and writing articles for the supermarket website. This month's article focuses on a new line of *healthful artisan breads* the store is promoting. Research the background on making artisan breads, identify healthful ingredients that can be added, and any techniques that make them unique. Write your article with a marketing focus to capture customer interest. What is so different about these artisan breads that will make customers *want* to buy them?

Critical Thinking

17. **Analyze.** What adjustment(s) might a baker need to make when preparing a yeast-raised product on an extremely hot and humid day? a hot and dry day? What factors enter in to the adjustment? Discuss in class.

18. **Identify cause and effect.** After kneading your dough, you let it sit for 2½ hours. You return to find that the dough has hardly increased in size. What conditions might have caused this result?

19. **Infer relationships.** Make a chart comparing the characteristics of a popular white sandwich bread with a hearty rustic bread. Next to each characteristic where the two differ, write a brief explanation of the step in the preparation or the ingredient(s) that might account for the difference.

20. **Create.** Develop a list of ingredients that you could add to a basic bread dough recipe to create specialty breads. Be creative.

Technology

Presume you are a pastry chef at a family owned bakeshop that is looking to expand. The owner of the shop has ask you to research proof boxes to speed up the bread-baking process and write a proposal for a new piece of equipment. Research at least three different models of proof boxes and double-check the information from vendors

through other sources. Remember that determining reliability is important. Before writing the proposal, ask yourself the following:

- **Information.** Is the information what you need? Is it current? Can you document the information from more than one source (for example, trade journals, professional organizations, or academic institutions)? Does the information carry endorsements that are reliable?

- **Author/writer.** Is the writer qualified to provide accurate information? What are his or her credentials? What is the intent of the research?

- **Bias/objectivity.** Does the research address different points of view? Is any important information omitted? Is the author/writer's bias obvious?

- **Quality.** Is the information provided in a logical sequence? Can you clearly identify key points of information? Does the text use good grammar and correct spelling?

After conducting your research, create an illustrated digital presentation to present your research and recommendations to the bakeshop owner (instructor/class).

Teamwork

Working in small teams, prepare the recipe for French bread included in this chapter. Divide dough in half before mixing or kneading. Mix or knead one piece of dough for the length of time called for in the recipe. Mix or knead the other piece of dough for 1½ times the length of time called for in the recipe. Finish following the recipe and bake both products. Evaluate the two breads for texture and appearance once they have cooled. Record your observations and compare with the class.

Chef's E-portfolio
Preparing Yeast-Raised Dough

Upload the video of your presentation in activity #12 to your e-portfolio. Ask your instructor where to save your file. This could be on the school's network or a flash drive of your own. Name your portfolio document *FirstnameLastname_Portfolio Ch#.docx* (i.e., JohnSmith_PortfolioCh43.docx).

While studying, look for the activity icon ➦ **to:**

- Build vocabulary with e-flash cards and matching activities.
- Expand learning with video clips, photo identification activities, animations, and interactive activities.
- Review and assess what you learn by completing end-of-chapter questions.

G-WLEARNING.com

Joshua Resnick/Shutterstock.com

686

Reading Prep

Skim the review questions at the end of the chapter first. Use them to help you focus on the most important concepts as you read the chapter.

Culinary Terminology Build Vocab

flaky pie dough, p. 689
mealy pie dough, p. 689
short dough, p. 693
sweet dough, p. 694
blind baking, p. 694
pastry glaze, p. 694
puff pastry, p. 695

Academic Terminology Build Vocab

mediocre, p. 687

Objectives

After studying this chapter, you will be able to
- prepare crust for pies and tarts.
- classify traditional fillings for pies.
- summarize how tarts differ from pies.
- recognize the characteristics and uses of puff pastry.

Pies and tarts are part of the repertoire of most bakeshops. The ingredients and preparation of the basic dough are simple, yet the many variations on forming and filling the dough give these pastries almost limitless possibilities. Though pies are based on some simple ingredients, the way in which these ingredients are combined and baked can make the difference between a **mediocre**, or ordinary, pie and a great one.

Piecrust

The foundation for a great pie is the right piecrust. The type of dough and mixing method must be appropriate for the intended filling. Then the crust must be properly rolled and formed so that it acts to highlight the filling.

Dough

Pie dough is a simple mixture of flour, fat, liquid, and salt. Though it may be simple, selecting the right type of ingredients will help produce a better finished piecrust.

Flour   To create a light and delicate textured pie, most bakers and pastry chefs use pastry flour. Piecrust made with pastry flour is delicate rather than dense and chewy because pastry flour has lower gluten potential and is higher in starch.

Fat   The choice of fat is the most important factor in creating a piecrust with an excellent texture. The melting point of the fat is key. Solid shortenings, fats that are solid at room

3-2-1 Dough

Pie dough is sometimes referred to as "3-2-1" dough. This name comes from the proportion of ingredients in the dough. Pie dough by weight is

    3 parts flour
    2 parts shortening
    1 part liquid

Most pie dough recipes are close to these basic proportions.

temperature, are best for creating flaky texture in the finished pie.

Butter is the choice of some bakers because it has good flavor. However, butter is an expensive ingredient and because it melts at a lower temperature it produces a crust that is not as flaky as one made with shortening.

Lard has been a favorite fat for pie dough for a long time. Its higher melting point creates flakier textured dough than butter. Some diners may find the flavor of lard objectionable. Additionally, some diners have dietary restrictions that prohibit them from eating lard.

Vegetable-based solid shortening is the most popular choice for making pie dough. It is reasonably priced, has a high melting point that creates a flaky crust, and has a neutral flavor, 44-1.

Mike Neale/Shutterstock.com

44-1 Sometimes a combination of fats is used in a piecrust.

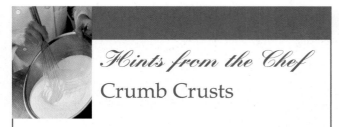

Hints from the Chef
Crumb Crusts

A simpler alternative to the traditional piecrust is a crumb crust. A bottom crust can be made by mixing dried crumbs with melted butter. The mixture is then pressed into a pie pan. Graham cracker crumbs and cake crumbs are the most popular ingredients for this type of piecrust.

Liquid The liquid used in pie dough can be water or milk. Water is most common. Some bakers prefer milk because a crust made with milk browns more quickly. Whether water or milk is used, it is important that the liquid is *ice cold*. Warm liquids might melt the fat during the mixing process.

Mixing

Mixing is an important stage in developing a particular texture in a finished piecrust. There are two distinct textures of finished piecrust—flaky and mealy.

To make **flaky pie dough**, the fat is mixed or cut into the flour until it is in pieces approximately the size of a pea. In other words, the fat is not fully mixed with the flour. The liquid is combined with the flour and fat. The fat and moistened flour form layers when the dough is rolled out, which create the flaky texture. Flaky pie dough is most commonly used for fruit-filled pies.

The ingredients are the same for **mealy pie dough**, but the shortening is cut into the flour until it resembles the texture of cornmeal. As with flaky pie dough, the liquid is added. Mealy pie dough is used for pies with liquid fillings because it resists becoming soggy.

Recipe No.	Name			Category
44.1A	Flaky Pie Dough			Pies and Tarts
Yield	**Portion Size**			**No. Portions**
2 lb. (900 g)	1¾ oz. (50 g)			18
US Quantity	**Metric Quantity**	**Ingredient**		**TCS**
1 lb.	450 g	pastry flour		
1 tsp.	5 mL	salt		
10 oz.	280 g	vegetable shortening		
5 oz.	150 g	cold water		
Method				**CCP**
1. Combine the flour and salt in a mixing bowl.				
2. Cut the shortening into pea-size pieces and add to the flour.				
3. Using the paddle, mix in the cold water.				
4. Mix only long enough to have the dough come together in a cohesive mass. Do not overmix.				
5. Refrigerate at 41°F (5°C) until ready to use.				CCP

Portion (g)	Calories	Fat (g)	Protein (g)	Carbohydrate (g)	Cholesterol (mg)	Sodium (mg)	Fiber (g)
50	235	16.35	1.95	19.53	0.03	133.11	0.72

TECHNIQUE
Forming a Piecrust

1. **Dust the work surface with flour to prevent dough from sticking. Place a 9 oz. piece of workable dough on the work surface and dust the top of dough with flour.**

2. **Apply even pressure with the rolling pin and periodically turn the dough 90 degrees to produce an even sheet of dough. Dust the dough and work surface with more flour as needed to prevent sticking.**

3. **Roll dough to ⅛-inch (2 mm) thickness. Either fold the dough in quarters or roll it over the rolling pin to transfer it to the pie pan without tearing. Lay the sheet of pie dough in the pie pan and gently press it into the corners.**

4. **Trim the excess dough from the edges by pressing the side of your hand against the rim of the pie pan.**

5. **After filling is added, the top crust is placed on the filling and the edges of the top and bottom crusts are crimped together to seal the pie.**

Do not overmix or overwork either type of dough to avoid developing too much gluten. Pie dough that is overworked becomes tough and chewy.

Rolling and Forming

The process of rolling out dough to form a piecrust requires some practice. However, there are a few steps that can make this task easier. First, the temperature of the dough is important. If the pie dough or the room is warm, the dough will be excessively soft and sticky. Allowing the dough to chill before rolling it is helpful. Alternatively, if pie dough has been refrigerated for a long time, it will be rigid and hard to roll. If that occurs, allow the dough to set out at room temperature until it is workable.

Do not try to roll out more dough at one time than is needed. It is easier to work with smaller amounts. About nine ounces of dough is enough to line a standard nine-inch pie pan.

Once the piecrust is formed, the raw pie shell is ready for the filling. After the filling is added, there are three options for finishing the pie. Many pies, especially those with liquid fillings, are left uncovered. Pies can also be finished with a solid top crust. With a top crust, it is necessary to cut holes or vents in the top layer of dough to allow steam to escape during the baking process. The most elaborate way to finish a pie is with a lattice top. For a lattice top, strips of dough are woven into a sheet. The woven sheet is then placed on the pie to create a decorative top crust, 44-2.

Egg wash is commonly used to seal the top and bottom crusts together. The edge of the pie dough can be crimped or decorated to better seal it and add eye appeal. Before baking, pies with a top crust are often brushed with egg wash to produce a brown shiny finished pie.

Draz-Koetke/Goodheart-Willcox Publisher

44-2 A lattice top piecrust takes more time to prepare than a solid top crust.

Recipe No.	Name			Category
44.4	Apple Pie			Pies and Tarts
Yield	**Portion Size**			**No. Portions**
1–9″ pie	⅛ pie			8
US Quantity	**Metric Quantity**	**Ingredient**		**TCS**
1½ lb.	680 g	cooking apples, peeled and cored		
6 oz.	180 g	water		
6 oz.	170 g	sugar		
1 Tbsp.	15 mL	lemon juice		
½ tsp.	2 mL	cinnamon		
¼ tsp.	1 mL	nutmeg		
1 oz.	30 g	cornstarch		
4 oz.	120 g	cold water		
as needed		flaky pie dough to line and cover a 9″ pie pan		
as needed		egg wash (beaten eggs)		•

Method	CCP
Filling	
1. Slice apples and combine with water, sugar, lemon juice, cinnamon, and nutmeg in a saucepot.	
2. Simmer until apples are tender but still firm. Test flavor and add more sugar if necessary.	
3. Combine the cornstarch with 4 fl. oz. water and stir into the apple mixture. Simmer to thicken.	
4. Remove from heat and allow mixture to cool to room temperature.	
Pie	
5. Roll out pie dough and line the bottom of a 9″ pie pan.	
6. Add the filling to the pie pan.	
7. Roll out a top crust. Cut vents in the crust.	
8. Brush the edges of the bottom crust with egg wash. Place the top crust on the pie and seal the edges well.	
9. Brush the top crust with egg wash.	
10. Bake the pie at 425°F (218°C) for 10 minutes. Lower heat to 375°F (190°C) and continue baking for 35 minutes.	

Portion (g)	Calories	Fat (g)	Protein (g)	Carbohydrate (g)	Cholesterol (mg)	Sodium (mg)	Fiber (g)
208	410	19.03	2.91	57.83	15.02	157	2.05

Pie Fillings

Pie fillings come in a variety of flavors and textures. Some are baked with the crust, others are added after the crust is baked. A successful pie filling must be properly thickened and paired with the appropriate piecrust.

Fruit Fillings

Traditionally, fruit fillings for pies are prepared using raw fruit. The fruit is mixed with sugar, spices, and a starchy thickener such as flour, cornstarch, arrowroot, or tapioca. The filling is placed in the pie shell and, as the pie bakes the moisture from the fruit and the starch create a thickened filling. This method is rarely used in foodservice because the final product is inconsistent. The degree to which the filling thickens can vary using this method. Underthickened fillings can result in a soggy pie. Fillings that become too thick are unappealing.

Most commercial operations prepare cooked fillings. In this method, either the fruit or juice from the fruit is sweetened and thickened on the stovetop. This method allows bakers to easily control the thickness of the filling before the pie is baked. When using delicate or frozen fruits, it is common to cook and thicken only the fruit juice and then mix the fruit back into the thickened juice. This keeps the pieces of fruit from disintegrating during the baking process.

Liquid Fillings

Many pie fillings are liquid before baking. Most contain eggs that coagulate and thicken the filling during baking. Some common examples of liquid pie fillings are custard, pumpkin, and pecan pies. Mealy pie dough should be used with liquid fillings.

Cream and Chiffon Fillings

Cream pies are made with a pudding or pastry cream filling. These fillings do not require baking, so it is essential to use a prebaked pie shell or a pie shell with a crumb crust. The consistency of the filling should be thick, so that slices of pie hold their shape when cut. Chiffon pies are a lighter version of cream pies. Gelatin and whipped cream are added to the base filling to make it airy and firm.

Tarts

Tarts are similar to pies because of the nature of their pastry crusts. However, tarts are much shallower at only ½ to ¾ inches (1.5 to 2 cm) deep. While the classical shape for tarts is round with fluted sides, tarts can also be square, rectangular, or oval. Tartlets are small individual tarts of any shape.

Dough

Depending on the type of filling, two different doughs may be used for making tarts. They are both rolled and formed in the same manner as pie dough.

Short Dough Short dough, also called *pâte brisée* (paht breez AY), is a dough used for savory tarts. It is similar to mealy pie dough. Butter is typically used as the shortening in this dough. This dough is used with savory fillings for items such as quiche, hors d'oeuvres, and canapés.

Sweet Dough Tartlets with sweet fillings are made with sweet dough, also called *pâte sucrée* (paht soo CRAY). **Sweet dough** is similar to short dough, but has the addition of sugar and egg yolks. Flavorings such as ground nuts, extracts, and cocoa powder are often added to sweet dough.

Blind Baking

As with cream pies, tarts and tartlets are often filled with ingredients that do not need further cooking or baking. Before being filled, the tart shells are prebaked. This prebaking is known as **blind baking**. To keep its shape and prevent the tartlet shell from bubbling or buckling, weights are placed in the shell during baking, 44-3 The dough is lined with parchment paper and then small, loose weights such as dried beans or ball bearings are placed on the paper. Many bakeshops keep a container of dried beans or bearings on hand for exactly this purpose.

Filling and Decorating

Pastry cream is the most common filling for tarts made with sweet dough. After the prebaked pie shell has cooled, a thin layer of pastry cream is spread over the surface of the shell.

The tart can then be decorated with pieces or slices of fresh fruit. In order to keep the fruit decoration in place and to keep it from drying out, a thin layer of apricot pastry glaze is brushed on the surface. **Pastry glaze** is a commercially prepared product made from fruit jelly and gelatin. The glaze must be heated so it becomes more fluid and easier to brush on the fruit, 44-4. As the glaze cools, it solidifies and coats the fruit to keep it fresh looking and in place. Apricot pastry glaze is the most common flavor used in bakeshops because its flavor is complementary to a wide variety of fruits.

Draz-Koetke/Goodheart-Willcox Publisher

44-3 Dried beans or other weights are placed on a piecrust prior to blind baking.

Draz-Koetke/Goodheart-Willcox Publisher

44-4 (A) Fresh fruit makes a beautiful presentation and (B) pastry glaze helps maintain its appearance.

Puff Pastry

Puff pastry is very flaky dough made by a complex process that creates over 1,000 extremely thin layers of dough and fat. This layering process creates dough that puffs to as much as eight times its original thickness when baked. The texture of baked puff pastry is light, delicate, and extremely flaky, 44-5. No other baked good has such a rich taste and flaky texture.

Puff pastry is a roll-in or laminated dough similar to croissant and Danish dough. First, a basic dough of flour, butter, and water is prepared. Then, a layer of butter shortening is spread onto the dough. The dough is folded and then rolled out. The process of folding and rolling the dough is repeated multiple times. This process creates many very thin layers of fat in the dough that give it a flaky texture when baked.

Many foodservice operations buy ready-made puff pastry because of the great amount of time and labor required to produce it. This product is frozen and comes in blocks, ready-rolled sheets, or squares.

Puff pastry has many uses. It is layered with pastry cream to create the classic dessert called a *napoleon*. Puff pastry is used for making pastry cases or containers that can be filled with various savory or sweet fillings. It is also used to wrap various products before they are baked. A product baked in a pastry crust is often described on the menu as *en croute* (ehn KREWT).

Draz-Koetke/Goodheart-Willcox Publisher

44-5 Puff pastry can be used in many creative ways.

Summary Points

- Pie dough is made of flour, fat, liquid, and salt. The way these ingredients are mixed can create a finished dough with either flaky or mealy texture.

- Fruit fillings for pies are commonly thickened with cornstarch or arrowroot on the stovetop before baking.

- Liquid fillings utilize eggs, which coagulate and thicken during the baking process.

- Cream fillings are a thicker version of pudding or pastry cream.

- Tarts are a shallower type of pie and can be made with short dough for savory applications or sweet dough for dessert.

- Blind baking is the process of prebaking a pie or tart shell. During blind baking, weights are placed on the dough to help it keep its shape.

In Review
Assess

1. True or false. Pastry flour is the best flour to use for piecrust because it has higher gluten potential and is lower in starch than other flours.

2. List three reasons vegetable-based solid shortenings are the most popular choice for making pie dough.

3. To create flaky pie dough, cut the fat into the flour until it is the size of _____.

4. Why is mealy pie dough preferred for liquid fillings?

5. What can be done to pie dough that is too soft or sticky to roll?

6. True or false. Egg wash is commonly used to seal the top and bottom piecrusts together and provide a brown shiny finish.

7. Pie shells must be _____ before filling them with a cream- or chiffon-type filling.

8. The type of shortening typically used for short dough is _____.
   A. butter
   B. lard
   C. omega-3 fatty acid
   D. vegetable-based shortening

9. What product is used to keep the fruit decorations in place and prevent fruit tarts from drying out?

10. Puff pastry has a flaky texture from the many thin layers of _____ in the dough.

Core Skills

11. **Math.** You need to make enough dough to line 12 nine-inch pie pans. How many pounds of pie dough should you make?

12. **Speaking and Listening.** In teams, prepare both flaky and mealy pie doughs with the recipe(s) obtained from your instructor. Roll them out and place in pie pans. Blind bake them using parchment paper and dried beans or ball bearings. Once piecrusts are baked, compare them for appearance, texture, and flavor. Record your observations and discuss them with the class.

13. **Speaking.** Use reliable resources to examine the history of pie across cultures. How did pie vary among cultures? How do pies today differ from the pies of the past? What information about the history of pie do you find most interesting? Do you think there is a market in today's foodservice industry for culturally and historically diverse pie? Why or why not? Use presentation software to create a digital report to share with the class.

14. **Writing.** Review an Internet video demonstration on the art of making puff pastry by such chef masters as Julia Child and Michel Richard. How does the text technique compare to that of the chef masters? Write a comparison summary of the video demonstration and the text instructions for puff pastry.

15. **CTE Career Readiness Practice.** Suppose you are interested in a career as a pastry cook in a large bakeshop. You have done your research in regard to educational requirements for such careers and think this fits with your personal goals and career goals. However, you feel you are missing the firsthand experiential knowledge necessary to commit to such a career. Locate a person with a local company or organization who

is an expert in your career of interest. Make arrangements to job shadow or work with this individual as a mentor as you pursue your career. How can you benefit by having such a mentor in your life?

Critical Thinking

16. **Identify evidence.** Use reliable Internet or print resources to research and write a short paper explaining what lard is and any evidence regarding health issues associated with it.

17. **Draw conclusions.** A wide variety of fruits can be used for creating fruit tarts. Draw conclusions about which fruits are poor choices for a fruit tart. Explain your reasoning.

18. **Critique technique.** You recently started using frozen cherries for your cherry pie filling which you sweeten and thicken on the stovetop before placing in the piecrust. However, the cherries are disintegrating during the baking process. Critique your technique. What would you do to correct this problem?

19. **Analyze cause and effect.** Your pastry chef has brought you a slice of the fruit pie recipe she is developing. You believe the crust is somewhat tough and chewy. What ingredients or procedures would you suggest she consider changing?

Technology

With a classmate, use a school-approved web-based video application to prepare a video demonstration on how to make tarts. Determine the type of tart you want to make—savory or sweet and obtain the appropriate recipe from your instructor for either a short dough or sweet dough. Write the script for the demonstration, explaining what you will say for each step of the process. Create the demonstration and upload it to the class website for class critique.

Teamwork

Divide into four teams and use the recipe for *Flaky Pie Dough* found in this chapter. Teams 1, 2, and 3 should prepare the recipe as is for a *flaky crust*. Team 4 should alter Step 2 of the method to cut in the shortening to the consistency of cornmeal for a *mealy crust*. Form the piecrust according to the text technique and fit it into nine-inch pie pans. (Note: Team 1 needs to reserve 9 ounces of dough for a top crust.) Then prepare fillings as follows:

- Team 1—prepare a cooked fruit filling as directed by your instructor, fill the piecrust, add a top crust, and bake as directed.
- Team 2—blind bake the crust and prepare a cream filling as directed by your instructor.
- Team 3—blind bake the crust and prepare a chiffon filling as directed by your instructor.
- Team 4—create a liquid filling (custard or pumpkin) as directed by your instructor and pour the filling into the unbaked mealy crust. Bake as directed.

After the pies are complete and cooled, plate the pies for class sampling. Compare the outcomes of the two types of crust—flaky and mealy. Were the crusts evenly browned, tender, and flaky? If not, what were the likely causes? Were the fillings prepared correctly? Were the flavors and consistency good and appealing? Discuss your findings.

Chef's E-portfolio
Tart Technique

Upload your video demonstration from the Technology activity to your e-portfolio. Ask your instructor where to save your file. This could be on the school's network or a flash drive of your own. Name your portfolio document *FirstnameLastname_Portfolio Ch#.docx* (i.e., JohnSmith_PortfolioCh44.docx).

While studying, look for the activity icon to:

- Build vocabulary with e-flash cards and matching activities.
- Expand learning with video clips, photo identification activities, animations, and interactive activities.
- Review and assess what you learn by completing end-of-chapter questions.

Cakes

45

Reading Prep

Before reading this chapter, review the objectives. Based on this information, write down two or three items that you think are important to note while you are reading.

Culinary Terminology Build Vocab

sponge cake, p. 700
genoise, p. 701

Academic Terminology Build Vocab

viscous, p. 701

Objectives

After studying this chapter, you will be able to

- recognize the functions of various cake ingredients.
- classify cakes according to the mixing method used to prepare them.
- apply cake pan preparation techniques.
- explain how to bake a quality cake product.
- apply proper techniques for mixing and baking quality cakes.
- recall the process for assembling and finishing layer cakes.

Many consider cakes to be the true measure of a pastry chef's skill. Cakes are widely appreciated because of their delicate texture and sweet taste. They often serve as the focal point of important celebrations such as birthdays, weddings, and anniversaries. Before a baker or pastry chef can begin to think about the elaborate decoration and structure of such cakes, he or she must first be able to create a flavorful and properly textured cake. Producing good quality cakes is a combination of accurately scaling the right ingredients, mixing and combining them in the correct manner, and baking them under the proper conditions.

Cake Ingredients

Cake ingredients serve either to form structure or tenderize. Flour, liquid, and eggs are the sources of structure, while fat and sugar make a cake tender. A good cake recipe is an exact blending of ingredients to create a balance between structure and tenderness.

Flour

As it does in other baked products, flour gives cakes their structure. The starch in the flour absorbs moisture. During baking, the flour's proteins coagulate trapping moisture and gases.

Cake flour has the lowest protein content and highest starch content of any type of flour found in the bakeshop. Its lower gluten potential results in a more delicately textured baked good than other types of flour. The higher starch content of cake flour also absorbs more moisture than other flours.

Shortening

Shortenings such as butter, vegetable shortening, and other fats tenderize cake batter by preventing too much gluten from developing. Shortenings also add richness and—in the case of butter—flavor.

Sweeteners

Sugar and other sweeteners provide cakes with their characteristic sweet taste. Sweeteners also help to absorb liquid, helping to keep the cake moist. Additionally, sweeteners act to tenderize the cake and contribute to a golden-brown crust.

Eggs

As they bake, egg proteins coagulate and help to give a cake structure. More importantly, eggs are the main source of leavening for many cakes though some recipes also include chemical leaveners. Air beaten into eggs becomes trapped in the structure of the batter. This accounts for the light airy texture of many cakes. The incorporation of air can be accomplished with whole eggs, egg yolks, or egg whites depending on the recipe.

Liquid

Flour must be mixed with liquid to form gluten, which provides structure. The most common liquids in cake recipes are milk and water. Milk provides nutrients and more flavor than water, therefore, the two are not always interchangeable. Besides adding moisture, liquid in cake batter helps to dissolve sugar and creates steam for leavening in the baking process.

Mixing Methods

Cakes can be categorized by the method used to combine the ingredients. There are many different mixing methods for preparing a variety of cakes. The two most important are the creaming method and the sponge or foam method.

Creaming Method

The creaming method is used for "butter cakes" or those cakes with a high proportion of butter or shortening. As you learned with cookies, the creaming method starts by mixing the butter or shortening with the sugar in an electric mixer with the paddle attachment. Eggs and liquid are added next, followed by dry ingredients.

Sponge Method

Another important method for making cake batter is the sponge or foam method. Sponge cakes are leavened by air whipped into eggs in the cake formula. **Sponge cake** recipes may call for whipping whole eggs, egg whites, or whites and yolks separately. The air that is incorporated into the batter expands when the cake is baked creating a light and airy sponge-like texture. To create this texture, sponge recipes contain a high proportion of eggs to flour.

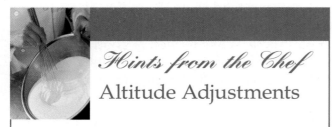

Hints from the Chef
Altitude Adjustments

When baking cakes at altitudes over 2000 feet (610 m), recipes must be adjusted to achieve the same texture as a cake baked near sea level. In general, less leavening is needed because of the lighter atmosphere at higher altitudes. A smaller amount of baking powder or soda is used in recipes that call for them. Also, eggs are whipped with less air. High altitude cakes require more structure, so the quantity of flour and eggs are often increased.

The cake recipes in this chapter are designed for lower altitudes. If you are baking in a location above 2000 feet, use recipes that have been tested in your locale or consult your local agricultural extension service for recommended adjustments.

Chapter 45 Cakes 701

Genoise (jehn WAHZ) is a classic European-type of sponge cake. It is distinct from most other sponge cakes because it contains some butter and no liquid. This recipe creates a rich and airy cake that can be made into many different forms. It can easily be cut into layers. If baked into a sheet, it can be rolled. Genoise contains less sugar than other sponge cakes so it is usually brushed with simple syrup after it is baked.

The sponge method begins with combining the egg products—whole eggs, whites, or yolks—with some or all of the sugar. The eggs and sugar are whipped at high speed to incorporate air. When preparing a genoise, the eggs and sugar are first warmed over a double boiler to help dissolve the sugar and incorporate more air.

When the egg and sugar mixture becomes more viscous, or thick, and forms ribbons as it falls from the beater, the other ingredients are incorporated. Sifted dry ingredients are folded into the egg mixture with a spatula to avoid losing any air in the mixture. Liquid or melted fat is added to the batter last. Care is taken to not overmix cake batter, 45-1. Overmixing can develop gluten or deflate the air bubbles resulting in a dense or tough cake.

Cakes made by the sponge method should be portioned into pans and baked immediately. Any delay in baking allows the air to escape from the sponge. The result is a dense and deflated cake.

Troubleshooting Cake Problems

Problem	Underwhipped eggs	Overmixed batter	Undermixed batter	Too much flour	Not enough flour	Too much sugar	Not enough sugar	Too much leavening agent	Not enough or weak leavening agent	Batter too stiff	Batter too loose	Baking temp. too high (overbaked)	Baking temp. too low (underbaked)
Lack of volume	●								●			●	
Dense texture									●				●
Coarse texture		●						●		●			
Tough		●		●		●							
Dark exterior						●						●	
Top bursts		●		●						●			
Crust too thick													●
Falls during baking					●								●
Shrinks when cooled			●								●		●

45-1 To correct problems with cake production, you must understand the reasons the problems occurred.

Copyright Goodheart-Willcox Co., Inc.

TECHNIQUE
Preparing Cake Batter: Creaming Method

1. Weigh all ingredients. Sift the flour along with any baking powder or baking soda.
2. Preheat oven and prepare cake pans.
3. Combine the butter or shortening with the sugar and any spices or flavorings in the mixer. Mix with the paddle attachment until well creamed.

4. Gradually add the eggs and any liquid. Mix until well incorporated.
5. Add the sifted flour and mix to form a smooth batter. Do not overmix.
6. Scale into prepared pans and bake immediately.

Pan Preparation

Before cake pans are filled with batter, they are often coated or lined to make the baked cake easier to remove from the pan. Not all recipes require a pan to be prepped before baking. The choice of how to prepare the pan may depend on the recipe and the preferences of the baker.

Baking

One key to proper baking is the ability to determine the doneness of a cake. The most common method for testing is to use a skewer or toothpick. When a skewer or toothpick is

TECHNIQUE
Preparing Cake Batter: Sponge Method

1. Weigh all ingredients. Sift the flour.
2. Preheat oven and prepare cake pans.
3. Combine eggs and sugar in the bowl of the mixer. For genoise, warm the eggs and sugar over a water bath until they reach 100°F (38°C).

4. Beat the eggs and sugar with the whip attachment until they are thick and ribbon-like. If using only whites, beat until the mixture reaches soft peaks.

5. Fold in the dry ingredients with a spatula.

6. Fold in any liquids or melted fats in the recipe.
7. Scale into prepared pans and bake immediately.

TECHNIQUE
Preparing a Cake Pan

1. Brush the inside of the pan with solid shortening.

2. Dust pan with a light coating of flour or sugar. Shake out excess flour or sugar.

To make the release of the cake from the pan even easier, some bakers line the bottom of the pan with a piece of parchment paper:

3. Fold a piece of parchment paper in half, then fold in half again.

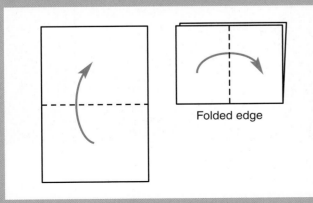

Folded edge

4. Fold parchment paper diagonally two times.

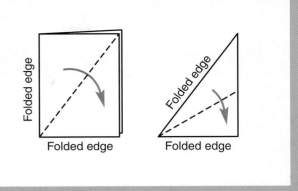

Folded edge   Folded edge   Folded edge   Folded edge

5. Position the tip of the parchment paper over the center of the cake pan. Cut the paper just inside the edge of the cake pan.

6. Open folded parchment paper and place in bottom of cake pan.

Recipe No.	Name		Category
45.3	**Basic Yellow Sponge Cake**		Cakes
Yield	**Portion Size**		**No. Portions**
2–10″ cakes	¹⁄₁₀th cake		20
US Quantity	**Metric Quantity**	**Ingredient**	**TCS**
8 oz.	225 g	cake flour	
1 tsp.	5 mL	baking powder	
10 oz.	280 g	sugar	
8 oz.	225 g	eggs	•
1 oz.	30 g	egg yolks	•
½ tsp.	3 mL	vanilla extract	
½ tsp.	3 mL	salt	
4 oz.	120 g	milk	•
2 oz.	60 g	butter	•
Method			**CCP**
1. Preheat oven to 375°F (190°C).			
2. Prepare cake pans by greasing and dusting with flour.			
3. Sift the cake flour and baking powder. Set aside.			
4. Heat the milk, salt, and butter until the butter is melted. Set aside.			
5. Combine eggs, yolks, vanilla, and sugar in the bowl of the mixer.			
6. Beat the eggs and sugar with the whip attachment until they are thick and ribbon-like.			
7. With a spatula, alternately fold in the dry ingredients and the milk.			
8. Scale into prepared pans and bake immediately for 20–25 minutes until done when tested with a skewer.			CCP

Portion (g)	Calories	Fat (g)	Protein (g)	Carbohydrate (g)	Cholesterol (mg)	Sodium (mg)	Fiber (g)
47	137.85	4.10	2.59	23.27	72.10	38.83	0.28

inserted into the center of a baked cake, it should come out clean, 45-2. However, if the skewer is coated with uncooked batter when it is removed, it means the cake has not yet fully baked. Along with a clean skewer, bakers also look for a springy feel to the cake when pressed. Another sign of doneness is when the cake pulls slightly away from the sides of the pan.

Finishing and Decorating

Once cakes are fully cooled, the process of filling and decorating can begin.

Draz-Koetke/Goodheart-Willcox Publisher

45-2 Many bakers use skewers to test cakes for doneness. Some prefer testing by touch or appearance.

Filling and Assembling Layers

Since most cakes are slightly rounded rather than level on top, a knife can be used to trim away any uneven shape. Flip the entire cake upside down before cutting layers and reassemble in this fashion once layers are cut. The top of the cake is now the smooth surface created by the bottom of the pan.

Most cakes are split into two or more layers and a filling or frosting is spread between the layers. To split the layers use a serrated knife. Keep the knife level and with a sawing motion, cut the cake horizontally into as many layers as desired.

Before filling the layers, it is common to brush the layers with simple syrup. This step creates a moist cake and adds sweetness. The syrup can be flavored with liquors or extracts for even more flavor.

The layers of cake are now ready to be filled. Place the bottom layer of the cake on a cardboard cake base that is slightly larger than the cake. The base makes the cake easier to move and decorate once it is assembled. A thin coating of filling should be placed on the bottom layer of cake, 45-3. The next layer of cake is then placed on top. Repeat this procedure with any other layers, leaving the top of the cake uncoated. The filling acts as an adhesive to hold the layers together for the next step—icing.

Chef Speak

Cake Glossary

Angel Food Cake—An airy white cake leavened with whipped egg whites and traditionally baked in a tube pan.

Baba—A yeast-raised cake that is baked in a special decorative pan or ring mold and soaked with rum syrup after baking.

Black Forest Cake—Chocolate sponge or genoise soaked with kirsch (cherry brandy) syrup. It is filled with cherries, iced with whipped cream, and decorated with shaved chocolate.

Bundt® Cake—Any variety of cake that is baked in a Bundt pan.

Carrot Cake—High shortening cake containing grated carrots in its batter. It is often iced with cream cheese frosting.

Chiffon Cake—Similar to angel food cake, but with the addition of yolks and vegetable oil.

Fruitcake—Any of a number of high fat cakes containing a large quantity of dried fruits and nuts.

Jelly Roll—A thin sheet of sponge cake spread with fruit filling and rolled into a log.

Devil's Food Cake—Rich chocolate sponge cake with chocolate buttercream.

Lady Baltimore—White cake leavened with whipped egg whites. It is filled and decorated with a white icing, dried fruits, chopped pecans, and brandy.

Lane Cake—A white cake made using the creaming method. It is split into four layers and filled with a cooked sugar icing that is mixed with raisins, cherries, pecans, coconut, and brandy.

Pineapple Upside-Down Cake—A butter cake made using the creaming method and baked in a pan lined with pineapple slices and brown sugar. After baking, the cake is inverted to display the pineapple on top.

Pound Cake—A high fat cake made using the creaming method with equal parts flour, butter, eggs, and sugar.

Red Velvet Cake—A rich chocolate cake tinted with red food color and iced with a white frosting.

Draz-Koetke/Goodheart-Willcox Publisher

45-3 Before a cake can be decorated, it is (A) cut into level, consistent size layers. The layers are (B) brushed with simple syrup and then (C) a thin coat of icing is applied.

Finishing and Decorating

After the cake layers are filled and evenly assembled, transfer the cake to a turntable. Center the cake on the turntable. Although the exterior of cakes can be decorated with many different icings and coatings, buttercream and whipped cream are most popular.

Place some icing on the center of the cake top. Spread the icing by dragging the blade of a palette knife across the cake while slowly rotating the turntable. Keep the palette knife level to create a smooth and level finish on the top of the cake. Excess icing around the edges is removed when the sides are iced. Many pastry chefs apply a very thin layer of icing over the entire cake before applying the final icing. This thin layer, called a *crumb coat*, prevents crumbs from spreading and appearing in the final icing application.

Begin to coat the sides by spreading out the excess icing from the top, 45-4. Apply

Draz-Koetke/Goodheart-Willcox Publisher

45-4 Apply icing (A) to the top of the cake first and, (B) then spread more icing on the sides.

more icing with the palette knife to coat the lower parts of the sides. Hold the knife vertically to the turntable and place it against the side of the cake. While applying light pressure and holding the knife stationary, slowly rotate the turntable and smooth out the icing on the sides. Remove any excess icing once the turntable completes one full rotation.

The sides of the cake may be left plain and smooth. Since it is often difficult to create a perfectly smooth surface on the sides, two other decorating techniques are often used. The sides may either be finished with a pastry comb or coated with crumbs and confections.

To finish the cake using the pastry comb, place the comb against the side of the cake at an angle. Apply light pressure while rotating the turntable. This technique gives the sides of the cake an appealing grooved pattern. Do not apply too much pressure with pastry comb, or the cake will show through from the icing.

Instead of the pastry comb, the sides of the cake may be decorated with crumbs, chopped nuts, shaved chocolate, or confections such as sprinkles or sanding sugar. Simply take a handful of the desired ingredient and gently press it against the icing on the sides. Let the material that does not stick to the sides fall away. Repeat this process moving around the circumference of the cake until it is evenly coated with the decoration.

Cakes are also decorated with icing piped from a pastry bag with a decorative tip. Borders of rosettes, scrolls, and shells are popular patterns when decorating with the pastry bag, 45-5.

Draz-Koetke/Goodheart-Willcox Publisher

45-5 Cakes can be decorated with (A) a pastry comb or (B) various ingredients such as chocolate sprinkles, and topped with (C) icing piped from a pastry bag. (D) Different tips and a variety of techniques can be used to create attractive patterns.

Summary Points

- Ingredients in cake recipes perform different functions. These ingredients must be in balance to create a quality cake.

- The creaming method of mixing cake batter is used for cakes with a high proportion of fat. The sponge method is used for cakes that use eggs as the leavener.

- Pans are often prepped to ensure that the finished cake is easy to remove.

- There are several ways to determine doneness of a cake.

- After cooling, cakes are often split into layers and filling is spread between the layers.

- Turntables make icing a cake easier.

- Icings are often piped with a pastry bag to create borders and designs on cakes.

In Review
Assess

1. Cake flour absorbs more moisture than other flours because of its higher _____ content.

2. What is the purpose of shortening in a cake?

3. List three ways sugar impacts the quality of a cake.

4. What is the purpose of eggs in making cakes?

5. True or false. Liquid helps to leaven a cake during the baking process.

6. The creaming method is used to mix cakes with a high proportion of _____.

7. How are sponge cakes leavened?

8. Genoise contains less sugar than other sponge cakes so it is usually brushed with _____ _____ after it is baked.

9. Describe the egg and sugar mixture of a genoise when it is ready to have the other ingredients added.

10. True or false. Sponge cakes should be baked immediately to prevent air from escaping the sponge.

11. In what ways can cake pans be prepped before adding batter?
    A. No prep at all.
    B. Brush pan with solid shortening.
    C. Brush pan with solid shortening and dust with flour or sugar.
    D. Line the bottom with parchment paper.
    E. All of the above.

12. Name three ways to test a cake for doneness.

13. List four tools and utensils that might be used to ice and decorate a cake.

Core Skills

14. **Math.** How many 3″ × 3″ pieces of cake does a full sheet pan (18″ × 24″) yield?

15. **Speaking and Listening.** With a teammate, demonstrate how to prepare a cake using the *Creaming Method*. Use a recipe of your choice or obtain one from your instructor. Prepare the script for your demonstration and gather the ingredients you need. Use the text technique instructions and the recipe as your guide. What will you say as you prepare the cake? Give your demonstration to the class. As one person mixes the cake, the other should prepare the pan(s). As an alternative, use a school-approved web-based application to create a movie of your demonstration to post to the class website.

16. **Reading.** Use Internet and print resources to read about the history of *cake*. Did cake exist in ancient times? How have cakes varied throughout history? How have ingredients changed? What did it mean to be honored with a cake? Use presentation software to create an illustrated digital report of your findings to share with the class.

17. **Speaking and Listening.** In teams, prepare the text recipe for *Basic Yellow Sponge Cake* using the *Sponge Method* of mixing. Assign tasks to each team member to prepare and bake the cake. Check the cake for doneness. Once cooled, teams should evaluate their cakes for appropriate appearance, flavor, and texture. Discuss differences among the teams' cakes. If any problems exist with

the cakes, discuss what should be done to rectify the problems.

18. **Math.** The *Basic Yellow Sponge Cake* recipe in this chapter makes two 10-inch cakes that yield 20 portions. You need to prepare three 10-inch cakes that yield 30 portions for a school banquet. Change the yield of the recipe and determine the new ingredient amounts needed to prepare 30 portions. (Use the following formulas for your calculations: *new yield ÷ old yield = conversion factor* and *old quantity × conversion factor = new quantity*.)

19. **CTE Career Readiness Practice.** Suppose you work in a bakeshop that specializes in various types of cake in all different shapes and sizes. You notice that there is a large amount of scrap waste from trimming the cakes before icing and finishing. You mention this to your supervisor who then asks you to come up with a creative way to use the scraps to eliminate waste and increase profitability. To develop a creative and innovative plan, use the following process.
    A. Analyze the problem.
    B. Apply past learning and brainstorm possible options.
    C. Gather new information for solving the problem.
    D. Organize your information and compare all the options.
    E. Choose one or two options for solving the problem
    F. Present the actions necessary to solve the problem.

    After working through the problem-solving process, write a proposal for your supervisor regarding your creative ideas for using the waste cake scraps.

Critical Thinking

20. **Create.** Use your creativity to describe four different finished cakes you could make using chocolate sponge batter. Your description should include the various pans, fillings, icings, and decorating techniques you would use to create each cake. Give an illustrated report showing your creative ideas.

21. **Analyze cause and effect.** Your pastry chef just finishes scaling his sponge cake batter into the cake pans when he slips and falls. After taking care of the pastry chef, you return to the bakeshop and place the cakes in the oven. The finished cakes are dense and tough. Analyze why.

22. **Problem solve.** Your younger brother enjoys baking and decorating layer cakes but complains that the top layers slide off or the cakes tilt to one side. What advice would you give him to correct this problem?

Technology

Tour a bakeshop or use the Internet to research the way pastry chefs create edible photos or messages on cakes. What technology is involved in producing edible photos? What ingredients make this possible? Use presentation software to create an illustrated report for the class. As an alternative, use a school-approved web-based application to create a digital poster of your findings to place on the class web page or blog.

Teamwork

Working in teams of two, prepare a cake recipe of your choice, fill and assemble the layers, and ice and decorate the cake. Half the teams should use the *Creaming Method* and the other half should use *Sponge Method*. Evaluate the finished cakes for appearance, texture, and flavor. Take this teamwork activity to the next level and invite several pastry chefs to class to evaluate the finished cakes and determine which team(s) prepared the best cakes.

Chef's E-portfolio
Creative Cakes

Upload your illustrated report from Critical Thinking activity #20 to your e-portfolio. Ask your instructor where to save your file. This could be on the school's network or a flash drive of your own. Name your portfolio document *FirstnameLastname_ Portfolio Ch#.docx* (i.e., JohnSmith_PortfolioCh45.docx).

While studying, look for the activity icon to:

- Build vocabulary with e-flash cards and matching activities.
- Expand learning with video clips, photo identification activities, animations, and interactive activities.
- Review and assess what you learn by completing end-of-chapter questions.

Custards, Foams, and Buttercreams

Reading Prep

In preparation for reading the chapter, visit or find a pastry shop online and obtain a copy of the menu. Read the menu descriptions and identify the use of the preparations discussed in this chapter.

Culinary Terminology Build Vocab

pastry cream, p. 711
tempering, p. 711
crème mousseline, p. 713
crème anglaise, p. 713
crème chantilly, p. 716
meringue, p. 716
mousse, p. 718
Bavarian cream, p. 718

Academic Terminology Build Vocab

infuse, p. 713

Objectives

After studying this chapter, you will be able to

- recognize the different forms of custards and their uses in the pastry kitchen.
- prepare a variety of foams used in dessert preparations.
- compare the two types of buttercream.

A study of baking and pastry would not be complete without an introduction to custards, foams, and buttercreams. Custards and foams are both used for making a wide array of desserts. Buttercream is used to ice cakes. Without custards, foams, and buttercreams, many popular desserts would not exist. Simply put, an aspiring pastry chef must be proficient at making different custards, foams, and buttercreams.

Custards

Custards come in many different forms and have very different applications in the pastry kitchen. These preparations are thickened with egg products and sometimes starch. Some custards are prepared on the stovetop while others are cooked in the oven.

Stirred Custards

Custards that are prepared on the stovetop are often categorized as stirred custards. Pastry cream and crème anglaise are both prepared on the stovetop.

Pastry Cream While pastry cream may sound unfamiliar, it is always recognizable by its more common name—custard. **Pastry cream** consists of milk that is thickened with starch and egg yolks, and sweetened with sugar. Egg yolks are first mixed with a small amount of hot milk before incorporating into the remaining ingredients to gently raise the temperature of the egg yolks and prevent curdling. This is called **tempering**. Pastry

TECHNIQUE
Preparing Pastry Cream

1. Whip egg yolks and sugar until the sugar is dissolved. During this step, the mixture becomes pale yellow and thickens. Flavorings, such as vanilla extract, are often added to this mixture.

2. Add flour and/or cornstarch to the egg yolk and sugar mixture. The mixture is whipped briefly to incorporate the flour or cornstarch.

3. Boil milk in a thick-bottomed nonaluminum saucepan. Flavorings, such as vanilla bean, are sometimes added to the milk.

4. Add half of the milk to the egg yolk mixture while stirring constantly with a whisk.

5. Pour the milk and egg yolk mixture back into the remaining milk in the saucepan. Stir until incorporated.

6. Place the saucepan over medium heat and stir continuously using a whisk. Be sure to scrape the bottom of the pot with the whisk to ensure that the custard does not stick to the bottom and burn.

7. Once the pastry cream has come to a full boil, reduce heat and simmer for 1–2 additional minutes. It is important that the pastry cream comes to a full boil so the starch thickens completely. If the pastry cream is not cooked enough, it will not thicken enough and taste starchy.

8. Remove the pan from the heat. Stir in butter until it melts.

9. Pour the pastry cream into a shallow container. Place plastic wrap directly on top of the pastry cream. This plastic wrap prevents a skin from forming. Chill on ice or in a blast chiller in accordance with local health department guidelines. Store the chilled pastry cream in the cooler until needed.

cream is also commonly referred to by its French name *crème pâtissière* (KREHM pah tis EEYHR).

Pastry cream is considered a potentially hazardous food. If improperly handled, it can become a breeding ground for pathogens. As a result, all dessert preparations containing pastry cream have a short shelf life and must be refrigerated until needed.

Pastry cream is a versatile preparation. It is generally flavored with vanilla, but can have many other flavors as well. For instance, spices can be **infused**, or introduced, into the milk before the tempering process. Once the pastry cream is cooked, chocolate can be melted into it. A splash of an extract or liqueur added to the chilled pastry cream will also change the flavor profile of the pastry cream. The addition of whipped cream creates a very light pastry cream that is called a **crème mousseline** (moo seh LEEN), 46-1.

Crème Anglaise While pastry cream has the texture of thick pudding, **crème anglaise** (KREHM ahn GLAYZ) has the texture of a sauce and is classified as a custard sauce. Aside from being used as a sauce, it is the base of important preparations such as Bavarian cream and many ice creams.

Draz-Koetke/Goodheart-Willcox Publisher

46-1 Folding whipped cream into a cold pastry cream produces a crème mousseline.

Crème anglaise is thickened solely by egg yolks, therefore it is a bit tricky to make and requires some practice. Unlike pastry cream which must be boiled to thicken the starch, crème anglaise cannot be boiled. When preparing crème anglaise, the temperature should not rise above 185°F (85°C). If it gets too hot, the egg yolks curdle and the sauce separates and becomes unusable. The starch in pastry creams prevents curdling during boiling. However, if crème anglaise does not get hot enough, the yolks do not thicken properly and the finished product is thin and watery.

When preparing crème anglaise, professional pastry chefs know the product is done when it is thick enough to coat the back of a spatula or wooden spoon. The other method to determine doneness is to monitor the temperature of the sauce. Once it reaches between 180°F and 185°F (82°C and 85°C), it is done. At this point, the sauce must be immediately removed from the heat and strained. If the sauce is not removed from the pan, the heat of the pan can be enough to raise the temperature of the custard a few

Hints from the Chef
Pudding

Pudding is a common dessert in America. Pudding uses a mixture of egg yolks and starch to thicken milk much like pastry cream does. The difference is that generally puddings use far less egg yolk and are thickened with a greater amount of starch. Cornstarch is the most common starch, although tapioca—a starch derived from the root of the manioc plant—is used to make tapioca pudding.

TECHNIQUE
Preparing Crème Anglaise

1. Combine egg yolks and sugar, and whip until the sugar is dissolved. During this step, the mixture becomes pale yellow and thickens. Flavorings, such as vanilla extract, are often added to this mixture.

2. Bring milk to a boil in a thick-bottomed, nonaluminum saucepan. Flavorings, such as vanilla beans, can be added to the milk.

3. Pour half of the milk into the egg yolk mixture while stirring constantly with a whisk.

4. Pour the milk and egg yolk mixture back into the remaining milk in the saucepan. Stir until incorporated.

5. Place the saucepan over medium heat and stir continuously using a heat-proof spatula or wooden spoon. Be sure to scrape the bottom of the pot with each stir.

6. Heat the crème anglaise just until it is thick enough to coat the back of the spatula or spoon, or until it reaches 180°F–185°F (82°C–85°C).

7. Immediately remove from heat and strain through a chinois. Chill on ice until completely cold and refrigerate until needed.

more degrees and cause the crème anglaise to separate.

Like pastry cream, crème anglaise is highly perishable. For this reason, it must be cooled immediately in ice water. Once cold, it must always be kept refrigerated and used within a couple days of preparation.

Baked Custard

Another common form of custard is baked custard. Baked custard is different from pastry cream and crème anglaise because it is cooked in the oven, not on the stove. Like crème anglaise, cooking a baked custard can be tricky as it must be cooked just to the point where it sets up or solidifies and no further. Baked custards start by combining eggs and dairy. The eggs can be either whole eggs or yolks. Using only yolks will produce a richer custard. The dairy product can be anything from milk to heavy cream depending on the desired richness of the final product. For instance, crème brûlée is a very rich custard made from egg yolks and a combination of half-and-half and heavy cream. To help moderate the cooking process, baked custards are cooked in dishes that are placed in a bain marie in the oven, 46-2.

Foams

Foams are created by incorporating large amounts of air bubbles usually into cream or egg whites. The trapped air creates a light, airy foam. These foams provide the base for well-known dessert preparations such as whipped topping, meringue, mousse, and Bavarian cream.

Whipped Cream

Whipped cream is one of the pillars of pastry. It is served on ice cream, spread on cakes, dolloped on shortbread, piped into éclairs, and added to many dessert preparations. Whipped cream is a foam that is made light by the incorporation of many tiny air bubbles.

Draz-Koetke/Goodheart-Willcox Publisher

46-2 Cups of custard are placed in a pan of water for baking to moderate the cooking process.

Draz-Koetke/Goodheart-Willcox Publisher

46-3 Whipping cream over a bowl of ice helps keep the cream cold in a hot kitchen.

Preferably, whipped cream is made from heavy cream with a minimum butterfat content of 36 percent. Without an elevated butterfat level, the cream is not able to hold the air for any appreciable length of time. To make whipped cream, the cream is simply beaten at high speed with a wire whisk. As the cream is whipped, more air bubbles become trapped in the cream. The cream thickens and gains volume.

One important rule when making whipped cream is that the cream must remain cold. If the cream warms even slightly, it will not hold the air bubbles. Whipping warm cream will eventually cause the cream to separate into solid fat particles and a watery liquid. At this point, the cream is unusable. To ensure the cream remains cold in a hot kitchen, use a chilled bowl and place the bowl of cream on ice during the whipping process, 46-3. It is also important to keep the whipped cream cold after it is made. Heat causes whipped cream to soften and eventually separate. Thus, desserts made with whipped cream must be held in the refrigerator until needed.

Knowing when to stop whipping the cream is an important consideration. Overwhipping the cream destroys the whipped cream. As the whipped cream is beaten, it becomes firmer and firmer. Most whipped cream is used between the soft and firm peak stages. Soft and firm peaks refer to the shape of the cream when the whisk is drawn from the bowl of whipped cream, 46-4. Whisking beyond firm peak causes the cream to separate.

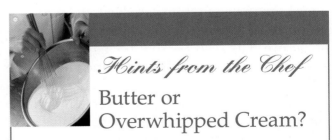

Hints from the Chef

Butter or Overwhipped Cream?

There is a name for overwhipped cream—butter. Making butter involves churning or beating cream until it separates into fat particles and buttermilk. If you overwhip cream or whip warm cream, essentially you are making butter.

Draz-Koetke/Goodheart-Willcox Publisher

46-4 Lift the whisk out of the whipped cream to judge if it is at (A) soft peak stage or (B) firm peak stage.

Whipped cream can be flavored in many different ways. For pastries, whipped cream is generally sweetened. Sugar is whisked into the cream when the whipped cream reaches soft peak stage. The classical name for sweetened whipped cream is **crème chantilly** (KREHM shahn tee YEE). In addition to sugar, other ingredients such as cocoa powder, liqueurs, and vanilla extract can be added. When adding any ingredient, whisk the cream just long enough to incorporate the ingredients. Overmixing can deflate the cream.

Meringue

Yet another foam, **meringue** (mehr AYNG), is made by beating egg whites with sugar. As the egg whites are beaten, large amounts of air are trapped in its protein structure. The result is that the egg white's volume increases substantially and the developing foam becomes increasingly firmer.

As with whipped cream, overwhipping destroys a meringue. As egg whites are whipped, they develop soft and then firm peaks. If egg whites are whipped beyond firm peak, they begin to break down. Overwhipped eggs look curdled and lose volume. Egg whites are also negatively affected by fat. If there is even a small amount of egg yolk in the egg

whites or fat on the bowl or whisk, the egg whites will not whip properly. Fat prevents the egg whites from gaining the necessary volume. Egg whites should be at room temperature to assist the whipping process.

Meringue is used in a variety of bakeshop preparations. Meringue can be used to top pies, add volume to soufflés, and lighten mousses or icings. When baked, it may function as a tart shell, layers in a cake, or simply eaten out of hand as a cookie, 46-5. The addition of ingredients such as nuts, chocolate, or flavorings to meringue develops its versatility and flavor even further.

Even if properly made, meringue is an unstable foam. If it is not cooked in some manner, the foam loses volume and eventually breaks down completely. There are three types of meringue—French, Swiss, and Italian. All three combine egg whites and sugar; but differ in how heat is applied to the meringue.

French Meringue French, or common, meringue is the most basic meringue. Egg whites are whipped until they have soft peaks. At this stage, some of the sugar is added to the whites. They are then whipped until they reach firm peaks. At this point, the rest of the sugar is folded into the meringue. Superfine sugar should be used in meringues because it dissolves quickly.

Recipe No.	Name		Category
46.4	French Meringue		Creams and Foams
Yield	**Portion Size**		**No. Portions**
1 qt. (0.95 L)	½ c. (120 mL)		8
US Quantity	**Metric Quantity**	**Ingredient**	**TCS**
4 oz.	115 g	egg whites (about 4 lg. whites)	•
9 oz.	255 g	sugar (preferably superfine)	
Method			**CCP**
1. Place egg whites in a stainless steel bowl. Verify there is no fat on the equipment and there is no egg yolk in the egg whites.			
2. Using the whip attachment on an electric mixer, whip the whites on high speed until soft peak.			
3. With the mixer running, add ⅓ of the sugar. Continue mixing at high speed until firm peak.			
4. Fold remaining sugar into the meringue using a spatula.			
5. Pipe meringue onto a parchment paper lined sheet tray. Bake at 200°F (93°C) until the meringues are completely dried and delicately crunchy. Once cool, store in an airtight container to prevent humidity from ruining meringue.			CCP

Portion (g)	Calories	Fat (g)	Protein (g)	Carbohydrate (g)	Cholesterol (mg)	Sodium (mg)	Fiber (g)
49	132	0.03	1.82	32.01	0	27.72	0

HLPhoto/Shutterstock.com

46-5 Baked meringue makes light, elegant tart shells.

French meringue needs to be baked to keep it from breaking down. Generally, it is piped into various shapes and then baked at very low oven temperatures, 46-6. Pastry chefs often refer to this low temperature baking as *drying*. Low oven temperatures ensure that the final product is white and not a shade of brown. Baked French meringue should be very light and brittle.

Swiss Meringue   Swiss meringue starts by combining the egg whites and all the sugar. This mixture is then mixed over boiling water until it reaches 100°F (38°C). It is then removed from the heat and whipped until it reaches firm peaks.

Swiss meringue is slightly heavier and more stable than French meringue. It is piped into shapes and baked at low temperatures as with French meringue.

Italian Meringue   Italian meringue preparation begins by preparing a hot sugar and water syrup. This hot syrup is slowly

46-6 Meringue is often piped into shapes that are baked at low temperatures until dried and crunchy.

poured onto the egg whites as they are beaten at high speeds using an electric mixer. The meringue is beaten until it is glossy, thick, and light.

The hot syrup cooks the egg whites. This makes the foam stable and heavier than either French or Swiss meringue. Italian meringue is often added to other pastry preparations

since it will not break down. It is also safe to consume without further cooking since the egg whites are cooked by the syrup.

Mousse and Bavarian Cream

Mousse (MOOS) and Bavarian cream are two dessert preparations that are served in many fine-dining restaurants. A **mousse** is a stable foam dessert that is solidified by fat or gelatin and lightened with whipped cream and sometimes Italian meringue. A well-made mousse should be light and airy. In fact, the word mousse is a French word that means "foam." A **Bavarian cream** is another stable foam dessert made from liquid custard sauce (crème anglaise) that is bound with gelatin and lightened with whipped cream.

There are many different flavors of mousses and Bavarian creams. Mousses and Bavarian creams can be served on their own either molded or scooped. However, mousses and Bavarian creams are often combined with other ingredients such as slices of cake and pieces of cooked fruit to make complex desserts, 46-7.

46-7 Mousses and Bavarian creams can be served in a molded shape or served scooped from a bowl.

TECHNIQUE
Preparing Mousses

Fruit-Based Mousse

1. Dissolve or melt bloomed gelatin in a small amount of fruit purée or other liquid using the tempering method. At this point, the gelatin is very concentrated. If it is not thoroughly and quickly stirred into the fruit purée, small hard balls of gelatin may form. This is a problem for two reasons—the gelatin balls are unpleasant to eat and no longer available to thicken the fruit purée.

2. Whisking constantly, add the fruit purée and gelatin mixture back into the remainder of the fruit purée.

3. Fold whipped cream into the fruit purée and gelatin mixture. Some chefs also add Italian meringue. Fold whipped cream into mixture gently while rotating the bowl. This folding technique keeps the whipped cream from deflating. Overmixing or mixing too energetically causes the whipped cream to deflate and results in a heavy mousse.

4. Once the mousse mixture is assembled, ladle it into containers. Refrigerate mousse for 12 hours before serving. In the refrigerator, the mousse sets up as the gelatin hardens.

5. Refrigerate mousse until service.

Chocolate Mousse

1. Melt chocolate in a bain marie.

2. Fold whipped cream and perhaps some Italian meringue into the melted chocolate. Fold the whipped cream into the melted chocolate quickly so that the cold whipped cream does not cause the melted chocolate to solidify into hard pieces. This would result in a poor mousse that is not smooth and silky. It should be noted that there is no gelatin in this recipe—the fat in the chocolate is sufficient to cause the mousse to set up.

3. Place chocolate mousse in the appropriate molds and refrigerate for 6 hours. Chocolate mousse sets up faster than gelatin-based fruit mousse.

4. Refrigerate mousse until served.

There are many different ways to prepare chocolate mousse. This is one of the easiest methods. Recipes containing raw whipped egg whites should not be prepared for food safety reasons.

TECHNIQUE
Preparing Bavarian Cream

1. Prepare a crème anglaise according to the instructions in this chapter.
2. Stir bloomed or softened gelatin into the hot crème anglaise until dissolved.
3. Chill the gelatin and crème anglaise mixture in an ice bath. Stir mixture often with a spatula so it does not solidify on the bottom of the bowl.
4. Fold in the whipped cream once the gelatin and crème anglaise mixture is cold but still liquid.
5. Pour the Bavarian cream into molds and refrigerate for at least 12 hours. During this time, the gelatin solidifies and sets up the Bavarian cream. Bavarian creams must be refrigerated until served

SCIENCE & TECHNOLOGY

When Gelatin Will Not Gel

Fresh fruits such as pineapple, papaya, and kiwi each contain an enzyme that dissolves gelatin. The enzyme in pineapple is *bromelin*, papaya's enzyme is *papain*, and kiwi contains an enzyme called *actinidin*. If gelatin is added to the purée of one of these fruits, the mousse will not set up. The solution is to first cook these purées. Heat destroys the enzymes in the fruits.

Buttercreams

In addition to custards and foams, pastry chefs must master buttercream preparation and use. Buttercreams are most often used as fillings between cake layers and frostings on the outside of cakes, 46-8. Unlike whipped cream and meringue, buttercream is very

Draz-Koetke/Goodheart-Willcox Publisher

46-8 Buttercream is used to frost cakes.

TECHNIQUE
Preparing Buttercreams

American Buttercream

1. Beat softened butter using an electric mixer fitted with a paddle attachment. Set mixer at a fairly high speed.
2. Once the butter is very soft, add powdered sugar a little at a time. If necessary, lower the mixer speed so powdered sugar does not splash out of the bowl. Flavoring is added along with the powdered sugar.

3. Once the buttercream is homogenous, it is ready to be used. Store buttercream in the refrigerator if it is not going to be used immediately.

French Buttercream

1. Prepare a syrup by boiling sugar and water.
2. Place egg yolks in the bowl of an electric mixer.
3. Run the mixer on high speed with the whisk attachment. Slowly pour the hot syrup on the egg yolks as the mixer is running. The hot syrup cooks the egg yolks, which become light and fluffy. Allow the mixer to continue on high speed until the egg yolk mixture is cool.

4. Turn the mixer speed to medium. Add softened butter a small amount at a time. If the butter is added too fast, the butter is too cold, or the egg mixture is too hot, the buttercream can separate. Add flavorings.
5. Once the buttercream is homogenous, it is ready to be used. Store buttercream in the refrigerator if it is not going to be used immediately.

stable. Unlike mousses and Bavarian creams, buttercream is not extremely sensitive to heat. Two common types of buttercream are American and French. Both American and French buttercreams can be flavored in many different ways with the addition of extracts or melted chocolate.

American buttercream, also known as *simple buttercream*, consists of softened butter and a large amount of powdered sugar. It is very sweet and stable even in hot conditions because of the large amount of sugar. American buttercream is also easy to prepare and therefore many pastry shops prefer to make it. Often, it is simply referred to as *frosting*.

French buttercream is more complicated to make, and richer and less sweet then American buttercream. In hot environments, it is less stable than American buttercream because of its higher fat content.

Summary Points

- Stirred custards, such as pastry cream and crème anglaise, are cooked on the stovetop and baked custards are cooked in the oven.

- Foams add volume and lightness to various desserts. Overwhipping destroys most foams.

- Meringue is a foam prepared by beating egg whites with sugar.

- Mousses are lightened by whipped cream and thickened by either gelatin or fat.

- Buttercreams are often used to spread between cake layers and to frost cakes.

In Review
Assess

1. Why is it essential for pastry cream to reach a full boil before it is removed from the heat?

2. Name two ways to flavor pastry cream.

3. Crème mousseline is pastry cream with the addition of _____ _____.

4. True or false. Crème anglaise is thickened with starch.

5. Why would a chef use only the egg yolks when creating baked custard?

6. List two reasons why whipped cream breaks down and separates into fat particles and a watery liquid.

7. Even a small amount of _____ coming in contact with egg whites during whipping will prevent the whites from gaining the necessary volume.

8. Why are French and Swiss meringues baked at very low temperatures?

9. What is the role of fat or gelatin in a mousse mixture?

10. How is a Bavarian cream different from a fruit-based mousse?

11. True or false. In hot environments, American buttercream is more stable than French buttercream.

12. List the two basic ingredients in American buttercream.

Core Skills

13. **Math.** Heavy cream doubles in volume when it is whipped. You need to prepare enough whipped cream to serve 48 guests a dessert topped with a ¼-cup portion of whipped cream. How much heavy cream will you need?

14. **Writing.** Conduct a search of the Internet for custards used in the pastry kitchen. Review several websites (especially those of professional chefs) for their creative use of different forms of custards. How do their custard techniques reflect the techniques in this text? Write a summary of your findings.

15. **Speaking and Listening.** In teams, prepare the chapter recipe for *French Meringue*. Once the meringues are completely dried and cooled, evaluate them for proper appearance, flavor, and texture. Remember, properly prepared French meringues should be white in appearance, have good flavor, and a light, airy texture. Discuss any differences in the teams' meringues, ways to ensure a quality product, and ways you might use them in desserts.

16. **Math.** Suppose your culinary class needs to prepare 164 portions of French meringue for a dessert for an upcoming school banquet. Change the yield of the text recipe for *French Meringue* to produce the needed portions. (*Use the following formulas*: new yield ÷ old yield = conversion factor; old quantity × conversion factor = new quantity.)

17. **CTE Career Readiness Practice.** Presume that you are the chef de cuisine at a fine-dining restaurant. Your new pastry chef is very creative and does fine work with other types of products, however, she is routinely producing curdled pastry creams and lumpy, unappealing mousses. What step in the preparation is she forgetting? How can you encourage her to produce a quality product? With a teammate, role-play your conversation with the pastry chef.

Critical Thinking

18. **Make inferences.** Bakeries often have refrigerated cases that contain items such as custard-filled donuts or éclairs. Why do these pastries need to be refrigerated while most other pastries are held at room temperature?

19. **Evaluate.** You have a recipe for a mousse that you would like to make. In reviewing the recipe, you note that it calls for meringue. Discuss with the class which of the three types of meringue you would use and why.

20. **Analyze criteria.** You need to prepare a wedding cake that will be served outside. There is a good chance that it will be a hot day. Should you coat the cake in French or American buttercream? Why?

Technology

Use Internet or print professional culinary resources to further investigate uses for the custards, foams, and buttercreams discussed in this chapter. Locate recipes for various bake-shop and dessert items in which these products are used. Add them to your digital recipe collection (remembering to credit the source of the recipes). Use presentation software and digital images to give a report of your findings to the class.

Teamwork

In teams, prepare a mousse following text guidelines. Take photos of your preparation at different stages as you work. Choose your own recipe or obtain one from your instructor. Refrigerate mousse until the next lab. Evaluate each team's mousse preparation for quality appearance, flavor, and texture. Record any differences in final products. Discuss explanations for any differences in the results.

Chef's E-portfolio
Mousse Preparation

Upload the recipe and images from the Teamwork activity to your e-portfolio. Ask your instructor where to save your file. This could be on the school's network or a flash drive of your own. Name your portfolio document *FirstnameLastname_Portfolio Ch#.docx* (i.e., JohnSmith_PortfolioCh46.docx).

While studying, look for the activity icon ↗ to:
- Build vocabulary with e-flash cards and matching activities.
- Expand learning with video clips, photo identification activities, animations, and interactive activities.
- Review and assess what you learn by completing end-of-chapter questions.

G-WLEARNING.com

RJ Grant/Shutterstock.com

Dessert Sauces and Frozen Desserts 47

Reading Prep

Skim the review questions at the end of the chapter first. Use them to help you focus on the most important concepts as you read the chapter.

Culinary Terminology Build Vocab

ganache, p. 726
caramel, p. 727
coulis, p. 728
overrun, p. 730
sorbet, p. 730
densimeter, p. 732
granité, p. 732
sherbet, p. 732

Academic Terminology Build Vocab

notable, p. 726

Objectives

After studying this chapter, you will be able to

- execute techniques to prepare common dessert sauces.
- explain the preparation of ice cream, sorbet, granité, sherbet, and other common frozen desserts.

It may seem odd to place dessert sauces and frozen desserts in the same chapter. After all, dessert sauces are served alongside desserts while frozen desserts are often scooped into bowls and cones. So what is the connection? The answer is that frozen desserts are largely made from dessert sauces. Therefore, if you learn how to prepare basic dessert sauces, you will know the first step in preparing frozen desserts.

Dessert Sauces

Savory sauces contribute flavor and moisture to a dish. Similarly, dessert sauces contribute flavor and moisture to a particular dessert. However, unlike many savory sauces, dessert sauces have a particular ability to improve the appearance of a dessert. This is true because dessert sauces come in a wide variety of vibrant colors. These sauces are used to create exciting plated dessert presentations.

Crème Anglaise

Crème anglaise is the thinnest of all custards. It is also considered a classic dessert sauce because of its pourable consistency. It

Chef Speak

Sabayon

Sabayon (sah bay OWN), known in Italy as *zabaglione* (zah bahg lee OHNAY), resembles the beginning steps of hollandaise sauce. To make sabayon, egg yolks, wine, and sugar are whipped over boiling water until hot and very fluffy. The sauce can be served hot or cold. It is often served with fresh strawberries and cookies.

can be flavored in many different ways by infusing flavors into the milk such as vanilla beans, spices, tea, or coffee. It can also be varied by adding other ingredients such as chocolate to the finished custard.

Crème anglaise is also versatile as an ingredient. It is used to make not only Bavarian cream, but also serves as the base for many ice creams.

Chocolate Sauce

Chocolate sauce is a very popular dessert sauce. There are many different types of chocolate sauce. Some are served hot and others are served cold. Some, such as hot fudge, are thick and solidify when poured onto a cold surface such as ice cream. There are two methods for making chocolate sauce.

One **notable**, or well-known, chocolate sauce is ganache (gah NAHSH). **Ganache** is a mixture of chopped chocolate and boiling hot heavy cream. Once a ganache has cooled, it can be used in many pastry specialties such as chocolate truffles, cake coverings, and cake fillings. This sauce is prepared using the Method Two technique.

Chocolate sauce can be flavored in a number of different ways. Adding ingredients such as vanilla extract, strong coffee, coconut, and chopped nuts changes the character of the finished sauce.

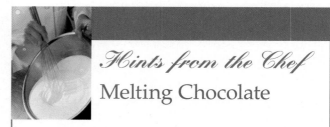

Hints from the Chef
Melting Chocolate

When melting chocolate, remember that chocolate burns easily. The safest way to melt chocolate is in a double boiler. This prevents the chocolate from heating above the boiling point of water. When a double boiler is unavailable, simply place a bowl of chocolate on top of a pot of boiling water. Be careful that no water comes in contact with the chocolate. A small amount of water added to melted chocolate will cause the chocolate to turn into a stiff mass. Never try to melt chocolate directly on a stove.

TECHNIQUE
Preparing Chocolate Sauce

Method One—Melted Chocolate and Hot Liquid

1. Melt chocolate in a bain marie.
2. Heat liquid to be added. The liquid may be water, sugar and water syrup, milk, cream, butter, or evaporated milk.
3. Stir the liquid into the melted chocolate until desired consistency is reached.

Method Two—Hot Liquid and Chopped Chocolate (Ganache Technique)

1. Bring the liquid (water, milk, or cream) to a boil.
2. Add chopped chocolate and remove from heat.
3. Stir until the chocolate has melted and the sauce is homogenous.

Caramel Sauce

Caramel sauce begins with the preparation of caramel. **Caramel** is sugar that is cooked to about 320°F (160°C), at which time it turns varying shades of brown and develops a rich flavor. To make caramel, place sugar and water in a saucepan over medium heat. Cook until the water evaporates and the sugar turns light brown. Avoid the temptation to stir the sugar as it cooks or after it has melted. If the caramel browns irregularly, gently swirl the pan over the heat.

Making caramel is only the first step in preparing caramel sauce. If the caramel were left to cool, it would become hard and brittle. A liquid must be added to the caramel to thin it out. This liquid is most often hot cream, but

could also be hot water or other hot liquids. The cream must be added to the caramel as soon as the caramel reaches the desired color. Waiting even a few extra seconds may cause the temperature of the caramel to rise further, which can cause the caramel to turn black. If this happens, the caramel becomes bitter and unusable.

When adding liquid to the caramel, two precautions need to be followed. First, be sure that your hand is not placed above the caramel, but rather off to the side of the pan when adding the cream. When the liquid is added to the very hot caramel, generous amounts of steam are produced and can result in serious burns. The second precaution is to add the liquid slowly to the caramel, 47-1. If the liquid is added too quickly, the

Recipe No.	Name			Category
47.2	Caramel Sauce			Dessert sauce
Yield	**Portion Size**			**No. Portions**
1 pt. (480 mL)	1 fl. oz. (30 mL)			16
US Quantity	**Metric Quantity**	**Ingredient**		**TCS**
7 oz.	200 g	sugar		
4 oz.	120 g	water		
8 oz.	240 g	cream		•
Method				**CCP**
1. In a saucepan, bring the cream to a boil. Remove from heat and keep warm until needed.				
2. In a saucepan, combine sugar and water. Bring to a boil over high heat. Continue cooking until the sugar turns medium brown. Do not stir the syrup while making caramel. If the syrup is browning unevenly, swirl the pan gently. *Be very careful when working with caramel because it is very hot and can cause serious burns.*				
3. As soon as the caramel turns medium brown, remove from heat and add the hot cream. Add the cream slowly as the sauce will start to boil furiously. If too much cream is added too quickly, the sauce can easily boil over. *Be careful when adding cream because the steam can cause serious burns.*				
4. Once all the cream is added to the sauce, bring the sauce to a boil to ensure the sauce is homogenous.				
5. The sauce can be served at room temperature or chilled. If the sauce becomes too thick, thin it with a small amount of water or cream.				

Portion (g)	Calories	Fat (g)	Protein (g)	Carbohydrate (g)	Cholesterol (mg)	Sodium (mg)	Fiber (g)
27	97	5.24	0.29	12.89	19.42	5.39	0

Draz-Koetke/Goodheart-Willcox Publisher

47-1 Adding hot cream to caramel produces intense boiling and steam.

caramel sauce can boil over onto the stove. Once the cream is added, stir the sauce to be sure the cream and caramel have dissolved. If portions of the caramel form lumps and do not dissolve, bring the sauce to a boil over medium heat. Stir until the sauce is smooth.

Fruit Sauces

Fruit sauces are as diverse as the fruits used to make them. They are also the easiest sauces to make. Some of the most popular fruit sauces include raspberry, mango, and apricot.

Fruit sauces are most often a mixture of puréed fruit, simple syrup, and, if necessary, lemon juice. Such fruit sauces are often referred to as a **coulis** (koo LEE). The quality of the coulis depends on the quality of the fruit. If perfectly ripe seasonal fruit is used, the quality of the coulis will be excellent. If the quality of the fresh fruit is poor, the coulis will lack the full flavor of ripe fruit. In such cases, frozen fruit purées should be substituted for fresh fruit.

Most coulis begin by blending fruit in a blender or food processor, 47-2. Some fruits, such as peaches and pears, should be cooked before blending. If these fruits are not first cooked, they will turn brown. The fruit purées are strained to remove seeds or any unblended pieces of fruit. After straining, simple syrup is added to taste. Often a small amount of lemon juice is added to the coulis to balance the sweetness and improve flavor. If the coulis is too thick, water or an appropriate fruit juice is generally added to adjust the consistency. Pastry chefs sometimes add other flavors to a coulis such as ginger, citrus, spirits, or a variety of spices.

Frozen Desserts

Frozen desserts are some of the most popular desserts. Frozen desserts are served

Draz-Koetke/Goodheart-Willcox Publisher

47-2 When using a blender, always start on low speed and secure the lid with your hand.

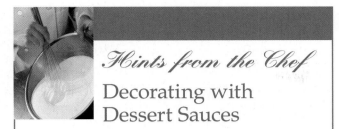

at all levels of foodservice. For instance, ice cream is served by vendors in the park, on top of a slice of apple pie in a casual restaurant, and next to a complex dessert in a four-star restaurant. Frozen desserts include ice cream, sorbet, sherbet, granité, and other miscellaneous frozen desserts.

Ice Cream

Traditional ice cream begins with crème anglaise. The amount of butterfat in a crème anglaise used for ice cream is often higher than the butterfat in a crème anglaise used as a sauce. To increase the butterfat, cream replaces a portion of the milk in the crème anglaise. As the amount of butterfat increases, so does the richness and quality of the ice cream.

As with other dairy products, the type of ice cream is defined by the amount of butterfat in the ice cream. Legally, ice cream must have at least 10 percent butterfat. Anything less than 10 percent must be labeled light, low fat, or reduced fat depending on the amount of butterfat.

To make ice cream, begin by pouring a cold custard mixture into an ice-cream maker. Ice-cream makers consist of a device that mixes or churns the ice cream inside a chilled metal container, 47-3. It is crucial that

Draz-Koetke/Goodheart-Willcox Publisher

47-3 A modern ice-cream machine churns ice cream at high speeds to produce very smooth ice cream.

the ice cream is continuously churned as it freezes. If it is not adequately churned, large ice crystals form. These crystals destroy the smooth, creamy texture of the ice cream.

Constant mixing also traps air within the ice cream as it freezes. This added air contributes to a light texture. Without this air, the ice cream would be unpleasantly dense. The name for the air that is frozen in ice cream is **overrun**. Some ice-cream manufacturers add large amounts of overrun to their ice cream. Very high amounts of overrun produce lower quality and less expensive ice cream.

Once the ice cream has been sufficiently frozen, it must be removed from the ice-cream maker and placed in a sanitized, prechilled container. The ice cream is covered and then stored in a freezer at 9°F (–12.8°C). Ice cream at this temperature can be scooped easily. Lower temperatures cause the ice cream to become hard and difficult to scoop.

Ice creams made with a rich crème anglaise, which contains eggs, are also called *French ice creams*. There are some ice creams that do not contain eggs. Generally, these eggless ice creams combine sugar, fruit purée, and cream.

Another popular ice cream is soft-serve ice cream. Soft-serve ice cream is ice cream that is served at warmer temperatures and immediately after churning. Many soft-serve ice creams served in commercial foodservice are made from mixes. If soft-serve ice cream is placed in a freezer after churning, it develops the more solid consistency of traditional ice cream.

Sorbet

As ice cream is closely related to crème anglaise, sorbet (sohr BAY) is most closely related to fruit coulis. **Sorbet** is the French name for a frozen mixture of fruit purée, sugar, and water, 47-4. As with a coulis, a simple syrup is added to the puréed fruit.

Sorbets are prepared by churning the fruit mixture in an ice-cream maker until solid. The product is then removed from the ice-cream maker and placed into a chilled container and stored in a freezer.

The amount of sugar in the sorbet determines the texture of the finished sorbet. In frozen desserts, sugar acts like an antifreeze. Therefore, the more sugar a sorbet contains, the softer the finished sorbet will be. Adding too much sugar results in a very sweet sorbet and might prevent the sorbet from freezing at all. Alcohol also behaves like an antifreeze. Adding too much alcohol can similarly prevent the sorbet from freezing correctly.

The proportion of water, sugar, and puréed fruit depends on the nature of the fruit. For instance, highly acidic fruits such as lemon and grapefruit require a large amount of water and sugar to offset the acidity of the fruit. The ripeness of the fruit also determines the proportion of ingredients. For instance, if one batch of raspberry purée is sweeter than another batch, less syrup is required. If the fruit is very ripe and thus very sweet, it may be necessary to add a small amount of lemon juice to balance sugar levels. Other fruits, such as pears and apricots, are most often cooked before being blended to produce a sorbet. If these fruits are not first cooked, they tend to turn an unattractive brown color.

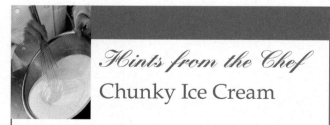

Hints from the Chef
Chunky Ice Cream

Many popular ice creams contain chunks of various ingredients such as chocolate chips, cherries, chopped cookies, chopped candy bars, or cookie dough. These ingredients are stirred into the ice cream as soon as the ice cream is removed from the ice-cream maker. At this stage, the ice cream is still soft enough to be stirred. Once the ingredients are added, the ice cream is placed in a freezer to harden.

Draz-Koetke/Goodheart-Willcox Publisher

47-4 A selection of sorbets can be a beautiful and light ending to a large meal.

Recipe No.	Name		Category
47.6	**Raspberry Sorbet**		Frozen Dessert
Yield	**Portion Size**		**No. Portions**
2½ qt. (2.4 L)	½ c. (120 mL)		20
US Quantity	**Metric Quantity**	**Ingredient**	**TCS**
25 oz.	700 g	sugar	
22 oz.	660 g	water	
32 oz.	960 g	raspberry purée, strained	
to taste		lemon juice	
Method			**CCP**
1. Combine sugar and water in a saucepan.			
2. Bring to a boil over high heat and simmer just until the sugar is dissolved. Let the simple syrup cool.			
3. When the syrup is cold, combine with the raspberry purée. Add lemon juice if additional acidity is necessary.			
4. Pour into an ice-cream maker and churn until frozen to a soft consistency.			
5. Remove from the ice-cream maker and place in a previously frozen container. Cover well and store in a freezer until needed.			

Portion (g)	Calories	Fat (g)	Protein (g)	Carbohydrate (g)	Cholesterol (mg)	Sodium (mg)	Fiber (g)
114	156	0.03	0.51	39.62	0	1.52	1.42

Professional chefs often use densimeters when preparing sorbets because of the different sugar levels in fruit. **Densimeters** are special instruments that measure the sugar levels in fruit purées and syrups, 47-5. The amount of sugar is measured using the Brix (BRIHKS) or Baumé (boh MAHY) scales.

Granité and Sherbet

Two unique types of frozen desserts are the **granité** (grah nee TAY) and sherbet. A granité is a style of sorbet that is often slightly less sweet than sorbet. To make a granité, a coulis is allowed to freeze in a shallow pan. At several points during the freezing, the mixture is stirred manually. As a result, the granité develops noticeable ice crystals.

Sherbet is a cross between sorbet and ice cream. It is a coulis-type mixture with the addition of a dairy product. Legally, it must contain 1 to 2 percent butterfat. It is churned in an ice-cream maker just like an ice cream or sorbet.

Other Frozen Desserts

Frozen desserts are more elaborate preparations than ice cream or sorbet. Indeed, ice cream and sorbets may be incorporated into some of these frozen desserts.

Baked Alaska To prepare baked Alaska, a piece of cake is topped with ice cream, coated

Draz-Koetke/Goodheart-Willcox Publisher

47-5 Densimeters enable chefs to produce more consistent sorbets.

Chef Speak

The Intermezzo

In fine-dining restaurants, an intermezzo (ihn tehr MEH zoh) is served between the fish and meat courses. An intermezzo is simply a small scoop of an acidic sorbet or granité that is attractively presented. Its purpose is to cleanse the taste buds, thus preparing them for the next course.

in Italian meringue, and then frozen until needed. When ordered, the baked Alaska is transferred from the freezer to a very hot oven. It is baked just until the meringue starts to brown. (Some chefs use a propane torch to brown the meringue instead of an oven.)

Banana Split A banana split consists of three scoops of ice cream placed on top of a banana that has been split lengthwise. The ice cream is finished with different toppings such as pineapple, hot fudge, strawberry, or caramel. Generous amounts of whipped cream, chopped nuts, and cherries complete the dish.

Bombes To make a bombe, a chilled mold is lined with a thin layer of ice cream and then filled with a special mixture called a *pâte à bombe* (paht ah BOHM). The mixture consists of whipped egg yolks into which hot syrup is slowly added. The mixture is whipped until light and cool and then whipped cream is folded in. The bombe is then placed in the freezer until completely frozen.

Parfait (pahr FAHY) Classically, parfaits are made almost identically to a pâte à bombe. They are often flavored with coffee. Unlike a bombe, parfaits are molded without a lining of ice cream. A parfait can also refer to layers of ice cream and other ingredients that are presented in a tall glass.

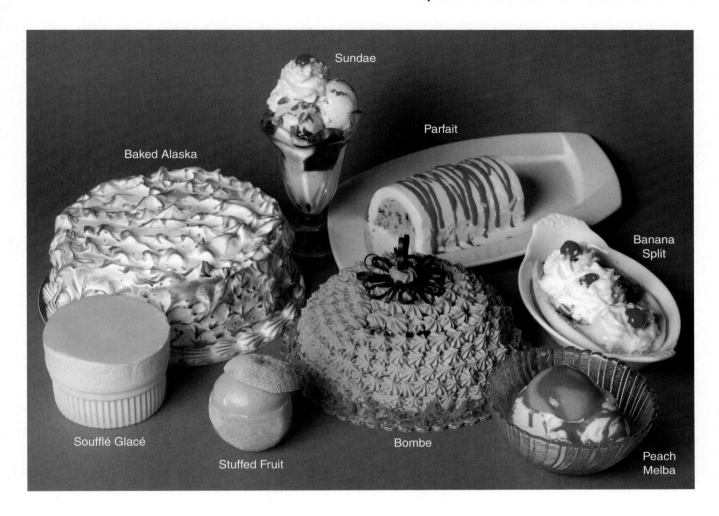

Peach Melba This dessert was invented by the famous chef Auguste Escoffier. It consists of a scoop of ice cream topped with a cold poached peach half. The dessert is finished with a coating of raspberry coulis.

Soufflé Glacé (soo FLAY glah SAY) A soufflé glacé starts with a mixture similar to the pâte à bombe, except the egg yolks are replaced by egg whites. A paper collar is tied to the soufflé mold so it rises above the mold. The soufflé mold is filled with soufflé glacé mixture until it reaches the top of the collar. The soufflé glacé is then frozen until needed. The collar is removed just prior to serving.

Stuffed Fruit This unique presentation serves fruit sorbet in the shell of the fruit. For instance, pineapple sorbet can be served in a scooped out pineapple half. Similarly, melon sorbet can be served in a melon half. To prepare stuffed fruit, simply fill the emptied fruit with sorbet and store in the freezer until needed.

Sundae There are many different types of sundaes. In general, a sundae is served in a bowl and consists of scoops of ice cream topped with various toppings, sprinkles, whipped cream, and a cherry.

Summary Points

- Many dessert sauces form the basis of frozen desserts. For instance, ice cream is classically made from crème anglaise and sorbet is made from fruit coulis.

- Dessert sauces are used to provide moisture, increase flavor, and create beautiful plate presentations.

- Frozen desserts include ice creams, sorbets, sherbets, granités, and a variety of other frozen desserts.

In Review Assess

1. List four types of dessert sauce.

2. Describe how to prepare a ganache.

3. When preparing caramel sauce, which of the following precautions should be taken?
   A. Stir sugar and water until mixture turns light brown.
   B. Once it reaches the desired color, cook caramel a little longer.
   C. Add cream quickly to hot caramel.
   D. Place hand off to the side of the pan when adding cream to hot caramel.

4. True or false. If ripe fruit is not available for making a coulis, a frozen fruit purée is a good substitute.

5. State the dessert sauce that is used to make each of the frozen desserts in the following list:
   A. Granité
   B. Ice cream
   C. Sorbet

6. List two reasons why ice cream must be continuously churned as it freezes.

7. Ice creams made with rich crème anglaise containing eggs are called _____ _____ _____.

8. True or false. High amounts of overrun produce a higher quality, more expensive ice cream.

9. The amount of _____ in a sorbet greatly determines the texture of a finished sorbet.

10. _____ is a cross between sorbet and ice cream.

11. Name four frozen desserts other than ice cream and sorbet.

Core Skills

12. **Math.** You place 32 fluid ounces of ice-cream mix into an ice-cream maker. When you stop the ice-cream maker, the ice cream has a final volume of 48 ounces. What percent increase in volume (overrun) is this?

13. **Speaking and Listening.** In teams, prepare the chapter recipe for *caramel sauce*. Once the sauces are complete and cooled to room temperature, evaluate them for proper appearance, flavor, and texture. Remember, properly prepared caramel sauce should have a creamy-brown appearance, good flavor, and a smooth texture. Discuss any differences in the teams' sauces and ways to ensure a quality product and ways you might use them in desserts.

14. **Reading.** Use reliable Internet or print resources to read about the history of *Baked Alaska* or another popular frozen dessert. What are the origins of this dessert? Share your findings in an oral report to the class.

15. **Writing.** Use reliable Internet or print resources to read about how professional chefs use *densimeters* (or sugar hydrometers) to measure sugar concentration and sugar density in making sorbet. Identify the difference between the Brix scale and the Baumé scale and how both might be used in the culinary kitchen beyond making sorbet. Write a summary of your findings for reference.

16. **Math.** Presume your culinary class is putting together a sundae bar for a school event. The principal has requested fresh chocolate and caramel sauces along with a variety of other toppings. You will need 300 portions of caramel sauce for the sundae bar. Use the text recipe and alter the yield to serve 300 guests. (Use the following formulas: new yield ÷ old yield = conversion factor; old quantity × conversion factor = new quantity.)

17. **CTE Career Readiness Practice.** A customer has ordered 10 of your bakeshop's highly prized cheesecakes for an anniversary party. The customer has requested a ganache covering for the cheesecakes. Your new assistants in the bakeshop have never made ganache. Prepare and give a demonstration to your assistants (the class) in the art of making ganache. Describe the procedure and the appearance, flavor, and texture of a quality finished product. Emphasize that preparing a quality product helps increase profitability.

Critical Thinking

18. **Draw conclusions.** Many restaurants do not have exact recipes for fruit coulis. Chefs often prefer to add sugar and lemon juice to taste. Why do you suppose pastry chefs do not use a recipe to ensure a consistent product?

19. **Make inferences.** Compare a coulis with a crème anglaise. Which is more likely to spoil? What facts support your inferences?

20. **Deconstruct evidence.** You are trying a new recipe for sorbet but it will not freeze. What ingredient(s) would you try adjusting? Would you increase or decrease the ingredient(s)? What evidence can you give to show your ingredient adjustments will help solve the problem?

21. **Draw conclusions.** The ice-cream machine has broken. A cook suggests freezing the ice cream in a freezer and stirring it from time to time as it freezes. Will this produce a quality ice cream? Explain your conclusions.

Technology

Use Internet or print resources to investigate the *anti-griddle* kitchen appliance. Who collaborated to develop this piece of equipment? What is the function of an anti-griddle? How does the anti-griddle benefit the professional kitchen? Use a school-approved web application to create a virtual poster about the anti-griddle to share on the class website.

Teamwork

In teams, prepare a raspberry sorbet using the recipe from this chapter. Evaluate each team's sorbet for appropriate appearance, flavor, and texture. Record your observations for each team's sorbet. Were there differences in the sorbets from team to team? Discuss what might account for the differences. Did your team have to adjust the recipe? Why or why not?

Chef's E-portfolio
Ganache Demonstration

Video your demonstration from the CTE Career Readiness Practice activity and upload it to your e-portfolio. Ask your instructor where to save your file. This could be on the school's network or a flash drive of your own. Name your portfolio document *FirstnameLastname_Portfolio Ch#.docx* (i.e., JohnSmith_PortfolioCh47.docx).

Unit Five
Beyond Cooking

B Calkins/Shutterstock.com

The Science of Preservation— Fermentation

While some bacteria are harmful and cause foodborne illness or food spoilage, others are beneficial. These beneficial bacteria are permanent residents on fruit and vegetable plants. Given the right conditions, these helpful bacteria "starve out" the bad bacteria. In the process of dining on available plant material, the good bacteria produce by-products such as lactic acid and carbon dioxide. These by-products not only make the environment even less friendly to bad bacteria, but also yield interesting aromas and flavors. This process is fermentation. Fortunately, the good bacteria consume such insignificant amounts of the actual plant material that there is plenty of food left for humans to consume. In fact, the bacteria sometimes enhance the quality or nutritional content of the food by adding vitamins or protecting those that occur naturally in the food. As a result of the unfavorable environment created for the bad bacteria, the food is protected from spoilage and contamination, and preserved in a wholesome state.

Common fermented plant foods include cabbage, olives, cucumbers, and radishes. Not limited to just plant foods, dairy and meats can also be preserved through fermentation. Yogurt, cheese, and salami are examples of fermented nonplant foods.

1. Summarize how fermentation preserves food.

2. In addition to preserving the food, what are other positive effects of fermentation?

While studying, look for the activity icon  to:

- Build vocabulary with e-flash cards and matching activities.
- Expand learning with video clips, photo identification activities, animations, and interactive activities.
- Review and assess what you learn by completing end-of-chapter questions.

G-WLEARNING.com

nakamasa/Shutterstock.com

Table Service

Reading Prep

Before reading this chapter, review the objectives. Based on this information, write down two or three items that you think are important to note while you are reading.

Culinary Terminology

Build Vocab

back-of-the-house staff, p. 739
front-of-the-house staff, p. 739
maître d'hôtel, p. 740
American service, p. 744
family-style service, p. 744
Russian service, p. 744
French service, p. 744
flambé, p. 744
flatware, p. 745
place setting, p. 746
crumber, p. 752

Academic Terminology

Build Vocab

pivotal, p. 740
point-of-sale (POS) system, p. 750

Objectives

After studying this chapter, you will be able to

- recall the roles of the front-of-the-house staff.
- apply successful strategies for handling reservations and inquiries.
- summarize the keys to quality front-of-the-house service.
- compare and contrast the three main service styles.
- recognize the steps necessary to preset a dining area.
- explain how to provide guests with a quality dining experience from start to finish.
- summarize common beverage options and their preparation.

Cooking is only one part of the larger foodservice environment. Every restaurant consists of the back-of-the-house and the front-of-the-house staff. The **back-of-the-house staff** refers to the kitchen personnel including chefs, cooks, dishwashers, and receiving clerks. The **front-of-the-house staff** includes the service personnel that work the dining room. The front-of-the-house is more than the servers who directly wait on tables. There are also hosts, cashiers, buspersons, and bartenders. Many people choose to make a career working in the front-of-the-house.

The service staff is crucial to the success of a foodservice operation because they can make-or-break the dining experience. The service staff interacts with both the customers and the kitchen staff. Great restaurants are made up of talented front-of-the-house and back-of-the-house professionals who work together seamlessly to provide the finest experience to the customer. Therefore, it is crucial that the back-of-the-house staff understands the needs and organization of the front-of-the-house.

Front-of-the-House Positions

Just as the kitchen is divided into different areas of responsibility, the dining room is also divided into different positions. The back-of-the-house must understand the role of each front-of-the-house worker so the entire restaurant functions efficiently, 48-1.

Not all restaurants divide their front-of-the-house staff into the same positions. For instance, in smaller or less formal restaurants, a restaurant manager would be in charge of the dining room. Also, smaller or less formal restaurants may not make the distinction between front and back servers. In these restaurants, each server performs all the duties of both front and back servers.

Handling Reservations and Inquiries

In many cases, a potential customer's first contact with a restaurant is to make an inquiry or a reservation. This pivotal, or crucial, interaction is often the determining factor in the customer's decision where to dine. An inquiry is simply a customer seeking information such as menu pricing or hours of service. Inquiries may be made by phone, e-mail, or via the restaurant's website. Staff whose job involves answering the phone must be trained how to do so properly. First and foremost, the staff must speak clearly, and be hospitable and friendly. It is a good policy for the restaurant to have a script for the staff to follow when answering phones. The script should include at least the following guidelines:

- Answer the phone with a greeting, name of the restaurant, and the staff's name.
- If the caller must be put on hold, first ask for permission to do so and wait for a response.
- Thank the caller for holding when you return to the call.

Front-of-the-House Positions	
Position	**Duties**
Maître d'Hôtel (mehtr doh TEHL)	The maître d'hôtel, or dining room manager, is responsible for the entire dining room operations. This position is to the dining room what the chef is to the kitchen.
Host	The host, or greeter, is generally the first person with whom the customer interacts. The host is positioned near the entrance of the restaurant and welcomes the guests to the dining area. In many restaurants, the host also leads the guests to their table and manages the reservations.
Front server	The front server, or captain, welcomes the guests, presents menus, takes orders, serves the food, provides beverage service, and is responsible for the bill. The front server has the greatest responsibility for the well-being and quality of service provided to the guests. To accomplish this task, he or she must coordinate the needs of the guests with back servers, buspersons, and kitchen staff.
Back server	The back server aids the front server and is responsible for coordinating timing with the chef and delivering food from the kitchen to the dining room.
Busperson	The busperson, or service assistant, is principally responsible for clearing dirty dishes, changing linens, and resetting tables. The busperson is also responsible for butter, bread, and water service.
Reservationist	The reservationist is responsible for taking reservations and booking parties via the telephone and Internet.

48-1 Distribution of duties among the front-of-the-house positions may differ from one restaurant to the next.

INDUSTRY INSIGHTS

The Importance of Good Grooming

Members of the waitstaff are constantly in the public eye, therefore it is crucial that their personal hygiene is impeccable. Before starting a shift, be sure to

- shower or bathe daily
- shave daily or neatly trim any facial hair
- use deodorant or antiperspirant
- avoid excessive perfume or cologne
- comb and arrange clean hair neatly, keeping long hair pulled back
- trim fingernails and be sure to clean under them
- brush teeth and use mouthwash or breath mints frequently
- avoid excessive jewelry

If reservations are taken via e-mail, be sure to send a response quickly confirming or denying the reservation request. Additionally, when communicating through e-mail, be sure to use a more formal style rather than a trendy, abbreviated format.

- *Restaurant website.* Many restaurants have websites where potential customers can learn about the restaurant, menu, chef, special events, and so on. It is important to keep the website up-to-date and to list alternative ways to contact the restaurant.
- *Reservation websites.* There are an increasing number of companies that provide reservation services for restaurants. Before hiring a company to provide this important service, research should be done to verify the company is reliable and capable.
- *Social media.* Social media is a critical communication avenue for many restaurants and an important way to

- When taking a reservation, record the guest's name, number of guests, time of the reservation, and a contact phone number.
- Repeat the details of the reservation back to the guest to confirm accuracy.
- Close the call by thanking the caller for his or her interest in the restaurant.

Customers also seek information about restaurants through digital media. Close attention must be paid to these means of communication as well.

- *E-mail.* The key to successful e-mail communication is to answer inquiries as quickly as possible. Individuals who use digital media expect a rapid response. If potential customers experience an incomplete or slow response, they may become disappointed or even angry with the restaurant and decide to dine elsewhere.

CHEF'S ETHICS

Ethics and Absenteeism

Ethical employees arrive to work on time and prepared to perform duties efficiently and effectively. In the foodservice industry, a high rate of employee absenteeism puts a strain on the business and coworkers. What happens when employees fail to show up to work? Other employees take on additional tasks or those tasks go unaccomplished. Suppose a restaurant server is absent on the busiest night of the week. Because of the server's absence, other employees must handle additional tables. This will likely have a negative impact on service levels at the restaurant. In addition, employees may not be able to accomplish the server's closing tasks, leaving them for the morning shift. Absenteeism negatively impacts foodservice establishments and the reputation of the business.

keep current customers interested in the restaurant and to introduce new customers to the restaurant. Social media must be managed like every other aspect of the business.

Keys to Quality Service

In most instances, cooks rarely interact with the customer unless they are working an exhibition cooking station, or action station. Conversely, the job of the front-of-the-house staff is mainly about interacting with customers and making sure that their experience is excellent. Individuals who are successful at providing quality service to customers possess a certain set of skills and characteristics. Front-of-the-house staff possessing strong interpersonal skills and welcoming demeanors are the keys to providing customers with a favorable dining experience.

Hospitable

Quality-oriented dining room staff members never forget that the customer is a guest and should be treated accordingly. Successful staff members have the ability to convey a sense of welcome and hospitality. Generous smiles and a friendly reception make the diner feel appreciated and valued. Front-of-the-house professionals maintain eye contact with the diner, are always personable and sincere, and address the customer by name when appropriate.

Poised

Experienced servers know how to stay calm and confident even if the restaurant is extremely busy or during service or kitchen problems. The ability to remain poised is important when working in the front-of-the-house. The customer should never feel as if the servers are too busy or distracted. The service staff should not appear stressed or nervous.

Knowledgeable

It is crucial that the front-of-the-house staff know as much as possible about the food being served. Customers ask questions as to the flavor of the food, how long it takes to prepare, what beverage best accompanies a certain dish, or if the food contains specific ingredients. While good servers try to anticipate questions, sometimes a guest may ask a unique question. If the server does not know the answer to a question, he or she should never try to bluff. This is especially dangerous if the customer has a food allergy and is concerned about ingredients in a dish. If the server does not know the answer, he or she should always ask the appropriate chef or manager.

Sense of Timing

The dining room staff is the link between the customer and kitchen. In most establishments, the dining room staff controls the timing of the meal. It is up to the server to ensure the kitchen is serving the food when the customer is ready for it. To accomplish this, servers must stay focused on what is happening in the dining room at all times, anticipate customer needs, and know how to prioritize tasks.

Communication Skills

No matter what position you work in foodservice, you must be able to communicate effectively. Front-of-the house must communicate with customers and the kitchen. Back-of-the-house must communicate with coworkers and vendors. Listening and speaking are the most basic communication skills and successful front-of-the-house staff use them well.

When listening, the server must give the customer his or her full attention. Servers use unspoken or nonverbal cues, such as maintaining eye contact and nodding, to let the customer know they are listening. Successful servers restate what the customer has said to be certain they understand the message. If a server is unclear about the message, he or she asks questions. The server should allow the customer to finish what he or she has to say before responding.

When speaking, thoughts should be organized and presented in a clear, logical manner. In addition to the words chosen, posture and tone of voice affect the message being communicated.

Ability to "Read" the Customer

The ability to "read" the customer is acquired with experience. Not all customers wish to be treated identically. Different customers have different expectations. Professional servers are able to determine a customer's expectations by carefully interpreting verbal and nonverbal cues, or body language. Initially, the server should interact formally with a new customer. After this initial interaction, a seasoned server adapts his or her style of service for individual customers. For instance, the server may decide to interact as little as possible

INDUSTRY INSIGHTS
Customer Complaints

Service staff members are usually the first ones to hear about a customer complaint. How they deal with complaints can make or break a customer's dining experience. The following pointers help deal positively with customer complaints:

- Never argue with a customer or make excuses such as "You know, the kitchen is very busy."
- Listen fully and compassionately to the complaint. Repeat the complaint back to the customer to be sure you understand the issue. This communicates to the guest that you take the complaint seriously and understand the complaint.
- If possible, solve small problems immediately. For example, if a dish is too salty, take it back immediately and get a new dish for the customer. Always report any problems to a manager.
- If the problem is beyond your ability to fix or the customer becomes aggressive, excuse yourself from the table and inform a manager.
- Once the guest's problem is resolved, thank the guest for bringing the complaint to your attention.

with customers that are in an intense business discussion. Other customers may better appreciate more informal conversation even to the point of good-hearted humor.

Efficient Time and Motion Techniques

Similar to cooks, servers are always analyzing how to maximize their productivity. This means being able to do as many different tasks as possible in a minimum amount of time. An inexperienced server may become stressed and move with lightening speed through the dining room and make his or her conversations with the customer as brief and expedient as possible. Unfortunately, these actions communicate the message that the guest is not important and that the server is overly stressed. Neither message contributes to a satisfactory experience. Instead, an experienced server analyzes what needs to be done and determines the most efficient way to accomplish the task. For instance, a server may visit a table, and then glance at two other tables to check on their progress and deliver a beverage order on the way to the kitchen. Likewise, a server positions a tray jack as close as possible to the table being served to reduce steps and increase efficiency.

Just like kitchens, dining areas must be designed to promote efficient service. For instance, a server station may be located near the ordering system or on the way into the kitchen. Server stations are stocked with items such as napkins, flatware, and glasses, which a server needs ready access to frequently throughout the meal service. In large dining rooms, server stations may also be strategically positioned in the dining area to limit server steps.

Types of Service

Through the centuries, a number of different types of table service have been developed. American service is the most common and basic type of service. Russian and especially French service require much more practice to master.

American Service

American service, or plated service, refers to a style of service in which the server delivers plates of food directly from the kitchen to the guest. American service is the norm in most restaurants throughout the United States. It can be an informal or formal service style depending on the restaurant.

A variation of American service is family-style service. With **family-style service**, the waitperson places serving platters of prepared food in the center of the table so the guests can serve themselves. This is an informal style of service that is common in restaurants and banquet halls across America.

Russian Service

When **Russian service** is used, the front-of-the-house staff serves food from a platter onto plates that are preset in front of the guests. In general, this style of service is practiced in upscale restaurants and hotels. The most common use of Russian service today is bread service. For example, in many restaurants dining room staff serve bread tableside to each guest. For Russian service, the server must learn to hold a large fork and spoon in his or her dominant hand. The fork and spoon are used like a pair of tongs to pick up and serve food. This same technique is used to serve most solid foods. Liquids, such as soup and sauce, can also be served Russian style using large spoons or ladles, 48-2.

French Service

French service is the most difficult style of service and requires much practice to learn. **French service** requires that the servers cook and prepare dishes in front of the customer. French service, often called *tableside service*, is a cross between the kitchen and dining room. It is a very formal type of service practiced only in some of the finest restaurants. Some of the more common items prepared tableside include

- sautéed pieces of meat or shellfish followed by the appropriate pan sauce (meat may be partially cooked in advance)
- Caesar salad
- guacamole
- flambéed dessert items

Flambé (flahm BAY) is a French term that means "to flame." A flambé dish is

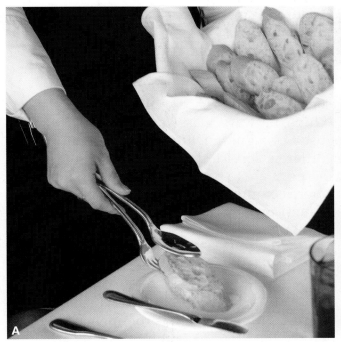

Draz-Koetke/Goodheart-Willcox Publisher

48-2 (A) Learning to use a fork and spoon in one hand for Russian service requires practice. (B) Russian service may also include serving soup from a tureen or sauce from a sauceboat.

finished tableside by a server setting it aflame, 48-3. The flaming process is attractive and makes a dramatic presentation.

Draz-Koetke/Goodheart-Willcox Publisher

48-3 Flambéed dishes are an example of French service.

Presetting the Dining Area

Before the guests arrive, many activities must be performed by the front-of-the-house staff. Readying the dining area for service begins by placing tablecloths—if used—on the tables and cleaning flatware and glassware. A tablecloth is placed on the table with creases pointing up. The hem of the tablecloth should be on the underside of the tablecloth and not visible to the customer. It is important that the tablecloth hangs evenly on all sides of the table. If a tablecloth is not used, all tables and placemats need to be inspected to be sure they are clean.

Knives, forks, and spoons are called **flatware** and must be polished before use. Polishing is the professional term for shining the flatware by wiping away any unsightly water spots. All flatware must be cleaned and sanitized prior to polishing. To polish flatware, simply wipe each piece with a slightly damp, clean cloth napkin. No cleaning products are used when polishing flatware. Flatware is always held by the handle end, not the food end. For sanitation reasons, do not touch the knife blade, fork tines, or the bowl of the spoon.

Glassware also needs to be polished. As with flatware, professionals refer to removing water spots as polishing. Glassware must be cleaned and sanitized before polishing. To polish glassware, place an inverted glass above hot steaming water. Once the glass has fogged with steam, wipe the inside and outside of the glass thoroughly with a clean cloth, 48-4.

Salt and pepper shakers or grinders also need to be inspected as part of the presetting activities. Servers should inspect the salt and pepper shakers or grinders to be sure they are clean and adequately filled with salt and pepper.

Menus should be carefully inspected not only for accuracy of information, but also to ensure the menus are clean, presentable, and not damaged.

The next step to readying the dining area involves setting the tables. There are many ways in which place settings can be arranged. A **place setting** includes the china, flatware, glassware, and napkin used by a guest. Different restaurants and different service styles dictate how the place settings are to be arranged. Three of the more common place settings include basic American, à la carte, and banquet.

Basic American Place Setting

This is the most common type of setting in restaurants today. It is routinely used in all but the finest restaurants. The setting consists of a dinner plate, one or two forks placed to the left of the plate, and a knife and

48-4 (A) Flatware and (B) glassware are polished to remove water spots.

spoon placed to the right of the plate. There is also a water glass placed to the upper right of the plate. Sometimes additional glassware is placed next to the water glass. A bread and butter plate (called a *B and B plate*), along with a butter knife, are placed to the upper left of the dinner plate. In some family-style restaurants a cup and saucer are also included in the basic table setting.

À la Carte Place Setting

À la carte service is reserved for upscale dining. Just prior to serving each course, the appropriate flatware and glassware are placed in front of each guest. The flatware is removed along with the plates from each course. The glassware is removed whenever there is a change of beverage. This type of setting requires maximum coordination

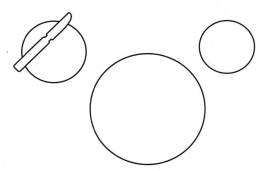

among the front-of-the-house staff. This table setting is sparse and consists only of a dinner plate, B and B plate, bread knife, and water glass. Often the dinner plate is a large decorative plate called a *charger*. The charger is for show purposes only and is removed before the first course is served.

Banquet Place Setting

When setting a table for banquet service, often all the glassware and flatware needed for the meal are placed at each place setting. This style of service is only possible because

Hints from the Chef
Folding Napkins

There are many ways to make beautifully folded napkins. To make these designs, cotton-rich cloth napkins must be used. Paper or polyester napkins are hard to fold or will not hold a fold. Many restaurants choose simple napkin folds because it takes too much time to make elaborate folds.

in banquet service, the menu is the same for every guest. When the plates are cleared after each course, the appropriate flatware and glassware are also removed.

Serving Guests

Once the dining area is completely set, the restaurant is ready to welcome its first patrons. It is critical that guests have excellent service from the moment they enter the restaurant to the moment they exit. Each step in service is an opportunity for guests to form either a positive or negative impression of the restaurant. Negative impressions might prevent these guests from returning to the restaurant, even if the food was very good. It is also probable these customers will tell other prospective customers about their negative experience. The following steps outline the best strategy for serving guests so they leave with a positive impression.

Welcoming Patrons

Patrons should be greeted the moment they enter the restaurant. This is most often the duty of the host or greeter, although every employee that comes in contact with a new guest should welcome him or her and ask if they can be of assistance. In many restaurants, coats are checked before the guests are escorted to their table.

After verifying a reservation, the host or maître d'hôtel leads the guests to their table and give them menus. Customers with disabilities may require special assistance. For instance, guests with vision impairment may need guidance to their table. Servers should be alerted to customers with hearing disabilities. Restaurants must provide suitable access for people in wheelchairs or using other mobility aids. In addition, dining rooms and bathrooms should be designed to meet the needs of these customers in accordance with the Americans with Disability Act (ADA).

Beverage Orders and Service

Once guests are seated, the front server approaches the table to welcome the guests and introduce him or herself. At this time, the front server can take beverage orders so the guests can enjoy their drinks while looking over the menu. It should be noted that this book describes service using the traditional distinction between the roles of front server, back server, and busperson. In many less formal restaurants, these roles are often blended into one position simply referred to as a *server*.

The busperson fills water glasses with water, if requested by the guest. In some restaurants, glasses already filled with ice water are placed on the table, although routinely pouring water for all guests can be a waste of water resources as not everyone wants to drink water. When pouring ice water in front of the guest, pour from the

SUSTAINABLE CULINARY
Water Service

In many restaurants, it is standard for the server to pour glasses of ice water for all guests shortly after being seated. Many times, the water is not consumed in lieu of other beverages that guests have ordered. While pouring water for everyone may seem hospitable, it can also be a tremendous waste of clean water. It takes resources to process and distribute clean tap water. Additionally, energy is used to make ice. When unused glasses of ice water are poured down the drain, these resources are wasted. Instead, offer your guests ice water and let them know why water is not automatically poured for everyone. This water service policy allows an operation to practice hospitality as well as sustainability.

right of the customer. Be careful that the ice does not pour abruptly from the pitcher as this could cause water to spill onto the table. To avoid this, special pitchers designed to prevent ice cubes from falling into a customer's glass are used.

The back server serves the beverage orders to the right of each guest. Glasses with stems should only be handled by the stem. Glasses without stems should be handled as close to the bottom of the glass as possible. The server's hand should never touch the rim of the glass, 48-5. While the guests are looking at the menu, bread and butter may be served. The bread may be in a basket that is placed in the center of the table or served Russian style. The butter is usually presented on a small serving plate. In some restaurants, the butter is already on the table when the guests are seated.

Selling the Menu

It is important that the front server be familiar with both the menu and specials as guests often ask questions concerning specific ingredients and possible allergens. In many restaurants, it is customary for the front server to inquire about possible food

Draz-Koetke/Goodheart-Willcox Publisher

48-5 When serving a beverage, hold the glass near the bottom half and never touch the rim of a glass.

allergies. The server can then help the guest avoid menu items containing possible allergens. The server must also inform the kitchen of any food allergies to prevent a life threatening situation.

The server's job is not only to take orders and serve food, but also to encourage sales and guide guests to certain menu items. These techniques are called *suggestive selling*. For instance, the chef may want to sell out a particular menu item before a long weekend. The owner may want the server to sell certain menu items that are particularly profitable. This strategy may include comments such as "Be sure to save room for our special house dessert." The display cases of desserts or restaurant-branded apparel that some restaurants place at the entrance is merchandising and also designed to increase sales. When a server presents raw steaks to the guest for approval and selection, or brings a display of desserts to the table, these are also examples of suggestive selling. All these strategies are designed to guide the customer to order these items. At this point in the serving process, the front server should dismiss him or herself from the table to allow the guests room for conversation.

Order Taking

Knowing when to take an order is a matter of practice. After a given period of time, the front server may inquire as to whether the table is ready to order. One clue that indicates the table is ready to order is when most of the guests have placed their closed menus on the table. Sometimes, a guest will signal that they are ready to order.

Each restaurant has a system for order taking. Many times, the front server has a piece of paper that lists position numbers and a table number. Each table in a restaurant's dining room is identified by a table number. Each seat at the table is also assigned a position number. Numbering tables and each position at the table is done to make communication easy. Thus, when ordering food, a server would say to the chef, "Fire table 33," which means start making the food for the table 33. Also, if one person at the table requests an iced tea, the front server would say to the back server, "Position two, table 33 needs an iced tea."

When taking an order, the front server writes the appropriate order next to each position number on the paper. It is important that there is no miscommunication

Front-of-the-House Terminology

Just like the kitchen, the front-of-the-house has its own jargon. Understanding these terms is important for both the kitchen and service staffs.

86—This term means the kitchen has run out an item, for example "86 T-bone steak" means there are no more T-bone steaks.

Comp—A comp refers to something that is free. For instance, if a person is not charged for dessert, it is referred to as being "comp'ed."

Cover—This is industry slang for a guest. For instance, if there are 30 reservations, the manager might say, "Tonight we will have 30 covers."

Deuce—A table of two guests.

Fire—Term used by the front-of-the-house to inform the kitchen that it is time to prepare the next course.

Pick up—This means a food order is prepared and ready to be "picked up" by a server and brought to the dining room.

Three-Top—A table of three guests or an empty table capable of seating three guests. A table of four would be referred to as a four-top and so on.

Ticket/Chit/Dupe—These are all references to the written food order for the guest.

Turn a Table—To clear, reset, and reseat a table with customers.

at this point or the entire pace of the meal may be endangered. As a result, the front server should repeat each order back to the customer.

The order is then submitted to the kitchen. In some restaurants, a copy of the front server's handwritten order form is submitted to the kitchen. Increasingly, orders are entered into a point-of-sale system, 48-6. A **point-of-sale (POS) system** is a computer-based ordering system that transmits the order to the kitchen, produces the customer's bill, and keeps track of important data. A POS system improves and speeds up communication with the kitchen. It also produces accurate bills and simplifies recordkeeping.

In some restaurants, the orders may be entered directly on a wireless device that immediately transfers the order to the kitchen and necessary information to the POS system. The advantage of these systems is that they make the order process faster and decrease errors when transferring information from the handwritten paper to the POS system.

Serving

Once the food is ready in the kitchen, a back server brings it to the dining room.

Draz-Koetke/Goodheart-Willcox Publisher

48-6 POS systems are common in most restaurants and help track valuable data.

Plates of food can be transported to the dining room in one of three ways.

- *Plates are carried by the server.* In this case, only several plates can be carried at one time by one server.
- *Plates are loaded onto a tray carried by the server.* Trays allow the plates to be stacked using plate covers. The tray is carried to the dining room where it is placed on a tray jack positioned near the table, 48-7. When picking up a tray of plates, the server should keep his or her back straight and bend at the knees to reduce the possibility of injury. Sometimes the tray can become quite heavy. Never attempt to lift or transport a tray that is too heavy to avoid injuring yourself or those around you.
- *Plates are loaded onto a rolling cart pushed by the server.* A cart allows a server to transport a maximum number of plates at once.

Before the food is placed on the table, the waitstaff should verify the appropriate flatware is at each place setting. For instance, if soup is to be served, the customer should have a soupspoon at his or her place setting. The server serves the women first and then the men. Food is served from the left of the customer. It is inappropriate to place a thumb on the rim of the plate when serving it to the guest, 48-8. The server should also announce each dish as it is placed on the table.

Once the food is served, the front and back servers carefully monitor the progress of the table. In some restaurants, it is customary for the server to check back with the table shortly after the guests start eating to be sure that everything is to their satisfaction. If there are problems with the food, corrective action should be taken immediately. For minor issues, it may be a matter of simply alerting the kitchen staff and manager. If there are larger problems with the food—cold, too salty, meat not cooked properly— the plate should be removed immediately and taken to the kitchen. Management should be informed so they can intervene and make sure the problem is resolved to the customer's satisfaction.

Draz-Koetke/Goodheart-Willcox Publisher

48-8 A server's thumb should not touch the top surface of the plate when serving the customer.

Draz-Koetke/Goodheart-Willcox Publisher

48-7 Plates should be stacked on the tray in a balanced manner for ease of carrying.

The waitstaff signals the kitchen when to have the next course ready. This is based on the speed at which the customer is eating.

Before the next course can be served, dirty plates are cleared from the table. Clearing plates is frequently the job of the busperson. No plates should be cleared until the entire table is done eating. It is wise to ask the customer's permission to clear dirty dishes, especially if there is still food on the plate. Soiled plates are cleared from the right of the customer. Depending on the course, some flatware and glassware may also need to be cleared from the table. The busperson then transports them to the dish cleaning area. The soiled plates may be transported by hand, tray, or cart. After handling dirty dishes, employees must wash their hands.

These steps are repeated as each new course is brought to the table. The servers alert the kitchen when the table is ready for their next course. Appropriate flatware and glassware are placed on the table, and the food is served.

During the course of a meal, the table often becomes messy. Servers periodically crumb linen tablecloths during a meal. A **crumber** is a tool used to scrape and scoop crumbs from the table onto a plate, 48-9. A crumber is a standard part of the servers' tools. If a customer spills a beverage, a cloth napkin may be placed on the table to cover the spill.

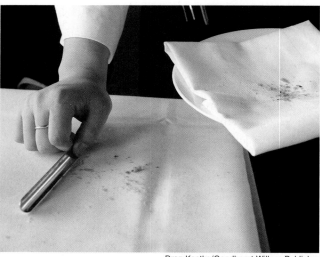

Draz-Koetke/Goodheart-Willcox Publisher

48-9 A crumber is used to remove crumbs from the table and should always be carried in the server's pocket.

Presenting the Check

At the end of the meal, a check is presented to the guests. It is usually placed on a check tray or in a folder. Generally, one person at the table—typically the host—asks for the check. The check should be given to the host. If the host is not known, place the check in the center of the table.

The guest pays with cash, check, or credit card. In most restaurants, payment is a function of the POS system. During the meal, the customers' orders were recorded and a check with the appropriate charges for the table was generated. The POS system, or even a cash register, is designed to make payments efficient and accurate.

- If the customer pays with cash, never ask if he or she wants change. The cash is given to the dining room manager along with the check that was presented to the customer. It is then entered into the POS system or a cash register. The amount of change to be returned to the customer is then indicated. It is important when dispensing change to count it out carefully to be sure it totals the correct amount. In some restaurants, the change is simply returned to the guest. In other restaurants, it may be customary to recount the money in front of the guest to be sure that it is accurate. The guest may then leave a tip on the table.
- If the guest is paying with a personal check, the check should be brought to the manager for processing. To verify authenticity of the check, it may be necessary to ask for the guest's identification.
- If the guest is paying with a credit card, the guest may elect to leave a tip on the credit-card bill. Credit-card charges are also processed by the dining room manager. In some restaurants, the

customer may swipe the credit card at the table with the aid of a small wireless devise. The guest's signature is needed to complete the payment process.

Once the check is paid, the customers may elect to leave the restaurant immediately or linger at the table. It is not good hospitality to try to rush guests out the door once they have paid. When leaving the restaurant, the last contact the customers have is often the same person who initially greeted them. This last point of contact is critical to complete the guest's positive experience. As the guests leave, thank them once again for their patronage and encourage them to return soon. It is important that these final gestures are not staged, but truly genuine.

After the guests leave the table, it is cleared and the tablecloth replaced with a fresh one. If the restaurant does not use tablecloths, the table should be cleaned and sanitized. The table is preset once again and is ready to receive new guests.

Beverages

Throughout the meal, numerous beverages are served. The simplest and most common beverage is ice water. Various soft drinks and juices are popular in restaurants from coast-to-coast. Flavored waters, coffee, and tea are typically prepared by the front-of-the-house staff and are served in many restaurants.

Water

Water is the most common beverage in restaurants. In sit-down restaurants, it is often assumed to be part of the dining experience and is thus served as soon as possible after the guest has been seated. This can lead to wasted water and ice as not everyone wants water. From a sustainability standpoint, it is preferable to offer water to the guests.

A range of bottled waters such as mineral waters, famous for their specific characteristics, or sparkling waters are also offered

INDUSTRY INSIGHTS

Customer Feedback

Customer satisfaction is essential for attracting and maintaining a loyal customer base. For this reason, restaurant owners and chefs want to know how satisfied customers are with their dining experience. What aspects of the experience delighted them? Which aspects were less than optimal? Customer feedback can be obtained using many methods including online surveys, wireless devices in the restaurants, and paper surveys. Surveys should include numerical ratings so results and progress can be measured and tracked.

in many restaurants. Increasingly, restaurants are menuing flavored waters that are prepared in-house. These waters can be infused with assorted fruit juices, vegetable juices, sweeteners, herbs, and even flowers. Some of these flavored waters may also be carbonated.

Coffee

Coffee is one of the most popular beverages in America. It is generally served with dessert, although some patrons may drink coffee throughout the entire meal. Preparing coffee always begins with ground coffee beans. The brewing method determines how the beans should be ground, ranging from fine to coarse grind.

Drip coffee is the most popular way to make coffee in America. To make drip coffee, ground beans are placed in a filter. The amount of ground coffee used for drip coffee depends on the machine, the amount of coffee being prepared, and the desired strength of the coffee. Hot water is then run through the ground beans and into a special container. In some restaurants, the brewed

SCIENCE & TECHNOLOGY

What Is Coffee?

Coffee beans come from a coffee tree that bears a fruit called a *cherry*. This fruit is both small and bright red similar to cherries traditionally eaten out of hand or used to make pies, but the similarities end there. Coffee trees grow in hot parts of the world. Most coffee is grown in Central and South America, east Africa, and Southeast Asia. There are two types of coffee trees—arabica and robusta. Arabica trees produce a higher quality and more expensive coffee bean.

Once the coffee cherries are picked, the fruit surrounding the bean is removed. The beans—actually a pit—are then dried. At this point, the coffee beans have a green color. The green coffee beans are then shipped and usually roasted in another country. Coffee can be roasted to varying degrees. Generally, the darker the color, the more intense, less acidic, and more bitter the coffee will be. Coffee beans which have had the caffeine removed from the beans are called *decaffeinated coffee beans*. Coffee beans can be decaffeinated using either a chemical or Swiss water method.

Draz-Koetke/Goodheart-Willcox Publisher

48-10 Vacuum pots are ideal for maintaining the temperature of hot coffee without turning it bitter.

coffee is held on a burner so the coffee remains hot. Coffee should not be held on a burner for more than 30 minutes because it can become unpleasantly bitter. More often, brewed coffee is being held in insulated vacuum pots, 48-10. These pots maintain the coffee temperature for a longer period of time while avoiding the bitterness.

Specialty coffee drinks have become popular in America and are served in many restaurants. Some of the most common coffee beverages include:

- *Espresso* (ehs PREH soh). Hot water is forced quickly and under pressure through finely ground coffee. The resulting cup of coffee is small but intensely flavored. A well-made espresso should have a light brown foam on top of the coffee. This foam is called a *crema*.
- *Cappucino* (cah poo CHEEN oh). This is a combination of espresso, steamed milk, and a topping of frothy milk foam.
- *Café au lait* (cah FAY oh LAY) or latte (lah TAY). This is a combination of espresso and steamed milk generally with little or no foam.
- *Iced coffee*. This specialty beverage is served in a glass over ice and is especially popular during the summer months. There are many ways to make iced coffee although most techniques tend to produce a rich and sweet product.
- *Mocha* (MOH kah). Mocha is a beverage that combines coffee and chocolate. This beverage often has a dairy product added.

A container of sugar and nonsugar sweeteners along with a pitcher of milk or half-and-half is served with coffee. A teaspoon should always accompany a cup of coffee. Some restaurants also serve a selection of small cookies or chocolates with the coffee.

Tea

Worldwide, tea is an extremely popular beverage. Tea is made from the leaf of the tea tree. Tea trees grow in countries such as India,

SCIENCE & TECHNOLOGY

What Is Tea?

To produce tea, leaves are first harvested from the tree. The tea leaves closest to the end of the branch are the most prized because they have the most delicate flavors. The leaves are then quickly transported to the production facility. There, they are manipulated so as to gently bruise the leaves. This begins an oxidation within the leaves that changes their color and produces new flavors. The oxidation can be stopped at any point by gently heating and drying out the leaves. How long the leaves oxidize defines whether the tea will be green or black tea. Green tea is 25 percent oxidized. Semifermented tea (also called *oolong* tea) is 30 to 70 percent oxidized. Black tea is 100 percent oxidized.

Chef Speak

Flavored Teas and Tisanes

Flavored teas are tea leaves that have been combined with other ingredients. Some flavored teas are extremely popular. For instance, Earl Gray is a black tea that is flavored with a citrus called *bergamot*. Rose tea is flavored with rose and jasmine tea is flavored with jasmine flowers.

There are other flavored infusions that are technically not teas because they do not come from the tea tree. These beverages are called a *tisane* (tee SAHN). Tisanes are an infusion of anything besides actual tea leaves. They tend to be delicately flavored. Customers often request them because they do not have the caffeine that tea and coffee have. Some of the more common tisanes include chamomile, lemon verbena, linden, and mint. Tisanes are made and served like tea.

China, Sri Lanka, and Japan. There are many types of tea sold in many different forms.

Tea is sold in bag or loose-leaf forms. Tea bags are often served in foodservice. They are advantageous because they are easy to use and infuse quickly. *Infusing* is the process of combining a hot liquid with a solid substance in order to dissolve the flavor of the solid into the liquid. To make tea from a tea bag, the bag is placed in a small pot filled with boiling water. The pot is brought immediately to the table along with sugar and possibly milk. The customer removes the tea bag after it is done steeping. In other restaurants, the tea bag is served alongside a cup of boiling hot water. The customer then is responsible to infuse his or her own tea.

Finer teas are sold as loose leaf. Loose-leaf tea is generally larger pieces of tea leaves that are sold packed in containers of different sizes. Such teas are brewed in a small teapot filled with boiling hot water. Generally, loose-leaf tea is infused for two to four minutes. The beverage must be strained to remove the actual tea leaves, 48-11. Some fine teas may have individualized infusing instructions.

Draz-Koetke/Goodheart-Willcox Publisher

48-11 Loose-leaf tea is placed in a teapot with boiling water, allowed to infuse, and then poured through a strainer into the teacup.

Summary Points

- As in the kitchen, the front-of-the-house staff is divided into different positions, each with its own set of responsibilities.

- Handling inquiries and reservations properly is key to an operation's success.

- Front-of-the-house staff members who are successful at providing quality service share certain skills and characteristics.

- There are three main types of dining room service—American, Russian, and French.

- Before the guests arrive, the dining area must be preset by the front-of-the-house staff.

- Once the guests arrive, staff should focus on providing quality service during each step of the dining experience so guests leave with a favorable impression.

- Coffee and tea preparation is usually the responsibility of the front-of-the-house staff.

In Review Assess

1. Which front-of-the-house position is responsible for dining room operations?

2. List the responsibilities of a front server.

3. True or false. The job of the front-of-the-house staff is mainly about interacting with the customer.

4. What guidelines should restaurant staff follow when answering the phone?

5. Name three forms of digital media through which restaurant customers might seek information.

6. What skills and characteristics should front-of-the-house staff possess that are key to quality customer service?

7. When food is arranged on plates in the kitchen and delivered to the guests by the server, it is called _____ _____.

8. Which style of service requires the server to cook and prepare dishes in front of the customer?

9. Which style of service requires the server to serve food from a platter onto the guest's plate?

10. List three types of commonly used place settings.

11. What is the proper way to handle a stemmed glass filled with a beverage?

12. What is suggestive selling?

13. Explain what a point-of-sale system is.

14. Plates of food are served to the customer from the _____ and cleared from the _____.

15. List three ways food can be transported to the dining room from the kitchen.

16. True or false. In the United States, espresso is the most common method used to prepare coffee.

17. Explain the process of brewing loose-leaf tea.

Core Skills

18. **Math.** The general rule for coffee making recommends 0.36 ounces (10 g) of ground coffee for every 6 fluid ounces (178 mL) of filtered water. If you are told to brew 2 gallons of coffee, how many ounces of ground coffee will you need?

19. **Writing.** Presume your job at a fine-dining restaurant involves answering the phone, responding to customer questions, and taking reservations. Use the text guidelines to write a script to use when answering the phone. Share your script with the class.

20. **Speaking and Listening.** With a classmate, role-play a customer calling a restaurant with questions and wanting to make a reservation. One person takes the role of the customer and the other takes the role of the restaurant worker. Share your role-play with the class. Discuss what aspects of the role-play were most effective and areas that could use improvement.

21. **Reading.** Use Internet or print resources to read the guidelines for creating different

napkin folds. Write a summary about what you learned. Then demonstrate one of the napkin folds you found most attractive for the class.

22. **Speaking and Listening.** In teams, demonstrate how to create the following place settings: basic American, à la carte, and banquet. After each setting, teams should rotate and evaluate the other teams' place settings for accuracy before moving on to the next type of place setting. Discuss ways to improve efficiency and accuracy.

23. **Math.** You are eating at a restaurant where the service has been excellent. Your bill is $25.48 and you want to leave an exact 20 percent tip on the credit-card bill. How much do you add to your $25.48 bill?

24. **Math.** Suppose you are a server at a small fine-dining restaurant that requires you to hand-calculate customers' checks. Your most recent table had the following charges: guest 1—$17.95 entrée, $2.25 soft drink; guest 2—$21.95 entrée, no beverage; guest 3—$18.25 entrée, $1.95 iced tea; guest 4—$21.95, $1.95 iced tea. Your state has a 9.5 percent restaurant sales tax. Calculate the guest bill including tax.

25. **CTE Career Readiness Practice.** Accurately applying technical skills in the workplace is something employers value. As a front-of-the-house employee you will need to know how to make coffee and tea and how to clean the equipment. Demonstrate how to make coffee using the classroom coffee maker and how to make tea using loose-leaf tea and a teapot. Have the class evaluate your technique. Discuss when, how, and how often coffee makers should be cleaned.

Critical Thinking

26. **Draw conclusions.** Why do you think French service is practiced in only finer quality restaurants? Discuss your conclusions.

27. **Evaluate.** Why is the role of the host one of the most important roles in the dining room? Explain your reasoning.

28. **Identify evidence.** In two teams, debate the following topic: Back-of-the-house staff is more important to a restaurant's success than front-of-the-house staff. Identify evidence to support your view.

Technology

Use Internet resources to investigate one of the following topics of your choice: wireless payment technology, online customer surveys, online reservation sites and apps. After gathering information about your topic, create an illustrated digital report about your findings to share with the class.

Teamwork

Working in teams of three or four, demonstrate the table-service skills discussed in this chapter. As a team, preset the dining table using the basic American place setting. Assign a team member to video each demonstration. One team member should be assigned the server role and the remaining members are "guests." The server should serve the guests following every step from welcoming the guest to presenting the check. The guests should give the server verbal and nonverbal clues as real customers would. As time allows, each student should rotate through the server role. Team members should model good grooming and hygiene standards. The team should review the videos along with their notes to evaluate how each server performed and make recommendations for improvement.

Chef's E-portfolio
Table-Service Skills

The ability to interact well with guests is highly valued by employers. Upload the video of your table-service demonstration from the Teamwork activity to your e-portfolio. Ask your instructor where to save your file. This could be on the school's network or a flash drive of your own. Name your portfolio document *FirstnameLastname_Portfolio Ch#.docx* (i.e., JohnSmith_PortfolioCh48.docx).

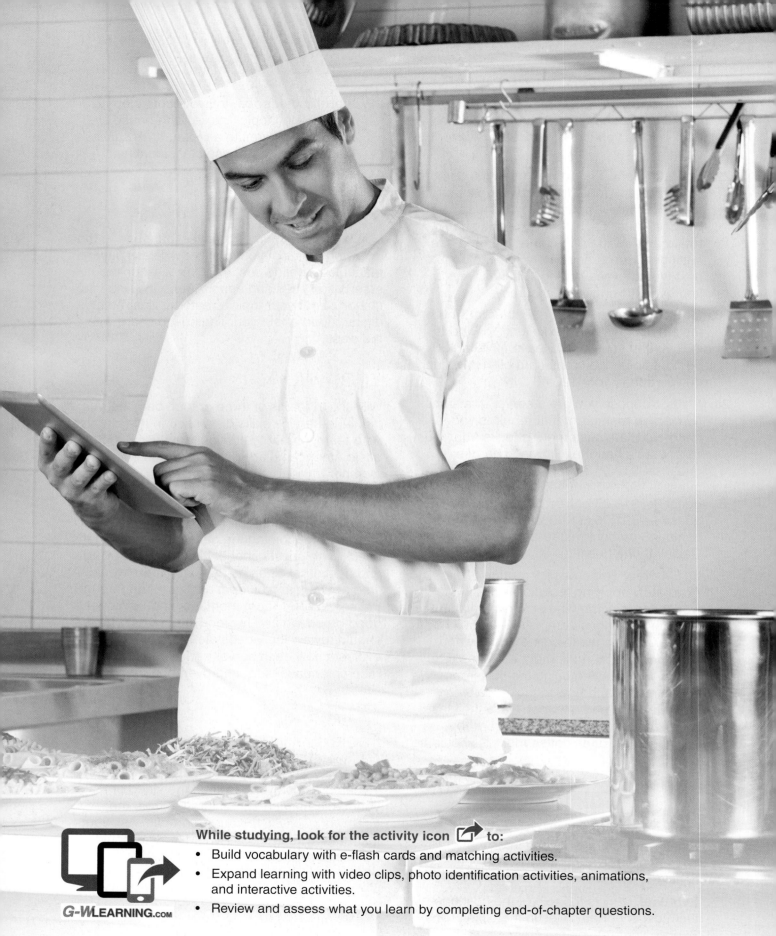

While studying, look for the activity icon ➚ **to:**

- Build vocabulary with e-flash cards and matching activities.
- Expand learning with video clips, photo identification activities, animations, and interactive activities.
- Review and assess what you learn by completing end-of-chapter questions.

G-WLEARNING.com

Reading Prep

Before reading this chapter, review the terms in red and definitions to preview the new content. Building content-related vocabulary is an important activity to broadening your understanding of new material.

Culinary Terminology Build Vocab

food cost, p. 759
forecast, p. 763
as purchased (AP), p. 765
edible portion (EP), p. 765
yield test, p. 765
yield percentage, p. 765
food cost percentage, p. 768

Academic Terminology Build Vocab

labor cost, p. 759
par stock, p. 760
purchase order (PO), p. 760
invoice, p. 761
issuing, p. 762
requisition, p. 762
profit and loss statement (P&L), p. 768
sales, p. 768
expense, p. 768
profit, p. 768
loss, p. 768

Objectives

After studying this chapter, you will be able to

- evaluate the processes a chef must monitor and control to manage food costs.
- demonstrate how to cost a recipe.
- summarize how labor costs are managed in a foodservice operation.
- calculate food and labor cost percentages.
- explain why food cost percentage is a measure of a chef's performance.

One of the most important responsibilities of a chef is to ensure that the establishment he or she works for is profitable. The owners of restaurants, hotels, clubs, and other operations set financial goals for their foodservice. If these goals are not met, the establishment may go out of business.

To meet the financial goals set for them, chefs must successfully manage a variety of resources involved in the operation. Resources used in the course of business become a cost to the establishment. The two most important cost areas are food cost and labor cost. **Food cost** is the cost of food used to make a menu item for a customer. **Labor cost** includes all the expenses involved in maintaining a foodservice staff such as wages, benefits, and payroll taxes.

Managing Food Cost

To manage food costs effectively, a chef must focus on a number of processes. How well the processes of purchasing, receiving, storage, production, and recipe costing are managed can affect food costs either favorably or unfavorably.

Purchasing

The goal of purchasing is to ensure that the kitchen gets the right product at the right price and in the right quantity. Purchasing the right product is the first step in managing the purchasing process. Product specifications for food products must be established together with standardized recipes. They ensure that the exact product called for in a recipe is always the product being purchased. This practice assures consistent quality, accurate purchase prices, and the desired labor cost.

Purchasing the right amount of product is key to controlling food costs. If too much product is purchased, there is a greater chance that food products will be wasted or spoil. Therefore, before deciding how much of various products to purchase, it's necessary to take an inventory of what is on hand. An inventory is taken by physically counting the amounts of various food products in house.

After an inventory is taken, the decision of how much product to purchase can be made. Many operations simplify this decision by setting a par stock. **Par stock** is a specific amount of product to be kept on hand in order to maintain a sufficient supply from one delivery to the next. With this method, when the amount of product on hand falls below a specified level known as an *order point*, a quantity of product is purchased to bring inventories back up to the par stock level.

Competitive Bidding   The prices of food products change regularly. The variability in food prices is due to seasonal changes in both availability of products and the demand for those products. Therefore, it is important for a chef or purchasing agent to know the latest price from vendors before ordering.

One of the key principles of purchasing is comparing prices. By checking the price of products to be purchased with at least two different vendors, the purchaser can be sure he or she is receiving the best price. Essentially vendors are competing against each other for business, which motivates them to sell at the lowest possible price. When comparing prices, it is important to be certain that prices quoted are for products of the same type and quality. Product specifications help to clarify product and price comparisons.

Receiving

Great effort is made to ensure that the right product and quantity at the best price is being ordered. Therefore, it is essential to verify that what has been ordered is what is delivered, 49-1. Procedures for receiving food products are a matter of inspection and verification.

Many establishments use a purchase order system to obtain food and supplies. A **purchase order (PO)** is a document listing the items ordered, quantities ordered, and the prices agreed upon. The chef or buyer fills out the purchase order, which is then used to order the products from the vendor. Most products are delivered with an invoice

CHEF'S ETHICS

Accepting Gifts from Vendors

Most foodservice organizations have strict policies prohibiting accepting gifts from vendors. This helps to ensure that buying decisions are made based on what is best for the establishment and not for the individual making the purchasing decisions. Employees should never make purchasing decisions based on vendor gifts or incentives. Some examples of gifts include those in the form of entertainment, travel, sporting events, personal discounts, and gift certificates. Accepting such gifts is unethical. Be sure to read, understand, and follow your employer's business ethics policies and procedures.

Draz-Koetke/Goodheart-Willcox Publisher

49-1 Verifying the delivery against the invoice is an important aspect of managing resources.

from the vendor. An **invoice** is a list of the quantities of products and their prices that are being delivered.

Products being delivered to the kitchen should be inspected to ensure they are of proper quality. Experience and training are required to recognize the quality signs of the numerous meat, fish, dairy, produce, and grocery products used in commercial kitchens. Packages are often opened so the receiver can see, touch, and smell the products to determine their freshness and quality. Receiving personnel should also inspect food for proper temperature. Frozen foods should be frozen. Foods that require time and temperature control for safety (TCS) must be received at or below 41°F (5°C) and refrigerated promptly. Food delivered in packaging that is dirty or damaged should be rejected.

Another goal of receiving is verifying that the order is correct. The items being delivered with their amount and price are listed on an invoice from the vendor. The individual who is receiving the delivery should check that the items listed on the invoice are actually being delivered in the quantities stated on the invoice. Items sold by weight should be weighed to be sure that the invoiced amount is being delivered. This is especially true with the more expensive items sold by the pound such as meat, poultry, and fish.

Good receiving practice involves checking the invoice against the purchase order to be sure the amount of product ordered is being delivered. The receiver also verifies the invoice price with the price noted on the purchase order. Any discrepancies should be corrected before the order is accepted.

Storage

Proper storage of food product is an essential aspect of sanitation and safe food handling. However, properly storing food products also helps to reduce costs. Correct storage of food reduces waste from spoilage and theft.

Spoilage   Spoilage is reduced by ensuring that products are stored under the best conditions for maximum shelf life. Temperature is key to product shelf life. Verifying that refrigerators and freezers are working properly is necessary for controlling spoilage. Additionally, foods should be stored in the temperature range that is ideal for that particular product. For instance, fish and dairy products should be stored at colder temperatures than lettuce and fresh herbs; and, celery should be refrigerated while potatoes are best stored in an unrefrigerated, cool, dry place.

Another key to reducing food cost is product rotation. Product rotation ensures that the oldest products are used first. This requires a certain amount of effort for kitchen and storeroom staff. The date a product is received is marked on the package. When new products are received the older products are moved to the front to be used first and newer products are moved to the back to be used last. This process of continually moving older product to the front or top and newer product to back or bottom is important for reducing spoilage.

Theft   If unchecked, theft or misuse of products can account for a great deal of lost food product. This has a negative effect on food cost.

Theft of food product is most often committed by a restaurant's staff. Employees do not always think of taking product from their place of employment as stealing. Nevertheless, it is a crime and should be grounds for dismissal.

Theft is best eliminated by removing the opportunity to take food product. Keeping coolers and storerooms locked when the kitchen is not open is a basic practice of good security. While the kitchen is operating, the most expensive and desirable items should be controlled so only accountable personnel have access to them. This includes meats, poultry, and liquor used in the kitchen.

Many operations go a step further by keeping a security camera aimed at food storage and production areas. These cameras can be readily viewed from the chef or manager's office and may also be recorded.

To further discourage theft of product, many foodservice operations apply certain employee rules and regulations. Many operations prohibit large bags or purses from being brought into the kitchen. Employees are often required to enter and leave the premises by an entrance that is monitored. The operation may reserve the right to inspect any package being brought in or out of the establishment. Though the purpose of many of these regulations may not seem clear, they are designed to reduce employee theft and help control costs, 49-2.

Issuing

Many larger foodservice operations have a process for drawing products from food storage. This process is called **issuing**. The storeroom is staffed by clerks who pull product from inventory based on formal requests from different departments. This written or electronic request for product is called a **requisition**. A requisition functions like an internal purchase order and invoice.

FIFO

Many foodservice professionals remember the principle of product rotation by using the acronym *FIFO*. FIFO stands for "first in, first out." This principle simply states the oldest product (first in) should be used first (first out). Avoid poor product rotation practices, which could be called *FILO* or "first in, last out."

Draz-Koetke/Goodheart-Willcox Publisher

49-2 Security plays an important part in controlling food cost.

The purpose of the issuing process is to control food used and also to account for food used by each department or area. As a way of managing food costs, only those who are directly responsible for the food cost of a department or area should be allowed to requisition product.

Production

Overproducing menu items wastes food. Underproducing may result in lost sales. Both instances have a negative effect on food cost. Every meal period, a decision must be made about how much food to prepare. That decision should not be left up to cooks, but should be made by the chef or kitchen manager who is accountable for the food cost.

Forecasting Before cooks can begin their mise en place, the chef must decide how many portions of each menu item to prepare. First the chef must try to predict, or **forecast**, how many diners will be served during the coming meal period and what menu items they will order.

As with weather, forecasting how much business will occur is not an accurate science. Still, it is more than simple guessing. Most restaurants keep records of important events that occur during each day's service. The number of customers served and notes on anything that might have affected business such as weather, special events, or holidays are noted. Chefs and restaurateurs interpret data from these databases to help predict how many guests they will serve for upcoming meal periods. Before forecasting the number of guests for an upcoming Saturday, the chef might look at sales reports from the last three Saturdays and the Saturday of the same week of the previous year. After reviewing these data, the chef can make an informed estimate of how much business to expect.

After estimating how many customers to expect, an estimate of what will be ordered must be made. Again, the chef or kitchen manager must rely on record keeping. Most

foodservice establishments keep track of the number of each menu item sold. These data can be used to determine a menu item's popularity.

Production Sheet The number of each menu item the chef wants prepared for meal service is often communicated to the kitchen staff with a production sheet, 49-3. A production sheet is posted in the kitchen before preparation for each meal begins. It shows the cooks how many portions the chef wants them to have on hand for the upcoming meal. Cooks refer to this sheet to know how many portions of the items on their station they need to prepare.

The production sheet is also used to note how many of each item is left at the end of the meal period. If the item is sold out, the time it ran out is noted. This information helps the chef forecast for the next meal period.

Costing Recipes

A standardized recipe is not only important for producing a uniform food product, but also for controlling costs. This cost control function is essential for the financial survival of any foodservice operation.

When a chef is developing or evaluating a recipe, knowing the cost of each ingredient can be helpful in controlling costs. If the recipe cost is high, the chef can readily see which ingredients are expensive and consider less costly substitutes that would not sacrifice quality or flavor. For example, a lower grade, less expensive tomato could be chopped up for a salsa recipe but would not be appropriate for tomato slices in a Caprese salad recipe.

Another reason to cost out a recipe is for accurate menu pricing. Without knowing the cost of producing a certain dish each time it is made, operators have no basis for pricing an item. Preparation of standardized recipes and calculating the cost of those recipes is a task that must be performed before prices are assigned to menu items.

The Grill Room

Day: _Tuesday_   **Supervisor:** _J. D._

Date: _April 5_   **Estimated Covers:** _165_

Shift: _Dinner_   **Actual Covers:** _152_

Menu Item	Station	Quantity needed	Inventory on hand	Need to prep	Leftover/ time ran out
Shrimp Cocktail	Pantry	30	6	24	3
Paté Maison	Pantry	16	8	8	4
Garden salad	Pantry	55	10	45	12
Caesar salad	Pantry	70	14	56	9
Onion soup	Prep	35	0	35	9:45 pm
Lobster bisque	Prep	30	8	22	6
Salmon fillet	Sauté	20	3	17	7
Tuna steak	Grill	15	6	9	8:10 pm
Chicken Diable	Grill	16	9	7	11
Veal cutlet	Sauté	25	2	23	4
Pork chop	Sauté	30	12	18	8
Strip steak	Grill	35	9	26	9
Tournedoes	Sauté	30	4	26	5
T-bone	Grill	35	16	19	10

49-3 The production sheet is an effective way for chefs to communicate with and receive information back from their cooks.

Mix In Math

Calculating Unit and Total Cost

Ingredients for foodservice are usually purchased in bulk units such as case, bushel, barrel, bag, or flat. In order to calculate the recipe cost, it is often necessary to convert the price of the purchase unit into a price that corresponds to the units used in the recipe such as pounds, ounces, or pieces. Once you know the unit cost, you can calculate the total cost for that ingredient.

Per Pound Unit Cost

Divide the cost of the purchase unit by the number of pounds in the purchase unit. For example, you purchase a 50 pound case of shrimp for $440.00

$440.00/cs. ÷ 50 lb./cs. = $8.80/lb.

Per Ounce Unit Cost

If the quantity used in the recipe is less than one pound, then the unit cost is usually expressed in ounces. Divide the per pound price by 16 (16 oz. = 1 lb.) to get the price per ounce. For example, if the recipe called for shrimp in ounces

$8.80/lb. ÷ 16 oz./lb. = $0.55/oz.

Per Piece Unit Cost

Divide the cost of the purchase unit by the number of pieces in the purchase unit. For example, you purchase a 140 count (ct.) case of lemons for $21.00

$21.00/case ÷ 140 lemons/case = $0.15/lemon

Total Cost

Multiply the number of units called for in the recipe by the unit price. For example, if a recipe calls for 6 ounces of shrimp

6oz. x $0.55/oz. = $3.30 total cost for shrimp

Chefs and foodservice managers calculate the cost of menu items on a regular basis to account for the changing prices of food products they buy. The costing process is simple math, but it can be time-consuming since the cost of every ingredient of every menu item must be calculated, 49-4.

Chefs often use standardized recipe cost sheets to calculate the food cost for a recipe. There are also many software programs available that can cost a recipe. Whichever method is used, accurate standardized recipes and current ingredient costs are essential.

Yield   Many times recipes call for a trimmed or prepared product. This complicates the costing process. When ingredients must be trimmed, peeled, boned, or cut, that loss of product must be added in to the cost of the recipe. The raw, unprepared product in the same form it is delivered from the vendor is called **as purchased (AP)**. The amount of food product that remains after cleaning, cooking, or other preparation is called **edible portion (EP)**. For example, a fresh, whole apple is as purchased, however, an apple that is peeled and cored is edible portion.

The process of determining and recording the usable amount, or edible portion, of a product is called a **yield test**, 49-5. The yield test may include the fabrication of meats or the cleaning and trimming of produce. Yield tests are regularly done on the most expensive ingredients in the kitchen, especially meat, poultry, and fish. Once the yield test is performed, the yield percentage can be calculated. The ratio of EP to AP is called the **yield percentage**. This percentage tells the chef how much usable product, or EP, he or she can expect from a given amount of AP product. Chefs keep a record of yield percentages to assist them in purchasing and to monitor the efficiency of the kitchen.

Recipe Costing Instructions

Steps		Information Source
①	Enter name of the recipe.	Recipe
②	Enter number assigned to the recipe for filing for computer purposes.	
③	Enter the serving size that is served to the customer (usually expressed in ounces, cups, or pieces).	
④	Note the number of portions the recipe yields.	
⑤	List ingredients using the names listed on invoice.	
⑥	List the amounts called for in the recipe (usually in pounds, ounces, or other unit).	
⑦	Calculate the cost per unit as noted in step 6.	Invoice
⑧	Calculate the Total Cost for each ingredient by multiplying the amount (step 6) by the unit cost (step 7).	Calculation
⑨	Calculate Total Recipe Cost by summing the Total Costs.	
⑩	Enter the date of current cost calculation.	
⑪	Calculate the Portion Cost by dividing Total Recipe Cost (step 9) by the number of portions (step 4).	
⑫	Enter date of previous recipe cost calculation.	Previous Recipe Cost Sheet
⑬	Enter previous portion cost.	

Sample Recipe Cost Sheet

① **Recipe name** Simmered Beef Short Ribs   ② **Recipe number** 30.2

③ **Portion size** 7 oz.   ④ **Number of Portions** 10

Notes _____

Ingredients		Ingredient Cost	
⑤ **Name**	⑥ **Amount**	⑦ **Unit Cost**	⑧ **Total Cost**
beef short ribs	4½ lb.	$6.29/lb.	$28.30
salt	1.0 oz.	$0.06/oz.	$0.06
turnips	6 oz.	$0.05/oz.	$0.30
carrots	8 oz.	$0.07/oz.	$0.56
celery	8 oz.	$0.09/oz.	$0.72
leeks	5 oz.	$0.14/oz.	$0.70
parsley	0.5 oz.	$0.10/oz.	$0.05
⑨ Total Recipe Cost			$30.69

⑩ **Date Costed** 11/19/2016   ⑪ **Portion Cost** $3.07

⑫ **Previous Date Costed** 9/20/2016   ⑬ **Previous Portion Cost** $2.98

49-4 Follow the steps in the Recipe Costing Instructions as you review the Sample Recipe Cost Sheet.

Draz-Koetke/Goodheart-Willcox Publisher

49-5 Yield tests should be performed often since yields of the same product can change over time.

Labor Cost

Along with food cost, chefs are charged with achieving financial goals for the cost of labor in the kitchen. After food, labor is the largest cost in most operations.

The most important tool in controlling labor cost is the staff schedule. Most operations schedule kitchen staff on a weekly basis. Before creating the schedule, the chef or kitchen manager needs to forecast the expected volume of business for the week. Much like forecasting production, historical data is the source for the forecast.

After the chef assigns workers for each shift, the number of hours for each employee is totaled and then multiplied by each employee's respective pay rate. By totaling the labor cost of each employee, the chef or kitchen manager can calculate what the labor cost for the week will be. If the amount is

Mix In Math

Using Yield Percentage to Find EP Price

Calculating Yield Percentage

A restaurant serves fillet of sole on its menu. They purchase whole fish and cut the fillets themselves. To determine the yield percentage, you must know the AP weight and the EP weight.

EP ÷ AP x 100 = Yield Percentage

The fish cook receives 15 pounds of whole sole (AP) from the vendor. After filleting, the finished fillets weigh a total of 6 pounds (EP). Now, you can determine the yield percentage.

6 lb. fillets ÷ 15 lb. whole fish = 0.4
0.4 x 100 = 40% yield

Calculating EP Price

Before you can cost a recipe using the sole fillets, you must calculate the EP price.

AP Cost ÷ Yield Percentage = EP Price

The restaurant purchases whole sole for $3.80/lb. (AP cost). You already determined that the yield percentage is 40% (hint: remember to convert percent back to decimal before dividing).

$3.80/lb. ÷ 0.40 = $9.50/lb. for sole fillets

You should use $9.50/lb. EP price for sole fillets when calculating the recipe cost.

higher than the amount budgeted, adjustments in the schedule must be made.

After employees are scheduled for the week, the actual labor cost is kept in check by enforcing rules regarding the time clock or time sheet. Employees should not be allowed to punch in early or punch out late without the approval of their supervisor. If the amount of business forecasted does not materialize, chefs or kitchen staff may need to send staff home early or adjust the schedule during the week.

Chefs must have a clear understanding of labor laws and, in some cases, union work rules when scheduling and managing labor cost. All the decisions made in scheduling and pay rates must be in accordance with federal labor laws and the laws of the state in which the business operates. Violation of these laws can result in sizable fines for the foodservice establishment.

Measuring Performance

Chefs may be doing all they can to control their costs but how will they know if their efforts have been successful? They must be able to measure their results.

Profit or Loss?

As in any other business, chefs must know how well their foodservice operation is performing. That performance is ultimately measured in the **profit and loss statement (P&L)**. The profit and loss statement (P&L), also called an *income statement,* is a business report that lists the sales and expenses incurred to make those sales during a given period of time. Many foodservice operations organize their P&L according to the Uniform System of Accounts for Restaurants (USAR), an accounting classification system established by the National Restaurant Association (NRA). Using the USAR enables foodservice professionals to organize sales and expense data in a consistent, efficient manner. As a result, chefs and managers are better able to compare and evaluate performance when making business decisions.

Sales are the dollars received in payment for the meal. **Expenses** are the costs incurred to prepare and serve the meal. When the sales are greater than the expenses, the business is said

to have a **profit**. If the expenses are greater than the sales, the business is operating at a **loss**. The term "bottom line" is often used to refer to the profit or loss of a company because it is the last, or bottom, line on the profit and loss statement. Every line on the P&L is also calculated and recorded as a percentage of sales, 49-6.

Food and Labor Cost Percentages

Food cost percentage shows the portion of food sales that was spent on food expenses. This statistic measures how

Profit and Loss Statement			
For Month Ending April 30, 2014			
Sales			
Food Sales	$92,650		100.0%
Cost of Sales			
Food Cost	$32,570		35.2%
Gross Profit		$60,080	64.8%
Operating Expenses			
Labor	$30,776		33.2%
Direct	$6,252		6.7%
Occupancy	$12,900		13.9%
Total		$49,928	53.9%
Profit			
Profit Before Taxes		$10,152	11.0%

49-6 Chefs use P&L's and other financial statements to measure the performance of their operation.

efficiently the operation is generating food sales. Because the amount of food an operation uses varies with the amount of business it does, the cost of food used is typically measured against food sales. The formula used to calculate food cost percentage is

Food Costs ÷ Food Sales = Food Cost Percentage

For example, suppose a restaurant's food costs for the month of April were $32,570 and food sales for that time were $92,650. The food cost percentage for April is

$32,570 ÷ 92,650 = 0.352 x 100 = 35.2%

Food cost percent is closely monitored in most foodservice establishments. It can be calculated daily, weekly, monthly, or annually. It is an important measure of how well a chef is managing the kitchen operation.

Similarly, labor cost percentage measures the amount of food sales that was spent on labor during a specific period of time. Labor cost includes the cost of payroll, payroll taxes, and employee benefits such as insurance.

Labor Costs ÷ Food Sales = Labor Cost Percentage

For example, if a restaurant's labor costs for the month of April were $30,776 and food sales for that time were $92,650. The labor cost percentage for April is

$30,776 ÷ 92,650 = 0.332 x 100 = 33.2%

Restaurant Management Software

Measuring a foodservice operation's financial performance involves many—and sometimes frequent—calculations. To make the task easier and deliver information to chefs and managers in a timely manner, most operations use computer software. Software for tracking food and labor cost is often integrated with the restaurant's point of sale (POS) system. An integrated software package can help manage sales receipts, recipes, food and beverage inventory, ordering, receiving, scheduling, time keeping and labor cost, 49-7. As with any system, results are only as accurate as the information that is inputted. While a software system can assist the process of managing resources, it still takes a trained and diligent manager to ensure successful performance.

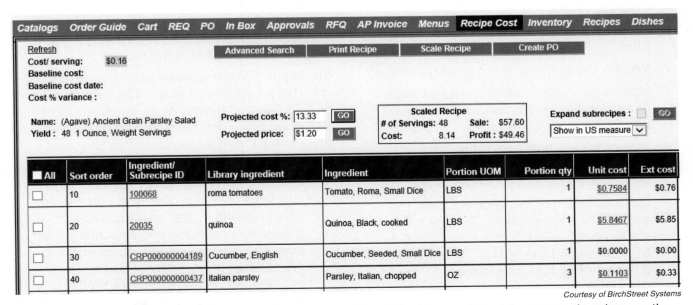

Courtesy of BirchStreet Systems

49-7 Using foodservice management computer programs like this recipe costing software greatly enhances the chef's ability to manage food cost and profitability.

Summary Points

- Chefs must manage costs for a foodservice establishment to be profitable.

- Food and labor costs are the two most significant costs chefs and kitchen managers are charged with managing.

- To manage food costs effectively, chefs must focus on purchasing, receiving, issuing, storage, production, and recipe costs.

- Staff scheduling is key to controlling labor cost.

- A chef's ability to control costs is reflected in the profit and loss statement.

- Food cost percentage is closely monitored in foodservice and measures how well a chef is managing his or her costs.

In Review Assess

1. Contrast food cost with labor cost.

2. True or false. Par stock is a specific amount of product to be kept on hand in order to maintain a sufficient supply from one delivery to the next.

3. Why is it important for the chef or purchasing agent to compare prices?

4. During the receiving process, the purchase order is checked against which document from the vendor?

5. Proper storage reduces food waste resulting from _____ and _____.

6. What is the purpose of the issuing process?

7. How does kitchen staff find out how many of each menu item to prepare for the next service?

8. True or false. Chefs and foodservice managers calculate food costs for a recipe only once because it is difficult to do.

9. Indicate if each of the following is an example of *as purchased (AP)* product or *edible portion (EP)*:
   A. raw ground beef
   B. peeled and cubed potatoes
   C. whole cantaloupe
   D. seasoned, cooked boneless chicken breast

10. What is the most important tool in managing labor cost?

11. If a company's expenses are greater than its sales, it is operating at a _____.

12. True or false. The amount of food used in most foodservice operations is constant with little variation.

Core Skills

13. **Math.** After taking an inventory, a chef determines $1,275 in food was used to produce customer meals this past week. In that same week, the restaurant made $4,150 in food sales. What is the food cost percentage for that week?

14. **Math.** The restaurant at which you work has several salads on the menu that require tomatoes. The chef receives two 10-lb. cases of regular tomatoes at $27.50 per case. After cleaning and slicing, the tomatoes yielded 17.4 lb. Calculate the yield percentage and the edible portion (EP) price for the tomatoes.

15. **Math.** Choose one of the text recipes and demonstrate the process of costing the recipe using the method shown in this chapter. You can locate ingredient costs from several sources including: school foodservice purchasing agent, your instructor, or via online or print food advertisements. How would the edible portion cost vary if you doubled the yield of the recipe?

16. **Math.** For a one-week period, a restaurant had a payroll cost of $31,184, payroll taxes of $6,236 and payments for employee benefits of $5,613. Food sales for that same week were $118,450. Calculate the labor cost percentage for the week.

17. **CTE Career Readiness Practice.** A restaurant sous chef is in charge of purchasing food products for the operation. A salesperson for one of the suppliers offers the sous chef free tickets to a major sporting event. Should the sous chef accept the gift? Discuss in class the implications of the sous chef accepting this gift. What would accepting such a gift say about the chef's

integrity? If word got out about this among employees, how could such an action impact the chef's leadership and management? What does such a practice say about the vendor? Is this an ethical way to get business? Is it legal?

Critical Thinking

18. **Analyze cause and effect.** Can a chef or manager be responsible for food cost if he or she has no authority over purchasing? Analyze the cause and effect of this situation. What are your conclusions? Use the text and other reliable resources to cite evidence to support your thinking.

19. **Generate procedures.** The chef is hiring a new receiving clerk with no previous experience. You have been asked to develop a brief training manual on proper procedures for receiving and compile a list of tools he or she will need to perform the job.

20. **Generate a solution.** After taking inventory, the chef determines that five portions of steak are missing. Identify possible reasons for this product to be missing and corresponding solutions for controlling loss.

21. **Analyze evidence.** You have been hired to manage an existing restaurant. The owner has expressed concerns about food costs in the kitchen. You discover that each cook decides how many menu items he or she will prepare. There has never been a problem running out of menu items. Analyze the evidence. Would you make any changes to this practice? Explain your answer and cite your reasoning.

22. **Interpret data.** You are responsible for determining how many servings of Spinach Stuffed Chicken Breasts to tell the cooks to prep for this Friday's dinner service. You review sales reports for the past four Fridays and learn sales of this menu item were as follows: Jan. 1st–23 sold; Jan. 8th–9 sold (note: major snowstorm on this date); Jan. 15th–22 sold; Jan. 22nd–20 sold. How many Spinach Stuffed Chicken Breasts would you tell cooks to prepare? Explain your decision.

Technology

Use Internet or print resources to research one or more restaurant management software products. Review any case studies, videos, or testimonials about the software. Identify the business solutions and benefits such systems have for a food-service operation. How does the software work? Are there different levels of software available to meet customer needs? What do customers have to say about the software? Write a summary of your findings to share with the class.

Teamwork

You have been hired as a consultant to develop a plan for a new restaurant's purchasing, receiving, storage, and issuing process. Before the restaurant opens, the owner wants a process identified that ensures her inventory is secure and managed in a cost-effective manner. Assemble a small team to help you develop the plan. Your team's plan should outline the steps in the process and identify the staff member who will be responsible for each step. Include a brief rationale for each step in the process. Be sure to note any equipment necessary for the staff to be able to perform their jobs. As a team, present your plan to the restaurant owner (the class).

Chef's E-portfolio
Researching Restaurant Management Software

Upload your summary of findings from the Technology activity to your e-portfolio. Ask your instructor where to save your file. This could be on the school's network or a flash drive of your own. Name your portfolio document *FirstnameLastname_Portfolio Ch#.docx* (i.e., JohnSmith_PortfolioCh49.docx).

While studying, look for the activity icon  to:
- Build vocabulary with e-flash cards and matching activities.
- Expand learning with video clips, photo identification activities, animations, and interactive activities.
- Review and assess what you learn by completing end-of-chapter questions.

Nutrition

50

Reading Prep

In preparation for this chapter, research the new federal menu labeling requirements compelled by Section 4205 of the Patient Protection and Affordable Care Act of 2010. As you are reading the chapter, keep in mind the goal of this law.

Culinary Terminology Build Vocab

nutrition, p. 773
nutrients, p. 773
essential nutrients, p. 774
calorie, p. 774
protein, p. 774
complete protein, p. 774
incomplete protein, p. 774
carbohydrate, p. 775
lipids, p. 776
saturated fat, p. 776
unsaturated fat, p. 776
trans fat, p. 777
hydrogenation, p. 777
cholesterol, p. 777
phytochemicals, p. 781
probiotics, p. 781
prebiotics, p. 781
nutrient-dense food, p. 782

Academic Terminology Build Vocab

bonds, p. 776
preclude, p. 789

Objectives

After studying this chapter, you will be able to

- explain how the six nutrient groups affect health.

- compare nonnutrients to nutrients.

- summarize the recommendations from *Dietary Guidelines for Americans* and MyPlate food guidance system.

- interpret ingredient lists and nutritional facts on food labels.

- apply nutrition principles to create healthful menu selections and accommodate special needs.

Understanding how different foods and food preparations affect health is important for all chefs. A chef can apply this knowledge during menu planning, and food purchasing and preparation to provide more healthful options for diners.

Nutrients

Nutrition is the study of foods, their components, and how the body processes and utilizes them. While this may sound unrelated to the study of cooking, nutrition is affecting the chef's profession more and more. A chef must consider not only the appearance and flavor of a dish, but also the nutritional impact of a dish. Customers are interested in how the foods they eat may benefit or harm them.

Nutrients are the substances in food that the body uses for energy, growth, and to regulate various functions. Nutrients are divided into six groups—proteins, carbohydrates,

SCIENCE &
TECHNOLOGY

Calorie or Kilocalorie?

The scientific definition of a calorie is the heat required to raise the temperature of one gram of water one degree Celsius. When measuring the energy value of food, the term Calorie is used. A Calorie is the amount of heat required to raise the temperature of one *kilo*gram of water one degree Celsius. Another name for Calorie is *kilocalorie*. Dietitians and other health professionals use kilocalories when calculating the energy value of foods, however, individuals outside the scientific community generally use the term *calorie* with a lowercase *c* to measure their energy intake from food.

lipids, water, vitamins, and minerals. The human body can manufacture some nutrients. The nutrients that the body cannot make and must be supplied by the diet are called **essential nutrients**. Serious illness and even death can result if a diet is lacking or missing essential nutrients.

Proteins, lipids, and carbohydrates are the nutrients that supply the body with energy. A **calorie** is the unit used to measure the amount of energy contained in foods. The term *calorie* is commonly used when discussing nutrition.

Proteins

Proteins are the building blocks of the human body. A **protein** is a chain of various amino acids that form a molecule. How the amino acids are combined and in what sequence determines the type of protein. There are nine *indispensable amino acids* (also known as *essential amino acids*) that must be consumed to support life. *Dispensable amino acids* (also known as *nonessential amino acids*) can be manufactured by the human body. Some health issues can inhibit the body's ability to

produce a dispensable amino acid and then it must be obtained from a food source. Proteins contribute four calories of energy per gram.

Protein is found throughout the human body. For instance, protein is part of the skin, blood vessels, blood, inner organs, hair, nails, enzymes, hormones, and antibodies. Early in life, protein is essential to support a rapidly growing body. During adulthood, protein still remains an important part of the diet and is needed for growth, maintenance, and repair of body tissues. In addition, proteins are required to replace other proteins that are damaged or used up.

Food sources of protein can be either animal or plant based. Animal proteins, which include meats, poultry, seafood, eggs, milk, and cheese, are complete proteins. **Complete proteins** contain all nine indispensable amino acids in the correct proportions needed to support life. Plant-based protein sources include legumes, nuts, and grains. Most of these are **incomplete proteins** because they are missing one or more of the indispensable amino acids. Therefore, vegetarians must combine different vegetable protein sources to create the equivalent of a complete protein. Two traditional combinations that supply complete proteins are corn tortilla with refried beans and peanut butter on wheat bread, 50-1. Some plant-based protein sources do supply the indispensable amino acids and are

jabiru/Shutterstock.com
50-1 Many Central American dishes combine beans and rice to provide a complete protein.

considered complete proteins. They are quinoa and amaranth, which are grains and soybean, which is a legume.

Carbohydrates

Carbohydrates are the body's chief energy source. Carbohydrates are further divided into simple and complex carbohydrates. Simple carbohydrates are sugars and complex carbohydrates include starch and fiber. Carbohydrates contribute four calories of energy per gram. Plants are the principal sources of carbohydrates. Animals store carbohydrates as glycogen.

Simple carbohydrates consist of either a single sugar unit or two sugar units combined. There are six sugars that are considered simple carbohydrates, 50-2. Of these six sugars, *glucose* is the body's preferred source of energy. Milk contains a small amount of sugar called *lactose*. Some people have lactose intolerance and are unable to digest the lactose. When these individuals consume food containing lactose, it can lead to digestive discomfort. Another sugar, *fructose*, is the sweetest of all the sugars. Fructose is present in fruits and honey. The scientific name for common table sugar is *sucrose*. Sucrose is composed of glucose and fructose. Common table sugar is made from sugarcane or sugar beets.

Starch is one of two types of complex carbohydrate. Starch consists of long chains of glucose molecules. Starches provide the body with energy because these chains are broken into single glucose molecules during digestion. As a result, starches provide energy at a slower pace than simple carbohydrates. Common sources of complex carbohydrates include pasta, potatoes, bread, grains, and legumes.

Fiber is another type of complex carbohydrate. Fiber—like starch—is made of long chains of glucose. Unlike starch, these chains do not break down during digestion. As a result, fiber is not digested. Instead, it passes

SCIENCE & TECHNOLOGY

Nonnutritive Sweeteners

For the last 100 years, scientists have been inventing nonnutritive sweeteners (NNS). Nonnutritive sweeteners are intensely sweet chemicals that have very little or no caloric value. The *Dietary Guidelines* state "Substituting NNS for higher-energy foods and beverages can decrease energy intake, but evidence of their effectiveness for weight management is limited." Nonnutritive sweeteners approved for use in the United States include

- **Acesulfame–K** is 200 times as sweet as table sugar and can be used in baking.

- **Aspartame**, also called NutraSweet®, is 200 times as sweet as table sugar and cannot be used in baking.

- **Luo han guo**, also known as *monk fruit* extract is 150 to 300 times sweeter than table sugar.

- **Neotame** is 7,000 to 13,000 times sweeter than sugar and can be used in baking.

- **Saccharin** is 300 times as sweet as table sugar and can be used in baking.

- **Stevia** (Rebaudioside A or Reb-A) is 250 to 300 times sweeter than table sugar and can be used for baking and is more stable in liquid form than acesulfame K and aspartame.

- **Sucralose** is 600 times as sweet as table sugar and can be used in baking.

Simple Carbohydrates

- Fructose
- Glucose
- Galactose
- Lactose (glucose + galactose)
- Maltose (glucose + glucose)
- Sucrose (glucose + fructose)

Animation

50-2 Lactose, maltose, and sucrose are each composed of two sugar units.

through the body and is excreted. Sufficient amounts of fiber contribute to overall health by reducing the risk of various cancers and heart disease. There are two types of fiber—soluble and insoluble, 50-3. Soluble fiber absorbs large amounts of liquid during digestion. Oats, fruits, vegetables, and legumes are good sources of soluble fiber. Insoluble fiber, which is not soluble in water, absorbs far less liquid during digestion. Good sources of insoluble fiber include whole grains and the structural parts of various fruits and vegetables.

Lipids

Lipids are the most energy-dense nutrients that humans consume. **Lipids** include fats and oils, as well as other fat-like substances such as cholesterol. Fats and oils are chains of carbon atoms to which

hydrogen atoms are attached. The chains vary in length depending on the type of fat or oil. The chains of carbon atoms also differ in the types of **bonds**, or forces that hold the chains together, 50-4. Lipids contain nine calories of energy per gram. Compare that to four calories per gram for both carbohydrates and proteins.

Fats are found primarily in animal-based foods. This type of lipid is solid at room temperature and is called a **saturated fat**. Saturated fats contain only single bonds. Dietary sources high in saturated fat include fatty meats, poultry skin, eggs, and dairy products. Coconut oil and palm kernel oil are unusual because they are plant-based products that are high in saturated fat. Oils are liquid at room temperature and are **unsaturated fats**. These fats are found in plant-based foods. Unsaturated fats contain

50-3 Plant-based foods contain fiber, animal-based foods do not.

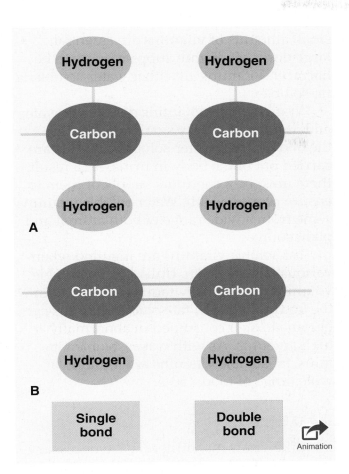

50-4 (A) Single bonds link carbon atoms to four other atoms. (B) When a double bond links carbon atoms, each carbon atom can bond to only two additional atoms. Double bonds are stronger bonds than single, but less stable.

one or more double bonds depending on the specific oil. Dietary sources of unsaturated fats include nuts, seeds, avocados, and olive, safflower, soybean, and sunflower oils, 50-5.

Lipids are often blamed for contributing to obesity and heart disease, but not all lipids are the same. Some oils are healthful and essential for the body to function. Lipids play a critical role in the body. Lipids are needed for normal growth and development, provide a concentrated source of energy, and transport fat-soluble vitamins. Lipids that are stored in the body tissue provide insulation for the body, supply energy when food is unavailable, and protect the body's organs.

Trans **fat** is a type of lipid that is created when an unsaturated oil is chemically changed to resemble a saturated fat. The chemical process that changes liquid oil to a solid fat is called **hydrogenation**. *Trans* fats are often created when oil is partially hydrogenated. Some of the most common partially hydrogenated oils are margarine and deep-fryer oils. *Trans* fats have adverse health effects and intake of them should be as low as possible.

Another type of lipid is cholesterol. **Cholesterol** is a white, pasty, fat-like substance found in the bloodstream and cells that is essential for many of the body's functions. For instance, cholesterol is needed for cell membrane structure and to construct various hormones. It is not necessary to consume food sources of cholesterol because the body is able to make it. Cholesterol is found only in animal tissue and never in plant tissue.

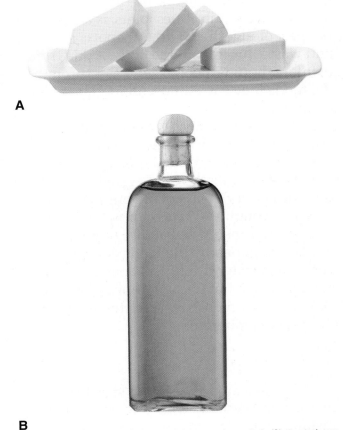

50-5 (A) Butter is solid at room temperature and a saturated fat. (B) Olive oil, an unsaturated fat, is liquid at room temperature.

Cholesterol is transported in the blood by high-density lipoprotein (HDL) and low-density lipoprotein (LDL). LDL circulates cholesterol in the body. High levels of LDL in the blood can deposit excess cholesterol on artery walls that feed blood to the heart and brain. If the arteries are narrowed and a clot forms, it could result in a heart attack or stroke. HDL has the opposite effect of LDL. HDL takes cholesterol to the liver which then removes it from the body. Thus, high levels of HDL and low levels of LDL in the blood are desirable.

Water

Water is the single greatest component of the human body. Water accounts for 50 to 60 percent of the weight of the human body. Without water, humans can only survive a short while. While water provides no energy, it is part of almost all bodily functions. For instance, water lubricates joints, is an essential part of digestion, and transports nutrients and waste throughout the body. Aside from drinking liquids, people get water through the foods they eat. Almost all food has some amount of water in it.

Thirst is the body's way of signaling that the body is starting to dehydrate and that more water is needed quickly to maintain optimal water levels. Beverages should provide about 75 percent of your daily water needs, or roughly 8½ cups for women and 11½ cups for men. The balance of your water needs is supplied by the foods you eat. The body loses water through evaporation and excretion. In a hot kitchen, cooks may likely need to drink more to replace the water lost through perspiration.

Vitamins

Vitamins are necessary to support many of the systems within the body. For instance, vitamins ensure proper vision, support the immune system, aid in the formation of healthy bones and teeth, and are part of the blood-clotting process. While small amounts of vitamins are essential, large doses of vitamin supplements can be harmful. Vitamins are either water-soluble or fat-soluble.

Water-soluble vitamins dissolve in water and are stored in very small amounts in the body. Excess water-soluble vitamins are carried out of the body in urine. As a result, there must be a continual supply of them to ensure proper health. Water-soluble vitamins come from a wide range of both animal and plant sources.

Fat-soluble vitamins are ingested when various fats are eaten. Unlike water-soluble vitamins, fat-soluble vitamins are stored in the body. Therefore, fat-soluble vitamins can become toxic if consumed in abnormally high amounts. As with water-soluble vitamins, fat-soluble vitamins are found in a wide range of foods, 50-6.

Minerals

Like vitamins, minerals are necessary for many body processes and become part of the body's bones, tissues, and fluids. Minerals are necessary for many important functions such as energy metabolism, water balance, bone formation, and proper functioning of the nervous system. Minerals are divided into major and trace minerals. Major minerals are those that are needed in the diet in amounts of 100 milligrams or more per day. Trace minerals are required in amounts of less than 100 milligrams per day. Both major minerals and trace minerals are important for good health, 50-7.

Nonnutrients

Other substances are found in foods that provide benefits to the body but are not classified as nutrients. These nonnutrients do not supply energy, but play useful roles throughout the body. Phytochemicals, prebiotics, and probiotics are examples of nonnutrients.

Vitamins and Their Functions

Vitamin	Function
Fat-Soluble Vitamins	
Vitamin A	Aids normal vision, helps body fight infections, needed for normal growth and development Sources: beef liver, sweet potato, broccoli, cantaloupe, spinach, peaches
Vitamin D	Needed for proper development of bones and teeth, controls cell growth Sources: produced by the body when exposed to sunlight, cod liver oil, fortified milk
Vitamin E	Protects cells from possible damage due to exposure to oxygen Sources: vegetable oils, whole-grain breads and cereals, eggs, organ meats, leafy green vegetables
Vitamin K	Helps blood clot Sources: green leafy vegetables, cauliflower, liver, egg yolk
Water-Soluble Vitamins	
Thiamin (vitamin B_1)	Needed for energy production; aids proper heart, nerve, and muscle function Source: whole-grain products, pork, legumes
Riboflavin (vitamin B_2)	Needed for growth and red blood cell production; aids energy production Sources: eggs, green leafy vegetables, lean meats, milk, legumes, nuts
Niacin (vitamin B_3)	Aids digestion, contributes to healthy skin and nerve function, aids energy production Sources: meat, fish, poultry, whole-grain products
Pantothenic acid (vitamin B_5)	Aids growth and development, helps body break down and use food Sources: broccoli, avocado, mushrooms, potatoes, oatmeal, sunflower seeds
Pyridoxine (vitamin B_6)	Needed for production of proteins and red blood cells, aids energy production, promotes healthy nervous system Sources: fortified cereals, bananas, potatoes, liver, garbanzo beans
Biotin (vitamin B_7)	Aids growth and development, helps body break down and use food Sources: cauliflower, liver, cheese, peanuts
Folate (vitamin B_9)	Promotes healthy cell growth, critical for healthy development of fetus Sources: dark-green, leafy vegetables, orange juice, liver, sunflower seeds, legumes, fortified cereals
Cobalamin (vitamin B_{12})	Helps body break down and use food, aids development of red blood cells and healthy nerve function Sources: beef, milk products, shellfish
Vitamin C	Protects cells from possible damage due to exposure to oxygen, aids skin and bone health, helps body use iron, aids healing Sources: oranges, strawberries, broccoli, raw spinach, banana, cauliflower

Lists of food sources are not all-inclusive.

50-6 Eating a variety of foods helps supply your body with the vitamins needed for health.

Minerals and Their Functions	
Mineral	**Function**
Major Minerals	
Sodium	Helps with nerve and muscle function, maintains fluid balance in the body Sources: table salt, processed foods
Magnesium	Helps with energy production and transport, needed for protein production, aids nerve and muscle function Sources: dark green, leafy vegetables; bananas; avocados; almonds; legumes; whole grains
Phosphorus	Needed for tooth and bone formation, needed for energy storage and protein production, aids body's use and storage of carbohydrate and fat Sources: meats, milk products
Sulfur	Helps maintain acid-base balance in body, aids in removing drugs from the body Sources: all foods containing protein
Chloride	Maintains fluid balance in the body, needed for proper digestion Sources: table salt, tomatoes, lettuce, celery, olives
Potassium	Needed for growth, helps regulate acid-base balance in body, aids in production of proteins, needed for normal heart function Sources: meat, poultry, salmon, cod, soy products, broccoli, sweet potatoes, cantaloupe, bananas, milk, nuts
Calcium	Supports structure of bones and teeth, needed for muscle movement and proper nerve function, helps move blood throughout body, aids in release of hormones and enzymes Sources: dairy foods, broccoli, Chinese cabbage, canned sardines and salmon, fortified foods
Trace Minerals	
Flouride	Supports the structure of bones and teeth Source: drinking water
Chromium	Involved in body's use and storage of carbohydrate, protein, and fat Sources: meat, whole-grain products
Manganese	Serves as key part of enzymes involved in preventing tissue damage Sources: fresh pineapple, oatmeal, brown rice, tea, coffee
Iron	Helps carry oxygen throughout the body, part of many proteins in the body Sources: Dried beans, dried fruits, lean red meat, dark meat poultry, salmon, whole grains
Copper	Helps red blood cell formation; needed for healthy bones, nerves, blood vessels, and immune system Sources: oysters, shellfish, whole grains, beans, nuts, potatoes
Zinc	Needed for immune system to work properly, aids cell growth and healing, required for senses of taste and smell Sources: meats, dark meat poultry, nuts, whole grains, legumes
Selenium	Helps prevent cell damage Sources: vegetables, fish, meat, grains, eggs
Molybdenum	Required for production of some important enzymes in the body Sources: Peas, beans, some breakfast cereals, liver
Idoine	Helps convert food into energy, required for normal thyroid function Sources: iodized table salt, seafood, dairy products
Lists of food sources are not all-inclusive.	

50-7 Both animal and plant foods can be sources of minerals.

Phytochemicals

Phytochemicals are substances produced by plants that may provide health benefits for humans. Plants make phytochemicals to protect themselves from such things as bacteria, fungi, and high levels of damaging light from the sun. When plant-based foods containing phytochemicals are eaten, people benefit from the phytochemicals in much the same way as the plants do. Research has shown some phytochemicals may help prevent heart disease and some types of cancer. Eating a wide variety of colorful plant foods is the best way to include phytochemicals in your diet.

Prebiotics and Probiotics

Some bacteria can make you sick. Other bacteria can help protect you from disease. **Probiotics** are foods containing live, beneficial bacteria that help to counteract the "bad" bacteria in your gut. The presence of "good" bacteria in the gut is believed to improve digestion, enhance immune function, and reduce risk for developing allergies. Food sources of probiotics include yogurt containing live culture, fermented vegetable preparations such as sauerkraut or kimchi, and fermented soybean products such as tempeh or miso, 50-8.

HLPhoto/Shutterstock.com

50-8 Yogurt containing live culture is a source of "good" bacteria.

Prebiotics are nondigestible food products that encourage the growth of good bacteria in the gut. Foods containing prebiotics include whole grains, honey, bananas, garlic, onions, leeks, and artichokes.

Government Guidelines

The Food and Nutrition Board of the Institute of Medicine, National Academy of Sciences developed dietary reference intakes (DRI) to help plan and assess the diets of Americans. The dietary reference intakes (DRI) are a set of recommended nutrient intake values for healthy individuals and groups. The DRIs are very comprehensive and provide recommended intake levels or ranges based on age group and gender for each nutrient. Many of the nutrient recommendations address the needs of pregnant and nursing women.

The DRIs include four types of nutrient standards
- Estimated Average Requirement (EAR)
- Recommended Dietary Allowance (RDA)
- Adequate Intake (AI)
- Tolerable Upper Intake Level (UL)

DRIs are quite technical and are used mainly by health and nutrition experts. These standards are too complex for most people to use in their daily lives. The DRIs serve as the basis for other nutrition-related guidance such as the *Dietary Guidelines for Americans* and MyPlate food guidance system.

Dietary Guidelines for Americans

Revised every five years, the *Dietary Guidelines for Americans* is a publication that provides information and advice to promote health through nutrition and physical activity. The *Guidelines* serve as
- authoritative advice on proper dietary habits to promote health and decrease risk for major chronic diseases in individuals two years and older.

Nutrition Connection

Other Dietary Recommendations

While the USDA's *Dietary Guidelines for Americans* and MyPlate are among the most well-known recommendations, there are other sets of dietary guidelines. Other important sets of recommendations come from organizations such as the American Heart Association and the American Cancer Society.

- the basis for nutrition education programs, federal nutrition assistance programs, and dietary guidance provided by health professionals.
- assistance for development and implementation of nutrition-related programs.

The *Dietary Guidelines for Americans* promote two leading principles:

- Maintain calorie balance over time to achieve and sustain a healthy weight.
- Focus on consuming nutrient-dense foods and beverages.

Achieving and maintaining a healthy body weight across the life span is critical for good health and quality of life. A healthy weight results when calories consumed are balanced with calories expended during physical activity. Additionally, it is much easier to take steps to avoid unhealthy weight gain than to lose weight.

Nutrient-dense foods provide vitamins, minerals, and other substances that may have beneficial health effects, but supply relatively few calories. Conversely, foods that contain many calories from solid fats or added sugars should be limited or avoided. Examples of nutrient-dense foods include green leafy vegetables, whole-grain breads, fat-free milk, and soybeans. In contrast, a calorie-dense food may supply many calories but little nutritional value. Examples of calorie-dense foods include candy, soft drink, cream, butter, and cake.

MyPlate Food Guidance System

The USDA developed the MyPlate food guidance system to help people apply the *Dietary Guidelines*. MyPlate is a simple visual message communicating how a healthful meal should look, 50-9.

MyPlate divides commonly eaten foods into five main groups—fruits, grains, vegetables, protein foods, and dairy. Foods from each of these categories, as well as oil, are necessary for a healthy diet. Oils are not represented on the MyPlate symbol because they are not a food group.

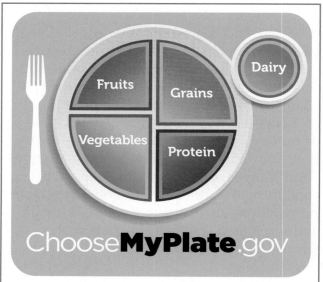

Balancing calories
- Enjoy your food, but eat less.
- Avoid oversized portions.

Foods to increase
- Make half your plate fruits and vegetables.
- Make at least half your grains whole grains.
- Switch to fat-free or low-fat (1%) milk.

Foods to reduce
- Compare sodium in foods like soup, bread, and frozen meals—and choose the foods with lower numbers.
- Drink water instead of sugary drinks.

USDA

50-9 MyPlate encourages key behaviors for more healthful eating.

Fruits   The fruit group is rich in nutrients and fiber. Fresh, frozen, canned, and dried fruits and fruit juices are included in this group. Whole fruits should be selected more often than fruit juice. Whole fruits supply fiber and are more nutrient dense than juice.

Grains   This group includes foods made from wheat, rice, oats, cornmeal, barley, and other grains. The grains may be either whole or refined, but it is recommended that half of the grains you eat be whole grains. Examples of whole grains include oatmeal, quinoa, brown rice, whole-wheat breads, and whole cornmeal. White breads, white rice, and other white flour products often used in crackers and cakes are examples of refined grains.

Vegetables   Vegetables provide a variety of nutrients and fiber. This group includes fresh, frozen, canned, and dried vegetables as well as vegetable juices. Vegetables are further divided into the following subgroups:

- *dark green vegetables* such as broccoli, spinach, and kale
- *red and orange vegetables* such as carrots, red peppers, tomatoes, and sweet potatoes
- *beans and peas* such as black-eyed peas, soybeans, and lentils
- *starchy vegetables* such as green peas, corn, and potatoes
- *other vegetables* such as celery, onions, and zucchini

MyPlate recommends eating vegetables from each group weekly. The amounts vary based on individual need.

Dairy   The dairy group includes foods high in calcium such as milk, cheese, yogurt, and milk-based desserts. Foods in this group supply other nutrients such as protein, potassium, and vitamin D. Calcium-fortified soymilk is a dairy group option for individuals with lactose intolerance. However, calcium-fortified foods and beverages may lack some of the other nutrients that milk-based foods in this group supply. Select fat-free and low-fat dairy foods

to reduce calories and saturated fats. Milk products that contain little or no calcium, such as cream cheese and butter, are not in this group.

Protein Foods   In addition to protein, foods in this group supply a variety of nutrients such as essential fatty acids, B vitamins, iron, zinc, magnesium, and vitamin E. Protein foods include fish, seafood, meats, poultry, eggs, nuts, seeds, beans, and peas. Choose lean meats and poultry to limit saturated fats and cholesterol. MyPlate recommends consuming fish or seafood at least twice a week and incorporating plant-based proteins more often.

Recommended Amounts   The amount of food you need changes across your life span. The food you eat supplies you with energy and many factors affect your energy needs. For instance, an individual's age, gender, height, and weight influence his or her energy requirements. Physical activity levels, health conditions, and pregnancy also affect energy needs.

As energy needs increase or decrease, the amount of food consumed must also increase or decrease if balance is to be maintained. However, not only the amounts of food you eat are important, but also the types of foods. As the *Guidelines* suggest, you should strive to select nutrient-dense foods more often. Choosing nutrient-dense foods ensures you are supplying your body with the vitamins, minerals, and other nutrients it requires for health. The MyPlate food guidance system provides tools to help individuals create personalized food plans, 50-10.

Understanding Food Labels

Food labels contain a large amount of information in a small amount of space. US laws and regulations require certain information on the label of all processed, packaged food products. Information required includes

- name and form of the food
- amount of food in the package in both US and metric units of measure
- name and address of the manufacturer, packer, or distributor

In addition, a list of ingredients and a Nutrition Facts panel must be provided. Understanding how to read these labels allows a chef to make nutritionally informed decisions.

Ingredient Labeling

In the United States, food product labels must include a list of ingredients. The ingredients must be listed in descending order by weight. Including the actual percentage of each ingredient is voluntary. Manufacturers are not required to list flavorings by their common or usual names. Often, these ingredients are listed as "flavorings" or "natural flavors."

You may have noticed special statements underneath the ingredients list such as "Contains wheat ingredients." This note is to alert individuals who have wheat allergies. Food manufacturers are required to include the name of the food source of any major food allergens contained in their product. Major food allergens include milk, eggs, fish, crustacean shellfish, tree nuts, wheat, peanuts, and soybeans.

My Daily Food Plan

Based on the information you provided, this is your daily recommended amount from each food group.

GRAINS 6 ounces	**Make half your grains whole** Aim for at least **3 ounces** of whole grains a day	
VEGETABLES 2½ cups	**Vary your veggies** Aim for these amounts **each week**: **Dark green veggies** = 1½ cups **Beans & peas** = 1½ cups **Other veggies** = 4 cups	**Red & orange veggies** = 5½ cups **Starchy veggies** = 5 cups
FRUITS 2 cups	**Focus on fruits** Eat a variety of fruit Choose whole or cut-up fruits more often than fruit juice	
DAIRY 3 cups	**Get your calcium-rich foods** Drink fat-free or low-fat (1%) milk, for the same amount of calcium and other nutrients as whole milk, but less fat and calories Select fat-free or low-fat yogurt and cheese, or try calcium-fortified soy products	
PROTEIN FOODS 5½ ounces	**Go lean with protein** Twice a week, make seafood the protein on your plate Vary your protein routine–choose more fish, beans, peas, nuts, and seeds Keep meat and poultry portions small and lean	

Find your balance between food and physical activity Be physically active for at least **60 minutes** each day.	**Know your limits on fats, sugars, and sodium** Your allowance for oils is **6 teaspoons** a day. Limit extras–solid fats and sugars–to **260 Calories** a day. Reduce socium intake to less than **2300 mg** a day.

Your results are based on a 2000 calorie pattern.   Name: _____

This calorie level is only an estimate of your needs. Monitor your body weight to see if you need to adjust your calorie intake.

USDA

50-10 Use the MyPlate food guidance system to create an individualized food plan.

Ingredient lists are not only crucial for people with allergies, but also for those who carefully monitor what they consume for religious or cultural reasons.

Nutrition Labeling

A Nutrition Facts panel must also be displayed on a product label, 50-11. This panel provides easy-to-use nutrition information.

Serving size. This section tells you the serving size and how many servings each container supplies. All the nutritional information listed on the Nutrition Facts panel is based on one serving size. Therefore, if a person consumes two servings, all the nutritional information must be doubled.

Amount of calories. The number of calories per serving and the number of calories from fat are shown next. This information

Nutrition Facts
Serving Size 1 cup (228g)
Servings Per Container about 2

Amount Per Serving

Calories 250 Calories from Fat 110

	% Daily Value*
Total Fat 12g	**18%**
Saturated Fat 3g	**15%**
Trans Fat 3g	
Cholesterol 30mg	**10%**
Sodium 470mg	**20%**
Total Carbohydrate 31g	**10%**
Dietary Fiber 0g	**0%**
Sugars 5g	
Proteins 5g	
Vitamin A	4%
Vitamin C	2%
Calcium	20%
Iron	4%

* Percent Daily Values are based on a 2,000 calorie diet. Your Daily Values may be higher or lower depending on your calorie needs:

	Calories:	2,000	2,500
Total Fat	Less than	65g	80g
Saturated Fat	Less than	20g	25g
Cholesterol	Less than	300mg	300mg
Sodium	Less than	2,400mg	2,400mg
Total Carbohydrate		300g	375g
Dietary Fiber		25g	30g

1. Serving Size
2. Amount of Calories
3. Limit these Nutrients
4. Get Enough of these Nutrients
5. Percent (%) Daily Value
6. Footnote with Daily Values (DVs)

FDA

50-11 The Nutrition Facts panel provides useful information for making healthful food choices.

can be used to compare similar products for caloric and fat content.

Limit these nutrients. Chronic consumption of too much total fat, saturated fat, *trans* fat, cholesterol, and sodium has been linked to elevated risk for certain diseases such as heart disease, some cancers, or high blood pressure. It is recommended that the total percent Daily Value for each of these nutrients be less than 100 percent.

Get enough of these nutrients. Dietary fiber, vitamin A, vitamin C, calcium, and iron are often lacking in the American diet. Increasing these nutrients in the diet may improve health and reduce the risk for some diseases and conditions.

Percent (%) Daily Value. The percent Daily Value is based on a 2,000-calorie diet. It states what percentage of the recommended daily intake for each nutrient is contained in one serving size. For example, if the percent Daily Value for total fat is 20 that would mean that for an individual on a 2,000-calorie diet, one serving meets 20 percent of his or her daily fat allowance.

Footnote with Daily Values (DV). This section supplies information about the DVs for important nutrients. Information is provided for both 2,000-calorie and 2,500-calorie diets. The amounts identified for total fat, saturated fat, cholesterol, and sodium are maximum amounts.

The Chef's Role in Nutrition

With the rise of obesity in the United States and the continued interest in nutrition, the need for chefs to prepare and serve healthful food has never been greater. The professional organization of chefs—American Culinary Federation—requires its members to study nutrition as part of its certification.

Chefs are increasingly called on to assume a leadership role in defining America's eating patterns. Through educating the general public, chefs can promote healthful eating styles that do not sacrifice the enjoyment of eating. Therefore, chefs need to create dishes that not only look and taste great, but also are healthful. Chefs must also be prepared to make accommodations for diners with special dietary needs such as food allergies and intolerance, vegetarianism, and health conditions.

Offer Healthful Menu Selections

When developing the menu, offering healthful selections should be a consideration. A number of factors influence the nutritional quality of a menu item—the ingredients, cooking method, proportion, and portion size.

Ingredients A healthful menu item begins with healthful ingredients. Select nutrient-dense ingredients more often and limit or reduce the use of solid fats and added sugars. More healthful alternatives can be found

for any ingredient. For instance, replacing refined, highly processed grains with whole grains adds interest as well as beneficial nutrients to a dish. Whole-grain flour can replace a portion of refined flour in baked goods. Any number of colorful, appealing whole-grain rice varieties can be used to enhance a meal. Consider whole-grain pastas for salads and Italian dishes.

High-fat dairy products can be replaced with low-fat options. Use low-fat milk instead of full fat. Select cheeses that are naturally lower in fat than others. For instance, Parmesan cheese contains about 25 percent less fat than cheddar cheese. Feta cheese is another lower-fat option that is also packed with flavor.

Some protein ingredients are more healthful than others. Leaner cuts of meat such as those from the round or loin primals can replace cuts with greater fat content. Ground meats and poultry should have less than five percent fat content. Simply trimming visible fat off meat before cooking can reduce calories from fat. The *Dietary Guidelines* encourages Americans to incorporate more fish and seafood into their diets. Many people are unsure how to prepare these proteins, but are eager to try fish when prepared by a chef, 50-12. Some diners are interested in plant-based proteins either due to health, religious beliefs, or other reasons. Dishes featuring dried beans or legumes provide a healthful and possibly more profitable alternative.

Whole, unpeeled fruits and vegetables often retain more of their nutrients. Processing these ingredients on-site may assist in providing healthful menu selections. Nutritional value of fresh produce declines as the fruit or vegetable ages. Using produce as close to harvest as possible translates to more nutrients in the meal. Consider serving seasonal, locally grown fruits and vegetables to shorten the time from farm to the table. Many times, frozen or canned produce are processed shortly after harvesting, which aids in high nutrient retention. Consider

SCIENCE & TECHNOLOGY

Seeking Valid Information

Every day, consumers are barraged with nutritional information from many different sources. It is important to evaluate the source of the information. Beware of product sponsored information or information from unknown institutions or individuals. Verify that information is not outdated. Credible sources include prominent universities, medical schools, and professional organizations such as the Academy of Nutrition and Dietetics (AND) formerly known as the *American Dietetic Association*. Beware of information contained on Internet sites that promote or sell nutritional products.

canned or frozen as healthful options when fresh is not available.

Fat, sugar, and salt should be used more sparingly. Replace butter, lard, or shortening with healthier fats such as oils. When decreasing salt or sugar in a dish, consider filling the flavor void with herbs, spices, lemon juice, chiles, or flavored vinegars. Marinades and rubs can be used to enhance the flavor of meats and poultry.

Cooking Methods How food is cooked affects its nutritional value. Certain cooking methods such as deep frying and panfrying add large amounts of fat to a dish. Boiling can dissolve water-soluble vitamins from vegetables. Other cooking techniques such as grilling, sautéing, roasting, baking, and steaming maximize nutrient density by decreasing fat. With braising, the nutrients that leach out of the food during cooking are captured and served in the sauce.

Poaching fish in flavorful liquid is a more healthful option than deep frying or panfrying. Reduce fat content by grilling marinated chicken rather than deep-fat frying it. Remove unnecessary fat by refrigerating braised dishes and then skimming the fat off the surface once it hardens.

Feature reduction sauces on the menu in place of sauces thickened with fats and starches. Reduction also acts to concentrate the flavors and produce a superior sauce.

Cook fruits and vegetables with as little surface area exposed as possible. This can be done by cutting them into large pieces and avoiding peeling when practical. Less surface area means fewer nutrients are leaching into the cooking liquid. Additionally, using as little cooking liquid as possible helps preserve water-soluble nutrients. Heat-sensitive nutrients, such as vitamin C and folate, benefit when cooking time is kept as brief as possible.

Proportion Ideally, restaurant menus should reflect the eating patterns recommended in the *Dietary Guidelines* and MyPlate. Restaurants often serve large amounts of protein and

ElenaGaak/Shutterstock.com

50-12 Fish should be prepared using healthful cooking methods such as poaching or grilling.

Nutrition Connection

Safe Weight Management

For many reasons, many Americans battle unwanted weight gain. While there are many different strategies for losing weight, they are not all equal. Some fad diets are unproven and may have negative health effects. When evaluating a strategy for weight management, avoid diets that

- prohibit certain nutrients while allowing only large amounts of other nutrients.

- do not also include physical activity.

- prescribe medicines or dietary supplements as a sole source of weight loss.

- do not address long-term lifestyle changes.

- claim to have extremely rapid weight loss.

- are based on scientific studies that have been performed by questionable sources and that have not been verified by a credible institution.

- treat all individuals as having the same nutritional needs.

small amounts of grains and vegetables. This is contrary to the recommendations of the *Guidelines* and in MyPlate. Creating healthier meals means that menus should contain larger amounts of whole grains, fruits, and vegetables, and smaller amounts of protein and fat.

Portion Size Moderation is key when the goal is healthful eating. Excess portion sizes should be avoided. In keeping with the goal of moderation, chefs need to evaluate their portion sizes. Serving appropriate portion sizes not only promotes good health, but also reduces wasted food. However, chefs are often caught between the nutritional goal of smaller portions and the customer's desire for the perceived value of large portions.

Make Accommodations for Special Needs

Chefs must also be prepared to respond to the special dietary needs of customers. Customers may have conditions that prohibit them from eating certain foods or ingredients. Making sure waitstaff and kitchen staff alike are aware of the importance of responding to these needs is critical.

Food Allergies and Intolerances A *food allergy* is an immune system response to a specific food. The response can range in severity from mild to life threatening. The amount of food that triggers the response can vary from person to person. A *food intolerance* is a digestive system response. This occurs when a food irritates the digestive system or the body is unable to break down the food properly. Symptoms of food intolerance may include nausea, vomiting, heartburn, headaches, or diarrhea.

Waitstaff must know and be able to communicate to the customer, which dishes contain potential allergens, 50-13. Understanding how dishes are prepared and their ingredients enables the waitstaff to aid the customer in identifying dishes that may precipitate a reaction. Waitstaff can

encourage customers to select simpler, more straightforward menu items that are easier to describe. Some foodservice operations list allergens contained in certain dishes on the menu. Meals for customers with food allergies should be delivered to the table separately from the other meals to avoid accidental contact.

In the kitchen, staff must ensure that allergens are not transferred from one dish to another by accident. For instance, using the same sauteuse to sauté first shrimp and then chicken can transfer the shrimp allergens to the chicken. Allergens can often survive cooking temperatures. Using the same deep fryer to cook foods that contain potential allergens and foods for customers with food allergies can result in transfer of the allergens. Foods for customers with food allergies should be cooked in a separate deep fryer.

50-13 Foodservice staff must be trained to respond appropriately to customers with special dietary needs.

All equipment and utensils must be washed, rinsed, and sanitized after coming in contact with a food allergen and before being reused. Food handlers should wash hands and change gloves to avoid transferring food allergens to food that does not normally contain these allergens. A separate area should be designated for preparing food for individuals with food allergies.

Vegetarian Diets People choose to follow vegetarian diets for a number of reasons. There are also different types of vegetarian diets.

- **Vegans** eat no food from animal sources and limit their diets to plant-based foods only.
- **Lacto-vegetarians** eat milk, cheese, and other dairy products, but do not eat meat, fish, poultry, or eggs.
- **Ovo-vegetarians** do not eat meat, poultry, or dairy products, but will eat eggs.
- **Lacto-ovo vegetarians** eat dairy products and eggs, but do not consume meat, fish, or poultry.
- **Pescetarians** consume vegetables, fruits, nuts, beans, and fish or seafood, but exclude animal and poultry products.

Understanding the restrictions of various vegetarian diets is essential so a chef can respond to customers' special requests. Many operations routinely offer vegetarian selections on the menu.

Health Conditions Individuals with various health conditions may be following more healthful eating patterns. This should not **preclude**, or prevent, these individuals from being able to enjoy a meal at a restaurant. Offering healthful menu choices has been a growing trend in foodservice. More and more operations are providing the

Nutrition Connection

Diabetes and Hypoglycemia

Both diabetes and hypoglycemia are disorders characterized by the body's inability to metabolize carbohydrates properly. Diabetes results when the body cannot properly absorb glucose. Insulin is a chemical messenger produced by the body. It is needed for glucose metabolism. If the body does not produce enough insulin, high levels of undigested glucose result. This condition is called *diabetes* and can be fatal if untreated. Hypoglycemia results from abnormally low levels of glucose. Hypoglycemia can also be very serious if untreated, but is generally very rare.

nutritional analyses for menu items so diners can make informed selections.

Individuals with diabetes, heart disease, or who are simply trying to manage their weight can often meet their special needs with menu selections such as fruits, vegetables, whole grains, lean meats and poultry, plant-based proteins, fish, and seafood. Healthful selections with little or no added solid fat, salt, and sugar and served in moderate portion sizes can address many diet restrictions. Individuals who are trying to improve their overall eating habits will welcome these options as well. Consider options such as

- broiled or grilled meats served without rich sauces
- steamed or sautéed vegetables seasoned with lemon juice or vinegar
- poached fish seasoned with herbs
- seasonal fresh fruits for dessert
- salads served with vinegar and oil dressing

Summary Points

- There are six groups of nutrients that provide energy to the body, and are necessary for growth and repair and bodily functions.

- Nonnutrients are substances in foods that provide benefits to the body but are not classified as nutrients.

- The *Dietary Guidelines for Americans* is a publication that provides information and advice to promote health through nutrition and physical activity. MyPlate is a food guidance system that helps people apply the *Guidelines*.

- Understanding how to read food labels helps a chef make nutritionally informed decisions.

- The chef's role is expanding to include educating the public about sound nutritional choices and creating nutritionally balanced meals.

In Review
Assess

1. True or false. Essential nutrients cannot be made by the body and must be supplied by vitamin supplements.

2. Contrast indispensable amino acids with dispensable amino acids.

3. _____ are the body's chief energy source.

4. Which nutrient provides the greatest number of calories per gram?

5. What is the difference between saturated fats and unsaturated fats?

6. _____ _____ is a type of lipid that is created when unsaturated oil is chemically changed through hydrogenation to resemble a saturated fat.

7. List three body functions in which water is involved.

8. Name two ways that vitamins support many body systems.

9. What are two ways minerals are necessary for body processes?

10. What are *nonnutrients*?

11. What are the two leading principles of the *Dietary Guidelines for Americans*?

12. Name the five main food groups that are part of MyPlate and give a healthful food example for each group.

13. True or false. Ingredients are listed on food labels by weight in descending order.

14. True or false. The information on the Nutrition Facts panel is based on the total amount of food in the package.

15. What factors influence the nutritional quality of a menu item?

Core Skills

16. **Math.** Suppose the restaurant in which you work serves a 9-ounce sirloin steak. The steak has 69 grams of protein and 45 grams of fat. Calculate the total calories for the sirloin steak. (*Note:* protein and carbohydrate = 4 calories per gram, fat = 9 calories per gram.) The steak is served with a baked potato with butter, which contains 15 grams of protein, 11 grams of fat (from 1 Tbsp. of butter), and 51 grams of carbohydrate. Calculate the total calories for the baked potato. If you want to serve a similar menu item that is lower in fat and total calories, what changes could you make?

17. **Speaking.** Use the text and Internet or print resources to conduct further research into nonnutrients such as phytochemicals, prebiotics, and probiotics. As a chef, how would you include more flavorful and appealing foods on the menu that provide these nonnutrients? Share your findings in an oral report to the class.

18. **Writing.** Select a meal from one of your favorite restaurants. Next, generate an individualized food plan at ChooseMyPlate.gov. Evaluate the meal based on your food plan. Write a summary of your findings. The summary should include: your food plan, a list of the items served in your restaurant meal, an estimate of the amounts of each of

the five food groups it supplied, the percent of your day's allowances for each food group the meal provided, and your suggestions to make the meal more healthful.

19. **Math.** Presume you work in a sandwich shop. To simplify portioning, your shop sells 2½ oz. bags of classic potato chips to accompany sandwiches. The Nutrition Facts panel on the chips indicates a serving size is 1 oz. There are 165 calories and 10 grams of fat in one serving. If the customer eats the whole bag, how many calories and fat grams is the customer consuming?

20. **CTE Career Readiness Practice.** The breakfast/lunch restaurant for which you are chef is updating the menu to include a selection of healthful breakfast and lunch options based on customer request. The manager has asked you to write an article for the restaurant website about these new options. What will you tell your customers about these new healthful breakfast and lunch options? Give several examples in your article.

Critical Thinking

21. **Differentiate.** Cholesterol is often in the news. Is it fair to say that cholesterol is dangerous and should be avoided at all costs? Differentiate between facts and opinions on this topic. Use the text and additional reliable resources for further information on the topic. Discuss in class.

22. **Identify evidence.** You have requested whole-grain bread from your bakery vendor. How would you verify that the packaged bread delivered to you is indeed whole grain?

23. **Debate.** Form two teams and debate the following topic: Chefs have a responsibility to promote healthful eating by offering nutritious dishes. Be sure to cite your teams' rationale during the debate.

Technology

For one of your favorite restaurants, locate the menu nutrition information on the website. Choose your favorite menu item and look up the nutrition information. How can the nutrition information available help you choose a more nutrient-dense meal? Write a summary of your findings to share with the class.

Teamwork

Divide into teams. Each team should plan two, nutrient-dense menus: a healthful meal menu for the health-conscious diner and a healthful meal menu to accommodate a special dietary need (food allergies, vegetarianism, or health conditions such as diabetes or heart disease). As a class, evaluate the teams' menus for healthfulness and diner appeal. Discuss how the menus meet the nutrition guidelines discussed in this chapter.

Chef's E-portfolio
Writing Healthful Menus

Upload the menus you created for the Teamwork activity to your e-portfolio. Ask your instructor where to save your file. This could be on the school's network or a flash drive of your own. Name your portfolio document *FirstnameLastname_Portfolio Ch#.docx* (i.e., JohnSmith_PortfolioCh50.docx).

While studying, look for the activity icon ⬈ to:
- Build vocabulary with e-flash cards and matching activities.
- Expand learning with video clips, photo identification activities, animations, and interactive activities.
- Review and assess what you learn by completing end-of-chapter questions.

G-WLEARNING.com

Menus

51

Reading Prep

In preparation for this chapter, use the Internet and visit restaurants to locate a variety of menus. Can you find any commonalities in these menus? As you read, identify key chapter concepts that are employed in the menus.

Culinary Terminology Build Vocab

static menu, p. 793
cycle menu, p. 795
market menu, p. 795
table d'hôte menu, p. 795
à la carte menu, p. 796
prix fixe menu, p. 796

Academic Terminology Build Vocab

value, p. 796

Objectives

After studying this chapter, you will be able to

- classify menus by format.
- explain how good menu planning is achieved.
- summarize the elements of menu mechanics.
- recognize the need for nutritional considerations when menu planning.

A menu is more than simply a list of a restaurant's offerings. A menu is how a chef or restaurateur communicates about his or her creations with diners. A menu sells the restaurant's products and is key to the profitability of a foodservice operation. Keep in mind as you read this chapter that the term *menu* is used when discussing both the list of dishes a restaurant offers, as well as, the physical object used to communicate that list. This chapter explores the different types of menus and looks at some of the elements that make an effective menu.

Menu Formats

The menu is an expression of a restaurant or foodservice operation's identity. The type of menu presented to customers varies depending on the type of operation. For instance, a menu for a fast-food operation is quite different from a fine-dining operation serving French cuisine. The same operation may have different menus for different meal periods, different times of the year, and special events. All foodservice professionals should be familiar with the basic menu formats.

Static Menu

Static means still or unchanging. An operation with a **static menu** offers the same items every day. There are several advantages of a static menu. With a static menu, customers know their favorite items are always available. Also, it is easier for the kitchen to perfect the preparation and service of the menu items. One disadvantage of a static menu is that repeat customers might become bored with the same menu offerings and lose interest in dining at the establishment. Static menus are common in fast-food and ethnic restaurants, 51-1.

PHOENIX RESTAURANT

TEL :312/328/0848

FAX :312/328/0850

萬壽宮酒樓

DIM SUM DAILY:
MON - FRI 9AM-3 PM
SAT - SUN 8 AM-3 PM

2131 S. ARCHER AVE
CHICAGO IL 60616
WWW.CHINATOWNPHOENIX.COM

猪肉，牛肉 Pork & Beef

501	菠萝咕噜肉	Sweet and Sour Pork with Pineapple	12.95
502	梅菜扣肉	Haka Style Pork Belly(Pork Belly with Preserved Mustard Greens)	12.95
503	京都焗排骨	Pork Loin with House Special Sauce	12.95
504	酒香椒盐焗排骨	Pork Rib with Spiced Salt	12.95
505	咸鱼蒸肉饼	Steam Minced Pork with Salt Fish	16.95
506	鲜吊片马蹄蒸肉饼	Steam Minced Pork with Squid	12.95
507	木须肉	Moo Shu Pork	12.95
508	西兰花牛	Beef with American Broccoli	12.95
509	干葱牛柳粒	Beef Tenderloin w/ Shallots	15.95
510	沙爹牛肉	Beef with Satay Sauce	12.95
511	蚝油牛肉	Beef with Oyster Sauce	12.95
512	时菜牛肉	Beef with Seasonal Chinese Vegetable	12.95
513	鬼马牛肉	Beef w/ Fried Dough and Water Chestnut	12.95
514	陈皮牛肉	Orange Beef (Stir Fried Beef with Dried Orange Peel, Dried Chilies & Garlic)	12.95
515	柱候牛筋煲	Beef Brisket Stew	12.95
516	蒙古牛	Mongolian Beef (Stir Fried Beef w/ Scallions & Shredded Carrots in Sweet & spicy Sauce served on a Bed of Crispy Noodles)	12.95
517	橙牛	Crispy Orange Beef (Crispy Beef Glazed in a Sweet & Spicy Orange Sa	12.95
518	香港士的	Angus Steak with Chinese Broccoli	25.95
519	脆烧牛柳球	Chef's Special Crispy Beef Tenderloin	18.95
520	芝麻牛肉	Sesame Beef	12.95
521	凉瓜炒牛肉	Beef with Bitter Melon	12.95
522	沙茶脆牛片	Crispy Satay Beef	12.95
523	X.O.酱牛柳	Shredded Beef Tenderloin in X.O. Sauce	15.95
524	花菇牛扒	Steak with Mushroom Sauce	35.95

Courtesy of Phoenix Restaurant, menu designed and printed by Azteca Photography

51-1 This Chinese restaurant menu is an example of a static menu.

Cycle Menu

A **cycle menu** rotates a set number of items over a certain period of time. After that time period, the daily menu offerings repeat. The cycle for repeating the menus might be a week, month, or longer.

Cycle menus are effective in operations that serve the same customers day after day, such as schools or hospitals. The changing menu keeps diners from getting bored with the menu offerings. The fact that menu items repeat allows the kitchen to control inventory and ordering. Over a period of time, the kitchen staff has the opportunity to prepare menu items repeatedly and perfect them.

Market Menu

The market menu is a traditional European model for menus. This menu format thrives in a culture where chefs visit the local market daily to purchase food. A **market menu** is composed daily based on what food products are available in the market, 51-2. This menu format allows chefs to use the best products available at any given time. It requires an experienced chef and well-trained staff to continually adapt to seasonal products and new preparations. Market menus are most often found in fine-dining establishments.

Baloncici/Shutterstock.com

51-2 A market menu features foods that are in season and at their peak of flavor.

Table d' Hôte Menu

Table d' hôte (tahbul DOHT) is French for "table of the host." A **table d'hôte menu** offers one set meal to all guests with no choices or substitutions. This format comes from the tradition of hotels and inns offering a set meal to lodgers, which was included in the price of the room. Today, a banquet is the most common use of the table d'hôte format, 51-3.

Menu Formats Based on Pricing

In addition to classifying menus by the frequency with which offerings change, menus are classified by the method used to price the

The Hatfield – McCoy Wedding
Congratulations Julie and Ken

Hors d'Oeuvres

Deviled Eggs with Caviar

Skewered Tomato and Mozzarella with Pesto Vinaigrette

Marinated Shrimp in Tortilla Cup with Avocado Salsa

Dinner

Chicken Consommé with Petite Mushroom Ravioli and Julienne Vegetables

Hearts of Boston Lettuce with Pimento and Asparagus, Tarragon Vinaigrette

Seared Filet of Sea Bass with Fennel and Lemon Butter Sauce

Rack of Colorado Lamb Roasted with Dijon Mustard and Herb Crumbs

Potato Gratin Dauphinoise

Medley of Baby Carrots, Turnips and Sugar Snap Peas

Wedding Cake

Coffee and Tea Service

Chocolate Truffles

51-3 This wedding banquet menu is an example of table d'hôte format.

meals. The most common menu formats based on pricing are à la carte and prix fixe.

À la Carte   The phrase *à la carte* (ah lah KAHRT) means "from the card or menu." An **à la carte menu** prices each course separately. In a true à la carte menu, side dishes and accompaniments cost extra.

In the United States, modified à la carte menus are popular. A modified à la carte menu prices each main course separately, but that price includes other courses such as soup or salad and accompaniments.

Prix Fixe   *Prix fixe* (pree FEEX) means "fixed price." A **prix fixe menu** has one set price for the total meal but allows the customer to make his or her own selection from each course offered.

Combining Formats

Restaurateurs often combine different menu formats to offer choices for their guests. Many restaurants with static menus offer daily specials on a cycle or market format. Often a restaurant with an à la carte menu also offers a tasting menu on a prix fixe basis. This menu offers small portions of the chef's specialties for tasting.

CHEF'S ETHICS
Ethics and Social Media

Many foodservice establishments use social media to market their services. It is an easy, inexpensive tool managers use to communicate special deals or updates to their menus. Individuals who write communications for their organizations to post on various social media sites must be cautious. It is unethical to send unsolicited messages to customers that have not requested to be on the establishment's mailing list. Remember, when using social media, you are representing the establishment so use good judgment at all times.

Menu Planning

Menu planning includes composing and pricing the menu. The goal of good menu planning is to create a mix of menu items that satisfies diners while maximizing profits.

Menu Mix

Chefs and restaurateurs must be in tune with the likes and dislikes of their customers. A successful menu lists items that appeal to an operation's diners. The term *menu mix* refers to the combination of items offered on a menu.

The amount diners are willing to spend, regional tastes, and current trends in food all need to be considered when choosing the right menu mix. An adequate variety of menu items is necessary to satisfy a range of tastes and to maintain the interest of repeat diners. Additionally, a combination of menu items that distributes the workload in the kitchen is desirable. The ultimate goal of menu mix is a combination of items that generates the most sales and the greatest profits, 51-4.

Menu Pricing

Managers must keep in mind the customer's perceived **value**, or worth, of the item and providing for profit when establishing menu

©BananaStock Ltd.

51-4 Some restaurants post their menu by the entrance to attract new customers.

prices. There are a number of ways that food-service operations can set prices for menu items. Some operations research their competitors' prices and simply charge the "going rate" or what their competitors are charging. This method is not recommended because it fails to take into account the actual costs of the items being sold.

Competent operators base their menu price on the actual cost of the menu item. Two of the most common pricing methods used to calculate menu price based on food cost are markup and food cost percentage.

Markup The simplest cost-based pricing method is the markup method. This method simply involves adding a set amount to the cost of the menu item.

$$\text{Food Cost} + \text{Markup} = \text{Menu Price}$$

The markup amount is determined by management. The markup is the amount that remains after the food cost is subtracted from the menu price. This markup must be sufficient to pay for labor and other expenses, as well as, provide a profit. Typically, different markups are determined for various menu categories. For example, salads may be assigned a markup of $1.25; entrées, a markup of $5.50; and desserts, a markup of $1.00. To price a menu item using markup method for an entrée with a food cost of $3.75, the calculation would be

$$\$3.75 + \$5.50 = \$9.25$$

Food Cost Percentage By far, the most common method of setting menu prices is to base the price on the operation's standard food cost percentage. The standard food cost percentage is determined during the financial planning and budgeting process. Taking into account operating costs and labor costs, the standard food cost percentage is the percentage of sales an operation budgets to spend on food products.

To calculate a menu price using the standard food cost percentage method, the food cost of an item is divided by the food cost percentage.

$$\frac{\text{Food Cost}}{\text{per Portion}} \div \frac{\text{Standard Food}}{\text{Cost Percentage}} = \frac{\text{Menu}}{\text{Price}}$$

For example, the manager of an operation that wishes to maintain a 32 percent standard food cost needs to set a menu price for a shrimp cocktail appetizer. The recipe cost sheet performed on shrimp cocktail shows a portion cost of $2.37. The manager calculates the menu price as follows:

$$\$2.37 \div 0.32 = \$7.41$$

The minimum menu price for achieving a 32 percent food cost is $7.41. Most restaurateurs would round up the price to $7.50.

Menu Mechanics

Menu mechanics addresses the physical characteristics of the menu. The goal of good menu mechanics is to create a menu presentation that communicates effectively to the customer and maximizes sales.

Chef's Ethics

Truth-in-Menu Laws

Federal Truth-in-Menu laws exist to protect consumers from fraudulent menu claims. Foodservice establishments' menus must truthfully describe the food's

- origin
- grade or quality
- preparation method
- level of processing
- ingredients
- portion size
- nutrition and health claims

For example, if a restaurant owner advertises a burger that is made from grass-fed beef, but serves beef from grain-fed cows, it would be a Truth-in-Menu violation. Inaccurate menus can lead to liabilities regarding food allergies or may result in customers seeking legal action due to misrepresentation.

Chefs and restaurateurs have an ethical and legal obligation to guarantee that what they say they are serving on the menu is actually delivered to the diner. Truth-in-Menu laws vary from locality to locality, so check with your state restaurant association to learn the regulations in your area.

There are varied types of misrepresentation found in menus. The most common violations are

- *Substitution violation.* Serving food that is of lesser quality or is different than advertised. For example, serving select instead of prime steaks; serving a generic product instead of a stated name brand.
- *Point of origin violation.* Using food that is not from the geographical region advertised. For example, designating Alaskan salmon but serving Chilean salmon instead.
- *Merchandising term violation.* Advertised food that is not accurate or is exaggerated. For example, "homemade pasta" is stated, but boxed product is used.
- *Freshness violation.* Products advertised as fresh but are previously frozen, canned, or preserved.

A good policy to follow when writing a menu is, "If you say it, serve it!"

Menu Descriptions

All menus state the names of the dishes being offered. Most menus also describe each item. The description of the dish is designed to both inform the customer about the ingredients and preparation of the dish, as well as, help sell the item.

Menu text should

- be accurate and truthful
- be descriptive but as brief as possible
- avoid culinary jargon and be written in language that customers can understand
- include the portion size of the main protein source
- describe the cooking method
- highlight unique ingredients that make a dish special—Tahitian vanilla beans, organic baby vegetables, farmstead cheese

Menu Design and Layout

Many restaurants choose a professional graphic designer or a printer that specializes in menus to design and produce menus. With the rising popularity of desktop publishing, there is a growing trend toward producing menus in-house. Computerized desktop publishing is often less expensive and allows greater flexibility to change menu items and prices. Whichever method an operation chooses for creating menus, decisions must be made about the following:

- size, shape, and color of the menu card, 51-5
- type of paper
- whether to use a holder or menu cover
- layout or arrangement of items on the menu card
- size, color, and typeface of menu text
- illustrations and graphics to be used

Nutrition on the Menu

As public awareness of nutrition and health rises along with the number of meals eaten outside the home, there is a growing demand for foodservice operations to share nutrition information with customers and to offer more healthy options.

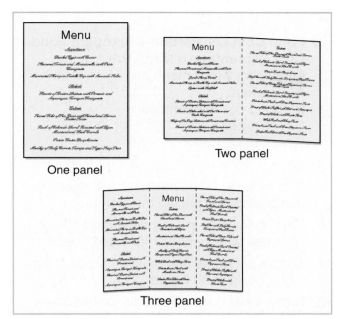

One panel

Two panel

Three panel

51-5 Menus may be one, two, or three panels, or multiple pages similar to a book.

For diners to make healthy choices when dining out, there is a growing trend toward including nutrition data on menus. Federal menu labeling requirements were included in the Patient Protection and Affordable Care Act of 2010. In some cities and states, laws are already enforced that require larger restaurant chains to post specific nutrition information on menus. Many other restaurants voluntarily include nutrition information. It is becoming increasingly common to see menus that list the calorie content for each menu item.

Some menus list content for multiple nutrients such as calories, fat, saturated fat, carbohydrates, protein, and cholesterol. If a menu makes a nutritional claim, the restaurant must be able to provide evidence to support the claim. Evidence might be a standardized recipe with a nutritional analysis and proof that restaurant staff practices portion control and adherence to the recipe.

Another strategy is to highlight menu items that are below a certain calorie content. Some restaurateurs believe that labeling items as healthful diminishes their appeal to some customers and opt for a strategy of

"stealth health." Using this strategy, an operation prepares most of its menu offerings to meet certain dietary parameters, but do not mention this on the menu.

Regardless what information is shared on the menu, chefs and restaurateurs must be mindful of nutrition when composing menus. The following are some of the nutrition considerations that should shape menu offerings:

- *Portion sizes.* Serve moderate portion sizes and deliver value to customers through the quality of the food rather than size of the portions.
- *Balance.* Offer menu items that include larger amounts of vegetables and whole grains to balance proteins and fatty sauces.
- *Freshness.* Offer fresh ingredients rather than processed when possible.
- *Vegan options.* Address the growing demand for vegan options.
- *Special dietary needs.* Plan menus with the ability to easily adapt items to special dietary requests such as gluten free, food allergies, or sodium reduced.

Nutrition Connection

Nutrition Considerations in Menu Planning

Chefs and restaurateurs have many factors to consider during menu planning. One issue they may encounter is addressing consumer demand for more health-conscious menu items. For some consumers, food choices are based on dietary restrictions. For instance, consumers who have diabetes may desire options containing more complex carbohydrates and less sugar. Consumers with cardiovascular disease look for healthful cooking techniques and leaner protein options such as fish and poultry. In addition, they request foods low in sodium, fat, and cholesterol. Many establishments post nutrition information or have it readily available to help consumers who have dietary restrictions make the appropriate choices.

Summary Points

- Menu formats differ based on how often menu items change and how they are priced.

- Menu planning includes choosing the right assortment of menu items at the right price to satisfy customers and maximize profits.

- Markup and food cost percentage are cost-based pricing methods used for pricing menu items.

- The goal of menu mechanics is to create a menu with a physical presentation that enhances communication with customers and maximizes profits.

- Growing awareness of nutrition influences choices on menu offerings and labeling.

In Review
Assess

1. Name the types of foodservice establishments most likely to employ the following menu formats:
   A. market menu
   B. static menu
   C. cycle menu
   D. table d'hôte

2. Name the menu format associated with each advantage described below.
   A. Customers know their favorite items will be available every day.
   B. Chef can use the best products available at any given time.
   C. When the same customers are served day after day, it keeps them from getting bored with menu offerings.

3. True or false. An à la carte menu charges for each course separately.

4. The combination of items offered on a menu is called _____.
   A. menu mechanics
   B. prix fixe
   C. cycle menu
   D. menu mix

5. List two considerations for achieving good menu mix.

6. List two cost-based menu pricing methods.

7. **Food Cost per Portion ÷ Standard Food Cost Percentage = Menu Price** is the formula for which menu pricing method?
   A. markup
   B. food cost percentage
   C. going rate
   D. prix fixe

8. What is the goal of good menu mechanics?

9. True or false. Menu mechanics involves composing and pricing the menu.

10. What guidelines should restaurant operations use when writing menu text?

11. List six decisions that must be made during menu design and layout.

12. Name three nutrition considerations chefs and restaurateurs should consider when shaping menus.

Core Skills

13. **Math.** If a chef wants to maintain a standard food cost of 28 percent, what is the minimum price to charge for a main course with a food cost of $3.72 per portion?

14. **Reading.** Use Internet or print resources to read about classical menus from a source such as Escoffier's *Le Guide Culinaire*. Choose a specific menu. Identify the menu format. Write a summary about the type of event or setting, style of service, kitchen staffing associated with that menu, and type of culinary business in which this menu might be used.

15. **Math.** Suppose the restaurant manager of the facility in which you work determined the markup on entrées will be $5.75 and the markup on desserts will be $1.25 on the new menu. You are adding a *Home-Style Meatloaf* entrée with a food cost of $3.74 and a *Strawberry-Rhubarb Pie* with a food cost of $2.25. Use the markup method to determine the menu price for each.

16. **Writing.** Use Internet or print resources to obtain a restaurant menu. Identify a special dietary need—such as vegan, food allergy, or health related—that is not addressed by

the current menu selections. Apply nutrition principles to current menu selections or add new menu selections in order to provide options to meet those needs.

17. **Math.** A menu item is priced at $18.50. The chef has calculated the food cost from the standard recipe as $7.03 per portion. What is the food cost percentage for this menu item?

18. **Speaking.** As a class, brainstorm and list the pros and cons of using a market menu format.

19. **CTE Career Readiness Practice.** Select one of your family's favorite home-cooked meals. Using the guidelines for menu descriptions from the chapter, write a menu description for your meal. Be sure to address the Truth-in-Menu laws in your description. Create a *table d'hôte* menu design and layout for the meal.

Critical Thinking

20. **Analyze criteria.** What criteria should chefs and restaurateurs take into account when determining the number of menu offerings for an operation? Analyze and discuss the importance of proper menu planning to overall operation and profitability of the facility. Cite the text and other reliable resources to support your response.

21. **Infer motive.** A small fine-dining establishment decided to switch from having menus printed by a professional printer every six months to designing and printing menus in-house on a daily basis. Infer reasons that may have motivated the restaurateur to make this decision.

22. **Generate a solution.** You are the newly hired chef at a restaurant that uses a static menu format. The owner is concerned that customers are becoming bored with the menu but he does not want to go to the expense of creating a new menu. What would you suggest as a possible solution? Write a proposal noting your solutions for the owner.

Technology

Some restaurants offer customers menus that are loaded on digital tablets rather than printed on paper. Discuss with your class the advantages and disadvantages of this practice.

Teamwork

Working in small teams, choose a concept (service style, cuisine, and atmosphere) and location for a restaurant. Design an *à la carte menu* for your concept. Explain why your menu choices, layout, and design are appropriate for your team's restaurant concept. Use a school-approved web-based application to create a report that displays your menu choices, layout, and design.

Chef's E-portfolio
Menu Planning and Layout

Upload your report from the Teamwork activity to your e-portfolio. Ask your instructor where to save your file. This could be on the school's network or a flash drive of your own. Name your portfolio document *FirstnameLastname_Portfolio Ch#.docx* (i.e., JohnSmith_PortfolioCh51.docx).

While studying, look for the activity icon ⬈ to:
- Build vocabulary with e-flash cards and matching activities.
- Expand learning with video clips, photo identification activities, animations, and interactive activities.
- Review and assess what you learn by completing end-of-chapter questions.

G-WLEARNING.com

Tupungato/Shutterstock.com

802

Analyzing Cuisines

52

Reading Prep

Before reading, observe the objectives for this chapter. As you read, focus on how the chapter is structured. Does this structure make points clear, convincing, and engaging?

Culinary Terminology Build Vocab

terroir, p. 804
foodways, p. 806
kosher, p. 807
halal, p. 807

Academic Terminology Build Vocab

authentic, p. 803
prohibit, p. 807

Objectives

After studying this chapter, you will be able to

- summarize how chefs develop a better knowledge and understanding of cuisines.
- identify factors that influence the development of national and regional cuisines.
- differentiate between the basic elements of a cuisine.
- summarize ways chefs learn about different cuisines.
- recognize notable dishes of various international cuisines.

The world of food is immense. The number of meals prepared worldwide daily is endless. Additionally, the variety of dishes is vast. Where the same ingredients are prepared in a similar manner repeatedly, a cuisine develops. This repetition of dishes over time can create an internationally recognized cuisine.

The world of cuisine is so broad and vast that no single chef could possibly master it all. Chefs rely on cookbooks, recipes, the Internet, and other resources to help recreate dishes from around the world. International cuisine is a source of creative inspiration. Chefs also need to respond to customer requests for new and exotic flavors or memorable international dining experiences.

Creating Authentic Cuisine

Diners today have been exposed to a wider variety of dishes and food from around the world. Through media, travel, and restaurant dining, diners have become more discerning than ever, 52-1. Still, a recipe is often not sufficient for a chef to create an **authentic**—or genuine—dish, meal, or menu. Because of this demand for greater authenticity, chefs need to develop a better knowledge and understanding of cuisines. How do chefs do this? First, a chef must understand the various factors that shape the cuisine of a region—both environmental and human influences. Next, a chef dissects a cuisine by breaking it down into its basic elements—ingredients, cooking methods, and dishes. However, the process does not stop there.

Kzenon/Shutterstock.com

52-1 Today, more diners are interested in experiencing authentic cuisines.

A chef must continue to pursue knowledge about different cuisines throughout his or her life. This lifelong learning can take a variety of forms ranging from reading cookbooks to travel.

Factors That Shape Cuisine

A number of factors shape a cuisine. These factors can be classified as either environmental or human. Both categories are important for gaining an understanding of a cuisine.

Environmental Factors

A cuisine starts with its ingredients. Certain ingredients can only be produced under certain conditions. Even when ingredients are produced in a wide area, those from a specific place may have unique characteristics. **Terroir** (ter WAHR) describes a special set of characteristics in a food product that results from the local environment. These influences of the local environment include the climate and geography of the place where the food ingredient was produced. Terroir is a term that was first used to describe unique qualities of wines, but is now used for many other foods.

Climate The climate of a location is affected by its latitude, terrain, altitude, and nearby bodies of water. Knowing about the climate of a region is helpful in understanding cuisine in two ways—its effect on ingredients and on the appetite.

Food ingredients are profoundly influenced by, and subject to, the limitations of the region's climate. Fruits, vegetables, grains, and other food plants require a certain climate to grow. Animals, birds, and fish used for food can only live and thrive in a favorable climate.

In addition to its effect on ingredients, knowing about a region's climate is helpful to chefs in another way. The climate affects diners' appetites. Consider how foods that are appealing on a humid, ninety-degree day differ from those that are appetizing on a frigid winter evening. Worldwide, it is generally true that the cuisines of colder climates are milder in flavor, but heavier and more calorie dense. Alternately, foods consumed in hotter climates are more highly seasoned. For instance, contrast the food products and flavors of Scandinavia with those of North Africa.

Geography

Whether it is coastal wetlands, rolling prairies, or snow-capped mountains, the geography of a region has a great effect on the food ingredients found there. The types of crops that can be grown and livestock that can be raised are a result of the land formation. The location, terrain, geology, and sources of water all affect food of the region. In addition to agriculture, game and foraged foods are a product of geography. The foods of the coastal regions of Southeast Asia differ from the mountain cuisine of Switzerland in a large part due to differences in geography, 52-2.

Agriculture

Agriculture is an outgrowth of both climate and geography. The food products that are historically raised in a region are often the foundation for the region's cuisine. Understanding some of the basics of a region's farming practices allows chefs to identify food ingredients and their relative importance to a particular cuisine. Understanding agriculture encompasses both crops and livestock. For example, having knowledge of the historical importance of corn in the American South gives chefs an appreciation of ingredients derived from corn such as corn meal, hominy, corn-fed pork,

Xiong Wei/Shutterstock.com

52-2 Sheep and goats are suited to regions with mountainous terrains.

and corn whiskey. Increasingly, the concept of "farm to table" is important to chefs. This concept is important in international cuisine as well.

Fisheries

Knowledge of a region's bodies of water and the fish or shellfish they supply is an essential part of understanding a cuisine. Oceans, rivers, estuaries, lakes, and wetlands provide each cuisine with specific varieties of fresh fish and seafood. Traditionally, fish and seafood were not transported very far from their source. For instance, a sturgeon fish may be a mainstay of Russian cuisine, but is an inauthentic ingredient in Caribbean cuisine, 52-3.

Ingrid Maasik/Shutterstock.com

52-3 Scandinavia's extensive coastlines shape that region's cuisine.

Human Factors

Just as important to a cuisine as the environment in which it is formed are the people who harvest and prepare its foods. Chefs can better understand the origins and importance of a cuisine's unique dishes when they know the history, ethnic groups, and religious food traditions of a region.

History   Historians and social scientists have a growing appreciation of foodways as a meaningful way to study cultures and their history. Foodways can be defined as the eating habits and culinary practices of a people, region, or historical period.

Learning the history of a region or country's foodways is a way for chefs to understand a new cuisine. Historic events, trade routes, exploration, conquests, occupations, and

migration are all historic events that shape a culture and its cuisine. Dishes, menus, holiday meals, and food festivals often commemorate historic events. For instance, how well could a foreign chef understand the meal shared by North Americans at Thanksgiving without knowing the story of the Pilgrims offering thanks for surviving their first year in a new homeland?

Ethnic Influences   Food and cuisine are important ways people express their ethnic identity. The cuisine of most ethnic groups is molded by their native environment. Throughout history, people have migrated taking their foodways with them. In their new homes, those dishes and customs are adapted to a new environment and ingredients. For example, the cuisine of the Chinese island of Macau features both

A SERVING OF HISTORY

Cooking in a Hole in the Ground

Earthen ovens are one of the oldest ways to cook large amounts of food for communal feasts. Typically, a hole or trench is dug and a layer of rock is placed in it. A fire is built on the rocks. As the fire dies to embers, the rocks continue to hold a surprising amount of heat. Food is placed on the rocks and covered or buried allowing the heat from the rocks to bake or steam the product. This method is repeated in many different regions of the world. In Peru, a variety of meats and vegetables are cooked in an earthen oven called a *huatia* for a feast called a *pachamanca*. In Mexico, meats cooked in the manner are called *barbacoa* or *cohinita pibil*. Polynesians cook whole pigs, fish, and root vegetables in an oven called an *imu* or *umu*. The Maori people of New Zealand call this method *hāngi*. In New England, fish, lobster, clams, corn, and potatoes are cooked this way for a traditional clambake.

BoyKov/shutterstock.com

the Cantonese cuisine of Southern China and Mediterranean dishes and techniques brought by Portuguese traders who colonized the island in the 16th century.

Cuisines are often a mixture of numerous ethnic influences. Over time, different ethnic groups living in the same region adopt and blend elements of each other's cuisines. This blending of different cuisines is called *fusion cuisine*. Chefs often intentionally create fusion cuisine. They blend ingredients from different cuisines to create new and novel dining experiences.

Religion Religious practices often dictate for followers what foods can and cannot be eaten, when they can be eaten, and how they should be prepared. Understanding the basic food guidelines for major religious groups represented in a region or nation is one of the most important factors in understanding a cuisine. It is also a practical necessity for chefs that may need to accommodate patrons' religious food customs. The most common religious dietary rules are derived from Judaism, Christianity, Islam, Hinduism and Buddhism.

Judaism has some of the oldest dietary laws. Foods that are acceptable under Jewish dietary law are called **kosher**. Jews who keep kosher do not eat pork. Only forequarter cuts of meats are consumed. Meat and poultry must be slaughtered under religious supervision. Only finfish with scales are acceptable. Kosher cooking also **prohibits**, or forbids, mixing of meats and dairy foods.

Some Christian religions have a tradition of fast days on which meat is not consumed. This is most common on Fridays and fast days during Lent, the forty days leading up to Easter.

Islam also has dietary regulations. Pork and alcohol are prohibited. Meats must be slaughtered according to ritual. In Islam, acceptable foods are called **halal**. During the Islamic month of Ramadan, Muslims fast from sunrise to sunset.

Hindus do not consume beef or uncooked meats and many Hindu groups are vegetarians. Many followers of Buddhism also maintain a vegetarian diet.

Elements of International and Regional Cuisines

To analyze a cuisine, it is first broken down into its basic elements—ingredients, cooking methods, and dishes. These elements are often specific to that culture. Of course, different cultures may have elements that are similar or overlap.

Ingredients

Familiarization with unique ingredients is key to understanding a cuisine and producing authentic flavors. Even seemingly familiar ingredients can be distinctive. For instance, any American chef is familiar with rice, but making Japanese sushi with the common American variety of white rice does not work well. The starch content and texture of Japanese-style rice is key to making good sushi.

Talking to chefs who are familiar with a particular cuisine and to vendors of ethnic food products is the best way to learn about important ingredients. Understanding how to select, purchase, store, and prepare these ingredients is necessary to achieve an authentic dish. Most chefs enjoy visiting ethnic markets and learning about new ingredients.

Learning the details of even basic ingredients can be the difference between a successful dish and a failure. When exploring a foreign or unfamiliar cuisine, a checklist of ingredients to consider includes:

- vegetables
- fruits
- grains
- herbs and spices
- meat and poultry
- fish and seafood

Unique Cooking Methods

Aside from learning recipes, chefs should also understand the preparation and cooking methods that are representative of a particular cuisine. These methods are often essential for authentic flavors.

Preparation methods such as curing, pickling, and fermenting have been used for centuries as a method of preserving foods and are often done today for the flavor and texture they impart. They are used with local variations throughout the world. Consider that European sauerkraut and Korean kimchi are both cabbage fermented by essentially the same process, but the flavors are distinctly different because of the ingredients used.

Some cooking methods are based on a specialized cooking vessel. Asian dishes acquire unique flavors and textures when cooked in a wok. In Portugal, shellfish and other ingredients are cooked in a special tightly closed pot called a *cataplana*. Many North African dishes owe their texture and flavor to being slowly cooked in a *tagine*, a clay pot with a cone-shaped lid. A number of Asian dishes are simmered in broth at the table in a vessel called a *Mongolian hot pot*, 52-4.

Many cooking methods impart a distinctive flavor on foods by using locally available plants and trees as wrappings or fuel

CHEF'S ETHICS

Global Diversity

Foodservice is a global industry and workers have an ethical responsibility to understand and respect others from diverse cultures. This may mean learning more about other cultures' customs. It also means acting in an appropriate way when dealing with customers or fellow employees from different cultures. You may work with someone who has beliefs or customs different from yours, but you should always treat them as you would like to be treated. Respect should be given to others regardless of race, religion, or ethnicity.

vvoe/Shutterstock.com, Oligo/Shutterstock.com, Hassel Sinar/Shutterstock.com

52-4 Specialized cooking vessels such as a (A) cataplana, (B) tagine, or (C) Mongolian hot pot lend a unique flavor to dishes

for roasting or grilling. Banana leaves and ti leaves are used in Polynesian cuisine to wrap food for baking. In Mexico, leaves from the maguey cactus lend a unique flavor to slow roasted meats. Chinese cuisine uses tea leaves to smoke foods in a wok. There are a wide variety of hardwoods used for grilling, roasting, and smoking around the world.

Dishes

How a culture's signature ingredients are prepared and cooked creates the specialty dishes for which a cuisine is known. A repertoire of popular dishes defines a particular cuisine. Diners recognize this collection and have expectations for them.

Professional culinarians trained in classical methods and techniques have an advantage when working in foreign cuisines. Often, the cooking processes of foreign cuisines are similar to classical method and technique. Knowing the desired outcome in terms of texture, flavor, and presentation of dishes is the key to reproducing international cuisines with authenticity.

Home-Style Versus Professional Dishes
Dishes in international and regional cuisines can be divided into two categories—home-style and professional. Home-style dishes are the meals families cook at home, typically more simple and rustic. They may also be prepared in small, local restaurants or sold as street food. Professional cuisine prepared by trained cooks and chefs utilizes more expensive ingredients, complex cooking techniques, and refined presentations that paying diners expect.

Most dishes in a cuisine's repertoire start as dishes cooked in the home. Some are elevated and refined as they are prepared in the professional setting of restaurants, hotels, resorts, and clubs. Other dishes are distinct creations of the professional kitchen requiring specialized techniques or equipment. For example, two famous dishes of Naples, Italy originate from different sources. *Ragú Napolitana* is a slow-simmered blend of meat sausage, tomatoes, and herbs served over pasta. It is a typical home-cooked dish popular in the region. The region's most famous dish is pizza. This dish is eaten in pizzerias and is rarely prepared at home because Neapolitan-style pizza is baked in a wood-burning oven.

Learning About Cuisines

Chefs are not born with knowledge of all cuisines. And, it is not possible for culinary schools to provide instruction on all cuisines.

Culture & Cuisine

Street Food

Street food is ready-to-eat food sold on the street or other public place. In many cultures, it is a convenient snack or light meal. Street food vendors may operate from a stall, cart, or truck and usually specialize in one particular food item. Street foods are usually highly flavorful and one of the best ways to experience authentic flavors of a new culture.

testing/shutterstock.com

Chefs must take the initiative to teach themselves about various cuisines. They do this with cookbooks, magazines, the Internet, visiting restaurants, and travel.

Cookbooks and Magazines

The obvious place to start when learning about a new cuisine is a cookbook. However, the range of expertise of cookbook authors can vary greatly. Trained culinarians can distinguish between books that are simply a collection of recipes by a home cook and those that are broadly researched and include information on cultural factors, ingredients, and detailed cooking techniques.

Food magazines regularly feature articles on international and regional specialties. Travel magazines frequently explore both the cooking and restaurants in locales they feature.

Internet

The Internet enables chefs to research foreign cuisines with ease. Not only can one find recipes, but also pictures and videos of chefs and cooks preparing their native specialties. The Internet is also a great resource for finding specialty ingredients.

The accuracy and reliability of this information ranges from highly expert to blatantly incorrect. For this reason, it is important to be discerning about the sources of the information posted.

Ethnic Restaurants

Dining at restaurants that specialize in a particular cuisine is one of the best ways to learn about that cuisine. The ability to see and taste dishes is more than books and the Internet can offer. Chefs are conscious of the fact that not all ethnic restaurants produce food that is equally authentic. Some alter dishes to suit American tastes. Ethnic restaurants that cater to diners of the same ethnic background tend to be most authentic.

Travel

Culinary tourism is growing in popularity, 52-5. This experience offers total immersion in the cuisine of a particular region. Visits to markets and local restaurants combined with cooking classes by local experts deliver an immediate and thorough understanding of local cuisine. Whether in an organized tour or just seeking out local specialties, vacationing chefs rarely leave their curiosity and passion for food at home.

AJP/Shutterstock.com

52-5 Thailand's floating food markets are a popular destination for culinary tourists.

Additionally, the career paths of many chefs include work in locations around the world. Chefs working for hotels, resorts, and cruise lines are commonly offered the chance to move up the career ladder when willing to relocate to a new country. Living and cooking professionally in a region offers an unmatched level of expertise. Chefs with this type of experience are an excellent resource.

World Cuisine Overview

Consider the factors that influence and shape the following regions' cuisines. As you examine the images of each region's geography, resources, and notable dishes, analyze the interrelationships. These overviews provide only an introductory analysis of cuisines around the world.

Western Europe

Characteristics of Cuisines

Western Europe has a continental climate which is tempered by the Atlantic Ocean. It is a rich agricultural area. The region is historically Christian and maintains many food traditions related to Christian holidays.

Roasted, braised, and stewed meats featuring beef, pork, and lamb are the focus of much of the region's cuisine. Sausages and cured meats are traditionally important. Dairy products from cows' milk are widely used for cooking, pastries, and cheesemaking. Potatoes, root vegetables, and cabbages are foundational vegetables. Seasonally, vegetables such as beans, squashes, and greens are popular. Freshwater fish and seafood from the Atlantic Ocean and North Sea play a key role. Wheat and other grains are staples used in numerous varieties of breads, pasta or noodles, and dumplings.

Pâté de Campagne (France)
Country-style pork pâté.

Roast Beef with Yorkshire Pudding (Great Britain)
Large pieces of roasted beef served with an egg- and
flour-based popover that incorporates the rendered fat
from the roast.

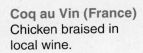

Irish Stew (Ireland)
Lamb and potato stew.

Gigot (France)
Roast leg of lamb.

Bangers and Mash (Great Britain)
Fresh pork sausages with mashed potatoes and
gravy.

Coq au Vin (France)
Chicken braised in
local wine.

Mediterranean

Characteristics of Cuisines

The Mediterranean basin encompasses lands surrounding the Mediterranean Sea. Due to similarities in climate and geography, the cuisines of this region share many characteristics. The Mediterranean enjoys a temperate climate with hot, dry summers and mild, wet winters. The region is ringed by mountain ranges with desert regions on the African side. Throughout history, European Christian and North African Muslim food traditions have influenced foodways of this area.

The region's agriculture is a legacy of the crops that the ancient Greeks and Romans spread through the region, including wheat, olives, and grapes. Summer vegetable crops such as tomatoes, peppers, beans, squash, artichokes, and eggplant grow well throughout the region. Generous use of garlic and herbs is characteristic. Mediterranean orchards provide oranges, lemons, figs, almonds, and pistachios. Rice is also a staple of the Mediterranean cuisine. Lamb and pork are the most common meats and the sea provides an abundance of fish, shellfish, and crustaceans.

Ratatouille (France)
Eggplant and zucchini stewed with peppers, tomatoes, onions, herbs, and garlic.

Pasta Marinara (Italy)
Pasta mixed with tomato sauce flavored with garlic and herbs.

Souvlaki (Greece)
Cubes of pork or lamb skewered and grilled.

Harira (North Africa)
Spiced legume soup usually with lentils or chickpeas and tomatoes.

Paella (Spain)
Short-grain rice flavored with saffron and cooked in an open pan with vegetables, chicken sausage, and shellfish.

Middle East and Central Asia

Characteristics of Cuisines

A region stretching from Libya to Pakistan shares similar cuisine forged by the rugged desert, mountain terrain, and arid climate. A small portion of the region is suitable for growing crops, so much of the foodways are based on the customs of nomadic herders.

Though numerous religions are practiced in the region, Islamic dietary law has the largest influence.

Chicken, lamb, beef, and goat are common meat sources. Yogurt is used in a large number of dishes. Coastal areas of the Arabian, Black, and Caspian Seas enjoy an abundance of seafood.

Wheat is a staple of the region, as is rice. Cucumbers, tomatoes, peppers, okra, beans, and chickpeas are common to the region's recipes. Melons, grapes, and orchard fruits especially, citrus, apricots, figs, and dates are cultivated. Nuts and sesame seeds are staples.

Historically, the region was part of the spice route from East Asia to Europe. Most of the region's cookery uses generous amounts of spices. Olive oil, garlic, parsley, and mint add their distinctive flavor of many dishes.

Tabbouleh (Syria, Lebanon)
Bulgur wheat, tomato, and parsley salad with lemon juice and olive oil.

Dolma (Balkans, Middle East)
Grape leaves stuffed with a filling or seasoned rice and sometimes ground meat.

Baklava (Turkish)
Filo pastry filled with chopped nuts and syrup or honey.

Shawarma (Arabic), Döner Kebap (Turkish)
Marinated meat or poultry stacked and roasted on a vertical spit.

Hummus (Arabic)
Dip made of pureed chickpeas with sesame, garlic, and lemon.

Scandinavia

Characteristics of Cuisines

Since the time of the Vikings, Scandinavia has depended on the sea. With its coastlines along the Norwegian, North, and Baltic seas, fish have long been a staple of the Scandinavian diet. Salmon, herring, cod, and eels are essential to the region's cuisine.

The southern part of the region—Denmark and Sweden—has rich rolling green pastures that produce wheat, oats, barley, and rye. These areas have grazing land for dairy herds. Beef and pork are important proteins. Potatoes and other root vegetables are also staples.

Much of Norway, northern Sweden, and Finland are mountains and/or forest providing an abundance of game, wild berries, and mushrooms. Freshwater lakes provide fish and crayfish. Above the Arctic Circle, native Laplanders' cuisine relies on reindeer herds.

Reinsdyrsteik (Norway)
Reindeer steak.

Smörgåsbord (Sweden)
Buffet with multiple cold offerings.

Gravlax (Sweden)
Cured salmon.

Inlagd Sill (Sweden)
Pickled herring.

**Frikadeller (Denmark),
Köttbullar (Sweden)**
Meatballs of ground beef and pork.

South Asia

Characteristics of Cuisines

The geography of South Asia is a study in extremes ranging from the highest points on earth in the Himalayas to low lying tropic coastal regions. This range gives the region's cuisines a wide variety of ingredients and cooking styles. In the northern region, wheat and barley are staples. In the southern part of the region, the tropical climate produces rice as a staple and provides a wealth of spices and tropical fruits.

A wide range of ethnic groups influence the region's cuisines. The region is home to Muslims, Hindus, and Buddhists. It is the place of origin for many of the world's spices including peppercorns, cloves, ginger, cinnamon, fenugreek, cardamom, nutmeg, and mace. Historically, the Chinese, Portuguese, Dutch, and British all came to the region to trade for these spices and left their mark on the foods of South Asia.

Dairy products such as ghee (filtered clarified butter), paneer (cheese), and yogurt are used. Lamb or mutton, goat, and chicken are the center of many dishes, while vegetarian meals are also common. The coastal areas depend on fish including kingfish, pomfret, and mackerel as well as crabs, prawns, rock lobster. and squid.

Lentils, chickpeas, onions, tomatoes, eggplant, spinach, and cauliflower are used regularly. Chili peppers, often referred to as sambal, are a key ingredient in the tropical regions. Mangoes, bananas, coconuts, and other tropical fruits are plentiful.

The region also produces a great deal of tea. Tea is often flavored with the region's spices and called *chai*.

Chutney (various)
Any of numerous condiments or dipping sauces that usually contain a mixture of spices, vegetables, and fruits.

Rendang (Indonesia, Malaysia)
Beef, lamb, or goat slow cooked with coconut milk, spices, lemon grass, and chiles.

Dal (Bangladesh, India, Pakistan)
Thick stew of split lentils or peas.

Naan (Bangladesh, India, Pakistan)
Leavened wheat flat bread baked in a clay tandoor oven.

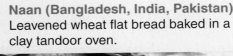
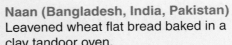

Tandoori Murgh (North India)
Yogurt and spice marinated chicken cooked on skewers in a clay oven.

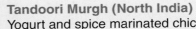

Australia and Oceania

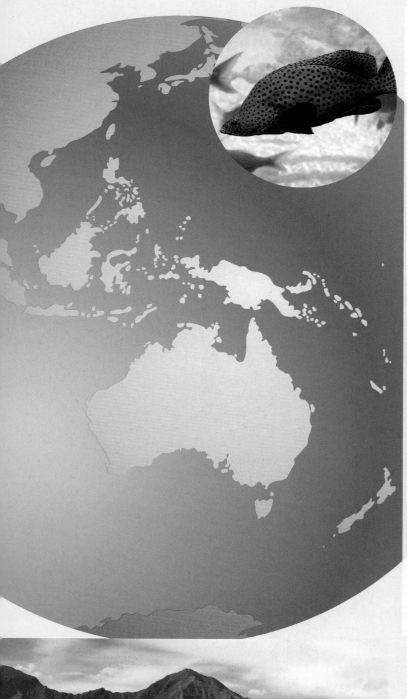

Characteristics of Cuisines

Australia and New Zealand share not only proximity in the Southern Hemisphere, but also in the development of their cuisines. The cuisines are heavily influenced by the food traditions of the British colonists and the region's prominent sheep and cattle production. Dishes such as meat pies, sausage rolls, roast dinners, and soda bread are some of the region's culinary icons. These Anglo foods were added to the bush foods of the Aborigines and Maori. Later, Chinese and other Asian traders and immigrants brought their food customs to create today's unique fusion cuisine.

Indonesian, Filipino, Micronesian, Polynesian, and Melanesian cuisines are enriched by Malay, Chinese, Spanish, American, and other Asian and Latin influences adapted to indigenous ingredients.

All of Oceania is made up of islands and, therefore the sea provides the majority of the regions sustenance. Both wild caught and aquaculture provide the region with ingredients such as salmon, tuna, barramundi, kingfish, pomfret, marlin, mahi mahi, wahoo, lobster, shrimp, crabs, oysters, and mussels.

The region's tropical climate produces an abundance of fruits such as mangoes, coconuts, papaya, bananas, and breadfruit. The islands of the South Pacific have traditionally relied on starchy root vegetables such as taro and yams. Pork and chicken are the most common meats in island cuisines.

Poke (Hawaii)
Diced raw tuna marinated with soy sauce and sesame oil.

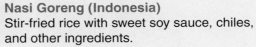

**Ota Ika (Samoa, Tonga),
Poission Cru (French Polynesia)**
Raw fish marinated in citrus juice and coconut milk.

Nasi Goreng (Indonesia)
Stir-fried rice with sweet soy sauce, chiles, and other ingredients.

Pavlova (Australia, New Zealand)
Baked meringue dessert topped with whipped cream and fresh fruit named for ballerina Anna Pavlova.

Kalua Pig (Hawaii)
Roast whole pig rubbed with sea salt and roasted wrapped in banana leaves.

**ANZAC Biscuits
(Australia, New Zealand)**
Cookies containing oats and coconut, named for the Australia New Zealand Army Corps.

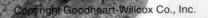

East Asia

Characteristics of Cuisines

East Asia is one of the most densely populated regions of the world and its cultures originate many centuries BC. Historically, China has been the greatest influence in this region, bringing its culture, religion, and foodways to its neighbors. The region's food customs are shaped by the customs and celebrations of Buddhism, Taoism, and Shinto. The cuisines of Asia are varied according to wealth. Cuisines range from the rich cuisine practiced in imperial palaces to the modest meals of poor peasants.

The region is also influenced by a variety of climatic conditions from the subarctic of Manchuria to the temperate regions of China and Korea to the tropical jungles of Vietnam, Thailand, and Cambodia.

The northern tier of East Asia depends on wheat as a staple using it in a wide range of noodles, dumplings, and pancakes. In the south, rice takes on a sacred importance as the staff of life.

Vegetables make up a large portion of the diet. The soybean provides nutritious protein in the form of tofu and adds distinct flavors as soy sauce, bean paste, and miso. Cabbages, onions, and a multitude of greens and root vegetables are common. Brought to the region from the West, chile peppers are widely used. Kelp and seaweed are important in Japanese and Korean cuisine. Animal protein, usually pork or chicken, is used sparingly.

The method of stir-frying in a wok is used in many East Asian cuisines. For centuries, the wok has allowed people to cook with intense heat while using a small amount of fuel.

Sashimi (Japan)
Thinly sliced raw fish.

Kimchi (Korea)
Spicy fermented cabbage or radish.

Pad Thai (Thailand, Vietnam)
Rice noodles stir-fried with vegetables, meat, poultry, or seafood.

Pho (Vietnam)
Beef or chicken in broth with rice noodles.

Larb (Laos)
Minced meat or poultry flavored with fish sauce, lime juice, toasted rice, chiles, and mint.

Peking Duck (China)
Crisp-skinned roast duck sliced and served on pancakes with scallions and sweet bean sauce—a specialty of Beijing.

Sub-Saharan Africa

Characteristics of Cuisines

Africa, the second largest continent, is home to a multitude of cultures. Most countries in Africa are home to multiple tribal cultures and a great diversity of cuisines and foodways. Much of the continent is undeveloped and many people's livelihoods as farmers, herders, and fishermen put them close to their source of food.

The cuisines of North Africa are dominated by Mediterranean and Arab foods. Cooking in East Africa and the Horn of Africa is influenced by centuries of interaction with Arab traders and European colonizers. Spices are used to great extent in East African cooking. The region is home to many Muslims and the influence of Islamic dietary law is evident.

West Africa's numerous regional cuisines rely on grains, starchy vegetables, and nuts as their foundation. Local recipes make great use of rice, millet, sorghum, cassava, yams, black-eyed peas, okra, and peanuts. Central and Southern Africa's cuisines are influenced by English, Dutch, and Portuguese colonists, as well as, Indian and Malay cultures. Southern Africans rely on porridges made from cornmeal or starchy vegetables. Wild game often called *bush meat* supplements domesticated meats and poultry.

Braai (Southern Africa)
Barbecue of various foods grilled over a wood or charcoal fire.

Fufu (West and Central Africa)
Boiled starchy vegetables such as cassava, yams, and plantains pounded into a dough.

Bobotie (South Africa)
A spiced, minced meat baked with a savory custard topping.

Jollof Rice (Western Africa)
Basmati rice cooked with tomatoes, spices, and peppers; often includes vegetables, meat, or fish.

Wot (Ethiopia, Eritrea)
A stew of chicken, beef, or lamb and vegetables, seasoned with a spice mixture called *berberé*.

USA and Canada

Characteristics of Cuisines

The United States and Canada share many of the same dynamics in the development of their cuisines. Their foodways are dominated by Northern European immigrants adapting their cuisines to the new conditions of North America and the food of the Native Americans. Each country also has a strong influence from Asian immigrants on the Pacific Coast and in urban centers.

Both the United States and Canada are economically developed and have rich agricultural production. That production yields large amounts of corn and soybean that is used as feed for beef, dairy cows, pork, and poultry. These proteins are plentiful and are the center of the typical North American diet. Both countries have extensive coastlines on both the Atlantic and Pacific oceans where seafood dominates the cuisine.

Regions within the United States and Canada have produced unique dishes and cooking styles resulting from the local terroir and the predominant ethnic influences in the region. For instance, the cuisine of Quebec is based on the manner in which French settlers adapted their cuisine to the conditions in northeast Canada. New England cuisine is a blend of English foodways with the seafoods and farm products of rural New England. A cuisine developed in the southeastern United States based on the ingredients and cooking methods of African slaves and European planters. These methods were applied to the region's fisheries and agriculture. The cuisine of the Southwest is a blending of native food staples and the influence of Spanish settlers. Though the history of American cuisine is more recent than many other parts of the world, each region can claim unique local specialties.

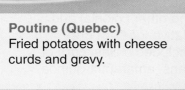

Poutine (Quebec)
Fried potatoes with cheese curds and gravy.

Baked Beans (New England)
Dried beans rehydrated and baked with salt pork and sweetened with molasses or maple syrup.

Planked Salmon (Pacific Northwest)
Salmon fillet roasted on cedar or alder wood plank.

Meat Loaf (Midwest)
Seasoned ground meat baked and served with gravy or tomato-based sauce.

Chile con Carne (Southwest)
Chopped beef stewed with onions, red chiles, and spices often served with pinto beans.

Jambalaya (Louisiana)
Rice and ham dish, flavored with bell peppers, celery, onions, and spices. Other meats, poultry, or seafood can be used in place of the ham.

Latin America and Caribbean

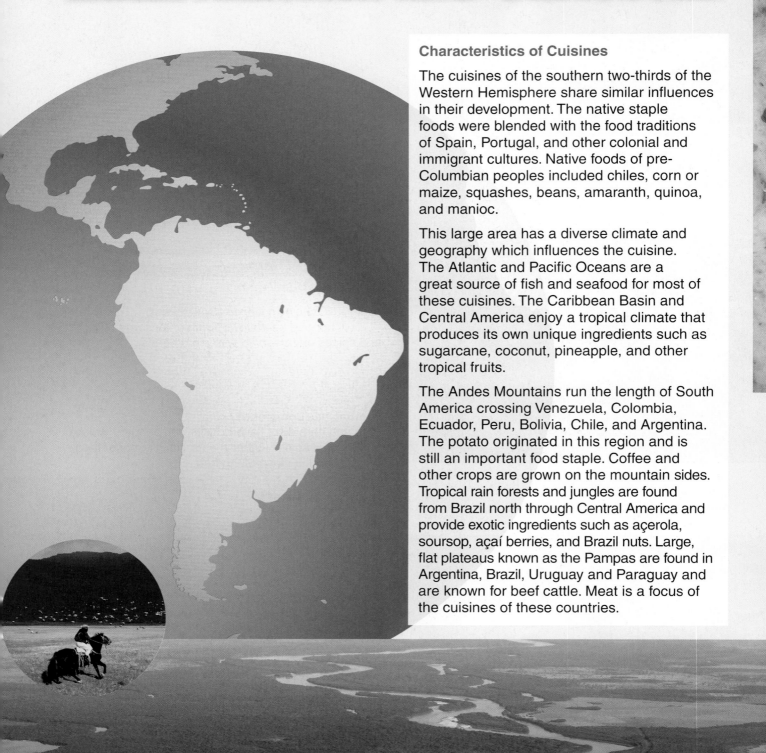

Characteristics of Cuisines

The cuisines of the southern two-thirds of the Western Hemisphere share similar influences in their development. The native staple foods were blended with the food traditions of Spain, Portugal, and other colonial and immigrant cultures. Native foods of pre-Columbian peoples included chiles, corn or maize, squashes, beans, amaranth, quinoa, and manioc.

This large area has a diverse climate and geography which influences the cuisine. The Atlantic and Pacific Oceans are a great source of fish and seafood for most of these cuisines. The Caribbean Basin and Central America enjoy a tropical climate that produces its own unique ingredients such as sugarcane, coconut, pineapple, and other tropical fruits.

The Andes Mountains run the length of South America crossing Venezuela, Colombia, Ecuador, Peru, Bolivia, Chile, and Argentina. The potato originated in this region and is still an important food staple. Coffee and other crops are grown on the mountain sides. Tropical rain forests and jungles are found from Brazil north through Central America and provide exotic ingredients such as açerola, soursop, açaí berries, and Brazil nuts. Large, flat plateaus known as the Pampas are found in Argentina, Brazil, Uruguay and Paraguay and are known for beef cattle. Meat is a focus of the cuisines of these countries.

Enchiladas (Mexico)
A corn tortilla rolled around savory fillings and coated with chile sauce.

Ceviche (Peru)
Seafood marinated in citrus juices.

Feijoada (Brazil)
A stew of black beans, pork, beef, and sausage.

Jerk (Jamaica)
Meat or poultry marinated in a mixture of spices and Scotch bonnet peppers.

Arroz con Pollo (Puerto Rico, Colombia, Venezuela, Ecuador, Panama, Peru, Cuba, Costa Rica, Honduras, the Dominican Republic)
Bone-in chicken braised with rice, often colored with annato.

Tamales (Mexico, Guatemala), Pasteles (Puerto Rico, Dominican Republic, Colombia, Panama)
A corn masa or other starchy dough often filled with meat or other ingredients, then steamed in corn husks or banana leaves.

Asado (Argentina)
Meats, poultry, or sausage roasted over a charcoal fire.

Central and Eastern Europe

Characteristics of Cuisines

East of the Alps, Europe is predominantly a large fertile plain. Throughout history it presented easy terrain for various armies to march through and conquer. From the Mongols and Tartars of the 13th century to the Germans in the 20th century, the region experienced continuously shifting nations, alliances, and borders. The result was an unusually large region that shares the same ingredients and styles of cooking.

Pork is an important meat, used in numerous sausages, cured and smoked. Beef is also common. Lamb meat and sheep's milk cheese are staples in the Carpathian Mountains which cut through the region. Saltwater fish from the Baltic, especially herring, are important. Inland lakes and rivers provide carp, pike, perch, and other freshwater fish.

Cabbage, both fresh and fermented, is widely used. Potatoes are a staple along with other root vegetables. Peppers, both fresh and in the form of paprika, are important in Hungary and the Balkans. Grains such as wheat, barley, buckwheat, and rye are key to the breads, dumplings, and noodles found throughout the region.

Wiener Schnitzel (Austria)
Breaded, panfried veal cutlet.

Goulash/Guylás (Hungary)
Rich meat-based soup or stew flavored with paprika.

Stuffed Cabbages (various)
Cabbage leaves rolled around a savory filling and braised.

Borscht (various)
A soup made from beets, cabbage, and other vegetables; served either hot or cold.

Pierogi (Poland), Perohy (Ukraine)
Ravioli-like dumplings with various savory and sweet fillings.

Dobos Torte (Hungary)
Multiple layers of sponge cake and chocolate.

Kielbasa (Poland)
Pork sausage in both fresh and smoked forms.

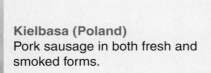

Summary Points

- Cuisines are influenced by a combination of environmental and human factors. Understanding these factors helps chefs create more authentic renditions of foreign cuisines.

- Environmental factors that influence cuisine include climate, geography, agriculture, and fisheries.

- Some characteristics of cuisines are a result of human influences such as historic events, ethnic traditions, and religious practices.

- The elements of a cuisine can be categorized as ingredients, important dishes, and unique cooking methods.

- Chefs learn about new cuisines through cookbooks, magazines, the Internet, dining, and travel.

In Review
Assess

1. How do chefs create authentic cuisine?

2. What concept explains why the same variety of grape grown in two different locations develops unique characteristics?

3. What are two ways that climate can affect a cuisine?

4. True or false. Generally, cuisines in colder climates are spicier and more highly seasoned.

5. The eating habits and culinary practices of a people, region, or historical period are also known as _____ _____.

6. Give an example of cuisine dish, menu, or holiday meal that commemorates a historic event.

7. True or false. Acceptable foods under Islamic dietary law are called *halal*.

8. Compare home-style dishes with professional dishes.

9. Give two reasons a unique cooking method may impart distinctive flavors or textures to dishes.

10. Name three ways chefs can learn about an international cuisine.

11. Why does much of Central and Eastern Europe share the same ingredients and styles of cooking?

Core Skills

12. **Writing.** Choose an international cuisine and find a topographical map of the country from which it originates. What correlations can be made from the map regarding the country's agriculture and fisheries? Write a one-page paper of your analysis.

13. **Reading.** Read an article in a food or travel magazine about an international or regional specialty discussed in this chapter. Research further to identify how the culture and its traditions are related to this food. Prepare a brief summary including your source.

14. **Listening.** Interview someone who grew up in another country about the foods they ate. What unique ingredients were used? What cooking methods were employed? What was his or her favorite dish? Does the dish have historical or religious significance? Prepare a summary of your interview.

15. **Math.** While researching foreign menus, you find a British pub menu listing Fish and Chips for £8.45. (£ is the symbol for the British pound sterling.) If the current exchange rate is £0.65 to $1.00, what is the cost of fish and chips in US dollars?

16. **CTE Career Readiness Practice.** You may have been taught to treat others how you would like to be treated. This is often referred to as *the golden rule*. Productively working with others who have a background different from yours may require that you learn to treat others as *they* wish to be treated. Conduct research on the Internet about cultural differences related to personal space, time, gestures/body language, and relationship toward authority figures. Create a T-chart that show the difference on the left and ways you would adapt your interactions to account for that difference.

Critical Thinking

17. **Analyze.** Describe the climate and geography of the place where you live. How do these factors influence what foods are locally produced?

18. **Compare.** Choose recipes for two dishes from different cuisines that utilize the same basic method and main ingredient. Which recipe's method is closer to the classic technique you have learned? How do the supporting ingredients differ?

19. **Predict.** What foreign cuisine do you think will gain the most popularity with American diners in the next five years? Why? What dishes or cooking methods will be most popular?

Technology

Choose a dish from an international cuisine and search the Internet for video demonstrations of that dish preparation. Critique two of the videos for presentation and culinary technique. Prepare an electronic presentation of your analysis for the class. Include the video demonstrations in your presentation.

Teamwork

Working in small groups, research a foreign cuisine. Write a five-course menu for a meal of dishes representative of that cuisine. Include recipes, a description of service, and décor to complement the menu.

Chef's E-portfolio
Analyzing International Cuisine Preparation

Upload your electronic presentation from the Technology activity to your e-portfolio. Ask your instructor where to save your file. This could be on the school's network or a flash drive of your own. Name your portfolio document *FirstnameLastname_Portfolio Ch#.docx* (i.e., JohnSmith_PortfolioCh52.docx).

While studying, look for the activity icon ↗ **to:**

- Build vocabulary with e-flash cards and matching activities.
- Expand learning with video clips, photo identification activities, animations, and interactive activities.
- Review and assess what you learn by completing end-of-chapter questions.

G-WLEARNING.com

Developing Taste

53

Reading Prep

Before reading this chapter, review the objectives. Based on this information, analyze the author's purpose for this chapter.

Culinary Terminology Build Vocab

gustation, p. 840
umami, p. 840
piquant, p. 840

Academic Terminology Build Vocab

olfaction, p. 838
retronasal pathway, p. 838
propelled, p. 838
tactile, p. 840

Objectives

After studying this chapter, you will be able to

- contrast eating with tasting.
- explain how the senses of sight, smell, taste, and touch contribute to how a person interprets food.
- recall subjective and physical factors that affect taste perception.
- summarize how chefs use and analyze taste combinations.
- implement a technique for tasting food critically.

Much time is spent learning how to present food attractively. However, appearance is only the first step in appreciating a dish. The ultimate success or failure of a dish depends on flavor. Taste is the artistic arena in which chefs function. Therefore, it is important that all chefs understand how they and their customers perceive taste.

Eating Versus Tasting

There is a difference between eating and tasting. Eating refers to the general process of ingesting food. Eating does not require thought. Tasting is different and requires concentration. Tasting is the process of thoughtfully analyzing foods and beverages using your senses.

Taste is the chef's most powerful tool for quality control. Chefs who walk around the kitchen constantly tasting do so to verify the quality of the food being prepared. Without tasting, there is no way to accurately judge the quality of a particular dish, especially in a fast-paced kitchen.

Painters develop an artistic eye capable of evaluating different colors and shapes. Singers and musicians develop their sense of hearing so as to distinguish differences in tone, rhythm, and harmony. Likewise, foodservice professionals must develop their sense of smell and taste. Developing these senses requires work and practice. For instance, the last time you ate a hamburger, did you think about how each of the ingredients contributed to the overall flavor balance of the burger? Did you consider how the sweet and tangy quality of the ketchup, the salt and acidity of the mustard, the crunch of the lettuce, the intensity of raw onion, the complexity of the pickle relish, the meaty texture and flavor of the burger, and the sponginess of the bun all combine to make a complex dish?

Tasting is work and requires effort. As you take the time to concentrate on the foods you eat, you will begin to form a taste memory. A taste memory is a library of taste sensations and combinations that are catalogued in your brain. Professional chefs have large taste memories. They draw on their taste memory when creating and evaluating dishes.

Taste Physiology

Many people think that taste is only a matter of what happens in your mouth when eating food. This is just part of the story. Taste physiology refers to the mechanisms of how our bodies perceive taste. Taste physiology is about more than just what happens when food is in your mouth. Interpreting food involves the eyes, mouth and the nose.

Sense of Sight

In almost all instances, food is first interpreted visually. In other words, you most often see the food before the other senses register its presence. When you see food, strong messages are sent to your brain including whether the food is edible or if you want to eat it. Chefs work hard to make food visually appealing so the customer wants to eat it on sight. In fact, attractive food sets up a certain expectation level that the food will smell and eventually taste delicious.

Sense of Smell

The sense of smell is referred to as **olfaction** (ohl FAHK shun). Olfaction interprets airborne molecules that enter the nasal cavity and

come in contact with the olfactory bulb. The olfactory bulb is a small area (about the size of a postage stamp) in the sinus region of the nasal cavity. The information gathered by the olfactory bulb is then transmitted to the brain via the olfactory nerve.

There are two avenues by which aromas reach the olfactory bulb. The first is simply through the nose, or nasal pathway. The second avenue is the **retronasal pathway**. The retronasal pathway is the route aromas travel up the back of the nasal cavity from the back of the throat cavity, 53-1. Aromas are **propelled**, or pushed, into the nasal cavity retronasally during swallowing.

Heat also has an effect on olfaction. Hot foods produce more aromas, or molecules, that travel to the olfactory bulb. Therefore, a soup served hot tastes stronger and more flavorful than if it were served lukewarm. Conversely, ice cream must be strongly flavored because it is served cold and therefore produces fewer aromas.

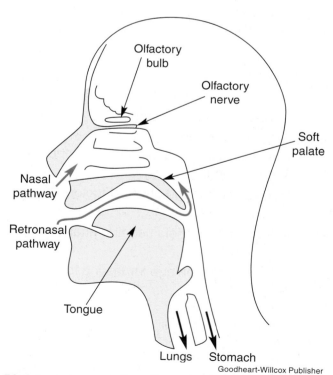

Goodheart-Willcox Publisher

53-1 Aromas reach the olfactory bulb by two different routes.

INDUSTRY INSIGHTS

Tasting with Your Ears?

Hearing is not often thought of as part of tasting food. Hearing does play a limited role in food appreciation. Consider the following food sounds—sautéing food, sizzling fajitas, a carbonated beverage being poured into a glass, the crunch of food as it is chewed, and the pop of a champagne cork.

Draz-Koetke/Goodheart-Willcox Publisher

53-2 Olfaction is crucial to appreciating and analyzing food.

Olfaction is an integral part of tasting food. The sense of smell recognizes well over 10,000 different smells at various levels of intensity. It is the sense of smell that accounts for food tasting complex. For example, the flavor of herbs, spices, ripe fruit, and smoky bacon are all "tasted" in the nose. If aromas cannot reach the olfactory bulb, food tastes boring. Remember the last time you had a stuffy nose and could not taste food? The swelling inside the nasal cavity and excess amount of mucus simply kept aromas from reaching your olfactory bulb. For instance, if you ate a chocolate bar while suffering from a head cold, you might only perceive a sweet and slightly bitter substance that melts in your mouth and has a fatty sensation. You would not be able to perceive the flavor of chocolate. In a similar way, bacon would only taste crunchy, salty, and slightly sweet if you were unable to smell it.

If you watch professional chefs or wine tasters, they often smell a product by inhaling quickly and intensely, 53-2. There is a reason behind this. They inhale deeply so as to propel as many molecules as possible to the olfactory bulb. They do not inhale many times in a row because the sense of smell fatigues easily. This means that as you repeatedly smell the same aroma, you perceive it less and less. At some point, your sense of smell may no longer even recognize the aroma. For instance, perhaps you have stepped into an elevator with someone wearing too much perfume. At first, the aroma is strong and obnoxious. However, the more time you spend in the elevator, the less you perceive the perfume. The reason is simple—your nose has become fatigued with smelling the same aroma and no longer perceives it. In essence, your nose only smells *changes* in aromas.

Sense of Taste

Gustation (guh STAY shun) refers to the sense of taste. The mouth cavity perceives only five basic tastes—sweet, salty, sour, bitter, and umami (u MAH mee). These five basic tastes are critical to appreciating and evaluating food.

Taste buds are concentrated mostly on the tongue. A smaller number of taste buds are found throughout the mouth and throat. People are born with about 10,000 taste buds that are clustered on small bumps on the tongue called *papillae* (pah PIHL ee). Different taste receptors on taste buds interpret particular tastes. In other words, there are sweet-, salty-, sour-, bitter-, and umami-specific taste receptors. Taste buds are replaced on average every 10 days. This explains why taste is not permanently lost after you burn your tongue.

The tongue interprets sweet from various sugar compounds and alcohol. Salty impressions result from the tongue coming in contact with chemical salts. Table salt, or sodium chloride, is the most common salt consumed. Sour sensations arise from acidic substances. In the kitchen, the most common acids are lactic acid from dairy products, citric and malic acid from fruits, and acetic acid from vinegar. Bitter compounds are common in many foods such as chocolate, artichokes, tonic water, cruciferous vegetables, coffee, tea, and olives. The bitter taste is a taste humans learn to like with repeated exposure. In general, intensely bitter foods are not appreciated in the same way sweet sensations are from birth. Mildly bitter foods can successfully add to the complexity of a dish. Some people are acutely repulsed by bitter sensations.

The fifth basic taste, **umami**, results from a type of protein called a *glutamate*. While the concept of umami has been understood by chefs for centuries, it was only labeled a basic taste in the last 100 years. Its scientific discovery happened in Japan, which accounts for its Japanese name. This fifth basic taste is critical to producing delicious food. Umami is perceived as a satisfying richness or meatiness. It is especially evident in fermented soy products, certain ripe vegetables, sea vegetables such as seaweed, aged cheeses, aged meats, long cooked stocks and braised meats, and monosodium glutamate, 53-3.

Sense of Touch

In addition to the sense of taste, the mouth registers the sense of touch. The mouth perceives **tactile**, or physical, sensations and temperature changes just as the skin on the rest of your body does.

The sense of touch allows your mouth to perceive differences in texture. As you chew, the inside of your mouth registers how crunchy, hard, soft, slimy, fatty, or smooth a food is. The ability to interpret texture allows you to gauge the tenderness and juiciness of a steak, or whether a vegetable is cooked to the correct stage of doneness.

Piquant (pee KAHNT) refers to the spicy hot sensation. Like texture, piquant is a tactile sensation. Piquant is the result of a chemical irritation of the lining of the mouth. A small amount of piquant adds interest to a dish.

Draz-Koetke/Goodheart-Willcox Publisher

53-3 These are some foods that convey the taste of umami.

Large amounts of piquant can make food difficult to eat—although this can become an acquired taste. Some of the most common piquant ingredients are chiles, peppercorns, onions, garlic, and mustard, 53-4.

Factors Affecting Taste

While humans share the same physical mechanisms for perceiving food, they do not perceive or interpret food identically. For instance, a plate of steaming brussels sprouts may make one person's mouth water, while another person might be completely repulsed. Similarly, one person may believe a well-seasoned dish to be flavorful while another person may think it overly salty.

Subjective Factors

Taste is a highly individualized and complex topic that reflects the diversity of human beings. It is shaped by our genetic makeup, life experiences, and culture. People may like and dislike certain foods because those foods are not part of their culture. In some cultures, plates of barbecued chicken feet would be warmly received. In other cultures, such a dish would be reviled. Food preference is often linked with memory. For instance, a particular food that was eaten during a vacation may elicit positive feelings. On the other hand, a food consumed while one had the flu may create negative feelings.

Physical Factors

Aside from subjective interpretation of food, there are physical explanations as to how or why people perceive taste differently. The ability to taste food may be negatively affected for many reasons. Colds and illnesses can make food taste boring. Head trauma and certain medicines and medical treatments such as radiation and chemotherapy can impair the ability to taste. Some medicines can make food taste radically different.

Age also affects taste perception. Children have a heightened sense of taste. As people age, the number of taste buds decrease, and the olfactory bulb can become less sensitive to certain aromas.

Draz-Koetke/Goodheart-Willcox Publisher

53-4 The spiciness in piquant foods is perceived by the sense of touch.

Culture & Cuisine

Comfort Foods

Comfort foods are those foods that are associated with childhood. Most often, comfort foods are simple foods that were prepared frequently at home. These foods cause a strong positive emotional response. Chefs often consider comfort foods when planning a menu since they are typically well liked by the customer. It should be noted that comfort foods are strongly linked to culture. Macaroni and cheese may be one person's comfort food, while raw fish dipped in soy sauce may be another's comfort food.

Some people are born with a heightened ability to taste. These people are called *supertasters*. They are genetically wired to taste foods more sensitively than the rest of the population. As a result, what may be slightly bitter to most people may be too bitter to eat for a supertaster.

Taste Combinations

Chefs spend their careers focusing on taste. They use their senses to evaluate the quality of the products they purchase. They use their senses to combine and balance the flavors of diverse foods. They use their senses to understand how the cooking process affects the flavor of the food. Understanding taste is at the heart of the professional chef's art.

When chefs want to create a new dish or analyze a menu item, they often break down a dish into its most basic taste components. This allows them to better analyze a certain preparation. Once a chef has considered the different aromas, tastes, and textures, he or she will be able to evaluate the overall success of the flavor combination. For instance, a chef would break down barbecue sauce into the following components:

- *Acid.* The acidity in the sauce comes from the tomato, vinegar, and citrus.
- *Sweet.* The sweetness comes from sugar, honey, tomato, and molasses.
- *Salt.* Salt comes from actual salt or salty ingredients such as mustard, soy sauce, or ketchup.
- *Bitter.* Some barbecue sauces may contain bitter spices or coffee.
- *Umami.* Tomatoes and fermented soy products contribute to umami.
- *Piquant.* Chiles, and possibly onion and garlic, contribute to the piquant impression.
- *Texture.* Barbecue sauces range from very thick to thin.
- *Olfaction.* Barbecue sauces can contain a wide variety of aromas that lead to

the complexity of barbecue sauce. For instance, onion, garlic, spices, herbs, mustards, tomato flavors, and smoky flavors are all olfactory sensations.

Once the chef has isolated each element, he or she evaluates the relative intensity of each ingredient. The goal is to achieve a balanced barbecue sauce.

Another key to understanding taste combinations is to consider basic taste pairings that complement each other. Chefs often employ these pairings when designing a new dish. Some of the most basic combinations are

- sweet and sour
- fat and sour
- sweet and bitter
- salt and sour
- sweet and salt

To better understand how these pairings work, consider the fat and sour pairing. Imagine a small bowl of oil. If tasted at this point, the oil would simply coat the mouth with a fatty sensation. Slowly, vinegar is added to the oil. Tasting periodically, the fat coats the mouth less and less as more vinegar is added. Eventually, a balance is struck between the fat which pleasantly coats the mouth and the acid that perks up the taste buds and cuts through the fat. As more vinegar is then added, the impression of the fat diminishes and is replaced by an overpowering acidity.

Tasting like a Chef

Chefs must be able to taste accurately and make quick decisions in a fast-paced kitchen. The ability to taste critically is the most important skill for controlling the quality of food being served, 53-5. When a chef tastes food, he or she must ask the question "Is this dish really as good as it can be?" Each taste of food is compared to the many different taste experiences a chef has had previously. A technique developed at the Kendall College School of Culinary Arts in Chicago helps students learn to taste critically. The technique, called *TAAT*

(Taste, Analyze, Adjust, Taste), includes the following steps:

Step 1 **T**aste the food. The first step is to see the food, smell it, and place it in your mouth. Many times cooks do not taste the food before serving it to the customer. This is comparable to a painter painting a canvas with his or her eyes closed. This seems foolish, but occurs frequently in many kitchens.

Step 2 **A**nalyze the food. This step requires work and concentration. During this step, thought is focused on how the food looks, smells, tastes, and feels. Consideration is also given to the balance of the dish. Are all the components of the dish in proper balance? Is something missing or too strong? Is it too dry or too moist? Is it sweet, bitter, or salty when it should not be? Is it too crunchy or not crunchy enough? There are many, many questions that must be asked at this point. When first learning to taste critically, it is very helpful to write down your impressions or discuss them with classmates.

Step 3 **A**djust the food. Based on your impressions in Step 2, it may be necessary to adjust the dish. This may take many forms. Perhaps more salt, liquid, sugar, or lemon juice is added. Maybe it is inedible and must be discarded. Whatever the specifics, Step 3 requires action. You do something to make the dish more perfect.

Step 4 **T**aste the food again. Adjustments made in Step 3, have changed the way the food tastes, so the process starts over. You must taste, analyze, and adjust again. It may take many times through this process to get the dish to be as perfect as possible. Eventually, the process finishes with Step 2 when you analyze the dish and determine that it is correct. At this point, the food can be served.

When first learning the *TAAT* technique, it seems slow and methodical. As you master the process, it moves faster. Over time, this process helps you build a taste library in your brain of many different taste experiences. Eventually, you will taste critically and quickly like a professional chef.

mangostock/Shutterstock.com

53-5 A chef must taste dishes before they are delivered to customers to ensure quality food is being served.

Summary Points

- Tasting is the process of thoughtfully analyzing foods and beverages using your senses. Analyzing food over time creates a taste memory that is crucial for all chefs to develop.

- The body perceives taste with the eyes, nose, and mouth.

- Taste is highly individual and is the result of genetics, life experiences, and culture. Illnesses, medicines, medical treatment, and age can reduce the ability to taste.

- Chefs use their developed sense of taste to combine flavors in a balanced and creative way. Chefs often break a dish down into its basic taste sensations so as to better analyze it.

- The ability to taste critically is an important skill for controlling the quality of food served.

In Review
Assess

1. What is the difference between eating and tasting?

2. How does the sense of sight impact taste?

3. What are the two ways that aromas can reach the olfactory bulb?

4. Select the effect temperature of food has on olfaction.
   A. Temperature has no effect on how many aromas reach the olfactory bulb.
   B. Hot foods produce more aromas that reach the olfactory bulb.
   C. Cold foods produce more aromas that reach the olfactory bulb.

5. The sense of smell recognizes over _____ different smells and the sense of taste registers _____ basic tastes.

6. How is the flavor or perception of umami best described?

7. List three different piquant foods.

8. A fondness for sourdough pancakes with huckleberry syrup first eaten while on your favorite vacation in the mountains is an example of a _____ factor affecting taste.
   A. subjective
   B. physical
   C. piquant
   D. objective

9. List four physical factors that could affect a person's ability to perceive taste.

10. Into what components might a chef break down a barbeque sauce?

11. Name three of the basic taste combinations that chefs use to design a new dish.

12. What are the steps in the *TAAT* technique?

Core Skills

13. **Math.** When the chef tasted your dish, she noted that the flavor from the thyme was overwhelming. You told her the recipe called for 2 tablespoons of fresh thyme but you substituted 2 tablespoons of dried instead. The chef tells you to remake the dish and adjust the amount of herbs because dried herbs have more concentrated flavor. She informs you that when substituting dried herbs for fresh, you should use one-third the amount of dried herbs as called for fresh. How much dried thyme should you use when you remake this recipe?

14. **Writing.** Create a simple chart with three headings—sense of smell, sense of taste, sense of touch. Bring this chart to your next meal and as you eat, be aware of the taste sensations you are experiencing. Make notes in the appropriate columns about your perceptions. Then write a summary of your experience to share with the class. What did you learn about developing taste?

15. **Reading.** Use the text and reliable Internet or print resources to read further about physical factors that can impair the sense of smell and taste. Choose one of the following topics and explore its impact on the sense of smell and taste: age, illness, medication, or a specific medical treatment such as chemotherapy. How

do these items impact smell and taste? What can a chef do to enhance the visual appeal, smell, and flavor of food to meet the varying needs of individuals? Write a summary of your findings to share with the class.

16. **CTE Career Readiness Practice.** Presume you are a chef at a local retirement community. The residents have the choice to either participate in group meals in the dining room or prepare their own meals. Many choose the latter. Because eating should be enjoyable as well as sustain life, a number of residents have requested a class on making foods more appealing and flavorful. The facility manager knows your expertise and has asked you to make a presentation to the residents. Develop a presentation/demonstration that will teach residents how to

- create visually appealing food
- enhance the aromas and flavors of foods to make them more appealing to eat

Critical Thinking

17. **Make inferences.** Form two teams and debate the following topic: Tasting is fun and, therefore, perfect for social parties. Each team should make inferences about the statement and cite reasons for their team's opinion. Use the text and other reliable sources to support your team's inferences.

18. **Generate a proposal.** Select three of the basic taste pairings discussed in this chapter. Propose a combination of ingredients or foods that demonstrate each pairing.

19. **Draw conclusions.** Consider all factors as to why a chef is interested in mentally breaking a dish down into its various basic taste sensations. Draw conclusions about the value in doing so. How can this impact food quality? How can this benefit customers? benefit the foodservice operation?

20. **Critique effectiveness.** You are a chef instructor and observe a culinary student smelling his food product by taking repeated, long inhalations. Critique the effectiveness of this student's technique. What feedback would you give the student?

Technology

In teams, develop a 10 to 15 question survey to evaluate how people taste food. Your survey should focus on how the following impact taste: visual appeal, sense of smell, and sense of taste as outlined in this chapter. Create a rating system to use with your questions such as 1 to 5 (with one being the least appealing and 5 being the most appealing). Choose a recipe to prepare and adjust the yield of the recipe to make at least 25 portions. Invite 25 guests to sample your food. Have each guest take your survey. Use spreadsheet software to tabulate the results of your survey and create a pie chart or bar graph to display your results. Discuss your findings in class. Were the other teams' findings about how people taste food similar or different from your team's findings?

Teamwork

Learning how to taste critically is an important skill for a chef. In teams, select a soup recipe to prepare or obtain a recipe from your instructor (alter the yield of the recipe to suit the number of members of your team). Prepare the soup. Then use the steps in the *TAAT* (Taste, Analyze, Adjust, and Taste) technique to critically analyze your soup. As a team complete Steps 1 and 2 and discuss what adjustments should be made to make your soup more flavorful and appealing. Then complete Steps 3 and 4. Discuss the results of Steps 3 and 4. At what point, does your team think its soup would be ready to serve to customers? Why?

Chef's E-portfolio
Analyzing Taste Sensations

Upload your chart and summary from the writing activity #14. Ask your instructor where to save your file. This could be on the school's network or a flash drive of your own. Name your portfolio document *FirstnameLastname_Portfolio Ch#.docx* (i.e., JohnSmith_PortfolioCh53.docx).

Appendixes

A–Measuring and Converting Weights

	Unit of Weight	Abbreviation	Equivalent
US System	ounce	oz.	
	pound	lb. or #	1 lb.=16 oz.
Metric System	gram	g	
	kilogram	kg	1 kg=1000 g
Conversions*			

1 oz.=28 g   1 lb.=454 g

1 g=0.035 oz   1 kg=2.2 lb.

*US/metric conversions are approximate

B–Measuring and Converting Volumes

	Unit of Volume	Abbreviation	Equivalent
US System	fluid ounce	fl. oz.	
	teaspoon	tsp.	1 tsp.=⅙ fl. oz.
	tablespoon	Tbsp.	1 Tbsp.=3 tsp.=½ fl. oz.
	cup	c.	1 c.=8 fl. oz.
	pint	pt.	1 pt.=16 fl. oz.=2 c.
	quart	qt.	1 qt.=32 fl. oz.=4 c.=2 pt.
	gallon	gal.	1 gal.=128 fl. oz.=16 c.=8 pt.=4 qt.
Metric System	milliliter	mL	
	liter	L	1 L=1000 mL
Conversions*			

1 fl. oz.=30 mL   1 qt.=0.95 L   1 gal.=3.8 L

1 mL=0.033 fl. oz.   1 L=33.8 fl. oz.

*US/metric conversions are approximate

C–Scoop Sizes

Scoop number*	Capacity (ounces)	Capacity (cups)
4	8	1
5	6	¾
6	5⅓	⅔
8	4	½
10	3⅕	⅖
12	2⅔	⅓
16	2	¼
20	1⅗	⅕
24	1⅓	2⅔ Tbsp.
30	1⅕	2⅖ Tbsp.
40	⅘	1⅗ Tbsp.

*Reflects the number of these scoop serving sizes in a quart.

D–Standard Foodservice Can Sizes

Can Size Number	Approximate Volume (cups)	Approximate Weight (ounces)
No. 1 picnic	1¼	10½
No. 300	1¾	14
No. 303	2	16
No. 2	2½	20
No. 2 ½	3½	27
No. 3	5¾	46
No. 10	12	6½ pounds

E–Common Fraction to Decimal Equivalents Used in Foodservice

Fraction to Decimal Equivalents
⅛ = 0.125
⅙ = 0.166
¼ = 0.25
⅓ = 0.333
⅜ = 0.375
½ = 0.50
⅝ = 0.625
⅔ = 0.666
¾ = 0.75
⅚ = 0.833
⅞ = 0.875

F–Produce Yield Percentage

Item	Yield	Item	Yield
Apples	91% (unpeeled) 78% (peeled)	Kohlrabi	73%
Apricots	93%	Lettuce	66%
Asparagus	53%	Mushroom	98%
Avocado	69%	Okra	87%
Bananas	64%	Onion	83%
Beans, Green	88%	Papaya	67%
Beans, Lima	44%	Parsnips	83%
Berries	96%	Peaches	76% (medium, pitted)
Bokchoy	77%	Pears	92% (unpeeled) 78% (pelled)
Broccoli	81%	Peas, Green	38% (shelled)
Brussels Sprouts	76%	Peppers, Bell	80%
Cabbage, Green	87%	Pineapple	54%
Cabbage, Red	83% (shredded)	Potato	81% (peeled)
Cantaloupe	47%	Radishes	94%
Carrots	83% (peeled, sliced)	Rhubarb	86%
Cauliflower	62%	Rutabagas	85%
Celery	83%	Spinach, Fresh	88%
Corn	34% (with husk) 54% (without husk)	Squash, Summer	96%
Cucumbers	84% (peeled, sliced)	Strawberries	88%
Eggplant	81%	Sweet Potatoes	80%
Endive	78%	Tomato	98% (wedges)
Grapefruit	74% (peeled)	Turnip	79% (peeled)
Grapes	97%	Watercress	92%
Kale	73%	Watermelon	61%
Kiwifruit	87% (peeled)		

*US/metric conversions are approximate

Glossary

A

abundant. Plentiful. (33)

acidulation. The process of adding acid to an item. (21)

active listening. An effective communication technique that signals to the speaker that what he or she is saying is understood. (5)

aerobic bacteria. Bacteria that require oxygen. (7)

aging. The time meat is allowed to rest after slaughter. (30)

airline breast. Chicken breast that is a boneless chicken breast with the first joint of the wing still attached. (31)

à la carte (ah lah KAHRT). A system in which food is prepared only when an order is received from the service staff. (22)

à la carte (ah lah KAHRT) menu. A menu that prices each course separately. (51)

al dente (ahl DEN tay). An Italian term used to describe a product being fully cooked but not soft or mushy. (27, 29)

allergen. A protein that is misinterpreted by the body and causes an immune system response. (7)

alternative. Option. (31)

American Culinary Federation (ACF). The largest professional organization for culinarians in the United States. (5)

American service. A style of service in which the server delivers plates of food directly from the kitchen to the guest, also referred to as *plated service*. (48)

anaerobic bacteria. Bacteria that thrive without oxygen. (7)

anchovies. Small, oily ocean fish preserved by salting that is a popular ingredient in Mediterranean cuisines. (17)

apprenticeship. A method of training in which a person learns a trade under the guidance of skilled tradespeople. (5)

aquaculture. The farming of fish and shellfish. (34)

aromatic. Distinctive smell. (26)

as purchased (AP). Raw, unprepared product in the same form it is delivered from the vendor. (49)

asymmetry. A sense of balance achieved by artistically arranging items without creating two identical sides of a center point. (39)

attitude. How a person thinks and feels about other people and situations. (5)

attribute. Characteristic. (42)

authentic. Genuine. (52)

authority. Control over. (2)

automated external defibrillators (AED). Devices that automatically detect the type of heart rhythm and deliver an electric shock if appropriate. (9)

B

back-of-the-house staff. The kitchen personnel including chefs, cooks, dishwashers, and receiving clerks. (48)

bacteria. Single-celled organisms that reproduce by dividing. (7)

baguette (bah GEHT). A long, thin French bread. (22)

bain marie (bay mahr Ee). A hot water bath used to cook foods gently. (13)

baker. The position responsible for preparing and baking breads. (40)

baking. The method used to cook foods with a certain amount of added moisture in the oven, similar to roasting. (18)

baking powder. A chemical leavener used in baking that consists of baking soda premixed with an acid chemical, such as cream of tartar. (40)

baking soda. An alkaline powder, also known as *sodium bicarbonate*, which is used as a chemical leavener in baking. (40)

banquet chef. Oversees a staff of cooks that prepares meals for large groups. (4)

bar cookies. Cookies made by portioning and forming dough into an approximate one-pound (454 g) log, flattening the log, and baking it. Once cooked, the warm log is sliced into one-inch segments and baked again. (42)

barding. The process of covering an item with a thin sheet of fat. (31)

base. A concentrated instant powder or paste that dissolves in hot water to make a stock-like liquid. (23)

basted eggs. Eggs fried in butter while the hot fat in the pan is spooned over the top to lightly cook the yolks. (38)

batonnet (bat ohn AY). A stick cut measuring $2 \times \frac{1}{4} \times \frac{1}{4}$ inches ($50 \times 6 \times 6$ mm). (12)

batter. A mixture of flour and liquid with greater proportion of liquid, which makes it pourable. (41)

Bavarian cream. A stable foam dessert made from liquid custard sauce (crème anglaise) that is bound with gelatin and lightened with whipped cream. (46)

béchamel (bay shah MEHL) sauce. A mother sauce that is a white sauce consisting of milk thickened with a white roux and flavored with onion, bay leaf, and a small amount of nutmeg. (24)

benefits. The non-wage, financial extras provided by employers to their employees such as paid time off, retirement plans, and health and life insurances. (6)

beurre manié (BEHR man yay). A mixture of softened whole butter and flour used to thicken liquids. (24)

beurre noisette (BEHR nwah zhet). A classical preparation made from browning butter that is used as a sauce for fish and seafood. (35)

biodegradable. A substance that can be broken down into harmless products by living things such as worms, insects, and bacteria. (10)

biodiversity. The variety of forms of animal and plant life in a particular area. (10)

biological hazards. Harmful organisms that cause foodborne illness. (7)

biscuit method. A process that combines dry ingredients first, then solid shortening is "cut in," or mixed with the dry ingredients until it breaks into small pieces, and finally, the liquid ingredients are added and mixed just long enough to combine with the other ingredients. (41)

bisque. A seafood-based soup that is thickened traditionally with rice, although modern methods use a roux. (25)

bivalves. Shellfish that have two shells, which clamp shut tightly to protect the tender interior flesh. (34)

blanching. The process of briefly cooking an item in boiling water. (21, 27); the process of boiling bones and then discarding water to remove impurities which could cause stock to be cloudy. (23)

blind baking. Prebaking a pie or tartlet shell that has weights placed in it to prevent bubbling or buckling. (44)

blooming. Softening gelatin in cold water. (40)

boiling. Cooking in liquid at its highest possible temperature. (18)

bolster. A thick, metal collar running from the heel of the knife blade to the handle that strengthens the blade. (11)

bonds. The forces that hold chains of carbon atoms together. (50)

bouillon (BOOL yohn). A stock-like preparation that is made with a larger proportion of meat than bone and a greater variety of vegetables than stocks. (23)

bound salad. A salad composed of cooked items mixed with mayonnaise or similar ingredient such as Greek yogurt. (19)

bouquet garni (boo KAY gar NEE). A bundle of fresh herbs tied to a piece of celery, leek, or carrot. (23)

braising. A combination cooking method that first browns the food on all sides and then simmers it in a liquid. (18, 33)

bran. The first layer of the grain kernel that is rich in fiber. (28)

brigade. A large kitchen staff that uses a chain of command—each workstation has a leader and each leader reports to the head chef—to complete a task. (4)

broiler. A device that uses a radiant heat source placed above the food to cook. (14)

broiling. A cooking method that uses radiation from a heat source located above the food. (18)

broth. A stock-like preparation that is made with a larger proportion of meat than bone and a greater variety of vegetables than stocks. (23)

brown rice. Whole-grain rice or rice sold with the bran layer left attached; other colors of rice can also be whole grain as long as the bran layer is left intact. (28)

brown stock. Stock made from roasted bones and roasted or sautéed mirepoix resulting in rich roasted flavor and caramel color. (23)

brunoise (broon WAHZ). A dice cut measuring $\frac{1}{8} \times \frac{1}{8} \times \frac{1}{8}$ inches ($3 \times 3 \times 3$ mm). (12)

buffalo chopper. A machine used for chopping large quantities of food. (13)

C

calorie. The unit used to measure the amount of energy contained in foods. (50)

canapé (kan ah PAY). A small, bite-sized hors d'oeuvre that resembles an open-faced sandwich and is well garnished and attractive. (22)

capers. The buds of a bush that grows near the Mediterranean that have been pickled or simply packed in salt to preserve them; used to garnish sauces, salads, and entrées. (17)

caramel. Sugar that is cooked to about 320°F (160°C) at which time it turns varying shades of brown and develops a rich flavor. (47)

caramelization. The browning that occurs when sugars are heated, resulting in a richer, more complex aroma and flavor. (18)

carbohydrate. The nutrient that is the body's chief energy source. (50)

carbon steel. The material used to make knife blades that is easiest to sharpen to a finely honed edge, but loses its shine and discolors quickly after its first use. (11)

cardiopulmonary resuscitation (CPR). A rescue procedure that combines chest compressions with blowing into the victim's mouth, simulating the beating of the heart and breathing of the lungs. (9)

carryover cooking. The cooking that continues after food is removed from the oven. (32)

catering. Providing food and service for groups in a hall or banquet facility. (2)

cellulose. The microscopic fibers that make up the rigid tissue of plants. (27)

cephalopods. A category of mollusks that are known for their long arms that are covered with suckers, well-developed eyes, and sac which holds and ejects ink. (34)

certification. A confirmation that a culinarian possesses certain knowledge, skill level, and experience. (5)

chafing dish. Decorative covered stand that keeps food hot. (39)

chain restaurants. A group of restaurants owned by the same company that use the same menu, décor, and management practices in each location. (2)

chemical hazard. Any chemical that contaminates food. (7)

chiffonade (shif on AHD). Thinly cut strips of leafy greens. (16)

china cap. A cone-shaped strainer used to remove lumps and particles from liquids such as sauces. (13)

chinois (SHEEN wah). A type of china cap that has a finely woven, metal mesh. (13)

chlorophyll. The chemical that gives green vegetables their color. (27)

cholesterol. A white, pasty, fat-like substance found in the bloodstream and cells that is essential for many of the body's functions. (50)

chop. A steak that always contains a bone. (31)

chowder. An American seafood-based soup that is flavored with dairy product, bacon, and potato; and thickened with flour. (25)

churning. The rapid mixing of cream that causes lumps of butterfat to emerge and begin to stick together to form larger and larger pieces of butter. (37)

chutney. A condiment made of preserved fruits and vegetables with an acidic, sweet and spicy flavor. (17)

clamshell griddle. A piece of cooking equipment that consists of two hot, smooth surfaces that close on the top and bottom of the sandwich, cooking both sides at once. (36)

clarified butter. The fat portion of the butter, which has been separated from the water and milk solids. (16)

classic cuisine. A style of cooking defined by orderly menus organized by courses, served tableside by waiters in hotels and restaurants. (3)

clean. A condition of being free of dirt, grease, or grime. (8)

clearmeat. A mixture of ground meat, vegetables, and egg whites added to stock to add flavor and remove impurities to clarify the stock. (25)

coagulant. Thickening agent. (37)

coddled eggs. Eggs cooked in their shells for one to three minutes. (38)

cohesive. Unified. (38)

colander. A large bowl-shaped strainer used to drain large quantities of product. (13)

collagen. A protein found in bones and other connective tissue from which gelatin is derived. (23); the most prevalent connective tissue in meat. (30)

combination oven. An oven that uses a combination of convection heat and steam to cook foods. (14)

commercial foodservice. Businesses with the primary goal of preparing and selling food to make money. (2)

compensate. Make up for. (32)

complete protein. Protein that contains all nine indispensable amino acids in the correct proportions needed to support life. (50)

composed salad. A finished salad that has ingredients assembled in a particular arrangement, also known as *plated salads*. (19)

composting. The process by which some food and other organic matter (leaves, grass clippings, paper, and so on) decay to form a highly fertile growing substance. (10)

concassé (kon kah SAY). A rough dice or chop of a product. (16)

concentration. Removal of water to make a liquid less dilute. (37)

condiment. Flavoring or seasoning served with foods to enhance their flavor. (17)

conduction. How well pots and pans transfer heat from the burner or oven to the food they contain. (13); the transfer of heat energy from one object to another through direct contact. (18)

confer. To grant. (34)

conflict. Disagreement. (5)

connective tissue. Protein that bundles muscle tissue together and connects muscle to bones, joints, and skin. (30)

consommé. A perfectly transparent and intensely flavored soup that is made by clarifying a stock. (25)

constitute. Make up. (30)

contamination. The presence of unsafe substances or levels of dangerous microorganisms in food. (7)

convection. The manner in which heat energy travels through liquids and gases. (18)

convection oven. An oven that uses a fan to circulate the air inside the oven allowing for faster cooking at lower temperatures. (14)

conversion factor. A multiplier that adjusts the quantity of each ingredient in the original recipe to determine the quantities needed for the revised recipe. (15)

converted rice. Rice that has been parboiled to remove surface starch. (28)

cooking. The process of preparing food for eating by applying heat. (18)

corporation. A business that is granted a charter from the state recognizing it as a separate entity with legal rights; ownership is divided among investors. (2)

coulis (coo LEE). A sauce made from puréed fruits or vegetables. (24, 47)

court bouillon (kohr BOO yohn). The preferred liquid for deep poaching fish, seafood, and vegetables that is made by simmering aromatic vegetables, herbs, and spices in water with an acid. (35)

cover message. A letter or e-mail that introduces yourself, indicates why you are contacting a potential employer, and provides a sample of your writing ability. (6)

craft. Occupation. (43)

creaming method. The process that first mixes the butter or shortening with the sugar and spices until smooth, then eggs and liquids are added and mixed until incorporated, and finally, the flour and leavening agent are added and blended. (42)

cream soup. Soup consisting of milk or stock, thickened with both flour and puréed ingredients, and often finished with cream. (25)

crème anglaise (KREHM ahn GLAYZ). Custard sauce that is the base of important preparations such as Bavarian cream and many ice creams. (46)

crème chantilly (KREHM shahn tee YEE). Sweetened whipped cream. (46)

crème mousseline (moo seh LEEN). A very light pastry cream resulting from the addition of whipped cream to pastry cream. (46)

crêpe (KRAYP). A very thin pancake. (41)

critical control point (CCP). A step in food handling at which control can be applied to prevent or eliminate a food safety hazard. (8)

cross-contact. When an allergen is transferred from its food of origin to a food that does not contain the allergen. (7)

cross-contamination. When harmful microorganisms are transferred from one product to another by hands, utensils, equipment, or other physical contact. (8)

cross training. Teaching staff to do more than one job in the kitchen. (4)

crumber. A tool used to scrape and scoop crumbs from the table onto a plate. (48)

crustacean(kruhs TAY shuhn). An aquatic species that has a hard and segmented exoskeleton, or shell. (34)

cuisine (kwih-ZEEN). the French word for "kitchen," but in English it means a style of cooking. (1)

culinarian. A cook or someone who prepares food. (1)

culinary. Matters related to the preparation or cooking of food. (1)

culinary apprenticeship. An entry-level job in foodservice combined with a formal training program. (6)

curdle. When the liquid and solid portions of milk or egg mixtures separate from each other and ruin a sauce. (24)

curds. The cubes containing the casein proteins that thickened milk is cut into for cheese making. (37)

cutlet. A thin, boneless steak. (31)

cycle menu. A menu that rotates a set number of items over a certain period of time. (51)

D

Danish sandwich. A neat, open-faced sandwich that often includes strongly flavored foods. (22)

deep frying. Cooking food in enough hot fat to fully cover the item. (18)

deglaze. The use of liquid to dissolve the browned bits off the bottom of a pan in which food has been roasted or sautéed. (23)

demi glace (DEH mee glahs) sauce. A mother sauce that is classically made by reducing espagnole sauce to proper nappé consistency. (24)

densimeter. A special instrument that measures the sugar levels in fruit purées and syrups. (47)

derivative sauce. A sauce that is made from a mother sauce. (24)

detract. Diminish the effectiveness. (39)

diversity. Composed of or including different elements. (5)

docking. The act of cutting small slashes in the surface of risen dough. (43)

dough. A mixture of flour, liquid, and other ingredients that is stiff enough to form into shapes for baking. (41)

dredging. The process of coating foods with flour. (32)

drop cookies. Cookies made by placing (or dropping) small amounts of dough onto a sheet pan. (42)

E

eclectic. Composed of the best aspects. (3)

ecofriendly. Products or practices that do not damage the environment. (10)

edible portion (EP). The amount of food product that remains after cleaning, cooking, or other preparation. (49)

eggs over. Eggs that are fried on one side and then flipped, without breaking the yolk, so they can continue cooking on the other side. (38)

elastin. A flexible but tough connective tissue found in ligaments and tendons. (30)

emulsion. A mixture of two liquids that do not naturally mix such as oil and vinegar. (19)

endosperm. The largest part of a grain kernel, which is a good source of carbohydrate (starch) and plant protein. (28)

energy efficient. Used to describe equipment and systems that use less energy to perform work than conventional alternatives. (10)

entrails. Guts. (35)

entrepreneur. Someone who organizes a business and assumes the risk for it. (2)

enzyme. A complex protein produced by living cells that brings about many different reactions in the body. (30)

epitome. Ideal example. (25)

Equal Employment Opportunity Commission (EEOC). A US agency responsible for the oversight and coordination of all federal equal employment opportunity regulations, practices, and policies. (6)

espagnole (ehs pan YOHL) sauce. A mother sauce made by slowly reducing brown stock, a small amount of tomato product, mirepoix, and brown roux for hours. (24)

essential nutrients. Nutrients that the body cannot make and must be supplied by the diet. (50)

executive chef. Coordinates the operation of the restaurants and departments in a large hotel or resort. (4)

expedite. Speed up. (41)

expense. The cost incurred to prepare and serve the meal. (49)

extract. An alcohol-based flavoring. (40)

F

fabrication. Cutting meat or poultry into serving portions. (31)

facultative bacteria. Bacteria that can grow either with or without oxygen. (7)

Fair Labor Standards Act. Legislation passed in 1938 to protect workers from unfair treatment by employers. This act establishes minimum wage, overtime pay, and child labor standards. (6)

family-style service. A style of service in which the waitperson places serving platters of prepared food in the center of the table so the guests can serve themselves. (48)

fermentation. When yeast feeds on any carbohydrates that are present in a dough and produces carbon dioxide and alcohol to leaven baked goods. (40, 43)

finfish. All species of fish that have an internal skeleton and swim in water. (34)

finger sandwich. A category of sandwiches that are attractive and slightly larger than canapés. (22)

fire extinguisher. A pressurized canister filled with a substance that puts out fires. (9)

flaky pie dough. The pie dough that results when fat is mixed or cut into the flour until it is in pieces approximately the size of a pea and then liquid is added. (44)

flambé (flahm BAY). A French term that means "to flame" and refers to a dish that a server finishes by setting it aflame tableside. (48)

flatfish. Fish that have two eyes on one side of their head and none on the other side and typically swim or lay on the ocean bottom. (34)

flats. The trays that eggs are packed in for foodservice. Each tray holds 30 eggs. (37)

flattop range. A cooktop with a heavy cast-iron top which has a heat source located underneath it. Pots and pans are placed on the flattop. (14)

flatware. Knives, forks, and spoons. (48)

focal point. The point or item to which the eye is first drawn when looking at a plate presentation. (39)

foodborne illness. Sickness caused by eating unsafe food. (7)

food-contact surface. Any surface such as a table, cutting board, or piece of equipment that comes in contact with food. (8)

food cost. The cost of food used to make a menu item for a customer. (49)

food cost percentage. The portion of food sales that was spent on food expenses. (49)

food miles. A measure of the amount of energy needed to move food from its point of harvest to its final destination. (10)

foodservice. The business of making and serving prepared food and drink. (1)

foodways. The eating habits and culinary practices of a people, region, or historical period. (52)

foraged. Searched for and gathered by hand. (26)

forecast. Predict. (49)

fork-tender. An indication of doneness for large cuts of meat or poultry when a long-tined fork or skewer is inserted into the cooked product and it easily slides off the fork. (33)

franchise restaurant. An independently owned restaurant that is part of a larger restaurant chain and pays for the right to use the brand name, concept, logo, and advertising. (2)

free enterprise. A system that recognizes and promotes a person's right to own a business and manage it with little intervention by the government. (2)

French service. A style of service which requires the servers to cook and prepare dishes in front of the customer. (48)

French toast. A breakfast preparation that is made from bread soaked in a milk and egg mixture and then fried. (38)

frittata. An Italian-style omelet that is cooked on both sides and served open rather than folded or rolled. (38)

fritter. Small individual fried pastries. (41)

front-of-the-house staff. The service personnel that work the dining room. (48)

full-service restaurant. Foodservice operation that employs servers to take the customers' orders and bring the meals to their tables. (2)

fumet (foo MAY). The French name for fish stock. (23)

fusion cuisine. The merging of two or more ethnic cuisines into one cooking style. (3)

G

ganache (gah NAHSH). A sauce made by mixing chopped chocolate into boiling hot heavy cream. (47)

garnish. A decoration added to a dish to make it attractive. (21, 39)

gaufrette (goh-FRET). Waffle-shaped, deep-fried potatoes. (29)

gelatin. An animal protein that when dissolved in a hot liquid adds to a rich mouthfeel. (23)

gelatinization. When starch combines with hot liquid and swells, acting to thicken the liquid. (18)

genoise (jehn WAHZ). A classic European-type of sponge cake that contains some butter and no liquid. (45)

germ. The smallest part of the grain and a good source of protein, vitamins, minerals, and oils. (28)

giblets. The offal meats that are commonly obtained from poultry. (30)

glaze. In cooking, it means to give it a shiny coating. (27)

gluten. A rubbery substance responsible for giving baked goods structure. (40)

goals. The aims a person strives to reach. (6)

grading. Evaluating a food against a uniform set of quality standards. (20)

grande cuisine. An elaborate and time-consuming style of cooking popular in the early 1800s that was often practiced in the homes of the rich. (3)

granité (grah nee TAY). A style of sorbet that is often slightly less sweet than sorbet. (47)

gratiner (grah tehn AY). A finishing process that browns the top of a food product. (18)

gravy. The jus from a roast that has been thickened. (32)

griddle. A polished stainless steel cooktop on which food is cooked directly without the use of pots or pans. (14)

grill. A cooking appliance that uses a radiant heat source located below the food. (14)

grilling. A cooking method that uses radiation from a heat source located below the food. (18)

gustation (guh STAY shun). The sense of taste. (53)

H

halal. Foods that are acceptable according to the dietary regulations of Islam. (52)

harbor. Be home to. (8)

haute (OHT) cuisine. The highest level of the culinary arts in which the most challenging dishes are prepared. (3)

Hazard Analysis Critical Control Point (HACCP). A system that identifies and manages key steps in food handling where contamination is most likely to occur. (8)

heat exhaustion. A heat-related condition that results when the body loses too much water and salt. (9)

heatstroke. A severe heat-related condition in which the body's usual ability to deal with heat stress is lost. (9)

heirloom variety. A plant grown from seeds that have been unchanged for several to many generations. (10)

herbs. The green leafy parts of aromatic plants that are used to flavor foods. (17)

hierarchy. An organization based on rank and ability. (4)

high-carbon stainless steel. The material used to make knife blades that combine the best properties of both carbon and stainless steels. (11)

hollandaise (hahl an DAYZ) sauce. A hot emulsified sauce that combines egg yolks and warm clarified butter. (24)

home meal replacements. Meals that are consumed at home but professionally prepared elsewhere. (1)

homogenization. The process that permanently and evenly distributes the butterfat in the milk. (37)

homogenous. Uniform throughout. (24)

hospitality. Welcoming guests and satisfying their needs. (1)

hotel pans. Rectangular stainless steel pans used to hold food in steam tables, warmers, and refrigerators; also called *steam table pans*. (13)

hybrid. The offspring of two different plant varieties. (20)

hydrogenation. The chemical process that changes liquid oil to a solid fat. (50)

I

icebox cookies. Cookies made by forming cookie dough into a log, square, triangle, or other shape. The dough is wrapped in plastic wrap or parchment paper and refrigerated. When fully chilled, the dough sliced into individual cookies and baked. (42)

incomplete protein. A protein that is missing one or more of the indispensable amino acids. (50)

indigenous (ihn DIH gehn us) food. Foods that are native or traditional to the particular geographic region or ethnic population. (3)

individually quick frozen (IQF). Fruit or fruit pieces that are flash frozen before packing so that they retain their original shape. (20)

induction burner. A cooktop that uses electromagnetic energy to heat special pots and pans made from magnetic metals such as steel, iron, nickel, and alloys. (14)

infection. Illness resulting from ingestion of live bacteria. (7)

infuse. Introduce. (46)

inspection. An assurance of safety and wholesomeness, not an indication of quality. (30)

instant rice. Rice that has been fully cooked and then freeze-dried. (28)

intoxication. Illness resulting from ingestion of toxins left behind by bacteria. (7)

invoice. A list of the quantities of products and their prices that are being delivered. (49)

issuing. A process for drawing products from food storage. (49)

J

julienne (joo lee EHN). A stick cut measuring $2 \times 1/8 \times 1/8$ inches ($50 \times 3 \times 3$ mm). (12)

jus (zhoo). The deglazed drippings of a roast that are strained and seasoned. (32)

jus lié (JOO lee AY). A reduced brown stock that is thickened with a cornstarch or arrowroot slurry. (24)

K

kitchen hood fire suppression system. An installed, comprehensive fire-fighting system that automatically puts out a fire before it spreads. (9)

kneading. Repeatedly folding and pressing dough after it is mixed to develop gluten. (43)

kosher. Jewish dietary law. (52)

L

labor cost. All the expenses involved in maintaining a foodservice staff such as wages, benefits, and payroll taxes. (49)

lactose. The main carbohydrate in milk that can cause digestive problems for some people. (37)

large dice. A dice cut measuring ¾ × ¾ × ¾ inches (2 × 2 × 2 cm). (12)

leach. Seep. (7)

leavening. The process in which gases are trapped in dough creating small bubbles that give baked goods a light and airy texture. (40)

legumes. A group of vegetables that includes beans, peas, and lentils. (26)

liaison (lee AY zun). A mixture of egg yolks and cream that is used to thicken liquids. (24)

lipids. Energy-dense nutrients that include fats and oils, as well as other fat-like substances such as cholesterol. (50)

living wage. A rate of pay that allows someone working full-time to support his or her family above the poverty level. (1)

loss. When expenses are greater than the sales. (49)

low-flow aerators. Reduce the amount of water that comes from a faucet while directing the water stream so as not to reduce its effectiveness. (10)

lucrative. Wealth producing. (2)

M

maître d'hôtel (mehtr doh TEHL). The position that is responsible for the entire dining room operations; also called *dining room manager.* (48)

mandoline. A device used to slice food by pushing the food onto and across a sharp metal blade. (13)

marbling. The streaks of fat that develop within a muscle and a key factor in meat grading. (30)

marinade. A liquid that is infused with different ingredients, in which foods are soaked in order to impart flavor before cooking. (17)

marinated salad. A salad composed of cooked foods mixed with a vinaigrette. (19)

market menu. A menu that is composed daily based on what food products are available in the market. (51)

material safety data sheet (MSDS). A document that lists the composition of a chemical product, proper procedures for storage and handling, and what to do in the case of an emergency. (7)

mayonnaise. A cold sauce that is an emulsion of oil and vinegar stabilized with egg yolk and mustard. (19)

mealy pie dough. Pie dough that results when the shortening is cut into the flour until it resembles the texture of cornmeal and then liquid is added. (44)

mealy potatoes. Potatoes that are high in starch, commonly called *baking potatoes.* (28)

mediocre. Ordinary. (44)

medium dice. A dice cut measuring ½ × ½ × ½ inches (13 × 13 × 13 mm). (12)

meringue (mehr AYNG). A foam made by beating egg whites with sugar. (46)

mesclun. A mixture of baby lettuces, sometimes referred to as *spring mix* or *field greens.* (19)

mincing. The process of chopping food into very fine pieces. (12)

minimum wage. The lowest hourly rate of pay that an employee can be paid legally. (6)

mirepoix (mir eh PWAH). A vegetable-based seasoning made of two parts chopped onion, one part chopped carrot, and one part chopped celery. (16)

mise en place. Having all foods and equipment ready for a specific preparation before beginning it, as well as being mentally prepared. (16)

mold. A large family of single-cell fungi. (7)

mollusk (MOHL uhsk). A family of shellfish that includes univalves, bivalves, and cephalopods. (34)

mother sauces. The base sauces from which other sauces can quickly be made. (24)

mousse (MOOS). A stable foam dessert that is solidified by fat or gelatin and lightened with whipped cream and sometimes Italian meringue. (46)

mouthfeel. The sensation created in the mouth by the body, texture, and temperature of a food as it is eaten. (23)

N

nappé. A sauce consistency that is thick enough to coat the back of a spoon. (24)

new potato. An immature potato of any variety. (28)

New World. The continental landmass of the Americas. (28)

noncommercial foodservice. Operations providing foodservice as a secondary activity for the business in which it is found, also referred to as *institutional foodservice*. (2)

notable. Well known. (47)

nouvelle cuisine. A style of cuisine that high-lighted individual ingredients that were simply prepared and served in small portions on artistic plates. (3)

nutrient-dense food. Food that provides vita-mins, minerals, and other substances that may have beneficial health effects, but supplies relatively few calories. (50)

nutrients. The substances in food that the body uses for energy, growth, and to regulate various functions. (50)

nutrition. The study of foods, their components, and how the body processes and utilizes them. (50)

O

Occupational Safety and Health Administra-tion (OSHA). The governmental agency that defines and enforces safe working condi-tions. (9)

offal. The term given to the internal organs and extremities that are removed before an animal or bird is butchered. (30)

olfaction (ohl FAHK shun). The sense of smell. (53)

olives. The fruit of the olive tree that is native to the Mediterranean region, may be green (picked underripe) or black (picked mature). (17)

omelet. A fluffy sheet of scrambled eggs served folded or rolled. (38)

onion piqué (pee KAY). A small onion with a bay leaf speared to it by several whole cloves. (24)

on-the-job training. Instructing new employees on the specific skills or procedures that are unique to the operation while they are working. (6)

open-burner range. A cooktop with open gas burners over which pots or pans are placed on trivets giving this range the advantage of instant heat control. (14)

oscillate. To move back and forth very rapidly. (14)

overrun. The air that is added into ice cream during the constant mixing and is trapped as the ice cream freezes. (47)

oxidation. The reaction that causes many fruits to brown once they are cut and exposed to the air. (21)

P

palate. The roof of the mouth. (19)

pan. A cooking container that is wider than it is tall. (13)

panfrying. Cooking food in enough hot fat to cover it halfway. (18)

panini grill. Cooking equipment similar to a clamshell griddle except the hot surfaces have ridges that leave grill marks on the cooked sandwich. (36)

parasite. An organism that lives in and feeds on the body of another live creature. (7)

Parisienne scoop. A utensil that is available in a variety of sizes used to form foods into appealing ball-shaped garnishes; also known as a *melon baller*. (11)

par stock. A specific amount of product to be kept on hand in order to maintain a sufficient supply from one delivery to the next. (49)

partnership. A business in which ownership is shared by two or more people. (2)

pasteurize. To heat at a temperature and for a period of time that destroys unsafe organ-isms, but does not cause major changes to the food itself. (19)

pastry chef. The head of the bakeshop who is responsible for supervising the preparation of all breads, cakes, pies, pastries, ice creams, and candies. (40)

pastry cook. The position responsible for preparing sweet dessert items. (40)

pastry cream. Sweetened milk that is thickened with starch and egg yolks. (46)

pastry glaze. A commercially prepared product made from fruit jelly and gelatin that is brushed on the surface of a tart to keep the fruit decoration in place and to keep it from drying out. (44)

pâte à choux (POHT ah shoo). The paste or thick batter used to make cream puffs and éclairs. (41)

pathogen. An organism that causes illness in humans. (7)

paysanne (pay ZAHN). A dice cut measuring ½ × ½ × ¼ inches (13 × 13 × 6 mm). (12)

perforated. Having holes punched through. (36)

permeate. Spread throughout. (17)

Persia. An ancient kingdom within Iran. (29)

pest control operator (PCO). A licensed professional who uses various chemicals, sprays, and traps to prevent or eliminate infestations. (8)

pH. The measure of acidity or alkalinity of a substance. (7)

physical hazard. A solid material that poses a danger to the consumer when present in food. (7)

phytochemicals. Substances produced by plants that may provide health benefits for humans. (50)

pickles. Foods that have been saturated with acid, usually vinegar, in order to preserve them, or have been fermented. (17)

pilaf. A cooking method that sautés grain in hot fat, then hot liquid is added, and the grain is simmered without stirring. (29)

pin bones. The small bones that are imbedded in the fillet and must be removed with pliers or tweezers. (35)

piquant (pee KAHNT). The spicy hot sensation that is the result of a chemical irritation of the lining of the mouth. (53)

pith. The white, spongy inner part of citrus skin that tastes bitter. (21)

pivotal. Crucial. (48)

pizza. A flatbread that is cooked in a hot oven with an assortment of toppings. (36)

pizza peel. A long-handled, large spatula that is used to slide the pizza in and out of the oven. (36)

place setting. The china, flatware, glassware, and napkin used by a guest. (48)

plumping. To reconstitute or return some of the liquid removed from the fruit during the drying process. (21)

poached eggs. Eggs that are removed from the shell and cooked in liquid at gentle heat. (38)

poaching. Cooking food in a liquid at temperatures from 160°F to 180°F (71°C to 82°C). (18, 33)

point-of-sale (POS) system. A computer-based ordering system that transmits the order to the kitchen, produces the customer's bill, and keeps track of important data. (48)

portion size. The serving size the chef expects to be served to the customer, frequently expressed in ounces, cups, or by count. (15)

pot. A cooking container that is as tall, or taller, than it is wide. (13)

potential. Capability. (40)

prebiotics. Nondigestible food products that encourage the growth of good bacteria in the gut. (50)

preclude. Prevent. (50)

prevalent. Widely accepted. (15)

preventive maintenance schedule. A list of tasks to be performed to ensure that equipment stays in proper working order. (14)

primal cuts. The major divisions of the carcass. (30)

principal. Most important. (23)

prix fixe (pree FEEX) menu. A menu with one set price for the total meal but allows the customer to make his or her own selection from each course offered. (51)

probation period. A length of time during which a supervisor observes a new employee to see if he or she is able to perform the job. (6)

probiotics. Foods containing live, beneficial bacteria that help to counteract the "bad" bacteria in your gut. (50)

product specification. A detailed description of a product used in a foodservice operation, called a "spec" for short. (15)

professionalism. Positive behaviors and appearance exhibited by an individual who is committed to a career in the culinary arts. (5)

proficient. Skilled. (12)

profit. When the sales are greater than the expenses. (49)

profit and loss statement (P&L). A business report that lists the sales and expenses incurred to make those sales during a given period of time; also called an *income statement*. (49)

progressive discipline. A method for dealing with unacceptable job-related behavior in a step process. The goal of this process is to give the employee feedback so he or she can correct the problem. (6)

prohibit. Forbid. (52)

proofing. Allowing yeast dough to rise after it is shaped and before it is baked. (43)

propelled. Pushed. (53)

protein. A nutrient made up of a chain of various amino acids; needed for growth, maintenance, and repair of body tissues. (50)

prudent. Wise. (9)

puff pastry. A very flaky dough that puffs to as much as eight times its original thickness when baked and is made by a complex process that creates many thin layers of dough and fat. (44)

Pullman loaf. A finely textured bread that cuts into perfectly square slices. (22)

punching. Folding dough to allow carbon dioxide gas to be released. (43)

pungent. Sharp. (22)

purchase order (PO). A document listing the items ordered, quantities ordered, and the prices agreed upon. (49)

purée soup. Soup that is thickened with a purée of well-cooked, typically starchy ingredients such as legumes, potatoes, winter squashes, or rice. (25)

Q

quality grade. For meat, a ranking based on an evaluation of traits related to tenderness, juiciness, and flavor. (30)

quick bread. A baked product that is chemically leavened. (41)

R

radiation. The transfer of heat energy through waves. (18)

raft. The coagulated clearmeat containing trapped impurities that floats on top of the consommé. (25)

recipe. A list of products and the amounts needed to prepare a dish followed by preparation instructions. (15)

recycling. The process by which something is reformulated to be used again. (10)

reduce. To boil a liquid, such as a stock, to evaporate water and concentrate flavor. (23)

reference. A person that knows and can discuss your work history and personal qualities. (6)

registered dietitian (RD). A nutrition professional that has completed at minimum a bachelor's degree in dietetics, an internship, and passed a national exam. (5)

rehydrate. To add water back to a product. (29)

relish. A condiment made of a mixture of chopped or diced ingredients preserved in an acidic liquid. (17)

remedy. To correct. (16)

Renaissance. A period marked by the end of the Middle Ages known for changes in science, art, thought, and music that transformed Europe. (3)

render. To extract by melting. (30)

requisition. A written or electronic request for product used to control food and account for food. (49)

resource. The supplies, money, or staff that a company needs to do business. (5)

résumé. A summary of the important information about an applicant, such as work history, education, and other relevant information such as awards, certificates held, and languages spoken. (6)

retronasal pathway. The route aromas travel up the back of the nasal cavity from the back of the throat cavity. (53)

reusable. An item that can be repurposed and kept out of the waste stream. (10)

rigor mortis. The state a carcass passes through shortly after death when muscle tissue temporarily becomes extremely hard and stiff. (30)

risotto. Rice that is simmered while hot seasoned liquid is continually added in small amounts with constant stirring. (29)

roasting. A method that cooks food by surrounding it with hot air. (18)

rolled cookies. Cookies formed by spreading dough out into a thin sheet and then cutting cookies into the desired shape and baking. (42)

rondeau (rahn DOH). A wide pan with 6 to 8 inch (15 to 21 cm) sides and two looped handles. (13)

rondelle (rahn DEHL). A round slice cut from round food such as carrots. (12)

round fish. Fish with one eye on each side of their head that swim through the water with their dorsal fin upright. (34)

roux. A mixture of equal parts flour and fat by weight that is cooked to varying degrees of doneness and used to thicken liquids. (24)

rub. A combination of seasonings that are massaged into a food product to impart flavor. (17)

Russian service. A style of service in which the front-of-the-house staff serves food from a platter onto plates that are preset in front of the guests. (48)

S

sachet (sa SHAY). A small cheesecloth bag containing herbs and spices. (23)

salamander. A smaller, less powerful broiler used for browning food rather than fully cooking it. (14)

sales. The dollars received in payment for the meal. (49)

sandwich. A number of ingredients placed on, in, or between bread. (22)

sanitary. An environment that is free from pathogens. (8)

sanitation. The creation and practice of clean and healthy food-handling habits. (7)

saturated fat. A type of lipid that contains only single bonds and is solid at room temperature. (50)

sauce. A thickened liquid that complements other foods. (24)

sautéing. Quickly cooking an item in a small amount of hot fat over high heat. (18)

sauteuse (saw-TOOZ). A sauté pan with sloped or rounded sides. (13)

sautoir (saw TWAHR). A sauté pan with straight sides. (13)

scaling. Portioning dough by weight. (43)

Scoville heat units (SHU). A measure of the heat of chile peppers. (26)

searing. The process of browning meat to form an even crust, which produces an appealing brown color and a richer flavor. (32)

semolina. The flour milled from a hard variety of wheat that is favored as a pasta ingredient because its texture allows pasta to stay firmer for longer. (28)

sexual harassment. Any unwelcome sexual advance, request for sexual favor, and other verbal or physical conduct of a sexual nature that affects a person's ability to work. (6)

sheet cookies. Cookies that are made by evenly spreading dough or batter onto a sheet pan, the dough is then baked and cut. (42)

sheet pans. Large, shallow pans used for baking and food storage. (13)

shellfish. Water creatures that have no bones, but have bodies covered by hard external surfaces such as the bony body of a lobster or the hard shell of a clam. (34)

sherbet. A coulis-type mixture with the addition of a dairy product that is a cross between sorbet and ice cream. (47)

shocking. Plunging a blanched vegetable or fruit into ice water; also called *refreshing*. (27)

short dough. Dough that is similar to mealy pie dough and used for savory tarts. Butter is typically used as the shortening for this dough. (44)

shortening. Fats used in the bakeshop. (40)

shrinkage. The loss of water during the cooking process. (30)

shucked. The act of separating the contents of the bivalve from the shell. (34)

simmering. Cooking food in liquid at temperatures between 185°F and 205°F (85°C and 96°C). (18, 33)

simple salad. A term used to classify a salad of greens and various raw vegetables such as cucumbers, carrots, tomatoes, and others. (19)

simple syrup. Equal parts of water and sugar by weight that is brought to a boil and simmered just until the sugar dissolves in the water. (40)

slurry. A mixture of cold liquid and starch used to thicken liquids. (24)

small dice. A dice cut measuring ¼ × ¼ × ¼ inches (6 × 6 × 6 mm). (12)

smallwares. The pots, pans, and other hand tools used to prepare food. (13)

sole proprietorship. A business in which one person owns and often operates the business. (2)

sorbet (sohr BAY). The French name for a frozen mixture of fruit purée, sugar, and water. (47)

spices. The woody parts of plants, including seeds, bark, berries, buds, and roots that are used to flavor foods. (17)

spider. A long-handled tool used to strain items or lift them out of liquid. (11)

sponge cake. Cakes that are leavened by air whipped into eggs in the cake formula. (45)

spore. A thick-walled, "supersurvival unit" produced by a bacterium to survive conditions that might otherwise kill the bacterium. (7)

spritz cookies. Cookies made from a soft cookie dough that is forced through a pastry bag to form shapes such as rosettes, shells, and scrolls and then baked. (42)

stainless steel. A material used to make knife blades that does not pit, rust, or discolor, and does not affect the flavor of foods. (11)

standardized recipe. An accurate list of the ingredients, their quantities, and the preparation methods needed to prepare a particular menu item in a consistent manner every time. (15)

static menu. A menu that offers the same items every day. (51)

steak. A portion-sized piece of meat that is cut from a larger muscle or group of muscles. (31)

steaming. A moist method that cooks a food product by surrounding it with steam vapor. (18)

steam-jacketed kettle. A permanently fixed, large pot with double-walled construction. The gap between the two walls fills with steam and heats the inside surface of the kettle. (14)

steel. A rod used to keep the knife blade sharp as you work. (11)

stewing. A cooking method that simmers or braises bite-sized pieces of meat or poultry in sufficient liquid to fully cover the ingredients. (33)

stock. A highly flavored liquid made by simmering bones with vegetables, herbs, and spices. (23)

stress. A physical, mental, and emotional response to external pressures. (5)

sunny-side up eggs. Fried eggs that are not flipped over during cooking. (38)

suprême. An individual segment without skin, pith, seeds, or membrane from any citrus fruit. (21)

sustainability. The adoption of practices that either preserve or improve the condition of Earth for future generations. (10)

sustainable products and practices. These can be produced or carried out over a long period of time without a negative effect on the environment. (1)

sweating. Cooking food in a small amount of fat using low heat in order to soften the food without browning. (18)

sweet dough. Tart dough that is similar to short dough with the addition of sugar and egg yolks. (44)

symmetry. A balanced arrangement that is identical on opposite sides of a center point. (39)

synthetic. Man-made. (11)

T

table d'hôte menu (tahbul DOHT). A menu that offers one set meal to all guests with no choices or substitutions. (51)

tactile. Physical. (53)

tang. The term used to describe the portion of the knife blade that extends into the handle of the knife. (11)

tare weight. The weight of the container holding the ingredients being measured. (15)

tea sandwich. A small, neatly made sandwich that is served during afternoon tea. (22)

temperature danger zone. The temperature range [41°F and 135°F (5°C and 57°C)] in which bacteria reproduce rapidly. (7)

tempering. The method of gradually warming the temperature of egg yolks with small amounts of hot liquid before adding into a large amount of hot liquid to avoid curdling. (24, 46)

terroir (ter WAHR). A special set of characteristics in a food product that result from the local environment. (52)

thermostat. A device that responds to temperature changes and either turns the burner on or off. (14)

three-compartment sink. Three adjacent sinks used to clean, rinse, and sanitize small equipment and utensils. (8)

time and temperature control for safety (TCS) foods. Any foods that require the control of factors including time and temperature to limit the growth of pathogens or the formation of their dangerous by-products; formerly called *potentially hazardous foods.* (7)

tourné (toor NAY). A vegetable that has been pared into a seven-sided football shape. (12)

toxin mediated infection. Illness resulting from ingestion of bacteria that then produce harmful toxins while in the human digestive tract. (7)

trans **fat.** A type of lipid that is created when an unsaturated oil is chemically changed to resemble a saturated fat. (50)

trends. New practices or conditions that point to the way things will be in the future. (1)

trussing. Tying poultry or other food in order to give the cooked product a pleasing appearance and to ensure even cooking. (31)

tuber. The enlarged part of an underground root that is eaten. (28)

U

ultra high temperature (UHT) pasteurization. The process of heating milk to 280°F (138°C) for 2 to 6 seconds, and then it is sealed in sterilized containers. (37)

umami. The fifth basic taste that is perceived as a satisfying richness or meatiness. (53)

United States Department of Agriculture (USDA). The federal agency that imposes standards for the quality and safety of food products in the United States. (20)

univalves. Shellfish that have only one shell. (34)

unsaturated fats. Fats that contain one or more double bonds and are liquid at room temperature. (50)

V

vacuum. A void. (3)

value. Worth. (51)

velouté (vehl oo TAY) sauce. A mother sauce made by thickening a white stock with a blond roux. (24)

vinaigrette. A mixture of oil and vinegar used to dress salads. (19)

virus. A very small organism that invades another cell and causes it to reproduce the virus. (7)

viscous. Thick. (45)

W

wash. A coating of liquid such as beaten eggs, milk, or water applied to risen dough before baking to give color and texture to crust. (43)

water activity (a_w). The amount of water available for microbial growth in a product. (7)

waxy potatoes. Potatoes that are relatively low in starch; also called *boiling potatoes.* (28)

whetstone. A flat, abrasive stone used to sharpen a knife once its edge is dull and worn. (11)

whey. The watery portion of the milk that contains the whey proteins. (37)

white mirepoix. A vegetable-based seasoning made of two parts chopped onion, one part chopped leek, and one part chopped celery. (16)

white rice. Rice that has had the bran layer removed during the milling process. (28)

white stock. Stock made from raw or slightly cooked bones and white mirepoix resulting in a light pale to deep golden color. (23)

whitewash. A slurry made with flour used to thicken liquids, often used when making American-style gravy. (24)

work ethic. How you feel about your job and how much effort you put into it. (6)

workplace diversity. Valuing and respecting the contributions of coworkers who are different from you. (6)

wrap. Various ingredients rolled in a tortilla. (22)

Y

yeast. A microscopic fungus that consumes sugar and expels alcohol and carbon dioxide gas. (7)

yield. The quantity or number of portions a recipe will produce. (15)

yield grade. An evaluation of the amount of lean, closely trimmed boneless cuts a carcass will produce. (30)

yield percentage. The ratio of EP to AP, which tells the chef how much usable product, or EP, he or she can expect from a given amount of AP product. (49)

yield test. The process of determining and recording the usable amount, or edible portion, of a product. (49)

Z

zest. The colorful, outermost part of the skin of citrus fruits. (21)

Index

P

R

radiation, 288
raft, 407
ranges, 220–221
rasp, 212
ratios, 310
rattail tang, 174
RCA, 70
RDs, 71
reach-in refrigerator, 229
receiving, food cost management, 760–761
recipe costing, food cost management, 763–766
recipes, 235–245
    definition, 235
    measuring ingredients, 238
    standardized, 238–244
        anatomy, 240–243
        product specification, 243–244
        value of, 240
    units of measure, 235–238
        volume, 236–237
        weight, 235–236
        weight and volume correlation, 238
    yield conversion, 244–245
recreation segment, hospitality industry, 6
recycling, 167–168
reduce, 375
reduction, 390
reference, résumé, 76–77
refrigeration, 229–230
registered dietitian (RD), 71
regulations and laws, 22–23
    employment, 88–89
    government role, 113–114
    Truth-in-Menu laws, 789
regulations
    fish, 555
    health inspection, 130
reheating, safety, 117–118
religion
    factors in cuisine, 807
    influence on cooking, 32, 34
relishes, 279–280, 399
Renaissance cooking, 35
render, 505
rennet, 595
repetitive motion injuries, 142
research, 786
    using reliable information, 68
research chef, 69
Research Chefs Association (RCA), 70
reservationist, 740
reservations, 740–742
resource, 55
resource management, 759–769
    food cost, 759–766

        issuing, 762–763
        production, 763
        purchasing, 760
        receiving, 760–761
        recipe costing, 763–766
        storage, 761–762
    labor cost, 767–768
    performance measurement, 768–769
respect, 57
restaurant consultant, 71
résumés, 77–80
    definition, 77
    submitting, 79–80
    writing, 77–79
retronasal pathway, 838
rigor mortis, 490
risotto, 478–480
roasting
    definition, 290
    meat and poultry, 526–529
        determining doneness, 528–529
        equipment, 528
        pan sauces and gravy, 529
    temperatures, 528
    vegetables, 451
rock salt, 264
rodent and insect control, 128–129
rolled cookies, 670–671
rolled sandwich, 360
Rome, ancient, 32–34
rondeau, 203
rondelle, 192
room service, 48
root vegetables, 417–419
rotisserie cooking, 526
rotisseur, 44
round fish, 544–546
    definition, 544
    filleting, 560–561
roux, 388–389
royale, 615
rub, 272
Russian service, 744

S

sabayon, 725
sachet, 375
safety, 135–149. *See also* sanitation hazards; sanitation
        procedures
    availability, 37
    blender, 408
    botulism, 104
    caramel, 728
    chiles, 429
    dress, 136–137

Photo Credits

Ballogg Photography: VII

Draz-Koetke/Goodheart-Willcox Publisher:

X, XI, XII, XIII, 121, 123–125, 127, 178, 181, 183–185, 190–196, 202–214, 223, 226, 226, 228, 229, 251–257, 264–271, 274, 276, 278, 280, 289–293, 301, 303–305, 309, 311, 321, 322, 324–328, 330, 331, 333, 334, 344–348, 351, 352, 375, 376, 378, 381, 389, 393, 396, 397, 404, 406–408, 416–426, 429, 430–434, 447, 456, 459–461, 464–468, 474–478, 480, 482, 483, 494–503, 505, 506, 512–516, 525, 526, 535, 538, 539, 545–548, 550, 552, 553, 561–565, 567, 570–572, 598–600, 609, 610, 613, 630, 631, 644–646, 648–653, 660, 662, 663, 682, 683, 690, 702, 703, 712, 714, 719, 726, 729, 733

Shutterstock.com:

III wavebreakmedia; VIII CandyBox Images; IX Bocharev Photography; XIV Kzenon; 58 (Chef's Ethics sidebar) Ilin Sergey; 120 (Sustainable Culinary sidebar) Mediagram; 212 (rasp grater) PRILL; 214 (slicer) fotoedu; 224 (microwave) trailexplorers; 268 (cayenne pepper) Carroteater; 322 (lemon) 327 (apricot) Dionisvera; 327 (nectarine) Nattika; 332 (cantaloupe) Viktar Malyshchyts; 332 (honeydew) eurobanks; 332 (watermelon) Maks Narodenko; 334 (fig) kaband; 334 (kiwifruit) Roman Samokhin; 335 (mango) Tim Ur; 335 (papaya) Yeko Photo Studio; 335 (pineapple) Maks Narodenko; 335 (star fruit) jigkofoto; 336 (cherimoya) picturepartners; 336 (guava) Vinicius Tupinamba; 336 (kiwano) Viktar Malyshchyts; 336 (kumquat) Nattika; 336 (lychee) Viktar Malyshchyts; 336 (passion fruit) Serhiy Shullye; 337 (persimmon) photolinc; 337 (pomegranate) Roman Samokhin; 337 (prickly pear) marco mayer; 418 (beet) Madlen; 419 (jicama) Mau Horng; 421 (broccoli rabe) GVictoria; 426 (acorn squash) Pham's photo, (butternut squash) Elena Schweitzer, (spaghetti squash) Darryl Brooks, (pumpkin) victoriaKh; 427 Hong Vo, Oliver Hoffman; 434 (lentils) Ivaschenko Roman, (okra) Le Do; 435–436 AN NGUYEN, Levent Konuk, nito, Ekaterina Lin, Ekaterina Lin, AN NGUYEN, Jan-Dirk Hansen, Ekaterina Lin, johnfoto 18, iampuay, Elenadesign; 437 Stephen B. Goodwin, eAlisa, Andrii Gorulko, picturepartners; 438 Elizabeth Chapman, Sally Scott, Dan Kosmayer, JIANG HONGYAN, picturepartners, JIANG HONGYAN; 457 Elena Schweitzer, nuttapong; 465 eye-blink (amaranth), WimL (quinoa); 545 (haddock) picturepartners, (mahi-mahi) holbox, (marlin) photomatz; 546 (monkfish) ANCH, (swordfish) Luis Carlos Torres, (tuna) holbox; 458 (catfish) Volosina, (perch) Keith Publicovre, (sturgeon) bergamont, (walleyed pike) Vladyslav Danilin; 550 (spiny lobster) Eric Isselee, (shrimp) antpkr, (oysters) Andrjuss, (scallops) deamles; 660 (baked biscuits) Marie C. Fields, (baked muffins) Charlene Bayerle; 812 (sheep in meadow) majeczka, (cheese) MaraZe, (Abbey Month Saint-Michel) Vasilyev, (fish) sisqopote; 813 (roast beef and Yorkshire pudding) Joe Gough, (Pate Campagne) Monkey Business Images, (Irish stew) Joerg Beuge, (gigot) jabiru, (bangers and mashed potatoes) Joe Gough, (cog au vin) Radu Dumitrescu; 814 (vegetables) jopelka, (olive grove) nito, (village of Manarola) JeniFoto; 815 (ratatouille) marco mayer, (souvlaki) smoxx, (pasta) Contrail, (haria) travelight, (paella) Sergio Martinez; 816 (mosques) Pecold, (sheep) Paul D Smith; 817 (Tabbouleh) Lilyana Vynogradova, (dolma) jabiru, (baklava) Dimitrios, (shawarma) Levent Konuk, (hummus) K. Miri Photography; 818 (house) Serge Lamere, (mushrooms) FotograFFF, (man with reindeer) A.B.G., (town of Reine) Harvepino; 819 (smorgasbord) steamroller blues, (reindeer steak) Alias Stuidot Oy, (gravlax) Foodpictures, (herring) B. and E. Dudzinscy, (meatballs) ivylingpy; 820 (goat) Alis Photo, (flag and mountain) Katarina Hoglova; 821 (chutney) Monkey Business Images, (rendang) Paul_Brighton, (dal) bonchan, (naan flatbread) Joe Gough, (tandoori chicken) WITTY234; 822 (fish) Ian Scott, (mountain) Jeanne Provost, (poke) the808; 823 (ota ika) FedorKondratenko, (nasi goreng) Hywit Dimyadi, (pavlova) p.studio 66, (roasted pig) GOLFX, (biscuits) Robyn Mackenzie; 824 (Mt Fuji) syearth, (rice field) Jun Baby; 825 (sashami) Dan Peretz, (kimchi) 54613, (Pad Thai) Piyachok Thawornmat, (pho) robertlamphoto, (larb) Hassel Sinar, (Peking duck) Kittipojn Pravalpatkul; 826 (fishermen) Louie Schoeman, (gazelles) Oleg Znamenskiy; 827 (braai) Anke van Wyk, (fufu) Paul D Smith, (bobotie) Ehrman Photographic, (jollof rice) Adriana Nikolova, (wot) Dereje; 828 (farm) MaxyM; 829 (poutine) bonchan, (meatloaf) Andrea Skjold, (chili) tacar, (baked beans) Robyn Mackenzie, (jambalaya) rj lerich, (salmon) Olga Lyubkina; 830 (gaucho) Galina Barskaya, (rainforest) Frontpage; 831 (enchiladas) Joe Gough, (ceviche) rj lerich, (feijoada) bonchan, (arroz con pollo) bonchan, (jerk chicken) Chiyacat, (asado) ermess, (tamales) Andrea Skjoid; 832 (mountain) Brykaylo Yuriy, (pig) Martin Pateman, (pike) Kletr; 833 (goulash) Tobik, (wiener schnitzel) ElenaGaak, (stuffed cabbage) stocknadia, (pierogi) B. and E. Dudzinscy, (dobos torte) Giuseppe Parisi, (borscht) Lisovskaya Natalia, (kielbasa) jurasy